The Catholic Family: Image and Likeness of God

VOLUME 1

Family Life

To dear Yvonne and Heinz.

Yours with prayers and blessings

Deacon Dr Bob McDonald

The Catholic Family: Image and Likeness of God

VOLUME 1

Family Life

Deacon Dr. Bob McDonald

Queenship

PUBLISHING COMPANY

P.O. Box 220 • Goleta, CA 93116

(800) 647-9882 • (805) 692-0043 • Fax: (805) 967-5843

Library of Congress Number #, Pending

Published by:
Queenship Publishing
P.O. Box 220
Goleta, CA 93116
(800) 647-9882 • (805) 692-0043 • Fax: (805) 957-5843

Printed in the United States of America

ISBN: 1-57918-118-X

Dedication

*"Now a great sign appeared in
the sky, a woman clothed with
the sun, standing on the moon
and on her head a crown of
twelve stars."*

(Rev. 12:1)

This book is dedicated to the Queen of Heaven, on whose feast day I was ordained a Permanent Deacon.

For my ordination gift I asked her that I would always preach and teach the truth with love. *"Veritatem facientes in caritate"* (Eph. 4:15). May this work give her the honour she is due as the Mother of Jesus and may it give glory to God in the hearts of Catholic couples everywhere.

Acknowledgements

A book such as this can never be the work of one person alone. I am so grateful for the love, the work, the countless hours, the support and the dedication of my wife, Rita, without whose wisdom and patience this book could never have been completed. She typed and retyped, read and reread the manuscript, always suggesting modifications with wisdom and tact. She never lost faith in the importance of the task and she never lost faith in me. Above all, she never lost faith in God and continued to believe in his holy will for this work.

My very special gratitude to Mark Sebanc, author of the wonderful novel *Flight to Hollow Mountain,* for his fearless editing and the expertise which he generously shared with regard to grammar and my poor literary style. It is not easy to make a silk purse out of a sow's ear.

My heartfelt thanks to my equally talented friend and mentor Michael O'Brien, artist and author of *Father Elijah* and numerous other works of literature, for his reading of the manuscript, pointing out errors and the need for clarification of many points which might otherwise have been misunderstood.

I am deeply grateful for the expert editing by Chris Zakrzewski, former editor of *Nazareth Magazine.* His input was given with such gentleness, yet at the same time he was firm in his conviction that the book should be brought to completion.

A special mention must be made to my fellow Secular Franciscan, Eric MacDonald, who was the expert "glitch-remover" for my computer. He made himself constantly available at all hours to assist, to advise, and to correct. I am sure that St. Francis is delighted with his spiritual son.

Above all, I humbly give *all* the glory to the Holy Spirit, Spouse of Mary, to whom I have prayed throughout the entire task of writing, and I also pray that this work reflects his guidance and inspiration.

Feast of Pentecost and the Visitation
May 1998.

CONTENTS

CHAPTER 1

The Story of Becky and John:
The Anatomy of a Catholic Marriage

*"You hate those who pay regard
to worthless idols but I trust
in the Lord. I will exult and
rejoice in your steadfast love,
because you have seen my
affliction; you have taken heed
of my adversities."*
(Ps. 31:6-7)

Becky and John were both baptised as infants into the Catholic Church. This would have been a wonderful thing except that they were raised with the lukewarm idea that one only needs to do the minimum for one's own salvation. True, they had to go to Mass on Sundays, but apart from that, there was no real sense of loving God or growing in holiness. These things were for saints only! In all honesty, they found Church to be boring and they were always glad when Mass was over, because then they could play with their friends. Becky's parents were modern liberal thinkers, who saw no problem with rejecting some of the teachings of the Church, especially if these were inconvenient or difficult. As a result, once Becky reached fifteen years of age, they decided to have her take the birth-control pill "as a precaution." They believed that this was a rational and intelligent thing to do, given the growing temptations out there in the world. After all, what could be worse than getting pregnant? That would bring shame to their good family name in the community. Becky meanwhile, quickly came to believe that if it was alright to be on the pill, then pre-marital sex must be no big deal. She assumed her parents could hardly disapprove.

John's parents were middle-class, educated people, who considered comfort and status to be more important than loving. They were determined that John should have a good education but this was so important to them that they tied their love to John's academic performance. If his grades were good, they showed him their love by buying him a coveted toy. If his grades were poor, they punished him. There were rarely any hugs or kisses for John. He soon learned that his value as a person depended upon his achievements and so he set about excelling in his studies. Deep within, he craved his parent's love, but he knew he had to earn it. As a result, he eventually entered university to study economics and with sheer hard work was turning out straight A's. In spite of his academic excellence, he never really experienced any profound sense of peace or joy, but he simply put this down to his personality. It never entered his head that this emptiness was connected to the way he had been raised. Somewhere deep within, there lurked a sinister feeling that he could never be good enough.

Unlike John, Becky never had any excessive demands made on her by her parents. They were too busy with themselves, enjoying trips, friends and pleasures. Becky had to fend for herself and enjoyed all kinds of freedom to do as she pleased with her peers, especially now that she was "protected" by the pill. She lost her virginity at age sixteen and from then on, sex was not so much a joy as just something a girl had to do in order to keep a boyfriend. Her school grades were never good, and by age seventeen she had dropped out and was drifting from job to job. By the age of twenty-one she was working in a café as a waitress and life was going nowhere. She did not seem to have any firm direction or purpose, but simply clung to a vague notion that somehow things would get better.

John dated a few girls while at university and even lived with one for a few months, but that ended in a very bitter break-up. He continued to go to Mass on Sunday, but only if he did not have something more important to do. He thought nothing of receiving Jesus in communion even though he had not confessed his sexual sins. No one had ever told him what a sacrilege was, and worse still, he had no notion of the state of his own soul. For him, religion was simply a habit, not a vital source of love and life. He would have scoffed at the suggestion that true religion could have anything to do with peace and joy, the very things he yearned for in his heart.

After graduation with full honours, he landed a job with a marketing firm and the prospects were excellent. He soon impressed his superiors with his competence and his personable nature, with the result that he began to climb the corporate ladder at a rapid rate. He was now twenty-six years old.

It was a bright spring morning when John wandered into the café where Becky was working, and as soon as he laid eyes on her, he was smitten. He could hardly drink his coffee, he was so intent on drinking in Becky. Her smile, her eyes and everything about her made him feel weak at the knees. He desperately wanted to speak with her, but all he could manage was a useless stammer. After that, he ate lunch there every day for two weeks before he plucked up enough courage to ask her for a date. Meanwhile, Becky was wondering if he would ever ask her out. She had been dreaming about him ever since he first walked in.

The romance blossomed at such an exciting pace that within three months, John had proposed to Becky and she joyfully accepted. They were deeply in love and they decided on a short engagement. John's parents did not really approve of Becky, but then no girl would really have been good enough for their son. Becky's parents seemed pleased enough, but really they were just relieved that she might settle down at last. Now they were both plunged into a flurry of arrangements. It was a given, that they would be married in a Catholic Church, but they had very little idea of marriage as a sacrament. They were more interested in the glitter of the ceremony than in its substance, and they spent all their energies planning the wedding reception, the cake, the limousine, the speeches and of course, the honeymoon in the Caribbean. By the time they had planned the perfect wedding, it was going to cost close to twenty thousand dollars and that did not include the absolute necessity, by their way of thinking, of a brand-new fully furnished bungalow. They were going to start married life at the top and they did not worry that such a start meant a huge debt load.

The wedding day was a dream. The sun was shining brightly, the wedding guests were beautifully turned-out, and while John was handsome in his tuxedo, Becky was stunning in her designer wedding dress. In all their careful planning, they never thought to include the Sacrament of Reconciliation prior to the great day, so they both received Jesus in a state of serious sin. In actual fact, neither of them had ever confessed their previous sexual adventures. Why should they, when they had always been told that God loved them so much that he would always understand? But that was not going to spoil their day. The priest delivered a beautiful homily on the solemn nature of marriage as a sacrament and as a covenant. He talked about true love as a willingness to sacrifice oneself for the other. Sadly, Becky and John never heard it. They were both too caught up with anticipating the reception, the honeymoon and their future life together.

Not long after settling into their perfect little bungalow, it began to lose its attraction for them and so they talked about buying a bigger, more opulent house in the suburbs, preferably with a swimming pool. Naturally, this meant that Becky would have to work, in order to save for the down-payment and meet the higher mortgage payments. It seemed logical then, to postpone having children, and so Becky continued to take the birth control pill.

They both still went to Sunday Mass, but occasionally they would skip it if they felt too tired or if they had planned an outing. They never thought to ask themselves why they should go to Mass at all; that was just something that Catholics did. Naturally, it never entered their heads to pray together.

After a couple of years, they had saved enough for the down-payment on their dream-home and they triumphantly moved in, believing that now they would be really happy. Sure enough, they were, for about four months, and then Becky pointed out that she needed to have her own vehicle. John readily agreed. They wanted children eventually, but that could wait until they became a two-car family. Before long, they were able to boast of having two shiny brand-new vehicles in the driveway and, to themselves at least, these were a sure sign of their success in life. Now they expected to be content.

John was by now rising very fast in the company and had to be away from home a lot, at seminars, sales meetings and picking up contracts. He was more and more wrapped up in his work, with the result that when he was ever home, he was withdrawn and uncommunicative, and spent more time in front of the computer screen than with Becky. Not surprisingly, Becky began to realize that the romance was losing its former lustre and she felt increasingly lonely and frustrated. They hardly ever made love these days since John seemed to be so tired all the time. He had decided that they needed to acquire a boat and in spite of her misgivings, he assured Becky that it would be the perfect answer. They could cruise on the lakes, sleep on the boat under the stars, and really get closer to one another. It would give them both a break from work and from the house, which by now had become more of a dormitory than a home. Becky wanted so much to believe in John's promise and so she continued to work and to put off having a baby. Maybe the boat really would be the answer to the emptiness she felt inside.

Eventually, they purchased a twin-engine cruiser, which meant taking out a loan from the bank, but it also meant purchasing a contract for docking facilities, and the boat was eating up gasoline at a phenomenal rate. John seemed to brighten up for a while, enjoying his new toy for three whole weekends that summer. But his work was becoming more pressing and soon he did not have the time or the energy for the boat anymore. It ended up being a major frustration to get the thing out of the water and into dry dock for the winter. From a plaything and a source of pleasure, the boat had become another drudge.

In the next few months, Becky experienced two episodes of unexpected heavy bleeding, and her doctor was convinced that these had been miscarriages in spite of her being on the pill. She was deeply wounded by this revelation. All of a sudden, she realised how empty her life had become and she knew she desperately wanted a baby. It was with a growing feeling of alarm that she also knew John had other priorities in his life. Gradually, she became more and more discouraged, more and more unfulfilled, and to make matters worse, John did not seem to notice. He was too busy saving money for his latest solution to all their problems. He was now fixed on buying a luxurious motor home. They were going to have a lot of fun with that.

They were fighting a lot these days and it slowly dawned on John that Becky never seemed to be content. She was complaining most of the time and exploded into anger or burst into tears at the slightest provocation. This really hurt him a lot. After all, he was working day and night to give her everything she could ever want. He told himself he was doing his very best to make her happy, and from time to time, he even wondered why he had ever married her. Becky began to drink too much.

One awful day, they had a huge fight. It was over a very trivial matter, but the years of pent-up frustration soon erupted into rage and all the resentment came pouring out. Becky accused him of not loving her anymore, while John completely lost his temper, threatened her, and almost struck her. They were both stunned at the power of their own feelings and they knew that something was terribly wrong. How had this ever happened? Where had they lost their way? Here they were, successful, with a beautiful house, a swimming pool, two cars, a luxury cruiser and the prospect of a top-of-the-line motor home, and yet they had become strangers to one another. John thought that Becky was no longer the wonderful girl he had met in the café fifteen years ago, while Becky could not understand how John had changed so much. All their striving and all their hard work seemed to be for nothing. What had happened to the wonderful dreams they had once dreamed together?

It took a couple of days for the anger and hurt feelings to settle down, and during that time, they did not speak a word to each other. Then Becky, realising her marriage was in serious trouble, decided it was time to have a heart-to-heart talk with John. Anxiously, she asked him to sit down and listen to what she had to say. He felt very uncomfortable and he was not sure that he really wanted to hear this. Becky, her voice trembling, then said, "John, we have everything, yet we have nothing. We are losing our love for each other and that scares me. Surely our love is the most important thing in our lives." Then, not being able to keep it in any longer, she blurted out in a pleading sob, "I want a baby!" John snapped back, "Oh sure! A baby will solve everything. If the two of us can't get along, how will three of us make things any better?" It was as though Becky had been stabbed with a knife. All of her dreams were shattered. Her hope of happiness had slipped through her fingers, and she had no idea how to recapture it. In desperation, she had a crazy thought, and like a drowning man clutching at a straw, she gave voice to it. "John, I love you and I don't want us to split up. We have tried to make it on our own and it isn't working. How about we ask God for some help? Maybe it wouldn't hurt to pray." By now, John was too defeated to argue. He just nodded his head.

Becky rummaged in a drawer and found a white mother-of-pearl rosary which one of her aunts had given her on her wedding day. It had never been used, but better late than never. They quietly recited the beads, each praying from the heart that their marriage could be saved. It was awkward at first, but as they progressed, they began to feel an unfamiliar sense of peace. The gentle rhythm of the prayers seemed to give them some hope that God really did want to be included in their troubles. Afterwards, Becky put her arms around John and they hugged one another for a long time. Then they just sat out the evening in silence, not really knowing where to go from there.

Two days later, there was an unexpected knock at the door. The new parish priest had decided to do the rounds and was calling on his parishioners in order to introduce himself to his flock. He was quite young and when Becky answered the door, she noted that he was wearing his Roman collar. They had never had a priest in their home before, so they felt a little embarrassed, nor had it even entered their heads to have their home blessed, and they both were feeling a little guilty for not having attended Mass the previous Sunday. They wondered if he had noticed. But before long, they knew they really liked Fr. Bill. He seemed so relaxed and genuinely interested in them, and it was soon clear that he had not called to take them to task.

After the usual formalities and good-mannered preliminaries, Fr. Bill looked around and asked, "Do you two have any children?" Becky and John felt immediately uncomfortable, but after a moment of embarrassed silence, Becky glanced at John. He nodded and she opened up. She told Fr. Bill about their problems, how they had been slowly drifting apart and how they had avoided having children for the sake of a better standard of living. She was surprised that she found it so easy to bare her soul to this man who seemed to genuinely care about their happiness. Fr. Bill listened intently to every word and it was clear to the unhappy couple that he was silently praying through it all. When Becky had finished, Fr. Bill thought for a while and then he said, "Becky and John, you are two beautiful people. You have so much to offer to the world, but you have gotten lost along the way. It seems to me that your priorities in life have been disordered and therefore you inevitably became more and more unhappy. Disorder always ends up in misery. Would you allow me to help you re-arrange those priorities so that you can have a second chance at the happiness you both long for?"

He had thrown down the gauntlet, and Becky and John eagerly accepted the challenge. John, with a resigned shrug, said, "Fire away, father. At this stage in our marriage I'm ready for anything."

Fr. Bill then settled down more comfortably in the plush chesterfield and he began to speak. "You two, whether you remember it or not, entered into a solemn covenant with each other and with God to be a holy people for his kingdom. This may come as a surprise to you, but your primary calling was not to pursue happiness in earthly wealth, but to find it in God and God alone. Your second calling was to have children and raise them to be children of God since they would be his as well as yours."

Becky and John sat up more attentively at that. They had never heard this before and they were eager to hear more. What they did not realize was that they *had* heard it before. They had been told the same thing in the homily given on their wedding day, but they were not listening then. They were definitely listening now.

Fr. Bill talked some more about what true love is, and how love demands self-sacrifice, rather than mere self-gratification. He gently pointed out, "Falling in love does not mean that you will satisfy all my needs. That is of little importance. What it means is that I desire to give myself completely to you with no strings attached. Even if you do not meet my needs, I still love you and will always place your well-being above my own. Meanwhile, both partners always place God first in all things."

For Becky and John, this was like a completely new revelation, and yet deep in their hearts, it had the ring of pure truth. It was as though the very thing they needed most had been right there all along, but they had been too blind to see it. How could they have missed something so obvious? In the ensuing silence, they could hear the monotonous tick-tock of the big grandfather clock out in the hall.

Fr. Bill sensed their eagerness and excitement, and knowing this was the moment of truth, he took a deep breath and said, "There is something more which you need to understand, but you may not like it. Please, at least accept that I value your immortal souls so much that I have to be honest with you." They both signalled for him to continue. What had they to lose? They were miserable enough as things stood. "Well," Fr. Bill ventured, "you really have been walking down the broad, easy road away from God. How could Almighty God help you two, when you had cut him out of your lives?" Becky, feeling the need to defend herself, jumped in and said, "But we go to Mass on Sundays, father." Father nodded. "Yes, but was that ever enough? When did you last clean house and go to Confession?" The resultant silence said it all.

"Now, listen carefully. It is clear, in the short time I've known you, that you are as ready as you will ever be to hear this, so here goes. The first serious disorder in your lives has been that you made success and things your first priority. You allowed them to displace God in your hearts and so they became false gods — empty idols. Such things can never bring true peace and you have both discovered that. Does that make sense to you?" Becky and John already realised this deep within, but this was the first time anyone had had the courage to tell them. They felt they could trust this Fr. Bill and they could sense the love he nurtured in his priestly heart for them and for the pain of their predicament.

John then spoke up, "Father, what you say is absolutely true. I take the burden of blame for that. Becky wanted to have children, but I always wanted to put it off in order to acquire more toys. I have denied her, and so I suppose I have been a rotten husband." Becky reached out, touched his hand and threw him a smile which radiated forgiveness, understanding, love, and above all, the light of a dawning hope. As he saw the look in her lovely eyes, the very look for which he had longed all these years, his heart seemed to crack open and he began to sob. Fr. Bill sat quietly, allowing them to minister to each other as only a wife and husband can.

After a few moments, John managed to choke out, "Fr. Bill, you said that was our first serious disorder. Is there a second?" And he replied, "Yes, John. There is. You have been using artificial contraception in order to promote your selfish life-style. Forgive me for being blunt, but you have both cut God out of your Covenant. It is God's right to bless you with children and his alone, but when you began to contracept, you usurped God's holy prerogative and reserved it for yourselves. That saddens God very much. I know it all looked very logical and reasonable at the time, but I can see that you are both bereft of the greatest blessing God could give to you. That gift is a child. Ask yourselves this. What has been the fruit of your love for one another? It looks to me that the answer is a big house and some expensive toys. Surely, the most sublime fruit of love between a husband and wife is a new life, a precious little soul to be raised for God's Kingdom." Now, it was Becky's turn to sob and the tears ran down her cheeks and splashed onto the hardwood floor.

John wanted to defend Becky and so he blurted out, "We were never told about this stuff. How were we to know this? Why were we not told?" Fr. Bill looked sad and said, "You're probably right John. But there is little to be gained by pointing the finger at anyone. What matters is that you are hearing it now and God willing, if you both have a child, you can ensure that he or she is not deprived of the truth. You can see to it that your little one is raised in the fullness of the Faith. Surely that is a marvellous thought."

By this time John had his head in his hands and he quietly said, "There is more isn't there?" The priest looked intently at him and nodded. "This is the worst part. You have both been receiving Jesus, the very Son of God, in Holy Communion, with mortal sin on your soul. You have been bringing great sadness to Jesus, inviting him into an unclean place. Think about it. If you knew Jesus was coming here tonight, you would rush around cleaning and tidying up the house to make it fit to receive the King of kings. Well, what about the house of your soul? It needs cleaning up even more than this mere building."

Now both Becky and John were in tears. The good priest allowed them to sob it out, knowing that it was not the moment for more words. He just prayed quietly inside, asking the Holy Spirit to fill their hearts and enlighten them with the love of God. The grandfather clock kept up its steady tick-tock out in the hall, marking out the relentless passing of these precious seconds. Becky was the first to compose herself. "You know Father, John and I were so desperate the other night, we actually said a Rosary together. We had never done that before and as we prayed, I knew that we had somehow lost God's blessing, but I did not know how to put it into words. Worse, I didn't know how to get it back. I am beginning to think that your visit was God's answer to our prayers. What would you advise us to do?"

The worst was over. Father Bill let out a deep sigh and with a sparkle in his eye, he said, "Now, that is the easy part. The first thing is to make a good general confession, and if you'd like to take a few minutes to examine your conscience, I can hear your confessions individually right now. Why put it off? The next step is to get to Mass as soon as possible and experience the joy of receiving Jesus into a soul that is free of sin, a soul as pure as it was on the day of your Baptism. The third step is to commit yourselves to a life of daily prayer together, asking God to take his rightful place once more in your marriage. One more thing. Stop the pill!" Becky was stunned. She hadn't told Fr. Bill that she was actually on the Pill. "How did you know that, Father?" He smiled knowingly. "It wasn't too difficult to figure out. You'd be surprised how many Catholic couples think it is OK to be on the pill."

That evening, Becky and John made a heart-felt confession. They were astounded at their overwhelming feelings of relief, cleansing, peace and joy. It was as though fifteen years of baggage had been lifted from their shoulders and their hearts. They profusely thanked Fr. Bill and it was obvious to all three of them that they were going to become fast friends.

After that, Becky and John grew rapidly in a whole new understanding of what it means to be Catholic. They became faithful to prayer, and to the Sacraments. They began to go to Mass on weekdays, whenever possible, in addition to Sundays. To their great delight, Mass was no longer an obligation, but the sheerest joy. They received the Sacrament of Reconciliation faithfully once a month, and became involved in lay ministry to young married couples in the parish. Fr. Bill came round for dinner every week and their wonderful conversations centred on God and their new-found faith. After dinner, they always said a Rosary together.

John sold his boat and never did buy that motor home. Six months later, Becky announced that she was expecting a baby. She and John both knew that this child was the most precious of all possible blessings from God and at last, after all these years, they experienced the joy they had been searching for in all the wrong places.

CHAPTER 2

Husband and Father:
Real Men Do Cry

"That men may appreciate wisdom and discipline, may understand words of intelligence."

(Prov.1:2)

There is a great and growing distortion in our society today. The battle of the sexes has now become open and total warfare, thanks, of course, to the unrelenting efforts of Satan to destroy the sanctity of the family. As a result, our world is peopled by the walking wounded, broken men who do not know how to be real men, and broken women who have rejected everything that is feminine. A powerful spirit of misogyny (that is to say, a hatred of the female) has taken a hold of our souls, so that men believe that the only way they can survive is to dominate and abuse women, while women, who also would like to survive, are denying the best of what it means to be female, in order to embrace the worst of what it means to be male. Misogyny has become so prevalent, that men hate and suppress their own femininity, while women try to escape from their femininity by becoming competitive, aggressive and power hungry.

This distortion between the sexes was prophesied by God after the sin of Adam and Eve in the garden. God said to the woman, "Your yearning will be for your husband, and he will dominate you" (Gen. 3:16). The power struggle between men and women, the so-called battle of the sexes, is a direct consequence of original sin. Satan is cashing in on this perversion, and is successfully setting men against women and women against men, thereby destroying family peace. Even more alarming is the fact that he is leading us to raise children who no longer know what true love is all about.

The great majority of men today do not have a clue what it means to be a real man. They have been raised by broken fathers, and so their masculine image is distorted by their own inadequate fathering experience. Dad was never really present to them. He was away at work all the time, or he was drunk most of the time, or he was caught up in his own selfish pursuits. Whatever the problem, he was emotionally a thousand miles away from his son. And even when he was physically close, he likely indulged in anger, physical beatings, or relentless put-downs of his children. With such a role model, what sort of image of manhood is a boy likely to internalise? Because he desperately wants his father's love and admiration, he either imitates dad and becomes another bully or he seeks his father's love in other men and commits himself to a homosexual life style, trapped in the prison of gender confusion. Others are so destroyed by dad's put-downs, they really believe that they will never amount to anything. They develop a crushing sense of worthlessness and go through life in constant fear, often totally controlled by their wives, their bosses at work, and even by their own children. They never knew a real man, a man whom they could have as a hero and who, in turn, could love them, encourage them, teach them and spend time with them. When dad is not a hero, men turn to other men to be their heroes. If they are fortunate, it will be a good model, a man of goodness and honour. If not, they will fashion themselves in the image and likeness of an anti-hero, whose example leads them farther and farther away from Jesus. So often they choose another dysfunctional man, such as Rambo the killer, or James Bond the womaniser, or Joe Big Bucks, the ruthless business man. If we do not have a father, we will invent one. Our need for fathering is that great. It is a built-in drive.

Nowadays, many men think that being a man means never to show emotions, other than anger, of course. Real men never ever cry. Real men get drunk on weekends. They hunt and fish, play endless golf, and neglect their families. They never indulge in tender hugs for their wives or children. They leave child-rearing to their wives. A real man never does housework. He must never be romantic, unless he is sexually aroused. Also, he must pretend to be a gold medal Olympic sexual athlete and brag about it to his male friends. His religion is sports, and his gods are hockey and football stars. He must succeed in the workplace, dominate his wife, and conquer the world. Naturally, real men must always indulge in some form of prejudice, because it makes them feel superior. Accordingly, a Hispanic becomes a Spic and a Caucasian becomes a Honky. A Catholic might be derogatorily referred to as a Papist, while a Protestant is labelled a Heretic. The ugly mind of a prejudiced man has to reduce a person to a single epithet, in order to cope with those who are "different." Prejudice makes no room for the love of Jesus Christ, which embraces all men and women regardless of race or creed. On top of this, of course, a real man never prays with his family. Prayer is only for women!

The tragedy is that such men are truly miserable and unhappy creatures. They become more and more neurotic, unable to understand why their wives become unhappy too. They fail to make the connection between their own behaviour and the disobedience of their children. When their kids become powerful teenagers, into drugs, alcohol, sexual pleasure and maybe even crime, they blame everything and everyone else but themselves. And if they ever suspected for a moment that they were actually dysfunctional, they would never come to a therapist for help, because that would be a sign of weakness, and real men can never admit to a weakness.

No wonder there is feminism in today's world. No wonder women are lashing out at men who are abusing them. No wonder more and more women are turning to each other for love and opting for lesbian relationships, given the risks they run in seeking true love from men. Something is seriously wrong. There is a major sickness in our world. In a word, it is the breakdown of God's order. God's design for men is being mutilated, which means that they must rediscover what God intended them to be. In fact, I would hazard a prediction right now. If men will turn around and become obedient to God's vision of who they are, not only will men become real men, but feminism will disappear from the face of the earth. It will simply become obsolete.

When men live out their true vocation of manhood, women will once again become secure, loved, respected, protected and provided for, and they, in turn, will rediscover their God-given role as receivers and nurturers of life and love. They will once again become man's helpmate, as God intended. The family will be restored to its holy order, and God will reign in our families as he should.

For men to reclaim their manhood, they would do well to take a good look at three heroes, three role models vastly different from the kinds of heroes they are exposed to by movies and television. Forget Archie Bunker and our over-paid sports stars. We need to open our hearts and look at God the Father, Jesus Christ the Redeemer, and St. Joseph the Foster-Father. Each of them is a treasure house of wisdom for men.

God the Father

"This then is what I pray, kneeling before the Father, from whom every fatherhood in heaven or on earth takes its name. In the abundance of his glory, may he, through his spirit, enable you to grow firm in power with regard to your inner self, so that Christ may live in your hearts through faith" (Eph. 3:14-17). From this we learn that, first and foremost, our fatherhood derives from the fatherhood of God. Our paternity is a gift from the paternity of God. A man is indeed the head of his household, but he is not given human power. He is given *divine* power, which he must exercise in accordance with the Father of fathers in Heaven.

"Whoever does not love does not know God, for God is love" (1 John 4:8). Love is the key to the Fatherhood of God. Love, therefore, must also become the key to our human fatherhood. If a man does not know how to love, he has not yet discovered what real manhood is all about. But what is love? St. Paul tells us, "Love is patient, love is kind, love is not envious or boastful or arrogant or rude. It does not insist on its own way. It is not irritable or resentful. It does not rejoice in wrong doing but rejoices in the truth. It bears all things, believes all things, hopes all things, endures all things" (1 Cor. 13:4-7). That does not seem to fit with today's ideas about manhood. This kind of manly loving is a far, far cry from the angry, fury-driven, hard drinking, wife abuser of today. The man who follows St. Paul has, as his model, God himself. The angry, fury-driven man models himself on Satan. That is the difference, and it makes all the difference.

"My son, do not disdain the discipline of the Lord or lose heart when reproved by him, for whom the Lord loves, he disciplines" (Heb. 12:5-6). As fathers, men stand in for the Lord and so they have the duty to discipline their children. This duty is not to be dumped onto their wives. It is true that wives must also discipline the children, but they derive that authority from their husbands. Husbands derive their authority from God the Father himself. It is a man's job, and he shirks it at his peril. God the Father disciplines and he expects earthly fathers to do the same. It goes with the job. If fathers do not take this task seriously, then their own immortal souls will be in grave danger. Read the Old Testament and see what happened to Eli the Priest, when he failed to discipline his sons. God said, "I condemn his family for ever, since he is aware that his sons have been cursing God and yet has not corrected them" (1 Sam. 3:13). Eli failed in his duty towards his sons and so deserved to be cursed by God. All fathers, therefore, are duty-bound to give godly discipline to their children.

A wise man once said, "Fathers are pals nowadays, because they don't have the guts to be fathers." Faithful Catholic men must decide to become true fathers and bring discipline to their homes. They begin this task by disciplining themselves. If they demonstrate obedience to God the Father in Heaven, then they have a right to demand obedience from their children. God the Father has rights over earthly fathers and they, in turn, have rights over their families. That is God's order. But just as God exercises his rights with love and mercy, so fathers must show love and mercy to their wives and to their children. "And parents, never drive your children to resentment but bring them up with correction and advice inspired by the Lord" (Eph. 6:4).

A real man knows his Father-God in heaven, and in turn, becomes a godly father in his own home.

Jesus, The Christ

Jesus, to be sure, was the perfect model of manhood, and he modelled his Father in Heaven perfectly. Indeed, Scripture tells us that we are to put on the mind of Christ. He said, "Learn from me for I am gentle and humble of heart" (Matt. 11:29). Jesus did not say, "Learn from me for I am powerful and arrogant of heart." If we are to be like him and become real men, we are to give up all notions of power or violence, and become gentle-men, humble in our relationships with our wives, our children and our neighbours. Rambo will waste you. Jesus will bless you. Violence is Rambo's way. Meekness is Jesus' way. We must not think that being meek or gentle is only for weaklings. On the contrary, meekness is for very brave and courageous men. Which is easier, to shoot a man or to allow him to shoot you? Jesus allowed violent men to nail him to a cross. Was that the action of a coward or a real man? When evil men come to kill my wife and my children, perfect conformity to the example and lessons of Jesus, as found in the Gospel, would require me not to kill them. This would be the heroic, Christ-like course of action. The consistent teaching of the Church, however, allows us to take life in extreme situations of self-defence. I am not sure what I would do in such an instance, but I do know this: they would have to climb over my dead body to get to my family. My manhood would demand this sacrifice for my wife and children. As a husband and father, I must be prepared to lay down my life for my family. That means dying to self every day, and it may one day mean a sacrificial death in reality. This is not just a lofty theory. This is the very life blood of my vocation as husband and father.

"You have heard how it was said, eye for eye and tooth for tooth, but I say this to you. Offer no resistance to the wicked. On the contrary, if anyone hits you on the right cheek, offer him the other as well" (Matt. 5:38-39). This, of course, goes against all of our natural, animal instincts and all of our training as males. Yet Jesus demands that we rise above any immediate urge to violence or retaliation against others. He teaches us that the most effective response to evil is goodness. If we punch the man who punches us, we only add to the evil in the world and we give Satan more power, because he feeds on evil. But if we give back goodness for evil, we neutralize it, there is rejoicing in heaven and Satan retreats in frustration.

Jesus also told us he came to save the world, not to condemn it. He never condemned sinners. He always encouraged them, built them up, and called them to a higher good. We too must never condemn others. We must also imitate Jesus and build others up, calling them always to bring out the best in themselves. This is especially pertinent in the case of our wives and our children.

"Love one another as I have loved you" (John 15:12). Once again it all comes back to love. God *is* love, and Jesus commands us to love. Love, then, is the foundation of true manhood. Men must become lovers, real lovers, which might even mean laying down their lives for their families, just as Jesus laid down his life for all of us. They are to sacrifice their own selfish desires and needs for the sake of their loved ones. They are to die to self if they are to truly find the happiness they desire as men.

In Michael O'Brien's novel, ***Plague Journal,*** one of his characters declares with great insight: "I didn't know it then, but the cost of a happy family is the death of selfishness. The father must die if he's to give life to his spouse and his children. Not a pleasant thought, but a true one. An entire life-time can be spent avoiding it. It's simply not enough to provide and protect. In themselves, of course, providing and protecting are good and necessary things. That's our responsibility. But a father can provide a mountain of material goods for his family and defend it against all kinds of inconveniences, thinking he can rest easy, having done his part, and still have missed the essential thing: he is called to be an image of love and truth."

Jesus tells us how to be happy as men, how to have a happiness which endures, not fleeting earthly pleasure. In the Sermon on the Mount, he preached on the richness of the Beatitudes, and there he said, "How *happy* are the poor in spirit ... happy the gentle ... happy those who mourn ... happy those who hunger and thirst for what is right ... happy the merciful ... the pure in heart ... the peacemakers." If men read this passage over and over again and truly welcomed these wonderful words into their hearts, they would be guaranteed a deep, abiding happiness within. Jesus promised it and he, as we all know, is the Prince of promise-keepers. The world tells us that we can only be happy if we strive to amass money and power, or if we frantically seek pleasure, if we accumulate things, get a bigger house, a bigger boat, and drink the right beer. Jesus had very different ideas.

Happiness is not to be found in the world and its trinkets, but in following his way, which is the way of the heart. And if we follow his way, we will also become the beneficiaries of the fruits of the Spirit, which St. Paul tells us are: "Love, joy, peace, patience, kindness, goodness, trustfulness, gentleness and self-control" (Gal. 5:22-23). Is there any man who does not want these treasures? If we do not follow Jesus, we are doomed to reap the opposite of these wondrous fruits. Once again, as St. Paul says, "When self-indulgence is at work, the results are obvious: sexual vice, impurity, and sensuality, the worship of false gods and sorcery, antagonisms and rivalry, jealousy, bad temper and quarrels, disagreements, factions and malice, drunkenness, orgies and all such things" (Gal. 5:19-21). The man who opts for these is indeed an unhappy man.

Is this the life a real man wants? Is this the life any man wants? Sin and misery come out of self-indulgence. Peace and happiness come out of being the husbands that God calls men to be. "Happy the man who trusts in the Lord" (Ps. 84:12). This is a profound truth. If men really trusted that God will take care of them, even in the little things, they would give up their neurotic, masculine need to control their own little world. They would relax and stop worrying, believing that all things are being worked towards their good by a wise and loving God. It is not by conquering the world that men will find peace. It is only by becoming like little children and placing all their trust in their Abba, their Papa-God, that they will find peace. Man cannot control the world, but our Father God can and it was Jesus who showed us how.

St. Joseph

St. Joseph was the step-father of Jesus. He was well aware that Mary, his wife, was the special gift of God to him. He knew he had been chosen by God to care for Mary and her Son, and he joyfully took on the task.

The Gospel of Matthew tells us that Joseph was a just man. Scripture is full of references which explain what it means to be a just man. "Wisdom comes from the lips of the just and his tongue speaks what is right. The law of God is in his heart, his foot will never slip" (Ps. 37:30-31). "The just always lend generously, and their children become a blessing" (Ps. 37:26). "He speaks truth from his heart. He keeps his tongue under control" (Ps.15:2-3). "The path of the just is like the light of dawn, its brightness growing to the fullness of day" (Prov. 4:18).

Good St. Joseph was all of these things. He loved Mary, his betrothed, and refused to hand her over to the law, even when it looked like she had become pregnant by another man, which must have struck him as the only natural explanation. His actions were informed by the law of love engraved deep within his heart and not by the human demand for vengeance. In spite of his hurt, he returned mercy for hurt. He decided to legally divorce Mary rather than openly condemn her, which he had every right to do under Jewish law. That is the mark of a just man. A real man knows how to be merciful.

St. Joseph exhibited eight singular qualities, which constitute a shining example to all who would become real men: loving man, chaste spouse, protector, provider, worker, teacher, faithful husband and servant. St. Joseph knew how to love. He sacrificed his own natural desires for fatherhood in order to do the Will of God. He loved God first and after that he also loved Mary and Jesus. He was chaste, but chastity is not to be confused with celibacy. Husbands are not all called to be celibate although some couples may generously choose this holy sacrifice later in life after having raised their family. They are free to enjoy a loving sexual life, but at the same time all men are called to chastity in their sexual lives. St. Joseph protected his little family, especially when he had to flee to Egypt to save them from Herod's murdering soldiers. He provided food, clothing, and shelter for Mary and Jesus by doing good, honest, hard work every day, excepting the Sabbath, which he insisted on keeping holy in accordance with the commandment of Yahweh. He taught Jesus carpentry, and he also taught him the Scriptures. St. Joseph was utterly faithful to Mary, his wife. There was no room for any other woman in his heart and, of course, he placed himself totally at the service of Mary and Jesus for their well being and happiness. How many of today's husbands know how to serve their wives and children? How many husbands today dedicate themselves to making their wives happy and content? How many husbands today spend time with their children? A real man understands his priorities in life. He puts God first, his wife second and himself third. That is God's order. It is God's design for husbands. Of course, for a wife it is God first, husband second, and herself third.

St. Paul calls on married couples to serve each other. My job as a husband is to put my wife ahead of myself, to love her as I love myself. I am called to do everything in my power to make her feel secure and loved. Then and only then do I have the right to expect her to serve me, building a home for me and my children. This sounds like a tall order, especially if I do not acknowledge one thing as certain: I am never going to succeed in doing this under my own power. I am going to need the power of God, which is God's grace, to accomplish this. That is why I am called by God to be holy and to pray every day, calling down upon me and my wife all the graces of our marriage sacrament. Prayer is not primarily for women. Prayer is in fact the fundamental obligation of the man of the house. I must be the prayer leader of my family, summoning my family to regular prayer time in the home. I am the *intercessor* before God for my wife and my little ones. God looks to me to guide my family in the ways of truth and holiness. If I fail in this task, I must answer for it before the Lord just as Eli the Old Testament priest had to do. My eternal happiness depends on my being the holiest husband and father possible. Marriage demands no less.

The family Rosary is a powerful prayer for unity, love and protection, and it is the man who should lead it. The man must constantly ask God the Father to give him the grace he needs to be a godly husband and father. He must see to it that his children are brought up in the faith and that they attend Mass, always on Sundays, and during the week if possible, and that they go to regular confession and communion. Such a man will be able to stand one day before Jesus, confident that he has lived out his Christian duty in the eyes of the Lord. But such a man is also promised great blessings by God even in his earthly life. "Your own labours will yield you a living. Happy and prosperous will you be. Your wife a fruitful vine in the inner places of your house. Your children round your table like shoots of an olive tree" (Ps. 128:2-3). God is promising that the faithful and holy husband will be blessed and that this will be manifested in fruitful work, in happiness, prosperity, in a contented wife and in godly children. This is an offer too good to refuse.

In chapter 10, it is pointed out that a father models an image of God to his young child. But the role of father becomes even more powerful when the child becomes older. He will model an image of *manhood* to his children, and this has major implications for their sexual development. From the age of ten to sixteen years, the most indispensable person in the child's life is father. It is especially during these years that a child desperately needs dad to model ideal manhood. If a child is deprived of fathering during these years, either by dad being physically absent, emotionally withdrawn or consistently drunk (which is the same thing), then dire consequences can ensue.

A male child needs dad to be his hero. He craves dad's love, and if he does not get it, he is devastated. This need is so great that he will search elsewhere for it. Indeed, the need may express itself in a homosexual preference whereby he may invite another man to give him the love he never received from his dad. His need for his father's love is that powerful.

Daughters who feel unloved by their fathers will come to hate dad for not loving them. From this they may come to hate all men in as much as they represent dad to them, turning to lesbian relationships as the only reliable source of love in their unhappy world.

The "gay" subculture refuses to accept the psychodynamics of its own disorder. Indeed, most of them try to prove that homosexuality is genetic. But even if that could be proven, which I seriously doubt, it is still a disorder. A genetic mutation cannot be used to justify an immoral lifestyle. The fact is, I have treated many homosexual patients, and in all cases I have found absentee or dysfunctional fathering in their critical years. Many also found healing when they came to experience the perfect fatherly love of God, the Father of all fathers.

When it comes to family relationships, a man needs to understand the "feminine" within himself. To accomplish this, he so often needs to overcome his own conditioning. Our parents meant well, but so often they raised us in their own image of what a man should be. Add to that the Hollywood brainwashing of boys and men to be a one-man army, and it is easy to see how the inborn feminine nature of the male can be crushed. We may believe that the macho image is the only valid way to be a real man, but that is absurd. It is interesting to look at Rambo after he has brutally killed scores of other men. He stands with the smoking gun in his hand surveying the mayhem he has created. Does he look happy? On the contrary, he looks alone, isolated, and unfulfilled. His vengeance did not bring him peace of mind. That is just as true for all of us men. When we follow the paths of the world, in violence and in denial of our own tenderness, we too will find ourselves alone. We will cut ourselves off from the life-giving love of our wives, our children will grow to despise us, and we will end up killing our own capacity for love.

The real man is the one who has discovered the God-given balance within and is not ashamed of it. He recognises that all men are really scared little boys inside. Men are expected to go to war, but they do not want to die. We are afraid. The real man has come face to face with his true inner self, the self that is loving, tender, gentle, self-giving, forgiving, understanding, and filled with compassion for lesser men. He faces the truth about himself and, like any other little boy, he is eager to rush into the protecting arms of his mother when he is frightened. The Blessed and Great Mother of God is ready to throw her arms around him, if only he will come to her. She of all people understands the heart of a man, from whom so much is expected and needed by his wife and children. She also understands the demands made on him by a perverse and sinful society. After all, Mary understood her Son and his Sacred Heart in all its beauty, its weariness, its deprivations, and even its fears. Jesus asked his Father to take the chalice away from him, but immediately submitted to his Father by asking that his will be done. This is the perfect model of how men, as husbands and fathers, should pray. Like Jesus we should admit that we are often "sorrowful unto death" (Matt. 26:38). We should kneel before the Father and tell him so.

Then, like Jesus, we can ask for what we want. "Father, if it be possible, let this cup pass me by" (Matt. 26:39). A real man then goes all the way in generosity and prays, "Not my will but thine be done" (Matt. 26:39).

A true husband knows how to be gentle with his wife. He offers her the words, "I love you" more than he needs to, but not just the empty words. He proves what he says by his loving actions. He knows when she is tired, or discouraged or sad and willingly gives her the strength of his arms. Nothing speaks more eloquently to a woman than a manly hug. He listens to her concerns. He never scorns her apparent lack of logic. To his delight, when he does listen, he usually finds that what he thought was illogical was actually wisdom. He knows how to sacrifice his own needs for her, and he learns that best from seeing the way she constantly sacrifices her needs for him. He indulges her little demands of him, as best he can, and thinks of her before he thinks of himself. He never criticises her or judges her, and absolutely never allows anyone else to do so.

On a certain occasion, when he was eleven years old, a holy priest whom I know defied his mother in angry and petulant rebellion. He and his mother were standing at the foot of the stairs in their house at the time. This good priest says that his father was upstairs, but came from out of nowhere, as if he had been shot out of a cannon, and planted himself in front of the boy. He took him by the lapels and said, "Don't you ever speak to your mother like that again. But never mind that, nobody speaks to *my wife* like that. Nobody." That young boy never ever forgot this lesson, even after he had grown up to become a priest. His father was a real man and he rushed to defend his wife as all real men should. He was teaching his son that the relationship with his wife was paramount and took precedence over all other relationships, even his relationship with his son. A man's wife is God's precious gift to him and him alone. God expects him to defend her against all-comers, including and perhaps especially, the children.

A real man is not ashamed of his tender heart. He is able to feel the pain of those he loves and to weep with them. So many men refuse to do this and see themselves as fixers. When his wife comes to him with her pain, he dispassionately offers her five solutions to "fix" her feelings. This is not what she is asking for. She merely longs for him to understand her, to accept her feelings without judging them, and to give her that magic manly hug. Again, the real man knows this and does it.

At the same time, a Christian man shares all of his income and his goods with his family. He does not hold back money for his own selfish pursuits at the expense of his wife and children, and especially not at the expense of their necessities. He does not hide money in a separate bank account and he never insists on "mine and yours." He rejoices that all of the family assets are "ours." Such a man recognizes his wife as his true partner in life in all things, and that she has equal right and access to the family goods and property.

As a father, the real man is willing to have his need for leisure and rest challenged. Children are spontaneous and in great need of affirmation. A good father is willing to submerge his own needs, to sit down, listen to their ideas and dreams and give them the wisdom of his gentle direction. His words have power in their little hearts, because they see him live out those words. He is a living example of his own wisdom. He knows how to play with them, to have fun, to let them jump all over him, even if he is tired. He sets aside time to take them to a ball game or to ballet or to a concert. He does not discriminate between one child or another, nor does he show a preference for boys over girls. I remember once organising a fishing trip for my son. This was to be the big father-son bonding experience. My daughter Kirstie was listening to our plans and with a kind of pleading look on her face, quietly said, "Dad, I like fishing too." It was like a bombshell to me. My lovely daughter also wanted to be a part of this special time with me. She was paying me the ultimate compliment of a daughter to a father and showing me the yearning in her heart for her father's love. So I happily took her along on the fishing trip, and it turned out she caught the biggest bass of the day, my son caught a couple of keepers and I caught the one that measured all of two inches from nose to tail. I have a snapshot to prove it. I know that a powerful and beautiful bonding was given expression on that memorable day. My daughter still loves to talk about it and we all chuckle at my mighty tiddler. It is one of those memories which will never lose its flavour. A good father knows how to give his children memories to be stored forever as priceless treasures.

A real man never backs down from his duty to discipline the children he loves. Indeed, it is because he loves his children that he takes the time to discipline. He knows his own strength, and so he always disciplines with love, never with anger. He appreciates that anger is by its very nature violent and can lead to abuse. He corrects, admonishes and instructs his child with the authority of God himself. Therefore, he knows that he is not imposing his own will on his children, but rather calling them to be obedient to the will of God, the Father. At all times, he supports his wife in the discipline of the children. He never contradicts her in front of them, although he may in private, later on, gently ask her to reconsider a harsh punishment.

Real men do cry. A manly man knows when to let the tears flow. He is not ashamed to show his wife and his children that the true heart of a man is capable of such tenderness. His tears are the silent sign of a compassionate heart. "Happy are those who mourn" (Matt. 5:4). Such a man is not stingy in offering comfort to those who need it, nor is he too proud to ask for it when he is the one in need.

My daughter Fiona once composed a little poem for me when she was a small child. She wrote,

> Pops are tops.
> My dad is too.
> He plays with me
> and takes me places.
> But best of all he loves me.

For me, that was a wonderful testimony to my own fatherhood and I will treasure it for ever. Could any father ask for more?

So now it is easier to appreciate the awesome responsibility that goes with being a husband and a father. Life does not come with an instruction manual. That's why we have fathers to instruct their families. A wife needs love and security. A child needs love, security and training. A man needs to provide all of these things to fulfil himself and to draw his family closer to God.

So what is a real man?

A real man is a lover, a great and wonderful lover, who follows God's way of love and not the world's way.

He is God-centred and never self-centred.
He is gentle and never violent.
He is peaceful and never angry.
He is kind and never mean-hearted.
He is firm and never controlling.
He is just and never unfair.
He is available and never absent.
He is humble and never proud.
He is faithful and never adulterous.
He is a promise-keeper and not a renegade.
If married, he is a husband and never a bachelor.
And he is a father in accordance with God the Father.
Above all he is a living model of Jesus Christ.

CHAPTER 3

Wife and Mother: Real Women are Mystery and Masterpiece

*"A gracious woman does
honour to her husband."*
(Prov. 12:4)

The Church is very often accused these days of having oppressed women down through the centuries. She is perceived as a male-dominated hierarchy, deliberately structured so as to keep women from realising their full potential and dignity. This is simply a lie, but then if a lie is repeated often enough, most people soon come to believe it. Satan understands this very well and so he keeps on telling and re-telling the lie. But it is a lie for the simple reason that the Bible from its beginning to its end honours the role of women in salvation history. It not only places woman firmly in a position of equal dignity with men, but it also highlights her very special feminine charisms. These are gifts from our loving God who, on the one hand, emphasises her equality with men, but at the same time rejoices in that which makes her irreplaceable and unique. The Catholic Church is the Bride of Christ and, as such, is obedient to Jesus who is the Word of God and the Bible is the Word of God. The Church therefore in that spirit of obedience has always elevated woman to her proper God-given dignity. She could do no less. Countless holy women have been recognised and canonised by the Church. Numerous seminaries for young men aspiring to the priesthood were run and taught by holy, highly educated women. It could not have been otherwise, since the Church models herself on Mary the Mother of Jesus and he founded the Church in the first place. Certainly there are countless examples of women being oppressed and dominated by men, even by priests who ought to have known better, but this was always contrary to the teachings of the Magisterium of the Church. Domination was never preached by the Church. Pope Paul VI, who conferred the title of Doctor of the Church upon St. Teresa of Jesus and St. Catherine of Siena, thus recognising their powerful contribution to the clarification of the truths of the Catholic Church, said, "Within Christianity, more than in any other religion, and since its very beginning, women have had a special dignity of which the New Testament shows us many important aspects ... it is evident that women are meant to form part of the living and working structure of Christianity in so prominent a manner that perhaps not all their potentialities have yet been made clear." In other words, the mystery of what it means to be female has not yet been fully revealed, and this is precisely because being female is indeed a profound and wondrous mystery. We can never fully understand a mystery. Both men and women need to explore this hidden reality in ever greater depth, because the more we learn about woman as God intended her to be, the more we learn about God himself. Men should be overawed at the beauty and the truth of women. The more they discover, the more they will revere their wives and all women and the less likely they will be to dominate, abuse and use women for their own selfish purposes.

The Second Vatican Council states: "The hour is coming, in fact has come, when the vocation of women is being acknowledged in its fullness, the hour in which women acquire in the world an influence, an effect and a power never hitherto achieved. That is why, at this moment when the human race is undergoing a deep transformation, women imbued with a spirit of the Gospel can do so much to aid humanity in not falling."

Are these the words of a Church which oppresses women? On the contrary, the Church is suggesting that much of the salvation of the human race is in the hands of godly women who choose to live out the Gospel of Jesus. The Church recognises that it is the quiet strength, courage, fidelity, wisdom and above all the love of women which will call men to be true disciples of Christ and, together with men, to change the world.

The Bible is a treasure house of insights into the mystery of woman and femininity. Right at the beginning in the book of Genesis we are told, "God created man in his own image, in the image of God he created him: male and female he created them" (Gen. 1:27). Therefore both male and female are human beings to an equal degree. Both are created in God's image. But while male and female are equal in dignity, they are not identical. God created real differences, not only to distinguish the sexes, but also that together we might be better equipped for our unique and special roles in the formation of family and community life. These differences are not simply in our physical bodies, but rather are more profoundly spiritual, psychological and emotional. There is therefore a God-given complementarity between men and women. "This is why a man leaves his father and mother and becomes attached to his wife and they become one flesh" (Gen. 2:24). Man is not complete without woman and she is not complete without man. But together they become one flesh, united in giving glory to God. God understood this emptiness within Adam and said, "It is not right that the man should be alone. I shall make him a helper fit for him" (Gen. 2:18). "Then Yahweh God made the man fall into a deep sleep. And while he was asleep, he took one of his ribs and closed the flesh up again forthwith. Yahweh God fashioned the rib he had taken from the man into a woman and brought her to the Man. And the man said, 'This one at last is bone of my bones and flesh of my flesh. She is to be called woman because she was taken from man'" (Gen. 2:21-24). We can therefore conclude that man and woman are made *for each other.* Each needs the other. Eve is a vital part of Adam, being made out of his rib and she is there to be his helper and to be one with him. It is important to note that God made her to be a helper "fit for him," which means she was the perfect mate for the man in every possible way. She was to be a helper, not in the sense of a slave jumping to his every command, but in the sense of sharing with him in "subduing the earth" (Gen. 1:28). She is his life's companion and Adam's highest calling on earth is to exist in relationship, first with God and then with the woman. Yet at the same time, it is in his relationship with woman that he finds his true relationship with God. Before the Fall, this union of Adam and Eve was so perfect that "Both of them were naked, the man and his wife, but they felt no shame before each other" (Gen. 2:25). Therefore, even their sexuality was totally pure and free from the darkness of lust. They both lived as truly equal persons, giving of themselves totally one to the other, and that is still the secret of any happy and successful man-woman relationship today. It was and still is God's intention for us and it is the only way in which we will find peace and happiness with one another.

Unfortunately, the tragedy of the apple spoiled the perfection which before had come so easily to them. Now they were both distorted by the Original Sin and all of us, to this day, share in that distortion. God himself pronounced the sentence upon them both. "To the woman he said, 'I shall give you intense pain in child-bearing, you will give birth to our children in pain. Your yearning will be for your husband and he will dominate you.' To the man he said, 'Because you listened to the voice of your wife and ate from the tree of which I had forbidden you to eat, accursed shall be the soil because of you. Painfully will you get your food from it as long as you live'" (Gen. 3:16-17).

Therefore the unity of the two was now disrupted. A woman would be the victim of her own emotions, *yearning* for her husband, that is to say, needing more from him than he could ever give, knowing that he could never fully satisfy her deepest self. As a result, she is often tempted to become a seductress just like Eve in order to get what she yearns for, thereby denying her own holy femininity. She may use her beauty to get what she thinks she wants or become demanding or complaining. She may begin to value trinkets because she cannot have what she truly values, namely a deep and abiding intimacy with her husband. As a result, she destroys her true self in order to satisfy her false self. A man on the other hand tends to dominate his wife and stifle her womanhood. The very thing he needs in order to be complete and happy is the very thing he destroys by his drive to dominate. This terrible consequence is in full swing today, dividing male and female, destroying marriages and families. The original God-given equality of man and woman is now violated and while it is clearly to the disadvantage of the woman, it also diminishes the true dignity of the man. The more he lords it over his wife, the more he violates himself. The battle of the sexes becomes total war. It is interesting to note that in this all-out battle, men do not try to win it by becoming like women. Instead it is women who take on the men on their own ground by trying to become like men. Pope John Paul II in his letter *Dignity and Vocation of Women* said, "Consequently, even the rightful opposition of women to what is expressed in the biblical words 'He shall rule over you' must not under any condition lead to the masculinization of women. In the name of liberation from male domination, women must not appropriate to themselves male characteristics contrary to their own feminine originality. There is a well-founded fear that if they take this path, women will not reach fulfilment but instead will deform and lose what constitutes their essential richness. It is indeed an enormous richness." The one and only hope for the human race is not militant feminism (although a woman's cry for equal dignity is a perfectly valid Christian principle) but to rediscover what God originally intended, to honestly face our post-original sin distortions, to repent of them and to strive to become true children of God, fully male and fully female.

It is true that St. Paul says, "Wives be submissive to your husbands as to the Lord" (Eph. 5:22), and Peter, the first pope, echoes this when he says, "You wives should be obedient to your husbands" (1 Pet. 3:1). Taken out of context, it looks like God is demanding a master-slave relationship. That is why it is vital to take the *whole* passage of Scripture and not a quotation in isolation, because therein lies the serious risk of misinterpreting the holy Word of God. First of all, as soon as St. Paul asks for wives to submit to their husbands, he immediately commands that "Husbands love your wives as Christ loved the Church" (Eph. 5:25). This passage demands our fullest understanding. We must ask ourselves, "How did Christ love the Church?" He *submitted* himself to it. He *obeyed* it. Did he not say, "Whatever you bind on earth will be bound in Heaven? Whatever you loose on earth will be loosed in heaven" (Matt. 16:19)? Therefore Jesus deliberately chose to be *obedient* to his own Church. Not only that, but he washed the feet of his disciples, powerfully demonstrating his desire to *serve* the Church. Husbands therefore are also called to submit to their wives and to serve them, to obey them and to be at their disposal. Likewise, when St. Peter asked wives to submit to their husbands, the whole passage reads, "You wives should be obedient to your husbands. Then if there are some husbands who do not believe the Word, they may find themselves won over, without a word spoken, by the way their wives behave, when they see the reverence and purity of your way of life" (1 Pet. 3:1-2). In other words, wives are indeed called to be submissive just as husbands are called to be submissive, but in a wife's silent submission and good example, she can draw her husband closer to God and truth. In fact, St. Paul makes this interpretation very clear when he says, "Be subject to one another out of reverence for Christ" (Eph. 5:21). Pope John Paul II re-emphasises this truth in the *Dignity and Vocation of Women,* when he writes, "In the relationship between husband and wife the subjection is not one-sided but mutual." Therefore, a husband governs and his wife rules. He is the king and she is the queen. He is the head and she is the heart. *He is the moral authority. She is the love authority.* This is equality in diversity. Catholics must reorganise their thinking. Jesus calls men and women to be equal before God and one another. The age of male domination must come to an end if humanity is ever to be restored to its original harmony and blessing.

Am I obedient to my wife? Yes I am. I recognize that she has wisdom in so many things and I listen to that wisdom. Her wisdom and intuition have saved me from many a rash and ill-considered decision. At a more mundane level, she has wonderful managerial skills with money and finances. I do not. I therefore am totally obedient to her in all matters to do with spending or saving money. In fact I often blissfully walk around with no money in my pocket, knowing that all such things are being prudently and wisely cared for by my life's partner. She runs my medical office and without her, my work would be a shambles and so I obey her in everything that has to do with organization. In turn she obeys me in all things medical because those are my skills. Likewise, she defers to my ministry as Permanent Deacon and does everything in her power to support that ministry. We have discovered each other's gifts and deficiencies and we have learned how to bring them together in a beautiful complementarity. Together we have found oneness and wholeness.

When we are of one mind and heart on an issue, we know that the Holy Spirit is present in and approves of our decision. But what does a Christian couple do when there is a stalemate? If man and wife cannot agree on an issue, how should they handle it? First of all they should set aside useless feelings of hurt, pride or anger. Bad feelings only cloud our reason and block our access to wisdom and truth. Then the couple should kneel down together and ask the Holy Spirit for guidance. If the Lord answers them, the next step is simple. Obey the Lord. If there is no obvious answer then God wants to test our love commitment to one another. At such an impasse one of the two must *defer* to the other. This is a test of humility, to submerge one's own opinion out of love. Because the woman is love, it is in fact easier and more likely that she will defer to her husband. Her having done so, the husband, as head of the household and deriving his authority from God the Father, has the right to lovingly override her act of submission and to submit to his wife, but if he chooses not to, then his decision stands. In submitting, the wife is fulfilling her role as helper or helpmate to her husband and in submitting, the husband is fulfilling his role as loving husband. If the wife defers to her husband, then he and he alone has to take full responsibility before God for the consequences of his decision. Such situations are a powerful test of love between man and woman and that is God's order for marriage. Love, for it to be true, has to be constantly tested.

Yet, as was stated earlier, this equality does not eliminate the essential differences between male and female. God ordained these differences and they must be better understood if we are to live more fully in the brilliant light of God. Woman is a mystery created out of *love,* by love and for love, and she is God's masterpiece of love. The sublime perfection of womanhood in the mind of God was, of course, the Blessed Virgin Mary, who attained the awesome perfection of both *virgin* and *mother*. She was *entrusted* by God with carrying and giving birth to the Son of God. After Adam, no man has ever been born without original sin, apart from Jesus, who was both God and man. Only a woman has been given that privilege and this is rooted in the very nature of Mary's womanhood and femaleness. If we are to come anywhere close to an appreciation of the mystery of woman, we must understand these four great feminine characteristics of love, virginity, motherhood and trustworthiness.

While it is true that both men and women are called by Jesus to love, there is a huge difference in the way that they do. Men have to learn how to love. They stumble over it because it goes against their sin-nature, which is to dominate, and love and domination cannot co-exist. Therefore man constantly has to strive to defeat his sin-nature if he is ever to become a true lover. Women, on the other hand, instinctively embrace love. Love pulsates deep within their very essence so powerfully that one could say, "A real woman is love." Love is what drives a woman. Love is what she lives for. Love is what she is created for. Love is her very breath and without it she withers and dies inside.

Men are capable of survival without love by sinking all their energy into work, power, domination and success. They are capable of *feeding* on these sad substitutes for love. A woman simply cannot do this without destroying herself as a woman. To do so, she has to renounce her femininity and become a sad imitation of a man. A woman feeds on love, not power. There is an old proverb which says, "What a woman wants, God wants." This saying recognizes that when a woman is fully female, she intuitively wants the things of God because God is love and the woman wants love above all things. When she is not loved, she becomes unhappy and it is her unhappiness which leads her to become self-absorbed, demanding, complaining, taking refuge in meaningless things like clothes or jewellery or expensive trips. These become poor substitutes for what she really wants, mere soothers to replace her real food, which is love itself.

A man who withholds love from his wife is slowly killing her and will answer to God for destroying that which is most beautiful and precious in her, namely her likeness to God, who is love. She is the very heart of the home, and for a man to abuse that heart, which was personally given to him in marriage by God, is to abuse himself. He needs a heart for him to be complete and his wife is that heart. A man should treat his wife as his most precious jewel because that is what she is. He should make her feel cherished and special. He should delight in her femaleness, loving to adorn her, taking a holy pride in what he is able to provide for her.

When I was in Ethiopia during the great famine of 1985, an Afar tribesman, when faced with the prospect of starvation, would first sell his weapons. For him these guns, swords and daggers represented his masculine pride because that is how he earned respect from other men. Among Afars, a real man had to be able to defend his family and his tribe, yet his weapons were the first to go in order to obtain food for his family. The very last thing to be sold was his wife's jewellery and this was the ultimate tragedy and defeat for that man. The wife knew this and she would humbly and sadly hand over her poor trinkets to her husband, knowing it was tearing him apart and that it was his last resort for survival. She, as a woman of love, set about comforting her crushed husband, building up his defeated ego and continuing to trust in his manliness. She was willing to stand by his side even to death itself. Is that not something which can only be done out of love? A woman, because she is loved, becomes a fountain of love which she shares generously with others, especially her husband. He is a creature of *action* and so he instinctively provides and protects. She has to *nurture* to be a woman and so she can quietly accept her husband's flaws and failings, never destroying his need to feel like a man and always encouraging and building him up.

The woman's highest calling of love is to love God above all. It is she who intuitively understands what it means to love God and so she draws her husband closer to that same calling. She fills her heart and her home with God. Prayer comes easily to her or at least, more easily than it does to a man. For a woman, prayer is like breathing, while for a man, prayer has to be a project. As a result of his wife's quiet blessing, the husband finds himself freed to become the spiritual leader of his family as he should. It is his duty to be that spiritual leader, but he needs his wife to sanction it, otherwise he is likely to falter and lose courage. If a wife blesses her husband's holiness and quietly calls him higher, he will respond in a manly way, but if she showers him with scorn, he will be tempted to give up. If she mocks him when he takes out his rosary, he is likely to put it down.

Recent research has shown that when a baby is being formed in the mother's womb, numerous rich connections develop between the right brain and the left. This is true of both male and female babies. At thirteen weeks, when the baby's sexual characteristics are being formed, the females retain these rich connections between right and left brain while in the male, many of them cease to function and they atrophy. In other words, men are mostly left brain creatures. They can still access the right brain, but it is not easy for them. This is not too difficult to understand, since they need to operate from the left side of the brain for most of their time. Out in the world, they need uncluttered logic, mathematical skills, and mechanical skills in order to solve problems and to survive. They cannot afford to be trammelled by emotions. Women, on the other hand, are in a way more complete. They are in equal touch with both sides of their brain. The right hemisphere is responsible for such wonderful qualities as intuition, wisdom, poetry, creativity and music. The result is that men focus more on problem-solving while women, like the Blessed Mother, ponder things in their hearts. Of course men can be great poets and musicians and artists but to accomplish this they must learn to quieten the left brain and listen to the right.

God built these differences into our very brains with the result that women find it much easier to tap into wisdom and intuition and to be creative. To do this well, they need their husbands to be out there doing left brain things because this frees her up to build that which we call a home. A man can build a house but only a woman can build a home. She should not have to build the house because that will drain her energy for making the home. That is why it is such a tragedy that there are so many single mothers and working mothers these days, who have to go out to work in order to build the house. They have little or no energy left to build a home for their children. The husband also pays a high price for insisting that his wife contribute to building the house by going out to work. He desperately needs a home too. He needs a sanctuary to which he can escape after his day's work, where he can take delight in his wife and his children, where he can take off his false mask of invincibility and admit to his weakness, where his flaws are accepted, where his wife encourages and compliments him and where he can be a true king hidden from the world. This is not intended to imply that a woman cannot assist her husband with regard to income and the promotion of a better standard of living for her family. This is a legitimate pursuit but it must never take precedence over her primary duties as wife, mother and heart of the home.

Needless to say, if a mother of young children has to enter the work force, then her children are also robbed of their birthright, which is to be loved and taught the faith by their very own mother. This is what fulfils a wife who is loved. It is she who creates the loving space. She chooses the colours, she chooses the furniture, she puts her mark and her love in all the corners of the home with pictures, mementoes, and signs of her Christian faith. Her smile decorates that space and her arms are always ready to receive her troubled husband and to scoop up her frightened children. Where else can man tap into the mystery of love but in the arms of his wife? Where else, apart from prayer, can he find solace and renewed energy?

Men like to think that a woman is more emotional than a man. This is not true. Certainly she is more in touch with her emotions than a man and is therefore more comfortable with emotional language. It is also true that when a woman allows herself to be dominated by her feelings instead of her wisdom, then things go seriously wrong. But that is just as true of men. If a man allows his angry feelings to rule his head, then he too can do a lot of damage. For both men and women, the will must dominate our feelings. Feelings are fickle and inconstant and should never be allowed to override the higher faculty of the will.

It is a fact that a woman quivers less than a man to a sudden explosion. In regard to pain and suffering she is much less cowardly than many a soldier. She can bear suffering without complaining. She is not disturbed by sickness. She does not give in to her own sickness as easily as a man does, nor does she flinch at the sickness of others. Rather, she rolls up her sleeves and gets on with the job of nursing, no matter how disgusting or exhausting it may be. It is as though her capacity for the pain of childbirth gives her the strength to face other forms of pain. It is a well known fact that a real woman tends to be serene, sure and deep-rooted.

This mystery of the feminine applies equally to the priest and the nun who have entered a different kind of marriage. The priest is married to the Church and it is only in the arms of his bride that he will find his true manhood. He needs the love of his flock, which is the Church, as much as a man needs his wife. I therefore appeal to all Catholics to love their priest. They should treat him as they would their very own husband or father. He should be invited to our homes and given the encouragement and love which help him to persevere, so that he can be for us the "other Christ," the *alter Christus,* the dispenser of the sacraments, which we all so desperately need. Never criticise a priest. That is the same thing as a wife criticising her husband and a man is easily crushed by a woman's scorn. The priest needs his parish to build him up and appreciate his efforts, otherwise he becomes defeated and discouraged. He needs the love of his bride. The religious sister on the other hand is married to Jesus, not to the Church. She is his bride and he looks to her for the love that he craves for, just as he does to the entire Church which is also his bride. She is most fulfilled by her divine husband, who never stops treating her as his most precious jewel. She is the apple of his eye, and so she can be a true lover also, totally loved and able to love the whole world in return.

This leads into the role of virginity for all women. Virginity is badly misunderstood if it is envisioned as something merely physical. The virginity of our Blessed Mother was much more than simply a body which did not know a man. It was for her a mental, emotional and above all a spiritual reality. She was literally married to the Holy Spirit and therefore her entire being was focussed on and dedicated to God. She was a perpetual virgin. She had to be, because of her spiritual marriage. She could never have had relations with St. Joseph because that would have been infidelity to her Divine Spouse. Likewise, all women are called to a spiritual virginity. This is of course, a physical thing in the unmarried, but that physical virginity becomes transformed by marriage. This spiritual virginity of woman should not be abandoned just because she is now united in one flesh with her husband. In fact she must nurture her spiritual purity all the more. She must be totally faithful to her husband and must be totally faithful to God. She must preserve, not only her body for her husband, but must preserve her soul for God, in purity and in chastity.

A man must see this reality in his wife if he is to delight in her and be constantly amazed at her mystery. Many women today refuse to see Mary as their ideal. They reasonably say that there is no way they can be both virgin and mother, and so they put Mary aside as irrelevant to their practical lives. But this is a serious mistake. It is true that God elevated the Mother of Jesus to the fullest perfection of virginity and motherhood, but in doing so, he wanted her to be the shining example of perfection to all women. In a deeply spiritual sense, all women are called to preserve within their deepest essence, that spiritual virginity for their husbands and for the Lord, just as they are called to motherhood, whether that be physical or spiritual motherhood. A real woman intuitively knows this, and when her husband sees the secret smile of knowing on her face, he can only gaze in wonderment at the secrets stored in her heart.

Scripture tells us that Mary "pondered these things in her heart" (Luke 2:51). That means she treasured the mysteries of God deep within her being and marvelled at them. All women are able to do this. They may not often be able to put the mystery into words because it is so profound, but they are able to let that mystery fill them with life. A man can only stare at the mystery, as something outside of himself. A woman lives it in her very heart. This is spiritual virginity and it truly reveals a woman as God's secret. She is his mystery given to him for his delight, to wonder at, and to explore.

The highest of all vocations for a woman, which at the same time is what makes her fully female, is motherhood. This does not necessarily mean having a child of her own, although that is the usual meaning. It also includes the motherhood of all women to all humanity. That is why Mary was not only the physical mother of Jesus in the fullest sense, but she was also given as mother to the entire world when she stood at the foot of the cross.

While Eve was given to Adam as a helper, woman is not merely a helper to her husband alone but is also a helper to God in the mystery of motherhood. God creates. Woman procreates. The distortion that occurred in the Garden of Eden took place because Eve wanted to become like God and to do her own creating. She wanted to devise her own rules of good and evil. The ultimate tragedy of that disorder is seen in those women of today who not only want to be like God and to create, but who also want to un-create by killing their own babies in the womb. Naturally, fathers who aid and abet in the crime of abortion are equally guilty. A real woman relishes her privilege to procreate, which means to cooperate with God in carrying and giving birth to new souls for God. In welcoming new life within her she says, "Fiat" to God. "Let it be done unto me according to thy word" (Luke 1:38) and to rejoice in it.

It is very important to understand that pregnancy is almost entirely a womanly experience. The father has planted his seed and certainly must now create a safe place for his wife so that she can give herself over completely to the new life growing in her, but he can never be plunged into the experience of pregnancy in the same way as his wife. Once more, he can only stand and stare at the mystery of what she is "pondering in her heart." He can never truly know. She is experiencing a profound change in her body, which is now directing all of its energies to the welfare of the baby. More importantly, she undergoes a transformation in her spirit and in her soul as she touches on the mystery of new life. Her entire being becomes expanded and it pulsates with its God-given purpose, which is to become love itself. Only a woman truly knows this. I can talk about it, but I have to eventually run out of words, because as a man, I do not know and I can never know. As a father, a man can rejoice in his paternity but try as he might, he still stands outside of his wife's profound and total transmutation.

The woman will, like Mary, give birth and she will hold the world in her arms, a living breathing miracle which she and God have given to the human race. Of course it was her husband who lovingly planted the life-giving seed, but there is an emptiness within him as he feels he is on the outside looking in. This is the critical time when he must conquer an urge to be jealous. He may be a proud father but he has to recognize that a bond has been forged between his wife and this child, into which he can never be fully absorbed. For the wife, this is also a critical time. While she rightfully rejoices in this deep bonding with her infant, she must remember that her husband may feel out in the cold. She has to have a heart big enough to reach out to him, to love him, to express her gratitude to him, to include him and to nurture his right to feel like a proud father. After all, he is the father of the miracle in whom she now delights.

Both mother and father must now set about the most important and valuable career in the world, which is to raise their child to be a godly child and ultimately a godly man or woman. Mothering cannot be compared to being a doctor, or a president of a corporation. It is laughable to even try. The future of the world and the future of the Church depends on mothering and fathering. No doubt, doctors and business people are important, but their fruits can never be compared to the fruits of godly parenting.

Even the woman who cannot have children of her own body, either by infertility or because of consecrated virginity in the religious life, must learn to become a mother if she is to be fulfilled. She too is created with the power for love, and so the childless woman can mother children by adoption. Likewise the religious sister can mother countless children by her love, her smile, her womanly understanding, her work, her prayer and the hospitality of her heart. Hospitality of the heart is the mystery of motherhood and motherhood is the supreme sign of what it means to be a woman. We as men should stand in awe and in wonder as we gaze upon the miracle of motherhood in our wives and in other women. It is his wife's motherhood which calls a man to be a real man. Motherhood is the life-blood of the human race and this priceless role has only been given to women. Women are indeed God's masterpiece.

The last, but not the least, of the quartet of womanly mysteries is the quality of trustworthiness. At the Annunciation, God entrusted the Virgin Mary with the care of his only son, Jesus the Messiah. God trusted the woman, who was still a mere human creature, even though she was immaculately conceived, to nurture him in her womb, to be a living monstrance of Jesus-incarnate for nine months. He trusted her to raise that divine and human child in holiness and in wisdom so that she might release him one day to the cross of Calvary. God's trust in her was well placed, as all mankind knows. "From this day, all generations will call me blessed" (Luke 1:48). At the same time he entrusts all of his human children to his human mothers. Each one of us had to trust the mother to whom God entrusted us. As Karl Stern, a great psychiatrist and convert to the Catholic faith observed, "The paradox of being human resides in the fact that, while we are the summit of God's creation, each one of us must, in order to enter this life, pass through a period of utter helplessness and dependence." We must trust our mothers because we are given no alternative. That is why abortion is so horrible a crime, because it utterly destroys the trust that the unborn child must invest in its mother to care for him, to welcome him and to protect him. In killing her child, a woman murders not only her child but murders all that is good in herself. She cannot be entrusted. But a real woman is trustworthy. Her children are entrusted to her in order that she can enable them to entrust themselves to others, initially their father and then ultimately, their eternal Father, God. Because the mother is trustworthy, she can also protect her children from all that is not trustworthy, namely malicious people or bad friends, unsuitable television programs, unholy music, false teaching and occasions of sin.

Satan understood this realm of trust and knew, that if he could distort it in Eve, then Adam would be no problem. So he sowed suspicion in Eve's heart. He directed her trust away from God and towards himself and his own lies. Eve then believed that the serpent was to be more trusted than God and so she ate the apple. Mary, the second Eve, entrusted herself fully to the truth of God and therefore was herself trustworthy. Likewise, if any woman wants to be fully woman, and to rejoice in her total femininity, she too must trust completely in God. In so doing, she also lures her children and her husband into a deeper and deeper trust in God. The entire family then, becomes more and more like the image and likeness of God in which it was made. It becomes akin to Adam and Eve before the fall, ever more pure, and ever more resistant to sin.

The book of Proverbs has a great deal to say about who a real woman is and how she behaves. "The truly capable woman, who can find her? She is far beyond the price of pearls. Her husband's heart has confidence in her, from her he will derive no little profit. Advantage and not hurt she brings him all the days of her life. She selects wool and flax. She does her work with eager hands. She is like those merchant vessels bringing her food from far away. She gets up while it is still dark giving her household their food, giving orders to her serving girls. She sets her mind on a field, then she buys it. With what her hands have earned, she plants a vineyard. She puts her back into her work and shows how strong her arms can be. She knows that her affairs are going well. Her lamp does not go out at night. She sets her hands to the distaff, her fingers grasp the spindle. She holds out her hands to the poor, she opens her arms to the needy. Snow may come, she has no fear for her household, with all her servants warmly clothed. She makes her own quilts, she is dressed in fine linen and purple. Her husband is respected at the city gates, taking his seat among the elders of the land. She weaves materials and sells them, she supplies the merchant with sashes. She is clothed in strength and dignity, she can laugh at the day to come. When she opens her mouth, she does so wisely; on her tongue is kindly instruction. She keeps good watch on the conduct of her household. No bread of idleness for her. Her children stand up and proclaim her blessed, her husband too sings her praises. 'Many women have done admirable things, but you surpass them all.' Charm is deceitful and beauty empty; the woman who fears Yahweh is the one to praise. Give her a share in what her hands have worked for and let her works tell her praises at the city gates" (Prov. 31:10-31).

This is a hymn to womanhood and to what a real woman is all about. It is not too difficult to translate this Old Testament passage into the realities of the modern woman. A woman is capable and priceless to her husband. He has the utmost confidence in her and because of her prudence with the family income, he will find that she can always make ends meet. The good woman works for her husband's advantage because his good name is her good name. She works hard and does it eagerly. She rises early to take care of her loved ones before they go off to work and to school. She decides what would be good for the family and what the family needs. She saves her money out of the budget and then joyfully goes out to purchase it. She is strong in her work, as strong as a man and never shirks it. She takes a deep personal pleasure for herself when things are going well for the family, because she knows that she has played her part in their good fortune. She is generous to those worse off than herself. She always gives to the poor and those in need and does it out of her means, and always with love. She sees to the material needs of her husband and children, making sure she buys the proper clothing for them, the best affordable nutritional food, and the items they need for their work and school. She is creative. She dresses modestly and within her budget. Because of her goodness, her husband is respected in the community. She has strength, dignity and a light heart in the face of the day's worries and challenges. She has control of her tongue. She speaks with wisdom and is always ready to instruct her children with kindness. She is not a gossip or a slanderer. She watches over her loved ones constantly with the concern of a wife and mother. Because of her love, her children cannot help but love her in turn, and they bless her and bless God for her. Her husband is proud of her and is eager to sing her praises to others. Above all she fears God, and since the fear of God is the beginning of wisdom, she is wise in all she does.

Is this too tall an order? Not according to God. It is an ideal, and surely we all fall short of the ideal, but if we do not know what is perfect then we will never know what to strive for. I recommend that both men and women should read Proverbs 31 over and over again. It will lead a woman to understand her own nature more clearly, and it will lead a man to see the beauty in his wife, never take her for granted, and to appreciate the wonderful gift that she is in his life.

So what is a real woman?

A real woman is love.
She loves God, her husband, her children and the whole world.
She is wisdom and she is intuition.
She is a receiver of life and not a contraceptor.
She is a nurturer of life and not an abortionist.
She is trustworthy and not fickle.
She is the heart of the home and not its head.
She is a queen and not a king.
She is a forgiver and not a grudge-bearer.
She loves and never rejects.
She is obedient and deserves obedience.
She is content and not a complainer.
She is gentle and not a tyrant.
She is courageous but never rash.
She is strong but never masculine.
She is sacrificial but never a victim.
She is humble but never a doormat.
Above all she is the mystery and masterpiece of God.

CHAPTER 4

Relationships:
Woman Wounded; Man Maimed

*"Then the eyes of both of
them were opened and they
realized that they were
naked."*

(Gen. 3:7)

As soon as Eve believed the lie of Satan and as soon as Adam believed the lie of Eve, the terrible original sin was committed. From that moment on, Adam and Eve and the entire human race were condemned to a ***sin-nature***. It is very important to understand what it means to have a sin-nature. It means to fall from innocence, and to become twisted and deformed. Before the fruit of the Tree of Life was violated, Adam and Eve were not conscious of any darkness in their relationship with one another. "Now both of them were naked, the man and his wife, but they felt no shame before each other" (Gen. 2:25). When Adam looked at Eve, he felt only delight and wonder at the miracle of her as God's gift. There was no lust in his heart but the great and first sin changed all of that. "Then the eyes of both of them were opened and they realized that they were naked" (Gen. 3:7). This terrible realization of their nakedness not only made them prey to shame and lust, but it also revealed to them their spiritual and psychological nakedness.

Humanity would, from then on, be prone to dark deeds, driven by lust for sex, money, power and things, while all of these excesses would fill the human soul with shame. What a shame that we must suffer shame! Shame is the sword which repeatedly stabs our human hearts and it leads to woman-wounded and man-maimed. Shame is the legacy of the Original Sin.

All men and women are damaged. We are damaged by our very genetic structure, which we inherited from our equally damaged parents who ultimately inherited their characteristics from Adam and Eve. Starting with our genetic distortions, we are then further damaged by life's experiences. We can have negative and frightening experiences in the womb. We are then further damaged by our parents (even by parents who love us and do their very best), our teachers, our relatives and friends and by strangers. And so we adults all have a storehouse of memories of being unloved or put down or used or discounted or scared. Our own sin-nature becomes further distorted by the sins of others and this is the human tragedy.

Give thanks to our loving God who never gave up on us. Praise him for his redemptive action which restores us to our inheritance as sons and daughters and which makes it possible for us to grasp heaven. But, while the Sacrament of Baptism washes us and makes us new creatures in Christ, we are still victims of our sin-nature and it is this which makes our marital relationships so difficult to perfect. It is because we act out of our own hurt, self-centeredness, anger, jealousy, greed, lust and pride that we experience relationship breakdown. We are so blind to this truth that we usually blame our partner for what we ourselves have done.

I remember as a little boy asking my mother how I came to be born and she delighted in telling me that one day she was lying in a hospital bed. Suddenly the window opened and a beautiful little angel flew in to the room. It was a boy angel and he flew up and down the ward till he finally recognized my mother and came and nestled into her arms. She told me how happy she was that the angel had chosen her. The angel was of course me! I loved that story and would ask her to repeat it to me over and over again. Often I would wonder what had happened to my wings and I know I grieved a little over their loss and longed to have them back again so that I could fly.

When I discovered how babies were really born, I was hurt. I "knew" that my mother had lied to me and I felt foolish in being so naive as to believe such a story. How could I ever have believed that I was once an angel? For many years after that, if ever I thought of the angel story, I felt a deep and strange mixture of delight and embarrassment. As a more mature Christian, I am able to re-evaluate my mother's little story, and I realize that she was trying to teach me a truth which she instinctively knew in her soul. She had a simple faith and was much closer to wisdom than I have ever reached with all my book learning. She intended to instill within me the important truth that we all come from God. God creates our immortal soul and human parents cooperate with him in creating the physical body of their child.

There is one fundamental truth upon which we should agree; all of us are born into post-Adam-and-Eve *dysfunctional* families. There is no escape from the perpetuated consequences of original sin, which are sickness, sadness, death and an attraction to sin. Nevertheless, it is still possible for parents to provide a reasonably healthy environment for their children. This should consist of being welcomed into the family and of being loved. It should include cherishing, touching, relationships, warmth, food, protection from harm, permission to explore the environment and to return to safety when it hurts or bites, encouragement in learning and praise for achievements.

Unfortunately for the majority of us, the child is soon disillusioned. We are all too quickly robbed of our birthright. We are neither freely loved, nor perfectly nurtured. We are abandoned, rejected and often increasingly abused by physical violence, emotional violence and sexual violation. Fifty percent of girls and twenty-five percent of boys are sexually abused. We are distorted by broken parents who were raised by broken parents. We find ourselves less and less focussed on our legitimate needs because we must focus on the most fundamental need of all, which is survival at all costs. We all learn different ways to survive and they all usually work for a while. Most of us survive to adulthood, but sooner or later, these same survival techniques will come back to haunt us. Somewhere in our adult lives our grieving, angry, brutalised child will at last break through. What was once Innocence-personified has now become sadly distorted.

There are many different survival techniques which children adopt. Because they know they are being cheated of their birthright, they may become hard of heart, overly timid and compliant, afraid to speak up, over-demanding, chronically depressed, angry, disobedient to authority or chronic complainers. In their teenage years they may also become sinfully involved in sex, drugs, alcohol or crime. Whichever of these dysfunctional survival techniques they embrace, the result will be unhappiness deep within. This is why so many adults, sooner or later, wind up in a therapist's consulting room. Ultimately, the only healing is to recognize that the survival technique is itself a disorder, to take it to the cross of Jesus Christ, renounce it and follow his way of love, forgiveness and peace.

In the light of all this, let us consider woman-wounded and look at how things were meant to be and how they became disfigured. *The Poem of the Man-God* by Maria Valtorta is a novel about the life of Jesus. She puts words into the mouth of the Lord and while these are not to be read as authentic private revelation, nevertheless they provide a penetrating insight into woman's reality. At one point, the women disciples are growing in numbers and Jesus is compelled to give them a teaching on their particular ministry. In the interest of clarity I have paraphrased a little, and so Jesus says: "In the closed religion of Israel, all the shame fell upon women, the origin of sin. In the universal religion of Christ, all that is changed. All the grace was assembled in one woman and she delivered it to the world that it might be redeemed. Woman therefore is no longer the anger of God but the help of God. How great is the necessity of woman near the altar of Christ. The infinite miseries of the world can be cured much more and much better by a woman than by a man ... woman must receive the broken as if they were dear children led astray, who are coming back to their father's house and dare not face their parent. You are the ones who will comfort the sinner and placate the judge.

"Many will come to you seeking God. You will welcome them as if they were tired pilgrims saying, 'This is the house of the Lord, he will be here at once and in the meantime you will envelop them with your love. A woman knows how to love. She was made to love. She might degrade love into sensual lust, but true love, the gem of her soul, is still imprisoned in the depths of her heart, a love made of angel wings, of pure flame and remembrances of God, of its origin from God and its creation by God. Woman is the *masterpiece of goodness* near the *masterpiece of creation* which is man, 'And now I will make Adam a help-mate that he may not feel alone.' Woman must take the faculty of loving and make use of it in the love of Christ and for Christ among her neighbours. She must be charitable to repentant sinners. She should tell them not to be afraid of God. How often a mother's little ones or a sister's young brothers were ill and needed a doctor and they were afraid. But with caresses and loving words, they relieved them of their fear and so, no longer terrified, with their little hands held by the women, they let the doctor cure them. Sinners are your sick brothers and children who are afraid of the Divine Doctor's hand and of his sentence. Since women know how good God is let them tell sinners that God is good and no one must be afraid of him.

"Be sisters and mothers to holy people. They too need love. They will become tired and worn out in evangelising. They will not be able to do all that is to be done. Help them, discreetly and diligently. Women know how to work at home and in everything that is needed for everyday life. The future of the church will be a continuous flow of pilgrims to the places of God. Be their kind hotel-keepers, taking upon yourselves all the most humble work so that the ministers of God may be free to continue the work of the Master. When cruel times come, man is never very strong in suffering. Women instead, as compared to men, enjoy the true kingliness of being able to suffer. Teach men, supporting them in the hours of fear, discouragement, tears, tiredness and bloodshed. Women are heroines of sorrow, the solace of martyrs and martyrs themselves, who can be silent priestesses who will preach God by their way of living and who with no other consecration but the one they received from the God-Love, will be consecrated and worthy of it."

A whole book could be written on these words and the exalted role of women in the eyes of God. However I want to emphasize the very first statement made by Jesus. "In the closed religion of Israel, all the shame fell upon women, the origin of sin. In the universal religion of Christ, all that is changed. All the grace was assembled in one woman and she delivered it to the world that it might be redeemed. Woman therefore is no longer the *anger* of God, but the *help* of God."

This is crucial to a fully Christian understanding of woman. The Old Testament religion viewed woman as the originator of man's downfall and so women were disdained and regarded with fear as though they were constantly primed to lead innocent man into sin. Thus man's control over woman was self-righteously justified. But Mary, the second Eve, has changed all of that. All of the grace, that is to say, Jesus, was assembled in one woman, who was Mary, and she delivered it to the world. Woman was therefore fully redeemed along with man, and ought to have been restored to her rightful place and role in the New Testament religion and indeed the Catholic Church has consistently taught this truth. Unfortunately to this day it is as though woman had never been redeemed, at least in the hearts of many men. Deep down in the male psyche, woman is still looked upon as the first Eve, still preferring the apple to innocence, still the temptress. Man blindly distorts the Genesis story. He continues to believe that he was basically a victim, artfully seduced by scheming woman. He believes that if it had not been for Eve there would have been no Fall. But Scripture makes it abundantly clear that Adam was a full cooperator in Eve's sin. If he had exercised his rightful authority as husband and said, "no" then none of us would be under the curse. Adam was even cowardly enough to blame Eve when he was challenged by God and to this day he continues to blame woman for his woes, and even for his sins. By the same token, Eve could only say, "The devil made me do it" and since in modern times, she has been duped by militant feminism into believing that man is the devil, she continues to say, "The devil made me do it." The stage is therefore set for a deep life-draining wound between the sexes. Man believes he is a victim of the seductive woman. Woman believes she is a victim of the devil-man.

Woman is the gifted mystery of God's loving creation. She does not need to become a priest. She is already the "silent" priestess of new life, just as Mary was the "silent" priestess who brought Jesus to us. She is made for love. She is our love teacher, the human archetype of love, the indispensable repository of the love memories of the race. Destroy her and we destroy love on the face of the earth. We fail her when we do not treasure her for herself, protect her in birth-giving, or provide for her mothering. Only she can teach our children how to love. Do we prostrate ourselves at the altar of God in gratitude and thanksgiving for the gift of such a jewel? Only a man who perceives the truth of the mystery can do so, and he is as rare today as he was yesterday.

Many women today are deeply damaged. If they escape being aborted, they face being rejected, not just because they are human, which is bad enough, but often because they are female. Un-nurtured and un-cherished, they are puzzled and devastated by their parents' broken-ness. Violence is perpetrated upon them. They are sometimes sexually invaded as little children, deeply damaged by the self-hatred of their raging fathers or brothers and undefended by their own mothers, who are so often conspirators of silence. Thus abandoned and violated, they grow into caricatures of womanhood. They become sleepwalkers in a nightmare, smouldering volcanoes of anger, hosts to the devouring worm of self-loathing and worst of all, death-dealing deniers of new life. Abortion is a lot easier for a woman when her precious femininity has been violated as a child. Violence begets violence. The damaged become damagers and so become impervious to love, both in giving it and in receiving it. As a child she craves her father's love, but perceives that somehow she is flawed and not worthy of it. So she goes through life searching endlessly trying to fulfil this deepest of needs. She either punishes herself for her own unworthiness or punishes her father in an endless rejection of all men. She may even embrace the counterfeit love of other women since a pretend love is much better than the terror of emptiness.

Likewise many men, equally flawed, respond by despising the shrew. They are terrorised by the new woman castrator and so they defend themselves by retaliation. They abuse their natural strength by rejecting, despising, using, beating and raping. They dominate and thereby confirm that they are right. They are no longer certain of women. They no longer perceive their male role with clarity.

Instead of offering men one apple, women are shaking the tree and hundreds of apples are falling down about their heads. Men are becoming scared out of their minds, but think it would be unmanly to admit it. We are discovering a new reality today or perhaps resurrecting a very old one, that if we add woman's fear to man's fear, we incarnate Satan's hatred.

Men try to explain away the woman wound with fatuous cliches such as, "It's her hormones." This is a terrible rejection of the female experience. If it is indeed her hormones, then as a doctor, I can tell you there is something very wrong with her hormones. She is ill. Men have no right to opt out of their duty to heal the woman-wound by naively explaining away her pain as merely hormonal. That is a lie to women and an insult to God.

Worse still, when woman is broken, impaled by violence, robbed of her birthright of love, men have no idea how to heal because the onus of loving them back to life falls on them and they are poor lovers. It is much easier to reject her, to dominate her, to call her names like shrew or nag and to abandon her to the coldness and loneliness she feels. But in so doing, men banish themselves into their own painful world of domination, which they use to hide their own terror. Men need to know that if women are wounded then the whole race is wounded.

If woman today is wounded, then man is maimed. He is also a victim. He has been tempted by Eve and found to be willing. Deprived of his birthright, he has also been distorted by his parents and by a society which idolises egoism, pride, impurity, money and power. Trained by playing with war toys, he has learned that might is right. Battle is the only valid arena in which disputes can be settled. Whoever is left standing must have been in the right, regardless of the issue. He has been robbed of his God-given sonship which calls him to grow in peace, strength, courage, gentleness, fortitude, perseverance and work. Instead he has become a grotesque caricature forced to wear a macho mask to conceal his terrifying inner darkness. "I am a man. I must at least pretend to be brave. I must not weep. I must take what I want even if that means taking a woman. I must bludgeon my enemies into submission and that includes any woman who challenges my assumptions. I am angry but it is justified." But how can that be when anger is a sin against justice? "Keep this in mind dear brothers. Let every man be quick to hear, slow to speak and slow to anger. For a man's anger does not fulfil God's justice. Strip away all that is filthy, every vicious excess. Humbly welcome the word that has taken root in you, with its power to save you. Act on this word" (James 1:19-22).

Some men are so threatened by the new aggressive female that they run and run and seek their solace in the arms of other threatened men. Mother damaged and unfathered, they confuse their gender identity and cannibalise other men in a frantic search for their true maleness, which is never to be found. They miss the mystery of Christian life which is to seek their wholeness in the very pain which terrifies them. Sooner or later, they must turn their face to woman, confront their fear and trust in Jesus if they are ever to find lasting peace.

Since secular psychology teaches that all of us must *self-actualise* and realize our full potential without God, then society concludes that it must be morally right to be self-centred. My greatest good, therefore, is to survive, not to love. A man can now justify beating his complaining wife and a woman feels no guilt in crushing her wimpish husband. Today many men despise women for not being women and women despise men for not being men and this is called society. What we call community or civilisation is nothing more than a thin veneer, easily rubbed off. It is predator and prey in an endless after-the-Fall survival of the fittest. Now we must contracept, because new life is too burdensome. We must abort, brutalise and euthanise if we are to survive. We in effect join forces with Satan, to de-create with him, to de-value life, to destroy the good within us. We cry out in our pain, proclaiming our tragedy but we cannot hear the pain of the other over our own din. I have a right to be hurt but you do not. We have forgotten how to father and mother each other. We have lost our compassion for our wounded partner in life because we have not learned how to be other-centred and so we persist in being self-centred.

If healing of this depressing wound is ever to occur, we must all turn to Jesus Christ. He was immersed in this wound when he lived among his fellow humans and he understood it very well. He also offered us the medicine for it and *he is that medicine.* We must stop devouring each other. Men must renounce their brutality and risk the healing of women. Women must give up being victims and stop avenging themselves on men.

The truth will set us free and the truth is that there is no difference in our wounds. They have the same sick root and Satan would like us to believe that it is not so. He cries in triumph, "You can never be reconciled" but God whispers to us, "You are both wounded by lack of love, but I can heal you." This lack of love is a sin and we sin when we blame each other. Man blames woman and becomes a woman-beater, while woman blames man and becomes a man-eater.

The fact is that no man and no woman causes our anger or deserves our disdain. We cause our own anger, we dance with our own disdain and both are sins. We may be distressed, distorted and twisted out of shape, but we are redeemed none-the-less. We lost our paradise by our sin but Jesus proved we can regain it. Since he did all the work, can we not then reclaim our former beauty?

The healing can and must begin. We can restore God's love in our marriage relationships. We must rediscover what it means to be fully woman and what it means to be fully man. Woman-love plus man-love equals God-love. It is in communion that we reflect more brightly the perfection of God's love. We are made in God's image and likeness but if the sexes remain divided, it is only half an image. We both need the complementarity of the other in order to be whole. We may therefore delight in our differences but recognize our fundamental equality as children of God. We modern Christians must affirm that what Jesus promised to the brothers, he also promised to the sisters. We are all entitled to love, respect and education in the fullest sense of these words. If we deny women's right to equal dignity, then we still regard woman as the post-fall seductress, the unredeemed first Eve. Our healing as husband and wife begins when we open our eyes and see woman as the post-resurrection mediatrix of love called forth by Jesus himself and perfectly incarnated in his Blessed Mother. Shall we act as if Jesus was mistaken?

This is not meant to imply that healing is for one or the other of the protagonists. Both sexes need healing. This is not a war, or at least there is no need for it. As long as we see only the enemy in each other we will never heal. If instead, we see the victim, then we can rescue one another from the battlefield. Healing must begin with **both** of us. Feminism is not wrong when it asks for healing, but it becomes terribly disordered when all it does is point the finger at men and remains blind to woman's own need for healing. "Why do you observe the splinter in your brother's eye and never notice the log in your own?" (Matt. 7:3). Healing begins when we all, men and women alike, cry out without shame to each other, "I am broken. I am a distortion of what the good God created. I need you. Could you not also need me? Let us hold each other in the dark and call upon the Lord." Man must rush into the arms of the broken woman and beg for comfort. Woman must lovingly melt her heart and joyfully receive the broken man. You comfort me and I will treasure you. God's life can then be re-kindled as it becomes re-incarnated in the re-union of male and female.

The real soul-healing takes place when we rival each other in the service of each other. Serve and you will be served. Serve and marriage will be restored no matter how distorted it may have become.

There are seven basic steps to the healing of marriage relationships.

1. Open your eyes to the miracle of yourself. You are totally and passionately loved by God. Love what God loves. If you do not, you reject his gift.
2. Open your eyes and see in your spouse a miracle of creation. The one with whom you fight so much is totally and passionately loved by God. Love what God loves. He or she is not an enemy but a fellow victim of original sin. Compassion is called for, not criticism.
3. Pray out your anger and self-loathing. Own it. Do not justify it by blaming the skeletons in your mental cupboard; mother, father, all men or all women. This is a cop-out. Reclaim your gift of free will. You are free to choose to refuse to be angry with your spouse. You are free to choose to refuse to abuse your spouse. This is the message of Jesus. He affirms our free will. My spouse does not make me angry. I choose it. Rediscover and rejoice in your freedom to do otherwise.

4. Have some one pray over you and over you and over you. We all desperately need prayer and it is good and powerful to have other Christians lay on hands and beg God to heal our marriage wounds.

5. Listen to the pain of others. Set your own pain aside for a time and enter into the heart of your neighbour. His or her pain is just as real. This activity brings you out of your own suffering and helps you to appreciate the suffering of the other. It stimulates compassion, empathy and identification. If the other's pain only causes impatience or scorn within you, then you are not listening. You do not have to offer fatuous advice. In a sense you only have to hold the other and soothe him or her by your attentive presence. Let what little strength you possess flow out and strengthen the one who is weak. Remember, it will be the other way around when it is your turn to feel weak. Strangely enough, when we do forget self by loving our brother or sister, our own pain becomes easier to bear.

6. Fearlessly proclaim your needs but without self-pity. If you are healing the other with love, the other will heal you. So take the risk and tell of your needs, give the other an opportunity to hear your pain and to perhaps meet those needs. Pain is pain. Hurt is hurt. You have every right to grieve, so comfort each other, hold each other, rock and cradle each other. You are all treasures of God, so treasure each other. Tell woman it is holy to be feminine, tell man it is holy to be masculine, but let us return to God's truth about what feminine and masculine are supposed to be.

7. Finally, there is no wholeness without holiness. Jesus knew that. But holiness is a lonely climb if we try it alone. Man, take woman by the hand and together climb the mountain. If you climb separately, then when you fall, no one can hold on to you. But, roped together, you can stop the fall and regain your foothold. Paradise awaits you but you need not suffer hell on earth. The good news is that for us Catholics, we are not cast adrift without help. Jesus is in the boat with us, waiting to rush to our aid in the storm. If we call out to him, he will rise up and command the wind and the waves to be still. We

have the Sacraments and the Sacrifice of the Mass by which we can confidently ask Jesus to enrich us with his grace. As St. Paul tells us, it is in our own flawed human weakness that we find the very strength of God. By grace and with Jesus we can defeat our failings and rise ever higher towards that perfection which God the Father intended for us. Surely we are deformed by sin, but Jesus can unravel that deformity for us if only we say, 'Fiat' to his will.

This chapter has focussed on the wound of our nature as male and female beings. The next chapter will look at those mental and emotional characteristics which mark out the differences between men and women. It will also help, not only to know what the differences are, but also to understand one another in joy instead of frustration. We *can* live in happiness with each other because we are followers of Jesus Christ who conquered sin and death. In restoring us to our inheritance as sons and daughters of God, he is able and eager to give us all the help we need to be revived as an image and likeness of God.

CHAPTER 5

Relationships: The Difference Makes all the Difference

"The husband must give to his wife what she has a right to expect, and so too the wife to her husband."

(1 Cor. 7:3)

It is self-evident that men and women are different. They are different physically, which is obvious, but they are also different psychologically, emotionally, socially and spiritually. This is simply a scientific fact verifiable by observation. Numerous psychologists have grappled with the problem of describing these differences in an orderly way but while they may often disagree with one another about the nature of these, they have always agreed that indeed men and women are very different. This may seem like flogging a dead horse since most of us know deep down that male and female are not identical, but there is a distorted faction in our time which is trying to eliminate gender altogether by moving towards an **androgynous** society, that is to say, a willful and distorted attempt to eliminate our unique sexual nature in order to create one sex out of the two. This usurps and denies God's holy intention when he created both male and female. Such people deliberately dress in such a way as to make it difficult to distinguish men from women and of course the end-point of their disorder is that they come to condone bisexual acts. But our escape from the battle of the sexes will never be found by eliminating our gender differences. It can only be regained by accepting our God-given sexual nature as male and female and rejoicing in it.

Let it be abundantly made clear that God decreed the differences and these are life-giving and good. As pointed out in chapter 3, God laid down our male and female characteristics in our very brains. Men find it easier to follow the left brain, given that it is neurologically difficult for them to access the right half of the brain. Women are comfortable using both sides of the brain and this simple anatomical fact helps us to understand one another's unique approach to life. The separate characteristics of male and female are therefore *genetic* in nature.

This genetic diversity between the sexes is then further entrenched by parents and by society. Boys and girls are socialised differently, with the result that they tend to think, feel, act and interact, play and pray differently. Unfortunately, men and women who fail to appreciate or understand these natural features react to one another, thereby provoking unnecessary fights and arguments. Those who do understand make allowances for their spouse, eliminate their adversarial attitudes and are less likely to fall into fighting. As any couple will admit, fighting resolves nothing and always leads to hurt feelings whereby love is eroded. Christians should do everything to avoid bitter wrangling, because both husband and wife adopt a stance of self-righteousness, a self-centred belief that their opinion is right, a determination to prove that the other is wrong and therefore stupid. It always includes criticism and judgement of the other, which is directly opposed to the commandments of Jesus Christ. "Love your enemies, do good to those who hate you, bless those who curse you, pray for those who treat you badly" (Luke 6:27). "Do not judge and you will not be judged because the judgements you give are the judgements you will get and the standard you use will be the standard used for you" (Matt. 7:1-2). How many Catholic couples believe in their faith and yet make a mockery of it by fighting with one another and telling themselves that it is not sinful? If I have a vicious, no-holds-barred fight with my wife, I am violating the woman who is a temple of the Holy Spirit and who has been given to me by God as pure gift. That is a sin for which I should rush to Confession.

There are many ways to help couples give up this disordered behaviour and not all of these can be covered in this book. Perhaps the most helpful strategy is to bring the reader to an understanding of why a spouse thinks and speaks in the way that he or she does. Montaigne, a French philosopher, once wrote, "To understand all is to forgive all." Understanding then, is the key to marital peace and harmony. Once we understand, it becomes easier to forgive. To achieve this new vision of each other, I have borrowed heavily from the work of Deborah Tannen, *You Just Don't Understand Me,* and the classic work of John Gray, *Men are from Mars, Women are from Venus,* Both of these books are straightforward, easy to read, very informative and for the most part are "easily baptised" into a Christian view of who we are.

This is not to imply that this is the only valid way to describe male/female differences. It is also important to understand that such attempts can only be generalisations at best. Every human being is unique and so the following observations can never be true of every man or every woman. Nevertheless, they can help us towards a better understanding and appreciation of ourselves as male and female.

The fundamental cause of strife between a husband and a wife is the fact that a man assumes his wife should think like him while she believes that he should think like her. Since both do not think alike, this illogical belief makes discord inevitable. The fact is, as Dr. Gray asserts, men and women might as well come from different planets. Each has his or her own reality, and each sees the world in a different way. More importantly, each has a different objective in relating to others. The world is not the same for men as it is for women. But just because they see reality differently, this does not mean that one is right and the other is wrong. Both are in their own way right. It is in accepting each other's separate realities that harmony is to be found. It is arrogant to assume that my reality is the only valid reality.

First of all, a man tends to be concerned about his *status* when he is interacting with others. He is constantly evaluating the pecking order and will do almost anything to avoid feeling inferior to someone else, especially a woman. He will always try to have the upper hand, not because he desires to crush another person, but simply because he hates to feel or to be perceived as inadequate. That is why he is driven to competition, power and success. He may not understand that, he may not even want to understand that, but it is true nonetheless.

A woman has very little interest in status. She desires *intimacy*. For her, connectedness and closeness bring inner feelings of warmth and security. The psychologists who have verified these truths are merely confirming the prophecy of Yahweh who said, "You will *yearn* for your husband and he will *dominate* you" (Gen. 3:16). Man therefore is driven by the need for independence while woman is driven by the need for intimacy.

This was perfectly demonstrated by my own experience. Some years ago, my wife and I were driving for the first time through the city of Barcelona in Spain. Neither of us spoke Spanish and so we could not understand many of the road signs. I was driving. I got lost, of course, and we found ourselves back in the city centre. I tried again and once more we were back in the centre. My wife pleasantly suggested we stop and ask for directions. I boorishly ignored that suggestion and kept on driving. Eventually, I was heading deeper and deeper into the suburbs of Barcelona, thoroughly lost, but the last thing I was going to do was stop and ask. My wife was by now very upset that I would not do the thing which was logical to her and ask a passerby for help. I became more upset with her, and before long we were into the inevitable shouting match. By now we were getting low on gasoline, but I was determined to find the airport under my own steam and at all costs. No pleading from my wife would make me pull over and ask a passerby. I did manage to find the airport in the end, but the next morning while apologising to my wife for my behaviour, I was really struggling with how I could have been so stupid and stubborn. I did not understand at the time the dynamics of that experience, but I do now, and my wife and I chuckle at it to this day.

As a man, I found it repugnant to ask for directions from anyone because that would have automatically placed me in an inferior position. I would have been the ignorant one needing help from someone who knew what I did not. Therefore, rather than accept the simple truth, I was unconsciously and irrationally willing to drive all night rather than lose status. For my wife, it was an entirely different situation. Since status is not important to her, she would have cheerfully stopped to ask the way and would have enjoyed it, because she could thereby connect with a stranger and feel warm feelings of gratitude for his or her help. Now that I understand this, I have learned not to feel so threatened by asking for advice. But I did have to work at it and I still get a vague feeling of discomfort when I do. I am certain that if my wife had been driving, we would have reached the airport a lot sooner. Needless to say, my wife loves to tell that story around the dinner table.

Since a man is driven by a need to be independent, he will often make arrangements without consulting his wife. He believes he is being generous when he announces the big surprise that he has purchased tickets for a show. He wants to delight her and to feel strong in his decision. She however is hurt and this deeply puzzles him. She would never dream of doing such a thing, not because she needs her husband's permission, but because she wants to feel united and close to him as they make plans together. She wants him to share in her excitement. Because of his independent decision, she feels left out.

A man likes to make his own decisions while a woman prefers consensus. Since a man is a being of action and needs to *act,* he feels trapped by lengthy discussions, especially on what he considers trivial matters. When his wife says "What do you think?" he assumes he is being asked to decide. He fails to understand that what she wants is a cosy intimate interaction. He prefers to believe "We are separate and different." She wants to believe "We are close and the same." He prefers to act. She prefers to interact.

Women generally want to do what is asked of them. Men will reflexively resist when they feel they are being told what to do. That is why army officers feel they must train soldiers by physical exhaustion and by humiliation in order to break their independent spirit, so they will automatically obey an order in battle. If a man offers to help a woman, she will gratefully accept. If a woman offers to help a man, his first impulse is to refuse because it makes him feel inferior. For her, she is saying "I want to be close to you and in helping you I feel connected." He does not hear that at all.

When she tries to help him he hears "You need my help because I am more competent than you."

A woman who displays a need for intimacy is easily misunderstood by the man who is only seeing the world through the eye-glasses of status. He sees her as insecure and incompetent, while she sees him as unfeeling and distant. This is not to say that men only want self-determination and women only want interdependence, but it is a matter of degree.

It is very informative to watch children at play. Boys tend to play in large groups which are structured according to status. They constantly brag about their skills and bravery. They usually have a leader and their games have winners and losers. In my own group, I was the leader. I was Robin Hood and the others were Little John, Will Scarlet, Friar Tuck and Allan-a-dale, and we always thoroughly defeated the evil sheriff of Nottingham. But while I was flattered to be the leader, I was secretly uneasy inside because I had to give orders and the orders always had to be right. A woman would do well to understand, that in spite of her husband's need to appear strong, independent and resourceful, he is probably very scared deep down. He lives in fear of being exposed as incompetent or cowardly. She should never let him suspect that she knows the awful truth behind his mask.

Girls play very differently. They tend to play in small groups or in pairs. The key to their activities is intimacy. Everybody gets a turn and there are no winners or losers. Girls do not boast of their talents. They do not give orders but prefer to make suggestions and to listen to the suggestions of others.

As might be expected, boys are more competitive in play while girls are more cooperative.

There is a funny story, told by men of course, which relates that if a dinner guest asks a man "Where did you get the beef?" the man will say "at the supermarket." If he asks the woman, she may say "Why? Don't you like it?" The story is meant to be a humorous put down to women. But there is a beautiful truth hidden in it. For the man, he felt superior in being asked a question and so he was able to give a straight forward answer. The woman however was motivated by her desire to please her guest, and so she asked a perfectly reasonable question in return. She needed to know if the beef was to his satisfaction because it was important to her that he enjoy his meal.

The difference between men and women is poignantly illustrated by the following interactions, first between two women, and then between one of the women and her husband.

1. **Woman:** "I feel violated by my breast surgery."
   Woman friend: "I know just how you feel. I would feel less of a woman if that happened to me. In fact that is just how I felt when I had my hysterectomy."

2. **Wife:** "I feel violated by my breast surgery."
   Husband: "Its no problem honey. You can have a surgical implant and no one will know the difference."
   Wife: "So you don't like the way I look anymore."

In the first encounter, the two women were exercising their need for connection. When the woman expressed her devastation, the friend immediately accepted her feelings and tried to connect by sharing a similar experience. In the second encounter, the man equally felt his wife's devastation but he blew it by trying to fix it. His wife interpreted that as a rejection of her post-surgical appearance. She was hurt and he was puzzled.

This desire to be a fixer gets men into a lot of trouble with their wives. If a woman says "I feel depressed" her husband will jump to the wrong conclusion and assume that he is being asked to fix her depression. He will then reel off five solutions. This is the last thing she wants. In fact she feels rejected by his response. What she is asking for is that he understand and accept her feelings and perhaps give her a reassuring hug. She just wants to connect. A woman appreciates a man who can fix mechanical things but she resents him trying to fix her feelings.

This works two ways. If a man says to his wife, "I feel depressed" she will in her desire to show solidarity with him, say something like, "Oh, I know just how you feel. I was depressed last week." Now he is the one who feels hurt. He thinks she is trivialising his real feelings by comparing his experience with hers. What he really wants from her is encouragement, to be assured that he is still a man and not a weakling. He may even want a little mothering but he does not want what he perceives to be condescension. Strangely enough, he is hoping she might be able to *fix him.* It is an interesting thing that men give to women what they themselves would like to receive and vice-versa.

There was a marriage counsellor who was helping an elderly couple who, after many years of happy marriage, were now fighting constantly. After a few sessions, he was still puzzled by their bickering. In desperation, he asked Joe if there was anything which Sarah did which really annoyed him. He said, "Oh yes. Whenever I am sick in bed she insists on bringing me hot sweet tea. I hate hot sweet tea." Sarah then jumped in and said, "Well, while we are on that subject, whenever I am sick, he always gives me hot lemon and I hate hot lemon." The counsellor was stumped for a while and then in a moment of inspiration, he said, "Joe, when you were a little boy, what did your mother give you anytime you were sick?" Joe instantly replied, "Oh she always brought me hot lemon. It made me feel loved." Needless to say, when Sarah was asked the same question she reported that her mother always gave her hot sweet tea. The problem was solved. Joe loved Sarah and so gave her what made *him* feel good. Sarah loved Joe and gave him what made *her* feel good. But that never works. Joe and Sarah wanted to express care and concern for one another but they did it by giving what the giver would like, not what the receiver would like. Once this was pointed out to them by the counsellor, they were delighted with this new insight and put it into practice. The answer is always to find out what your spouse would like and give it generously, even if you yourself would hate it.

Many men object that women want to talk endlessly about their problems. Men prefer to deal with issues quickly, forget them and move on. A woman cannot quite do that. She needs to "ponder these things in her heart," to talk them out before bringing them to closure. For example, a man could insult his wife vehemently in the evening, then get up in the morning, give her a big kiss and cheerfully go out to work. She is stunned. "How could he just walk out of here as though nothing had happened last night?" He has put it out of his mind and for him it is over. For her it is not nearly over and she needs to talk about it. If she tries to do this, he reacts by accusing her of refusing to forgive and forget.

A woman, on the other hand, will often be heard complaining that her husband does not talk enough. She cannot understand why she has to do all the talking at home, yet when they are somewhere else, he is the life and soul of the party. The truth is that men and women both do plenty of talking but talking serves a different purpose for them. Men talk more at meetings, in groups or in classrooms. At a meeting is it not always a man who asks the first question? He enjoys relaying factual information in order to preserve his status and to show off his knowledge and skill. She talks to achieve rapport with others and so she prefers to talk in an intimate setting. He, on the other hand, prefers pontificating in large groups. He is a public speaker. She is a private speaker. As a result, men are uncomfortable with intimate talk at home and they find "small talk" unworthy of their attention. Men often do not know what women want and women often cannot understand why men find it so difficult to know what women want.

The classic scenario is the breakfast table where the husband is hidden behind a newspaper while the wife, who would like to talk, share and feel close, is staring at her non-present spouse. She may indeed talk, but all she gets is a disembodied "Humph" now and then. She feels he is not there at all and worse still she feels discounted. In fact, she feels the need to talk even more than usual when he is deep in his newspaper, precisely because of this sense of being invisible. She does not understand his need to withdraw while he does not understand her need to relate. I remember a very funny cartoon where a couple are at the breakfast table. He is holding up a newspaper so his wife cannot even see his face. She is clutching a set of bag-pipes and she says, "Bob, marriage is about communication and I am about to communicate!" This poor woman is going to try anything to get his attention.

Dr. Gray touches very well on this theme when he writes about how men and women deal with problems. When troubled, the man will go off "into his cave." He will disengage and withdraw to think out the problem alone. Not until he has decided on a solution or a course of action will he re-emerge from the cave and rejoin his wife.

She is often hurt by this, but if she understood that this behaviour is not an insult but a male strategy which he needs to indulge in, then she would be more likely to give him his space, knowing he will eventually come back. It is his way of solving his problem.

A woman rarely goes into her cave. Instead, she handles a problem by talking about it and so she needs someone to talk to, usually her husband. It is by talking around the problem and coming at it from a variety of directions that she brings it to resolution. If the husband does not understand this, then he will think it is stupid to go on and on about an issue (because it is not his way and therefore must be wrong). If he learns that this is a woman's problem-solving technique, then he will more likely be prepared to sit down with his wife, listen to her and allow her to give voice to her thoughts and her feelings. It is not that she needs any response from him, other than acceptance. She really only needs to hear her own thoughts out loud. Verbalising for her is a way of organising the problem. The solution is really not very difficult. A wife needs to respect her husband's need to go into his cave. He needs to respect his wife's need to be heard. Couples who take this advice to heart find that they greatly reduce the number of their arguments and have a lot more time left over to enjoy one another.

Men often complain that their wives rake up the past. As soon as they get into a disagreement, she will then bring up incidents from out of the dim and distant past, incidents long forgotten by him. He feels this is unfair and he is hurt that she has clearly not forgotten or let go of his past sins. But he is again misinterpreting what is going on in her mind. She is simply taking the opportunity of a particular offense, occurring in the present, to point out a wider pattern of his general behaviour by relating it to past examples. She deeply desires him to see the pattern clearly so that he can begin to work against it. It is not that she has not forgiven. For her it is a way of asking him to change an undesirable habit. Meanwhile, he can see no point in digging up a corpse to see if it is still dead. Again, if he can understand this strategy, he will be less likely to react, and by listening, may hear what he needs to hear about his way of behaving.

Women accuse men of not looking at them when they talk. This is not really an avoidance strategy on his part. It makes good sense to him. He avoids eye-contact because with another man, it could look like an aggressive challenge. He avoids it with a woman because it could be interpreted as flirting. In avoiding eye contact, he is expressing a desire for friendship.

When a woman sees her husband performing a task, it is the most natural thing in the world for her to offer to help. She is again expressing a desire to cooperate with him, to feel close and to make things easier for him. She may in her eagerness even jump in and take over, because she thinks her's is a better way of doing the task. Her intentions are admirable, but he is more likely to react by feeling utterly incompetent and inadequate. He wants to feel strong and independent and sees her offer of help as a put down.

Much of the misfiring of communication between spouses boils down to the use of language. A man is very literal in his interpretation of what is said to him. He hears the words being used and takes them at their face value. After all, that is how he thinks he speaks. A woman however, uses language in a very different way. There is meaning behind her words that is never immediately obvious to a man, although it always is to another woman. Therefore men and women need to learn how to interpret "man-ese" and "woman-ese" if they are ever to understand one another. They must learn each other's "gender-speak." After all, they do come from different planets!

The mistake we all make is in thinking that there is only one way to think (my way), one way to talk (my way), or one way to listen (my way). Nothing hurts more than to be told your intentions were bad when you know they were good, or being told you are doing something wrong when you are just doing it your way.

Dr. Gray's book covers this language problem very well, but I will give a few examples by way of illustration, together with some of my own.

Women like to use the words "never" or "always" and "should." Men take it literally and so they get it all wrong.

Mistranslation

Wife:	"We never go out."
Husband:	"That's not true. We went out last Wednesday. How can you lie like that?"

Wife:	"No one ever listens to me."
Husband:	"That's stupid. I listen."
Wife:	"I always feel tired these days."
Husband:	"You were full of beans at the Joneses on Sunday. I just don't understand how you can exaggerate like that."
Wife:	"You never give me flowers."
Husband:	"I bought you a new coat a month ago. Would you rather have flowers than a coat?"
Wife:	"You should do it this way."
Husband:	"You're saying I am incompetent."

If he had studied gender-speak, he would have heard something very different:

Translation

Wife:	"We never go out."
Translation:	"I'm feeling overwhelmed. I wish we could go out together and just be relaxed and close."
Wife:	"No one ever listens to me."
Translation:	"I feel un-cherished and discounted. Please be there for me right now."
Wife:	"I always feel tired these days."
Translation:	"I am emotionally drained. Just accept my feelings and do not judge me. Give me your strength."
Wife:	"You never give me flowers."
Translation:	"I feel unloved and lonely. I need a big warm hug."
Wife:	"You should do it this way."
Translation:	"I want to help. If you let me, I'll feel nice and close to you."

When a man learns "woman-ese" he finds it much easier to respond by understanding her needs and meeting those needs. He really does enjoy giving his wife what she wants because it makes him feel needed. The problem arises when he does not know what she wants. That scares him to death. It works the other way around too.

Mistranslation

Husband:	"I hate my job."
Wife:	"Oh no! If he quits, how will we survive?"
Husband:	"That makes me angry."
Wife:	"It's not my fault you are angry."
Husband:	"I'm too tired right now."
Wife:	"I know just how you feel. I get tired too."
Husband:	"It's nothing."
Wife:	"Yes, it is. Something is bothering you. Tell me what it is."

What did he really intend to convey?

Translation

Husband:	"I hate my job."
Translation:	"Sometimes I feel inadequate as a man. I need you to build me up."
Husband:	"That makes me angry."
Translation:	"I'm scared of my anger. Please don't provoke me."
Husband:	"I'm too tired right now."
Translation:	"I have things on my mind. Could you let me be alone for a while till I figure them out?"
Husband:	"It's nothing."
Translation:	"I'm in my cave. Don't follow me in there. I can handle it by myself."

A man is not as intimately aware of his emotional life as a woman is, except when it comes to anger or fear and so he is uncomfortable when his wife wants him to talk about his inner being. So when she asks, "What are you thinking?" he usually says, "I don't know." This may well be the truth for him. He feels that his passing thoughts are not worthy of mention. She, on the other hand, values all of her thoughts and likes to share them in closeness with her husband. She verbalises thoughts. He filters his. If she has negative thoughts about her husband she will tell him, assuming that he will not be hurt and that it will help him to change. He rarely tells her his negative thoughts about her (unless he is angry) because he does not want to be a bully and hurt her. Paradoxically his silence hurts her more.

The aforementioned differences do not reflect a *communication problem,* which these days has become the big excuse for couples to separate and give up on each other. They are merely signs of a different *communication style.* It is easily resolved once each spouse learns to translate the language. Why should I assume that my spouse is out to destroy me or to score points at my expense? It is far more logical to believe that he or she wants to be happy and that my spouse wants me to be happy also. My spouse may fumble it from time to time but he or she usually means well. I fumble it too and I *know* that I mean well.

The Bible book of *Jesu ben Sirach* (or *Ecclesiasticus*) instructs married couples how to interpret the Word of God in regard to relationships. "A man with no understanding has vain and false hopes" (Sir. 34:1). Such a man not only does not understand the things of God but he will also not understand his wife. He has "vain and false hopes," which means he will foolishly have expectations of her which she cannot meet, and because he does not understand her language, he will be hurt by her words.

"Blessed the soul of the man who fears the Lord.... He lifts up the soul and gives light to the eyes; he grants healing, life and blessing" (Sir. 34:15 and 17). A man who fears the Lord has the right disposition and so is inspired by grace to bring healing to his wife's hurts, to give her life (which is love) and to bless her in all she does. "He who acquires a wife gets his best possession, a helper fit for him and a pillar of support" (Sir. 36:24). A man's wife is his supreme boast. God gives him a "helper" fit for him, and so he must see her as a specially chosen gift from God himself. If he treats her as a treasured gift, then she will always lovingly support him and he deeply needs her support to boost his sense of manhood. "If kindness and humility mark her speech, her husband is not like other men" (Sir. 36:23). This speaks to the amazing power of a good wife to bring out the very best in her husband. By her kindness, her womanly humility and her way of speaking, she helps him to feel like a man, to feel strong and to interact with confidence in the workplace and elsewhere outside of the home.

Once we open our eyes and our ears to the separate reality of our spouse, once we realize that he or she does not think, feel, speak or act in the way we do, then the light bulb can go on. We quickly begin to come to a new understanding of one another and to a new appreciation of one another. This is a whole new level of loving. It is a deepening of the love we felt in courtship. It is a post-honeymoon awakening of the soul which now becomes the major player in our love interaction. When the soul is now in love with the soul of our spouse, we enjoy a love that cannot die. The roots of love now run deep and in turn nourish us as a covenant couple free from competition, free from the need to manoeuvre or to outsmart or play games. We are free to grow in spirit because we are immersed in a confident love. We can joyfully accept the differences between us, because the difference makes *all* the difference.

CHAPTER 6

Troubled Marriages:
From Conflict to Communion

*"Where do these wars and
battles between yourselves
first start? Is it not
precisely in the desires
fighting in your own selves?"*
(Jas. 4:1)

In the Scripture passage quoted above, the apostle James goes right to the heart of the matter. Conflicts and battles in a marriage really begin in our own hearts. As victims of a sin-nature we tend to be blind to our own sins and at the same time we are driven to blame our spouse or anyone else for our own bad behaviour. Therefore if I am yelling in a rage, it is only because my spouse "made me angry." If I seek illicit sexual gratification in the arms of another person, it is because my spouse "does not love me." If I am cold and withdrawn, it is because my spouse "does not understand me." On the other hand, if my spouse is angry with me then he or she is at fault for giving in to sinful anger against innocent me. If my spouse is unfaithful, how could I ever forgive such a betrayal? If my spouse is cold and withdrawn, there must be something wrong with him or her since I have done nothing wrong. Therefore if I am behaving badly, it is my spouse's fault. If my spouse is behaving badly it is also my spouse's fault.

This flawed mind-set is a prescription for conflict. It is founded upon a self-centred and disordered ego which is blind to its own defects and only too willing to allot blame to others (chapter 4). The Christian life calls us to renounce this unholy attitude, to examine and root out our own personal flaws and to respond to our spouse with understanding and compassion. A real Christian acknowledges and faces up to his sinful tendencies and repents of them. If anger is a problem, he works against it. If he has to struggle with lust or disordered sexuality he prays about it and engages his free will in the fight to overcome it. If he is cold and withdrawn, he can choose to become warm and loving.

So many of us justify bad behaviour by telling ourselves, "I can't help it." This is a lie which denies our free will, the very gift given to us by God, by which we either choose heaven or choose hell. To convince ourselves that we do not have free will does not make free will disappear. Even if we distort our intelligence to the point of being convinced that we can't help it, God will not be convinced. A fool can fool himself but never God.

Conflicts in marriage are therefore a serious risk if only by the fact that we are sinful by nature. But they also occur for several other powerful reasons. Men and women think and act differently. These differences lead to misinterpretations and misunderstandings which so often propel us into conflict. Another reason for arguments is that we too easily give in to our negative feelings. Thus, when our spouse is behaving in a non-loving way, we find ourselves experiencing hurt, rejection, failure, sadness or anger. If we allow these feelings to dominate our thinking, then we will act out of these feelings and in turn justify our own non-loving behaviour. Again, Jesus calls us to rise above our feelings, not to allow them to dominate our will and to continue loving no matter what. Surely Jesus was the perfect example of how to do that. If he had acted upon his feelings in the Garden of Gethsemane, he would have abandoned the painful work of redemption. If we act on our negative feelings then we will abandon the work of loving our spouse. True love stands on its own. It is not dependent on whether my spouse loves me back. Even if my spouse does not love me, I will still love. Anything less than that is conditional, and sends the message that "I will love you only so long as you love me."

A major cause of marital conflict is that somewhere after the bliss of the honeymoon, the partners come face to face with each other's flaws. The flaws were always there of course, but infatuation had blinded them. Now they are coming to the forefront and have to be dealt with. This is a very precarious time in a marriage and can lead to the destructive habit of "weather proofing" the relationship. The truth is that Christian love overlooks the flaws in my spouse rather than focussing on them. Weather-proofing is an arrogant attempt to change my spouse into the perfect fantasy in my mind of what a spouse should be, and that is a dangerous illusion. Love on the other hand accepts the other as he or she is, "warts and all!" Love is grateful to God for the priceless gift of the other and rejoices in the gift. Certainly I can lovingly provide the encouragement and the environment by which my spouse can grow, even to overcoming his or her weaknesses and defects, but I must not judge or demand. "Judge not that you may not be judged" (Matt. 7:1). Judging and criticising are not my God-given rights. In fact, it is sinful because only God has the right to judge. When I judge I am telling my spouse that I am a superior being and that he or she is not good enough for me. Husband and wife are equal partners, equal in dignity and equal before God.

A major stumbling block to peace in a marriage is the sudden, awful realization that my spouse cannot meet all of my needs all of the time. If, on my wedding day, I laboured under that naive illusion then I am in for a rude awakening.

My spouse is not my perfect fantasy and I have to undergo a reality check sooner or later. No human being can meet all of my needs, ever. We spouses are all finite beings struggling with our own baggage and now we are challenged to struggle with the baggage of our spouse as well. Not only are we male and female and therefore conditioned differently, but we come from two totally different family backgrounds and experiences. Now we expect to come together and create a harmonious and peaceful new family as though that should be automatic and effortless. It is more like trying to mix oil and water. Marriage is a sacrament, which means that it needs sanctifying grace in abundance for it to succeed in uniting two strangers in harmony. Human effort alone will never be sufficient.

It is bad enough that I must come to the realization that my spouse cannot meet all of my needs, but it is even more alarming to realize that perhaps my spouse also expects *me* to meet all of his or her needs. Broken marriages are littered with unrealistic expectations. So many immature persons get married and expect impossible perfection from the other. When the spouse turns out to be a poor flawed human creature just like them, they react with disproportionate anger or hurt or resentment. *Our spouse is not God.* Only God is God. We therefore do well to put our expectations of perfection onto God, who alone is perfect, and accept our spouse as merely human.

It is true that the badge of real love is self-denial and self-sacrifice for the other. Without this willingness to die for the other, it can hardly be called love at all. "Love one another as I have loved you" (John 15:12). But that does not mean that one can ever hope to meet all of another's needs. It simply means that one gives oneself completely and hopes that it will be enough. What more can a human lover do? This gift of self should be accepted graciously by the other and cherished as any other priceless treasure. I cannot give one ounce more than my complete self.

Many of us foster conflict by presuming malice in whatever our spouse does. In other words, if my spouse is critical, complaining, cold, demanding or childish, then it must be because he or she is out to get me. He or she cannot wish me well and so is deliberately trying to wound me. This is almost always not true. If my spouse is behaving in this way then he or she is feeling insecure and maybe even unloved. Insecurity leads to low moods and a low mood causes us to lose our warm feelings. It makes us lose our bearings and so we likely fall into habitual behaviour which, at first glance, is ugly and destructive. But it is really a cry for love. It is an appeal for us to respond, not with rejection, scorn or criticism, for that only engages us in battle, but with compassion for and understanding of our spouse's insecurity.

If we claim to love then we should be sensitive to our spouse's low moods and be eager to help him or her recover. Recovery will never take place if we try to talk the other out of the low mood or if we try to cheer him or her up. Humour in this situation only trivialises the other's low mood. Perfectly good logic appears to be totally illogical to the victim of the low mood. If I am in a low mood and my spouse tries to reason with me it will not work. In a low mood, I am no longer in touch with logic or reason. I am the victim of my own distorted thoughts and I cannot see reality for what it is. The only effective response is compassion. Compassion does not judge the other, it accepts the other's temporary low mood and it wraps the other in serenity, thereby promoting security. As one's spouse begins to feel more secure, his or her mood begins to rise and will once more break out into the sunlight where thoughts and feelings are once more logical, objective and warm.

Meanwhile how should we react to our spouse when he or she is in a low mood? Believe it or not, it is surprisingly simple. If the reader will take the following strategy to heart and put it into practice then I guarantee that arguments and conflicts will practically disappear.

Some years ago, I realised that I was often caught up in mind-games with my wife. I always had to guess whether she was in a low mood or not, just as she had to somehow read my mind and decide if I was in a low mood or not. Sooner or later our low moods would become obvious, because we were indulging in destructive behaviour, but even then I had no idea as to how to react, nor did my wife. I could also see that once we were expressing our low moods in a negative way, the damage was done and more difficult to recover from. There had to be a way to catch the problem and contain it *before* it became a source of argument. So one day, I shared my thoughts with my wife. Naturally, I chose to do this when we were both in a high mood. This was important because it is always easy to know when your spouse is in a high mood and it is only in a high mood that we are objective, logical, gracious to each other and willing to make things even better. It is only when we are in a high mood that we can have an intelligent and productive conversation. I asked her if she would be willing to tell me that she was in a low mood as soon as she was aware of it. She agreed and of course I also undertook to tell her when I was in a low mood. Now we would no longer have to guess at what was going on in the other's mind. At least we would now know that the other was in a low mood before it led to a fight. But it was not going to solve our conflicts to simply be aware that the other was feeling insecure. There had to be a way of helping the other *feel* more secure. So I asked my wife, "Whenever you are in a low mood, how would you want me to respond?" She thought about it and said, "Give me a hug. Then if you maybe could do some little thing that shows you love me, I would like that. Maybe you could make me a cup of coffee or sit down and listen to my thoughts." When she shared that with me, it all seemed too simple and yet it was like a gift from her to me. Now I knew what to do to help her at those times and I really wanted to help her. Then she asked me what I would like her to do when I am in a low mood. I replied, "leave me alone!" She instantly understood that this was how I cope with my own low moods. I need to "go into my cave." She agreed to give me that gift.

The result is, that whenever my wife informs me that she is in a low mood, I launch myself into hug-mode and help her feel more secure. She in turn allows me the space to deal with my own low mood knowing that my mood will eventually come back up, as it always does. Meanwhile, we never discuss serious subjects when one of us is in a low mood. The problem will keep till we are both in a high mood and it will then be an exciting challenge rather than a problem.

The rules then, are quite simple:

1. Agree to inform your spouse when you are in a low mood before it explodes. Your spouse is not a mind reader.
2. Tell your spouse how you would like him or her to respond when you admit to a low mood.
3. Be eager to find out how your spouse wants you to respond to his or her low moods.
4. Just do it.

You will be amazed and delighted at how arguments simply become unthinkable. Like every change in behaviour, it will take a commitment, but unlike other changes in life, this is much easier than you think, since the rewards are immediate and gratifying. If, as you try to put this into practice, you find yourselves in a major, hurtful yelling match, do not treat it as a huge tragedy or failure. Once you are both in a high mood again, you can think clearly once more, discuss what happened and then get on with practising your new strategy. Both spouses really want the same things. They want peace, love and harmony in the home and in their relationship, and when they begin to see it actually happen as they live out this new strategy, they will never give it up. It is too rewarding.

The above recommendations work when only one of the spouses is in a low mood and the other is in a secure high mood. But what should we do when both of us are in a low mood at the same time? This is a recipe for disaster if we both try to interact in such a state since neither of us is in a healthy frame of mind. We will be embroiled in a terrible fracas in no time. "If you go snapping at one another and tearing one another to pieces, take care; you will be eaten up by one another" (Gal. 5:15). There is only one answer and it is to *disengage.* Both spouses should agree beforehand, that if ever this happens, they will leave each other alone, deal with their own low mood by themselves and reconnect when they feel better. This is the only way to avoid unnecessary damage.

That is the "McDonald Technique," pure and simple, and I can attest that it works for my own marriage and I have recommended it to numerous couples who report on its effectiveness for them. It is a lot better than fighting.

When it comes to really troubled marriages, naturally one has to consider professional marriage counselling. There is nothing wrong with seeking the help of an objective and skilled counsellor. But before entering into a client-therapist relationship, it would be essential to know if the counsellor is really committed to saving your marriage. It is a sad fact that many counsellors give up all too easily and recommend separation and divorce. They often may pontificate and declare that the spouses are not compatible and therefore would be happier living apart. This is not therapy. It is certainly not Christian therapy. If you are fortunate enough to have a Christian therapist, then he or she will usually believe in the sacredness of marriage and will counsel accordingly.

Another very important aspect of marriage counselling is that often the couple comes in with a hidden agenda. The husband or the wife may enter therapy earnestly desiring that the marriage get back on track. However, one of the partners may simply be there because he or she feels dragged into it and wants to pretend to be open to healing, when in fact this is not the case. Such a spouse is dishonest and merely engineers the failure of therapy so he can then say, "Well I tried and it did not work so I am justified in calling it quits." Another difficult problem in therapy is where one partner is convinced that there is nothing the matter with him or her and that the therapist's job is to "fix" the other. This never works because it is a lie. Both partners in a troubled marriage need to learn how to change if love is to be rekindled. Marriage counselling works best if both partners desire help and if both are willing to honestly look at their own responsibility in the relationship. Nevertheless, this is not an absolute rule. I have seen marriages recover simply because one partner decided to change. The other unwilling spouse then felt more secure and also began to change. The new loving behaviour in one spouse brought out the best in the other. Nonetheless, counselling is a lot easier when both partners are open. Christian counselling calls forth this necessary sense of responsibility and encourages the partners to reach for the goodness within.

It is very important to eliminate a misunderstanding about how marriage counselling works. The process is not a mere matter of problem-solving. In fact, this is usually bad therapy, although there is sometimes a place for it. Most couples, by the time they are desperate enough to seek counselling, are caught up in the pain of their own damaged feelings and they are focussed on their major areas of disagreement. They expect the therapist to come up with a magic solution to their problems and that is very wrong. Some therapists do get drawn into these problems, but it is a lost cause. A marriage will never be without problems, so if I as a therapist am merely a problem-solver, then I should move in with the married couple. I could be their live-in guru to be consulted every time a problem arises. This of course, would be laughable, but it is no more laughable than the therapist who restricts his role to mere problem-solving. It does not work in the long haul. The real skill of therapy is to help couples solve their own problems. If they do this with love, then their solutions will be far more ingenious than anything I could come up with. In the end, my solutions are only good for *my* marriage, not yours. If, as so often happens, the therapy focuses only on individual problems, it soon gets bogged down in recriminations, low mood feelings and in the futile search for solutions. The couple leaves the office in a lower mood and more discouraged than when they came in, only to return next time with a new set of problems for the therapist to solve.

There has to be a better way and there is. It is called "high mood therapy." The basic principle of high mood therapy is to offer hope to the distressed couple. Focussing on problems is low mood therapy and drags down the couple's spirits, thereby creating a deeper and deeper despondency which defeats the very purpose of therapy. A high mood therapist takes the "high-road," is optimistic about the couple's potential and calls them to greater confidence in their recovery. As a result, couples should leave the office with a deeper sense of closeness, a greater sense of hope and a willingness to come even closer together. They leave the office believing that it might be worth the risk to try again. If a couple were to go sight-seeing in a city, would they go and visit the town dump? Not likely! They would visit the gardens and the beautiful art galleries. So it is with therapy. Low mood therapy visits the dump. High mood therapy prefers the gardens.

There are a variety of schools of therapy. Some use Cognitive techniques, some use Gestalt, some use Behaviour Modification Principles, but whichever modality your therapist employs, success will still depend on the high-mood approach.

Good therapy therefore helps a couple to recall the heady days of what it was like to be in love with each other and to assure them that their love has not died. It has merely become paved over by the cares of life. This will mean re-examining one's priorities. After the honeymoon, a couple tends to settle down to the business of making money, striving for a bigger house or saving up for a better vehicle. This can become so all-consuming that years down the road, when the couple has successfully acquired all these signs of success, they wake up one day to the awful realization that they are living with a complete stranger. Just like Becky and John in chapter 1, love has been sacrificed for material gain. What a tragedy! The therapist will try to re-focus a couple's priorities so that their love once again becomes their primary goal, while all other objectives are given a proper secondary importance. Love was the reason for the marriage in the first place and if it is not nurtured, then in the midst of later affluence, the marriage is slowly dying.

The best way to achieve success in marriage counselling is to promote a real change of attitude in the husband and wife towards themselves and towards each other. If a spouse insists on seeing the other as malicious or as an enemy out to destroy his or her happiness, where is the hope in that? If, on the other hand, a spouse chooses to see his partner as well-meaning, desiring happiness as much as he does, and like him, given to low moods, then his attitude towards her behaviour becomes more understanding and more gracious. As a result of this healthy change in attitude, a wife can see her husband behaving badly, can hear him saying hurtful things, but instead of allowing these behaviours to wound her, she is immediately aware of her husband's insecurity and responds with compassion.

The basis of this style of counselling is the belief that couples can get a fresh start. It rightly emphasises that the problems in a marriage are not the cause of the marital discord, but are merely the symptoms. It emphasises that when two people are in a state of healthy psychological functioning, they will feel warmly towards each other and capable of loving acts. The good news is that healthy psychological functioning can be taught. As a result of learning about healthy thinking, moods, mind-sets and feelings, a couple begins to see the innocence in each other. The couple will learn how to forgive, how to overlook irritable behaviour in a spouse, and how to bring out the best in each other. A very important principle of high mood therapy is that when we are in a high mood we are like the good Dr. Jekyll. We are magnanimous, understanding, patient, forgiving and joyful. But when we are in a low mood, we are the horrible Mr. Hyde, aggressive or complaining, childish or mean. We are at our worst. If Mr. Hyde learns not to be drawn into his low moods, but wisely waits for his higher mood to return, he will automatically recover his real Dr. Jekyll self.

For marriage therapy to be effective, it is obviously ideal if both partners begin to change, but the surprising fact is that wonderful things can happen even if only one makes the effort. If one spouse decides to become the very best wife or husband possible and begins to live out the marriage vows as God intended, then miracles of change will usually occur in the other spouse. There is a very good adage in therapy. "If you want to change your spouse, change yourself." It only takes one Dr. Jekyll to move a marriage towards health. Nevertheless, I still find it a lot easier when both partners genuinely desire change.

If we are really honest, then the very things which irritate us today about our spouse are the very things which often attracted us to him or her in our courting days. For example, now I see my spouse as aggressive where only a few years ago I loved him or her for being confident and assertive. I can't stand my spouse for being critical yet not long ago I admired her for being so truthful. What is slovenly today was relaxed and laid back yesterday. The smothering intimacy I hate today was yesterday's wonderful loving hugs. What has happened here? Nothing has really changed except for my own attitude. I am seeing my spouse differently and that is my problem, not hers. The marvellous truth is that I can change my attitude in the blink of an eye. I can get in touch once again with my first love for her and re-claim my former appreciation for her qualities.

Bearing in mind that men and women come from "different planets" why should it surprise young married couples that they have different opinions on just about everything? If my attitude towards this discovery is that we are *incompatible*, then I will be despondent, maintain myself in a low mood and so I will be constantly poised for an argument. If my attitude is one of *excitement* at my wife's way of seeing the world, I will be in a high mood, constantly stimulated by her ideas and never threatened by them. It becomes a joy to discover the ways in which she sees the world. Instead of an irritant, her opinion stimulates me to reconsider my own opinion. Our life is then filled with interesting discussions. In the first scenario, I believe that my wife's contrary opinion accuses me of being wrong. Therefore I must prove that I am right and she is wrong. The battle is on. In the second scenario, I know that opinions are not important, that instead of one being right and the other wrong, we could easily both be right or both be wrong. It does not matter to me, because I love my wife and we enjoy the process of knowing each other more and more each day. Because it is exciting, the idea of fighting over it never enters our minds.

Our attitude towards a troublesome event changes the way we think and the way we feel.

ATTITUDE	THOUGHTS	FEELING
1. A tragedy.	This is terrible.	Depression/despair.
2. A big problem.	I can't cope.	Stressed out.
3. A challenge.	I can handle it.	Interested.
4. A lesson.	I needed this.	Grateful.
5. An opportunity.	I love this.	Exhilarated.

Dr. George Pransky, a practising psychologist, recounts a story which demonstrates how our attitude influences our thinking. "The scene is the lobby of a movie theatre. You are standing in line to buy tickets. Suddenly a burly man walks in front of you and steps on your toe. He offers no apology. In fact, he acts like you don't exist. Anger builds in you. Suddenly your anger turns to chagrin. You just noticed his white cane and black glasses. Turning to the man behind you, you relate your mistake. He laughs and says he knows this alleged blind man. "That man is not blind" he reports. "He's just a sadist who pretends to be blind to avoid punishment for his sadistic acts." Your embarrassment instantly turns to outrage. You ask yourself, "How could anyone be that low?" You consider taking a punch at him despite his size. An older man pulls you aside. He tells you that the man behind you is the sadist and the burly man actually is blind. Your outrage turns to confusion and then to levity when a middle-aged, bald-headed man comes over and says, "Smile, you're on Candid Camera!"

Notice how the man in the story romped through a variety of different feelings depending on the attitude he had at any given moment towards the blind man. Marriage is like that too. Therefore, we need to discard useless attitudes which breed conflict and take on a more philosophical attitude which leads us to warm feelings about our spouse.

We need to rise above our problems instead of fretting about them. If I have a sore on my arm, the last thing I should do is pick on it. Fretting about problems and giving them undue attention is like picking at a sore. It will never heal. For example, disagreement over money is a very common cause of marriage breakdown. Yet money seems to be a problem for some couples and not for others. This has nothing to do with whether the couple is wealthy or poor. It has to do with attitude. When financial matters are not a problem for a couple, they simply do not spend much time on it. Husband and wife share their resources without petty squabbles about "mine and yours." If they have the cash, they buy the item they always wanted. If they are short, they have no difficulty in refraining from a purchase. Money is not important to them. But if another couple sees money as a problem then the very thought of money fills them with insecurity. Any mention of the word "money" is a source of anxiety or despondency for the couple and sets them up for fights and an exchange of blame.

A perceived problem is in fact a *state of mind* which can manufacture a problem out of anything or even out of nothing. It is my attitude that will decide whether a life's issue is a problem for me or not. Certainly a major tragedy is a problem. That is not in dispute, but even there, my attitude will have a big impact on how well I handle it. If my bank collapses and I lose all my savings I can tell myself, "This is the end. My family will starve to death. I wish I were dead." I could equally well say, "What a mess. Well, we are not going to roll over and die. We can start over again."

Understanding is a powerful tool for saving a marriage. It is in fact the stimulus to a *change of heart* which is so necessary if we are to cast off previous hurtful behaviours. As a rule, people convince themselves that they cannot change. If that were true, then there is no hope either for our own personal salvation (I am a drunkard, or an adulterer. That is the way I am and I cannot change it), or for our marriages (I know you don't like me going out with the boys so much, but I can't help it). Believing one cannot change is a cop-out from mature Christian living.

Everyone has the ability to change. Change takes place when I act out of my real self, rather than out of my conditioning. If I feel insecure, I tend to fall back into my conditioned personality, which is full of bad habits. For example, if I was raised in a home where there was a lot of violence, then I have been conditioned to be violent. As a result, whenever I feel insecure (criticised, threatened, irritated, anxious), then I will be strongly tempted to fall into the old habit of violence. It is not however, a foregone conclusion. I can experience a change of heart whereby I renounce violence, see the wisdom of becoming a peacemaker and I become more understanding, tolerant and gentle. The way to facilitate a change of heart is to treat people with understanding and goodwill. Goodwill relieves insecurity. It invites my spouse to drop her old defence mechanisms and to become her authentic self. As a result, she quickly regains her built-in qualities of wisdom, creativity, humour and compassion.

As Dr. Pransky again writes "When Jim gets insecure at work he puts on an armour called 'frenetic.' By the time he gets home to Elaine he is wound up like a spring. She reacts to this tension by becoming irritable, forcing him deeper into his shell of tension. When Elaine sees that insecurity is causing Jim's freneticism, she becomes compassionate and warm toward him. He relaxes and the tension starts to dissipate. Soon, the contrast between his relaxed feeling at home and his overwrought feeling at work helps him to get his perspective. Gradually, he learns to keep his bearings under pressure. A human being can be likened to a flower. In a climate of emotional well-being a person grows towards his or her potential. Understanding and goodwill are the food and water that nourish the blossom."

All of this can be taught by a good therapist. In high mood therapy, the focus is on showing a couple that their behaviour so often depends on their thinking, their moods, their mind-sets and their old habits. It teaches healthy psychological functioning, how to think, how to deal with low moods and how to tap into our own natural resources of wisdom, understanding and creativity. Once a couple takes this teaching to heart, then a change of heart automatically follows. It may surprise many couples to be told, that regardless of years of bad habits and destructive behaviour, there is within each of us a perfectly natural mechanism for healthy psychological functioning. It is still there even if it is not being used and it can be activated at any time. All it takes is a teacher-therapist to show how to tap into your own built-in health resources and a willingness to learn on your part. As one learns how to think creatively, one automatically becomes more compassionate, more understanding and more gracious in dealing with one's spouse. My new psychological equilibrium leads to the same thing in my spouse.

For a Catholic, a change of heart means even more than simply mental and emotional health. It means more than a change in personal habits. It calls me to a higher *spiritual* change of heart, the kind of change which works miracles both in myself and in my spouse. This is the massive change of heart which prompts me to "lay down my life" for the other. Such a leap from the merely worldly to the sublime can only occur with the direct help of the Holy Spirit. It is, in other words, *conversion.* Conversion is not a once-in-a-life-time event. It is an on-going daily transformation by which we submit our lives and our will to the will of God. It means accepting Jesus Christ as my personal Lord and Saviour and following in his footsteps, carrying the cross. For this to occur, sanctifying grace is needed and that comes through the power of the Sacraments. As married couples, we can lay claim to the vast graces of Matrimony which are ours for the asking and we can receive an increase in grace as we attend regular Confession and frequent Holy Communion. Conversion, or a holy change of heart, transforms the ordinary, worldly, dual relationship of man and woman into the extraordinary, supernatural, three-way relationship of man, woman and God. All it takes is a decision by the couple to allow God to rule in their home and in their hearts.

As a result of such conversion, a husband learns to become a real man, while a wife becomes a real woman. "Real" in this context refers to the real world of the life of grace, not the illusory world of money, work and pleasure, which the majority of people mistakenly call real today.

The beauty and joy of this conversion lies in the fact that the husband begins to live for his wife instead of for himself, while his wife begins to live for him, rather than for herself. If I "lay down my life" for my wife and live for her happiness, I need never worry, since it is very likely that she will do the same thing in turn for me. The result is that my wife's needs will be met and my needs will also be met. Instead of living a self-centred life, I live an other-centred life, and I am empowered to do this because I live for God first. "If there is any encouragement in Christ, any solace in love, any participation in the Spirit, any compassion and mercy, complete my joy by being of the same mind, with the same love, united in heart, thinking one thing. Do nothing out of selfishness or vainglory; rather humbly regard others as more important than yourselves, each looking out not for his own interests, but everyone for those of others" (Phil. 2:1-4). This is the formula for a long, happy and satisfying marriage. It requires dying to self but the rewards are guaranteed by the Word of God. It is the royal road to real communion as a couple.

The truth is that we should discard all false notions of "incompatibility." That is a myth created by secular psychologists and psychiatrists. It is simply a feeble excuse to avoid real commitment and is a passport to separation and divorce when the going gets rough. Christianity does not teach incompatibility. In fact, it recognises and rejoices in the countless successful marriages where couples would never have been considered compatible by secular standards. Yet they found excitement in one another and stood by one another throughout a lifetime. Christians can love anyone whether they are compatible or not in the eyes of the world.

If your marriage seems troubled, do not give up. It is more than possible, if you both want it, to be transformed from conflict to lasting communion. "In everything you do, act without grumbling or arguing. Prove yourselves innocent and straight forward, children of God without reproach" (Phil. 2:14-15). God is the best of all marriage counsellors.

CHAPTER 7

Children: The Fruit of Love

*"He blesses the children
within you."*
(Ps. 147:13)

Children are the fruit of our love as husband and wife. Husband, wife and child form an earthly Trinity, contained in the mind of the Divine Trinity. As such, the family is created in the image and likeness of God (vol. 2, chap. 14). Just as God the Holy Spirit proceeds from the love between God the Father and God the Son, so also the child proceeds from the love between his father and mother. It is a sublime and wondrous mystery that God has given to human beings the privilege of co-creating new souls for his kingdom. Such a joy was not given to the angels and yet we, who are inferior to them, can help God to fill up heaven with holy souls. Surely this is the highest of all callings, to give life and to nurture it towards its supreme good, which is God himself. Priesthood is of course the most perfect of all vocations, but there would be no priests at all without fathers and mothers who first loved one another.

Children, being the fruit of love, therefore also thrive on love. Since they are created out of love, they feed on love and are made to love in return. Some argue that a child is not always created out of love but, rather, could be conceived in violence, drunkenness or lust and that the resultant child is not a fruit of love. This is not true. Even where a conception has occurred in disorder, the child is still created out of ***God's love***, since God cannot be unfaithful to his covenant with humanity, even if we are unfaithful to our covenant with him. "If we are unfaithful, he remains faithful, for he cannot deny himself" (2 Tim. 2:13). That is why there is no such thing as an unwanted child. A child may be unwanted by his selfish parents but he is always wanted by God. "Yahweh called me when I was in the womb, before my birth he had pronounced my name" (Isa. 49:1).

Children are a blessing from God. "He blesses the children within you" (Ps. 147:13). "And their children become a blessing" (Ps. 37:26). When God blesses, he bestows grace and so children are, as it were, grace incarnate. The child playing before us is an embodiment of grace, a sign of God's delight in our love. As such, the child is both a blessing and a responsibility, for grace always imposes the responsibility of nurturing it. Parents, therefore, are expected by God to cherish their child as a most precious gift from the heart of God, and are expected to devote themselves to the welfare of that child. This obligation of promoting welfare applies not simply to the basic bodily demands for food, clothing and shelter, but includes the higher demands for love, teaching, discipline and, above all, training in godliness. The last is indeed the first in importance, since eternal life for a child depends upon it. All the others foster earthly life and even quality of life, but without godliness, all our efforts will be wasted.

Children become what they learn. If they are taught about Jesus and his Blessed Mother and the truths of their faith from the cradle, they will become disciples of Christ. It is true that in the first flush of freedom from parental control, as young adults, they may decide to test the dark waters of sin, but they will not be able to fully escape from their training in the ways of goodness. Sooner or later, they will waken up to the fact that they have engineered their own misery, and they will turn back to the wisdom of their childhood joy in the Lord. This turning back, however, will depend on the nature of their faith experience when they were little. If all they received was cold, harsh religion, then religion will never be life-giving to them. If, on the other hand, they learned the love of God and the warmth of prayer and worship, then like a powerful magnet, it will always draw them back.

The most beautiful and endearing quality of a child is innocence. To God, innocence is his greatest delight since innocence does not know sin. A child has the ability to simply be. He is what he is. He is like a flower which blooms and gives off a marvellous perfume and without knowing it, gives us delight. He laughs, he plays, he explores, he falls down and always gets up again. If parents try to see the world through their child's eyes, they too will recapture the wonder, the awe and the excitement of all things. To a child all things are new and marvellous and the world has not yet taken on the dust-covered layers of experience and boredom.

One of the great attributes of a child is his curiosity. Children are delightfully curious about every thing. G. K. Chesterton wrote, "The most childlike thing about a child is his curiosity and his appetite and his power to wonder at the world." Children remind us that the very things we adults now take for granted are the very signature of God. The world around us is saturated with the love of God, crying out to us to see the handwriting of its Maker. The proof of the existence of God lies in his works and that idea is so simple to a child that it need not be questioned. It is adults who try to explain away the mystery of the universe as some cosmic accident, but in so doing, they rob themselves of their own meaning. God gives meaning to all things, especially to the lives of his people, and the childlike heart rejoices in it.

Innocence means freedom from corruption by evil. A child enjoys this innocence until the age of reason and it is then that he comes to that dreaded milestone of "knowing good and evil" (Gen. 3:5). It is at this point that his innocence is in grave danger, just as the innocence of Adam and Eve was corrupted by this "knowing." It is true that a very young child can be self-centred, even wilful, but that is not actual sin. As the Church teaches, actual sin is not possible until the child reaches the age of reason, which occurs when he attains the age of seven or thereabouts. From then onwards, he is accountable for his actions, thoughts and decisions. Wise parents understand this transition and so they are diligent in their duty to guide the child in the ways of holiness.

One day, when Jesus was in Judea on the far side of the Jordan, many loving parents brought their children to Jesus asking him to lay his hands on them and to pray over them. The disciples, full of their own importance and desiring to protect Jesus from such irritation, scolded the parents. It is amusing to imagine the apostles shooing the children away and telling them not to be pestering this important man. After all, Jesus had a mission to get on with and children would simply be a bother and a distraction from his real work. They were in for a shock. Jesus, without scolding his disciples, simply said with great love "Let the little children alone, and do not stop them from coming to me; for it is to such as these that the kingdom of heaven belongs" (Matt. 19:14). What a gentle and wonderful lesson Jesus taught us that day. God's love of innocence is so great that the kingdom of heaven belongs to children, that is to say, to the childlike heart.

"So he called a little child to him whom he set among them. Then he said, 'In truth I tell you, unless you change and become like little children, you will never enter the kingdom of heaven. And so the one who makes himself as little as this little child is the greatest in the kingdom of heaven'" (Matt. 18:2-4). We, as adults, are called to scrape off the barnacles of our sophistication and to rediscover the heart of a child within us, full of love, wonder, and simple acceptance of the mysteries of God.

Jesus went even farther in this discourse when he said, "Anyone who welcomes one little child like this in my name welcomes me" (Matt. 18:5). In other words we are to revere children as God's blessing, as the fruit of love, and in so-doing, we are giving honour to Jesus himself. In fact, Jesus is teaching that no one on earth is a closer facsimile to the mind of Christ than a little child and so childhood demands our respect and holy imitation. Therefore, we are bound to love all children in a very special way, for they are very special to God. No child should be deprived or starved or treated cruelly, otherwise we will be held to account. Strangely enough, our sinful society agrees with that statement and then uses it to justify the abortion of so-called unwanted children, as if killing a child were not the ultimate in cruelty.

To God, the innocence of a child is so precious that Jesus was compelled to indicate the dreadful consequences for anyone who violates that innocence. "Whoever causes one of these little ones who believe in me to sin, it would be better for him to have a great millstone hung around his neck and to be drowned in the depths of the sea" (Matt. 18:6). Therefore sexual abuse, physical abuse, mental cruelty and any other sin against innocence is one of the very worst crimes one can commit. Such corruption of the child also occurs when parents allow their little ones to watch immoral videos, to listen to music with satanic or evil lyrics or to keep bad company with their peer group. These sins mutilate the sacredness of a child and the consequences are terrible. The child loses his or her innocence, since it has now been breached, and so grows up to be distorted, disturbed and disconnected. The perpetrator, of course, is now horribly disfigured in his own spirit, and while he need not be damned if he repents, he must shoulder an enormous debt for atonement. Yet atonement is by far preferable to a millstone.

By the very fact of their innocence, little children seem to have no problem with the mysteries of God. Adults grapple with the things which are beyond their power to understand. Little children never do this but rather enjoy the wonderful ability to hear the truth and accept it no matter how profound. The critical factor for this acceptance is the degree to which they trust the person who tells them this truth. For a little child, the resurrection of Jesus from the dead is quite simple. He or she sees no difficulty with that idea whatsoever. The fact that volumes, if not libraries of books, have been written for and against the mystery of the Resurrection, is of no interest to the child. Jesus rose from the dead. Mother said so. Therefore it is true.

One day, St. Augustine was pondering upon the mystery of the Trinity while walking along the seashore. Suddenly, he noticed a little boy dipping a thimble into the ocean, then emptying it out on the beach. The child was very intent on this activity and repeated it over and over again. Finally the theologian asked him, "What are you doing my child?" The boy, without stopping his serious task replied, "I am emptying the ocean." The theologian smiled condescendingly and said, "Son, it is impossible for you to empty the ocean." The child quietly said, "Not nearly as impossible as you trying to understand the Trinity." He then disappeared. I love that story since it shrinks our proud adult ego down to its proper size, which is minuscule in the affairs of God, and the shrinking was done by a little child. "And a little child shall lead them" (Isa. 11:6).

This does not mean that in becoming like a little child, an adult must also become uninformed and renounce his experience and learning, but it does mean that an adult must become de-programmed from all his years of worldly conditioning. He needs to be bleached from the accumulated dirt of duplicity, guile, self-centeredness, pride and above all, the arrogant reliance on his puny reason as the only way by which he can *know* anything. "When I was a child, I spoke like a child, I thought like a child, I reasoned like a child; when I became a man, I gave up childish ways" (1 Cor. 13:11). Therefore, when Jesus tells us that we will lose the kingdom of heaven unless we become like a little child, he is not telling us to become *childish.* He is reminding us that so much of what we think of as adult and sophisticated is in fact childish and stupid. It is when we learn from our experience of life, grow in wisdom and *marvel* at the mysteries of God that we become like a little child, and thereby delight our Father-God. This childlikeness means facing our own limitations with fearless honesty, and that is humility. It also means an abiding gratitude to God for absolutely everything.

It is as though life is a kind of circle. We are born as infants and raised to adulthood by our earthly parents. Once released from their authority, we then allow ourselves to be raised by our heavenly parents who are God the Father and Mary the Mother. If we are docile to their discipline, they in turn will raise us to become children once more, true children of the kingdom. We have come full circle, from child to adult, to child again. In the spiritual sense, our adult is childish and our child is childlike and God desires all of us to embrace this childlikeness. "All your children shall be taught by the Lord and great shall be the prosperity of your children" (Isa. 54:13). It was Solomon, the man of wisdom, who prayed "And now, O Lord my God, you have made your servant king in the place of David my father, although I am but a little child; I do not know how to go out or come in" (1 Kings 3:7). Solomon asked Yahweh for the gift of wisdom, for it is wisdom which distinguishes the true child of God from the merely childish. "A wise child makes a glad father" (Prov. 15:20).

As soon as our child has language skills, we should teach him that he has a guardian angel specially appointed by God to be his constant companion. The child should come to know and believe that even when mother and father are out of his sight, he is never alone. His guardian angel is an unseen presence, hovering over him and protecting his soul. Wherever the child goes, his angel goes with him. Whatever the child thinks, his angel knows his thoughts. Whatever the child does, his angel observes it. The child must believe that his angel is not a parent and certainly not some kind of policeman, but is his very best friend who cares for his goodness and welfare. His angel is really a teacher as well as a guardian, and the child should come to a relaxed familiarity with his angel. He should be encouraged to give his angel a name and the angel will joyfully accept that name and wear it with love. It does not matter to the angel if the name is male or female since angels are not distinguished by sexual differences. The angel simply rejoices in whatever name is given, since it signifies that the child acknowledges him and desires to have an intimate relationship with him.

The child should be instructed never to do anything which will make his angel sad, and of course it is sin which saddens our angels. Jesus tells us, "See that you do not despise one of these little ones; for I tell you that in heaven their angels always behold the face of my Father who is in heaven" (Matt. 18:10-11). This is the ultimate testimony to the great innocence and sinlessness of a little child, that his guardian angel is given the privilege of constantly beholding the face of the Father. How sad that we usually lose that innocence, and thereby our angel is no longer able to gaze upon the face of the Father. If a child understands this truth, surely he will try not to hurt his best friend in this way, but will make every effort to avoid the sin which deprives his angel of the ultimate privilege. "My son, give me your heart and let your eyes observe my ways" (Prov. 23:26). This could equally well apply to our guardian angel, who strongly desires that we observe his ways, which are God's ways.

Apart from direct instruction from his parents, a child learns most of his skills from play. The child rehearses by meaningful role playing and hones his abilities by repetitive practice. In other words, he learns by imitating his parents or by imitating other heroes to whom he has been exposed. This is why parents must be very anxious to give the child holy and wholesome heroes, such as the great saints of the Church. He also learns physical dexterity by exercising his body, repeating the same manoeuvre over and over again until he gets it right. Once more, the parents must quietly observe these play activities and direct the child into good practices, and firmly distract him from those that are sinful, reprehensible or dangerous.

A child needs to play. Naturally, he needs also to learn how to work, and that will be discussed in more detail in chapter 9 of this volume. But he must be allowed to be a child. Adult knowledge should *never* be given to him before his time, since that is a sure way to corrupt his childhood. His innocence should be as valuable and precious to parents as it is to God himself. There is no place in a Catholic family for so-called sex education of a little child.

A very important concept for all of us, is that we desperately need the *Father's blessing.* This includes not only the blessing from God our heavenly Father but also the blessing from our earthly father. Gary Smalley in his book, *The Blessing,* explains this vital built-in need within every person. For both sons and daughters in the Old Testament, the father's blessing was a momentous event. Esau in his misery at selling his birthright for "a mess of potage" cries out "Bless me, even also, O my father" (Gen. 27:34). In losing the father's blessing, Esau realised that he had lost everything.

A father's blessing indicates that the child is highly valued, and it also denotes an abiding confidence by the parent in the child's unique future. It is both a blessing and a sign of trust. All of us desperately need this blessing even if we are not aware of it. So many children are never given the blessing and so they grow up to feel unworthy. They deem themselves to be flawed in the estimation of their parents, themselves and others. Because they were cheated of their earthly father's blessing, they believe they can never have their heavenly Father's blessing. This destitution leads to a fruitless search for acceptance and that can mean acceptance by anyone at all, so long as it is some kind of blessing, no matter how disordered. The result is, that so many of our teenagers, being starved for blessing, will associate with a sinful peer group and even fall into drugs, drunkenness and debauchery. The need to be accepted is so powerful that a child will accept a counterfeit blessing rather than none at all. Many grow up into adulthood and become workaholics and perfectionists, or withdrawn and dependent, or wallow in self-hatred, frantically searching for the blessing they never had. How hard it is to believe in the loving, gentle fatherhood of God when we were robbed of blessing by our own earthly father.

Esau was so devastated by his loss that he pleaded with Isaac, "Do you have only one blessing, my father?" (Gen. 27:38). The ancient Jewish custom was to reserve the father's blessing to a special time only, and it was usually reserved to the eldest son. Thankfully, this exclusive blessing has been transformed by Jesus in the New Testament to include all of God's children. All of us deserve blessing as our birthright by baptism, and all of us crave for it. Not only that, but this privilege of bestowing the blessing is no longer reserved to earthly fathers alone, but is a prerogative of both parents. We need our mother's blessing as much as we need that of our father. Do we Catholics not desire the gentle blessing of our Mother Mary as well as that of our God-Father? Likewise, we desire, deserve and desperately need the blessing of both our earthly parents. This is the fullness of blessing, which gives us the secure knowledge that we are the treasured offspring of our mother, our father and God. The blessing of the new covenant is so much more affirming than the old.

Today, there are so many cults seducing our children. These cults are very good at offering a counterfeit blessing to our children and those who have not known genuine blessing are very vulnerable to it. The cults provide a false sense of family, attention, affection and affirmation and that is very alluring indeed. Yet these are the very gifts which ought to have been bestowed by the child's own parents in the first place.

The family blessing also prepares the young adult for a true commitment to marriage. "For this reason a man shall leave his father and his mother and shall cleave to his wife" (Gen. 2:24). By dint of being blessed, the growing child is affirmed and is capable of leaving the comfort and security of his parental home and is empowered to love a marriage partner in a mature and holy way. Unblessed adults may ultimately leave home to marry, but they never emotionally leave it. They continue to be chained to their parents, constantly seeking blessing and therefore never able to enjoy a wholesome, committed intimacy with their spouse. If a man or woman feels unworthy, how can he or she feel that a spouse would value their total giving of self? The self is not worthy and so the gift of self is a worthless gift in its own estimation. Not only that, but if the parents themselves were unblessed, then they find it impossible to let their children go and they neurotically continue to disapprove of their child's freedom, of his choice of partner for life, and interfere sinfully in their child's marriage.

The solution is not so difficult. Parents must decide to bless their children and this blessing should be offered daily. It is so beautiful for parents to ask their child to kneel down at bedtime and receive a brief prayer of blessing, along with a reverent sign of the cross on his or her forehead. The little child feels the solemnity of that blessing and feels so affirmed by it, that he would not dream of going to bed without it. For the older child, it takes on the additional quality of trust. When I was a teenager and a university student, I earned my tuition fees by playing piano in a band. Naturally, that placed me in a regular atmosphere of late nights, revelry, drinking and opportunities for sexual adventure. Before I went off in my tuxedo to play, my father would place his big carpenter's hands on my shoulders, look me in the eye and say "Son, I trust you. I know you will not bring shame to the McDonald name." Whenever the opportunity for sin arose, my father's words would come back to haunt me and I remembered his holy trust. He did not try to stop me from encountering the world, but with his trust he stopped me from being seduced by it. I was a beneficiary of my father's blessing. Even when I did fall into sin, I had to first deliberately suppress my father's wise words, and then afterwards, I invariably was overwhelmed by remorse, which led to repentance, which led to confession of my sin, which led to atonement, which led to once more bathing in the blessing of my two fathers, my dad and my Abba-God.

The family blessing consists of meaningful touch, a spoken message, attaching a high value to the one being blessed, picturing a special future for the child, and an active commitment to help the child fulfil the blessing. The latter means that the parents need to be diligent in encouraging their child to realize all the potential of his being. This means the consistent interest in and involvement in the dreams and aspirations of the child, both in the world and in the life of faith. Blessing is the key to becoming a lover oneself in the holiest sense, and a lover of God and neighbour.

I am not sure who wrote the following poem, but it says so much about childhood. It is entitled *Little Jesus.*

Little Jesus, wast thou shy
Once, and just so small as I?
And what did it feel like to be
Out of Heaven and just like me?
Didst thou sometimes think of *there,*
And ask where all the angels were?
I should think that I would cry
For my house all made of sky;
I would look about the air,
And wonder where my angels were;
And at waking 'twould distress me,
Not an angel there to dress me!
Hadst thou ever any toys,
Like us little girls and boys?
And didst thou play in Heaven with all
The angels that were not too tall,
With stars for marbles? Did the things
Play *"Can you see me?"* through their wings?
And did thy Mother let thee spoil
Thy robes, with playing on *our* soil?
How nice to have them always new
In Heaven, because 'twas quite clean blue!

Didst thou kneel at night to pray,
And didst thou join thy hands, this way?
And did they tire sometimes, being young,
And make the prayer seem very long?
And dost thou like it best, that we
Should join our hands to pray to thee?
I used to think, before I knew,
The prayer not said unless we do.
And did thy Mother at the night
Kiss thee, and fold the clothes in right?

And didst thou feel quite good in bed,
Kissed, and sweet, and thy prayers said?
Thou canst not have forgotten all
That it feels like to be small:
And thou know'st I cannot pray
To thee in my father's way —
When thou was so little, say,
Couldst thou talk thy Father's way? —
So, a little Child, come down
And hear a child's tongue like thy own:
Take me by the hand and walk,
And listen to my baby-talk.
To thy Father show my prayer
(He will look, thou art so fair),
And say: "O Father, I, thy Son,
Bring the prayer of a little one."
And he will smile, that children's tongue
Has not changed since thou wast young.

Nothing is more powerful in moving the heart of God than the prayer of a little child. As the poem says, "O Father, I thy son, bring the prayer of a little one." As scripture says, "Your majesty is praised above the heavens; on the lips of children and of babes you have found praise to foil your enemy, to silence the foe and the rebel" (Ps. 8:1-2). It should be the most sublime delight of all parents to know that their child is the fruit of love and is truly God's blessing. If little children and babes can give the Most High God acceptable praise, surely we parents should joyfully protect and bless them as our highest treasure.

In learning what children are, we adults learn what we ought to be.

CHAPTER 8

Parenting: God's Design for Children

*"Honour your father and your
mother so that you may live
long in the land that Yahweh
your God is giving you."*
(Ex. 20:12)

The most valuable resource for understanding the Catholic family is the new *Catechism of the Catholic Church*. It is a gold mine of truth and probably Pope John Paul II's greatest legacy to the universal Church. It has much to say about God's design for good and godly parenting and all of it is thoroughly founded upon Scripture and upon the Holy Tradition of the Church.

Paragraph 2205: The Christian family is a communion of persons, a sign and image of the communion of the Father and the Son in the Holy Spirit. In the procreation of children, it reflects the Father's work of creation. It is called to partake of the prayer and sacrifice of Christ. Daily prayer and the reading of the Word of God strengthens it in charity.

Paragraph 2206: The relationships within the family bring an affinity of feelings, affections and interests, arising above all from the members' respect for one another. The family is a privileged community, called to achieve a sharing of thought and common deliberation by the spouses as well as their eager cooperation as parents in the children's upbringing.

Paragraph 2214: The Divine Fatherhood is the source of human fatherhood. This is the foundation of the honour owed to parents. The respect of children, whether minors or adults, for their father and mother is nourished by the natural affection born of the bond uniting them. It is required by God's commandment.

Paragraph 2215: Respect for parents derives from gratitude toward those who, by the gift of life, their love, and their work, have brought their children into the world and enabled them to grow in stature, wisdom and grace.

"With all your heart honour your father and do not forget the birth pangs of your mother. Remember that through your parents you were born; what can you give back to them that equals their gift to you?" (Sir. 7:27-28).

Paragraph 2216: Filial respect is shown by true docility and obedience.

"My son, keep your Father's commandment and forsake not your mother's teaching ... when you walk, they will lead you; when you lie down, they will watch over you; and when you awake, they will talk with you" (Prov. 6:20-22).

Paragraph 2217: As long as a child lives at home with his parents, the child should obey his parents in all that they ask of him, when it is for his good or that of the family.

"Children, obey your parents in everything, for this pleases the Lord" (Col. 3:20).

Children should also obey the reasonable directions of their teachers and all to whom their parents have entrusted them. But if a child is convinced in conscience that it would be morally wrong to obey a particular order, he must not do so. As they grow up, children should continue to respect their parents. They should anticipate their wishes, willingly seek their advice and accept their just admonitions. Obedience toward parents ceases with the emancipation of the children; not so respect, which is always owed to them. This respect has its roots in the fear of God, one of the gifts of the Holy Spirit.

Paragraph 2221: The fecundity of conjugal love cannot be reduced solely to the procreation of children, but must extend to their moral education and their spiritual formation. The role of parents in education is of such importance that it is almost impossible to provide an adequate substitute. The right and duty of parents to educate their children are primeval and inalienable.

Paragraph 2222: Parents must regard their children as children of God and respect them as human persons. Showing themselves obedient to the will of the Father in Heaven, they educate their children to fulfil God's law.

Paragraph 2223: Parents have the first responsibility for the education of their children. They bear witness to this responsibility first by creating a home where tenderness, forgiveness, respect, fidelity and disinterested service are the rule. The home is well suited for eduction in the virtues. This requires an apprenticeship in self-denial, sound judgement and self-mastery, the preconditions of all true freedom. Parents should teach their children to subordinate the material and instinctual dimensions to interior and spiritual ones. Parents have a grave responsibility to give good example to their children. By knowing how to acknowledge their own failings to their children, parents will be better able to guide and correct them.

"He who loves his son will not spare the rod. He who disciplines his son will profit by him" (Sir. 30:1-2).

Paragraph 2225: Through the grace of the Sacrament of Marriage, parents receive the responsibility and privilege of evangelising their children. Parents should initiate their children at an early age into the mysteries of the faith of which they are the first heralds for their children. They should associate them from their tenderest years with the life of the church.

Paragraph 2226: Education in the faith by the parents should begin in the child's earliest years ... parents have the mission of teaching their children to pray and to discover their vocation as children of God.

Paragraph 2227: Children in turn contribute to the growth in holiness of their parents. Each and everyone should be generous and tireless in forgiving one another for offenses, quarrels, injustices and neglect. Mutual affection suggests this. The charity of Christ demands it.

Paragraph 2229: As those first responsible for the education of their children, parents have the right to choose a school for them which corresponds to their own convictions. This right is fundamental.

Paragraph 2230: When they become adults, children have the right and duty to choose their profession and state of life. They should assume their new responsibilities within a trusting relationship with their parents, willingly asking and receiving their advice and counsel. Parents should be careful not to exert pressure on their children either in their choice of profession or in that of a spouse. This necessary restraint does not prevent them — quite the contrary — from giving their children judicious advice, particularly when they are planning to start a family.

The foregoing paragraphs beautifully give us the foundation of Catholic Family Life. However, it requires some expansion in order to fully appreciate the jewels which the church offers in its inspired wisdom.

Basically the Catechism teaches that ***good parenting is God-parenting.*** This means that parents must make every effort to teach their children the ways of God. In doing so they will automatically raise their children in virtue, in self-esteem (which is not to be confused with vanity), in responsible behaviour towards others, in tolerance, moderation and love. The ways of God will also include holy discipline and a recognition of the dignity of honest work. The family is expected to be united in prayer and sacrifice for one another. Parents are commissioned by God to joyfully put aside their own selfish needs and to put themselves out for their offspring. This cannot be properly done in the Catholic manner without daily prayer and a firm grounding in the teachings of Jesus. Mutual esteem must exist amongst all of the family members, without any exceptions. There is no place for favouritism in a Christian family. God has no favourites and neither should parents and if they fall into that trap, they create a selfish self-centeredness in one child and destroy the self-esteem of another.

Parenting can be said to pass through four stages or phases:

1. Pregnancy
2. Childhood
3. Teenage Years
4. Releasing the child into the world.

PHASE I. A child is a gift from God and is the incarnation of God's blessing to a couple. As such, the child enjoys a very special place in the Heart of Jesus. "Let the children come to me, and do not prevent them; for the kingdom of heaven belongs to such as these" (Matt. 19:14).

Parental responsibility actually begins with the act of sexual union. Ideally, this should be a moment of total communion, a true act of selfless love between husband and wife, with a generous openness that if God blesses their love with a new life, they will joyfully welcome it. They will accept and love this child whether it be male or female, intelligent or retarded, healthy or disabled. These are the proper dispositions of Catholic parents towards their sexual love and towards their children who are the fruit of that love.

From the moment that the couple is aware of a pregnancy, they should begin the task of parenting their child. This they do by praying together and by praying over the tiny life in the mother's womb, speaking words of love to the baby and planning together for the baby's welcome into the world. A husband has the indispensable manly duty to promote his wife's emotional, physical and spiritual well-being. Her whole being is focussed on the task of carrying the child growing within her. For her to be completely fruitful in her pregnancy, she should be as free as possible from stress and from having to worry about worldly things. She needs to feel protected, nourished and loved by her husband, whose duty it is to allow her to be fully female, fully mother, and fully free to give her whole self to the precious life she carries.

The as-yet-unborn baby should be welcomed as God's blessing with grateful hearts, and a pledge should be given to God by both parents that they will do their utmost to raise this new little soul in the love of God.

PHASE II. Once born, the baby is a blank blackboard, waiting for his or her parents to write on it. Many of the baby's future personality traits, ideas, dreams and most importantly his beliefs, will depend on what his parents will write on that blackboard. The newborn baby is not born angry or proud or jealous, or hate-filled or frightened or a worrier, nor does he loathe himself. These things are all learned from the parents, if that is what they teach him by their example. If mother worries, the child will soon come to worry simply by imitation. If dad is angry, the child will learn that anger is an acceptable response to frustration.

There is nothing more innocent than a newborn baby. The baby simply lies in his or her crib with total helplessness, waiting for his birthright, which is love, food, clothing, warmth, teaching, protection, and discipline. These are parental duties and this total dependence of the baby and the young toddler is *a dependency ordained by God the Father.*

During the first few years of growth, the child assimilates information and data at a phenomenal rate. This is the most important time for the parents to lay the foundations of the child's personality and beliefs. A Jesuit priest once said, "Give me a child from the age of three to seven and he will be a Catholic for the rest of his life." In other words, right from the beginning, the parents must teach their child about God, Mary, angels and the saints, because that teaching will remain deep in his heart for life, even if he chooses to stray later on. They must teach about love, self-esteem, sharing and friendship, not just how to drink from a cup and hold a spoon. These skills are so vital to the little one's subsequent adulthood, how can we hand over this job to a day-care centre? How can your child learn *your* standards and *your* faith from a paid professional? Certainly, once the child is at school, the mother may legitimately go to work if she wishes, but from the moment of conception to school, the child learns family values only from the mother's lap. Today, no stranger can be trusted to put God into your child's heart. Jealously reserve that duty to yourself, just as the Blessed Mother did. It was she who taught little Jesus everything from his first baby steps to God's Holy Scripture. There were no day-care centres in Nazareth. "Wisdom brings up her own children, so become wisdom and do the same" (Sir. 4:11). "Listen my child, to your father's instruction; do not reject your mother's teaching" (Prov. 1:8).

St. John Vianney said, "Virtue passes easily from the hearts of mothers into the hearts of children." How then can a child receive teaching from his mother, if mother is working an eight-hour shift during the child's most productive time of the day? Father's instruction of his child has to be different since he is the family provider and he must work. Therefore his instruction has to take place outside of his working hours. Even so, it is still a vital fatherly duty, and if he fathers in a slovenly manner, he will do untold damage, both to his child and to his own soul. He has so much to teach about life, about work, about practical survival skills and about manhood.

From conception to the age of around nine years, the most important person in a child's life is definitely the mother. But from the age of nine to sixteen years, the most needed person is the father. The child's healthy growth into a healthy sexual being depends on the presence of a loving and manly father. It is he who models the man his son would like to become, and it is he who models the kind of man his daughter will seek out as a future partner.

"Better die childless than have children who are godless" (Sir. 16:3). That says it all. The first and primary duty of parenting is to teach children about God and his truths. Regardless of what that child may choose to do in adult life regarding the faith, if the parents have not planted the seed of faith in his heart as a toddler, this will be held against them as neglect of the worst order. More will be written about this in chapter 10. It is God, then, who gives us the gift of becoming parents, and he expects that we will behave like parents, not like mere custodians. We must father and we must mother. Our model of father is God himself and our model of mother is Mary.

PHASE III. The teenage years have always been the most difficult challenge to parents throughout the entire history of the human race, but in these times, it is a much more difficult challenge.

Chapter 11 will be devoted to this difficult phase of parenting, but it need not be depressing. This can be a most rewarding time for parents who know how to love, who understand the marvellous changes a teenager is experiencing in his or her body, and who appreciate the struggle of coming to a fuller self-knowledge. Wise parents give their growing teenagers more and more good self-determination as they work towards Phase IV and finally leave home. Again, only love will conquer, together with a great deal of prayer for guidance as a parent. I deeply believe in the power of consecration to Jesus through the Immaculate Heart of Mary for the entire family. This is a great force for safe-guarding our young people from worldly temptations. In her locution to Fr. Gobbi of July 23, 1987, Our Lady said that when a family is consecrated to her, she will take care of the children. "When I enter into a family, I immediately look after the children; they become also mine. I take them by the hand; I lead them to walk along the road of the realization of a plan of God, which has from all eternity already been clearly traced out for each one of them. I love them. I never abandon them. They become a precious part of my maternal estate." Every Catholic parent should rejoice in the knowledge that the Blessed Mother is eager to personally help them in parenting their children and teenagers. The act of Consecration engages the Mother of God to do precisely that. We need all the heavenly help we can get, so it is wise to invite Mary to help us in these difficult years.

PHASE IV: The final act of parenting which all of us must accomplish is releasing the grown child into the world, to fend for himself and to take his rightful place as a responsible citizen in society. Many parents find it surprisingly painful to do so, and this is especially true of mothers. Some mothers completely fail to understand that the time for obedience is over and, as the Catechism tells us, while it is right that they continue to command respect from their adult children, they no longer can exercise legitimate *control* over their children. The umbilical cord must be severed. There are mothers who continue to manipulate their sons and daughters long after they have left home, disapproving of their career decisions, jealous of their choice of spouse, and flatly refusing to accept the spouse as a new son or daughter. Some mothers even insist that sons, for example, show more allegiance to them than to their wives. This is sinful behaviour on the part of parents. I am not denying the pain parents will face when the nest becomes empty, but this must be accepted as a part of life's inevitable cycle. It happens to all of us. "A man shall leave his father and mother and be united to his wife and the two shall become one flesh" (Eph. 5:31). He will be united to his wife, not to his mother.

One day, I was looking out of the kitchen window and I saw a female robin perched on the edge of my raised vegetable garden. She was looking intently at a spot on the lawn. When I looked down I saw a very young robin on the ground. He flapped his little wings, trying to fly, and when he got a couple of inches off the ground, mother bird immediately took to the air and hovered about two feet over the little bird, flapping her wings at high speed. He flopped to the ground again, obviously tired, and mother went back to her perch. This went on several times and I realised that she was, first of all, showing him how to fly by the furious flapping of her wings. By hovering over him, she was also making sure he could not get too much height, so that when he became tired and fell he would not be hurt. Then all of a sudden the little bird finally got it. He rose into the air and triumphantly flew to the upper branches of a large tree. And what did mother do? She flew away! Her last act of mothering had been completed. The little bird was now on his own and would have to fend for himself. Why is it that so many human parents do not seem to know what that mother robin obviously knew?

There are two indispensable ingredients for good Catholic parenting. The first is *love* and the second is *teaching.*

Love is the foundation stone of human parenting, just as it is the foundation stone of God's parenting. Therefore, just as God is love, so also human parents must strive to be love. A child cannot be spoiled with love. It is impossible. Spoiling a child is only done by lack of discipline and indulging his every whim with things. True love is never a sugar-coated indulgence. On the other hand, true love can never be too much. Love given can only result in love returned and love always bears fruit.

As Catherine Doherty said, "The home should be a school of love," that is to say, a place where children are taught what *sacrificial* love is all about. Love is not easy. It requires more than just a natural parental instinct, and it is much more than simple bonding. Love requires time, effort, thought and patience. It often demands sacrifice of our immediate personal needs or desires. A child needs my time, not my money. For a father, that may mean giving time out of his evenings or weekend hours when he might feel justified in taking his own leisure. It may even demand that he give up a promotion in the best interests of his family. A workaholic father is a neglectful father. A true father balances work and family. He recognises his need to be gainfully employed, but he subordinates that to his most important priority, which is his wife and children. He knows he works for them, not for money or a bigger fishing boat.

For a mother, it means long hours of dedication, often having to love even when she is tired and in need of rest. She may have had to give up a promising career in order to devote herself to the more important career of mothering. The career of a nurse or the president of a big company pales before the awesome career of raising godly children to become responsible citizens and evangelisers for Jesus.

Both parents have to love, often when they do not feel like it, and yet, they must have enough love left over to love each other. How is this possible? It can only be done by constantly asking for the graces freely offered by God through their sacrament of Matrimony. Human effort alone is doomed to failure but, "With God all things are possible" (Luke 1:37). Therefore, parental love must be founded on prayer of petition and intercession, holding up the children to the Father of all children, begging for their well-being and especially for their holiness.

Touching is an indispensable part of loving. There can never be enough hugging in a loving family. Mommy's and daddy's lap should be a safe and familiar place to a child. Where better to hide from a scary world and to feel safe than on a parent's knee? Never deny a frightened child the security and love of your physical closeness. Remember, you were frightened yourself once.

Words of love need to be spoken with sincerity and joy, without strings attached. Never tie love to the child's performance, otherwise the child comes to believe he is only loveable if he is good. This was the unhappy experience of John in the story outlined in chapter 1. It is a parent's duty to make sure the child knows he is loved no matter what he may have done. Discipline should be seen by the child as an act of love, not as a vicious act of vengeance.

Parents should always be willing to listen attentively and to show interest in their child's dreams, problems, career choices, boyfriends or girlfriends, activities, their music, and their growing sexuality. Children need to know they can come to their parents with anything, and that it will be heard with love and fairness. This means that they should be able to come to their parents with **absolutely** anything, even something of which they are ashamed.

It is love which fuels all the desirable outcomes which we cherish for our children. Responsible adults were once loved children. If love is not given in this way, we should not be surprised if the children start to look for their love needs elsewhere. They will look for it in someone else's home, with their friends, of whom you may not approve, or later on in drugs and alcohol, and of course in sex, which is so easily confused with love.

Catherine Doherty once wrote this, "I knew a lady whose housekeeping was so impeccable that all the women of the neighbourhood extolled her, and whose cooking was so perfect that all the men wished their wives could cook so well. Yet, the strange thing was that both her husband and her children were seldom home. Mr. X preferred to spend his evenings 'with the boys,' and the children could invariably be found a few doors away, where the lady of the house and her husband, and her brood welcomed them happily, and gave them the front living room for themselves. Mr. & Mrs. Neighbour spent much time in an old fashioned large kitchen, to which everyone eventually gravitated for cookies and milk, of which there was always an inexhaustible supply. Now Mrs. Neighbour was not a perfect housekeeper. How could she be, with youngsters running in and out all day? With records covering the tables, chairs, not to mention skates, sweaters and such. But the whole house smelled of the wondrous cookies she seemed always to be baking. And the lazy big smile of her husband just drew crowds of boys to talk about anything and everything from fishing to dating."

Is this not a wonderful sketch of a home filled with love and with memories a child will cherish for life? A child does not need worldly things for happiness. He needs love, but if the parents are irritable, quarrelsome and led by a materialistic spirit, then the fire of love will simply die out and the family will find itself living in the cold. The cute little toddler will surely grow up to be a problem teenager and ultimately a problem adult.

Teaching children is a major responsibility for parents. "Train a child in the way he should go, and when he is old he will not depart from it" (Prov. 22:6). As Christians, we believe in the mystical Body of Christ, and just as in any body, each individual cell has a specific function. By carrying out that function, each cell contributes to the health and well-being of the body. If, however, a cell rebels, then it becomes a threat to the integrity of the body. Children, as individual cells in the Body of Christ, need to be taught by their parents in order that they will take on full responsibility for their own unique function in the Body of Christ and as future citizens in our society.

Parents must be sensitive to the fact that all of their children are uniquely different, with various gifts according to the will of the Holy Spirit. Parents have the duty to nurture and develop those gifts, respecting the differences between their children, because one child may be studious, another good with his or her hands, another artistic and so on. Parents must beware of imposing their ambitions and desires onto a child. That is a sinful parental dictatorship which will destroy a child's self-image and can easily kill God's gifts to that child. Years ago when I used to take my little boy to hockey practice, I was often shocked to see a father and mother screaming at their own little boy (who clearly had no hockey talent) to score, to body-check and to skate beyond his ability. What an intolerable burden on a child who, deep in his own heart, knows he cannot meet such expectations. He was robbed of his right to find joy in play. In the early days of my son's hockey career, he spent a lot of time falling down but he and I both had a great time. Today, we can both laugh about it, but we also know that he learned a lot about his own abilities and about team spirit. My son knows how not to let the side down in life and he learned this well, precisely because he had fun learning it.

Teaching means thorough instruction in all necessary things, from moral values to good manners. However, the child has to **understand clearly** what is asked of him and must be shown gently how to carry out a command correctly. If the child is confused, then he will blow his assignment and come to think of himself as a failure. A parent has no right to expect good workmanship in a child if the parent does not invest time and effort to instruct him clearly. It will save hours of heartbreak if parents properly train the first one or two children well. The later children will observe the older ones applying themselves, and so they will follow by imitation.

Parents must also teach their children moral values as well as work. **Truthfulness, faith and modesty** are three vital virtues for children. Parents should demonstrate a deep disgust for lying, for unbelief in God, and for immodesty, and instill these principles into their children. Lying is a sin, and children must very quickly come to understand this. Lying arises out of pre-meditation, cunning and cold calculation, and is therefore deserving of a more severe punishment. Satan is the prince of lies, and he must not be allowed a foothold in your child's heart. The truth, and nothing but the truth, must rule in your home.

Children must be taught to have a firm unswerving belief in God and his doctrines. Lack of faith leads to the modern heresy of doubting everything, of scepticism, which is extolled today in our schools and universities. Scepticism is the devil's tool. Faith is our weapon against it. Teach your children to put on the armour of God every morning to protect them from the onslaughts of Satan.

"Stand your ground, with truth a belt around your waist and uprightness for a breastplate, wearing for shoes on your feet the eagerness to spread the gospel of peace and always carrying the shield of faith so that you can use it to quench the burning arrows of the Evil One. And then you must take salvation as your helmet and the sword of the Spirit, that is, the Word of God" (Eph. 6:14-17). Have your child imagine himself putting on this powerful armour every morning and he will likely be strong in the Lord for the rest of the day.

Modesty is under vicious attack these days and it seems people have become shockproof. Young people today embrace the most insulting immodesty in manner of dress, speech, and body language, and they display these on the street, in school, and often in church. This cannot be justified by saying that because the rest of the world is immodest, our youngsters must conform to the world's standards. The world is not interested in modesty. A Christian must swim against the current and establish God's standards of modesty if he is to follow Jesus at all. If the Queen of England were to be introduced to me, would I receive her in cut off shorts and a revealing shirt? More likely I would rush to put on my very best clothes in an effort to be "presentable." How much more, then, should we make a supreme effort to be presentable to the King of kings at all times. If a Christian mother dresses provocatively, which not too long ago was done only by women of loose virtue, then will she be shocked to see her teenage daughter go off to school, inviting boys to lust by her same manner of dress? Does this mother realize the consequences of such immodesty? Her daughter has lost respect for the miracle of her body and so will think very little of losing her virginity, and once that is lost, she may think very little of promiscuity.

Boys, who are so easily aroused and often think that their manhood depends on being a successful sexual hunter, will be only too willing to take advantage of this cheaply available sex-without-responsibility. That sets the scene for venereal disease, H.I.V. infection, illegitimate pregnancy, contraception, abortion, and loss of the Christian vision of each other as holy children of God. It cheapens that vision by reducing women to mere objects of unholy desire and tempts men to use them for their own selfish pleasure.

A Christian household must have rules, but the rules must be reasonable. It is just as destructive to have too many rules as to have none at all. Too many rules confine a child to a rigid stifling environment in which he cannot grow or explore, while no rules create anarchy in the home and violate the divine order. While children may kick against the rules because they want to do as they please (don't we all?), they fail to realize that they depend on their parents to establish order in their lives and to render their world manageable. I often hear nonsense from parents who say, "I can't do anything with little Johnny." Of course they can. What they are really saying is, "I can't do anything with little Johnny because I can't be bothered to do anything with little Johnny. I don't want to put out the effort. I don't want to give up some of my comfort or pleasure. I don't want to be unpopular." Well, take the time and be unpopular now or regret it later. The rewards will be multiplied a thousand-fold in the end. What a child thinks of you when he is being chastised is irrelevant. What the child thinks of you twenty years down the road is much more important.

Here is what one young housewife wrote about her mother (with a lot of tongue in cheek, but a lot of wisdom): "I had the meanest mother in the world. While other kids ate candy for breakfast, I had to have cereal, eggs or toast. When others had cokes and candy for lunch, I had to eat a sandwich. As you can guess, my supper was different from the other kids also. But at least I wasn't alone in my sufferings. My sister and two brothers had the same mean mother as I did. My mother insisted upon knowing where we were at all times. You'd think we were on a chain gang. She had to know who our friends were and what we were doing. She insisted if we said we'd be gone an hour, that we be gone one hour or less, not one hour and one minute. I am really ashamed to admit it, but she actually struck us. Not once, but each time we had a mind of our own and did as we pleased. That poor belt was used more on our seats than it was to hold up daddy's pants. Can you imagine someone actually hitting a child just because he disobeyed? Now you can see how mean she really was. We had to wear clean clothes and take a bath. The other kids always wore their clothes for days. We reached the heights of insult because she made our clothes herself just to save money. Why, oh why, did we have to have a mother who made us feel different from our friends?

"The worst is yet to come. We had to be in bed by nine each night and up at eight the next morning. We couldn't sleep till noon like our friends. So while they slept, my mother actually had the nerve to break the child-labour law. She made us work. We had to wash dishes, make beds, learn to cook and all sorts of cruel things. I believe she lay awake at night thinking up mean things to do to us. She always insisted upon our telling the truth, the whole truth and nothing but the truth, even if it killed us, and it nearly did. By the time we were teenagers, she was much wiser and our life became even more unbearable. None of this tooting of the horn of a car for us to come running. She embarrassed us no end by making our dates and friends come to the door to get us. If I spent the night with a girlfriend, can you imagine she checked on me to see if I were really there? I never had the chance to elope to Mexico. That is if I'd had a boyfriend to elope with. I forgot to mention, while my friends were dating at the mature age of twelve and thirteen, my old-fashioned mother refused to let me date until the age of fifteen and sixteen. Fifteen, that is, if you dated only to go to a school function. And that was maybe twice a year.

"Through the years, things didn't improve a bit. We could not lie in bed 'sick' like our friends did, and miss school. If our friends had a toe-ache, a hang-nail or other serious ailment, they could stay home from school. Our marks in school had to be up to par. Our friends' report cards had beautiful colours on them, black for passing, red for failing. My mother, being as different as she was, would settle for nothing less than ugly black marks. As the years rolled by, first one and then the other of us was put to shame. We were graduated from high school. With our mother behind us, talking, hitting and demanding respect, none of us was allowed the pleasure of being a drop-out.

"My mother was a complete failure as a mother. Out of four children, a couple of us attained some higher education. None of us has ever been arrested, divorced or beaten his mate. Each of my brothers served his time in the service of his country. And whom do we blame for the terrible way we turned out? You're right, our mean mother. Look at all the things we missed. We never got to march in a protest parade, nor to take part in a riot, burn draft cards, and a million and one other things that our friends did. She forced us to grow up into God-fearing, educated, honest adults. Using this as a background, I am trying to raise my three children. I stand a little taller and I am filled with pride when my children call me mean. Because, you see, I thank God, he gave me the meanest mother in the world."

This lady has learned, on looking back to her childhood, just how dedicated, loving, and wise her mother really was. Her negative opinion of her mother, when she was a mere child, did not matter at all. What mattered was that as an adult she was able to appreciate mother's wisdom. Mother did not try to win a popularity contest with her young daughter. She hung in for the long haul and won her daughter's admiration years later. We should take the same delight in raising our children to become responsible citizens and disciples of Jesus Christ.

Catholic parents would do well to remember one most important thing. Many, many parents come to me and complain that their son is alcoholic, or their daughter is living with her boyfriend, or their kids have all left the church. They constantly ask themselves where they went wrong. God left lots of room for free enterprise. He gave us a very wide margin for error. Most of us parent according to our best ability and if I am a bad parent, I know it in my deepest heart. But the vast majority of us are good parents, and we should comfort ourselves with the thought that most of our rebellious teenagers eventually grow up to be responsible people. It is a fact that, no matter how much we have done imperfectly, most kids do grow up. What they have learned as little children usually comes back to them later on, once they have checked out the sinful side of the tracks. So give up feeling guilty. If your children are now of legal age and are choosing rebellion, they are now God's job. All you are asked to do is pray for them. You do not need your child's permission to do that. Call on God to perfect that which we all do imperfectly.

Most parents would like to know how they are doing and how they stack up against other parents. I have printed here a "Spiritual Check-up for the Married." It is not my invention, but it is a wonderful little tool for Catholic couples. It might help some to recognize a flaw and take steps to correct it while there is still time.

Duties Toward God and Each Other:

1. Am I in earnest about saving my soul, as well as my husband's (or wife's) and children's souls?
2. Do I go to Confession and receive Holy communion at least once a month, realizing that it is the best thing I can do to bring happiness and blessing upon my family, because I thereby bring God into it?
3. Do I try to attend Holy Mass and receive Holy communion even on weekdays if it is possible?
4. Do I recite my Rosary daily and invoke the blessing and protection of the Blessed Virgin upon my family?
5. Do I permit mortal sin to harm the peace and happiness of my home and bring down God's judgement upon it by missing Mass on Sundays and holy days, by drunkenness, by giving scandal to my children, by not keeping my marriage chaste and holy?
6. Do I avoid in my language vulgarity and cursing?
7. Do I speak to my husband (or wife) in a way that betokens love, or am I in the habit of nagging, complaining, arguing or refusing to talk?
8. Do I lose my temper easily and frequently, want to have my own way, and always consider myself right?
9. When differences arise, do I discuss them with my husband (or wife) calmly and honestly?
10. Do I overlook the shortcomings of my husband (or wife) or do I hold grudges against him (or her)?
11. Do I discuss the faults of my husband (or wife) with others?
12. Have I made it a point to do those little things for my husband (or wife) which keep love alive in the human heart, or have I given my love to another?
13. Am I neat in appearance to please my husband (or wife)?
14. Do I keep things secret from my husband (or wife) which he (or she) ought to know?
15. Am I happy about sharing the intimacies of married life, or am I selfish and inconsiderate, thinking only of my personal satisfaction?

16. Have I shirked motherhood (or fatherhood) and yet taken the pleasures connected with my state of life, or offended God by the terrible sin of birth prevention?
17. Have I given my husband (or wife) a good example, especially by frequent reception of the Sacraments and prayer?

Duties Toward Their Children:

1. Am I conscious of the sublime dignity of parenthood and its grave responsibility?
2. Do I give my children a good example in the matter of frequenting the Sacraments, praying, keeping from sin?
3. Do my children ever hear me use improper language, tell questionable stories, talk unkindly about others?
4. Am I impatient and irritable in dealing with my children?
5. Am I loving but firm in correcting my children, and do I discuss their development and progress with my husband (or wife)?
6. Do I send my children to a truly Catholic school, if possible, or at least to Catechism classes? If not, do I see to it myself that they are given true Catholic education?
7. Do I know my children's companions, reading, types of recreation?
8. Am I interested in their school work and in preparing them for their future?
9. What would be, or has been, my reaction to a religious vocation in the family?
10. Is my outside work and recreation depriving my children of proper care and protection?
11. Is there any questionable literature in my home?
12. Do I do everything possible to make my home a clean, happy, and pleasant place for my children to live in, or do I waste much of my money and time outside my home?
13. Are my children proud of their mother (or father)?
14. Do I pray fervently each day for my husband (or wife) and children?

If we took this to heart and lived it out, we would be rightfully proud of our children as they grow to become wholesome and holy adults. We would one day be able to stand before Jesus and say, "I was not a perfect parent but, by the grace of God, I was a Catholic parent."

CHAPTER 9

Parenting: God's Discipline for Children

*"Children, obey your parents
in the Lord, for this is right."*
(Eph. 6:1)

The Oxford Dictionary defines discipline as "instruction, mental and moral training, the maintenance of order, ***chastisement and mortification by penance.***" In other words, discipline can be achieved by a variety of strategies such as good example, teaching, explanation, repetition of lessons, encouragement and if necessary, punishment. Punishment can mean different things for different situations and different children.

For today's permissive society, discipline is a forbidden word, and our godless culture naively believes that it can raise disciplined children by giving them no discipline at all. Discipline is fundamental to a Christian. The Bible mentions discipline fifty-eight times, so it can safely be concluded that, since God took the trouble to talk about discipline in fifty-eight different ways, discipline is very important to God's order.

God's order is founded on obedience. It was Jesus who decreed that the Holy Father obey Jesus Christ. The bishops are to obey the Holy Father, the priests obey the bishops, parents obey the priests and children obey their parents. This is the moral hierarchy of obedience. God disciplines us and we in turn discipline our children.

It is very important to appreciate that by disciplining our children we are *not* imposing our *will* upon our children, rather we are being *obedient* to the word of God. As was emphasised in chapter 8, *good-parenting is God-parenting.*

> *"So you must realize that the Lord your God disciplines you, even as a man disciplines his son."*
> (Deut. 8:5)

> *"Whoever loves discipline, loves knowledge. Stupid are those who hate correction."*
> (Prov. 12:1)

> *"Discipline your children while there is hope; Do not set your heart on their destruction"*
> (Prov. 19:18)

From these scripture passages, it is evident that:

1. We discipline because God disciplines.
2. Without discipline, a child can have no worthwhile knowledge. So discipline and learning go hand in hand.
3. We must discipline children while there is hope. That is to say, we must begin to discipline a child at the earliest possible age.
4. The obedience of a child is not *optional.* It is *demanded* by God.

Great care must nevertheless be exercised. While discipline may at times use correction, not all correction is true discipline. Correction or punishment can sometimes be brutal, excessive, and cruel, and that constitutes child abuse. Christian discipline is principally a fatherly prerogative, since it is derived from God the Father, and it is always designed to save, to purify, and to heal. "Not for vengeance did the Lord put them in the crucible to try their hearts, nor has he done so with us. It is by way of *admonition* that he chastises those who are close to him" (Judith 8:27). As it is for God, so it is for Christian parents. Punishment is an act of *love,* not an act of *vengeance.*

"If you wish it my child, you can be taught. Apply yourself and you will become intelligent" (Sir. 6:32). Are these not the words of a loving and gentle Father? Yet, love must not be confused with permissiveness. "Pamper your child and he will terrorise you, play along with him and he will bring you sorrows?" (Sir. 30:9). This is exactly what we are seeing in our society today. We are being terrorised by a whole generation of pampered children. I have seen a family utterly controlled by a five-year-old child running riot. He spits, he stamps his feet, he screams for what he wants, and his distraught parents give it to him. He breaks his toys then throws a tantrum till he gets a replacement. He is in fact a child abused by neglect, who is trying to find the boundaries, but can never reach them because his parents do not give him any. It is so easy for parents to lose or relinquish their legitimate and God-given authority. How can parents take back what has been lost and give back to children what they do not know they have lost? It is accomplished by means of loving discipline and just discipline.

The first and most fundamental prerequisite for just discipline is to *know* your child. All children are unique and different, they come in all shapes and sizes, and what is good discipline for one child may be disastrous for another. A rebellious child may respond to more severe correction, while a sensitive child may be totally crushed by it.

Many parents make the mistake of trying to treat all of their children exactly alike, in the belief that equality is the same thing as justice. It is not. A father once told me that he was disturbed that his two very young daughters seemed always to be fighting with each other. As an experiment he bought them two identical toy cribs with identical little comforters and identical little dolls. He gave one set to Susan and one to Melissa. They were delighted at first, but within a half hour, they were fighting over one crib. Susan screamed, "It is mine!" while Melissa yelled back, "No, it isn't. It is mine." Meanwhile, the other crib was lying over in the corner being ignored. Treating children identically does not work. Their very uniqueness demands individualised parenting.

Only the parents can know their own children and it is the duty of parents to observe their children, to know how sensitive each one is, and to respond accordingly. A day-care attendant cannot understand your child and his special needs. God gave your children to *you*, not to paid professionals.

All of us have moods both good and bad, both high and low, and our children do too. But little children do not understand their low moods, and they will often express their bad feelings with bad behaviour. As grown ups, however, we must understand that hidden behind every low mood there is a temporary insecurity. Whenever we feel insecure, we will experience a low mood, and a low mood tempts us to give in to anger, anxiety, fear, sadness, hurt, jealousy and other negative feelings.

Imagine little Johnny. He is angry. He is sitting on the rug and he is demolishing his dump truck. He is tearing the wheels off it and throwing them away, and is pounding the truck into a shapeless pulp. If all you see when you observe this is his destructive behaviour, then you will feel justified in yelling at him, "Who do you think you are? Don't you know I had to work hard to get the money to buy that dump truck? How dare you show such ingratitude. Well, you are grounded, mister. Go to your room." Little Johnny will have to react to your punishment and he will react by having his mood plummet even lower. He will therefore feel even more insecure, and so he is likely to throw a major, out-of-control tantrum. Instead of attacking his dump truck, he is more likely to start trashing your house! However, if instead of merely judging his behaviour, you look beyond that and see that he is feeling insecure and that what he is doing is expressing his low mood, then you might react very differently.

In the light of this insight, you could distract him from the useless truck demolition enterprise by lifting him up onto your knee. Then you might say, "Johnny. Let's just sit here for a while and let me love you." There is no need for words at this point. A silent hug will speak volumes. Then when Johnny is feeling more secure, you can talk. "Johnny, you were feeling really bad there, weren't you?" "Yes, mom." "You sort of wanted me to know that, right?" "Yes, mom." "Well, do you think that it was a good idea to smash up your dump truck just to let me know how bad you feel, because now you don't have a dump truck to play with any more?" (Notice I did not say that you would rush out and buy him a replacement. He trashed it so he will have to do without. A child must learn that there are consequences to actions.) "No mom." "So what are you upset about Johnny?" "I heard daddy say he was leaving us." "Oh, that's the problem! No, Johnny. Dad is only going away for a couple of days on business. He isn't leaving us. He is coming back on Tuesday. Why don't you and I do something special for daddy when he comes home? So listen, Johnny, the next time you are feeling bad, instead of breaking your toys, why don't you tell me you're feeling bad, and we'll work something out, OK?" "OK, mom." And off he goes to play. First of all, he is reassured about his fear; secondly, he is learning there is a better way to express his insecurity; and thirdly, he has learned that some behaviours merely end up by hurting himself. In this case, he no longer has a dump truck. Naturally, this takes time, but it is time well-spent. It means dropping some agenda of your own in order to listen to your child, but only you, the parent, can understand that what Johnny was doing was not out of malice, but out of a low mood. Another of your children may do the same thing with his dump truck, but you know that with him it is not a mood but *rebellion,* and that must be handled differently.

The second most important tool for discipline is *love*, because effective discipline is loving discipline. There is no other way. It is loving discipline which we receive from our heavenly parent, God the Father, and he expects us to discipline in like manner. "For the Lord disciplines those whom he loves" (Heb. 12:6). Likewise, we who love our children are to discipline them also. In fact, discipline and love go hand-in-glove. Discipline without love is nothing more than tyranny, and love without discipline is indulgence. Loving discipline generates love in the child. Loveless discipline generates fear which renders the child incapable of performing almost any task. Disciplineless love generates disobedience, which reaps the whirlwind of an out-of-control child. Needless to say, this concept of love is so often misunderstood by parents and they wonder why they are raising aliens from outer space, instead of children.

Gary Smallery, a well known counsellor, identifies four types of parents: **Dominant, Neglectful, Permissive, Firm Lovers.**

Dominant parents tend to have excessively high expectations of their children. They expect them to be perfect in everything. They seldom offer warm, loving support and they seldom help the child understand why the rules have to be so rigid. The result is that when the child does not know why something is wrong, he will tend to secretly do that wrong thing. A major study out of Columbia County, New York, found that high aggression in younger children is often caused by overly dominant parents. This aggression usually lasts a lifetime and can lead to major violence. The study also showed that harsh punishment, such as washing out a child's mouth with soap, coupled with rejection will always lead to aggressive behaviour.

Neglectful parents neither give loving support to their children nor do they exercise control over them. They isolate themselves from their children by excessive use of baby-sitters, and they forever indulge in their own selfish activities. Neglect of children in our society occurs for four reasons:

1. Divorce

The current high divorce rate leads to single parent families. The divorce rate has increased seven hundred per cent since the beginning of the century, and as a result a single mother has to be both provider and parent. While it does not absolutely have to happen, it is difficult for a single mother not to be emotionally distant from her children, simply because she is so burdened and exhausted. In spite of that risk, numerous courageous and dedicated single mothers should be applauded for their often awesome commitment to their children. They are heroines in a broken society.

2. Absentee Parents

Dr. Amand Nicholi, a psychiatrist at Harvard Medical School, warns that by going out to work, mothers are less accessible to their young children. One study he quoted shows that American parents spend less time with their children than parents in any other nation in the world, except England. A Russian father said he would not think of spending less than two hours a day with his children. By contrast, the average father in the U.S. spends about thirty-seven seconds a day with his children! I still have difficulty believing that statistic, but there it is, like it or not.

3. Television

Television has become a major child rearing resource, and not for the better. The problem with television is that even though people are physically together in a room, there is no meaningful and emotional interaction going on. As parents neglect their children by watching T.V. or other activities, children experience a powerful emotional loss similar to that of losing a parent through death. The child can come to believe that the reason for this is that he is bad and so his self-esteem is seriously wounded. He needs more than just your physical presence — he needs loving interaction.

4. Frequent Relocation

Society today is increasingly mobile. Moving house every three to five years robs children of a stable, manageable and predictable environment. They become isolated from their extended family and school friends, and if mum and dad are simply dragging their children all over the country without helping them to understand, then the children become insecure and uprooted.

Permissive parents are often warm, supporting persons, but are very weak when it comes to establishing and enforcing rules and limits for their children. They live in fear of confronting their children, not realizing that failure to confront will produce the very things they fear. Good parents know that a certain degree of permissiveness is healthy. They accept that children will be children, that a clean shirt will not stay clean for long, that a mirror is for making faces, and puddles are for splashing. But over-permissiveness cuts children loose, allowing them to beat up other children, to break valuable objects, and to write on walls. The child learns that the rules are not rules at all. They are simply there to be ignored.

Firm loving parents combine loving support with loving discipline. They take time to help their children understand the rules. They are flexible and willing to listen so that they themselves understand fully why their child has done something and, as a result, the child is more content. He has learned to control himself. He is more secure because he knows he is loved. He knows that his parents are investing time and effort in him, that they are strong, and thus he is safe in their care. Study after study confirms that children of loving and firm parents rank highest in self-respect, and obedience to authorities at school, church and society. They also have a greater interest in their parents' faith in God, and a greater tendency not to join a rebellious group. "How blessed are all who fear Yahweh, who walk in his ways. Your own labours will yield you a living, happy and prosperous will you be. Your wife a fruitful vine in the inner places of your house, your children round your table like shoots of an olive tree. Such are the blessings that fall on those who fear Yahweh" (Ps. 128:1-4).

Ed Piorek, who has done a powerful work on the meaning of fatherhood in God's design, tells of a distraught father who came to him one day and said, "Ed, I am at my wits end. My son is out of control. He is into drugs, sex, defying my curfews, you name it! I yell at him, threaten him, and impose bigger and bigger punishments on him, but it is all to no effect. What can I do?" Ed looked at him for a minute in silence, then softly said, "Dan, how has your heavenly Father fathered you?" Dan was stunned. Tears filled his eyes and he said, "God has always graced me. He has always loved me and I have not done this with my son. God forgive me." Dan repented, went off and began to treat his son with love and with respect. He began to *listen* to his son's heart. As a result, the boy began to turn around and come back to the family love he always desired, and which he felt forced to seek outside of his home.

The third tool of discipline is *prayer*. Ask the Holy Spirit to come into your heart in every situation related to your children. The Holy Spirit is available free of charge every moment of every day so why rely on your own limited notions when you can have the inspiration of Wisdom itself? Before you utter a word of correction to your child, breathe a prayer to the Holy Spirit for wisdom in your discipline. You will receive that wisdom. It is promised in Scripture by Jesus himself. "If you, then, who are wicked, know how to give good gifts to your children, how much more will the Father in Heaven give the Holy Spirit to those who ask him?" (Luke 11:13).

The fourth tool of discipline is *example.* There is no use in asking your child to do something if you do not do it yourself. It is pointless to say, "Don't drink, son" while you are slurring your speech with a beer in your hand. Parents must show order in their lives if they are to expect order from their children. If you demand that your little daughter pick up her toys or that your teenage son tidy his room, you must also be a model of tidiness. If you expect your child to obey the ten commandments, you had better be seen to obey them also. If you expect him to go to Mass, you must be faithful to it. But it is not enough just to do those things, you must demonstrate joy in them. Show your child how happy you are in obeying God and the Church. The child will pick up on your enthusiasm and try to please you too. Good example justifies your demands. The message to the child is, "Do as I say, because I also do as I say."

Dr. David Posen, a psychotherapist, recounts how he helped a father who was very anxious about his son's disobedience. The man said, "Doctor, I can't do anything with him. He comes home from school and drops his satchel on the hall floor. No matter how much I tell him, he just will not change his slovenly habit." Dr. Posen thought for a moment and said, "Joe, where do you leave your briefcase when you come home from the office?" Joe's face was a sudden picture of surprise. "Oh no!" he said, "I drop it in the hall and it stays there all night till I go out to work in the morning." The solution was obvious. Dad had to learn to change his bad habit before he had the authority to demand the same from his son.

There are some practical guidelines for effective and loving discipline — for true Christian discipline. In order to do this, I will give examples of how to handle specific situations, but most importantly I want to empower parents with an understanding of the principles in order to gain the best results from a child rather than unwittingly bringing out the worst in him or her.

In the Catholic tradition, the first principle is that liberty for a child means the *freedom to do what is right,* but the child must defer to authority at all times in determining what is wrong. This is fundamental to good Catholic parenting. Parents would do well to write this out, stick it up on the door of the fridge and memorise it. It would avoid many power struggles and pain for both the parents and the child.

A child has the right to do what is pleasing and interesting to him, provided that what he is doing is not wrong or dangerous or destructive to property. Parents often make the mistake of diverting a child from some activity which he finds fascinating, but which the parent sees as useless. In so doing, that parent is choking off the child's initiative to explore his environment and to achieve a task which he believes to be important. For example, dad notices his child is carefully taking a small spoon and scooping up some sand to put it in his bucket. Dad can see that this is going to take hours and hours. The child is totally absorbed in the task, but dad, a) desires to help him and, b) is impatient at the obvious waste of time of this pointless task. So dad, with the best will in the world, goes over, picks up a man-sized shovel and with one scoop fills the bucket. The child collapses in tears of frustration and dad, totally puzzled, becomes angry with the child. "After all," thinks dad, "the object was to fill the bucket and I was only showing him how to do it more quickly." Dad is also thinking how dumb it was for his child to be using a spoon. But dad has missed the point. The object in the child's mind was not to fill the bucket. The object for him was to repeat a complicated manoeuvre over and over again so as to train his muscles, eyes and balance, and to do it well. As an adult, dad was goal-oriented. As a child, little Johnny was method-oriented. Johnny is not yet old enough to figure out the *why.* He is too busy figuring out the *how to.* Johnny had a right to play for hours with the spoon, the sand, and the bucket. He was not doing anything wrong, and he should have been given the freedom to do what was right, even if it seemed pointless to the parent. It is rarely pointless to the child.

The second principle of discipline is that a child must come to gradually understand the difference between *good and evil.* That understanding, of course, must become more and more sophisticated as the child grows older. "When I was a child, I spoke like a child, I thought like a child, I reasoned like a child. When I became an adult, I put an end to childish things" (1 Cor. 13:11). Therefore, *do not give adult information to a little child.* The child is not ready for these things, and will be seriously damaged by such premature information. That is why I am not a supporter of current sex-education programs in Catholic schools. The children are not ready for the information given. The system completely fails to recognize that children, like little Johnny with the spoon, the sand and the bucket, learn by imitation, by rehearsing and by repetition. A child will try to make sense of this sex-education information by doing it, not by reflecting on it. The sex class becomes a "How-to" class, at least that is how the child will *perceive* it.

This will no doubt shock many Catholic parents, but I believe that *premature sex-education is child sexual abuse.* Everyone agrees that any adult who exposes himself to a little child, or touches a child intimately, or has intercourse with a child, is *sexualizing* that child. That is called sexual abuse. Providing premature sex education to a young child also sexualizes that child, and so it too is a form of sexual abuse. They are little innocents and deep within, they know that their innocence is being violated. Educators do this with the best will in the world, and I am sure many will be offended by what I have written, but these remarks are not meant to be offensive. Rather, they are meant to promote an honest re-assessment of what has become an unchallenged assumption. I believe that the well-intentioned efforts of Catholic educators often betray a sad lack of understanding of child psychology. A child will ask questions when he is ready for the answers. He should not be robbed of his precious childhood.

Illegitimate pregnancy and sexually-transmitted diseases (S.T.D.'s) are not prevented by sex education, but rather are promoted by it. They are prevented only by abstinence and by teaching the child about the virtue of modesty. *Education in modesty is the only sound Catholic sex-education.* It is a frightening fact that illegitimate pregnancies and S.T.D.'s are increasing at an alarming rate in spite of widespread sex-education programs. Is it not possible that these very programs are contributing to this increase? Only by returning to instruction in chastity and the sanctity of the body can we ever hope to protect our cherished children. Wise parents instinctively know how to wait for the right moment, which will be different for each of their children. Only the parents know enough to discern this right moment for their child. But classroom sex education mass-processes children, as though they were all at the same stage of receptivity. Pope John Paul II has solemnly announced his opposition to current sex-education programs and it is encouraging for me as a Catholic therapist to know that my foregoing remarks are in accord with the teaching of the Holy Father.

The third principle is that Christian discipline consists of *silence and activity*. A little child should be given repeated lessons in silence, but in *active silence*, not *forced immobility*. The very young child should be engaged in a game that teaches him how to be silent. Make it an adventure. Ask him to show you how silent he can be so that not a sound or a movement is made. Ask him to listen in the silence to see if he can hear a whispered word or name. Show him how to be silent. This is vital. Do not command him to be quiet and sit still. Show him how to get up without making a sound, without scraping the chair on the floor. Then ask him to do it. Show him how to walk silently. Then ask him to do it. Make it a fun game. This is silence in action, not enforced inertia. Encourage him to repeat these actions till he can be silent and attentive, then congratulate him on a job well done. You will be amazed at how he will learn, not only to hear a whispered or quiet command, but will be delighted to obey it to show you how clever he is. Alternate periods of silence with activity and the child will learn about his body, how to control his movements, and so will learn self-discipline.

He will also learn the value of silence when he comes to meditate later on in prayer. Many young people today are afraid of silence and so they assault their ears continually with blaring music from stereos and radios. Silence is vital if we are ever to contemplate the mysteries of God. Such a child will instinctively feel his success, and will grow in self-esteem as he learns to conquer both himself and his environment and he will come to value his own thoughts.

This kind of discipline should begin at the earliest possible age. A child is never too young. From birth, he is absorbing information at a phenomenal rate. Before he can use language, he is watching you and preparing to imitate you. Apart from the words "mama" and "papa" one of the first words he will learn is "no." If he is doing something harmful or undesirable, no matter how young, let him hear a gentle but firm "No." Then distract him from the undesirable behaviour and into another activity.

Effective discipline must be active. A child is not disciplined who is rendered mute or totally immobile by force. Rather, he is annihilated. A disciplined person is one who has learned to master himself, and who regulates his own conduct. Give him the freedom to move and in so doing, he will learn to perform easily and correctly the simple acts of community and social life. However, the limit or boundary to the child's liberty is the common good. We must check in the child any rough or ill-bred actions, or whatever offends or annoys others. All the rest should be permitted. We often do not appreciate the consequences of suffocating a child's spontaneous action at a time when he is just becoming active.

Believe it or not, a parent has to learn a certain passive role, observing the child's behaviour, rather than dominating it. Parental duty is to discern which are the acts to hinder and which to leave alone. For example, a little girl gathered her friends around her in class and began talking and gesticulating. The teacher rushed forward and told her to be still and to keep quiet. What the teacher did not take the time to find out was that the child was taking the role of teacher and was teaching her friends the Hail Mary and the Sign of the Cross.

Mother is tidying up the living room. The child comes and picks up things. Mother says sternly, "Leave those alone." As a result the child is crushed. He learns that it is not good to try and imitate mummy and to help her. Mother has missed an opportunity to give a lesson in tidiness, a lesson the child was clearly ready for.

A child is watching others. He cannot see what they are doing, so he gets the brilliant idea of bringing over a chair. He intends to climb onto it in order to see. Suddenly a well-meaning adult comes along and lifts him up and says, "There you are. Now you can see." That adult has stifled the child's inventiveness in conquering a problem. Instead, the child is being taught that others will solve all his problems. *The child who does not do, does not know how to do.* How often have you seen a parent dress a child as though the child were a doll or a puppet? Much better to encourage him to experiment with dressing himself, and if he puts the right shoe on the left foot, do not scorn him or ridicule him. Tell him how good he is for trying, then show him the difference between a right shoe and a left one. Mark the shoes with two coloured laces, red for right, yellow for left. He will get the hang of it. He wants to.

The fourth principle is that as soon as possible, it is vital to give your child a sense of *work*. Work was decreed by God, because God himself worked, and God continues to work. In six days, he worked at creating the universe, and he works constantly at his ongoing creative process, making new souls and revealing his face to us in research, new knowledge and new discoveries. We must inculcate work into our children right from the beginning. A working child is not getting into mischief. A working teenager is not hanging out on the street corner looking for trouble.

Give the young child a role to play in the organization of the house. He must be shown that you expect him to do his assigned job but, for him to do it well, he must understand what is expected of him. So show him. Do the job yourself and show him how you want it done. Hang in there with him, encouraging him, congratulating him and gently correcting him till he gets it right. This whole exercise of learning a new skill should be made into an exciting adventure. Do not just say, "Do it" and then give him heck when he is confused and messes up. He has no idea, on his own, what is a good performance and what is bad.

While he is learning, do not focus on what he does wrong. Focus, rather on what he does right. Congratulate him and hug him. Show him your pleasure at his efforts. Where he is not doing things quite right, encourage him, show him again and he will put his little heart into it, because instinctively he wants to please you and to be loved by you. Once he masters one job, start him off on another and work at that till he gets that one right, and so on. Work teaches discipline and work is discipline. In taking time to do this, you are teaching your child responsible work habits. Later, as an adult, he will expect to work, he will take pride in his work and he will accept responsibility.

If you inculcate good work habits in your children as soon as you can communicate with them, they will come to accept that responsible behaviour is preferable to sloth, and is a great deal more satisfying. Delinquents have too much free time. As one judge put it, "Football players don't get into trouble during football season. They are too tired at night to do anything but fall into bed. After the season, they start to roam around and some of them turn up at Juvenile Hall." Thelma Hatfield, an educator, once wrote, "Parents, you must teach and train your children so they will like to work or at least when faced with a piece of hard work, be able to get in and do it without suffering oppression. A lazy Christian never did anything for God. When you get your child to do a long and tedious piece of work, do not permit him to dispute and enlarge upon redundant details in order to build obstacles, or to be just generally irritable, because he must work, thinking he will wear you out and soon be able to leave the job undone. If you are not firm here, this spirit will possess him, and when he is an adult and expected to make something of himself, he will fail, because he was trained to avoid and oppose that which is unpleasant."

Note that a lazy adult is only doing what he was allowed to do in his childhood years. A child who is permitted to play, play, play from morning to night for eighteen years will expect to play for the next fifty years. All work and no play will surely make Jack a dull boy, but all play and no work will make him a grown-up slob. How can such a person ever face the challenge of weariness and the duty of the moment? It is too late. "Whatsoever a man sows, that also shall he reap" (Gal. 6:7).

Thelma Hatfield also wrote, "I have in mind a family where the child was not obligated to do anything, but what pleased his fancy. He was made the centre of attraction, and when small, was allowed to indulge in all sorts of wee-sized vandalism throughout the house and grounds. When an interested person saw what was taking place in that child, he tried to speak to the parents. However, they could not be approached. The friend had scarcely broached the subject when he was silenced by their angry and superior attitude. Years later, when this child was the literal embodiment of the Devil, and totally incorrigible, the parents in tears were ready to talk hours on end to the same friend regarding their trouble. The kindly man did not have the heart to shake his finger under their nose and say, 'Remember when I tried to tell you.'"

Work is a holy thing. Play is only holy when it is justified by work.

The fifth principle is that a child needs to know what *goodness* is and that goodness is to be preferred over sin. Take every opportunity to teach the child about goodness, about such things as modesty, consideration for others, his prayers, reverence in Church, and respect for authority. Teach him about Jesus and the Blessed Mother. Tell him how good Jesus was and is, and how obedient he was to his parents. Tell him how much he is loved. Read stories to him about Jesus and about the saints. Ask him never to embarrass his guardian angel.

Keep him away from television, the corrupter of innocent minds. By all means show him a good Christian video, but avoid regular programming. It is disguised to instill worldly values. T.V. is not a baby-sitter. It is an idol, so do not bow down before it. Apart from the actual hypnotic effect of television, which leads the child to uncritically soak in and internalise whatever message is being peddled, there is also the "jolt effect." Any T.V. producer will tell you that for a visual input to be really effective, the picture has to be continually changing. These changes are referred to in the trade as "jolts." The child who is glued to the set is receiving a preplanned number of jolts per minute. As a result he begins to need his jolts. He will start to look for them in his world, in his parents, his siblings, in Church and at school. Since jolts are not built in to these encounters, he becomes bored with them and they lose their power to mould him. He will therefore find Church boring (how many jolts do we receive in a homily?), school becomes a chore, and his parents will lose their authority to command.

The four watch words for discipline, therefore, are: Silence, Activity, Work, and Goodness.

If you have asked a child to do some work, do not sit around idle yourself. That discourages the child. For example, if he is doing homework, at some point make him some hot chocolate and cookies, and get on with a useful task of your own. Do not flop on the couch and watch the ball game. That is a contradictory message.

Imagine that the child is playing in the sand box, and he starts to throw sand around. He is giggling with delight at this exciting new discovery. As a parent, you know this is undesirable and dangerous behaviour, so you must put a stop to it. Since the child is not knowingly doing evil, it is cruel to punish him. Go immediately to him and distract him from his behaviour. You can say, "Johnny, instead of throwing sand around, why don't we dig. Let's dig." If he throws some more then you can explain that this might get sand into someone's eyes and that would hurt a lot. In other words, if you distract him from the undesired behaviour, that is usually enough. This is a good time to tell him a story about a little bird in his nest. Parents are often shocked at this story and think it cruel, but children understand it fully.

"A little bird's mother told him she had to go and look for food and that he must stay in the nest till she got back. He decided not to obey his mother and after she was gone, he climbed out of the nest, fell onto the ground and a big cat came and ate him up." This will not terrify your child. He will listen wide-eyed and immediately get the point. You are teaching Johnny that mummy knows best, and that is a very good lesson for Johnny to learn at an early age.

It is vital to avoid a power struggle. A child will often try to pull you into one, and if he wins you lose. This only leads to more power struggles, because he loses respect for you. If you win, then while you may have control, the child feels weak and defeated. A power struggle is a losing game, so always try to avoid it. The best way to deal with a temper tantrum is to remove yourself. In this way, the child has nobody to perform for. By all means use humour to get him to quit, but never be sarcastic. Watch your language with a power-hungry child. Don't say, "You will go to bed now." That is only setting yourself up. Rather say, "Bedtime in ten minutes, Johnny, so let's play one more game." If he throws his coat on the floor, say, "Oh, you forgot to hang up your coat. Let me show you where it goes." Then show him. The next time he drops his coat on the floor you say, "Johnny, can you show me where your coat goes?" And in so doing, you give the child input into the solution. This is the way to avoid the authority which threatens and to share the authority with the child. Another example is if you want the child to learn how to set a table, you say, "Johnny, I'm having a problem setting the table. How can you and I do this?" Then Johnny may say, "Well, you do the forks, mummy, and I'll do the spoons." In other words respect the child, but use firmness and determination. In this way, the child becomes part of the solution instead of part of the problem.

Children, of course, often get into expressing their need for attention. They can do this passively or actively. Passive attention-getting occurs in the child who says, "I can't do it" or "I'm not good at that." It is his way of saying, "I am discouraged. I don't want to fail again." If you, as a parent find yourself throwing up your hands and saying, "I give up" then you are simply reinforcing his discouragement. Try to build up this child's self-esteem by giving him tasks which you know he can do. He needs to experience some successes in his efforts to conquer his environment. Encourage a lot and try not to criticise him or her since criticism really crushes a child who is in this frame of mind.

The active attention-getter is the child who gets into the power play, and is prone to the classical temper tantrum. This child does not obey the first time, because the payoff is he will get more attention. He will try to get mum and dad involved, or he will refuse to eat or to go to bed, or he will fight other kids. So be firm but kind. Do not pay attention when he is trying to get attention. Instead let him take the consequences of his negative behaviour. Give him good attention, and not self-defeating attention. That is to say, if his behaviour is not in and of itself harmful, then ignore the bad and compliment the good. However, if the behaviour is sinful, then the parent must step in. If the child is destroying property, then it must be stopped and he must clean it up.

An excellent way to deal with deviant behaviour is to isolate the child. Place him where he can see the normal loving activity of the rest of the household. He will calm down eventually and want to return to the warmth and activity of the others. *Always be consistent.* Inconsistency will cause a child to test the limits. A child without boundaries panics and starts to frantically try and find out where these boundaries are. He will simply run out of control, and that is anarchy.

When my son was about six years old, he was sitting very quietly on the rug looking very thoughtful. Suddenly he looked up and said, "Dad, which would you rather be, a frog or a snake?" I replied, "I don't want to be either." He looked disturbed and said, "No dad! You have to choose one. Which do you want?" I said again that I preferred to remain a man, and my son became even more agitated and kept on insisting that I had no choice but to select one of his two options. The idea that there could be other possibilities never seemed to enter his mind. Reflecting on that, I realised that young children can only hold on to two choices at a time. They cannot hold onto three or more options. Use this knowledge when dealing with a disobedient child. Give him two punishment options and let him choose whichever one he wants. For example, if little Johnny spits at you, first of all let him know firmly but kindly that this is not acceptable behaviour. He spits at you again, so you give him a choice. "Alright Johnny, until you are ready to be with people you can either go to your room or you can sit in the corner on that chair. It's up to you." Johnny will instinctively opt for one of the two choices presented. Either way he is being punished. Do not put a time limit on it by saying, "OK, you will sit there for fifteen minutes." That will only set you up for another power struggle. Instead, after a little while you say, "Are you ready now to be with people?" He will say, "yes" or "no." If he says "no" leave him a little while longer, then don't ask again. Just say, "It is time to get up now." If he says "yes" then welcome him back with love.

It is time to address the controversial and difficult problem of physical punishment. Is there a place for it in a Catholic home? The new Catechism seems to imply that at times discipline will demand the rod. In *paragraph 1804,* it places two biblical quotations together. "He who loves his son will not spare the rod" (Sir. 30:1). "Fathers, do not provoke your children to anger, but bring them up in the discipline and instruction of the Lord" (Eph. 6:4).

The Church recognises that parents aren't to choose between the rod of the Old Testament or the love of the New. Rather, we are to seek a Christian balance between the two. The Old Testament was the time of the law and of justice, and so discipline was seen mainly in terms of physical retribution. With the New Testament, we have Christ incarnate and the spirit of the law which is mercy, love and gentleness. Certainly the effects of original sin are there in us, but Baptism makes available God's grace whereby we are able to love God and to more clearly discern what is good.

Two thousand years ago, a child was born and he grew up to say: "Suffer little children to come unto me" (Mark 10:14). "I give you a new commandment: Love one another as I have loved you" (John 13:34). Yet, the same gentle Jesus was capable of being stern when it was called for: "Whoever causes one of these little ones who believe in me to sin, it would be better for him to have a great millstone hung around his neck and to be drowned in the depths of the sea" (Matt. 18:6). Jesus loved innocence so much that he threatened unspeakable punishment on those who would corrupt the little ones. Is this not another very good reason for parents to avoid anything which they know would corrupt their children, or lead them into sin?

"Making a whip out of cord, he drove them all out of the temple, sheep and cattle as well, scattered the money changers' coins, knocked their tables over" (John 2:15). Clearly Jesus was not afraid to discipline those who offended his Father in heaven. We too must not be afraid to discipline our children if they offend God.

"You serpents, brood of vipers, how can you escape being condemned to hell?" (Matt. 23:33). The ultimate punishment from God is to be lost forever. We, as parents, must correct our children while the correcting is good, otherwise, they may grow to a life of offending God with its awful consequences. What parent would choose such an eternity for their child? Therefore, choose now and discipline now. Eternity does depend upon it.

"My son do not disdain the discipline of the Lord or lose heart when reproved by him, for whom the Lord loves, he disciplines. He scourges every son he acknowledges" (Heb. 12:5-6). God's discipline is founded on love and so should ours as parents. Yet God *scourges* his own when they need it. As parents, designated by God, we may also have to show our love in a physical way to our children if they need it.

Bishop Fulton Sheen once said, "A spanking is just a pat on the back that is low enough and hard enough to let the child know you love him." Therefore, the only motivation for spanking is love. It must never be an act of vengeance. A loving parent will use the rod in obedience to the word of God, not as a merciless avenging angel. A child should never be physically punished in anger. Anger always results in harshness and unnecessary pain, and always provokes a child to resentment. *Physical punishment out of rage is always child abuse.*

One child may need a swat and react well to it. Another may be too easily crushed and be totally defeated. Only a parent can truly know his or her own child well enough to punish appropriately. Let the rod be reserved as a last resort, and only for outright rebellion. The parent must be sure that the child is deliberately and with malice choosing to rebel, to tell lies, to take the name of the Lord in vain, to be stealing, or breaking any of the other commandments. The rod is reserved for open rebellion against God.

The discipline must be administered immediately. There must be a direct connection in the child's mind between his action and the consequences. Do not say, "Well, just you wait till your father gets home. You're going to get it then." This makes no sense to a child. Do it and do it there and then. "Because sentence against an evil told is not executed speedily, the heart of the sons of men is fully set to do evil" (Eccl. 8:11). A threat of punishment followed by no punishment is a waste of breath. Absolutely never use threats that cannot be carried out. Some parents make threats which would make one's hair stand on end, but the child is clever enough to know that this will never happen, so he ignores them. Never scream or yell or get out of control. A child soon learns to tune you out, and all you will achieve is high blood pressure. The child will also learn that it must be acceptable for him to scream and yell in order to get what he wants. Meanwhile, the child continues blithely to do whatever he was doing which irritated you in the first place. It is far better to remain serene and demand what you want from the child in a calm, quiet, but firm voice. If you have taught him silence he will already be primed to hear a quiet command. If that is ignored, then as Scripture tells us, punishment should be immediate. Never ask a child over and over again to do something. He soon learns that he can safely ignore the first dozen or so commands. Ask once only and then act. Thereby, the child soon learns to obey a request immediately. Punishment should be administered in a calm, quiet and firm manner. Scriptural discipline with the rod is not child abuse. Today's misguided "authorities" try to tell us that discipline is child abuse, but that is absurd. *Lack* of discipline is child abuse.

Always bear in mind the size of the child who is about to be spanked. The size of the rod must match the size of the child! A firm tap on the back of the hand for a three year old will get his attention and get the message across. A nine year old may need something more convincing. If you are firm and loving and you discipline your child right from the beginning, you will soon realize that you do not have to get physical with your child as time goes on. A slap on the wrist at age two will avoid dozens of ineffective blows later on. Your word simply becomes a corrective presence in the back of your child's mind. He now carries in him a memory of discipline, and his instinct is to continue to obey a quiet command right away. He knows that if he ignores the first command there will not be a second.

This is the best way to discipline effectively. Ask the child to do what you want him to do. If he does not, then punish him *appropriately and immediately.* Appropriate punishment, more often than not, means being banished from the family for a while or being deprived of some privilege or other. If, however, the child's behaviour is outright rebellion, then it is valid to use a physical attention-getter. Rebellion must not be tolerated. After the punishment is over, and a short time is allowed for the child to think about it, that is the moment to kneel down with him and ask him to ask God for forgiveness. After all, he must know that it is God whom he has offended here. You are only being obedient to God by punishing him. You are imposing God's will on him, not your own. After he has repented before God, then you pray over him, thanking God for giving you such a wonderful gift in this child. Tell God and the child how much you love him. Then it is time to hug and kiss and put the whole incident into the past. The prodigal son or daughter is welcomed back to the love of the family.

My father spanked me only twice in my life. The first occurred when I was seven years old, when I had refused to stop interrupting him when he was in serious conversation with his brother-in-law. The second time was when I was caught out in a deliberate and flagrant lie. When it was over, I was left to lick my wounds and I was given a little time to reflect on my sins. Then my father came and apologised for having had to resort to this, but he insisted that before God, he had no choice. He then hugged me. He said, "The pain will go away, but the lesson you have learned never will." He was right.

For a teenager, spanking time is definitely over. It is ludicrous. They are usually bigger than you are. All you can do is let them know what you expect and what God expects. It is vital that their actions be directly linked with the consequences. The consequences usually become longer-term, since the adolescent is capable of understanding more. It should take the form of some kind of deprivation, such as not going to a dance, or not going out for a bike ride. You have the keys to the car, not your child. You have the money, not the child. You can ground your child. He cannot ground you. You pay for the mortgage, not your child, and so you can refuse to accept certain types of behaviour in your home. In fact, it is a duty of parents, commanded by God, that you must not allow mortal sin to occur under your roof. If a young man wants to bring his girlfriend home to sleep with her, the answer is very simple. You may not be able to control a lot of what he does outside of the home, but you surely can control what goes on inside it. He might get drunk in someone else's house, but never in yours.

Never try to be a buddy or a pal to your teenager, or try to win a popularity contest with him. You will regret it. You are a parent and you owe it to your child always to be a parent. The Catechism tells you to command both respect and obedience from your child. If you are only a pal, then I may respect my pal, but I need never be obedient to him. So watch for this trap. God the Father will always be a loving Father to us, never a buddy.

A tired teenager cannot get into trouble. So tire him out! He has limitless stores of energy and if allowed to become bored or idle, he will find some mischief with which to relieve it. In addition to his school work and homework, involve him in extra-curricular activities which interest him, such as sports or camping. During the summer vacation, encourage him to find a job. Whatever you do keep him busy. He needs it and it will save you and him from the grief which is born of boredom.

If a teenager is being disobedient in a major way, then something was wrong with his childhood discipline. Thomas Millar in his book, *The Strong-willed Child,* states that in the old days parents were strong on discipline and weak on affection. The child grew up to be strong in character but unhappy. Modern parents, on the other hand, are strong on affection and weak on discipline, so the child grows up happy with his own disorder, but also unmotivated and irresponsible. Real parenting gives a child both affection and discipline. This does not mean that it is hopeless to try and discipline an unruly teenager. God and you can do anything, but it is just harder!

Good, non-threatening, civilised communication is essential. Take time to *listen* to your teenager and to offer good advice. Emphasize his choices and give him more control of his life. Help him to choose his friends, or if you have problems with that, at least stop him from having bad friends. Encourage him to bring his friends to the house so you can observe them. Encourage the good. Forbid the bad. Let your home be a place of welcome to his friends. Talk to them and let them feel accepted.

One day recently, I was seeing a young man in my office. His girlfriend sat in the waiting room talking to my wife. At one point the girl admitted that most of the teenagers in her high school were into crime, drugs, sex, alcohol and defying curfews. Rita asked her why she thought this was so. The girl replied, "Because their parents do not love them." Rita said, "But they have everything, the best of running shoes, leather jackets, cars, and spending money." "Yes" said the girl, "Their parents are just buying them off."

Another tenth-grade girl said to me, "There is violence in my school. But that is because parents either don't care or are too strict. We need limits. I have limits, but I have a lot of freedom within my limits."

So it is a question of balance — balance between permissiveness and stifling control. Moderation will have far better results.

All of the foregoing material has been directed at the "normal" child who is by nature disobedient, but who will respond to love and balanced discipline. There are two abnormal situations, however, which must be mentioned and understood. The first concerns those children who suffer from Attention-Deficit Disorder (ADD), Depression or Fetal Alcohol Syndrome. Such children will be often angry, exhibit very poor concentration, perhaps be aggressive, and certainly will always be disobedient. They will be unresponsive to the frantic efforts of their parents to bring order into their lives. In fact, the more the parents discipline, whether by stern admonition or physical punishment or both, the child will react by becoming even more unmanageable. His energy for resistance seems to feed on punishment. These are very unhappy children, and because they are dysfunctional, punishment becomes unjust and ineffective. They need help. The good news is that these conditions are treatable. They should be referred by a family doctor to a child psychiatrist for confirmation of the diagnosis, and then excellent results can be expected from good therapy. I have treated a number of such children, and it is a cause for praise to God to see many of them become calm, reasonable, manageable and functioning well in their studies and in their relationships. If you have an unmanageable child, then have him checked out by a professional. He or she may have a treatable disorder. You will not regret it.

The second situation is a very disturbing phenomenon which has surfaced in our modern society and is, to say the least, extremely alarming. "You must understand this, that in the last days, distressing times will come. For people will be lovers of themselves, lovers of money, boasters, arrogant, abusive, *disobedient* to their parents" (2 Tim. 3:1-2). These are words of prophecy from St. Paul. Why would he mention children being disobedient to their parents? After all, ever since Cain and Abel, children have always tried to be disobedient to their parents at times. St. Paul emphasises this because he foresaw that in the last days, a new kind of disobedience would show itself. It would be total and very widespread and not curable by ordinary disciplinary measures. Is this not what we are witnessing in our own day? Little children are running riot and big children are into sex, drugs, alcohol and sinful pleasure. It seems that practically a whole generation is now defying discipline, and it is making them into very miserable souls indeed.

I was talking recently to a distraught couple in my office. They began to suspect that their fifteen-year-old daughter was sneaking out of the house during the night, and they had no idea what she was up to. These were very intelligent, very loving, and very holy Catholic parents. Eventually they found out that the girl was using marijuana. They found a supply of birth control pills and condoms in her satchel. When they searched her bedroom, they found Satanic posters, and they discovered that the music she listened to was full of lyrics encouraging suicide, mutilation of women, and worship of evil. To their horror they also found a box in which was concealed black candles, incense and other paraphernalia for witchcraft rituals. They also found a book on how to practice Wicca.

Mother and father confronted the girl and were devastated to find that instead of repenting or feeling ashamed or desiring to be accepted back into the love of the family, she took on a cold, mask-like look. It was a look they had never seen before on her face. It was then that they realised that their daughter did not want to be taken back into the love of the family and into goodness. She *wanted* evil.

This scenario is much more common than Catholic parents realize. I advise all parents of teenagers to exercise their rights to go into and to search their youngster's bedroom. They must listen carefully to the music the child is listening to and trash anything Satanic or evil. The teenager's bedroom should never be allowed to be locked. Parents have a right to know what is going on in that room. Never allow a television set in a teenager's bedroom. How can you know what they are watching? Beware of the Internet. Pornography of all kinds is easily available, and it is a parent's duty to know which web sites are being visited by their teenagers. Their bedroom should be a bedroom, not a place where they can hide away for hours and do dark things. If a teenager is bringing Satan into his or her bedroom, then Satan is being allowed into your home. This must be stopped at all costs. Satan, given a foothold, will do everything possible to destroy family peace, harmony and love.

Naturally, the good parents of that girl asked me what they could do. They wanted their daughter back, knowing that she no longer wanted goodness and love, and that she had chosen the very opposite of all that was good. I told them that ordinary, reasonable discipline would no longer be effective. There were only two things they could do, and it was Jesus himself who told us, "This kind can only be driven out by *prayer and fasting*" (Mark 9:29). I told these worried parents that their child was beyond the reach of their love and wisdom. She could only be helped by a dedicated program of prayer and fasting. Needless to say, her parents were praying, but in such a case, prayer alone would never be enough. It needed the powerful sacrifice of regular fasting by the parents on behalf of their daughter.

Fasting can be done in a variety of ways. We can fast for an extended period or we can fast one day a week. The nature of the fast also varies. One may fast on bread and water, on water only, or on fruit juices and so on. Fasting, however, need not simply be confined to depriving ourselves of food. It can be a decision to avoid other things which we find pleasurable. We could abstain from smoking, alcohol, entertainments, and other pleasures. Some couples I know abstain from sexual intercourse, and offer that up as a holy gift to the Lord. Whatever way you choose, do it with love and if possible with joy, and during the fasting period pray like you have never prayed before. I can think of no other weapon against this new type of disobedience, which is sweeping our society today.

The police department in Houston, Texas once drew up a list of twelve rules for raising *delinquent* children! Follow these and you can be guaranteed that you will suffer from the tyranny of a problem teenager.

1. Begin with infancy to give the child everything he wants. In this way he will grow up to believe the world owes him a living.
2. When he picks up bad words, laugh at him. This will make him think he is cute. It will also encourage him to pick up "cuter" phrases that will blow off the top of your head later.
3. Never give him any spiritual training. Wait till he is twenty-one, and then let him "decide for himself."
4. Avoid the use of the word "wrong." He may develop a guilt complex. This will condition him to believe later, when he is arrested for stealing a car, that society is against him and he is being persecuted.
5. Pick up everything he leaves lying around, books, shoes and clothing. Do everything for him so he will be experienced in throwing all responsibility onto others.
6. Let him read any printed matter he can get his hands on. Be careful that the silverware and drinking glasses are sterilised, but let his mind feast on garbage.
7. Quarrel frequently in the presence of your children. In this way they will not be too shocked when the home is broken up later.
8. Give a child all the spending money he wants. Never let him earn his own. Why should he have things as tough as you had them?

9. Satisfy his every craving for food, drink and comfort. See that every sensual desire is gratified. Denial may lead to harmful frustration.
10. Take his part against neighbours, teachers and policemen. They are all prejudiced against your child.
11. When he gets into real trouble, apologize for yourself by saying, "I never could do anything with him."
12. Prepare for a life of grief. *You are likely to get it!*

There is no such thing as perfect parenting, so it is a futile exercise to beat up on yourselves for mistakes. God does not expect you to be perfect parents, but you are the best parents for your children because God gave them to you and not to anyone else. The only perfect parenting ever accomplished on the earth was done by Mary and St. Joseph in the Holy Family. Nobody else is a perfect parent and no one else has all the answers. So relax.

God parents the universe. The Holy Father parents the Church. The bishop parents the Diocese. The priest parents the parish. Parents parent their children, while single adults also parent, in that they are to bring life and love and give birth to Jesus in the community around them. Parenting is for all of us, and so it is vital that we study God's plan for parenting and live it out. God's design for parenting is the only design which will work.

CHAPTER 10

Parenting: God's Instruction in the Faith

*"Take to heart these words
I enjoin on you today. Drill
them into your children.
Speak of them at home and
abroad, whether you are
busy or at rest."*

(Deut. 6:6-7)

The Catholic Catechism states,

Paragraph 2223: Parents have the first responsibility for the education of their children. They bear witness to this responsibility first by creating a home where tenderness, forgiveness, respect, fidelity and disinterested service are the rule. The home is well suited for education in the virtues. This requires an apprenticeship in self-denial, sound judgement and self-mastery, the preconditions of all true freedom. Parents should teach their children to subordinate the material and instinctual dimensions to interior and spiritual ones. Parents have a grave responsibility to give good example to their children. By knowing how to acknowledge their own failings to their children, parents will be better able to guide and correct them.

Paragraph 2225: Through the grace of the Sacrament of Marriage, parents receive the responsibility and privilege of evangelising their children. Parents should initiate their children at an **early age** into the mysteries of the faith of which they are the **first heralds** for their children. They should associate them from their tenderest years with the life of the Church.

Paragraph 2226: Education in the faith should begin in the child's earliest years. Parents have the mission of teaching their children to pray and to discover their vocation as children of God.

Paragraph 2227: Children, in turn, contribute to the growth in holiness of their parents. Each and everyone should be generous and tireless in forgiving one another for offenses, quarrels, injustices and neglect. Mutual affection suggests this. The charity of Christ demands it.

Paragraph 2229: As those first responsible for the education of their children, parents have the right to choose a school for them which corresponds to their own convictions. This right is fundamental.

This is the framework for understanding how to impart the faith to our children. But it must not be confused with the mindless teaching of cold religion. Many parents believe that by merely delivering religious facts to their children, they are doing their duty. This is wrong. Anybody can hand a child a Penny Catechism and have him recite it by rote, but this does not nourish a lively faith. It is true that the child has to learn facts about Jesus and the salvific mandate of the Church, but if that is all he is given, then later on, when he is attracted to the sinful trinkets and glitter of the world (as we all are at some point), he will be likely to abandon the faith. The word of God will have fallen on shallow soil and the weeds of the world will find it easy to choke it. Rearing children in the faith is a much more awesome responsibility than some might think. It is not just classroom pedagogy. *It is a way of life.* The faith has to be something in which the child is immersed. He must swim in the faith, he must breathe the faith, and he must find the Catholic faith to be in front of him, behind him, to his right and his left, above and below him. Only by this can the child be immunised against the plagues of the world and its allurements. The faith must be brought to life in his heart, must be nurtured in his heart, and the child must be constantly encouraged to grow towards that perfection which is union with Jesus Christ. "You must be perfect as your heavenly Father is perfect" (Matt. 5:48).

To parents falls the wondrous task of this evangelisation. But how can good parents, who desire this result with all their hearts, help their little ones to pulsate with the spirit of God? At first glance this can appear too daunting, and could lead to a throwing up of the hands in discouragement. Many parents do just that. They look at the desired end-point, see it as too lofty an ideal, and then, aware of their own deficiencies, give up before they even begin. This is a defeatist posture and defeatism comes from listening to Satan's lies. He wants to discourage us, and he puts a lot of effort into it because, by getting parents to give up, he is assuring himself of yet another soul or souls who will grow up with little or no faith.

God built in a lot of margin for error in our parenting. While we may not be perfect parents, we should take heart in knowing that for our children, we are the best parents possible. God decreed it to be so. God has faith in you and so you should have faith in you, and you can be sure that your child has faith in you. You are not alone, for the simple reason that God is with you. You are Catholics, so you have access to sanctifying grace through the Sacraments. You are not raising your children with your own limited human strengths. On the contrary, you are only able to fulfil this mission by your human weakness, for as St. Paul reminds us, "For power is made perfect in weakness" (2 Cor. 12:9). God did not give you this assignment without also giving you all that you need to do it. You have each other and parents should come together with other parents to provide mutual support, praying together, encouraging one another and exchanging those useful ideas which you have discovered, about which no educator could ever tell you.

When a child is born, he has intrauterine memories and has already been formed by events which had an impact on him while he was in the womb. It may come as a surprise to realise that teaching religion to your child should ideally begin at the moment of conception. This means that even if you are not aware of your pregnancy for a few weeks, you should already be living out your faith, faithfully. You should always be ready to welcome new life. Your sexual loving should be ever holy and self-giving, one to the other, not tarnished by lust or drunkenness or violence. Then the womb in which the new life will be placed is at all times a holy place, ready to impart holiness to that tiny single cell. As soon as they become aware of the pregnancy, both mom and dad should know that they are now parents. So often, pregnant couples say, "We are going to be parents." This is erroneous thinking. They are *already* parents, and should immediately begin a lifelong campaign of prayer for their child. This should be prayer of thanksgiving and gratitude to God, the Father of all children, and to Mary, the mother of all children. It should also be prayer of supplication and intercession for the holiness of the child. Parents would do well, as soon as possible, to consecrate that new little life to Jesus through the Immaculate Heart of Mary. In this way, the Blessed Mother will be given permission to regard this child as her own, and she will take that task very seriously indeed. She will then orchestrate the child's life, always drawing him or her ever closer to the Sacred Heart of her Son Jesus. She will do all in her power to protect her little consecrated one from the snares of the Devil.

As stated in chapter 9, every day of the pregnancy, mom and dad should pray over that tiny growing life for its protection and to minimise one of the effects of original sin, which is the trauma of labour pains to the mother and the trauma of painful progress through the birth canal for the baby. This daily habit of prayer should be maintained after birth, every day of the child's life, by praying over him, and by praying together for him even when he is absent from the home.

I believe that raising a child in the faith can only be done well by *prayer and fasting.* If Jesus has shown us that fasting can cast a demon out from someone who is possessed, can fasting not also keep Satan away from our children, fortify them against daily temptations, and protect them from the poisonous influence of their peer group and the world? It can and it does. The power of fasting in dealing with a very disturbed child has already been addressed in chapter 9. The Church calls parents to empty themselves for their children. What could be more powerful than to fast for their souls?

Fasting, quite simply, is giving up something good in order to experience a higher good. Obviously we are to fast from all that is bad. We should fast from sin. But while it is good to eat food, or to enjoy a holiday, it is a higher good to deny ourselves some of these things, because such fasting not only storms heaven to grant our request, it also strengthens our spiritual muscles, giving us the virtues of fortitude and perseverance. Fasting is spiritual gold, both for our children and for our personal sanctity. If you are feeling discouraged in your efforts as regards teaching the faith to your child, then begin to pray and fast, asking Jesus and Mary to change things around. They will. Jesus promised it and he always keeps his promises. Never be afraid to remind Jesus of his promises for he loves to be reminded. He loves a confident faith. If you are willing to offer him the rather small gift of your mortification and penance, he in turn, will refuse to be outdone in generosity and so will respond with a "good measure pressed down, shaken together and running over" (Luke 6:38).

Once the baby is born, he or she enters a new phase of education in the faith. A newborn baby will learn at a rate which will never be matched again as he grows older. Now is the time to instill holy things into the baby's mind. For example, he should consistently hear and feel mom and dad praying over him as he lies in his crib. Prayer is a harmonic rhythm which penetrates and affects the subconscious. Even if the baby cannot understand your words, he can absorb the holy and peaceful vibrations of his parent's prayer. He will make deep and rich interior connections between the energy of prayer and his own inner sense of peace and love and security. His guardian angel will be empowered by prayer to protect him more effectively. Likewise sing hymns to your baby instead of lullabies. Baby will again make profound associations of tranquillity with the music of praise to God. He cannot help it. He was built that way by a loving Father. It is in his very nature to absorb holy things. As parents, you will never have more power than during your child's infancy to be a sanctifying influence for him, and of course you must convey love. You cannot love enough. The child needs touching and soothing. The more you do this, the more the child will recognize you as his source of love and the more credence he will give later on to your instructions in the faith. He will be able to accept that God is the source of all love, even the very love he is receiving from his parents.

The most important principle of all in religious education is that you yourselves must live it. The child must see you practising what you preach. That is what makes your commands authentic and believable. You cannot tell him not to be angry if you yell and scream at each other whenever you have a disagreement. You cannot direct your child away from lust or promiscuous sex if you have pornographic magazines lying around the house. You cannot demand that your child pick up his toys if you are a disorganized slob. You cannot ask him to give up television and do his homework if you spend hours in front of the one-eyed monster watching ball games and immoral sitcoms. Your most powerful educational tool is your example. Let your lives be a living homily and your children will eagerly imitate you. In fact, during the child's earlier years, he will eagerly imitate you anyway, so beware of what you role model. The manner of your life will instruct your child more surely than instruction itself.

When you see your child misbehaving, ask yourself if you are not doing the same thing. Observe your child and you will be amazed at how perfectly he imitates your behaviour in word, gesture, action and play. If one of your gestures is a clenched fist, do not be surprised that your child clenches his fist. If one of your gestures is the Sign of the Cross, you should not be surprised that your child readily and joyfully does the same. Long before you are able to explain to him that the Sign of the Cross is the sign of our faith and a ritual of blessing, your child will somehow know that it is a powerful and solemn thing to do. He knows in his heart much much more than you think he does.

Many of today's fathers have a very impoverished view of what their function should be. That is not God's opinion. It may come as a surprise to fathers to know that to a very young child, dad is god. To an older child dad is all men. In fact, the role of father in the religious education of children ought to be paramount. It is not a responsibility to slough off onto mothers. As fathers, we reflect the fatherhood of God, and for this reason we are required to father our children as God fathers us. Certainly fathers are providers and protectors of the family entrusted to them, but fathering means much more than that. As fathers we carry the awesome responsibility of the moral authority over our family, and this is no mean duty. We must model tenderness, gentleness, manly firmness, generosity and willingness to listen to our children. The children must see mother deferring to dad's authority in holy things. That does not mean that wives must obey when dad wants to quit his job for no good reason, nor must she buy him alcohol when he is going to get drunk.

St. Paul is very clear on this. "Husbands should love their wives just as Christ loved the Church and sacrificed himself for her to make her holy" (Eph. 5:25). Therefore husbands must be like Jesus to their families. Fathers must serve their wives and their children, they must instruct their little "domestic church" in the faith, and they must lay down their lives for it. Fathers cannot and must not abdicate their vocation as religious and life-educators for their children. They must be involved, and they must do it in one mind and one heart with their wives. This is God's order, and if we ignore it, we create disorder.

Whatever image a father portrays, that is exactly the image a young child will have of God. In fact, one child psychologist has said that if you could creep into your child's mind while he is saying his night prayers and see the visual image of the God he is praying to, you would find your own face there. A father is the only way a child can relate to God in his early years. Therefore, if dad is stern and aloof and unaffectionate, the child will have a problem believing that God is loving and merciful. If dad is a rigid and punitive disciplinarian, then the child will see God as a giant cruel policeman waiting to punish him. If dad is a strict controller, the child will see God as the great controller, who is responsible for the death of his pet dog or the rain that ruined his day at the beach. If dad is an indulgent weakling who spoils his children they will grow up to be moral weaklings also. They will see God as "nice" and believe that he would never censure them for doing as they please, even if it is sinful.

If, on the other hand, dad is gentle, kind, playful, considerate and forgiving, then the child's vision of God will be true and good. While mother is the constant presence to the young child, and dad has to be out at work all day, nevertheless, dad is present because his spirit orchestrates the family and he role-models for God. Many dads *play* god in their families, instead of *reflecting* God to their families. Fathers, therefore, should take back their God-given role as religious educators of their children, by leading their families in prayer. They should insist on God's discipline in their homes, and their wives will find their efforts blessed as they too play their part in teaching the faith.

The most powerful educational tool that we can use with children is the story. Jesus modelled that perfectly for us by teaching his disciples by means of parables. "Give ear, oh my people, to my teaching: incline your ears to the words of my mouth. I will open my mouth in a parable, (The N.A.B. renders this, 'I will open my mouth in story.') I will utter dark sayings from of old, things that we have heard and known, that our ancestors have told us. We will not hide them from their children: we will tell to the coming generation, the glorious deeds of the Lord, and his might, and the wonders that he has done. He established a decree in Jacob, and appointed a law in Israel, which he commanded our ancestors to teach to their children: that the next generation might know them, the children yet unborn, and rise up and tell them to their children, so that they should set their hope in God, and not forget the works of God, but keep his commandments" (Psalm 78:1-7).

God therefore, wishes us to teach our children with parables and stories, just as he himself does, and as Jesus his obedient Son did. He knew that people remember stories much better than facts, and so he used powerful, beautiful and captivating stories to make his doctrinal points. We only have to think of the parable, of the prodigal son and the good Samaritan in order to realize the power of the story. By means of these, all of us understand the forgiveness and love of the Father even when we have squandered our inheritance in sin, and we also learn the way in which we are to act towards our neighbour who is in pain. The moral theological point could not have been so well remembered if it had not been delivered in story format. In my own preaching I always try to find or to write a story which will emphasize the readings of the day. There is no doubt that people's hearts ring with the truth if they can link it up with a narrative. They remember the story first and then infer the moral after.

So it is with children. They, even more than adults, love a story. Not only do they love it, but they eagerly demand that it be repeated over and over. Children learn by repetition and so we as parents should be ever willing to tell good stories as many times as the children want to hear them. When they have assimilated the point of the story, they will drop their demands and move on to the next one. But it is not just the story itself which has power: *Story-telling* has power. The children love to cuddle up close to mom or dad and feel connected, intimate and loved. Story-time is a source of warm memories well into adulthood. My own grown up children still reminisce with me about my stories when they were little, as though they need to recapture the warmth and security of those days. Tell your children the stories of the Bible. Tell them about the lives of real heroes — the saints of the Church. Never mind sports idols or movie stars. They are hardly role models for a good moral life, nor even of achievement in life, apart from those who have remained strong in their faith. If we teach our children to look up to the saints who lived and died heroically, our children will inevitably try to model their own lives to their favourite saint. This firmly puts them onto the path of their own call to sainthood.

Another exciting method with which to re-enforce a story is through activities. In this way the child learns to take what he has heard in the story and "make it his own." Naturally the activities, whether discussion, drawing, dramatizing or writing, should be selected according to the age and ability of the child. A very young child finds it much easier to express himself with drawing than with verbalising. As he retells the story with crayons, he is thinking through the story again, mulling it over and interpreting what he has heard from his parents. Also, a parent will be able to assess what the child has learned when he is asked to talk about his picture.

For example, after reading the story of the prodigal son, ask the child to answer the following questions:

a) How was the younger son selfish?
b) How did the father show love for his son throughout the whole story?
c) What do we learn about our Father God from this story?
d) When are we like the prodigal son?

Ask the child to draw the main characters in the story. Then cut them out and paste each one onto a popsicle stick. These can then be used as puppets, and the child can retell the story by acting it out in his own puppet play.

If the day's theme is Baptism, then after talking about the Sacrament, you could show your child photographs, slides or a home video of his Baptism. Tell him about his Baptismal day, who was there, the priest who baptised him, who his Godparents were and what they said. Compare his birth and growth in your own family to birth and growth in the family of God. Help him to understand the responsibility each member has towards the others if there is to be peace and harmony in the family. Tell him how happy you were on that great day, and why it was the greatest day in the life of his soul. Have him mark the date of his Baptismal anniversary on the calendar. Plan with him how you will celebrate that day. His Baptismal candle could be the centrepiece for the family meal. The child should be given the privilege of saying grace, and the family can thank God for the gift of this child and that they all have been admitted through Baptism to God's family. Ask him to draw a picture of his Baptism and have him send it along with a note of gratitude to his Godparents.

I did not think up these activities. I took them from a wonderful little book called, *Will Religion Make Sense to Your Child?* by Earnest Larsen and Patricia Gavin. If you could locate a copy, you would find it most helpful in teaching your child about the faith.

As pointed out earlier, religious training is not just the imparting of facts or doctrinal truths, but is a way of life. The child must therefore be immersed in the faith, he must be made to see that the faith affects everything in his life, and he must see that it works, as opposed to all the other systems to which he will be exposed in life. All of us are a man or woman, a spouse, a parent, an aunt or uncle, a cousin and a son or daughter, but we are much more than that. We are a *Catholic* man or woman, a Catholic spouse, a Catholic parent, a Catholic aunt or uncle, a Catholic son or daughter. That makes all the difference in the world, and your child must come to know why. A Catholic parent should never be indistinguishable from a pagan parent. A Catholic teenager should never be a clone of his non-Catholic peers. Everything we do, and everything we teach our children to do, must be stamped with a unique Catholic character.

To become effective teachers of the faith, parents must educate themselves as to what it means to be Catholics and followers of Jesus Christ. They must show their children how mommy and daddy love each other, and they must show their children that they too are humble of heart, mutually forgiving and obedient to their master, Jesus Christ. Ideally they avoid harsh words, anger and yelling when trying to resolve disputes. They should show the children that differences of opinion are exciting opportunities to learn about each other. They demonstrate by action that it is better to find peaceful and respectful ways to come to loving closure of an issue. They should always, of course, show that there can be no compromise in matters of faith or morals.

Do not judge your success as parents by the results. Parents understandably get down on themselves when their children later abandon the faith of Jesus. By the time a child is old enough to choose to abandon the Church, he is old enough to take the consequences. The parental power in this matter has been taken out of their hands. All that is left is prayer and fasting, beseeching God to keep your grown-up children solidly in the Faith or to bring them back to it if they have fallen away.

Finally, since religious education is preparation for Catholic life, the child must come to think of church as his extended home. He must be taken to Church often, shown how to be reverent, shown the beautiful works of art in the Church, encouraged to walk the stations of the Cross, to recognize the True Presence of Jesus in the Tabernacle, and to take part in the Sacramental and Liturgical Life of the Church. A beautiful practice with a pre-communion child is to have him come up to the priest with you at Communion time, to cross his arms over his heart and to receive a blessing from the priest. This teaches a holy disposition and prepares the child to look forward to the wonderful day when he will be able to receive Jesus, Body, Blood, Soul and Divinity along with his parents and older brothers and sisters. When a child finds love, peace, joy, encouragement and friendship in Church and family, he will be eager to learn his faith and he will develop a proper sense of the holy. His heart will resonate with a deeper and deeper sweet chord of wonder and awe at God's perfect plan and he will find it impossible to imagine that anything outside of the faith could be life-giving. True religion is life. Give your child life, and God in turn, will give you eternal life.

CHAPTER 11

Teenagers: From Caterpillar to Butterfly

*"God, you have taught me from
my youth. To this day I proclaim
your wondrous deeds."*
(Ps. 71:17)

When I was a teenager, which according to my children was sometime before the Flood, but which to me seems like only yesterday, it never entered my head that God had "taught me from my youth." I was caught up in my own pain like a caterpillar writhing in its chrysalis, convinced I would never make a butterfly. On the one hand, I was arrogantly convinced of my own opinions on just about everything. On the other hand, I felt threatened and buffeted about by events beyond my control. My teenage life was a mix of youthful exuberance, periods of depression, moments of exultation, bouts of anxiety, feelings of dread, and self-loathing, alternating with intense conceit, a hormonal roller-coaster. And yet I was also imbued with a deep sense of destiny. I believed that I had a future and that belief probably saved my life. It is not that I had experienced a bad childhood. On the contrary, in spite of World War II and the sense of insecurity that went with those years, I was deeply loved by my parents and my extended family. We were poor but I really never knew that. I accepted my lot in life because that was just the way things were, and all my friends were equally poor. I was raised in the Catholic faith by a mother who was a convert and a holy woman, and by a hard working father who knew how to discipline with fairness.

The teenage years, however, exploded upon me, and like most teenagers, I was not ready. In spite of the fact that I was an "A" student and the high school sports champion, I mostly agonized over my perceived physical defects and was constantly preoccupied with being accepted by my peers. My self-esteem was near zero on a scale of one to ten, and I would have given anything to be me in a different body. What I did not realize at the time, and nobody pointed it out to me, was that *all* of my classmates felt exactly the same way. To me they looked self-assured, happy and confident and I longed to be like them, but if by some miracle I could have become one of them, I would have found the same pain, the same self-hatred and the same deep-seated insecurity.

It is very important for parents to understand that, while the teenagers of today are no different from the teenagers of yesterday, there is a huge difference in the environment within which they are being raised. In today's society, Christian parents are out-manned and out-gunned by the peer group and by a pagan culture. Teens are bombarded by a sex-obsessed environment, by friends who use drugs, by sin-filled messages on television, by pornographic magazines handed around by so-called friends and by satanic messages of rape, violence and suicide in today's heavy-metal music, punk rock and acid-rock. They are seduced by anti-Catholic articles in newspapers, by a self-centred consumerism, and by the New Age message that we are gods and so we do not need God, that sin does not exist and that whatever feels good must be good. How can parents combat this barrage of corrupting influences on their teenagers?

The teen years are the most morally vulnerable phase of their lives. They are not quite out of childhood and not quite into adulthood. They do not want to be children anymore but do not know how to be adults. They want to be treated like adults but are afraid of the responsibility which goes with being adult. They struggle with powerful sexual urges, yet emotionally are not mature enough to cope. They are amazingly impulsive and may fall into horrifying sin on a mere whim. Their egos are huge yet they are overly sensitive to rejection. They can spend hours grooming themselves and admiring themselves in front of a mirror. Yet they almost all hate some perceived minor physical imperfection. They feel too fat, too thin, their nose is too big or not big enough. They would rather have brown eyes instead of blue, blonde hair instead of red. They wish they were taller or shorter. The appearance of a single pimple on the chin is a life-threatening event. Enormous amounts of energy are expended on looking good on the outside, while they cover up their agonizing emotional pain on the inside. They feel they cannot confide in their parents because they believe that parents would never understand. So they confide in their peers and risk betrayal, or they secretly write their dark thoughts in a diary. They desperately need an outlet for their innermost angst and if they cannot find a healthy outlet, they will be drawn into destructive behaviour such as sex, drugs or alcohol.

There are numerous self-help books about raising teenagers. Many of them focus on problems and offer all kinds of strategies with which to deal with rebellion, defiance and deviant behaviour. These are all well and good, but such reading can lead us to believe that all teenagers are bad and need to be reined in ruthlessly. It is as though a perfectly good child is destined to become a teenage monster and parents must therefore become more like prison guards than parents if they are to survive the teen years. Teenage deviance is a stark reality, but we can get mired in pessimism if we focus solely upon it. I prefer to look at the wonderful potential of our youth and call them to find their true selves and therefore their true happiness in the love of God.

There is a wonderful light within teenagers which must be appreciated and which parents should always encourage. Teens are not all doom, gloom, sin and defiance. They are the adults of tomorrow and, as such, are bursting with potential. They are the scholars, statesmen, priests, sisters, marriage partners and parents of the near future. They are the Church. They are gifted by God with wonderful talents and are searching for ways to use these to the fullest advantage. At first, they will tend to use their gifts for their own vanity, as I did, but eventually they will realize the truth that these were given by God to be used for the building up of the community and the Church. Once they reach that moment of insight, it is then that they shed their adolescence and become mature, responsible, Christian citizens. They enjoy the energy and vigour of youthful life, discovering a bigger world than the one they have known. They test themselves against the demands of their expanding environment, often with a fearlessness that we adults have lost. Naturally they make mistakes but they do learn from the consequences. Adults never seem to comprehend why teenagers refuse to learn from the wisdom and experience of their elders, forgetting that they too learned in much the same way. It is as though each generation is a fresh new human creation driven to its own maturity by the process of trial and error. It would save a lot of pain and hurt for our youth if they did learn from their elders, but all of human history proves that for the most part they do not. They must dive into the shark-infested waters and find out for themselves. We adults can warn them about the sharks and pray that they will not test the waters, but to our dismay and hurt, we so often find our advice being ignored.

What is absolutely vital, however, is that when a teenager is bitten and comes home wounded, we never react with rage, self-righteous indignation or "I told you so," and absolutely never with sarcasm. We must be there like the Father for the Prodigal Son, to receive him, tend his wounds and be prepared to listen to what he has learned from his reckless adventure. This is not the same thing as condoning what he has done. Wrong is wrong and sin is sin. In spite of the urge of youth to find out the hard way, we must continue to offer our wisdom, to try to protect them from needless pain and especially from soul-destroying sin, but as in all things, we were not given the right to judge the sinner. We adults, no matter how difficult it may be, must put on the mind of Christ and respond as he would respond to the wayward child. That means love, compassion and firm admonition, always welcoming the prodigal son back into the family.

It would be well for parents to meditate on the parable of the Prodigal Son with especial emphasis on the way in which the Father behaved towards his self-willed son. The boy arrogantly demanded his share of the inheritance. He wanted it immediately and was not willing to wait until his father died. The Father did not hesitate. He did not demand to know what the lad was going to do with the money. He did not ask for any guarantees. He acknowledged his son's gift of free will and simply handed it over, which is to say he *blessed* his son, silently expressing his trust in the boy's future. The son, as is well known, squandered every penny on debauchery and lustful indulgence. Now it was time for the consequences. He had dived into the shark-infested waters and been badly mauled. Now he was forced to feed the pigs, the most humiliating job that any Jew could be made to perform. For a Jew, just being near pigs was to be ritually unclean. The son was brought so low, that his fall from grace was even worse than having to merely feed the pigs. He even longed to eat pig-food, he was so hungry. It was only when he had reached this most wretched state that he finally repented. Only when he had scraped the bottom and could not be degraded any further, did he turn around and decide to return to his Father's house. All pride was gone, and he resolved to beg that he be accepted as a servant in his Father's household. He did not believe for one moment that he could be reinstated as a son ever again.

Scripture tells us, "While he was still a long way off, his Father saw him and was moved with pity. He ran to the boy, clasped him in his arms and kissed him" (Luke 15:20). This is a most wonderful passage. The good father saw him from a long way off and so he must have been looking down the road every day, hoping and praying that his son would come home. He had given his son his freedom, even the freedom to renounce all the traditions of his family, but he still never gave up hope. When the longed-for day came, the father did not stand with his fists on his hips, a stern look on his face and wait for the boy to stagger up to him. Instead "he *ran* to the boy" and in his love he hugged him and kissed him. He did not indulge in righteous anger or recriminations nor did he ask his son to recount his humiliations and sins. He already knew that his son was defeated and so he simply welcomed him back.

The son of course launched into his prepared speech but his father would have none of it. He called for the best robe, the sign of wealth, he put the family ring on his finger, the sign of family authority, and he put sandals on his feet, the sign of a free man and not a slave. Then he killed the fatted calf and held a feast to let the entire community know that this son was fully reinstated into the family. "And when he found it, would he not joyfully take it on his shoulders and then, when he got home, call together his friends and neighbours, saying to them, 'Rejoice with me, I have found my sheep that was lost.' In the same way, I tell you, there will be more rejoicing in heaven over one sinner repenting than over ninety-nine upright people who have no need of repentance" (Luke 15:5-7).

Jesus wanted to teach us about the love of his heavenly Father and, by means of this new understanding, to teach earthly fathers how to father their own youth. Fathers must learn to love and to welcome a wayward teenager back into the household. It is useless to indulge in recriminations. The teenager is already punished and humiliated enough by the consequences of his foolishness and he needs to find his sure-point once more. He needs to know that there is one place where he can stand in security and safety and that must be in his father's house. "Yahweh is my rock and my fortress, my deliverer is my God. I take refuge in him, my rock, my shield, my saving strength, my stronghold, my place of refuge" (Ps. 18:2).

Naturally loving Catholic parents desire to save their adolescents from all avoidable harm, and it is right that they should make every effort in their power to do so. For there to be any hope of real success, this effort must begin at the moment of conception. It is a little too late to start doing this when the child has become a teenager. Parents have amazing power over a child during its dependent years and it is then that firm foundations of goodness and holiness must be laid down. Parents who teach a child what love really is, who inculcate good work habits, who discipline with fairness and who live out their own call to virtue and holiness, will prepare that child for the turbulence of adolescence. Such a child will be less likely to wander far from the narrow road of goodness when he is older and tempted by the sin of the world. An undisciplined child will become a nightmare teenager and trying to correct him at that point is like closing the stable door after the horse has bolted. This does not mean that it is too late to do anything fruitful with a teenager who has lost his way, but it is a thousand times more difficult. A teenager is a product of his childhood. As the poet Wordsworth wrote, "The child is the father of the man."

Many parents would agree that there is some kind of communication vacuum between them and their teenagers. They are convinced that youth does not listen to their advice, wisdom and commands. It may come as a surprise to know that teenagers feel exactly the same way. They believe that parents never listen to their ideas, thoughts and dreams. The truth is, that even well-meaning parents who want the very best for their youngsters fail to realize that they are no longer raising a child, but nurturing a fledgling adult. As a result they continue to talk down to the teenager, fully expecting him to obey everything without question, as though he were still in diapers. This is a parent problem, not a teenager problem.

As Father Hampsch put it, "What we think is dialogue is really an interrupted monologue." That is to say, parents often do not talk *with* their adolescents. They talk *at* them or worse still talk *down to* them. The result is that our youth, who are bursting with ideas and insights which are new to them but old-hat to us, feel they are discounted. They cannot get a word in, and even if they do, they know their parents do not hear it. Parents can so easily fall into the trap of talking and not listening. Therefore, they often unjustly assume that the youngster is wrong and they are right. Meanwhile the teenager is equally convinced that he is right and the parents are wrong.

Parents must begin to understand that their teenagers are intensely passionate on just about everything. They are constantly forming opinions about God, about themselves, about the world and about relationships and have a right to question their elders about their values. This is a built-in vital part of growing up. They recoil at the idea of being mindless clones of the past and desperately need to discover their own uniqueness. Parents usually do not like to be challenged by their own offspring but good parents accept it. They recognize that if a young man or woman is to grow to his or her fullness, it is healthy to question, to sift out the dross, to reject what is phony and adhere to what is true.

Young people must question our truths. They will not accept them simply because we say they are true. Teenagers are very sensitive to anything that is phony. In fact the worst insult a teenager can receive from his friends is to be called a phony. So he in turn, despises anything within his parents that is not honest and true. Therefore again, so much in successful parenting boils down to good example, consistently lived out. It takes a good and humble parent to accept an honest criticism from his teenager, to see the simple truth in it, to admit that he is wrong and to try to correct it. In doing so, he demonstrates respect for the teenager's perception and silently teaches him that he too can be wrong and correct it. This is very hard to do but it is just.

However, a parent will not hear these kinds of ideas if he does not listen. Teenagehood should be the automatic signal for parents to change gears. From a more or less autocratic power over the little child, they must now parent in a whole new way. They must shift into the adventure of *listening* and *guiding*. Failure to do so results in the futile attempt to enjoy their former unquestioned authority, and now the irresistible force comes up against the immovable object. That results in a battle of wills in which both the parents and the teenager lose.

Wise parents make the gear-shift as effortlessly as possible and enter this phase of raising their teenager by means of the new tools of listening and guiding. They are willing to sit down and truly listen to what the teenager is trying to say. They let him know that they *want* to understand even if they may not agree in the end. They do not treat him like a fool. They accord him the respect that is due to one who is trying to think for himself. They enjoy true dialogue which is the honest exchange of ideas between people who, though not yet equal in status, nevertheless respect each other. In this way, the teenager eagerly latches on to the respect he is accorded and feels like a significant contributor to the family. This is listening with an *open mind*.

A teenager may have ideas which are not yet refined and matured but they are his ideas nonetheless. That is why guidance is so invaluable. Adolescents do want *authority* but they do not want *authoritarianism*. If they feel that their parents are being authoritarian, they know that there is no hope for dialogue and so they will simply switch off. The well-meaning orders from above will be ignored and will not achieve the desired result. Teenagers, however, will be likely to respond to guidance. If they know they are being heard, they in turn will listen and will be more likely to accept wisdom and to see the sense in it.

They hunger for stability and inner security but they also have a fearlessness about truth. They do not want a raw statement about what is true. They need to know *why* it is true and they challenge parents to show why it is true. It is not enough to baldly state that God loves them. Teenagers will simply come back with ideas which question God's love. "If he loves us then why does he allow a child to die of leukaemia? If he loves us, why does he permit the atrocities of war?" Parents may not like this challenge to their most cherished of truths, but they must learn to transmit them in a way that meets the demands of young inquiring minds. A good response is to let the teenager express his doubts and questions and then to express your understanding as to how he might feel that way. Admit that it is not a simple issue. It is very complex and worthy of their examination. Direct them to relevant reading material which addresses their challenge.

Parents are not walking encyclopaedias and so must never try to pretend that they have all the answers. Teenagers spot that lie very quickly. It is far better to exchange views and together to search out wisdom from experts on the subject. It will never satisfy a teenager if you close the subject by saying, "The Church says so, so there!" To a teenager that is intellectual cowardice. Therefore, we must feed his hunger for a dynamic truth which he can confidently believe in. If our teenager is unafraid of truth, why should we parents be afraid? If parents do not guide in this way, then the adolescent will take his search for truth elsewhere. He will read books which lead him into false doctrine and he will absorb the worldly errors of his peers.

The teenager, being as yet immature emotionally and socially, is less interested in principles than in particular issues. He is passionate about issues. They may not be eager to learn about Church dogma but they do want to know what the Church is doing about the poor, war, justice and unequal distribution of wealth. I remember speaking with a group of teenagers at a well-known Catholic high school for boys. One outspoken young man challenged me by asking, "What is the Church doing for the poor? The Church is rich and yet there are so many poor in the world." It was a very good question. I did not respond by saying that the Catholic Church is the largest charitable organization in the world. I simply replied with another question. I asked, "What are *you* doing about the poor?" He stopped dead in his tracks, thought for a moment and said, "I am being a phony, aren't I?" He had the courage to admit his own dishonesty and all I needed to say further was, "Perhaps. But the important thing to realize is that you are the Church. You reach out to the poor in your own world and I will reach out to the poor in mine." That was listening, that was dialogue and that was guidance.

If there is any trick to this at all, it is to convince the teenager that he is forming himself rather than the parent forming him. Parents almost all love their teenagers but not all love is good. There are two ways by which love can be something disordered. Love can be over-possessive or it can be over-permissive. Over-possessive love imposes excessive restraints and so the teenager cannot breathe. He is suffocated by stupid rigid rules and so he has only two choices. Firstly, he can fight back, which results in a never-ending clash of wills. The more pressure the parents apply, the greater the resistance from the adolescent. As Sir Isaac Newton proved, "To every action there is an equal and opposite reaction." Secondly, he can choose to become overly compliant, stifling his own originality, and grow up to be timid and afraid.

Over-permissive love has no rules whatsoever. A teenager in such a home panics. He can never find the boundaries and so he tests for them by becoming more and more out of control. He searches for authority and finds none and so he becomes deviant, reckless and self-indulgent. In his destructive behaviour, he is crying for help but no one hears him. His parents have opted out.

This cry for help is a very important signal for parents to recognise. If all that parents focus on is the bad behaviour of their teenager then they will tend to react with shock, anger and punishment. If on the other hand, they see beyond the behaviour to the insecurity that the teenager is feeling, then they are more likely to respond with compassion, a desire to listen, talk it out and come up with helpful guidance. A teenager knows when he has betrayed the family honour. He feels shame and wants acceptance, but he will dig his heels in if he feels rejected. Rejection will only propel him into further deviant behaviour.

Another useless strategy is to tell a teenager what it was like to be a teenager in your own day. This is meaningless to him. He is not interested in past history. He is too interested in his present pain. I recall telling my youngsters, "When I was your age, I had to get up at six in the morning, get on my bicycle and ride two miles to Church for morning Mass. Then I had to ride home again to have breakfast and go off to school. You kids have it too easy." Needless to say, my son and daughters merely looked at me as though I had sprouted another head. They saw it as irrelevant to their present reality. Later, as they became adults, I could share these historical facts and they would enjoy hearing about them and even rib me about them, but as teenagers they saw it as utterly pointless.

While little children are very intuitive about whether they are loved or not, teenagers are equally intuitive about control. They know if parents are trying to restructure them or manipulate them. Parents often give out a contradictory message. On the one hand, they demand that teenagers "act their age" which means "act like an adult" yet at the same time they demand absolute obedience which means "act like a child." A teenager cannot cope with the contradiction. He needs to know what is expected of him and that his blundering efforts at adult behaviour are not being scorned.

Parents therefore must be helpful, not controlling. They must respect the adolescent's individuality and gifts and be available for loving listening, guidance and help. Teenagers are often too embarrassed to be open and to share feelings. Parents therefore can help by demonstrating openness first. They can share their feelings and dreams with their teenagers and they, in turn, will learn that it is safe to do likewise. Not only that, but the teenager will feel privileged and included in the family, being recognised as a person who has much to contribute. If such an atmosphere of acceptance pervades the home, then if the teenager gets into trouble, he will be likely to confess it to his parents, which is far better than struggling with it himself.

Sooner or later, it is likely that an adolescent will have to own up to some sin or other. This is when the parental reaction is crucial. Explosion, rage and condemnation will simply ensure that in future, the teenager will absolutely keep his secrets to himself. The only way to handle it is to acknowledge it as serious, to sit down and talk about it and see what can be done *together*. The teenager knows he has to take the consequences of his behaviour, but he will do that more bravely if he knows his parents will stand by him. My father always told me, "Son, if you have something coming to you, take it on the chin. Don't let them have to shoot you in the back." He meant that I should face up to the consequences of my actions and not run away like a coward. It helped enormously though, to know that my father would always be by my side. He never tried to bail me out, which would have ruined the lesson I needed to learn, but he had his manly hand on my shoulder when I faced the music. "You did it, you got caught, you've had your punishment, it is over, so move on." My father never raked up my past sins. He put them behind him and he expected me to do the same.

"Rejoice, o young man while you are young and let your heart be glad in the days of your youth. Follow the ways of your heart and the vision of your eyes, yet understand that as regards all this God will bring you to judgement" (Eccles. 11:9). Our loving Father-God blesses the vigour and excitement of youth, but like a good father, he firmly reminds them that he will call them to account for all that they decide to do with that energy. Parents should pray daily for their teenagers to direct their enthusiasm in the pathways of God, for therein lies true blessing. In fact, without prayer it is difficult to imagine that parenting of teenagers could ever hope to be successful. During this phase, the wisdom of Solomon is not enough. Parents need the wisdom of the Holy Spirit.

Many parents take on unnecessary guilt for the sins of their young people. They understandably blame themselves for their teenager's transgressions. There is no need for such self-flagellation. Parents would do well to remind themselves that teenagers are far beyond the age of reason and are fully accountable to God for their own decisions, both good and bad. "A son is not to bear his father's guilt, nor a father his son's guilt. The upright will be credited with his uprightness and the wicked with his wickedness" (Ezek. 18:20). Therefore an adolescent's sins may be a source of grief to his parents, but never a source of guilt. God will place the responsibility where it properly belongs. Surely this has to be of some small comfort to worried parents, who are scourging themselves for the bad behaviour of their young people.

Above all, parents must let their teenager know that they *believe* in him or her. This, in fact, is the natural continuation of the Blessing of the Child mentioned in chapter 7. Teenagers want your trust and they want to live up to it, but they can only do that if they believe in themselves, and that can never happen without the parents first believing in them. This declaration of trust is basic to the healthy future of the teenager. When he knows he is trusted to carry the family honour he will be a lot less likely to sully the family name. If he ever does, he will be a lot more likely to feel good honest shame at his actions and shame is the beginning of repentance and repentance is the beginning of a resolve not to repeat that behaviour.

The father and the mother must always be ready to embrace the Prodigal Son or the Prodigal Daughter. That is what Catholic family is all about. It is the desire to imitate the love of Jesus Christ, to counsel and instruct just as he did, to love just as he did, to listen and guide just as he did, to forgive always just as he did, and to assure our teenagers that their parents are willing to die for them just as he did.

The following poem was written by an anonymous poet, but it beautifully describes the teenage experience:

Please Hear What I'm Not Saying

Don't be fooled by me.
Don't be fooled by the face I wear.
For I wear a mask, a thousand masks,
masks that I'm afraid to take off,
and none of them is me.
Pretending is an art that's second nature to me,
but don't be fooled.
For God's sake don't be fooled.
I give you the impression that I'm secure,
that confidence is my name and coolness is my game,
that the water's calm and I'm in command,
and that I need no one.
But don't believe me.
My surface may seem smooth but my surface
is my mask, ever-varying and ever-concealing.
Beneath lies no complacence.
Beneath lies confusion and fear and aloneness.
But I hide this. I don't want anybody to know it.

I panic at the thought of my weakness and fear being exposed.
That's why I frantically create a mask to hide behind,
a nonchalant sophisticated facade, to help me pretend,
to shield me from the glance that knows.
But such a glance is precisely my salvation.
My only hope, and I know it.
That is, if it's followed by acceptance,
if it's followed by love.
It's the only thing that can liberate me from myself,
from my own self-built prison walls,
from the barriers I so painstakingly erect.
It's the only thing that will assure me
of what I can't assure myself,
that I'm really worth something.
I don't like to hide.
I don't like to play superficial phony games.
I want to stop playing them.
I want to be genuine and spontaneous and me,
but you've got to help me.
You've got to hold out your hand
even when that's the last thing I seem to want.
Only you can wipe away from my eyes
the bland stare of the breathing dead.
Only you can call me into aliveness.

Each time you're kind and gentle and encouraging,
each time you try to understand because you really care,
my heart begins to grow wings, very small wings,
very feeble wings,
but wings!
With your power to touch me into feeling
you can breathe life into me.
I want you to know that.

Who am I, you may wonder.
I am someone you know very well.
For I am every man you meet,
and I am every woman you meet.

"After this, I shall pour out my spirit on all humanity. Your sons and daughters shall prophesy, your old people shall dream dreams, and your young people see visions" (Joel 2:28). It is God's order for families that the elders will dream dreams and share them with the young, and that the young be allowed to have their visions for a better world. Teenagers may still be immature in so many ways, but they do have visions of their own. Parents must impart their wisdom (dreams) in such a way that the young can grow to realize their own visions. God says they shall prophesy which means to speak the Word of God, and it takes wise parents who know how to listen to hear the prophecies of their young.

One fine day your caterpillar will become a wondrous butterfly.

CHAPTER 12

Growing Older in Years:
Growing Bolder in Christ

*"In old age they will still bear
fruit, will remain fresh and
green to proclaim Yahweh's
integrity."*

(Ps. 92:14-15)

Perhaps the biggest problem the elderly face is that they are stereotyped by a society which has lost its reverence for old age. Strangely enough this is a relatively new phenomenon. Throughout history, the elderly were usually treated with respect for their advanced years and with respect for their wisdom and experience of life. The young were encouraged to consult their elders for advice and wise counsel. In many societies, it was the elderly who governed, who made the decisions for the community and who were consulted in times of crisis. Most villages had a council of elders who were given the last word on village affairs. If ever there was a very, very old person living in the community, that person was often held in some kind of awe, being regarded as "the ancient" and therefore to be accorded the utmost respect and deference. In the tradition of the Jewish people of the Old Testament, old age was regarded as a sure sign of God's favour. "For your part, you will join your ancestors in peace; you will be buried at a happy old age" (Gen. 15:15). Growing old and remaining happy and content were gifts given by God to his righteous ones.

As society has become more materialistic, more taken up with leisure and pleasure, more dependent upon technology and less religious, this respect for older citizens has dwindled. Instead of commanding more esteem from society, they are being regarded as "over the hill" and as economically unproductive. Society today is so obsessed with productivity and profit that anyone who is not productive and who is not generating profit for himself or for the corporation is relegated to the status of inferior or even useless. This disdain, of course, applies not only to the retired elderly but also to younger persons caught in the poverty trap. Unhappily, such an attitude is on the increase, since the number of elderly is growing as a percentage of the general population. The result is that fewer and fewer persons are working and providing the tax base to take care of those in retirement. Because of this shrinking tax base, governments are paring back the numbers of available hospital beds and other medical services necessary to an aging society. Social services such as home care, so vital for many elderly to remain independent in their own homes, are forced to be more concerned with their budgets than with the real needs of older citizens. Perhaps the most alarming development of all is the increasing erosion of respect for human life, reflected in the euthanasia debate. The high sounding words of compassion from those who advocate mercy-killing are nothing more than a front for the unspoken motive of eliminating unproductive and dependent citizens. The needy elderly are a challenge to society's capacity to love and to sacrifice, while the euthanasia movement is really about a refusal to love regardless of its protests to the contrary.

The fact is that a whole new education is needed to bring about a change of attitude towards our seniors. Society needs to rediscover the wonderful truth of what it means to grow older and the elderly need to show to the world what it means to grow bolder in Christ.

For a start, the general notion of aging is that it mysteriously begins somewhere around the age of forty to fifty years. This is untrue. As one gerontologist put it, "Aging refers to the process of change in the organism from the time of fertilisation of the ovum until the death of the individual." In other words from the moment of conception, life is a continuity of aging. So-called old age is nothing more than an advanced stage of the aging process.

Stereotyping is a major hindrance to the understanding of the elderly as unique and valuable persons. Human beings seem to find it much easier to cope when they cluster people into groups, rather than accepting each individual on his or her merits. This is the foundation of prejudice. The result is a whole list of beliefs about the elderly which are completely untrue.

Some of the common misconceptions are:

- "Most of the aged are sick or disabled."
- "Most of the aged are senile and useless."
- "Older workers produce less than younger workers."
- "Older people are like children and need to be treated that way."
- "Older people should be herded into their own group. They cannot relate to anyone younger."
- "Older people are totally dependent."
- "Older people cannot function effectively."
- "Older people cannot learn."

Given these kinds of convictions, it is little wonder that society has lost its way in caring for its elders, and the elders in turn, have lost the respected status they once enjoyed.

The truth needs to be proclaimed and the truth is that most elderly people are physically and mentally able to function well. It is true that many older persons may have to cope with chronic disorders such as arthritis, heart disease or diabetes, but they not only cope, they demonstrate the wonderful courage of the human spirit. If younger persons would take the trouble to acquaint themselves with their elders, they would learn a vital lesson in how to be uncomplaining, to live with physical losses and even to be joyful and at peace with these losses. The vast majority of the elderly are not senile. They enjoy mental and intellectual clarity throughout their lives, able to love, to laugh, to pray and to be of help to the younger generations. Happy elderly are those who, in spite of being forced to retire at the arbitrary age of sixty-five, are still productive and active, still full of purpose in their lives and still creating goals.

Such elderly do not retire and then sit down to await death. They view retirement as the end of one career and the beginning of a new one. Long before retirement has taken place, they have been planning ahead, setting objectives for this exciting new phase of their lives. They may decide to take on part-time work in a different field, they may at last indulge in a hobby which was impossible while they were working at their job, they may now donate their skills and expertise to community groups or take up volunteer work. Many become even more productive after so-called retirement than they ever were in the drudgery of their previous career. At last, they have the time and the freedom to take up crafts, woodworking, landscaping and countless other stimulating projects. The possibilities are endless. What matters is that the retirement stage must be embraced as a fascinating opportunity for new life rather than the beginning of the end.

Jean Maxwell in her book *Centres for Older People* states, "Aging is universal, aging is normal, aging is variable, dying is normal and inevitable, aging and illness are not necessarily coincidental, older people can and do learn, older people want to be more self-directing and older people are vital human beings."

Clark Tibbits, a gerontologist, described five needs which should be met if one is to grow old gracefully: the need for relationships and association with others; the need for creativity; the need for security; the need for individuality and recognition; and the need for an intellectual frame of reference. I would add to that a sixth need, which is the deepest need of the human heart. It is the need to have faith in something higher and more reliable than oneself. It is the need to believe that life persists after death. Old age must have meaning. This is the time when many people who have, till now, distracted themselves from any spiritual life because of the pursuit of career and the quest for material things are willing to ask themselves serious questions about God and eternity.

The elderly know that death is closer than it has ever been and so they are more likely to reflect on what death really means. Is it the end of all consciousness or is it the doorway to new life? The first option brings terror. The second option creates hope. Actually, these six needs apply to all human beings regardless of age, but they are more pressing and more immanent for the elderly.

It is not the intention here to imply that aging does not bring problems with it. Two researchers, Clark and Anderson, reported on their study of older people and concluded that there were seven main challenges for them.

1. A change in physical appearance.
2. Partial or total retirement from active duties.
3. Lower energy level.
4. Greater possibility of ill health.
5. Greater possibility of need of help.
6. Changes in cognitive and intellectual functioning.
7. Greater uncertainty about the duration of life.

Again, I would add an eighth problem. It is the problem of *homeostasis.* This is a medical term which refers to the natural ability of the body to keep everything in balance. For example, if a person's blood pressure goes up and is sustained for many years without treatment, the heart will compensate by growing larger, in order to more effectively pump the blood throughout the body. With aging this capacity for homeostasis becomes less and less efficient. The result is that a stress which might have been easily shrugged off in a younger person can be a major challenge to the elderly body systems. Since the major organs are deteriorating as one gets older, even a trivial stress, such as a cold, can trigger a domino effect whereby one organ after another collapses and goes into failure, possibly resulting in death. In other words, one of the problems of advancing age is that one is less resilient in reacting to a stressful event.

Most specialists in the field of gerontology define the problems of aging in terms of loss. As each person grows older, losses both small and large begin to occur and continue. Some of these losses are: loss of physical faculties, such as hearing and vision, loss of one's valued role in society usually through compulsory retirement, loss of prestige due to failing faculties, loss of authority with one's children, loss of close ties with loved ones due to death or relocation, loss of home and independence, and often loss of former optimum health due to heart disease, arthritis or organic brain disease.

These losses lead to one of the most difficult problems of aging, which is increasing dependency. For an aging person to remain in his or her own home as long as possible, there has to be a courageous acceptance of dependency needs. To deny the relentless and progressive loss of independence is to expose oneself to greater and greater risk of accidents in the home, or to the tragedy of falling ill without anyone regularly stopping by to see that all is well. Since there is often some loss of mobility, elderly persons will sometimes neglect grocery shopping due to the effort involved. Even where they are able to bring in their own groceries, they will often find cooking for one to be too irksome, and so they become malnourished and suffer from vitamin and mineral deficiencies.

Increasing dependency must be faced as a reality, especially since it is possible thereby to arrange for others to provide what one can no longer provide for oneself. For example, the home can be rendered safer by some simple adjustments such as a grab-bar in the bathroom, removal of slippery rugs, a speaker phone for the deaf, a raised toilet, or a more user-friendly kitchen where commonly used utensils are stored in the lower cupboards rather than high up out of reach. Where possible, arrangements should be made to have a neighbour, relative, or a caring church member undertake to check up on a senior by daily telephone calls or even visits. Too often an elderly person suffers a stroke and then lies on the floor for days before anyone thinks to call and check. This is easily avoided.

Where necessary, a healthy younger adult can do the grocery shopping. If one is becoming more disabled, then he or she may need to connect with the numerous available social services such as Meals-on-Wheels, home nursing, occupational therapy, physiotherapy and provision of house cleaning. Such strategies should not be seen by the elderly as "cold charity" or as a sign that one is a nuisance to others. These are common-sense solutions which prevent one from "being a nuisance" and help maintain one's independent living for as long as possible. The ultimate in dependency is when so many factors break down to the point where one cannot continue to live at home any longer, even with home-care services. That is when one may have no other choice but institutionalisation. Certainly, this last resort option is the final challenge to one's humility, to become completely dependent on nursing-home personnel for everything, from personal hygiene to food and laundry. As a practising family doctor, I never ceased to marvel at the cheerfulness and the humble resignation of so many of my aged patients who could no longer enjoy even a private bedroom, but who had to share with someone they would never have befriended in their earlier life. How adaptable and how courageous the human spirit can be.

Loneliness is a terrible reality for many elderly people. As mentioned earlier, all people need social interaction and relationships, and this applies just as much to older persons. We are gregarious by nature and so we crave for community. Until recently, families stayed together. It was not unusual for three generations to live together in the same house. As a result, grand-children had easy access to grandparents and vice versa. The little ones revered their eldest relatives and also knew that they could go to grandma or grandpa for advice, for acceptance, and most of all for love. Grandparents are not responsible for the outcome in raising grandchildren. That is the burden of the parents and so grandparents could afford to be indulgent, understanding and caring without anxiety. In addition, they were available as built-in baby-sitters, thereby allowing the parents to take time out for each other, and to escape from the relentless demands of parenting, for a few hours or even for a weekend. Such families, while they probably had their moments of frustration and personality clashes, nevertheless learned to live with one another and to enjoy the balance of having a three-generation household.

Much of that stability has been lost. Career demands have created increasing mobility. So often parents and children have to relocate to new or better paying jobs, leaving the grandparents behind. Although most elderly would never dream of complaining, and indeed would outwardly rejoice at their own children's good fortune, they feel a deep sense of loss of their dear ones. The family may do all in their power to maintain contact through phone calls and even visits on special holidays, but for most of the time, the grandparents feel isolated and lonely. They grieve and usually do it silently.

When I was a young doctor, I emigrated to Canada from Scotland, leaving my parents behind. I visited them every year until their deaths. For at least six months prior to my visit, they lived in excited anticipation and for the next six months they grieved over my departure. To this day I am haunted by the sad look on my mother's face and the stoic look of my father when I said my annual farewell at the airport. Each time, I know they wondered if they would ever see me again.

God is a family, a Trinity, and in creating us in his own image and likeness, he decreed that we too, should live in families. We need family as children, we create new families in marriage, and we still need family in our old age. Mother Teresa of Calcutta once wrote "Loneliness is only Jesus calling us to a deeper union with him. Perhaps then, we need to experience a loneliness for us to turn towards the only reliable remedy for it, which is Jesus Christ who will never stray from us. He is our constant companion if only we invite him into our hearts." "God gives the lonely a home to live in" (Ps. 68:6).

In view of this pain of loneliness and its devastating effects on the elderly, there are two solutions. The first is to have family nearby or even to be living with family. This, however, is a more and more rare phenomenon in today's society. The second strategy is for the elderly to create their own social contacts. They may belong to a senior citizens organization where social activities are available and varied. They may seek out friendships. They may choose to visit those who are also isolated, the sick, the poor or the marginalised. They may get involved in volunteer work, such as the food banks or driving others to hospital appointments. They can become more involved in Church as lay ministers, Eucharistic ministers, members of the Catholic Women's League or the Knights of Columbus. Since they usually have time, they can become more active in the Corporal and Spiritual Works of Mercy.

The Corporal Works of Mercy are:

1. To feed the hungry.
2. To give drink to the thirsty.
3. To clothe the naked.
4. To shelter the homeless.
5. To comfort the imprisoned.
6. To visit the sick.
7. To bury the dead.

Is it not true that our elders are in a wonderful position to do all of these things? They are no longer required to focus on an eight-to-five job. They are usually at a point in their lives where they have fewer wants. They have learned to be content with less and do not feel the former drive to get a bigger house or a bigger boat. Therefore, they are more able to share what they have with those who have less. They may well take someone into their home for the sake of a person in need, but also for their own need of relationship. They have time to visit the homeless and even the imprisoned if they feel called to that generous ministry. As to burying the dead, the elderly can reach out to grieving families with love, in practical support such as providing food for the funeral meal and most importantly in prayer.

The Spiritual Works of Mercy are:

1. To admonish sinners.
2. To instruct the uninformed.
3. To counsel the doubtful.
4. To comfort the sorrowful.
5. To be patient with those in error.
6. To forgive offenses.
7. To pray for the living and the dead.

Once more, the elders are in an excellent position to perform these works for the Body of Christ and for God. By dint of their long life's experience, they have learned so much in the way of wisdom, which they should be eager to share with the young. They can, with the authority of their years, lovingly call sinners to a higher way of life. They can give wise counsel to those who are troubled and give timely instruction to teenagers. They have had to face tragedy in their own lives, and so are well equipped to comfort others in their tragedy. Patience comes with wisdom and the elderly can astound us with their forbearance towards their own infirmities and towards the flaws of others. As to forgiving offenses, how many elderly go out of their way to look for the good in others, to overlook their faults and to excuse members of the family who never visit them? Old age is the last trumpet call from Jesus to grow in love.

The two greatest commandments are for us to love God above all and to love our neighbour as ourselves. Love is everything, and life's hard knocks not only challenge us to love more, but temper us in the crucible of love. The elderly have suffered and it is suffering which melts and expands the human heart to become patient, accepting, forgiving, compassionate and motivated by love.

One of the most powerful duties of the elderly is the seventh spiritual work of mercy, which is to pray for the living and the dead. "But a woman who is really widowed and left on her own has set her hope on God and perseveres night and day in petitions and prayer. The one who thinks only of pleasure is already dead while she is still alive" (1 Tim. 5:5-6). St. Paul is emphatically stating that those who are retired from the work force, whether widowed or not, now have a new job. They are called by the Lord to take up prayer in a committed and more powerful way. They have the time and the wisdom to devote themselves to the task of interceding for souls. Our grown-up sons and daughters are inevitably caught up in making their way in the world and in raising their own children. While it is expected that they will still attend Mass, receive the Sacraments and pray daily, they do not have the same time freedom which the elders have. The world is in desperate need of prayer of intercession and the causes are endless. We need to pray for an end to abortion, for the conversion of sinners, for the spiritual and material well-being of our young family members, for peace in the world and for equal distribution of food and resources to the poor. In days gone by, there were numerous cloistered orders of monks and nuns who offered continuous prayer of intercession for their nearby communities and for the world. These communities benefited incalculably from the graces called down by these holy contemplatives. Most of us do not enjoy the fruits of such prayer today, due to the regrettable decline of monastic life, and so more than ever, the world needs an army of elderly people who have the time, the generosity and the prayer power to bombard heaven on our behalf. The rosary should become a part of their right hand, constantly being offered up through the Blessed Mother to her Son Jesus for the benefit of the world. "Pray without ceasing" (1 Thess. 5:17). "The end of all things is near, so keep your minds calm and sober for prayer" (1 Pet. 4:7).

How many of today's elderly have grandchildren or, for that matter, children, who have left the Church? How many grandchildren are living with their partners without the blessing of marriage? How many grandchildren are being seduced by the world and led astray into drugs, alcohol and selfishness? There is no shortage of things to pray for. God gives to his holy elders the power to evangelise, and to convert the hearts of the young. They should therefore not give in to weariness but should battle on, proclaiming the truth, gently calling the young ones back to a moral life because, of all people, it is the elderly who know that only in an upright life, can peace of mind ever be found.

So often, society dismisses the aged as less than useful with the result that many seniors buy into that lie and think of themselves as useless. That is a treacherous deception. Old age can and should become the most spiritually powerful and effective phase of one's entire life. It is there for the taking.

As we grow older we are at an ever-increasing risk of the disease which is commonly called depression and this condition will be discussed at greater length in volume two, but at this point, it is helpful to know that if depression is confirmed it is treatable. Modern therapy can bring about very gratifying relief and can prevent the tragedy of suicide, which, sad to say, is on the increase in our elderly population. If after reading the chapter on depression, a person identifies with the symptoms or believes that an elderly relative has those symptoms, then a visit to the doctor is well worthwhile. The patient can be restored from the darkness of the disease and into the light of their normal outlook on life. Failure to recognize the disorder or a refusal to seek out medical help could result in an otherwise preventable loss of life.

"The young girl will then take pleasure in dance and young men and old alike. I shall change their mourning into gladness, comfort them and give them joy after their trouble" (Jer. 31:13). The mourning of depression can be changed into the gladness of health and this is a promise of God who guarantees a wonderful reward to those who remain faithful to him into their old age.

"After this, I shall pour out my spirit on all humanity. Your sons and daughters shall prophesy, your old people shall dream dreams" (Joel 2:28). What a wonderful grace to pray for. God is promising that he will transform the Church to the point where our young people will abandon sin and enjoy the gift of speaking God's word to the world. The elderly meanwhile, will dream dreams, which means they will expect to have a future, an eternal future, that for now we can only "dream about."

One of the beautiful traditions of the Catholic spiritual life is that we pray for the Holy Souls in Purgatory. Judas Maccabeus considered it profitable and good to pray for the dead. "For had he not expected the fallen to rise again, it would have been superfluous and foolish to pray for the dead, whereas if he had in view the splendid recompense reserved for those who make a pious end, the thought was holy and devout. Hence he had this expiatory sacrifice offered for the dead, so that they might be released from their sin" (2 Macc. 12:44-45).

We Catholics believe in the Communion of Saints and so we are called to pray for the souls in Purgatory, that their suffering will be shortened and relieved, and that they might sooner enter into the joys of Paradise. They cannot pray for themselves but they constantly pray for us on earth that we might not have to undergo their torment. Therefore, should we not in turn pray for them, especially for those who have no one to pray for them?

The elderly in their generosity can "adopt-a-soul" and direct much of their daily prayer energy towards his or her earlier release into heaven. In fact, very few Catholics realize that they can obtain a Plenary Indulgence every day. A Plenary Indulgence is a privilege granted by the Church whereby, if certain conditions are met, we can obtain the complete and instant cancellation of all punishment due to a soul who is suffering in Purgatory. The conditions are not all that stringent:

1. I must go to Mass on the day that I obtain the indulgence and receive Jesus in Holy Eucharist.
2. I must go to the Sacrament of Reconciliation within one week on either side of the day of indulgence. Therefore, if I went to Confession once every two weeks, I could obtain a Plenary Indulgence every day.
3. In addition to these two, I must either read Scripture for thirty minutes or say a Rosary or spend thirty minutes before the

Blessed Sacrament and I must add an Our Father, Hail Mary and Glory Be for the Pope's intentions.

That is all! For the elderly who are mobile and can attend Mass, surely these are not too difficult to perform. In truth, we could release a soul from Purgatory three hundred and sixty-five times a year.

Such is the generosity of the Church and such is the generosity of Jesus who promised, "Whatever you bind on earth shall be bound in heaven" (Matt. 16:19). In other words, since it was the Church which developed the privilege of indulgence, Jesus keeps his promise and honours that same privilege in heaven. Therefore, our Catholic elderly should never consider themselves to be retired. They can now be employed full-time in praying for the kingdom of God. As one wit put it, "The pay is not very good but the retirement benefits are terrific." This is highlighted by the Psalmist who wrote, "In old age, they will still bear fruit, will remain fresh and green to proclaim Yahweh's integrity" (Ps. 92:14-15). It is prayer which bears fruit and it is good works which proclaim God's integrity.

One of the most beautiful images of old age is to be found in the book of Zechariah, "Yahweh Sabaoth says this: Aged men and women will once again sit in the squares of Jerusalem, each with a stick to lean on because of their great age. And the squares of the city will be full of boys and girls playing there" (Zech. 8:4-5). What a marvellous image this is of holy community life. How wonderful it is for the old to watch the young at play, and how secure it is for the young to be watched over by the old. God promises us a great old age and he promises us the peace to enjoy it. It is holiness which secures it.

The New Testament also promises abundant life in old age. When the Angel Gabriel spoke to Mary, he said, "Your cousin Elizabeth also, in her old age, has conceived a son and she whom people called barren is now in her sixth month, for nothing is impossible to God" (Luke 1:36-37). This miraculous pregnancy was given to us, not solely to bring John the Baptist into history, but also to prove that God can do anything. It also confirmed that God loves his holy elderly people enough to work wonders through them. How many of today's elderly truly believe that? How many trust in the power of God to do great things in their own lives and in the lives of their loved ones? It is never too late to trust in God. Scripture says that ***nothing*** is impossible to God.

St. Paul echoes this theme when he writes, "It was equally by faith that Sarah, in spite of being past the age, was made able to conceive, because she believed that he who had made the promise was faithful to it. Because of this there came from one man (Abraham) and one who already had the mark of death on him, descendants as numerous as the stars of heaven and the grains of sand on the seashore which cannot be counted" (Heb. 11:11-12). God honours his friends and he honours his elderly who are faithful to his word. Sometimes though, the problem is that we do not have a generous enough picture of what God can do. We limit him by our own human limits and do not ask him for great things. We have to believe in miracles for miracles to occur.

A factor which is too often underplayed, especially by the youth of today and even by the elderly themselves, is that being old demands respect. "Listen to your father from whom you are sprung, do not despise your mother in her old age" (Prov. 23:22). This is a serious demand by God. He expects us to treat our elders with respect, honour and deference, acknowledging their venerable age. This does not mean that children, teenagers, and young adults only owe respect to those elderly who are clever or wise or competent. This respect is owed simply because a person is old and has survived many years of joy and sorrow, health and sickness, prosperity and grief. Old age is to be revered because God says so.

The fourth commandment of the Decalogue states, "Honour your father and your mother" (Ex. 20:12). We therefore are called upon to honour our elderly, for they are all our mothers and fathers. We honour them by our love, respect, tolerance, patience, kindness, caring and a willingness to give them our time.

Sadly, very few younger people seem to do this today, because they have been seduced by the myth of the "generation-gap" but that is no reason for discouragement. The world may shirk its obligation, but God at least, will always glorify his older friends and will always love and honour them. They will not be lacking in what is their right of seniority before him. "Never speak sharply to a man older than yourself but appeal to him as you would to your own father: treat younger men as brothers, older women as mothers and young women as sisters in all purity" (1 Tim. 5:1-2). Therefore, while it is a tragedy that seniors are so often neglected or relegated to loneliness, it is a major catastrophe for the adults and youth who reject them. God in his holy word is commanding us to treat all elders as though they were our very own fathers and mothers. Violation of this ordinance is a serious refusal to love. The Old Testament Jews understood this principle, even if the Pharisees and wealthy landowners often did not practice it. Jews always addressed an elderly woman as mother and an old man as father, even if they were meeting them for the first time. How transforming it would be if our society would adopt the same custom. As soon as I refer to someone as mother or father, I immediately display an attitude of reverence for their age and speak with respect, as I would to my own parents.

Yet, such a reclaiming of one's dignity as an elder is unlikely to happen if the elderly merely sit around hoping for it. If older persons become passive then this only convinces younger persons that indeed the elderly are good-for-nothing and should be set aside. Therefore it is time for our senior citizens to take back their dignity. It is time for seniors to learn where their dignity lies in order to become what they are in truth. Contrary to what is believed by some radical segments of society, the dignity of our elders will not be reclaimed by militant action or protests or the demanding of rights. True holy change can only occur through true and holy people. Seniors must first learn who they are before God and how the Almighty wants them to behave. By becoming a holy people, they will find to their amazement that God will provide in marvellous ways.

"Older men should be reserved, dignified, moderate, sound in faith and love and perseverance. Similarly older women should behave as befits religious people with no scandal-mongering and no addiction to wine; they must be teachers of right behaviour and show younger women how they must love their husbands and love their children, how they must be sensible and chaste, and how to work in their homes and be gentle and obey their husbands so that the message of God is not disgraced" (Titus 2:2-5).

This is a superb sketch of what God expects of his faithful elderly. With a few strokes of the pen, St. Paul describes an older man as one who should be manly in every way. He acts in a dignified manner. He is moderate in all things and therefore not a drunkard or a glutton and shows proper reserve in company. He has learned self-control, he believes in the truth of God and shows manly perseverance in that truth. Naturally, all that he does is prompted by love. It is as though St. Paul is suggesting that the hot-headedness, the anger, the pride and the violence of youth have all been laid aside, and that maturity has at last brought true freedom, the freedom to be a loving and peaceful man.

Elderly women are expected by the Lord to be more like religious in their behaviour than like women of the world. With age there should come the wisdom to know that malicious gossip and excessive drinking are never satisfying, and always do major evil. In addition to temperance and self-control, they also can, where possible, teach younger women in the family (or outside the family if the young girls will listen) how to be pure and good, how to love their husbands and how to nurture their children. What a privilege we have that God would give us the health and the grace to grow to a ripe old age. What a privilege it is to become a mother or a father to all the younger generations. What a joy it is to share one's experience, wisdom, time and skills with those in need. What a privilege it is to have the time to pray for souls, to attend daily Mass, to visit Jesus in the Blessed Sacrament, and to make one's eternal reward a top priority.

It is absolutely true that society has serious obligations with regard to the elderly and it is a tragedy that, for the most part, society is revoking these obligations. There is an erosion of respect for our elders. There is a regrettable tendency for modern society to banish the troublesome elderly into institutions, and no doubt the euthanasia debate will not go away. Nevertheless, if our older citizens could really learn to believe in who they are before God, if they would take up their cross and follow Jesus, if they would live a life of peace, moderation, faith and love, then not only will the elders themselves feel content and at peace, but society will slowly be transformed into a new vision of old age. Once more the elders will be given the respect and deference that is their due. It is not enough to grow older in years. It is necessary to grow bolder in Christ, for seniors to discover themselves and for society to rediscover them.

CHAPTER 13

Death and Dying: The Doorway to Life

> *"Death is swallowed up in victory. Death, where is your victory? Death, where is your sting?"*
>
> (1 Cor.15:54-55)

A friend of mine once attended a meeting of psychologists in a major city. During one of the presentations everyone was asked to write down what they would try to accomplish if they knew that they were going to die in five years time. Everyone wrote eagerly about their dreams, unfinished projects, trips they would like to take and so on. Then the professor asked them to write down their priorities if they knew they were going to die tomorrow. The effect was electrifying. Everyone soon realised that their priority list was totally different. The immediacy of death changed all. There were no more long-term projects. Instead, most realised they needed to gather their loved ones together, to speak the words that had not been spoken, to ask for and to give forgiveness, and to express love and gratitude to them. It was a powerful demonstration of the sad fact that we rarely live as though we would die one day and that death could come sooner than we think. In fact it would seem that death always comes sooner than we think.

Christians are reminded by the Church that death is a reality and that if we are in a state of grace it need not be feared. In fact it can be a peaceful if not a joyful experience as we confidently go to Jesus. "Look, I am old and do not know when I may die" (Gen. 27:2). This not-knowing does not postpone the appointed day and certainly denying death will not prevent it. As followers of Jesus, we can both live and die with hope. We know as no one else can that death is only a change of address. Death is not the end, but is the beginning of a new life and as such is really only a continuation of life into eternity.

"Precious in the eyes of the Lord is the death of his faithful ones" (Ps. 116:15). For God, death is not the tragedy that we consider it to be. For his Divine Heart, it is a moment of greatest joy for he can then delight in giving us our eternal reward in Heaven. The only time that it is painful to God's way of thinking is when we die in our sins. "Would I take pleasure in the death of the wicked, declares the Lord Yahweh, and not prefer to see him renounce his wickedness and live?" (Ezek. 18:23). Most of us, then, look upon death very differently from God. If only we knew what was waiting for us as disciples of Jesus, we would look forward with holy expectancy to see and experience the joy of our Creator God.

Most Christians already know all this, but when it comes right down to it, we really fear dying more than death. Death is not so bad since we can appreciate that it is an end to pain, the moment of final release from suffering. Dying however is a very different matter and all of us are uneasy about that. Naturally very few people, except for some exceptionally holy Christians, relish the idea of terminal suffering and pain. It is only natural to wish to avoid it or even to fear it, but this can lead us to miss an important truth. I very often hear people say something like, "When I go I want to go instantly and suddenly." This is understandable in that they do not desire to suffer, but to be honest, I am personally horrified at the thought of a sudden death. Should that happen to me, would I have any time to prepare my soul for God? Would I have time to tell Jesus I am sorry for my sins? Would I even have time to call upon the name of Jesus? This is a very important concept for me. I pray that I do not have an instantaneous death. On the contrary I pray that the Lord will grant me the grace of a *happy* death, one by which I am prepared and ready to meet him, a death which is preceded by the time needed to put my immortal soul in order.

Every day I pray a little prayer which I was taught as a child. It is the prayer for a happy death.

"Jesus, Mary and Joseph, I give you my heart and my soul.
Jesus, Mary and Joseph, assist me in my last agony.
Jesus, Mary and Joseph, may I breathe forth my soul in peace
with you." Amen.

Some may regard that as a selfish desire. After all, someone else will have to nurse me in my last illness and my illness would cost the taxpayer a lot of money in health care. My only answer is that I, for my part, am prepared to nurse any of my loved ones who are dying, and eternal life is worth it. Also, my salvation is of infinite worth to me and certainly much more than mere dollars and cents.

Having laid the spiritual groundwork, it is important to discuss dying and to promote some understanding of its effects both on the patient and upon his or her family. For this I am indebted to the wonderful work of Therese Rando, a clinical psychologist, who has devoted her life to the care of the dying and those who are grieving.

It is difficult to imagine a more devastating moment in anyone's life than to be told by the doctor that one has a fatal disease. All of a sudden, all illusions of immortality are stripped away and death is close at hand. It becomes real and the patient will be forced to deal with it one way or another. Understandably he or she will have a major emotional reaction, which will consist of initial shock followed by bargaining, anger, depression and ultimately acceptance. These reactions do not necessarily occur in that sequence and people will move in and out of any one of these at any given time. One moment she may feel angry, at another sad, then back to anger again or into a state of shock. It is a time of confused coming to terms with a deadly reality.

The stage of shock is marked by a sense of disbelief at the diagnosis. It causes an emotional numbness and the patient is in a kind of stunned daze unable to really accept that death is staring her in the face. She tends to have such thoughts as "This is not happening to *me*. The doctor has made a mistake."

The bargaining phase is an attempt by the patient to find a way out of her terrible reality. She may bargain with the doctor. "If I give up smoking now, surely that would cure the cancer" or she may completely reject the offer of conventional medical help. She may then latch on to magical concoctions which guarantee more than they can deliver, or worse still she may be duped by charlatans who offer phony miraculous cures. How many desperate people with cancer have ruined themselves financially by rushing off to Mexico for treatment with the new "wonder drug" which was nothing more than extract of apricot pits? No one can blame the patient who is only too ready to grasp at straws, but we should certainly despise those who cheat them.

While it is a good and holy thing to pray for a cure to Almighty God, nevertheless it can also take the form of bargaining with God. "If you heal me Lord then I promise to give up drinking. I will stop being nasty to my wife and children. I will go to daily Mass from now on." This is not so bad and certainly God understands one's desperation, but we must also allow God to be God and humbly accept his perfect will for us, otherwise we risk becoming unjustly angry with him or even blaming him for our plight.

Anger is of course a natural response to devastating news. The patient may have such thoughts as "Why me?" "What have I ever done to deserve this?" It can be directed towards others. "Why has this not happened to Amy? I am a better person than she is. Where is the justice?" When this anger is directed at God, we may find ourselves asking such questions as, "Why has God done this to me." "God does not love me." "There is no God." Family members must never rebuke their loved one for expressing such thoughts. At this time they must understand that it is a frantic effort to cope and it is a cry for help and for hope. The family needs to be there, to accept and to love. It is not the time for deep discussions about death and the afterlife. That may be appropriate later on but during the anger phase, the patient needs acceptance and hope, not doom and gloom.

At any point, the patient can plunge into a severe depression. This is a form of grieving for oneself and it is a deep sense of loss for one's former health and vigour. The patient mourns over her previous enjoyment of life, may regret not having lived it more fully and is anticipating her own death, seeing it as a tragedy. She is unable to see any hope. She may feel guilty over past transgressions and may become so overwhelmed that she feels condemned by God.

During this time, the family must allow the loved one to express her feelings, without judging them and to foster within her an attitude of hope. They need to emphasize that the patient is not dead yet, that there is time to realize some ambitions and that the patient still has some control over how events will unfold. All of us are frightened of losing control and a dying person needs to feel that, while control is shrinking, it is not all gone.

Hope is vital to a dying patient, but as the illness progresses, the hope has to change its focus. As hope of a longer life fades, it must be replaced by an increasing hope of life hereafter. This is absolutely fundamental to a Catholic. The key to a worthy death lies in the hope that there is a God and that Jesus will keep his promise to us of eternal salvation.

The last phase of emotional adjustment is acceptance. This is the time when the patient finally faces reality. The patient knows she is going to die and is at peace with it. She is now able to plan the time she may have left, to attend to her affairs, to communicate with her family and to prepare her soul for God. It is a relief to the patient. It is also a great relief to the family. There is no more need for pretend games. The family can now freely talk about the death of their loved one, about funeral arrangements, about the music for the Mass of the Resurrection and the many other details which the patient may wish to be carried out. In planning her own funeral, she is being given a necessary sense of control over her final rites. It is a way of holding onto dignity.

When the patient has been allowed to proceed through the initial emotional sequence, it is now time for her to face certain very important tasks. Again she should be given as much control as possible.

The first task is to cope with the progressive symptoms of the illness itself. All of us are afraid of pain and so the patient needs to understand that her pain can be relieved very effectively and still leave her in complete possession of her faculties. She can expect to have pain control and continue in a warm and realistic relationship with her family. She can expect to retain her full awareness and intellect. Patients do fear that they will be heavily drugged and thereby out of touch with their loved ones. This does not happen with modern palliative care. Not only that, but medical science can offer relief from distressing symptoms other than pain, such as vomiting or diarrhoea. Nevertheless, there is still going to be suffering in the sense of knowing that one is losing ground daily. There will likely be a drastic change in one's appearance if weight loss occurs, and ultimately, one may become confined to bed. Even though the patient may have reached a good acceptance level of reality following the initial shock of the diagnosis, nevertheless she has to adjust to each loss as it comes along, whether it be loss of former beauty or loss of ability.

The second task is dealing with the demands of often dramatic treatment interventions. The patient may have to face hospitals, medical personnel, chemotherapy, radiation, surgery and prosthetic devices. All of these put new demands on the patient to adapt. Adaptation requires energy and a dying person is losing energy. It is a major challenge and can only be met by means of spirit and sheer courage. Again, family is so vital in supporting the patient through these ordeals, driving her to appointments, being in the waiting room during surgery and helping her with medications.

The third task is to develop a good relationship with medical personnel. So often a patient feels helpless. For her, it is as though her body does not belong to her anymore. She feels at the mercy of the doctors and nurses who "do things to her body" as though it was their property and not hers. There is no need for this. The patient has the right to exercise her own unique dignity, and medical personnel need to understand that it is a profound privilege for them to be allowed to even lay a hand on a patient. Good doctors and nurses understand this, the patient automatically senses it and so she feels confident in placing herself into their care. Unfortunately, this is an ideal not always present since it seems to depend upon the philosophy and the sensitivity (or lack of it) on the part of the caregivers.

Two physicians by the name of Moos and Tsu wrote, "Consider the questions patients may ask themselves: Can I express my anger at the doctor for not coming to see me? How can I ask for additional medication for pain when I need it? How can I deal with the disagreements among different physicians regarding how I should be treated? How can I handle the condescension and pity I sense in the nurses who care for me? How can I tell the physical therapist not to give up on me even though my progress is disappointingly slow? How can I engage my doctor in a meaningful discussion of how I wish to be treated if I am incapacitated and near death? These are problems which plague patients and their families. The frequent turnover and change in personnel, particularly those staff who come into more direct contact with the patient, makes this an unusually complicated set of tasks."

The fourth task is to cope with feelings. As has already been mentioned, this is best done by fostering a sense of hope even where the hope is limited by the realities of the illness. Hope prolongs life, as the work of many researchers has shown and it prolongs quality of life, which is even more important. Loss of hope is despair and that only leads to withdrawal from life. Such a patient merely curls up and dies, which is a major and unnecessary tragedy. The family and the priest are vital agents of hope to a dying Catholic.

The fifth task is to preserve an acceptable self-image and to maintain some sense of control over events no matter how increasingly limited that control may become. For example, a patient may continue to have her hair done regularly. She may decide to have her bed moved downstairs so she can interact with her family. She may refuse to accept the offer of certain chemotherapy, because the side-effects may be unacceptable. She may decide to make a last trip. She may decide to write her life story as a legacy for her loved ones.

The sixth task is to preserve and to deepen family relationships and friendships. A dying patient really needs continued contact with loved ones in spite of the isolation caused by hospitalisation or the reluctance of others to be close to someone who is sick or dying. This is really more of a challenge to the family than it is to the patient. The patient needs this contact but having no control over others, she is dependent upon the love and caring of family and friends, to visit and talk or simply to be by the bedside. We all fear dying alone and no one should ever have to. This task falls onto the family's shoulders.

The seventh task is, if there is time, to put one's affairs into order. That means making sure the will is made out according to the patient's wishes and is properly legal and binding. Perhaps debts need to be paid and insurance policies checked on. Many persons choose to write letters to family, friends and co-workers to be opened only after their death.

The eighth task is spiritual. For a Catholic, death is the beginning of the great eternal adventure and so dying demands preparation of the soul. Arrangements should be made for the priest to visit regularly, to pray over the person, to hear her confession, to bring her Holy Communion and to administer the Sacrament of the Sick. The priest should encourage the patient to talk about life after death and to share with her the truths of Jesus about the promised resurrection. The family should gather around their loved one to pray the Rosary, asking the Mother of God to be present to receive her soul at the appointed time. St. Joseph is the patron saint of a happy death and so he too should be asked to be present at the moment of death so that both he and his spouse, Mary, can lead the soul with joy to Jesus. This is not pious pablum. This is raw spiritual truth.

I have had the privilege of being present many times at the death of a Catholic who, having had time to prepare, joyfully received the last rites. It was heart-warming to see the family gathered around the death-bed and praying the Rosary. On occasion I even heard the patient exclaim that she could see Mary, Jesus or St. Joseph waiting for her expectantly, and then she closed her eyes and died. Such Catholics experienced a truly happy death. I have seen other deaths which I can only describe as fear and terror-filled and it was a harrowing thing for me to witness their refusal to accept Jesus right to the last. They did not die in the peace of Christ, at least it did not appear so. I have always believed that our last hours are Satan's last chance to tempt us. This is the critical time when he makes his last frantic attempt to snatch our soul from heaven's grasp. Therefore it is critical that a patient be surrounded by family, friends and hopefully a priest, to fervently pray for the protection of the soul from this final onslaught. The Chaplet of the Divine Mercy has been proven over and over again to be a powerful weapon against Satan and his demons during this last battle.

The most difficult death for anyone to cope with is the death of a child. The reasons for this are not too difficult to understand. The death of a child is considered a greater loss because the child has not had the opportunity to live a full life as compared to an adult. The life of a child has great social value. We are moved by his or her childlike helplessness and we grieve for the loss of an innocent. Also, we find it very hard to see why a child should have to die. It may even lead us to question God. How can a loving God allow an innocent child to die of cancer or in an accident? The death of a child, even one we have never known, affects us all.

Until recently, families and care-givers alike have tended to withhold from the child the awful fact that she was dying. The adults around her understandably wanted to protect her from unnecessary hurt and they felt confirmed in that attitude by the fact that the child refrained from asking any disturbing questions. This approach is no longer considered to be appropriate. Recent research has shown that children, no matter how young, are very aware that they are dying. They do not ask questions because they quickly pick up on the pain of the adults around them and realize that it would hurt them to talk about death. The brave little soul sacrifices her own need to understand, out of consideration for her parents and family.

Nevertheless, the child suffers from fear of the unknown and really needs to be allowed to ask questions and receive answers. Any professional today, who works with dying children, will agree that children do have an awareness of their own condition and experience grief and anxiety as a result of it. Therefore communication with the child is indispensable. Naturally, parents who may be willing to communicate honestly will worry about how much the child can understand, especially if the child is very young. Again research has shown that terminally ill children can understand their dying in terms previously thought of as possible only in older children and that, surprisingly enough, their ideas and concepts are much more sophisticated than those of healthy children (Bluebond-Langrer 1977).

Fr. Kavanaugh in his book *Facing Death* wrote, "of the many children I visited near death, Tildy affected me the most. Burned beyond repair, her obvious pain and severe disfigurement were instrumental in keeping many friends away. I am ashamed at how frequently I manufactured excuses until she shared with me in our huddled confession her perplexity about how to handle her parents. This loveable nine-year-old could not tell them how much she knew and they would not tell her. Together, Tildy and I kept her secret. Only days before she died, she took my hand and said with smiling pride, 'We did it, Father, we did it! I don't think they know that I know.'" We often do not give our children the credit for their knowledge, insight and great courage.

Dr. Spinetta, writing in 1980, provides a list of topics which should be raised with a dying child and discussed at a level appropriate to the child's age. The care-giver should use the child's own language and should encourage the child to express her own worries, fears and concerns. This allows the parent, doctor or nurse to address the real struggles within the child. There are fourteen points. The first eleven points can be raised when the child may have months or years of life still ahead even though the diagnosis of a fatal disease has been established. It is recommended that points twelve through fourteen should be reserved for the time when the child is very close to death. I will paraphrase the fourteen points from the Catholic perspective.

1. Death is part of nature. In fact it is a part of life.
2. The death of the child is very important to her and it is very important to her family and friends.
3. Not only will the child lose those who are left behind but those left behind also lose her.
4. Death is not the end. The child will live on in the arms of Jesus in the most wonderful joy and she can help mom and dad and her brothers and sisters by asking Jesus to help them. She can also look forward to the day when her family will also die and they can all be reunited in heaven.
5. The child will not have to die alone. Her loved ones will be by her side praying with her and holding her hand.
6. The child needs to know that her life has had a purpose. Parents need to tell her what a precious gift she is from God to them and how much she has brought joy into their lives.
7. It is all right to cry and feel sad.
8. It is all right to sometimes be angry about dying.
9. It is all right not to want to talk about it anymore for a while.
10. When the child is ready to talk about it again, the adult will be there to listen and support. This is crucial.
11. It is all right to feel confused or to say things which you think are silly. Adults say silly things too.

12. Death will not hurt. Dying might be painful and the doctor will do everything possible to take the pain away, but death stops the pain. Children need to know that the pain will stop.
13. When someone you love dies it is important for you to be able to say good-bye. "So we parents will need to say good-bye to you and we do that at the funeral Mass where we give you to Jesus. This is very important for your mother and father and your brothers and sisters. So I hope you don't mind. You will be with Jesus in the joy of Heaven, but we have to stay here for a while longer."
14. The child needs to know that it is also hard for her family to face the separation of death. "If we talk to the doctor a lot and cry afterwards or if we cry when we talk to you about your illness, it is only because we love you and it will be hard to get along without you around, but we will always be with you. We won't be able to hear you talk to us from heaven but guess what! You will be able to hear us talk to you. That is the way it is in heaven so you will know when we are thinking of you and that will be a lot."

Gabrielle was a tiny, elderly, courageous lady who was a patient of mine many years ago. Right from the start, she insisted that I call her Gabby, so Gabby it was. She had been raised in a Catholic home, but had abandoned the Church a long time before I met her.

Shortly after I began to look after her, her husband developed a serious illness and it soon became clear that he was going to die soon. He became house-bound, then chair-bound, then bed-ridden and finally he passed away, leaving Gabby alone in the world. She did have a sick sister who lived too far away to visit. All during that time, Gabby nursed her husband with great love and tenderness. No task, no matter how intimate, was beneath her and she never uttered one single word of complaint.

During her husband's last days, I would make many house-calls, attend to her husband's needs and then Gabby and I would sit down to a cup of tea. I was able to talk to her about death, about life after death, about prayer and the love of God. Not long after her husband's death, she asked me to come and talk some more about the faith. I did, and one day I asked her outright if she was ready to make a long-overdue confession and return to the Church. She said a joyful "yes" and I arranged for her to see a good priest. She was instantly transformed and her natural exuberance for life became a joy that sparkled in her eyes.

After that I would take the Holy Eucharist to her when I made my house-calls and, whenever she received Jesus, she seemed so peaceful and happy. Her face would light up at the sight of the Sacred Host and she would say, "Oh! I am the luckiest girl in the whole world!" Some time later, Gabby's sister died and in her will she left Gabby a single dinner place-setting of Limoges china. For Gabby, who was very poor, this was a priceless treasure and it was with great excitement and pleasure that she carefully unwrapped it to show it to me. In all innocence she said, "Now my dream is to sit down at a table with my place-setting and to enjoy a tender filet mignon with mashed potatoes and garden peas, and maybe even a sip of good wine."

When I returned home that night, I told my wife, Rita, of Gabby's dream and it was no surprise to me that Rita immediately set about making the dream come true. A week later I picked up Gabby and her Limoges china and we went home, where Rita lovingly set out the china on the dining table and all three of us had a marvellous dinner with the filet mignon and all the trimmings and Gabby even had that sip of good wine. I do not know how many times she said, "Oh! I am the luckiest girl in the whole world!"

Not too long after that, Gabby began to complain of some very ominous-sounding symptoms. An X-ray revealed a rapidly growing cancer in her large bowel. She was so tiny and elderly and fragile that the surgeon wisely refused to be aggressive with treatment. So Gabby came home to face death. I continued to see her regularly and to bring her Holy Communion and I did all I could to keep her as comfortable as possible. Christmas was coming and so Rita and I invited her to share Christmas dinner with us. She was so excited, she kept on talking about it, telling all her neighbours in her apartment building. She could hardly wait for the big day. However, it did not work out as we had planned.

Around five o'clock in the afternoon of Christmas Eve, she called me in great pain. I went round to find her in complete bowel obstruction and I had no choice but to take her to hospital right away. She was so crestfallen that she would miss her longed-for Christmas with us, but we were not beaten yet. The next day, Rita and I loaded her presents into a colourful shopping bag and off we went to visit Gabby in the ward. Rita had bought about twenty little gifts, all beautifully wrapped and she piled the lot onto Gabby's bed. Needless to say, Gabby had already captured the hearts of all the doctors and nurses on the ward and soon they all gathered round to enjoy the big unwrapping ceremony. Again and again Gabby kept declaring, "I'm the luckiest girl in the whole world!"

The good doctors were able to temporarily relieve the bowel obstruction and so Gabby was allowed home for a little time. Her prayer life became more and more beautiful and fervent. She said her Rosary faithfully and continued to receive the Sacraments. However, it was clear that she was failing fast, losing weight and becoming weaker.

It was in March of the year that I had to admit her to hospital for the last time. When Rita and I went to see her, she humbly whispered to us that she was embarrassed to have to wear a hospital gown. She did not have a gown of her own. That was enough for Rita, who promptly took off to the shopping mall and purchased an exquisite white satin nightdress for Gabby. When Rita took it in to the hospital I could not be there but Rita reported to me that Gabby was beside herself with excitement and joy. She put it on and looked like a little bride, which is exactly what she was. She was a pure and holy little bride of Jesus.

While visiting, Rita noticed that some of Gabby's flowers were wilting badly and she innocently reached over to remove them. Gabby look up and said, "No! Leave them alone. They are not dead yet." Rita knew that Gabby was really saying, "Don't count me out. I'm not dead yet, either." So Rita just smiled and gently left well enough alone.

The following day, Gabby knew I was coming in to see her and so she put on her new gown, wanting to look her very best. Unknown to me, she also refused to take any morphine shots that day so that she could be fully alert for my visit. She looked like a little porcelain doll sitting up in bed. She must have been in severe pain but she never let out a whimper. She had received the Sacrament of the Sick and she told me quite matter-of-factly that she was ready to meet Jesus. She promised that she would pray for Rita and me when she got to Heaven. Before I left, she took my hand and whispered, "I'm the luckiest girl in the whole world!" I kissed her and said good-bye. She died the next day.

Little Gabby taught me more than years of study with books. She taught by her wonderful spirit of thanksgiving and gratitude to God for all her blessings. She thanked God for her life, for her Limoges china, for her filet mignon, for her friendship with Rita, but most of all she thanked God for calling her back to the rich life of the Church. She truly considered herself to be the luckiest girl in the whole world even in the midst of dying. Above all, I thank God for Gabby and for her happy death. She will never be canonised by the Church. She was too tiny to be noticed, but she is in heaven. "Remain faithful unto death and I will give you the crown of life" (Rev. 2:10).

Dying is not easy but it is the doorway to life.

CHAPTER 14

Grief: My World is Empty Without You

*"We want you to be quite
certain, brothers, about those
who have fallen asleep, to
make sure that you do not
grieve for them, as others do
who have no hope."*

(1 Thess. 4:13)

The virtue of hope is vital to every human being and it is hope which gives us the fortitude to bear our worst tragedies. It is indispensable to the person facing a terminal illness and it is indispensable to anyone who is grieving over a loved one. It should go hand in hand with being a Catholic, and that is why the funeral Mass is called the Mass of the Resurrection. The Church calls us at the time of death to remember that Jesus conquered death, to tap into our hope and to look to the heavenly reward which our relative or friend is now enjoying. It urges us to find our own joy in the fact that she who has died is now free from pain of any kind and is in the arms of the Lord. The Church also reminds us that our time of separation will be short and one day we will be reunited in Heaven in unspeakable joy. "Eye has not seen nor ear heard what God has prepared for those who love him" (1 Cor. 2:9).

While this message of joy is absolutely true, we still cannot escape from grief over the loss. All of us, in one way or another, will enter into a time of mourning which is painful, and for some it will be very prolonged indeed. Most people grieve acutely over a period of about one year, have a significant relapse at the anniversary date of the loved one's death, and only then begin to look forward to a new and meaningful life. It is as though the mind needs to go through the four seasons of the year before it can come out of the darkness. One of the reasons for this is, that during the first year following the bereavement, a person will often think, "Last year at this time Susan was alive and we were on holiday together." This triggers the acute sense of loss all over again. Once the anniversary date is past, this kind of memory is no longer so painful because, of course, last year at this time Susan was already gone.

The mourner may then do well for a time but have a bad grief experience at the next anniversary date and so on for a few years, but each time it is of less and less intensity.

Grief at the death of someone we love is often somewhat lessened if there has been a prolonged illness prior to the death. During the sickness we are able to do some grief work, bit by bit, as we see our loved one deteriorate and approach death. This is called *anticipatory grief* and it is not a bad thing. It can greatly reduce the intensity of the grief we are going to feel when death finally takes place.

However, there is a very difficult aspect of grieving which has been termed *The Lazarus Syndrome*. This refers to a situation where a loved one is clearly dying. We enter into anticipatory grief, expecting her to die very soon, and then the patient makes a dramatic recovery. This raises two problems for the family. First of all, if we have interiorly said good-bye to Susan then it can be incredibly difficult to welcome her back into the land of the living and give her once more a place in our hearts. Secondly, when Susan relapses, we find it very hard to let ourselves grieve again for fear she may recover unexpectedly once more. *The Lazarus Syndrome* is an extremely difficult emotional crisis for family members. If it occurs more than twice, people can find themselves wishing that Susan would get on with it and die. They then feel deeply guilty about entertaining such "dreadful" thoughts. A good therapist knows how to deal with that guilt and helps a family member to understand that very few people can cope with the roller-coaster intense feelings which attend such a problem. The need for relief from the overwhelming emotion is so great that one might entertain a death-wish, something one would never have dreamed possible before.

The truth is that grieving is a necessary process. Left alone, and allowed to proceed naturally, it will result in self-healing. A grief therapist will compassionately allow the bereaved person to go through the process in his or her own way and at his or her own speed. Grief is not healed by aggressive intervention, but by patience and compassion. It is vital that the therapist affirm a person's unique way of grieving and reassure him or her that what they are experiencing is normal. The only time that grief can be considered to be abnormal is when it becomes blocked and is no longer progressing towards resolution. Blocked grief definitely requires therapy, otherwise it will persist for many, many years. Some people do not recover at all. This blockage can occur where a loved one died a sudden or violent death, or where the loved one was a young child. It can also occur if the survivor experiences crushing guilt (because she feels responsible for the death) or where she had not given or received forgiveness from the loved one. Guilt is a powerful obstacle to the grieving process.

As a rule, normal grieving passes through the seven *"R's."*

1. Realization

It is essential for the bereaved to fully realize that the death has actually occurred and to make some kind of sense out of it. This can be very difficult where death was sudden and unexpected, such as in a motor-vehicle accident. It is much more difficult where the death was a suicide or a murder. The stage of shocked disbelief can be very paralysing and the bereaved simply refuses to accept that the loved one is really dead. It takes a lot of love to gently help her accept the terrible truth.

As the person gradually allows reality to sink in, then the floodgates of loss can be opened up and she can give herself permission to feel the pain.

2. Remembering

A grieving person should be given permission to reminisce about her past life with the deceased. She should be allowed to bring back all kinds of memories of what they did together, trips they enjoyed, humorous times, and even sad times. There is no agenda here. The bereaved can talk about any memory at all and we should be very patient in allowing her to go over a memory as many times as she needs to. She should never be cut off just because she has already told someone the same thing many times before.

3. Realistic Recall

This is very important to healthy grieving. Very often the bereaved will focus only on the good qualities of the loved one as though it would be disrespectful or somehow sacrilegious to do otherwise. Most people believe that one should not speak ill of the dead. Yet, there is a big difference between the sin of slandering the dead and simply accepting the truth. All human beings are the usual mix of good and bad. The loved one was all of that as well. To "canonise" the deceased, as it were, is not only unrealistic but can lead to blockage of the grief process. The bereaved should be encouraged to remember good times, but should also acknowledge that the loved one was no saint and be able to talk about past hurts or hard times. This keeps the memory balanced and rooted in reality.

4. Releasing

If the grief is progressing in a healthy way, then sooner or later the survivor has to let the loved one go. There has to come a point at which she accepts the death, and releases the deceased into his or her eternal life. The fact is, of course, that the deceased is already in eternity, but the griever still fiercely holds on to the loved one in her heart. For healthy progress, she must cut the cord and allow the loved one to be really dead. It is very important to understand that this releasing does not mean the severing of a *relationship* with the deceased. On the contrary, therapy encourages the one left behind to develop a new and meaningful relationship with the loved one. This is a more spiritual connection, understanding that the loved one is not only still alive elsewhere, but is able to be closer to the survivor than ever before. The loved one is not constrained by the physical limitations of the body and so is able to be close to the bereaved in a new and beautiful way. As Catholics we believe we can and should pray *for* the souls of the dead, that they will be released from Purgatory (if they stand in need of purification), and we can pray *to* them asking for their intercession with Jesus on our behalf. This is the wonderful doctrine of the Communion of Saints and it is a source of great consolation to anyone who is grieving. The relationship with the deceased is not over. It is simply transformed.

5. Reassessment

With the death of someone very dear, all our assumptions about the world are drastically changed. The survivor up to that point had lived in a world where the newly deceased was intimately present. Perhaps the deceased had been the principal breadwinner. Perhaps he had always cut the grass and tidied up the yard. If the bereaved is a woman, perhaps she enjoyed a world in which her husband took care of the garden, looked after the family budget and organized vacations. Whatever the survivor was used to, she can no longer make those assumptions. The world has now changed drastically and in order to survive, she will have to make a whole new set of assumptions. She must learn to live in a world which has changed dramatically, a world wherein the loved one no longer resides.

6. Readjustment

Once the bereaved is able to accept that the old assumptions are no longer viable, she can begin the process of adjusting to a world without the loved one in it. This means finding new ways to secure income, to begin to prepare one's own meals and to perform the many other tasks previously done by the other. This may mean having to learn new skills. It could mean enlisting help from others in the family or co-opting friends. Naturally, this readjustment to a new and frightening world is more difficult the older one is at the time of the bereavement.

7. Resolution

The final stage of grieving is reached when the bereaved is able to look forward to a new life, to have a sense of future without fear, and to formulate goals for a productive and happy life. She is able to give herself permission to be happy without feeling that it betrays the memory of her loved one. She will still experience some pain on the anniversary dates of the death, but as time goes by, the anniversary becomes more of a nostalgia than a pain. It becomes a day or two of quiet reflection and gratitude.

The effects of grief upon a person are profoundly psychological, physical and social. Psychologically, the immediate reactions are similar to those of any major crisis in one's life and were first described by Dr. Kubler-Ross. These are denial, anger, bargaining, depression and acceptance. Denial is a period of shock which functions as a defence mechanism against the overwhelming reality of the death. There may be a period of anger at a cruel world which would callously take the life of a loved one or anger at whoever was deemed to be the cause of the death, or even anger at God. Bargaining means to indulge in behaviours which try to avoid experiencing the awful pain of grief. This can be so intense that it leads to blockage and so healthy grieving cannot proceed. Acceptance is simply the point at which the survivor enters into the first of the seven *"R's,"* namely realization. She accepts that the death has actually occurred and now gradual movement towards resolution can begin.

A very important feature of early grieving is a phase of yearning and searching. The bereaved manifests a strong urge to find, recover and reunite with the lost person. Many bereaved persons will confide that they keep "seeing" the loved one going into a store, or getting onto a bus, or walking down the street. They feel alarmed at this and think they must be going mad. This is a perfectly natural part of grieving. The yearning is so great that the mind plays tricks on one's perception and so the bereaved will connect to anyone who looks like the deceased and want it to be him. The bereaved merely needs to be reassured that she is not going insane, that this is to be expected and that it will become less intense with the passage of time.

This phase is also characterised by restlessness and irritability directed towards the self or to others. She may sit down, then immediately get up and pace around, perhaps going from room to room in the house searching for the loved one. She then sits down again only to get up once more. She may think she hears the loved one's voice from the kitchen and respond to it only to be overwhelmed when she realises it could not have been him. If the phone rings it must be him. If the door opens and someone comes in, it must be him.

Everything seems to remind the bereaved of the loved one. Items of clothing, photographs on the dresser, garden tools, or the deck he built last summer, all take on a dramatic significance. The survivor will at first tend to hold fast to these reminders, hoping thereby to somehow keep the loved one "alive." It will usually take a long time before she can slowly release these items one by one. She might allow her son to have dad's fishing rod or might finally bundle up his clothes and give them away, but there will always be something she retains in an effort to keep his memory alive.

Some persons find it comforting to create a special kind of shrine to their loved one. They set up a corner of the house to display special photographs, trophies and mementoes, perhaps with a candle burning as a sign of remembrance. She may adopt little rituals such as kissing a photograph of her loved one every night before going to bed and greeting the loved one in the same way in the morning. She might adopt some of the habits of the deceased such as watching his favourite T.V. show on Tuesdays, or cooking his favourite meal on Sundays. She may play family videos over and over again or constantly go to the family photograph album and remember old times. These are necessary rituals and should never be discouraged.

After a while other people who were less attached to the deceased might become impatient with one who continues to grieve and remember. This is cruel and to remark on it or to tell them to snap out of it will only add pain to the pain already being experienced. Everyone grieves in their own way and should be allowed to do so. Only when it is clear that the grieving is unhealthy should one seek professional help and advice. I have been in therapy with grieving persons sometimes for years, but the process was able to proceed mainly because I validated their unique way of grieving.

A very important point to make is that while we have described the stages of grief in terms of the seven *"R's,"* these are not chiselled in stone, nor do they necessarily have to take place in a rigid sequence. Such thinking often causes care-givers to deal with a grieving person according to the stage she is "supposed to be in" rather than dealing with the stage she is actually in at any given moment. Grieving people do not read the text books and adhere to nice theories. They grieve and follow their own instincts. The theory is only a way of coming to a better understanding of the individual and must be applied uniquely to each individual. Grieving people will tend to move in and out of phases seemingly at random and a good care-giver recognises the reaction of the moment and accepts it.

The physical manifestations of grief can be many. The following is a list of the more common responses:

- Anorexia and other gastro-intestinal disturbances.
- Loss of weight.
- Inability to sleep.
- Crying.
- Tendency to sigh.
- Lack of energy or strength.
- Physical exhaustion.
- Feelings of emptiness or heaviness.
- Feelings of "something stuck in the throat."
- Heart palpitations.
- Tremor and shaking.
- Nervousness and tension.
- Restlessness and searching for something to do.
- Loss of sexual desire or increased sexual desire.
- Slow thinking.
- Shortness of breath.

These physical features can be very debilitating and may require medical intervention to bring about some relief. For example, insomnia may require some form of sleeping medication since prolonged insomnia merely intensifies the grief and could progress to utter exhaustion and collapse. If the picture becomes one of a deeply entrenched depression then again an anti-depressant medication may have to be considered. The depression may have to be lifted for the grieving to proceed normally.

The social consequences of grief can be quite devastating. The bereaved often finds it impossible to initiate or maintain useful activity. Her actions tend to be pointless, without purpose and seemingly random. She cannot do the budget where she had previously been skilled in this area. She does not plan the shopping and so runs out of food for the daily meals. The laundry piles up. She begins her housework and does not complete it. She may just sit and stare while everything around her demands attention.

Social withdrawal is a major problem for many. She may sever all contacts with others, never lifting the telephone, staying at home and taking no part in conversations. This prevents her from creating new relationships to offset the one she has lost. It also perpetuates the stress she is already feeling. Again, the only compassionate approach is to accept her inertia and to gently encourage her to make some small non-threatening forays back into society. This can only begin by visiting the bereaved in her home then hopefully enticing her to a brief outing, perhaps for a drive, then to the grocery store, and so on. She must never be overwhelmed by large crowds of people during this withdrawal phase.

One of the most potentially dangerous forms of grieving is known as pining. Pining is an extreme combination of the psychological, the physical and the social. All grief involves some pining for the loved one, but it can become so over-powering that it leads to a rapid wasting away in spite of the best efforts of the family and of the doctor. It can progress to death and in such cases it is referred to as "dying of a broken heart." It usually occurs between six months to a year after the bereavement.

Children who are grieving require special understanding and care. A child may exhibit some or all of the following reactions and some reactions may occur right away, while others may be delayed.

For the following I am grateful for the work of Theresa Huntley and her book, *Helping Children Grieve*.

1. Denial

This is not unusual. Death often comes as a shock and if the reality is too dreadful to face, a child will shut it down for a while. Often a child will resume playing as soon as she hears of a death. This does not mean that the child did not love the deceased. It is simply her way of coping. She may make such statements as "My daddy didn't really die. He is just away. He'll come back." "I want my mommy to come home."

2. Panic

Once a child accepts the reality of death, particularly the death of a parent, she may become fearful of her own survival or fearful for the survival of others whom she loves. She may become convinced that she will be bereft of all adults who care for her and so will starve to death or have no where to sleep or live. She may be heard to ask, "Mommy, are you going to die too?" "Who will take care of me?"

3. Anger

A child may find herself being angry at the death of someone whom she loved. She may see the death as an abandonment and rejection of her personally. She may be angry at the person who died, or she may be angry with the doctor or with God. The anger may be manifested by acting out, or by refusal to pay attention at school. Adults need to validate the child's feelings, letting her know it is normal to feel that way, then to listen to her concerns, and gently correct any misconceptions she may have. The angry child may make such statements as "Why did daddy leave me all alone?" "Why did God let him die?" "It's not fair."

4. Guilt

Children often feel responsible for the death of a loved one. They may blame themselves and believe that they must have been bad. This needs to be spotted by an adult as soon as possible before it becomes a deeply entrenched belief. They need to be told that they could not have caused the death and that the death was due to an accident, or a disease beyond anyone's control. It can be very difficult to shake that belief and the adult must be prepared to persevere with the child and keep on stating the truth. The signals from a child who believes she is responsible are such statements as, "If only I hadn't disobeyed him." "I shouldn't have said I hated him." "It's my fault. I was bad." "I was mean to my friend and so God took my daddy away."

5. Regression

A child who is experiencing shock may begin to exhibit infantile or childish behaviour. She may start to suck her thumb, she may soil herself, having been previously well toilet-trained, or she may indulge in baby-talk. This is simply her way of going back to a time when she was secure and lovingly provided for. She should never be scolded. Sooner or later, she will come out of it and get on with growing up. She needs to be reassured that her needs will be met and that she will be loved and looked after. Care should be taken to avoid adding any new stresses at this time. She has enough to cope with.

6. Anxiety and Physical Distress

A bereaved child may experience actual symptoms. These can be symptoms which the deceased exhibited during his last illness such as stomach pains or refusal to eat or headache. The child may also experience her own bodily distress because she is afraid that she is also going to die. She may say, "I can't sleep." "I'm not hungry." "My stomach hurts." This child needs to be reassured that she is safe and will always be loved.

7. Clinging

Some children are so fearful and threatened by a death that they become overly attached to an adult, usually the surviving parent. "I don't want to be with the baby-sitter." "Don't go out,

Mom." The adult needs to gently reassure the child that she will come back, but that she needs to go out at this time. Only reassurance will help, together with lots of demonstrations of love as in hugs, sitting closely together, reading a story and so on.

8. Preoccupation with the Deceased

Often a child will idealise the deceased. She becomes obsessed with the lost relative and is compelled to keep on remembering him or her as though not remembering was some kind of betrayal. "Mommy. Remember when dad and I went fishing?" "Dad would have done it this way." Each remembrance causes more pain for the child. She needs to be told that this is quite normal and that you too are remembering. By sharing your memories with the child, you help the child sort out her own memories.

Other manifestations of grief in a child include hyperactive behaviour, poor attention span, withdrawal from social contacts, assuming the mannerisms of the deceased and idealisation of the deceased.

One of the more profound consequences of grief in a child is that she feels she must fill the deceased's shoes in some way or another. As a result, a boy may feel compelled to become the "man of the house" to replace the father who was lost. Many well-meaning adults will say to a child at the funeral, "Well, you must take care of your mother now," or some similar call. The child hears these words and takes them to heart. He then gives up all playing and all childish things and tries to do what his father would have done. Likewise, a girl suddenly becomes a house keeper, a cook, and a laundry maid and forsakes her right to be a child. This loss of childhood can come back to haunt a person in later adult life. It can take the form of grieving for childhood, angry outbursts or bouts of depression. Adults of a grieving child must allow the child to be a child. She should never be robbed of her normal growth by being forced to become an adult before her time.

Just as in adult grieving, it is important for Catholic parents to encourage the child to rejoice that her loved one is still alive but in a better place and that she can still talk with that loved one at anytime. She can ask Jesus to take care of grandma and to believe that Jesus will do that. She should come to know that one day, she too will go to be with grandma in heaven and it will be a wonderful reunion.

The Incarnation of Jesus the Son of God changed the meaning of death for ever. Jesus died on the cross "that through death he might destroy him who had the power of death, that is, the devil" (Heb. 2:14). Death may be inevitable, but it need never be the end, "for since by man came death, by man came also the resurrection of the dead. For as in Adam we all die, even so in Christ shall all men be made alive" (1 Cor. 15:21-22).

St. Peter Damian, praying with a dying friend, put it so beautifully, "As your soul departs from your body, may the shining cohorts of angels hasten to greet you, the tribunal of apostles acquit you, the triumphant ranks of white-robed martyrs accompany you, the lily-bearing bands of glorious confessors surround you, the choir of virgins bring up your train with rejoicing, and in blest tranquillity may the patriarchs receive you into their loving embrace. May our Lord Jesus appear before you gentle and eager of countenance and assign you a place amid those who stand in his presence for evermore."

With thoughts such as these, grieving becomes bearable. We can latch onto Christian hope and while the present world may be empty for us without our loved one, it can be filled with anticipation of a far better world, one which lasts for ever and where there will be no more grieving for there will be no more death.

POSTSCRIPT

The major purpose of *Volume 1* has been to give Catholics a new and more exalted appreciation of what family life is intended to be in the mind of God. In particular, it is a call for Catholics to come to a new understanding of the Sacrament of Marriage, that it is a very lofty vocation indeed, much higher than most of us have realized in the past. It is true to say that, if anything, there is much more to be explored and revealed as the Church ventures deeper and deeper into the mystery of the marital union of a man and a woman. We will probably never ever reach the bottom of this mystery but surely, just as God continues to reveal himself to us in endless ways, he will also continue to shower the Church with ever new insights into the beauty and challenge of the married state.

Volume 2 will be concerned with the kinds of moral values and standards which a holy Catholic family should espouse. If we enjoy the privilege of belonging to a Catholic family, then we must also accept the responsibilities which accompany that privilege. This means learning, embracing and practicing good Catholic morality, which is founded upon the teachings of the Magisterium of the Church. When it comes to faith and morals, the Church can only teach the truth since it is forever under the inspiration and guidance of the Holy Spirit. As members of the Catholic Church, we stand on the Rock of Peter upon which Jesus built his Church and which therefore has God-given authority with which to impart his pure truth.

Volume 2 addresses some of the more important moral issues facing Catholic families in our time and is intended to provide not only good solid principles, but also to offer helpful practical advice on how to more easily live out these obligations.

Finally, the last chapter of all is really the very foundation upon which this whole work is built. The title of this book is *The Catholic Family: Image and Likeness of God,* and since God is a Trinity of three Persons, I make an attempt to explore the ways in which the Catholic family might also be seen to have "trinitarian" characteristics. This is by no means to suggest that the Divine Trinity and the human family are somehow comparable. That would be absurd. Nevertheless, since God informed us that he wished to make us in his own image and likeness, then we should be able to discern a "three-ness" about our individual natures and about our family relationships. If I have done this well, then the reader should develop a deeper appreciation of the awesome mystery and miracle of who we are and how we all, in some tiny way, reflect the infinitely greater mystery of who God is.

Aviation Maintenance Management

Aviation Maintenance Management

Harry A. Kinnison, Ph.D.

McGraw-Hill

New York Chicago San Francisco Lisbon London Madrid
Mexico City Milan New Delhi San Juan Seoul
Singapore Sydney Toronto

The McGraw·Hill Companies

Library of Congress Cataloging-in-Publication Data

Kinnison, Harry A.
    Aviation maintenance management / Harry A. Kinnison.
        p.   cm.
    ISBN 0-07-142251-X
    1. Airplanes—Maintenance and repair.   2. Airplanes—Management.   I. Title.

    TL671.9.K58 2004
    629.134'6—dc22

                                                    2004040267

9 10 11 12 13 14 15 16 17 18 19   DOC/DOC   1 5 4 3 2 1 0

ISBN 0-07-142251-X

The sponsoring editor for this book was Stephen S. Chapman and the production supervisor was Pamela A. Pelton. It was set in Century Schoolbook by International Typesetting and Composition. The art director for the cover was Anthony Landi.

Printed and bound by RR Donnelley.

McGraw-Hill books are available at special quantity discounts to use as premiums and sales promotions, or for use in corporate training programs. For more information, please write to the Director of Special Sales, Professional Publishing, McGraw-Hill, Two Penn Plaza, New York, NY 10121-2298. Or contact your local bookstore.

In memory of Dave Ross and Al Farris

Contents

List of Figures

List of Tables

Preface

I never read the "begat chapters" in the front of books until I became a writer myself. I wanted to see just what it took to write a book and was quite surprised to say the least. Although only one name appears on the book as "author" it takes many, many people (as well as numerous books, articles, and experiences) to produce the final, usable manuscript. This textbook is no exception.

The project began many years ago when the author was in Electronics School at Keesler Air Force Base, Mississippi where instructors have long since become nameless and faceless, but their efforts were not in vain. They planted the seeds for my future harvest. Next, I spent several years as an Airborne Navigation Equipment Repairman in Wiesbaden, Germany. Line, hangar, and shop maintenance activities were drilled into me by a Sergeant Gottlieb R. Schneider, who taught me the art and science of troubleshooting as well. My coworkers—Ron Wright, Tom Cummins, and Gene Hackett—helped immensely in my training. They taught me radar systems and I taught them navigation systems. We all gained from that.

After receiving a Bachelor of Science degree in Electrical Engineering, I spent several years on an Air Force Radar Site as a maintenance officer. Then it was on to civilian employment with the FAA and The Boeing Company. It was the latter experience—about 20 years worth—where I encountered the regulatory, management, and administrative aspects of the maintenance field. The people I worked with, and there were many, all contributed something to my knowledge and understanding of the maintenance field, which I have set forth in this book. Those most directly involved with my education at that level were Isaac Zere, Lloyd Wilson, and Lee McEachron, team leaders on many of my visits to airlines. Others who contributed in various ways were

Peter Ansdell	John Ota
James Bodie	Naval Ramdin
Terry Garris	Dr. William Rankin
Jim Glover	George That
Jose Gomez-Eligido	Bill Tsai
Gene Lange	Kurt Utterbach

Naseem Mahmood   Victor Wang

Ron Merry   R. Derek White

Lori Nakahara   Eric Wiseman

Hernan Normbuena

Special thanks should go to those at Embry-Riddle Aeronautical University (ERAU) Extended Campus. They not only hired me to teach the subject of this book, they allowed me to use my own materials. This book is an outgrowth of that original series of lectures. In addition, the staff at the Seattle Center of ERAU not only provided assistance on contacts and information when needed, several of them read and critiqued the manuscript. These people include Dr. Richard Glover, Center Director of Operations; Tom Glover, Center Faculty Chair and Safety Professor; and Dr. Ernie Damier, National Faculty Advisor, ERAU who read the manuscript not once but twice. And last but not least, Terry Cobb, Course Monitor for the Aviation Maintenance Management course for the entire Extended Campus. Their comments and suggestions were quite helpful.

Several airline people have also assisted in this endeavor. First are the employees of foreign and domestic airlines—too numerous to mention by name—who were the key figures of my airline technical visits which addressed various maintenance management topics. Special recognition goes to Dr. Karl Pape, Maintenance Supervisor at United Airlines, retired, now Associate Regional Academic Dean, ERAU Western Region, who read the first draft of the manuscript and provided much information and guidance. Thanks, also, to Les Ross, Aircraft Maintenance Supervisor, United Parcel Service, Ontario, California, for taking the time to discuss his organization's operation with me and for allowing me to measure the inside of one of his package freighters.

Additional information and discussion came from the Air Transport Association (ATA) of America: Victoria Day, Director, Publications and Technical Communications, and Rick Anderson, Director of Maintenance and Materiel. At the FAA, Northwest Region, Tom Newcomb, Aircraft Evaluation Group (AEG) and Kevin Mullin, Manufacturing Inspection District Office (MIDO), provided copies of FAA certificates to use as illustrations. The Boeing Company's Renton library allowed me to use their facilities for some basic literature research.

As with all such efforts with acknowledgments, this one has probably missed a good many names, and I sincerely want to apologize to those people. It should be understood that their efforts and contributions were just as important and just as appreciated as any of those mentioned.

Although many people have contributed and assisted in the production of this book, it is appropriate that the person whose name appears on the byline should take full credit for any errors or omissions within the text. For those inaccuracies, I humbly apologize.

HARRY A. KINNISON, PH.D.
Kent, Washington

Introduction

Aviation in the Beginning

The 24th International Air Transportation Conference was held in Louisville, Kentucky, June 5–7, 1996. One of the many evening activities available to the attendees was a tour of the main facilities of United Parcel Service (UPS) at the Louisville International Airport. About 15 people signed up for the tour. After watching the young college students hustle around unloading, sorting, and loading the packages and listening to the tour guide's explanation of this unique distribution system, we were escorted out to the flight line parking ramp to look at airplanes. Our tour guide led us up the portable air stairs into the huge chasm that was the Boeing 747 freighter. She stood there for a moment, silently looking around at the huge, empty airframe. Her tour guests did the same. Finally she spoke.

"The cargo area inside this 747 freighter is longer than the Wright brothers first flight," she said with some pride. "And the deck we are standing on is higher off the ground than that first flight was."*

Certainly aviation has come a long way since that windy December day in 1903 when Wilbur and Orville Wright made history at Kill Devil Hills near Kitty Hawk, North Carolina. Likewise, the field of aviation maintenance has made great strides. The early days of aviation were filled with experimenters, daredevils, and showoffs called barnstormers for obvious reasons. With their stunt flying and other antics, they were trying to prove to the public the safety and utility of this newfangled machine, the airplane. Selling "rides" to the curious became a side business. At first, aviation was more entertainment than transportation, but that soon changed. Just as modern jet liners boast dimensions greater than those of the first flight itself, the technological advances in aviation over the ensuing 100 years are equally impressive. And the approach to the maintenance of these complex vehicles has kept pace. Today, aviation is

---

*The Wright Brothers' first flight went 120 ft in about 12 seconds and reached an altitude of less than 10 ft. The Boeing 747 freighter is approximately 150 ft inside and the deck is 16 ft off the ground (unloaded).

the safest mode of transport in the world.[*] A considerable part of that safety record can be attributed to the efforts of mechanics, technicians, engineers, and managers who work in the field of aviation maintenance.

A Brief History of Aviation[†]

Aviation began as a pastime, a sport, a whimsy. Like so many new and "past-the-edge-of-reason" inventions, flying was considered a fanatic's sport. It would not last, people said. It is unnatural. "If God had meant for man to fly He would have given us wings." Well, in a sense He has given us wings.

Through the efforts of people like the Joseph and Jacques Montgofier, Octave Chanute, Otto Lilienthal, Samuel P. Langley, Glenn Curtis, Orville and Wilbur Wright, and many others, we have "earned our wings." We can fly.

All these men devoted time, thought and fortunes to resolving the problems of manned flight. Even men famous for other great works—Leonardo da Vinci, George Cayley, Hiram Maxim, Thomas Edison, et al.—made contributions. But it was two inquisitive bicycle makers and repairers in Dayton, Ohio, who brought man's longtime longings to "fly like the birds" to fruition. Much work was done by many people, but it was Orville and Wilbur Wright who are credited with the first controlled, manned flight.[‡] Although they covered a distance of only 120 feet and got no higher than 10 feet off the ground, their first flight was the result of a concentrated effort to master that which others had only courted.[§] Many experimenters in aviation—some of them with more academic or engineering credentials than the Wrights—had failed to meet the challenge. And some of them, unfortunately, lost their lives in the attempt.

The Wright Brothers were early systems engineers. They insisted that certain obstacles be surmounted, certain ideas be proven regarding manned flight before they would opt to get into their "airplane." An idea other experimenters should have heeded. Although Otto Lilienthal had done considerable work in aerodynamics and had published lift tables for others to use, the Wright Brothers found these tables to be in error and proceeded to make their own corrections. They built a small wind tunnel, made a few tests, and developed their own tables.

---

[*]In 1999, there were 17 commercial aviation deaths for 569 million miles flown. Or 0.003 deaths per 100 million miles. Contrast that with other transportation modes for that same year. Automobile: 20,763 deaths or 0.83 per 100 million miles; railroad: 14 deaths or 0.10 per 100 million miles; transit bus: 1 death or 0.005 per 100 million miles.

[†]Ray Bradbury probably wrote the shortest history of aviation in his short story "Icarus Montgofier Wright." It is recommended reading for aviation students. See Ray Bradbury, "S is for Space", Bantam Books, NY, 1970. Also available in other anthologies.

[‡]There were disputes as to who was actually first, but the credit is generally awarded to the Wright Brothers.

[§]The Wright Brothers made four flights in all that first day (December 17, 1903). The fourth one was up for 59 seconds and covered a distance of 852 ft.

Some of the first attempts to fly by the Wright Brothers involved essentially flying a kite.* They tied ropes to their craft, released it into the high winds of Kitty Hawk Beach and, by tugging on these ropes and thereby twisting the wing surfaces they assured themselves that this rig, this airplane, could not only fly with the wind strategically directed over and under its wings, but its direction of flight could be altered and controlled by a human operator. Then and only then would they climb into the contraption themselves. Satisfied that they could control their glider, Orville and Wilbur Wright set out to find an engine with the right power-to-weight ratio to successfully power their invention. They soon found that there was no such engine available so they designed their own with optimum specifications for flight.[†]

Next, the brothers needed a propeller. They thought the ship building industry would be the most likely place to solve this problem but they were disappointed. The shipbuilders told them that, for the most part, props were designed on a trial and error basis—there was no exact science. Undaunted by this, the Wrights designed and built their own propeller. They did not have time to use the trial and error method to develop a suitable propeller, so the Wrights used their newly developed aerodynamic tables to design the ideal device. And they were successful.

Although many others over the next few years after 1903 would make great advances in aviation and improve the performance, safety, and convenience of manned flight, it was the Wright Brothers' systematic process, their effort to design the whole system as a usable device (usable by people), that made the airplane a viable and important invention. The next step would be to convince the public of its value.

Promotion of Flying

Flying was for daredevils, at first. Numerous pilots showed off their skills and their new toys by performing for crowds—acrobatic stunts and other daring maneuvers—and often by selling joy rides to brave onlookers at three to five dollars apiece. But this showmanship soon gave way to those who wanted to see a more practical use for the airplane, and delivery of the U.S. Mail was considered the first down-to-earth application.

The first airline in the United States to carry passengers on a regular schedule was the St. Petersburg to Tampa Airboat Line, which started operations in January 1914 between the two cities, but they carried only one passenger at a time. Service ended after 3 months, however, due to the end of the tourist season and the onset of World War I.

---

*To this day, old timers in the Seattle area refer to The Boeing Company as "The Kite Factory."

[†]The Wrights had already designed and built a gasoline engine to run the drill press and lathe in their shop.

After World War I, airmail service began and dominated the aviation industry (such as it was). Entrepreneurs set up airline operations for that specific purpose. Occasionally, a passenger would ride along, sitting atop the mailbags if there was room. But later, additional seats were added to airplanes and passengers became more frequent sources of revenue. The U.S. government encouraged operators to use bigger planes and carry more passengers so they wouldn't have to rely solely on government mail contracts to stay in business.

Navigational aids were nonexistent in the early days of flying, and flyers used railroads, highways, and common automobile road maps to find their way. Nor could the first flyers fly at night until someone decided to light bonfires along the desired route to show the way. Weather conditions were received by observation and by telephone until air-to-ground radio came into use in the late 1920s. By the end of 1929, however, there were over 10,000 miles of lighted airways, 275 lighted airports, and 1352 rotating beacons.

While development of air travel in the United States lagged behind that of Europe after World War I, the opposite was true after World War II. Airplanes got bigger and flew "higher, faster, farther" and in 1958, we were introduced to the "jet age" with the Boeing 707, followed by the Douglas DC-8, and the Lockheed L1011. Navigational aids both on the ground and in the aircraft (later in earth-orbiting satellites) revolutionized the industry along with drastic improvements' in aircraft and engine technology. Today, 100 years after the Wright Brothers historic first flight, aviation has come of age. People can fly—and in immense comfort and safety.

Early Aviation Maintenance

In those early days of aviation, maintenance was performed "as necessary" and the machines often required several hours of maintenance time for every hour of flying time. Major maintenance activities consisted of overhauling nearly everything on the aircraft on a periodic basis. Even though the airplanes and their systems were quite simple at first, maintenance carried out in this manner became quite expensive. With the increasing complexity of the aircraft and their onboard systems over the following years, that expense rose accordingly.

The modern approach to maintenance is more sophisticated. The aircraft are designed for safety, airworthiness, and maintainability, and a detailed maintenance program is developed along with every new model aircraft or derivative of an existing model. This initial maintenance program can then be tailored by each airline to accommodate the nature of their individual operations. This ensures continued airworthy operation under any circumstances. Backing up that individual undertaking are the ongoing efforts by manufacturers, airlines, and regulators to improve design and maintenance techniques and to keep the aviation industry on the leading edge.

Of course, such a sophisticated approach to maintenance requires sophisticated management both in development of the initial maintenance program and at the airlines to accomplish all that is necessary to maintain that superior record of safety mentioned earlier.

Technical Management

It takes several disciplines to properly conduct the maintenance activities at an airline: (*a*) Maintenance: the hands-on, "nuts and bolts" labor required to accomplish the actual work; (*b*) Engineering: the design, analysis, and technical assistance required to support maintenance work; and (*c*) Management: the organization, control, and administration of the many facets of the maintenance operation. This book will not be about aircraft maintenance. Numerous courses and books relate to the details of the art and science of maintenance. This book will not be about engineering—electrical, mechanical, civil, aeronautical—because this field is too broad for one book to address it all. Nor will this book be about management, the handling of personnel, the organization of activities, the creation of case studies, program evaluation and review technique (PERT) charts, budgeting, and all the rest that comes under this title. Again, there are numerous books and courses to address this aspect of the professional life.

This book will be somewhat unique: it will cover all of these topics—maintenance, engineering, management—but in a more cursory manner than the individual courses would address them. We will be looking at the "big picture." We will be looking at maintenance, engineering, and management as an integrated whole. We will examine how all these disciplines combine and coordinate to accomplish the goals and objectives of airline maintenance. While some of the details of these three topics may be left out of the discussion, this text will emphasize the coordination of these three disciplines required to achieve the desired results.

The book is written for those who have background and experience in aviation maintenance and who wish to move into lower and middle level management positions within the airline's maintenance and engineering section. Those managers without a technical background, of course, can still benefit from the book by expanding their horizons to the technical realm. Mechanics and technicians who desire to move into the management of maintenance will gain valuable information about the overall operation of the maintenance and engineering unit.

Aviation Industry Interaction

The aviation industry is unlike any other transportation mode. In aviation, we cannot pull off the road and wait for a tow truck whenever we a have problem. We are required by Federal Aviation Administration (FAA) regulations to meet all maintenance requirements before releasing a vehicle into service. This is often not the case with other commercial transport modes. In aviation we have a relationship with gravity that differs considerably from that of any other transportation mode. We have problems with extremes of temperature (e.g., very hot engines and very cold air at high altitude).

In aviation we have an interactive group of people determined to make aviation a safe, efficient, and pleasurable activity. Aircraft manufacturers, makers of onboard equipment and systems, airline operators, industry trade associations, regulatory authorities, flight crews, and maintenance personnel all work together to ensure aviation safety from the design of the aircraft and its systems, through the development of maintenance programs and modifications, and continuing throughout the lifetime of the aircraft.

Working together and providing feedback at all levels and in all directions between and among these factions allows the aviation industry to provide continually improved systems and services to the public. The aviation industry was one of the first to employ this "continuous quality improvement" concept even before that catch phrase became popular.

Layout of the Book

This book has five parts. Part I contains information related to the basic philosophy of maintenance as well as fundamental requirements for an effective maintenance and engineering operation. Part I ends with the discussion of the organizational structure of a typical midsized airline. Parts II through IV give the particulars of each functional unit within that structure. Part V, Appendixes, provides information essential to various aspects of maintenance and engineering activities. These should be read and understood as background or support material for the rest of the book.

Part I: Fundamentals of Maintenance

Chapter 1, Why We Have to Do Maintenance, discusses some basic theory about designing and building complex equipment and why we cannot build perfect systems. This chapter also covers common failure patterns and failure rates of components and systems as well as methods for minimizing service interruptions such as line replaceable units (LRUs), redundant systems, and minimum dispatch requirements (MEL). It establishes the basic reasons why maintenance has to be planned, organized, and systematic.

Chapter 2, Development of Maintenance Programs, discusses the process of creating a maintenance program for a given model aircraft and how that program can be changed by an operator, as necessary, after entry into service. The chapter also defines basic maintenance intervals.

Chapter 3, Definitions, Goals, and Objectives, defines maintenance and a few other selected terms including goals and objectives. The chapter then establishes specific goals and objectives for maintenance. The text discusses how these were developed and what they mean to airline maintenance management.

Chapter 4, Aviation Industry Certification Requirements, addresses the Federal Aviation Administrations requirements for aircraft design and manufacture and the federal requirements with which a transportation company must comply to become an airline and operate the aircraft in commercial service.

Chapter 5, Documentation for Maintenance, discusses the manuals supplied by the manufacturers and vendors with the aircraft, the documentation required to be written by the airline for defining maintenance activities, and the regulations and advisories issued by the Federal Aviation Administration and other regulatory authorities relative to that maintenance.

Chapter 6, Requirements for a Maintenance Program, covers the regulatory requirements for a maintenance program outlined in FAA Advisory Circular, AC 120-16D and other FAA requirements: scheduled and unscheduled maintenance, inspection, overhaul, and recordkeeping. The chapter also discusses additional management requirements deemed necessary by airline managers: requirements for engineering, reliability, quality assurance, computer support, and training, for example.

Chapter 7, The Maintenance and Engineering Organization, covers the organizational structure of the maintenance and engineering function of a typical, midsized airline based on the requirements identified in Chap. 6. Variations of this structure for large and small airlines as well as operators with multiple maintenance bases and those who outsource some or all of the major maintenance work are also discussed.

Part II: Technical Services

Chapter 8, Engineering, covers the duties and responsibilities of the technical experts of the maintenance organization. This includes development of the airline's maintenance program from the airframe manufacturer's data and creation of the policies and procedures that govern the execution of that program. Engineering also provides assistance to maintenance for the solution of difficult problems and performs investigation of maintenance problems noted by the reliability program, as well as problems brought up by mechanics or by personnel from the quality control and quality assurance organization.

Chapter 9, Production Planning and Control, discusses the organization and workings of the department that is at the center of all maintenance activity. Production planning and control (PP&C) is responsible for all maintenance activities performed on the unit's aircraft. Duties and responsibilities of PP&C include forecasting future maintenance requirements and activities, planning and scheduling major checks for the current operational situation, and exercising control of the maintenance in progress. They are responsible for ensuring that personnel, parts, facilities, and special tools and test equipment are available for each planned maintenance event and that the activity is accomplished successfully and on time.

Chapter 10, Technical Publications, discusses the publication and distribution of all documentation required by the various maintenance and engineering departments. This includes documents provided by manufacturers, vendors, and regulatory authorities as well as those documents produced by the airline.

Chapter 11, Technical Training, covers the training requirements of mechanics, technicians, quality control (QC) inspectors, and quality assurance (QA) auditors. The chapter also discusses training conducted by the airline as well as that done by outside sources. The technical training organization is also required by the FAA to keep records of all training accomplished by each employee.

Chapter 12, Computer Support, discusses the various uses for computers within the airline and the maintenance organization. It also includes information on how to select computer software and hardware to meet those requirements.

Part III: Maintenance and Materiel Support

Chapter 13, Line Maintenance (on-Aircraft), discusses the activities of the line maintenance units that are responsible for maintenance and servicing on all aircraft in service. This includes maintenance activities at the home base, at outstations where the airline performs regular stops, and the organization and operation of a maintenance control center, the unit responsible for coordinating maintenance for all in-service aircraft.

Chapter 14, Hangar Maintenance (on-Aircraft), discusses the unit that is involved with maintenance activity on out-of-service aircraft (i.e., aircraft not currently on the flight schedule). The hangar group handles all major maintenance activities including major modifications. Both line and hangar maintenance are supported by the ground support equipment (GSE) unit that provides power units, work stands, and various other equipment and facilities for the efficient production of maintenance and servicing. These functions will also be addressed at the end of this chapter.

Chapter 15, Maintenance Overhaul Shops (off-Aircraft), discusses the organizations that perform maintenance on systems and components that have been removed from the aircraft during line or hangar maintenance activities. These shops are sometimes called back shops, and include avionics, mechanical, and hydraulic systems and various other specialty shops. They may also include third-party maintenance activities. The organization of these shops as well as their work and data collection efforts are discussed.

Chapter 16, Materiel Support for Maintenance, discusses the functions and processes of buying, issuing, and storing parts and supplies needed for the maintenance operation. Materiel establishes usage rates and reorder points to ensure adequate stock on hand at all times. Materiel is also responsible for processing defective units through maintenance and for handling warranty claims on equipment.

Part IV: Oversight Functions

Chapter 17, Quality Assurance, covers one of the primary oversight functions an airline needs to ensure top operation. Quality assurance (QA) is responsible for setting maintenance standards at the airline and also serves as M&E's point of contact with the regulatory authority. QA also performs yearly audits of all maintenance and engineering functions, including outside suppliers and contractors, to ensure compliance with airline and regulatory requirements.

Chapter 18, Quality Control, discusses the duties and responsibilities of those inspectors who provide direct oversight of the performance of maintenance actions. While QA looks at the overall compliance to rules and regulations, QC looks at the day-to-day work activities for compliance with good maintenance practices and procedures. The QC organization is also responsible for conducting nondestructive test and inspection activities and for the calibration of tools and test equipment.

Chapter 19, Reliability, discusses types of reliability and the concept of a reliability program to monitor the effectiveness of the airline's maintenance activity. Data collection on maintenance actions, such as failures, removals, etc., is monitored for trends. Investigation is made into possible problem areas so that corrective action can be implemented. Follow-up activities of reliability determine the effectiveness of that corrective action and the need (if any) for further action.

Chapter 20, Maintenance Safety, discusses the safety programs of the airline as they relate to maintenance and engineering. This includes smoking regulations, fire detection and prevention, fall protection, handling of hazardous material, etc. The chapter also discusses the material safety data sheets (MSDS) and the "right to know" program to alert workers to hazards.

Part V: Appendixes

Appendix A, Systems Engineering, discusses the concept of systems engineering and how it applies to maintenance and engineering in aviation. The text includes discussion of various system engineering terms such as internal and external components, inputs and outputs, system boundaries, and the changing of system boundaries for the sake of analysis. It also discusses the difference between the systems approach and the systematic approach.

Appendix B, Human Factors in Maintenance, discusses the application of human factors in the maintenance field. Since human beings constantly interface with the complex aviation equipment, those humans should be considered as part of the system when it is designed. This appendix discusses human factors in general and then discusses human factors as it relates to systems engineering. The appendix ends with a discussion of human factors activities at manufacturer and airline levels.

Appendix C, The Art and Science of Troubleshooting, discusses one of the fundamentals of a maintenance activity that is difficult and elusive. Troubleshooting requires a certain amount of experience for one to blossom fully in the art, but there are some basic concepts one should understand first. This appendix provides the fundamentals of the troubleshooting process, which can be used by maintenance mechanics and technicians, by engineering personnel, and by management to locate and pinpoint problems.

Appendix D, Investigation of Reliability Alerts, provides detailed information on how engineering would go about investigating maintenance problems identified by the reliability program. It is an extension of the troubleshooting process. While mechanics look at a specific system and its interfacing equipment, the engineer must look beyond the particular electrical, electronic, or mechanical system and include the entire aviation environment, if necessary, in his or her analysis of a problem. This appendix consists of a cross-functional chart showing the interaction of M&E organizations during the process of these investigations and a series of flow charts to guide the investigator through the process of determining the specific problem area.

Appendix E, Extended Range Operations (ETOPS), discusses the 60-minute rule for two-engine airplanes (FAR 121.161) and provides some historical background on the development of ETOPS. Requirements a carrier must meet to obtain FAA permission to deviate from the 60-minute rule (i.e., to fly ETOPS) are also covered.

Appendix F, Glossary, is a list of terms and abbreviations used throughout the book.

Fundamentals of Maintenance

"... maintenance is a science since its execution relies, sooner or later, on most or all of the sciences. It is an art because seemingly identical problems regularly demand and receive varying approaches and actions and because some managers, foremen, and mechanics display greater aptitude for it than others show or even attain. It is above all a philosophy because it is a discipline that can be applied intensively, modestly, or not at all, depending upon a wide range of variables that frequently transcend more immediate and obvious solutions."

LINDLEY R. HIGGINS
Maintenance Engineering Handbook;
McGraw-Hill, NY, 1990.

These opening chapters contain basic information related to the aviation maintenance field and should be considered background for the maintenance management effort. Chapter 1 begins with a discussion of the fundamental reasons why we have to do maintenance in the first place. After all, our skills and techniques have improved immensely over the 100-year history of flight, but we haven't quite reached total perfection. And, considering the number of components on a modern aircraft, we realize early on that maintenance is a complex, ongoing process. For that reason, we need to approach it systematically.

We need a well-thought-out program to address the diverse activities we will encounter in this endeavor, so in Chap. 2 we will study the industry procedures for developing an initial maintenance program. We will discuss the various maintenance check packages (the 48-hour and transit check, the monthly "A" check, the yearly "C" check, etc.)

used to implement the maintenance tasks. We then address the ongoing process of adjusting that program during the lifetime of the equipment. In Chap. 3, we establish the goals and objectives for an airline maintenance program that will serve the real-life operation.

Chapter 4 discusses the extensive certification requirements levied on the aviation industry from the original design of the vehicle to the establishment of commercial operators and the people who run them. The documentation for the aircraft, its operation, and its maintenance, is discussed in Chap. 5 and includes the documents produced by the equipment manufacturers, by the regulatory authorities, and by the airline itself.

Chapter 6 will identify those activities required by the FAA to accomplish maintenance as well as those additional requirements deemed necessary by operators to coordinate and implement an effective maintenance and engineering program. Chapter 7 defines a maintenance and engineering (M&E) organization for a "typical" midsized airline. Variations for larger and smaller airlines will also be discussed. Part I, then, can serve as background to the remainder of the book and can, if desired, be used as the basis for a first or introductory course in the subject of aviation maintenance management.

Why We Have to Do Maintenance

Thermodynamics Revisited

Nearly all engineering students have to take a course in thermodynamics in their undergraduate years. To some students, aerodynamicists and power plant engineers for example, thermodynamics was a major requirement for graduation. Others, such as electrical engineers for instance, take the course as a necessary requirement for graduation. Of course, thermodynamics and numerous other courses are "required" for all engineers because these courses apply to the various theories of science and engineering that must be understood to effectively apply the "college learning" to the real world. After all, that is what engineering is all about—bridging the gap between theory and reality.

There is one concept in thermodynamics that is often a puzzler to students. That concept is labeled *entropy*. The academic experts in the thermodynamics field got together one day (as one thermo professor explained) to create a classical thermodynamic equation describing all the energy of a system—any system. When they finished, they had an equation of more than several terms; and all but one of these terms were easily explainable. They identified the terms for heat energy, potential energy, kinetic energy, etc., but one term remained. They were puzzled about the meaning of this term. They knew they had done the work correctly; the term had to represent energy. So, after considerable pondering by these experts, the mysterious term was dubbed "unavailable energy"—energy that is unavailable for use. This explanation satisfied the basic law of thermodynamics that energy can neither be created nor destroyed; it can only be transformed. And it helped to validate their equation.

Let us shed a little more light on this. Energy is applied to create a system by manipulating, processing, and organizing various elements of the universe. More energy is applied to make the system do its prescribed job. And whenever the system is operated, the sum total of its output energy is less than the total energy input. While some of this can be attributed to heat loss through friction and other similar, traceable actions, there is still an imbalance of energy. Defining entropy as the "unavailable energy" of a system rectifies that imbalance.

The late Dr. Isaac Asimov, biophysicist and prolific writer of science fact and science fiction,[*] had the unique ability to explain the most difficult science to the layman in simple, understandable terms. Dr. Asimov says that if you want to understand the concept of entropy in practical terms, think of it as the difference between the theoretically perfect system you have on the drawing board and the actual, physical system you have in hand. In other words, we can design perfect systems on paper but we cannot build perfect systems in the real world. The difference between that which we design and that which we can build constitutes the natural entropy of the system.

A Saw Blade Has Width

This concept of entropy, or unavailable energy, can be illustrated by a simple example. Mathematically, it is possible to take a half of a number repeatedly forever. That is, half of one is 1/2; half of that is 1/4, half of that is 1/8, and so on to infinity. Although the resulting number is smaller and smaller each time you divide, you can continue the process as long as you can stand to do so, and you will never reach the end.

Now, take a piece of wood about 2 feet long (a 2×4 will do) and a crosscut saw. Cut the board in half (on the short dimension). Then take one of the pieces and cut that in half. You can continue this until you reach a point where you can no longer hold the board to saw it. But, even if you could find some way to hold it while you sawed, you would soon reach a point where the piece you have left to cut is thinner than the saw blade itself. When (if) you saw it one more time, there will be nothing left at all—nothing but the pile of sawdust on the floor. The number of cuts made will be far less than the infinite number of times that you divided the number by two in theory.

The fact that the saw blade has width and that the act of sawing creates a kerf in the wood wider than the saw blade itself, constitutes the entropy of this system. And no matter how thin you make the saw blade, the fact that it has width will limit the number of cuts that can be made. Even a laser beam has width. This is a rather simple example, but you can see that the real world is not the same as the theoretical one that scientists and some engineers live in. Nothing is perfect.

The Role of the Engineer

The design of systems or components is not only limited by the imperfections of the physical world (i.e., the "natural entropy" of the system), it is also limited by

---

[*]Dr. Asimov wrote over 400 books during his lifetime.

a number of other constraints which we could refer to as "man-made entropy." A design engineer may be limited from making the perfect design by the technology or the state of the art within any facet of the design effort. He or she may be limited by ability or technique; or, more often than not, the designer may be limited by economics; that is, there just is not enough money to build that nearly perfect system that is on the drawing board or in the designer's mind. Although the designer is limited by many factors, in the tradition of good engineering practice, the designer is obliged to build the best system possible within the constraints given.

Another common situation in design occurs when the designer has produced what he or she believes is the optimum system when the boss, who is responsible for budget asks, "How much will it cost to build this?" The designer has meticulously calculated that these widgets can be mass produced for $1200 each. "Great," says the boss. "Now redesign it so we can build it for under a thousand dollars." That means redesign usually with reduced tolerances, cheaper materials, and, unfortunately, more entropy. More entropy sometimes translates into more maintenance required. The design engineer's primary concern, then, is to minimize (not eliminate) the entropy of the system he or she is designing while staying within the required constraints.

The Role of the Mechanic

The mechanic (technician, repairer, or maintainer), on the other hand, has a different problem. Let us, once again, refer to the field of thermodynamics. One important point to understand is that entropy not only exists in every system, but that the entropy of a system is always increasing. That means that the designed-in level of perfection (imperfection?) will not be permanent. Some components or systems will deteriorate from use and some will deteriorate from lack of use (time or environment related). Misuse by an operator or user may also cause some premature deterioration or degradation of the system or even outright damage. This deterioration or degradation of the system represents an increase in the total entropy of the system. Therefore, while the engineer's job is to minimize the entropy of a system during design, the mechanic's job is to combat the natural, continual increase in the entropy of the system during its operational lifetime.

To summarize, then, it is the engineer's responsibility to design the system with as high a degree of perfection (low entropy) as possible within reasonable limits. The mechanic's responsibility, on the other hand, is to combat the continual increase in entropy during the operational lifetime of the equipment.

Two Types of Maintenance

Figure 1-1 is a graph showing the level of perfection of a typical system. One hundred percent perfection is at the very top of the y-axis. The x-axis depicts time. There are no numbers on the scales on either axis since actual values have

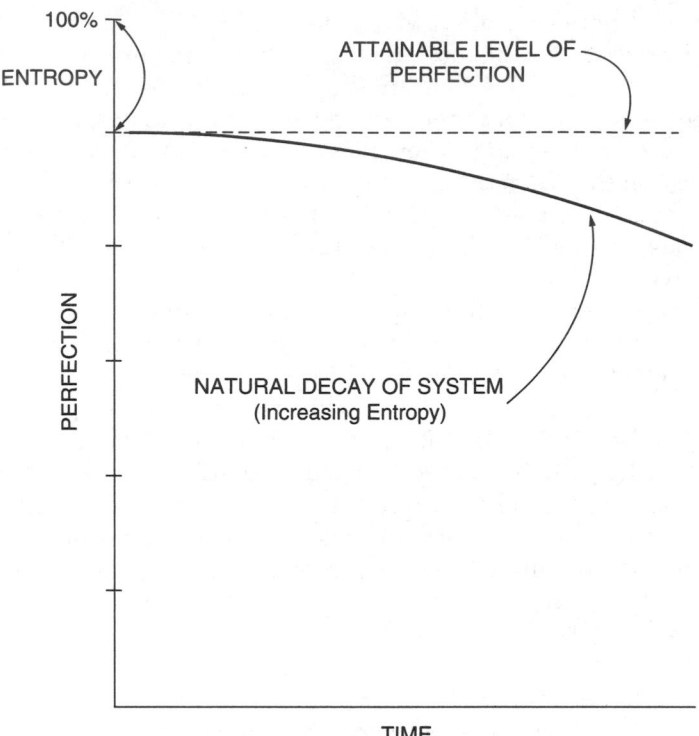

Figure 1-1   The difference between theory and practice.

no meaning in this theoretical discussion. The left end of the curve shows the level of perfection attained by the designers of our real world system. Note that the curve begins to turn downward with time. This is a representation of the natural increase in entropy of the system—the natural deterioration of the system—over time. When the system deteriorates to some lower (arbitrarily set) level of perfection, we perform some corrective action: adjusting, tweaking, servicing, or some other form of maintenance to restore the system to its designed-in level of perfection. That is, we reduce the entropy to its original level. This is called *preventive maintenance* and is usually performed at regular intervals. This is done to prevent deterioration of the system to an unusable level and to keep it in operational condition. It is sometimes referred to as *scheduled maintenance*. This schedule could be daily, every flight, every 200 flight hours, or every 100 cycles (a cycle is a takeoff and a landing).

Figure 1-2 shows the system restored to its normal level (curves a and b). There are times, of course, when the system deteriorates rather rapidly in service to a low level of perfection (curve c). At other times the system breaks down completely (curve d). In these cases, the maintenance actions necessary to restore the system are more definitive, often requiring extensive testing, troubleshooting, adjusting, and, very often, the replacement, restoration, or complete

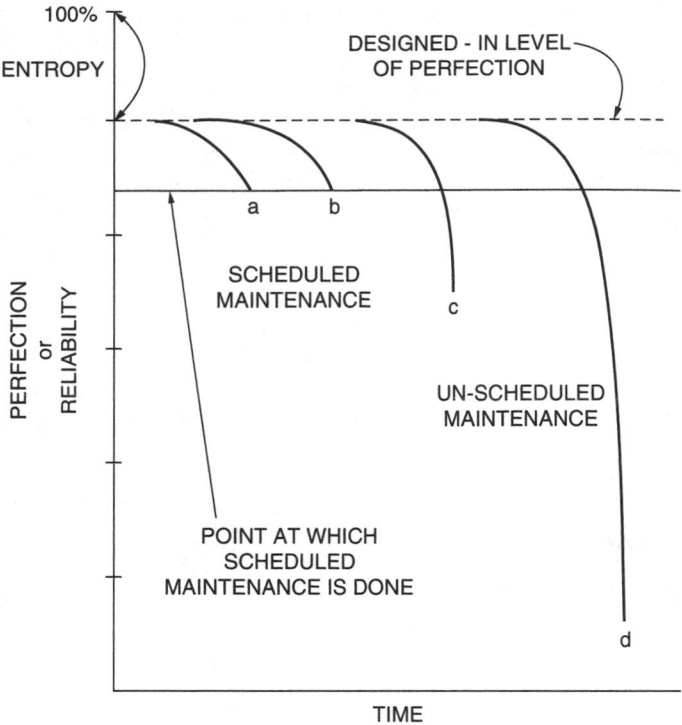

Figure 1-2 Restoration of system perfection.

overhaul of parts or subsystems. Since these breakdowns occur at various, unpredictable intervals, the maintenance actions employed to correct the problem are referred to as *unscheduled maintenance*.

Reliability

The level of perfection we have been talking about can also be referred to as the reliability of the system. The designed-in level of perfection is known as the inherent reliability of that system. This is as good as the system gets during real world operation. No amount of maintenance can be performed to increase the system reliability any higher than this inherent level. However, it is desirable for the operator to maintain this level of reliability (or this level of perfection) at all times. We will discuss reliability and maintenance in more detail in Chap. 19. But there is one more important point to cover here—redesign of the equipment.

Redesign

Figure 1-3 shows the original curve of our theoretical system, curve A. The dashed line shows the system's original level of perfection. Our system, however,

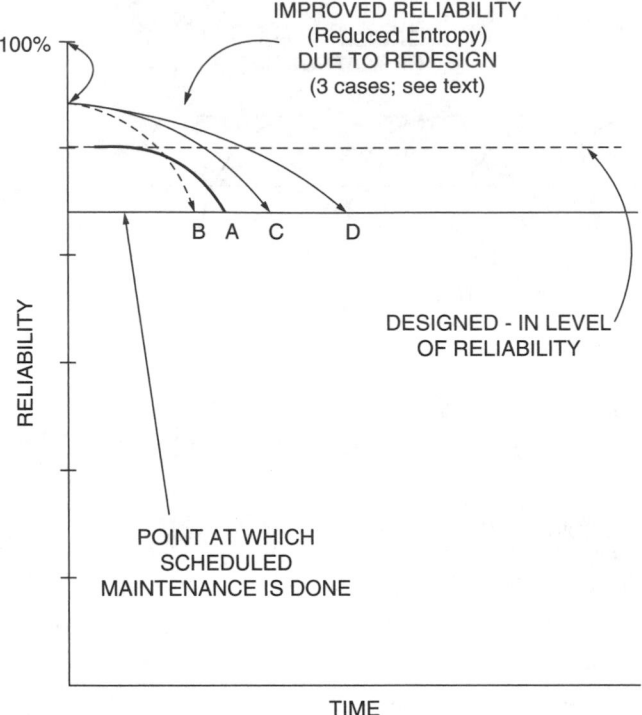

Figure 1-3 Effects of redesign on system reliability.

has now been redesigned to a higher level of perfection; that is, a higher level of reliability with a corresponding decrease in total entropy. During this redesign, new components, new materials, or new techniques may have been used to reduce the natural entropy of the system. In some cases, a reduction in man-made entropy may result because the designer applied tighter tolerances, attained improved design skills, or changed the design philosophy.

Although the designers have reduced the entropy of the system, the system will still deteriorate. It is quite possible that the rate of deterioration will change from the original design depending upon numerous factors; thus, the slope of the curve may increase, decrease, or stay the same. Whichever is the case, the maintenance requirements of the system could be affected in some way.

If the decay is steeper, as in (B) in Fig. 1-3, the point at which preventive maintenance needs to be performed might occur sooner, and the interval between subsequent actions would be shorter. The result is that maintenance will be needed more often. In this case, the inherent reliability is increased, but more maintenance is required to maintain that level of reliability (level of perfection). Unless the performance characteristics of the system have been improved, this redesign may not be acceptable. A decision must be made to determine if the performance improvement justifies more maintenance and thus an increase in maintenance costs.

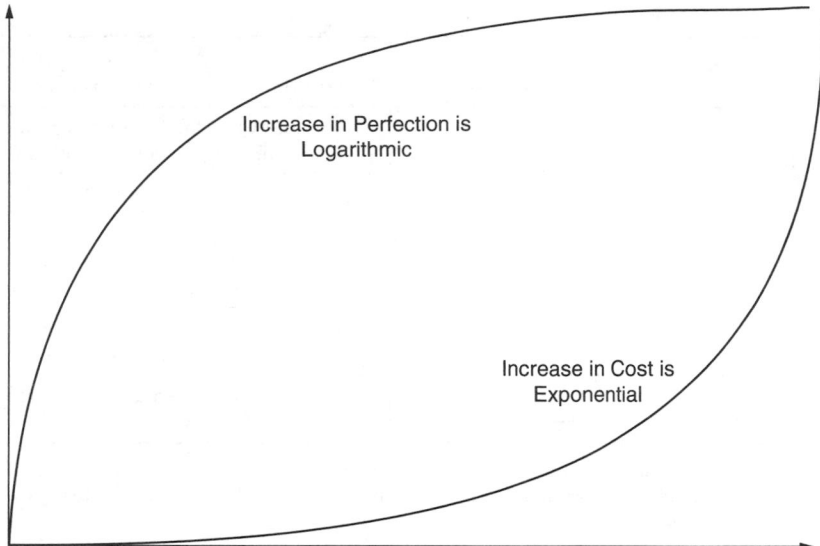

Figure 1-4   Perfection vs. cost.

Conversely, if the decay rate is the same as before, as shown in (C) of Fig. 1-3, or less steep, as shown in (D), then the maintenance interval would be increased and the overall amount of preventive maintenance might be reduced. The question to be considered, then, is this: Does the reduction of maintenance justify the cost of the redesign? This question, of course, is a matter for the designers to ponder, not the maintenance people.

One of the major factors in redesign is cost. Figure 1-4 shows the graphs of two familiar and opposing relationships. The upper curve is logarithmic. It represents the increasing perfection attained with more sophisticated design efforts. The closer we get to perfection (top of the illustration) the harder it is to make a substantial increase. (We will never get to 100 percent.) The lower curve depicts the cost of those ongoing efforts to improve the system. This, unfortunately, is an exponential curve. The more we try to approach perfection, the more it is going to cost us. It is obvious, then, that the designers are limited in their goal of perfection, not just by entropy but also by costs. The combination of these two limitations is basically responsible for our profession of maintenance.

Failure Rate Patterns

Maintenance, of course, is not as simple as one might conclude from the above discussion of entropy. There is one important fact that must be brought out: not all systems or components fail at the same rate nor do they all exhibit the same pattern of wear out and failure. And, as you might expect, the nature of the maintenance performed on these components and systems is related to those failure rates and failure patterns.

TABLE 1-1   Failure Rate Patterns

	A. Infant mortality; constant or slightly rising failure rate; definite wear-out period (4%)
	B. No infant mortality; slightly rising failure rate; definite wear-out period (2%)
	C. No infant mortality; slightly rising rate; no definite wear-out period (5%)
	D. Increasing failure rate at outset; constant or slightly rising rate; no definite wear-out period (7%)
	E. No infant mortality; constant failure rate throughout life; no definite wear-out period (14%)
	F. Infant mortality; constant failure rate throughout life; no definite wear-out period (68%)

Source: F. Stanley Nowlan and Howard F. Heap: *Reliability-Centered Maintenance*; U.S. Department of Commerce, National Technical Information Service, Washington, DC, 1978.

United Airlines did some studies on lifetime failure rates and found six basic patterns.[*] These are shown in Table 1-1. The vertical axes show failure rates and the horizontal axes indicate time. No values are shown on the scales since these are not really important to the discussion.

Curve A shows what is commonly referred to as the "bathtub" curve, for obvious reasons. This failure rate pattern exhibits a high rate of failure during the early portion of the component's life, known as "infant mortality." This is one of the "bugaboos" of engineering. Some components exhibit early failures for several reasons: poor design, improper parts, incorrect usage. Once the bugs are worked out and the equipment settles into its "pattern," the failure rate levels off or rises only slightly over time. That is, until the later stages of the component's life. The rapid rise shown in curve A near the end of its life is an indication of "wear out." The physical limit of the component's materials has been reached.

Curve B exhibits no infant mortality but shows a level, or slightly rising failure rate characteristic throughout the component's life until a definite wear-out period is exhibited toward the end.

Curve C depicts components with a slightly increasing failure rate with no infant mortality and no discernible wear-out period but, at some point, it becomes unusable.

Curve D shows a low failure rate when new (or just out of the shop), which rises to some steady level and holds throughout most of the component's life.

Curve E is an ideal component: no infant mortality and no wear-out period, just steady (or slightly rising) failure rate throughout its life.

Curve F shows components with an infant mortality followed by a level or slightly rising failure rate and no wear-out period.

---

[*]Nowlan, F. Stanley and Howard F. Heap, *Reliability-Centered Maintenance*. National Technical Information Service, Washington, DC, 1978.

The United Airlines study showed that only about 11 percent of the items included in the experiment (those shown in curves A, B, and C of Table 1-1) would benefit from setting operating limits or from applying a repeated check of wear conditions. The other 89 percent would not. Thus, time of failure or deterioration beyond useful levels could be predicted on only 11 percent of the items (curves A, B, and C of Table 1-1). The other 89 percent (depicted by curves D, E, and F of Table 1-1) would require some other approach. The implication of this variation is that the components with definite life limits and/or wear-out periods will benefit from scheduled maintenance. They will not all come due for maintenance or replacement at the same time, however, but they can be scheduled; and the required maintenance activity can be spread out over the available time, thus avoiding peaks and valleys in the workload. The other 89 percent, unfortunately, will have to be operated to failure before replacement or repair is done. This, being unpredictable, would result in the need for maintenance at odd times and at various intervals; i.e., unscheduled maintenance.

These characteristics of failure make it necessary to approach maintenance in a systematic manner, to reduce peak periods of unscheduled maintenance. The industry has taken this into consideration and has employed several techniques in the design and manufacturing of aircraft and systems to accommodate the problem. These are discussed in the next section.

Other Maintenance Considerations

The aviation industry has developed three management techniques for addressing the in-service interruptions created by the items that must be operated to failure before maintenance can be done. These are equipment redundancy, line replaceable units, and minimum aircraft dispatch requirements.

The concept of redundancy of certain components or systems is quite common in engineering design of systems where a high reliability is desirable. In the case of redundant units—usually called primary and backup units—if one unit fails, the other is available to take over the function. For example, in aviation most commercial jets have two high-frequency (HF) radios. Only one is needed for communications but the second one is there for backup in case the first one fails.

A unique feature of redundant units also affects the maintenance requirements. If both primary and backup units are instrumented such that the flight crew is aware of any malfunction, no prior maintenance check is required to indicate that incapability. On the other hand, if neither system is so instrumented, maintenance personnel would need to perform some check on both primary and backup systems (at the transit or other check) to determine serviceability.

Very often, however, one system (usually the backup) is instrumented to show serviceability to the crew. If a maintenance check is performed on the other (i.e., the primary) the crew can be assured that it is serviceable. In the case of failure, then, they already have a positive indication, through the instrumentation, that the backup system is available and useable. The purpose for this arrangement is to strike a middle ground between how much instrumentation is used and how much maintenance is required to ensure system serviceability. In some cases the backup system is automatically switched into service when the primary system fails. Flight crew needs during the flight are primary concerns in making such decisions.

Another common concept used in aviation is the *line replaceable unit* (LRU). An LRU is a component or system that has been designed in such a manner that the parts that most commonly fail can be quickly removed and replaced on the vehicle. This allows the vehicle to be returned to scheduled service without undue delay for maintenance. The failed part, then, can either be discarded or repaired in the shop as necessary without further delaying the flight.

The third concept for minimizing delays for maintenance in aviation is known as the *minimum equipment list* (MEL). This list allows a vehicle to be dispatched into service with certain items inoperative provided that the loss of function does not affect the safety and operation of the flight. These items are carefully determined by the manufacturer and sanctioned by the regulatory authority during the early stages of vehicle design and test. The manufacturer issues a *master minimum equipment list* (MMEL) which includes all equipment and accessories available for the aircraft model. The airline then tailors the document to its own configuration to produce the MEL (more on this in Chap. 5). Many of these MEL items are associated with redundant systems. The concept of the MEL allows deferral of maintenance without upsetting the mission requirements. The maintenance, however, must be performed within certain prescribed periods, commonly 1, 3, 10, or 30 days, depending on the operational requirements for the system.

The items are identified in the MMEL by flight crew personnel during the latter stages of new aircraft development. Thus, flight personnel determine what systems they can safely fly the mission without or in a degraded condition. These flight crew personnel also determine how long (1, 3, 10, or 30 days) they can tolerate this condition. Although this is determined in general terms prior to delivering the airplane, the flight crew on board makes the final decision based on actual conditions at the time of dispatch. The pilot in command (PIC) can, based on existing circumstances, decide not to dispatch until repairs are made or can elect to defer maintenance per the airline's MEL. Maintenance must abide by that decision.

Associated with the MEL is a *dispatch deviation guide* (DDG) that contains instructions for the line maintenance crew when the deviation requires some maintenance action that is not necessarily obvious to the mechanic. A dispatch deviation guide is published by the airplane manufacturer to instruct the mechanic on these deviations. The DDG contains information such as tying up cables and capping connectors from removed units, opening and placarding circuit breakers to prevent inadvertent power-up of certain equipment during flight, and any other maintenance action that needs to be taken for precautionary reasons. Similar to the MEL is a *configuration deviation list* (CDL).

This list provides information on dispatch of the airplane in the event that certain panels are missing or when other configuration differences not affecting safety are noted.

Although failures on these complex aircraft can occur at random, and can come at inopportune times, these three management actions—redundancy of design, line replaceable units, and minimum dispatch requirements—can help to smooth out the workload and reduce service interruptions.

Establishing a Maintenance Program

Although there has been a considerable amount of improvement in the quality and reliability of components and systems, as well as in materials and procedures, over the 100-year life of aviation, we still have not reached total perfection. Aviation equipment, no matter how good or how reliable, still needs attention from time to time.

Scheduled maintenance and servicing are needed to ensure the designed-in level of perfection (reliability). But, because the real world is as it is, some of these components and systems will, sooner or later, deteriorate beyond a tolerable level or will fail completely. In other instances, users, operators, or even maintenance people who interface with these components and systems can misuse or even abuse the equipment to the extent of damage or deterioration that will require the need for some sort of maintenance action.

We have seen that components and systems fail in different ways and at different rates. This results in a requirement for unscheduled maintenance that is somewhat erratic and uncertain. There are often waves of work and no-work periods that need to be managed to smooth out the workload and stabilize the manpower requirements.

Those components exhibiting life limits or measurable wear-out characteristics can be part of a systematic, scheduled maintenance program. Design redundancy, line replaceable units, and minimum dispatch requirements have been established as management efforts to smooth out maintenance workload. But there are numerous components and systems on an aircraft that do not lend themselves to such "adjustment for convenience." Occasionally, inspections and/or modifications of equipment are dictated—within specified time limits—by aviation regulators as well as by manufacturers. It is necessary, then, that the maintenance and engineering organization of an airline be prepared to address the maintenance of aircraft and aircraft systems with a well-thought-out and well-executed program. The remainder of this textbook will address the many-faceted process known as aircraft maintenance and engineering.

The program discussed herein has been created over the years by concentrated and integrated efforts by pilots, airlines, maintenance people, manufacturers, component and system suppliers, regulatory authorities, and professional and business organizations within the aviation industry. Not every airline will need to be organized and operated in the same manner or style, but the programs and activities discussed in this text will apply to all operators.

Chapter 2

Development of Maintenance Programs

Introduction

The maintenance programs currently in use in commercial aviation were developed by the industry using two basic approaches: the process-oriented approach and the task-oriented approach. The differences in these two methods are twofold: (*a*) the attitude toward maintenance actions and (*b*) the manner in which maintenance actions are determined and assigned to components and systems. Although the commercial aviation industry has recently gone to the task-oriented approach for the most recent airplane models, there are many older airplanes still in service whose maintenance programs were developed by the process-oriented approach. In recent years, McDonnell-Douglas (now part of Boeing) and Boeing have developed new task-oriented maintenance programs for some of these older model aircraft. The operators can purchase these new programs from the manufacturer.

The process-oriented approach to maintenance uses three primary maintenance processes to accomplish the scheduled maintenance actions. These processes are called hard time (HT), on-condition (OC), and condition monitoring (CM). The *hard time* and *on-condition processes* are used for components or systems that, respectively, have definite life limits or detectable wear out periods. These are the items in categories A, B, and C discussed in Chap. 1 and illustrated in Table 1-1. The *condition monitoring process* is used to monitor systems and components that cannot utilize either the HT or OC processes. These CM items are operated to failure and failure rates are tracked to aid in failure prediction or failure prevention efforts. These are the "operate to failure" items in categories D, E, and F of Table 1-1.

The task-oriented approach to maintenance uses predetermined maintenance tasks to avoid in-service failures. Equipment redundancies are sometimes used to allow in-service failures to occur without adversely affecting safety and operation. A reliability program is usually employed (similar to, but more elaborate than, the CM process) for those components or systems whose failure rates are not predictable and for those that have no scheduled maintenance tasks. Reliability is discussed in Chap. 19.

Both of these maintenance philosophies—the process oriented and the task oriented—are discussed in general below along with the basic method of generating the program. How the maintenance tasks and task intervals are determined will be discussed in detail in later sections.

The Maintenance Steering Group (MSG) Approach

The Boeing Company started the modern approach to maintenance program development in 1968 with the Boeing 747 airplane, then the largest commercial airplane. It was the start of a new era in aviation, the era of the "jumbo jets" and the company felt that this new era should begin with a more sophisticated approach to maintenance program development. They organized teams of representatives from the Boeing Company's design and maintenance program groups along with representatives from the suppliers and the airlines who were interested in buying the airplane. The FAA was also included to insure that regulatory requirements were properly addressed.

The process used involved six industry working groups (IWGs): (a) structures; (b) mechanical systems; (c) engine and auxiliary power plant (APU); (d) electrical and avionics systems; (e) flight controls and hydraulics; and (f) zonal. Each group addressed their specific systems in the same way to develop an adequate initial maintenance program. Armed with information on system operation, maintenance significant items (MSIs) and their associated functions, failure modes, failure effects, and failure causes, the group analyzed each item using a logic tree to determine requirements.

This approach to maintenance program development was called a "bottom up" approach because it looked at the components as the most likely causes of equipment malfunction. The purpose of the analysis was to determine which of three processes would be required to repair the item and return it to service. The three processes were identified as HT, OC, and CM as defined above.

This maintenance steering group (MSG) approach to maintenance program development was so successful on the 747 that it was modified slightly for use with other aircraft. The specific references to the 747 airplane were removed and the new generalized process could be used on all aircraft. It was renamed MSG-2 and applied to the development of maintenance programs for the Lockheed L-1011 and the McDonnell-Douglas DC-10 airplanes. Other slight modifications were made to the process in 1972 by European manufacturers and the resulting procedure used in Europe became known as EMSG.

The MSG-2 process was slightly different for the three maintenance areas studied: (a) systems and components; (b) structures; and (c) engines. Table 2-1 summarizes the steps for each:

TABLE 2-1 MSG-2 Process Steps

Step number for			
System/comp	Structure	Engine	Analysis activity
1		1	Identify the systems and their significant items
	1		Identify significant structural items
2			Identify their functions, failure modes, and failure reliability
	2		Identify failure modes and failure effects
		2	Identify their functions, failure modes, and failure effects
3		3	Define scheduled maintenance tasks having potential effectiveness relative to the control of operational reliability
	3		Assess the potential effectiveness of scheduled inspections of structure
4		4	Assess the desirability of scheduling those tasks having potential effectiveness
	4		Assess the desirability of those inspections of structure which do have potential effectiveness
	5		Determine that initial sampling thresholds were appropriate

SOURCE: Airline/Manufacturer Maintenance Program Document-MSG-2: R&M Subcommittee, Air Transport Association; March 25, 1970.

Step 1, identify the maintenance or structure items requiring analysis.

Step 2, identify the functions and failure modes associated with the item and the effect of a failure.

Step 3, identify those tasks which may have potential effectiveness.

Step 4, assess the applicability of those tasks and select those deemed necessary.

Step 5, for structures only, evaluate initial sampling thresholds.

The process flow diagram in the MSG-2 document is too complex to repeat here, especially since the MSG-2 process is no longer used. It is important, however, to understand how the maintenance processes were assigned to the tasks selected. Figure 2-1 is a simplified diagram of that process. Briefly, if failure of the unit is safety related (block 1) and there is a maintenance check available to detect a reduction in failure resistance (block 4), then the item in question is identified as on-condition. If no such check is available, then the item is classified as hard time. The student can follow the logic of Fig. 2-1 for the other conditions.

Once the maintenance action was determined, it was necessary to define how often such maintenance should be done. Available data on failure rates, removal rates, etc. of the item were then used to determine how often the maintenance should be performed.

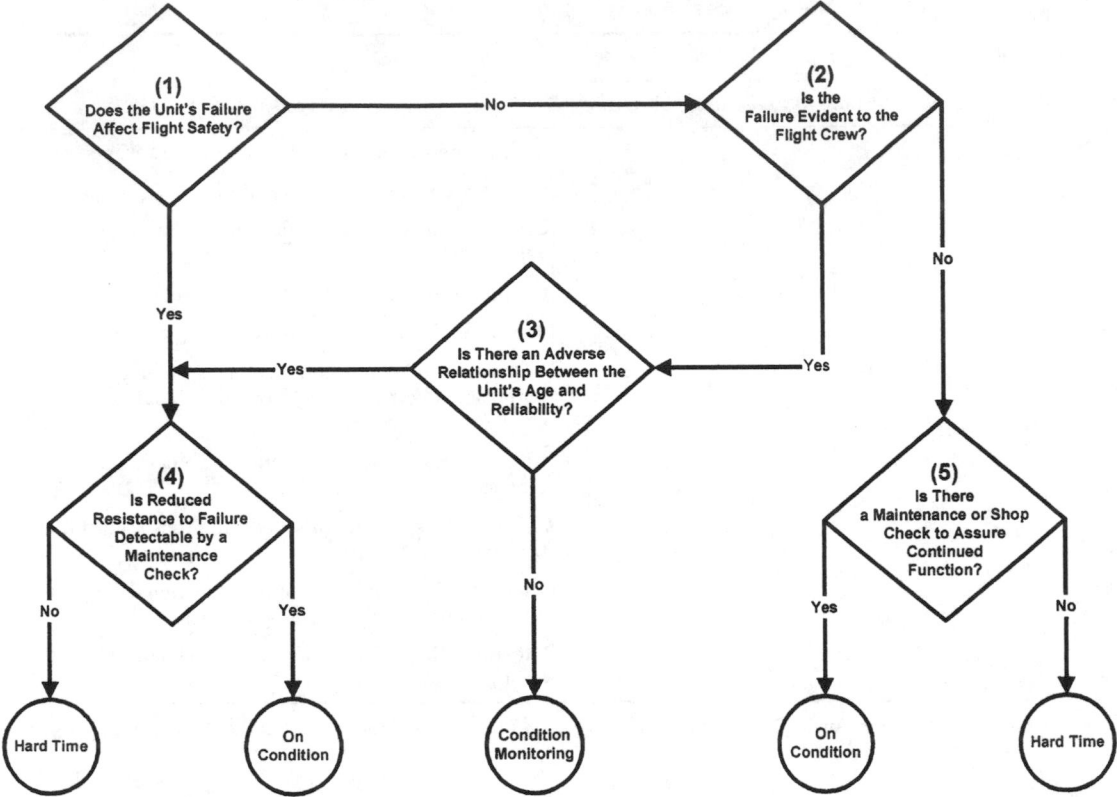

Figure 2-1   Simplified MSG-2 flow chart.

Process-Oriented Maintenance

Process-oriented maintenance programs are developed for aviation using decision logic procedures developed by the Air Transport Association of America (ATA). The MSG-2 process is a bottom up approach whereby each unit (system, component, or appliance) on the aircraft is analyzed and assigned to one of the primary maintenance processes, HT, OC, or CM.

In general, hard time means the removal of an item at a predetermined interval, usually specified in either so many flight hours or so many flight cycles. In some cases the hard time interval may be in calendar time. On-condition means that the item will be checked at specified intervals (in hours, cycles, or calendar time) to determine its remaining serviceability. Condition monitoring involves the monitoring of failure rates, removal rates, etc. to facilitate maintenance planning. Let us look at each process in more detail.

The hard time (HT) process

Hard time is a failure preventive process which requires that the item be removed from the vehicle and either completely overhauled, partially overhauled (restored), or discarded before exceeding the specified interval. The hard time interval may be specified by calendar time, by engine or airplane check interval (engine change, "C" check, etc.), by landing or operating cycles, by flight hours, by block hours, by specified flights (over water, terminating, etc.), or in conjunction with another process (OC for instance).

When HT is specified, the component will be removed from the vehicle and overhauled, restored, or discarded, whichever is appropriate. This will be done before the component has exceeded the specified time interval. The component overhaul or restoration will restore the component to a condition that will give reasonable assurance of satisfactory operation until the next scheduled removal. Ideally, hard time would be applied to a component that always fails at X hours of operation. This component would then be replaced at the last scheduled maintenance period prior to the accumulation of X hours; thus the operator would get maximum hours out of the component and the component would never fail in service (ideally).

Hard time is also applied to items having a direct adverse effect on safety and items subject to reliability degradation with age but having no possible maintenance check for that condition. The former components, as we will see later, are not eligible for condition monitoring because of the safety issue. The latter components, such as rubber products, do not lend themselves to any periodic check for condition; i.e., there is no OC check to determine how much serviceability is remaining.

As an example, structural inspection, landing gear overhaul, and replacement of life-limited engine parts are all controlled by hard time. Frequently, mechanical linkages and actuators, hydraulic pumps and motors, electric motors and generators, and similar items subject to a definite wear-out cycle will also be identified as hard time. For items having clearly defined wear-out periods, hard time is probably the most economical process. However, these items can also be OC or CM, depending on the operator, as long as they are not safety related.

The on-condition (OC) process

On-condition is a failure preventive process that requires that the item be periodically inspected or tested against some appropriate physical standard (wear or deterioration limits) to determine whether or not the item can continue in service. After failing an OC check, the component must be overhauled or restored to the extent of at least replacing out-of-tolerance parts. Overhaul or repair must restore the unit to a condition that will give reasonable assurance of satisfactory operation for at least one additional OC check interval. If the item cannot be overhauled or restored, or if it cannot be restored to a condition where it can operate one more OC check period, then it should be discarded.

On-condition must be restricted to components, equipment, or systems on which a determination of continued airworthiness may be made by measurements, tests, or other means without doing a tear-down inspection. These on-condition checks are to be performed within the time limits (intervals) prescribed for each OC check. On-condition determination of continued airworthiness is a "quantifying" check with specified tolerances and/or wear limits which must be set forth in the operator's maintenance manuals.

The periodically scheduled OC checks must constitute meaningful determination of suitability for continued operation for another scheduled OC check interval. If the check performed provides enough information regarding the condition and failure resistance of the item to give reasonable assurance of its continued airworthiness during the next check period, the item is properly categorized as on-condition. If the check constitutes merely a maintenance task—servicing, adjustment, or a go/no-go determination—and is not making a meaningful disclosure of actual condition, the item is, in fact, operating as a condition monitored item. It should be classified as CM and not OC. In some cases, it could even be classified as HT. A simple operational check is *not* an acceptable requisite for the on-condition process. On-condition checks must measure or evaluate the wear and/or deterioration condition of the item.

The on-condition process also encompasses periodic collection of data that will reveal the physical condition of a component, system, or engine. Through analysis and evaluation, OC data must be able to ascertain continued airworthiness and/or deterioration of failure resistance and imminence of failure. On-condition data must be directed to an individual component, system, or engine (by serial number). It is a priori (before the fact) failure data that can be used to measure decreasing life expectancy and/or predict failure imminence. Examples of OC checks are as follows: (*a*) tire tread and brake linings, (*b*) scheduled borescope inspections of engines, (*c*) engine oil analysis, and (*d*) in-flight engine performance analysis (i.e., engine condition monitoring or ECM). In each of the above stated cases, one can measure degradation and determine, from established norms, how much life or serviceability remains.

Most of the commercial airplane operators in the United States use the on-condition process to control engine overhaul. The determination of when to remove an engine is based on engine data collected by an ECM program. Data showing engine performance degradation, such as oil and fuel consumption, borescope inspection results, trends in recorded in-flight instrument readings, oil analysis, etc. are compared to standards to predict decreasing engine reliability and failure imminence. Engine data programs attempt to provide data to indicate the need to remove engines before an in-flight shutdown (IFSD) occurs; i.e., they are failure preventive processes.

Two points to remember about the on-condition process: (*a*) if a satisfactory on-condition check can be accomplished to ensure serviceability with reasonable probability until the next OC check, or if evaluation of the OC data collected will predict failure imminence, then the OC process will achieve close to maximum life on components and engines; and (*b*) on-condition applicability is limited by the requirement for a satisfactory condition measurement or pertinent failure predicting data.

Examples of components susceptible to the on-condition process are as follows:

1. *Brake wear indicator pins*: Compare brake wear condition against a specified standard or limit. Brake wear will vary considerably among operators due

to operational conditions and crew habits, but the wear indicator pin OC check will help attain near maximum usage out of each set of brakes.

2. *Control cables*: Measure these for diameter, tension, and broken strands.

3. *Linkages, control rods, pulleys, rollers tracks, jack screws, etc.*: Measure these for wear, end or side play, or backlash.

The condition monitoring (CM) process

The condition monitoring process is applied when neither the hard time nor the on-condition process can be applied. The CM process involves the monitoring of the failure rates, removals, etc. of individual components or systems that do not have a definite lifetime or a noticeable wear-out period. Condition monitoring is not a failure preventive process as are HT and OC. There are no maintenance tasks suitable for evaluating the life expectancy of the CM item and there is no requirement to replace the item before it fails. Neither time nor condition standards can be used to control CM items because these components do not have such attributes. Therefore, CM components are operated until failure occurs and replacement of CM items is an unscheduled maintenance action.

Since CM items are operated to failure, the ATA states that these items must comply with the following conditions:[*]

1. A CM item has no direct, adverse effect on safety when it fails; i.e., the aircraft continues to fly to a safe landing. Generally, CM items have only this indirect, nonadverse effect on safety due to system redundancy.

2. A CM item must not have any "hidden function" (i.e., a malfunction that is not evident to the crew) whose failure may have a direct adverse effect on safety. However, if there is a hidden function and the availability or operation of that hidden function is verified by a scheduled operational test or other nonmeasurement test made by the flight crew or maintenance crew, CM can still be used.

3. A CM item must be included in the operator's condition monitoring or reliability program; that is, there must be some sort of data collection and analysis for those items for maintenance to get a better understanding of the nature of failure for those components or systems.

In addition to the above ATA stipulations, CM items usually have no adverse relationship between age and reliability (i.e., no predictable life expectancy). They exhibit a random failure pattern.

The most appropriate application of the condition monitoring process is to complex systems, such as avionics and electronics components, and to any other components or systems for which there is no way to predict failures. Typical

---

[*] *Airline/Manufacturer Maintenance Program Development—MSG-2*; R&M Subcommittee of ATA, March 25, 1970. (*Note*: This document is no longer kept up to date by ATA.)

components and systems suitable for CM include navigation and communications equipment, lights, instruments, and other items where test or replacement will not predict approaching failure nor result in improved life expectancy. In aviation, CM is frequently applied to components where failure has no serious effect on safety or airworthiness, due to redundancy, and to items not affecting airworthiness at all, such as coffee makers, lavatories, passenger entertainment systems, etc.

Condition monitoring systems consist of data collection and data analysis procedures that will portray information upon which judgments relative to the safe condition of the vehicle can be made. A CM program includes those kinds of evaluation programs that utilize the disclosure capabilities of the airplane or its systems and components to the degree that such disclosure information can be used to make judgments relative to the continuing safe condition of the airplane, its systems, engines, and components. Evaluation based on reports by flight crews, on-board data systems, and equipment for ground check of system performance may be used for CM actions. The basic elements of a CM program may include data on unscheduled removals, maintenance log entries, pilot reports, sampling inspections, mechanical reliability reports, shop findings, and other sources of maintenance data. These and other data may indicate a problem area and thus the need to investigate the matter (see Chap. 19).

Condition monitoring, which is primarily a data collection and analysis program, can also be used on HT and OC components for verifying or adjusting the HT and OC intervals. For example, if a hard time item is removed just prior to its expiration date and overhaul activities reveal that little or nothing needs to be done to restore the component, then perhaps the HT interval can be extended. Likewise, if OC checks reveal little or no maintenance requirement or that the lifetime of the component is longer than originally expected, the OC check interval can be changed. However, without the collection of data over a period of time (several HT periods or OC intervals), there would not be any solid justification to change the intervals. By the same token, CM data collection may indicate that the HT or OC intervals need to be shortened for some components. The CM program also provides data to indicate whether or not components are being monitored under the most appropriate process.

Note for the technical purists

Condition monitoring does not really monitor the "condition" of a component. It essentially monitors the failure or removal statistics of the unit. You monitor the component's condition with the on-condition process.

Task-Oriented Maintenance

Task-oriented maintenance programs are created for aviation using decision logic procedures developed by the Air Transport Association of America. The process, called MSG-3, is a modification of and an improvement on the MSG-2 approach.

The MSG-3 technique is a "top down" or "consequence of failure" approach whereby failure analysis is conducted at the highest manageable level of airplane systems instead of at the component level as in MSG-2. The MSG-3 logic is used to identify suitable scheduled maintenance tasks to prevent failures and to maintain the inherent level of reliability of the system. There are three categories of tasks developed by the MSG-3 approach: (*a*) airframe systems tasks, (*b*) structural item tasks, and (*c*) zonal tasks.

Maintenance tasks for airframe systems

Under the MSG-3 approach, eight maintenance tasks have been defined for airframe systems. These tasks are assigned in accordance with the decision analysis results and the specific requirements of the system, component, etc. under consideration. These eight tasks are listed and defined below:

1. *Lubrication.* An act of replenishing oil, grease, or other substances used for the purpose of maintaining the inherent design capabilities by reducing friction and/or conducting away heat.
2. *Servicing.* An act of attending to basic needs of components and/or systems for the purpose of maintaining the inherent design capabilities.
3. *Inspection.* An examination of an item and comparison against a specific standard.
4. *Functional check.* A quantitative check to determine if each function of an item performs within specified limits. This check may require use of additional equipment.
5. *Operational check.* A task to determine if an item is fulfilling its intended purpose. This is a failure-finding task and does not require quantitative tolerances or any equipment other than the item itself.
6. *Visual check.* An observation to determine if an item is fulfilling its intended purpose. This is a failure-finding task and does not require quantitative tolerances.
7. *Restoration.* That work necessary to return the item to a specific standard. Restoration may vary from cleaning the unit or replacing a single part up to and including a complete overhaul.
8. *Discard.* The removal from service of any item at a specified life limit.

Maintenance tasks for structural items

Airplanes are subjected to three sources of structural deterioration as discussed below.

1. *Environmental deterioration.* The physical deterioration of an item's strength or resistance to failure as a result of chemical interaction with its

climate or environment. Environmental deteriorations may be time dependent.

2. *Accidental damage.* The physical deterioration of an item caused by contact or impact with an object or influence that is not a part of the airplane, or damage as a result of human error that occurred during manufacture, operation of the vehicle, or performance of maintenance.

3. *Fatigue damage.* The initiation of a crack or cracks due to cyclic loading and subsequent propagation of such cracks.

Inspection of airplane structures to determine if deterioration due to the above has occurred requires varying degrees of detail. The MSG-3 process defines three types of structural inspection techniques as follows:

1. *General visual inspection.* A visual examination that will detect obvious, unsatisfactory conditions or discrepancies. This type of inspection may require removal of fillets or opening or removal of access doors or panels. Work stands and ladders may be required to facilitate access to some components.

2. *Detailed inspection.* An intensive visual inspection of a specified detail, assembly, or installation. It is a search for evidence of irregularity using adequate lighting and, where necessary, inspection aids such as mirrors, hand lenses, etc. Surface cleaning and detailed access procedures may also be required.

3. *Special detailed inspection.* An intensive examination of a specific location. It is similar to the detailed inspection but with the addition of special techniques. This examination may require techniques such as nondestructive inspections (NDIs): dye penetrant, high-powered magnification, magnetic particle, eddy current, etc. (see Chap. 18 for details on these test methods.) The special detailed inspection may also require the disassembly of some units.

Zonal maintenance tasks

The zonal maintenance program ensures that all systems, components, and installations contained within a specified zone on the vehicle receive adequate surveillance to determine the security of installation and general condition. The program packages a number of general visual inspection tasks, generated against items in the system's maintenance program, into one or more zonal surveillance tasks.

The Current MSG Process—MSG-3

The MSG-2 process was modified in 1980 in a document released by the Air Transport Association of America.[*] The document states "MSG-3 did not

---

[*] *Airline/Manufacturer Maintenance Program Development Document*; issued September 30, 1980. Revised several times (March 1988; September 1993; March 2000; and March 2001). Latest version is called *Operator/Manufacturer Scheduled Maintenance Development*, revision 2000.1.

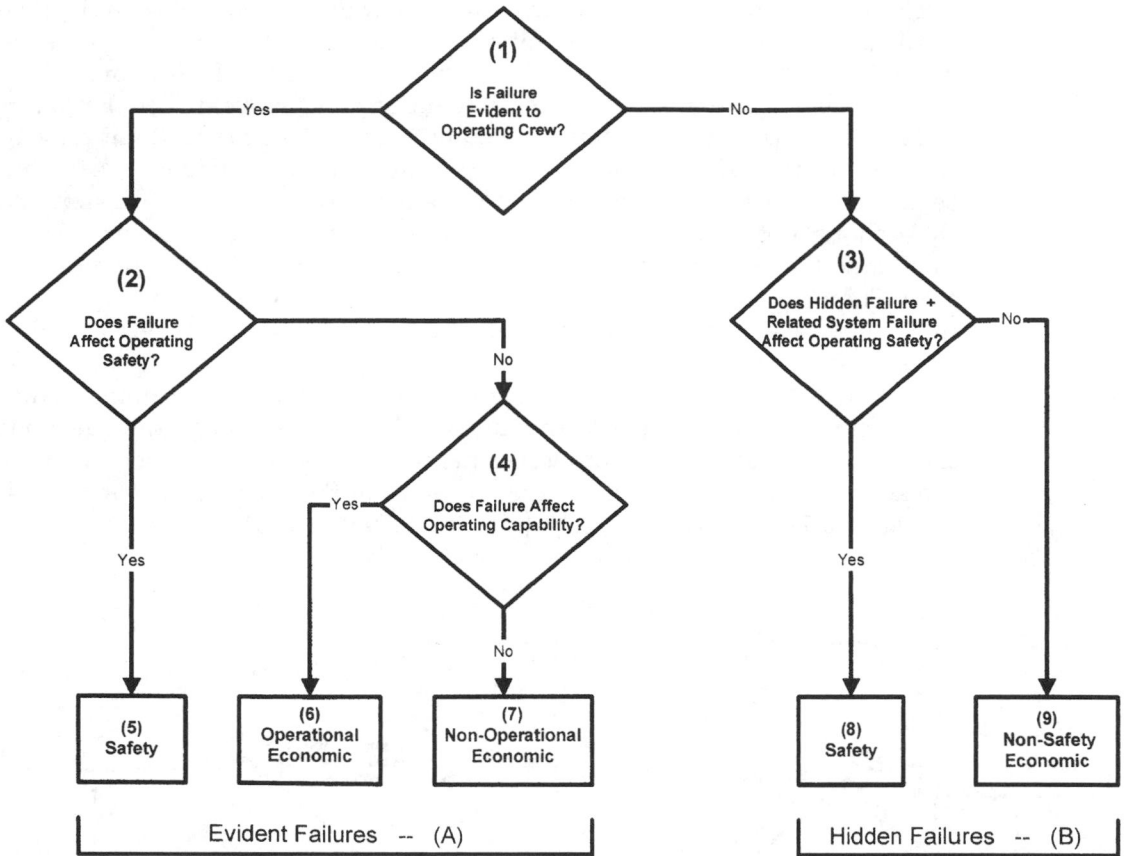

Figure 2-2 MSG-3 – level I analysis – failure categories. (*Courtesy of Air Transport Association of America, Inc. Reprinted with permission. Copyright © 2003 by Air Transport Association of America, Inc. All rights reserved.*)

constitute a fundamental departure from the previous version, but was built upon the existing framework of MSG-2 which had been validated by 10 years of reliable aircraft operation using the maintenance programs based thereon."

The MSG-3 program adjusted the decision logic to provide more straightforward and linear progression through the logic. The MSG-3 process is a top-down approach or consequence of failure approach. In other words, how does the failure affect the operation? It does not matter whether a system, subsystem, or component fails or deteriorates. What matters is how the failure affects the aircraft operation. The failure is assigned one of two basic categories: safety and economic. Figure 2-2 is a simplified diagram of the first step in the MSG-3 logic process.*

---

* Each block in Fig. 2-2 is numbered. The numbers on the output block (5 through 9) are used later to identify the category of the failure (hidden, evident, safety, etc.). These numbers will be referenced later in this discussion.

The maintenance tasks resulting from the MSG-3 approach may include hard time, on-condition, and condition monitoring tasks similar to those of MSG-2, but they are not referred to by those terms. The MSG-3 approach is more flexible in developing the overall maintenance program. The flow chart of Fig. 2-2 is used to determine if the failure is evident to the flight crew or hidden from them (level I analysis). Those failures that are evident are further separated into safety related and operationally related with the latter split into those that are of economic significance and those that are not. These types are numbered 5, 6, and 7. The significance of these categories will be addressed later. Those failures that are determined to be hidden from the crew are divided into safety related and nonsafety related items. These are designated as categories 8 and 9.

Figures 2-3 and 2-4 (level II analysis) are used to determine the maintenance tasks required to accommodate the functional failure. Although the questions are similar, there is a slight difference in the way evident and hidden failures are addressed. Note that some of the flow lines in Figs. 2-3 and 2-4 are identified as Cat 5 or Cat 8 only. This requires some explanation.

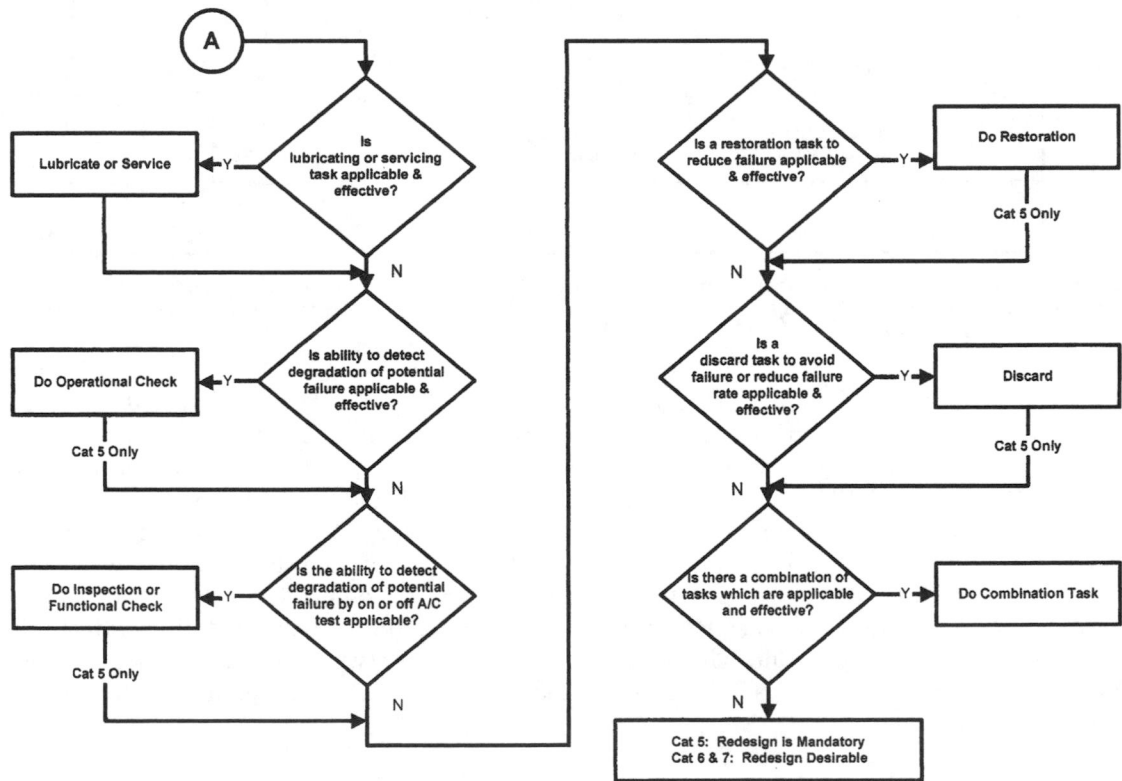

Figure 2-3   MSG-3 – level II analysis – evident failures. (*Courtesy of Air Transport Association of America, Inc. Reprinted with permission. Copyright© 2003 by Air Transport Association of America, Inc. All rights reserved.*)

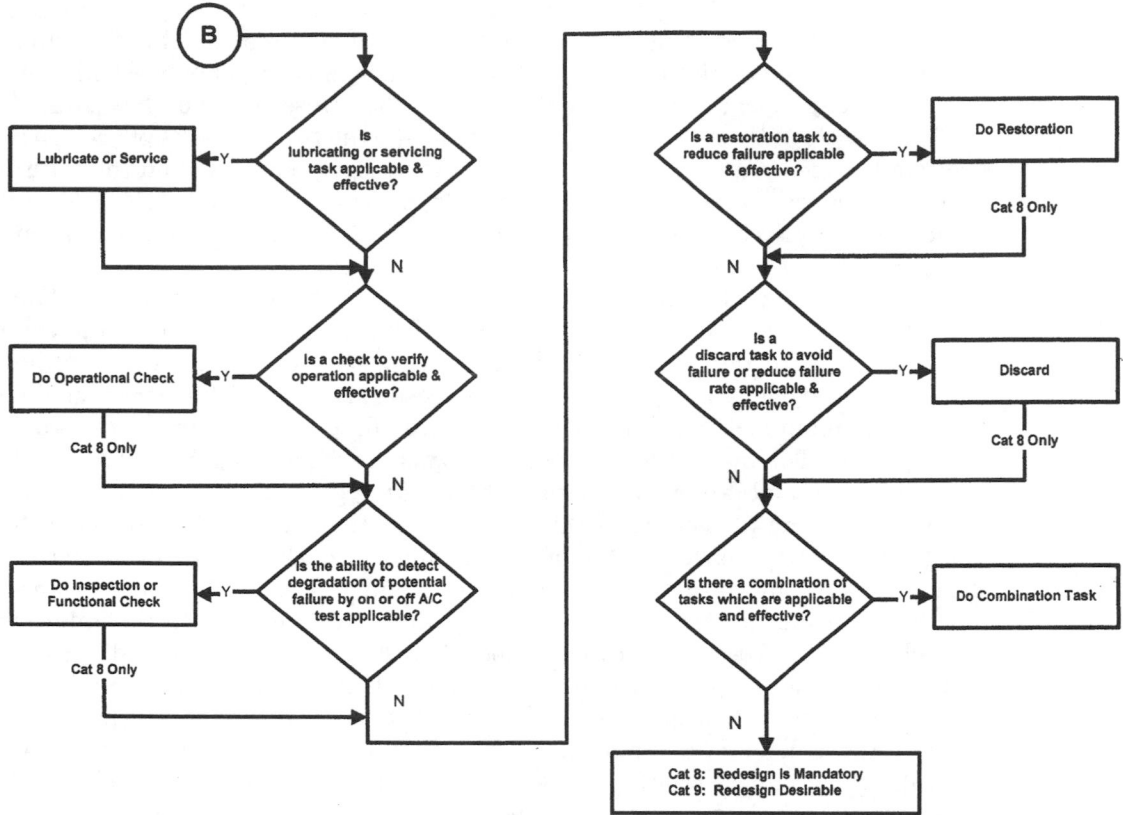

Figure 2-4 MSG-3 – level II analysis – hidden failures. (*Courtesy of Air Transport Association of America, Inc. Reprinted with permission. Copyright© 2003 by Air Transport Association of America, Inc. All rights reserved.*)

The first question in each chart, regarding lubrication or servicing, must be asked for all functional failures (categories 5 through 9). Regardless of the answer to this question (Yes or No) the analyst must ask the next question. For categories 6 and 7 in Fig. 2-3 and category 9 in Fig. 2-4, the questions are asked in sequence until a Yes answer is obtained. At that point the analysis stops. For categories 5 and 8 (safety related), however, all questions must be answered regardless of the Yes or No response to any of them.

The last block of Figs. 2-3 and 2-4 also requires some explanation. These flow charts are used for the development of a maintenance program for a new aircraft or derivative. If progression through the chart ends up in this block for categories 6, 7, and 9, then a redesign on the equipment involved may be considered by the design engineers. However, if the item is safety related—categories 5 or 8—then a redesign is mandatory. Once the initial maintenance program is developed, the airline mechanics will use that program. Mechanics do not have the option of redesign unless that is indicated by the reliability program as discussed in Chap. 19.

The MSG-3 process can be best understood through a step by step explanation of what the working groups would do for a given analysis. Each working group will receive information about the systems and components within their respective groups: (*a*) the theory of operation; (*b*) a description of the operation of each mode (if there is more than one mode); (*c*) the failure modes of each operational mode; and (*d*) any data available (actual or estimated) on the failure rates, removal rates, etc. [such as mean time between failures (MTBF) and mean time between unscheduled removals (MTBUR) for repairable parts; and mean time to removal (MTTR) for nonrepairable parts].

If the system is the same as, or similar to, that used on an existing model aircraft, the group members may only need refresher training on the operation and on the failure modes. If the equipment is new, or has been extensively modified for the new model aircraft, the learning process may take a little more time. The airframe manufacturer is responsible for providing this training to the working groups. The manufacturer is also responsible for furnishing any available performance and failure rate data to the working groups.

Once the group assimilates this information, they begin to run through the logic diagrams, answering the questions appropriately, and determining the maintenance approach that best suits the problem. Each failure in each operational mode is addressed. The working group first determines if the failure is hidden to the crew or is obvious (block 1 of Fig. 2-2). Then they determine whether or not the problem is safety related and, in the case of evident failures, whether or not it has operational impact. Next, they determine which maintenance tasks should be applied using Figs. 2-3 and 2-4 (level II analysis), and finally, the group determines at what maintenance interval that task should be performed. This latter exercise makes use of the failure rate data as well as the experience of the working group members.

The Maintenance Program Documents

The result of the MSG-3 analysis constitutes the original maintenance program for the new model aircraft and the program that is to be used by a new operator of that model. The tasks selected in the MSG process are published by the airframe manufacturer in an FAA approved document called the *maintenance review board* (MRB) *report*. This report contains the initial scheduled maintenance program for U.S. certificated operators. It is used by those operators to establish their own FAA approved maintenance program as identified by their operations specifications (see Chap. 4).

The MRB report includes the systems and power plant maintenance program, the structural inspection program, and the zonal inspection program. It also contains aircraft zone diagrams, a glossary, and a list of abbreviations and acronyms.

In addition to the MRB report, the manufacturer publishes its own document for maintenance planning. At Boeing, this document is called the maintenance planning data (MPD) document. McDonnell-Douglas called it the on aircraft maintenance planning (OAMP) document. At Airbus Industries, it is called the maintenance planning document (MPD). Hereinafter, we will use the acronym MPD/OAMP to refer to all such documents. These documents contain all the maintenance task information from the MRB report plus additional tasks suggested by the airframe manufacturer. The MPD/OAMP also sorts the tasks in various ways to aid in planning. This document often groups by letter check and by hours, cycles, and calendar time.

These manufacturer's documents also contain diagrams showing the location and numbering of access doors and panels, aircraft dimensions, and other information to aid the development of maintenance programs and the planning of maintenance checks. The latter includes man-hour requirements for each task. These are only estimates of the time required to do the actual work prescribed. They do not include the time required to open and close doors or panels, position work stands, to analyze or troubleshoot problems, or to correct any discrepancies found during conduct of the task. These estimated times must be altered by the operator to accommodate the actual task requirements when planning any given check activity.

Maintenance Intervals Defined

Various maintenance checks have been named and defined in the MSG-3 process and are considered standard. Individual airlines, however, can identify their own named intervals as long as they maintain the integrity of the original maintenance task requirements or receive FAA approval for deviations. The standard intervals are as follows.

Transit checks

A transit check is performed after landing and before the next takeoff; that is, while the airplane is in transit at the airport. It is also performed before the first flight of the day. The transit check consists of oil level check and fill actions and a general visual inspection, called a walk-around, to check for any fluid leaks, open or loose panels, and damage to the flight control surfaces or antennae. Although the oil check and fill requires opening of the engine cowlings, the remainder of the transit check is usually done with a minimum of stands or other tools and equipment. If a problem is found, however, the resulting action will be unscheduled maintenance (even if it is deferred). This check is often done jointly by maintenance and flight crew personnel. At stations where no maintenance is available, the flight crew will do a walk-around inspection; i.e., they will do everything except open cowlings and check oil levels.

One variation in the pattern is that the oil level check on the engines must be done between 5 and 30 min after the engines have been shut down to obtain an accurate reading. This means that the oil level cannot be checked and replenished prior to the first flight of the day. It can only be done soon after landing.

48-hour checks

A 48-hour check, for most aircraft models, replaces what used to be called a daily check. The 48-hour check is performed once every 48 hours. This check includes tasks that are more detailed than the transit checks; for example, items such as wheels and brakes as well as certain fluids such as oil levels for the auxiliary power unit (APU), the integrated drive generator (IDG), and the aircraft hydraulic fluid level.

Hourly limit checks

Certain checks determined by the MSG analysis have maintenance tasks assigned by the number of hours the unit or system has been operating: 100, 200, 250 hours, etc. This approach is used for engines, airplane flight controls, and numerous other systems that are operating on a continual basis during the flight or on the ground.

Operating cycle limit checks

Other airplane systems are maintained on a schedule determined by the number of operating cycles they have endured. Items such as tires, brakes, and landing gear, for instance, are used only during takeoffs and landings and the number of these operations will vary with the flight schedule. Airframe structures are also subject to cyclic stresses and will have numerous tasks in this category.

Letter checks

Until the development of the Boeing 777, all aircraft utilizing the MSG-3 processes for maintenance program development had various letter checks identified in the maintenance program. These checks were identified as A, B, C, and D checks. The Boeing 777, using a modified MSG-3 process (called MSG-3, Revision 2) eliminated the letter checks.[*] Every task that was not on the transit check was identified by hours or cycles only, and these tasks were not grouped into letter checks as was done for previous model aircraft. This produced an optimum maintenance program in that it allowed maintenance to be done at the most appropriate time for the equipment or system. For the operator, it makes the program more adaptable to their needs. Some operators, however, still schedule this maintenance in blocks at specific time or cycle intervals.

Changing Basic Maintenance Intervals

Operational conditions will often require that an operator change the basic maintenance program to better address the organizational needs and to accommodate the fifth objective of a maintenance program (see Chap. 3). As an

---

[*] The same is true for the Boeing 737, new generation (NG) airplanes, and other airplanes designed after the 737 NG.

example, operation in hot humid climates may require that corrosion control tasks be performed more often than the MRB report indicates while operating the same vehicles in a dry, desert climate may reduce the needed frequency for these tasks. In the latter situation, however, items sensitive to sand and dust will need increased attention in the maintenance program.

It is expected that an operator will change the original maintenance intervals for certain tasks or for entire letter checks whenever in-service experience dictates. However, to do this, the operator must have proof that a change is warranted. The accepted proof for such maintenance interval changes is in the form of data collected through the operator's condition monitoring program or reliability program. Details on this will be covered later in Chap. 19. As aircraft get older, task intervals for certain items may have to be shortened while others may be lengthened. Maintenance is a dynamic process.

Chapter 3

Definitions, Goals, and Objectives

Definitions of Important Terms

In the classic children's book *Through the Looking Glass*, a young girl named Alice (of Wonderland fame) is having an argument with Humpty Dumpty on the meaning of words.[*]

> "When I use a word," Humpty Dumpty said in rather a scornful tone, "it means just what I choose it to mean—neither more nor less."
>
> "The question is," said Alice, "whether you can make words mean so many different things."
>
> "The question is," said Humpty Dumpty, "which is to be the master—that's all."

They go on with further discussion about words which we will omit here but this dialogue illustrates an important point. All through the history of science and engineering it has been customary for authors to define, early in their texts, what they mean, specifically, by the words they use. This text will not be any different: i.e., a word means what we say it means—no more, no less—and will be so defined.[†]

This section discusses some basic terms used in aviation maintenance and engineering. Some of the conventional definitions will be modified or replaced by this text to better define the meaning and purpose that they serve. There are some word pairs used in aviation that are, in conventional usage, synonymous, but in the world of science and engineering—and especially aviation—they take on subtle differences. These word pairs will be defined and discussed, also, to ensure that the reader is aware of the precise meaning when the terms are used

---

[*] Carroll, Lewis, *Through the Looking Glass*, in *Alice in Wonderland and other Favorites*. Pocket Books, NY, 1974.

[†] In this text, conventional definitions will be shown in quotes. Definitions new to this text will be boxed.

hereafter. We will begin with the most important definition: the definition of maintenance.

Maintenance

We have talked about maintenance and how the approach to maintenance has evolved over the years; but just what is it that we mean when we use the term "maintenance"? In the front of this book, we have quoted a very elegant definition of maintenance by Lindley R. Higgins, defining maintenance as art, science, and philosophy. In this text, however, we will address the subject in less poetic and more practical terms.

Numerous other authors have defined the term maintenance but their definitions are somewhat unsatisfactory. Most of them are not incorrect but they are often inadequate to describe the full scope and intent of the maintenance effort. We will look at a few of these and discuss the differences. Then we will provide the reader with our own definition of maintenance which, as you will see, falls into place with other definitions and concepts discussed in the text.

Typical airline definition of maintenance

This one was taken from the text of a "typical" airline's technical policies and procedures manual (TPPM). *Maintenance* is defined as "those actions required for restoring or maintaining an item in a serviceable condition, including servicing, repair, modification, overhaul, inspection, and determination of condition."

This is not incorrect. However, it merely describes what maintenance people do; it is not descriptive of the intent or the result of maintenance activity.

Moubray's definition of maintenance

In the mid-1970s, a process was developed for use by the U.S. military to develop the initial maintenance program for their equipment similar to the MSG process used for civilian aircraft. The process was called reliability-centered maintenance or RCM.[*] The RCM process was primarily for scheduled maintenance and gives a definition of *preventive maintenance* only: "… the program of scheduled maintenance tasks necessary to ensure safe and reliable operation of the equipment."[†]

John Moubray, an industrial consultant in the United Kingdom, took the RCM philosophy and applied it to the maintenance of machines and equipment in a typical manufacturing plant. He presented the following definition of maintenance in his book on the subject.[‡] *Maintenance* is "… ensuring that physical assets continue to do what their users want them to do."

---

[*] Nowlan, F. Stanley and Howard F. Heap, *Reliability-Centered Maintenance*. National Technical Information Service, Washington, DC, 1978.

[†] Nowlan and Heap, p. 11.

[‡] Moubray, John: *Reliability-Centered Maintenance*, 2nd ed, Industrial Press Inc., NY, 1997.

Even though one can easily read into this definition what was intended, it is really rather wide open. It just so happens that, in some rare cases, users want a tool, machine, or system to do something other than what it was designed to do. Using a glass bottle for a hammer is a good example. All the maintenance in the world cannot ensure that the bottle will be an adequate hammer. This definition seems a bit ambiguous for our purposes.

FAA definition of maintenance

In the Federal Aviation Regulations, FAR part 1, *maintenance* is defined as "… inspection, overhaul, repair, preservation, and replacement of parts."[*] Again, this describes what maintenance people do but it is not a definitive description of what maintenance is intended to accomplish.

Hessburg's definition of maintenance

Jack Hessburg, former chief mechanic for the Boeing 777 design effort, has provided a definition of maintenance which gives a broader view of the field. "*Maintenance* is the action necessary to sustain or restore the integrity and performance of the airplane."[†] He goes on to say that maintenance "includes inspection, overhaul, repair, preservation, and replacement efforts." This definition is more accurate.

Kinnison's definition of maintenance

The author of this textbook feels that the above definitions—although well intended and, in most cases, adequate in general terms—are not fully descriptive of what the maintenance process is about. The definition in the box below will be used in this book.

> *Maintenance* is the process of ensuring that a system continually performs its intended function at its designed-in level of reliability and safety.

This definition implies the servicing, adjusting, replacement, restoration, overhaul, and anything else needed to ensure the proper and continual operation of the system or equipment, but it emphasizes the notion that the equipment was designed for a specific purpose (or purposes in the case of multifunction systems) with an inherent or designed-in level of reliability and safety. Not all systems and components, however, will require the same attention to accomplish the required maintenance. For example, some items need continual servicing and adjustment; others need oil, lubrication, or other fluids replaced or replenished;

---

[*] Federal Aviation Regulation part 1 contains definitions and abbreviations.

[†] Hessburg, Jack, *MRO Handbook*. McGraw-Hill, NY, 2000, p. 246.

still others may require overhaul, parts replacement, etc. to achieve this ultimate goal.

We cannot make a system any better than its designed-in capabilities no matter how much maintenance we perform. We can only restore it to its designed-in level after deterioration has occurred. This definition, then, is more descriptive of the purpose of maintenance and what maintenance is supposed to accomplish for the operator.

Inherent Reliability

Inherent reliability is a term used frequently in aviation and already discussed in this text (Chaps. 1 and 2). This term may require some clarification. Nowlan and Heap state that "the inherent reliability of an item is not the length of time it will survive with no failures; rather, it is the level of reliability the item will exhibit when it is protected by preventive maintenance and adequate servicing and lubrication."[*] The authors go on to say that the degree of reliability achieved depends upon design characteristics of the equipment and the process used for determining the maintenance requirements (i.e., the MSG process). In other words, the inherent reliability of a system or component is both a function of the design and a function of the maintenance program established for it. The two are interrelated.

Mechanics, Technicians, Maintainers, Engineers

The terminology used by the world's airlines to identify maintenance personnel varies. The terms mechanic, technician, and maintainer are often used to identify those who perform the scheduled and unscheduled maintenance tasks of the unit's aircraft. In some organizations, however, these same people are called engineers while in others, the term engineer is reserved for those personnel who have college degrees in one of the engineering fields. These people usually perform duties quite different from those of the line, hangar, and shop maintenance people.

In this book, for the sake of standardization of the discussion, we will define those who work on the scheduled and unscheduled aircraft maintenance tasks (line, hangar, or shop) as mechanics, technicians, or maintainers, while those who work in the technical services organization as specified in Chap. 7 will be called engineers.

Word Pairs Used in Aviation

There are a number of word pairs that we use in aviation that are assigned very specific meanings. These meanings are more precise than those addressed in the dictionary. Here are a few of them; there may be more.

---

[*] Nowlan and Heap, p. 103.

Verification and validation

These words are used in aviation, as well as in the railroad industry, in relation to determining the adequacy of maintenance processes and procedures. Although some dictionaries define one of these words with the other one, in the world of engineering and technology there are various definitions given depending on the application. In aviation, it is generally accepted that the two words have distinctly different meanings. Many procedures are written to test or measure the condition, accuracy, or availability of equipment and systems. The words verification and validation describe different approaches or concepts used to assure that maintenance has been properly addressed by such procedures.

Verification means that a test or procedure has been written and that, when read and understood by a knowledgeable person, is deemed to be correct, adequate, and acceptable for the purpose for which it was intended.

Validation, on the other hand, means that the written test or procedure has been performed by an appropriately trained maintenance person, and the procedure, as written, is understandable, adequate, and, most importantly, proven to accomplish the intended purpose.

In other words, verification means that the procedure exists and is acceptable based on the knowledge and understanding of the related equipment and on perusal of the procedure itself. Validation means that the procedure has actually been performed as written and has been deemed to be adequate and acceptable.

Operational and functional

Although these words are often used interchangeably in daily life, in aviation they are distinctly different. The terms are used in conjunction with the process of testing equipment, systems, or components; the difference is in the complexity of the testing.

Operational check means to operate the equipment, system, or component as usual (all modes and functions) and determine whether or not it is useable for its intended purpose. No special test equipment or tools are needed and no measurements are taken. An operational check is defined as "a task to determine if an item is fulfilling its intended purpose. This is a failure finding task and does not require quantitative tolerances."[*]

Functional check means that the equipment, system, or component has been checked out using the necessary equipment and tools to measure certain parameters for accuracy (i.e., voltages, frequencies, physical measures such as gap size, length, weight, etc.). The official definition for a *functional check* is "a quantitative check to determine if each function of an item performs within specified

---

[*] Air Transport Association of America (ATA); *Common Support Data Dictionary* (CSDD); revision 2001.1.

limits."[*] The term "limits" here implies a check or measurement against some standard.

As an example of the differences in these two types of tests, consider the check-out of a radio. If you turn on the radio, tune in a station (by ear) and check for clarity of reception and adequacy of volume control, you have performed an operational check. If you use additional equipment to check the accuracy of the frequency dial and the magnitude of the volume, the input signal strength, etc., you have performed a functional check. The operational check uses only the equipment itself; the functional check uses additional equipment or tools for a more accurate measurement of the various parameters of the unit.

Goals and objectives

There seems to be considerable confusion throughout the engineering profession, and perhaps other fields as well, about the similarities and differences between "goals" and "objectives." Some modern dictionaries, as they have done with so many pairs of similar words, define one word with the other one making the two nearly synonymous. But these two words—goals and objectives—have always had specific meanings to this author and to many other people in the technical fields. We have taken the liberty of writing our own definitions for these terms in order to establish a clear understanding and application of the two words for use throughout this book.

> A *goal* is a point in time or space where you want to be; a level of accomplishment you want to achieve.

> An *objective* is the action or activity you employ in order to help you achieve a specific goal.

In other words, a goal is where you want to be; an objective is how you plan to get there.

Example: Suppose a person living in Seattle, Washington wants to be in Dallas, Texas for Christmas with family members. First, the mode of travel must be determined (private auto, bus, train, or airplane) and then, depending on which mode is chosen, the desired dates of departure and return must be determined. Of course there are numerous decisions that must be made and each possible choice will have its own pros and cons. This must be worked out ahead of time. In this simple example, being in Dallas for Christmas is the goal. The objective is to make the trip happen and that involves the planning and decision-making activities, which would vary with the mode choice, that would be necessary to make the trip possible.

---

[*] ATA CSDD.

Goals and Objectives of Maintenance

We have already established the fact, in Chap. 1, that we cannot make perfect systems and that the systems we have will fail at various times and for a variety of reasons. We have also established, in Chap. 1, various management actions to minimize the effects of service interruptions caused by these failures (LRUs, redundancy, minimum dispatch requirements). Also, the manufacturer has established a maintenance program (see Chap. 2) that includes numerous tasks at scheduled intervals as well as references to other tasks and maintenance manual procedures for addressing the unscheduled failures. But these are not quite enough. To establish an effective airline maintenance program that will effectively implement these tasks, achieve the reliability and safety standards we desire, and still maintain an adequate flight schedule to stay in business, we must have some additional guidelines. Namely, we need to establish some goals and objectives for an airline maintenance program.

Goals of a maintenance program

The purpose of any transportation company is to move people and/or goods from one place to another, usually for a profit. This means, to some people, that the operational part of the unit is more important than the maintenance part. As you will see later, the two are actually on a par as far as management and administration are concerned. But, the fact remains that the maintenance organization is in business to support the unit's operation. Maintenance must ensure that the flight department has vehicles available to carry out the flight schedule, and this schedule should be met with all required maintenance completed. Therefore, the goals of an airline maintenance program can be stated as follows:

> 1. To deliver airworthy vehicles to the flight department in time to meet the flight schedule
> 2. To deliver these vehicles with all necessary maintenance actions completed or properly deferred

The FAA requires maintenance to be done at specified intervals and to accepted standards. The FAA also requires that this work be done at or before the appointed time. If there are circumstances that prevent work being done (lack of parts or qualified maintenance personnel, time constraints, etc.) the FAA allows such maintenance to be deferred to a more opportune time. Deferrals of certain items can be in accordance with the MEL; others can be deferred through the short-term time escalation program identified in the FAA approved maintenance program. The accepted standards include the manufacturer's, the regulator's, and the operator's standards of safety and reliability. The time limits refer to the maximum number of hours or cycles of operation and any calendar limits (days, months, etc.) as prescribed by the approved maintenance program. The repair must be completed within the specified deferral time and this cannot be extended.

Maintenance program objectives

To achieve the stated goals of a maintenance program, we need to identify the objectives we will employ. The Air Transport Association of America (ATA) has identified four objectives of a maintenance program.[*] The FAA, the airframe manufacturers, and the airlines repeat these objectives throughout their own literature. These objectives were developed in conjunction with the establishment of the initial maintenance program when a new airplane model was being developed (i.e., the MSG-3 process of Chap. 2). These objectives are not quite sufficient for a good, effective maintenance program at the operator's level once the equipment enters service. For this in-service activity, five objectives of a maintenance program are established and addressed in this textbook. The list below contains the ATA objectives, from the aforementioned document, with the addition of one very important objective—objective number three in this new list. The objectives of an airline in-service maintenance program are as follows:

1. To ensure the realization of the inherent safety and reliability levels of the equipment
2. To restore safety and reliability to their inherent levels when deterioration has occurred
3. To obtain the information necessary for adjustment and optimization of the maintenance program when these inherent levels are not met
4. To obtain the information necessary for design improvement of those items whose inherent reliability proves inadequate
5. To accomplish these objectives at a minimum total cost, including the costs of maintenance and the cost of residual failures

The ATA document cited above states the following:

These objectives recognize that maintenance programs, as such, cannot correct deficiencies in the inherent safety and reliability levels of the equipment. The maintenance program can only prevent deterioration of such inherent levels. If the inherent levels are found to be unsatisfactory, design modification is necessary to obtain improvement.

[*] ATA MSG-3—*Operator/Manufacturer Scheduled Maintenance Development*, Revision 2001.1. Air Transport Association of America, Inc., Washington, DC, 2001.

We need to modify that statement to accommodate the third objective above, the one we added. The maintenance program as developed by the manufacturer is only a general guideline intended for use by new operators of new equipment. In service, this program may have to be adjusted to fit specific airline operations in the field. Experience may show an operator that maintenance intervals established by the manufacturer may not be the best for that airline's operational environment. The results of maintenance may also be less than expected because of bad parts, improper or inadequate procedures, or even the lack of proper training of the mechanics. All of these could affect the overall reliability and safety of the equipment and they should be addressed by the airline before calling the manufacturer and requesting or demanding a redesign of that equipment as implied by objective 4. This is the reason for the added objective.[*]

Contrary to popular belief, the manufacturers cannot be blamed for all the problems occurring with the equipment once it is in the field. Therefore, the airline must look into its own operation first. Keep in mind, however, that any serious problems in any of the areas above relating to the airline's ability to meet its objectives could affect the operator's FAA certification. So these conditions should always be monitored closely and corrected if found to be lacking.

Maintenance Program Content

The ATA document cited above discusses what a maintenance program should be as stated below.

> The maintenance program consists of two groups of tasks: a group of scheduled tasks to be accomplished at specified intervals and a group of non-scheduled tasks which result from (a) conducting the scheduled tasks, (b) from reports of malfunctions, and (c) from data analysis.
>
> An efficient [maintenance] program is one which schedules only those tasks necessary to meet the stated objectives. It does not schedule additional tasks which will increase maintenance costs without a corresponding increase in reliability protection.

Thus, a maintenance program consists of scheduled maintenance tasks to keep equipment and systems in top operating condition (objective 1); unscheduled maintenance tasks to address in-service failures (objective 2); a continuing analysis and surveillance activity to optimize the total maintenance effort by improving the maintenance program (objective 3) or by requesting a redesign of equipment (objective 4); and an effort to minimize maintenance costs (objective 5).

Discussion of the Five Objectives

Objective 1.   To ensure the realization of the inherent safety and reliability levels of the equipment. This objective is satisfied by a series of scheduled maintenance

---

[*] More on the discussion of causes for not achieving the inherent level of safety and reliability can be found in Chap. 19.

tasks. The scheduled maintenance tasks may be developed by the manufacturer of the equipment, by the maintenance organization of the airline, a third party maintenance company, by some industry-supported organization (trade association), or by some combination of these. Usually, the manufacturer supplies the operator with basic information on how the equipment works and some basic troubleshooting techniques, as well as servicing, removal/installation procedures, and maintenance procedures.

In the commercial aviation industry, the manufacturers, the vendors, and the operators get together and develop a maintenance program for the scheduled maintenance. The program developed is based on knowledge of the equipment as well as knowledge and experience with the equipment in the operational environment. The process used to do this was discussed in Chap. 2.

Objective 2.   To restore safety and reliability to their inherent levels when deterioration has occurred. This objective is satisfied by unscheduled maintenance tasks developed by the MSG process and contained in the manufacturer's maintenance manual. Unscheduled maintenance tasks result from a combination of activities: (*a*) troubleshooting actions that determine the nature and cause of the problem; (*b*) removal and replacement of parts or components to effect repair or restoration; and (*c*) performance of certain tests and adjustments to ensure proper operation of the system or equipment after the "fix" has been implemented. Unscheduled maintenance tasks, developed by the manufacturer, are sometimes modified, in the field, by the operators through experience. Such modifications, however, must be approved by the FAA.

Reports of malfunctions come from operators and users through various means, usually a logbook kept in the airplane or by verbal or written reports from operators, flight crews, cabin crews, users, or maintenance personnel. Maintenance tasks that result from data analysis are usually actions that result from some form of reliability program or other failure rate analysis activities conducted by quality control (QC).

Objective 3.   To obtain the information necessary for adjustment and optimization of the maintenance program when these inherent levels are not met. This objective concerns the adjustment or optimization of a maintenance program by an operator. If it is not possible to meet the inherent safety and reliability of the system, or if failure rates or removal rates of certain items are considered to be too high, the problem must be investigated to determine the reason for this condition. The problem could be in the quality of maintenance performed, the inferiority of parts or components used in maintenance, the inadequacy of the maintenance processes and procedures used, or in the maintenance intervals themselves. In some cases, the problem may be electromagnetic or mechanical interference from other systems in the airplane or on the ground. As a result of such investigations, the airline may need to adjust its maintenance program, provide additional training to its personnel, or adjust its parts control procedures accordingly to achieve the equipment's inherent level of safety and reliability.

Objective 4.   To obtain the information necessary for design improvement of those items whose inherent reliability proves inadequate. This objective is applied when the operator cannot achieve the desired level of reliability due to some deficiency in the design. If the investigation associated with objective 3 shows no deficiency in the operator's program or in the performance of the mechanics, then objective 4 is applied. Coordination with other operators using the same equipment and with the manufacturer is usually involved here. A joint effort to resolve the problem usually results in redesign by the manufacturer and subsequent modification developed by the manufacturer and incorporated by the operator. Other operators of the same equipment, as well as regulatory authorities, may take part in the investigation and redesign process. (This objective can also be applied when, in the opinion of the operator, a higher level of performance is deemed desirable for a given system.)

Objective 5.   To accomplish these objectives at a minimum total cost, including the costs of maintenance and the cost of residual failures.[*] This objective is important to a good, effective maintenance program. A loose interpretation of this objective is "do not do any more maintenance than you have to, to meet inherent levels of safety and reliability; and do not do any less maintenance than necessary to meet those levels." In other words, a good maintenance program, to be effective, must provide airworthy vehicles to the operations department at a reasonable cost.

As an example, suppose a component or system is checked daily, in accordance with the scheduled maintenance program, and a problem is found maybe every 2 or 3 weeks (or even less often). It is sensible, then, to reschedule this check to perhaps a weekly or even a biweekly interval to reduce maintenance costs.

When it comes to maintenance, more is better but only up to a point. Too little maintenance may lead to early degradation and failure. But increasing the maintenance beyond that which restores the inherent level of safety and reliability will provide no additional benefit although it will cause increased maintenance costs.

Economy must also be considered when modifications are suggested by the manufacturer or others. Objective 5 requires that the airline weigh the cost of making the modification against the benefits derived from the modification. The benefits may result in increased operational capabilities and at the same time reduced maintenance costs. At times, however, the cost of modification may not be justified. If the cost of modification exceeds the savings, then the modification is not justified unless the measurable increases in performance and/or safety can justify the cost.

---

[*] Residual failures are those failures that would occur because the airline deemed that, for economic reasons, certain maintenance tasks were not employed or certain modifications were not installed. All costs must be considered when making such decisions: the cost of incorporation as well as the cost of continued maintenance (failures) resulting from not incorporating.

Summary

This chapter has addressed various terms relating to the maintenance effort which will be used or referenced throughout the remainder of the textbook. The use and understanding of these terms and definitions should become second nature to the student.

Aviation Industry Certification Requirements

Introduction

The aviation industry is the most heavily regulated of all the transportation modes. With the exception of certain requirements for a business license and licensing of the vehicles and drivers, one can enter the taxicab business quite easily. Trucking is pretty much the same. Transit buses, generally operated by nonprofit or government entities, have similar licensing requirements for vehicles and drivers but the vehicles themselves are built and sold with little government regulation except for safety and air pollution items. The railroads undergo more stringent controls, however, as do the operators of commercial water vessels. But in the aviation industry, there is a considerable amount of regulation, from the design of the vehicles through the manufacturing efforts to the operation and maintenance of the vehicles. There are also regulatory requirements for the business side.

Aircraft Certification

There are three certificates necessary for full certification of the airplane. These documents—the type certificate, the production certificate, and the airworthiness certificate—certify, respectively, the aircraft design, the manufacturing process, and the aircraft itself.

Type certificate (FAA form 8110.9)

To begin with, each aircraft designed and built for commercial as well as private operation must have an approved type certificate (TC). This certificate is applied for by the designers of the vehicle once the basic design has been determined. The TC defines the vehicle, its engines, and the various instruments, systems, and equipment that make up the model. If more than one engine type (i.e., derivatives of existing engines or engines from different manufacturers) is offered for the same vehicle, the TC must cover the characteristics and limitations of all of them. The same is true on other equipment, systems, and accessories. The TC also defines the capabilities and limitations of the vehicle such as passenger and cargo carrying limits, altitude limits, fuel capacity, and top speed as well as cruising speed. All of these parameters combined, which define the airframe/engine combination, must be identified on a data sheet attached to the certificate. The aircraft/engine combination is designed to exacting safety and airworthiness standards set by the FAA and this design must be proven to the FAA by means of inspections and test flights. A final FAA proving flight is conducted before the TC is awarded.

The TC is applied for early in the design stages but is not awarded until the aircraft is actually built, tested in flight, and proven to meet the standards of safety and airworthiness. As an example, the Boeing Company applied for the TC for the 757-200 airplane in 1978; it was awarded by the FAA's Aircraft Certification Office (ACO) in 1982.

For variations, or derivatives, of a given model, the TC can be amended. Suppose the manufacturer builds and sells a passenger airplane. After this model enters service, the manufacturer decides to produce an all-cargo version of the same basic airplane. The resulting design will be different: no passenger windows, different flooring (to handle cargo pallets), and other variations which change the basic characteristics of the vehicle. This will require further FAA approval but, instead of issuing a new TC, the FAA will supplement the original one. The model/type will be added to the certificate and an additional data sheet will be attached to delineate the new model's characteristics and differences. Flight test proving of the new configuration will be required and a supplemental TC will be issued. The FAA will only issue type certificates (design approvals) for products manufactured in the United States or for foreign made products intended for use under U.S. registry or by U.S. operators under lease or charter.

A sample of the TC is shown in Fig. 4-1. This is the first page showing the airplanes covered. Additional information concerning the design is given in the data sheets (not shown) attached to the TC. The TC remains in effect until superseded, revoked, or a termination date is established by the FAA. Figure 4-2 shows a supplemental type certificate (STC).

Production certificate (FAA form 8120-4)

Once the type certificate is awarded, the manufacturer must then apply to the FAA's Manufacturing Inspection District Office (MIDO) for a production certificate (PC). This certificate is awarded after the FAA is satisfied that the manufacturer has the necessary manufacturing facilities and has established an effective quality control program to ensure that each unit produced will be built to the TC standards. In other industries, it is possible to build a hand-made prototype of a

The United States of America

Department of Transportation

Federal Aviation Administration

①

Type Certificate

②

Number _____ ③

This certificate issued to   ④

certifies that the type design for the following product with the operating limitations and conditions therefor as specified in the Federal Aviation Regulations and the Type Certificate Data Sheet, meets the airworthiness requirements of Part   ⑤   of the Federal Aviation Regulations.

⑥

This certificate, and the Type Certificate Data Sheet which is a part hereof, shall remain in effect until surrendered, suspended, revoked, or a termination date is otherwise established by the Administrator of the Federal Aviation Administration.

Date of application: ⑦

Date of issuance: ⑧

By Direction of the Administrator

(Signature)_____

⑨

(Title) _____

This certificate may be transferred if endorsed as provided on the reverse hereof.

Any alteration of this certificate and/or the Type Certificate Data Sheet is punishable by a fine not exceeding $1,000, or imprisonment not exceeding 3 years, or both.

FAA FORM 8110-9 (2-82)(Representation)

Figure 4-1   FAA type certificate (sample). (1) Type of product (airplane, engine, propeller); (2) "IMPORT" if applicable; (3) TC number as assigned; (4) applicant's name; (5) applicable Federal Aviation Regulation; (6) product type designation: "Airplane Model 120." Additional models if applicable; (7) date of original application; (8) date TC is issued. When later models are added, retain original date and add new date; (9) signature of manager, FAA accountable directorate.

United States of America

Department of Transportation-Federal Aviation Administration

Supplemental Type Certificate

Number

This certificate, issued to

certifies that the change in the type design for the following product with the limitations and conditions therefor as specified hereon meets the airworthiness requirements of Part   of the Regulations.

Original Product-Type Certificate Number:

Make:

Model:

Description of Type Design Change:

Limitations and Conditions:

This certificate and the supporting data which is the basis for approval shall remain in affect until surrendered, suspended, revoked, or termination date is otherwise established by the administrator of the Federal Aviation Administration.

Date of application: Date reissued:

Date of issuance: Date amended:

By Direction of the Administrator

_____
(Signature)

_____
(Title)

Any alteration of this certificate is punishable by a fine not exceeding $1,000, or imprisonment not exceeding 3 years, or both.

FAA FORM 8110-2 (10-68)(Representation)

This certificate may be transferred in accordance with FAR 21.47.

Figure 4-2   FAA supplemental type certificate (sample).

product which often differs from the mass-produced units. This is then used to demonstrate the unit's capabilities. This is not the case in aviation. Each copy of the aircraft must be built to the type certificate standards.

A manufacturer usually gets one production certificate. Each subsequent aircraft manufactured by that company will be added to the original PC by the FAA. Figure 4-3 shows the first page of a typical production certificate. A production certificate may have a production limitation record (PLR), shown in Fig. 4-4, which lists all the TCs and supplemental TCs issued to that manufacturer as well as any limitations. The PC is effective for as long as the manufacturer complies with the requirements of the original issuance. For new technology, or for derivative or new aircraft, the FAA may conduct additional inspections of the manufacturer's facilities and processes if it deems that to be necessary. The FAA may cancel, suspend, supersede, or revoke the PC for just cause at any time.

Airworthiness certificate (FAA form 8100-2)

The third certificate, the airworthiness certificate (AC), is awarded by the FAA's MIDO to each aircraft produced by a manufacturer. This certificate confirms that the aircraft to which it is awarded has been inspected and found to conform with its type certificate and to be in airworthy condition. This airworthiness certificate is applied for by the manufacturer and awarded by FAA after the aircraft has passed all inspections and a successful flight test—when the aircraft "rolls out the door"—just prior to delivery to the customer. The airworthiness certificate contains the aircraft's unique serial (tail) number.

The standard AC remains in effect as long as the following conditions are met: (a) the aircraft meets its type design; (b) the aircraft is in a condition for safe operation; (c) all applicable airworthiness directives (ADs) have been incorporated; and (d) maintenance and alterations are performed in accordance with applicable FARs. The FAA can cancel, suspend, supersede, or revoke the AC if, in its opinion, any of the above have been violated.

Figure 4-5 shows a typical airworthiness certificate. FAA rules require that this certificate be prominently displayed in the aircraft. In passenger airliners, it is usually posted by the main entry door. Look for it the next time you board a commercial aircraft. If you do not see it, ask a crew member where it is.

Delivery Inspection

Prior to delivery to a customer, the aircraft usually undergoes an inspection by that customer to ensure that the vehicle has been built to the customer specifications and requirements. This includes basic design, options, and customer furnished equipment (if any), down to the shape, color, and positioning of the airline logo. This inspection by the operator may be cursory or detailed and often includes a test flight by their own flight and cabin crews. Any discrepancies found should be corrected by the manufacturer before delivery is taken.

The United States of America
Department of Transportation
Federal Aviation Administration

Production Certificate

Number   6CE

This certificate, issued to
ABC AIRCRAFT COMPANY
whose business address is
4954 AIRPORT DRIVE
KANSAS CITY, MISSOURI
and whose manufacturing facilities are located at
752 PRIMROSE LANE
St. LOUIS, MISSOURI
authorizes the production, at the facilities listed above, of reasonable duplicates
of airplanes
which are manufactured in conformity with authenticated data, including,
drawings, for which Type Certificates specified in the pertinent and currently
effective Production Limitation Record were issued. The facilities, methods, and
procedures of this manufacturer were demonstrated as being adequate for the
production of such duplicates on date of 5 May, 1999 .

Duration: *This certificate shall continue in effect indefinitely, provided,*
the manufacturer continuously complies with the requirements for original
issuance of certificate, or until the certificate is canceled, suspended, or revoked.

By direction of the Administrator

Date issued:
August 10, 1999

J.J. Jones . *J. J. Jones*
Manager, Manufacturing Inspection Office

This Certificate is not Transferable, AND ANY MAJOR CHANGE IN THE BASIC FACILITIES, OR IN THE
LOCATION THEREOF, SHALL BE IMMEDIATELY REPORTED TO THE APPROPRIATE REGIONAL OFFICE OF THE
FEDERAL AVIATION ADMINISTRATION

Figure 4-3   FAA production certificate (sample).

The United States of America
Department of Transportation

Federal Aviation Administration

Production Limitation Record

The holder of
Production Certificate No. 6CE
*may receive the benefits incidental to the
possession of such certificate with respect to*

**AIRCRAFT
(OR AIRCRAFT PROPELLERS,
AIRCRAFT ENGINES, AS APPLICABLE)**

*manufactured in accordance with the data forming the
basis for the following Type Certificate(s) No.*

Type Certificate	Model	Date Production Authorized
A 920CE	ABC 2047R	August 10, 1978
A 9CE	ABC 258D	August 10, 1978
STC 492CE	Drawing List HC-B2YK-6	August 10, 1978

(Note: Any number of columns may be used provided the material is neat and legible. Additional PLRs may be used when necessary. Additional PLRs shall be numbered "1 of 2," "2 of 2," as appropriate to the number of pages involved.)

LIMITATIONS:

   (if any)

August 10, 1999	**By Direction of the Administrator**
	J. J. Jones
Date of issuance	J. J. Jones
	Manager, Manufacturing Inspection District Office

FAA FORM 8120-3 (7-67)

Figure 4-4   FAA production limitation record (sample).

STANDARD AIRWORTHINESS CERTIFICATE

UNITED STATES OF AMERICA
DEPARTMENT OF TRANSPORTATION FEDERAL AVIATION ADMINISTRATION

1. NATIONALITY AND REGISTRATION MARKS	2. MANUFACTURER AND MODEL	3. AIRCRAFT SERIAL NUMBER	4. CATEGORY
N12345	**Boeing 747-400**	**197142**	**Transport**

5. AUTHORITY AND BASIS FOR ISSUE

This airworthiness certificate is issued pursuant to the Federal Aviation Act of 1958 and certifies that as of the date of issuance, the aircraft to which issued has been inspected and found to conform to the type certificate, therefor, to be in condition for safe operation, and has been shown to meet the requirements of the applicable comprehensive and detailed airworthiness code as provided by Annex 8 to the Convention on International Civil Aviation, except as noted herein:

EXEMPTION NO. 1013A FAR 25.471(b): Allows lateral displacement of C.G. from airplane centerline.

6. TERMS AND CONDITIONS

Unless sooner surrendered, suspended, revoked, or a termination date is otherwise established by the Administrator, this airworthiness certificate is effective as long as the maintenance, preventive maintenance, and alterations are performed in accordance with Parts 21, 43, and 91 of the Federal Aviation Regulations, as appropriate, and the aircraft is registered in the United States.

DATE OF ISSUANCE	FAA REPRESENTATIVE	DESIGNATION NUMBER
11/29/92	*John Q. Publican* **John Q. Publican**	**DMIR ANM 1234**

Any alteration, reproduction, or misuse of this certificate may be punishable by a fine not exceeding $1,000, or imprisonment not exceeding 3 years, or both. THIS CERTIFICATE MUST BE DISPLAYED IN THE AIRCRAFT IN ACCORDANCE WITH APPLICABLE FEDERAL AVIATION REGULATIONS.

FAA Form 8100-2

Figure 4-5 FAA airworthiness certificate (sample).

Commercial carriers will often fly the aircraft "around the flag pole" at the builder's delivery center to perform this check out. Some may take the aircraft on a "shakedown flight" from the delivery center to the carrier's home base. Once the customer accepts the aircraft from the manufacturer, that customer is fully responsible for maintaining the unit in airworthy condition in accordance with its own maintenance program and regulatory authority rules.

Operator Certification

An operator cannot just buy an aircraft and enter into commercial service simply by getting a license and petitioning the market for customers. In aviation, for a prospective operator to enter the business, he or she must meet the requirements of both the Department of Commerce, with respect to the business aspects of airline operation, and the Department of Transportation, primarily the FAA, with respect to the technical aspects. In short, the prospective operator must provide the necessary information to ensure that he or she understands the business of commercial aviation; understands the operational and maintenance aspects of commercial aviation operation; and has the necessary people, facilities, and processes in place that are needed to carry out that business.

The secretary of the Department of Transportation (DOT) issues a "certificate of public convenience and necessity" authorizing the recipient to enter into commercial transportation. The secretary determines that the applicant is "fit, willing, and able" to perform the service.[*]

An operating certificate (OC) is then issued by the Flight Standards District Office (FSDO) of the FAA to the airline company. This certificate authorizes the carrier to operate scheduled air transportation service under the Federal Aviation Act of 1958 as amended. The operating certificate is not transferable to another operator.

The OC remains in effect indefinitely unless it is surrendered by the operator, superseded by another certificate, or revoked by the FAA. The OC states, in part, that the airline is authorized to operate in accordance with the Federal Aviation Act and its rules and regulations, and "the terms, conditions, and limitations contained in the operations specification."

In part, the Federal Aviation Act of 1958 requires the airline to develop an operations specifications document (Ops Specs for short) for each type aircraft to be operated in commercial service. The Ops Specs is a parent document; that is, in addition to specific information listed in the document, it may identify other airline documents, by reference, that fully describes certain airline operations that apply to the model. The Ops Specs outlines such operational activities as (a) the type of service to be offered, passenger, cargo, or combination; (b) the type of aircraft to be used; (c) the routes to be flown; (d) the airports and alternate airports that will be used; (e) the navigation and communications facilities to

---

[*] Kane, Robert M. *Air Transportation*, 13th ed. Kendall/Hunt, Dubuque, IA, 1999.

be utilized on each route; (*f*) the way points used in navigation; and (*g*) the take-off and approach routes, including any alternate approach routes, at each airport.

The Ops Specs must also identify the maintenance and inspection program applicable to the model including the scheduled and unscheduled maintenance programs; the inspection program; and the engine and equipment repair program (off-aircraft maintenance). Other aspects of maintenance such as the quality assurance and reliability programs will also be defined. If any portion of the aircraft or systems maintenance is performed by a third party, that agreement must also be addressed in the Ops Specs.

The operations specifications document is a detailed document and is put together by the principal maintenance inspector (PMI) assigned to the airline by FAA and by the airline personnel. It is tailored to each operation.

Certification of Personnel

The minimum requirements for airline operations under part 121 state that the airline must have sufficient full time qualified management and technical personnel to ensure a high degree of safety in its operations. The basic personnel requirements are a director of safety; a director of operations, a director of maintenance, a chief pilot, and a chief inspector. This is only a suggestion, however. The FAA goes on to say that they may approve any other number of positions and any other titles as long as the operator can show that it can perform the operation safely.[*] The people in such positions must have the necessary "training, experience, and expertise"[†] for conducting the business of aviation and must be knowledgeable of the regulatory and airline policies and procedures as they relate to their specific jobs. The airline identifies the "duties, responsibilities, and authority"[‡] of these management personnel.

Maintenance personnel must be properly trained and licensed in basic aviation maintenance skills as well as on the specific equipment they are assigned to maintain. The FAA states that those personnel eligible for a mechanic certificate must be at least 18 years of age and be able to read, write, speak, and understand English.[§] Although it is not specifically stated in the FARs, it is reasonable to require that those who supervise or manage these maintenance personnel be equally versed in the English language. Flight crews must also be properly trained and licensed for the type of equipment being flown.

Aviation Industry Interaction

The aviation industry is made up of aircraft manufacturers; manufacturers and vendors of parts, systems, and accessories for the aircraft; airline operators;

[*] Federal Aviation Regulation 119.65 (a), (b).

[†] Federal Aviation Regulation 119.65 (c), (d).

[‡] Federal Aviation Regulation 119.65 (e).

[§] Federal Aviation Regulation 65.71 (a).

third party maintenance organizations; trade associations, such as the Air Transport Association of America (ATA) and the International Air Transport Association (IATA); flight crew, cabin crew, and mechanics unions; and regulatory authorities. This integrated group of professionals is constantly working together to develop and improve aviation both technically and operationally. This is somewhat unique compared to other transport modes. This continuous quality improvement (CQI) concept was in effect in the commercial aviation field long before it became standard procedure in other areas.

Chapter

5

Documentation for Maintenance

Types of Documentation

It has been said that the paper documentation required for the maintenance of a modern jet airliner would weigh about the same as the airplane itself. Whether this is true or not, there is a considerable amount of documentation required to understand, identify, and implement the maintenance requirements. There is additional paper required to report the activity. In recent years, for some of the effort, the computer has replaced the paper but the requirements for data and reporting are still there.

We will not be talking about maintenance forms here, for they are many and they vary widely from one airline to another. This chapter will focus on that documentation that identifies the aircraft, its systems, and the work to be done on them. Some of the documents will be customized for the operator by the supplier, others will be generic. Most of these documents have standard revision cycles and changes are distributed on a regular basis by the airframe manufacturer. Some documents are designated as "controlled" and some are "noncontrolled" documents. A controlled document is one that is used for operation and/or maintenance of the aircraft in accordance with FAA regulations. Such documents have limited distribution within the airline and require regular revision cycles with a list of revisions and active and rescinded page numbers recorded in the document. The operator is required to use only up-to-date documents.

This bounty of written information includes the documentation provided by the airframe manufacturer and the manufacturers of systems and equipment installed on the aircraft; the documentation provided by the regulatory authorities; and the documentation written by the airline itself for the purpose of detailing the individual maintenance processes. We will discuss each of these in turn.

Manufacturer's Documentation

Table 5-1 lists the documentation provided to an operator by the airframe manufacturer for the maintenance of an aircraft. The form and content of the documents sometimes varies from one manufacturer to another. The table identifies, basically, the type of information which airframe manufacturers make available to their customers. Some of the documents can be customized for the operator to include only the operator's configuration and equipment. These are called "customized documents" by the manufacturer and are marked in the table with an asterisk (*). Some documents, such as the illustrated parts catalog (IPC) may be customized at customer request (usually for a price). These are identified with the dagger symbol (†). The other documents are generic for all models or all airplanes of a specific model. This, too, may vary among airframe manufacturers. Each document and the type of information supplied is discussed below.

Airplane maintenance manual (AMM)

The AMM contains all the basic information on the operation and maintenance of the aircraft and its on-board equipment. It starts with an explanation of how each system and subsystem works (description and operation) and describes various basic maintenance and servicing actions such as removal and installation of LRUs; the various tests performed on the systems and equipment such as functional tests, operational tests, adjustments, the replenishing of various

TABLE 5-1   Manufacturer's Documentation

Title	Abbreviation
Airplane maintenance manual*	AMM
Component maintenance manual	CMM
Vendor manuals	VM
Fault isolation manual*	FIM
Fault reporting manual	FRM
Illustrated parts catalog†	IPC
Storage and recovery document‡	SRD
Structural repair manual	SRM
Maintenance planning data document	MPD
Schematic diagram manual*	SDM
Wiring diagram manual*	WDM
Master minimum equipment list	MMEL
Dispatch deviation guide	DDG
Configuration deviation list	CDL
Task cards*	TC
Service bulletins	SBs
Service letters	SLs
Maintenance tips	

*Customized to contain customer configuration.
†Customized on request.
‡Information may be included in AMM for recent model aircraft.

fluids, and other servicing tasks. Details of these components of the AMM are discussed later in the section ATA document standards.

Component and vendor manuals

Any components built by the airframe manufacturer will be accompanied by a component maintenance manual written by the manufacturer. Vendor manuals (VM) are written by the manufacturer of components and systems built by outside vendors who supply electronics, computer, and other systems to be installed on the aircraft. These components are either supplied to the airframe manufacturer for equipment offered as options (seller-furnished equipment, SFE) or purchased by the operator and installed by the airframe manufacturer before delivery or installed by the operator after delivery (buyer-furnished equipment, BFE). These component and vendor manuals are for components that have to be removed from the aircraft for maintenance in the shop. The manuals provide the same type of information on these components that the AMM provides for the aircraft and its systems.

Fault isolation manual (FIM)

The FIM contains a set of fault isolation trees for the purpose of pinpointing and fixing numerous problems related to the various systems and components on the aircraft. These flow diagrams are designed to locate many of the problems within the various systems but may not be inclusive. The FIM is sometimes used in conjunction with the fault reporting manual (FRM) discussed below.

Fault reporting manual (FRM)

The FRM was designed to be used by the flight crew to provide maintenance with advanced warning of malfunctions and an indication of where to begin looking (in the FIM and AMM) for a solution prior to the aircraft's arrival. The flight crew identifies their problem using a series of questions and diagrams of system operation and instrument indication. This leads to an eight-digit code which is reported to the ground station. Maintenance people then use this code to determine the appropriate solution. This can either be a "quick fix" listed in the FRM cross-reference list or it can direct them to a specific fault tree in the FIM for more detailed troubleshooting.

Illustrated parts catalog (IPC)

The IPC is produced by the airframe manufacturer and includes lists and location diagrams of all parts used on the aircraft model. This includes all parts for all systems and is usually not customized to the airline's configuration. It does, however, indicate applicability of parts (i.e., engine, airframe model, etc.) and also provides information on part numbers, vendors, interchangeability of parts, and whether or not the part can be used with or without certain service bulletin incorporation.

Storage and recovery document (SRD)

The SRD contains information needed to address maintenance and servicing of aircraft that are to be out of service and stored for long periods of time. This includes the procedures for draining certain fluids, moving the aircraft so that tires will not go flat, and protecting components from the weather. In the older model aircraft, this document was produced separately by the airframe manufacturer. For more recently manufactured aircraft, this information is included in the applicable AMM (ATA, Chapter 10).

Structural repair manual (SRM)

The SRM is a manual that provides the operator with information needed to effect certain repairs of the aircraft structure. These repairs are simple and are approved by the FAA for operator completion. Other structural repairs must be done by the airframe manufacturer or some other FAA designated repair facility.

Maintenance planning data document (MPD)

This document (called the on aircraft maintenance program by McDonnell-Douglas) provides the airline operator with a list of maintenance and servicing tasks to be performed on the aircraft. It contains all items of the MRB report along with other information. Some of these tasks are identified as certification maintenance requirements (CMRs) and are required by the FAA in order to maintain certification of the aircraft. All other tasks, which were developed by the MSG process (see Chap. 2) are included along with other tasks recommended by the manufacturer. The tasks are divided into various groupings for older aircraft models—daily, transit, letter checks, hourly limits, and cycle limits—and are used for planning purposes by the airline. Later models do not group the tasks by letter checks, only by hours, cycles, and calendar time.

Schematic diagram manual (SDM)

This document contains schematic diagrams of electrical, electronic, and hydraulic systems on the aircraft as well as logic diagrams for applicable systems. The diagrams in the AMM and other manuals are usually simplified diagrams to aid in describing the system and assist in troubleshooting. The schematic manual, however, contains the detailed information and identifies wiring harnesses, connectors, and interfacing equipment.

Wiring diagram manual (WDM)

The wiring diagram manual provides information on the wiring runs for all systems and components having such elements. The wiring diagram shows the complete run of wiring, including cable bundle numbers and routing, plug and connector numbers and locations, bulkheads, and other structural elements through which the wiring is routed.

Master minimum equipment list (MMEL)

The MMEL is identified by the airframe manufacturer and approved by the FAA to identify the equipment which may be degraded or inoperative at dispatch of the aircraft. These are systems that the flight crew, under certain circumstances, may agree to accept at dispatch in a degraded or inoperative condition, provided the system is fixed within the prescribed time limit set by the MMEL. The manufacturer's flight engineering group develops the MMEL. The MMEL contains information on all equipment available on the aircraft model to which it applies. It is the airline's responsibility to develop their own manual tailored to their specific equipment. This document, called the MEL, is discussed later, in the section Airline Generated Documentation.

Dispatch deviation guide (DDG)

Some of the MMEL items that are inoperative or degraded at dispatch require maintenance action prior to the deferral and dispatch. This may be the need to pull and placard certain circuit breakers, disconnect power, tie up loose cables for removed equipment, and various other actions to secure the aircraft and the system against inadvertent operation. The instructions necessary for these actions are provided in the DDG. This guide is written by the manufacturer's AMM staff and is coordinated with the MMEL.

Configuration deviation list (CDL)

The CDL is similar to the DDG but involves configuration of the aircraft rather than aircraft systems and equipment. The CDL provides information on panels, fairings, and similar variations in configuration that can be nonstandard at dispatch as long as it does not affect the safety of flight.

Task cards (TC)

Certain tasks in the AMM for removal/installation, testing, servicing, and similar maintenance items are extracted from the AMM and produced on separate cards or sheets so that the mechanic can perform the action without carrying the entire maintenance manual to the aircraft. (The Boeing 767 manual is about 20,000 pages.) These task cards can be used "as is" or they can be modified by the operator for reasons discussed in the section Airline Generated Documentation.

Service bulletins, service letters, and maintenance tips

Whenever the airframe manufacturer or the engine manufacturer have modifications or suggestions for improving maintenance and/or servicing, they will issue appropriate paperwork to the affected airlines. A service bulletin (SB) is usually a modification of a system that will provide improved safety or operation of a system and includes a detailed description of the work and parts required. An SB is usually optional and the airline makes the choice (see Chap. 8), except in certain cases involving an FAA airworthiness directive (AD) discussed below in Regulatory Documentation. A service letter (SL) usually provides information to improve maintenance actions without equipment modification. The maintenance tip is a suggestion for maintenance personnel to assist in their work or improve conditions.

Regulatory Documentation

The FAA issues numerous documents related to maintenance of aircraft and their systems. Table 5-2 lists the more significant of these documents.

Federal aviation regulations (FARs)

In the United States, Federal laws are collected into a document known as the code of federal regulations or CFRs. Those laws related to commercial aviation are under title 14 of this code, aeronautics and space, parts 1 through 200. The regulations relating to certification and operation of large, commercial aircraft—part 121—would be noted as 14 CFR 121. We usually refer to this as FAR part 121. In this book we will use the FAR terminology and form since it is so common in the industry. These FARs address all aspects of the aviation field including private, commercial, and experimental aircraft; airports; navigational aids; air traffic control; training of pilots, controllers, mechanics, etc.; and other related activities.

Advisory circulars (ACs)

An advisory circular is a document issued by the FAA to provide assistance to operators on meeting the requirements of various FARs. These ACs are not binding as law but are merely suggestions as to how to comply with other requirements. An AC often states that it is "a means, but not the only means" of complying with a regulation. The FAA allows some leeway in how its regulations are met in order to achieve the desired results without trying to micromanage the operator.

Airworthiness directives (ADs)

The airworthiness directives are substantial regulations issued by the FAA to correct an unsafe condition that exists in a product (aircraft, aircraft engine,

TABLE 5-2   Regulatory Documents

Title	Abbreviation
Federal aviation regulations	FARs
Advisory circulars	ACs
Airworthiness directives	ADs
Notice of proposed rule making	NPRM

propeller, or appliance) and a condition that is likely to exist or develop in other, similar products.[*] An AD, whose incorporation is mandatory, may be issued initially by the FAA when an unsafe condition is noted or it may result from FAA action after the airframe manufacturer has issued a service bulletin (SB) relative to some noted problem. Incorporation of an SB is optional but, if it is made into an AD by the FAA, incorporation becomes a mandatory requirement.

Aircraft owners or operators are required to maintain the aircraft in compliance with all ADs.[†] Typically, an AD will include (*a*) a description of the unsafe condition; (*b*) the product to which the AD applies; (*c*) the corrective action required; (*d*) date of compliance; (*e*) where to get additional information; and (*f*) information on alternative methods of compliance if applicable.

Notice of proposed rule making (NPRM)

Whenever the FAA intends to change or amend any FAR, it will issue an NPRM in advance in order for the industry to have ample time to study and comment on the proposed rule change. These documents allow the operators to participate in the change and assist the FAA in developing workable and acceptable rules.

Airline Generated Documentation

Table 5-3 lists the documentation that the airline will generate in order to carry out its maintenance activities. Again, these documents may vary in name and actual content from one operator to another, but the information identified here must be addressed by airline documentation.

---

[*] Federal Aviation Regulations 39.3 and 39.5.

[†] Federal Aviation Regulation 91.403.

TABLE 5-3   Airline Generated Documentation

Title	Abbreviation
Operations specifications	Ops Specs
Technical policies and procedures manual	TPPM
Inspection manual	IM
Reliability program manual	RPM
Minimum equipment list	MEL
Task cards[*]	TC
Engineering orders[†]	EOs

[*]May be manufacturer written, customer written, or a combination.

[†]Issued for maintenance not identified in standard maintenance plan.

Operations specifications

The operations specifications (Ops Specs) document has been discussed in Chap. 4 as an FAA requirement for airline certification. It is written by the airline in accordance with strict FAA requirements and usually with the help of an FAA representative. The Ops Specs is required for each aircraft type flown by the airline. It is a parent document, which refers to numerous other documents to avoid duplication and details the airline's maintenance, inspection, and operations programs.

Technical policies and procedures manual

The TPPM[*] is the primary document for the airline's M&E operation and, with other documents supplied by the airframe manufacturer, serves as the FAA requirement for a maintenance manual per AC 120-16D. It is usually written by engineering, to ensure technical accuracy, from inputs supplied by management of the various M&E organizations. It should define exactly how all M&E functions and activities will be carried out. The TPPM is a detailed document and may be several volumes. Personnel in all units of M&E must be trained on the TPPM, especially those parts that relate directly to that unit's operation, so that the operation will go smoothly. Details of the TPPM contents are discussed later in this chapter.

Inspection manual

The inspection manual (IM) may be a separate document distributed primarily to QC personnel, or it can be a chapter in the TPPM (usual approach).[†] Contents of the IM relate to all inspection activities within M&E: (a) mechanic inspection tasks from the MPD/OAMP or the MRB report; (b) QC inspector's tasks; (c) special inspections (hard landings, bird strikes, etc.); (d) the airline's required inspection item (RII) program; and (e) the paperwork, forms, and reports required to carry out these functions. Some IMs may indicate details on the calibration of tools and test equipment, since these are QC functions, or these may be in a separate chapter of the TPPM.

Quality assurance (QA) manual

The QA manual could be a special manual for QA auditors only, it could be part of the inspection manual, or it could be a separate chapter in the TPPM as desired. The QA manual defines the duties and responsibilities of the QA organization and defines the processes and procedures used in the annual quality assurance audits

---

[*] The TPPM is sometimes called the policies and procedures manual (PPM), general maintenance manual (GMM), or the maintenance organization exposition (MOE).

[†] The reason this and other documents listed below are often separate from the TPPM is so that changes can be made when necessary without issuing a change for the entire TPPM. In these cases, the TPPM merely identifies the detailed document as a reference, thus making the TPPM complete.

conducted on the M&E units, suppliers, and outside contractors. Forms used and reports are also covered along with the procedures for follow-up and enforcement of QA write-ups.

Reliability program manual

An airline's reliability program, under FAA rules, must be approved by the regulatory authority, so it is usually published as a separate document. This document defines the reliability program in detail (see Chap. 19) so that the FAA can evaluate and approve all its elements at one time.

Minimum equipment list (MEL)

The MMEL provided by the airframe manufacturer includes all equipment and aircraft configurations available for the model to which it applies. With up to three manufacturers supplying engines (customer option) on some models, and the multitude of auxiliary systems available as buyer options, this manual includes much information that is not applicable to some operators. To eliminate confusion, the operator is required to customize the MMEL for his or her particular airframe/engine configuration. This copy is referred to as the airline's minimum equipment list or MEL. The operator must carry copies of this MEL in each aircraft for flight crew reference. The applicable items in the DDG and the CDL should also be included with the MEL.

Task cards

The task cards produced by the airframe manufacturer are usually for one action only. These procedures may call for the mechanic to open panels, set certain circuit breakers "in" or "out," turn other equipment "on" or "off," etc., prior to the work and to reverse these processes at the completion. Much of the work done at an airline during an aircraft check, however, involves the combination of several tasks to be performed by the same mechanic or crew within the same area or on the same equipment. To avoid unnecessary duplication of certain actions, and the unnecessary opening and closing of the same panels, etc., most airlines write their own task cards to spell out exactly what to do, using the manufacturer's cards as a guide. This eliminates the duplicated or wasted efforts. Some airlines find it sufficient, or perhaps more expedient, to provide mechanics with all the manufacturer's task cards for a given work project and allow him or her to avoid the duplications during the work activity. Often there will be an airline task card attached to this package of cards with special instructions for working the group of cards. Whichever approach is used, the engineering section is responsible for creating these cards to ensure technical accuracy.

Engineering orders (EO)

Any maintenance work not covered in the standard maintenance plan developed by engineering from the MRB report or Ops Specs data must be made official by the issuance of an EO. This is official paper work, issued by engineering and approved by QA, and is usually implemented through the production planning and control (PP&C) organization. In some airlines, the document may be called simply a "Work Order." Details of the EO are discussed in Chap. 8.

ATA Document Standards

Line maintenance people for most airlines, especially those doing contract maintenance for other carriers, will have the opportunity to work on a wide variety of aircraft during the course of their shift or work week. Since aircraft manufacturers are independent, they each (in the past) had their own way of doing things. This meant that their maintenance manuals were as different as their aircraft (or perhaps more so). To reduce confusion on the line, the Air Transport Association of America (ATA) stepped in and standardized the overall format of the maintenance manuals so that all manufacturers' documents would be more compatible. Each system or system type was assigned a chapter number. For example, hydraulic systems are in ATA Chapter 29 for all manufacturers. Radio

TABLE 5-4   ATA Standard Chapter Numbers

ATA	Subject	ATA	Subject
5	Time limits, maintenance checks	37	Vacuum
6	Dimensions and access panels	38	Water/waste
7	Lifting and shoring	45	Central maintenance system
8	Leveling and weighing	49	Airborne auxiliary power
9	Towing and taxiing	51	Standard practices and
10	Parking, mooring, storage, and		structures—general
	return to service	52	Doors
11	Placards and markings	53	Fuselage
12	Servicing	54	Nacelles/pylons
20	Standard practices—airframe	55	Stabilizers
21	Air conditioning	56	Windows
22	Auto flight	57	Wings
23	Communications	70	Standard practices—engines
24	Electrical power	71	Power plant (package)
25	Equipment/furnishings	72	Engine (internals)
26	Fire protection	73	Engine fuel control
27	Flight controls	74	Ignition
28	Fuel	75	Air
29	Hydraulic power	76	Engine controls
30	Ice and rain protection	77	Engine indicating
31	Indicating/recording system	78	Exhaust
32	Landing gear	79	Oil
33	Lights	80	Starting
34	Navigation	82	Water injection
35	Oxygen		
36	Pneumatic	91	Charts (miscellaneous)

SOURCE: From Air Transport Association (ATA); iSpec 2200. Reprinted with permission.

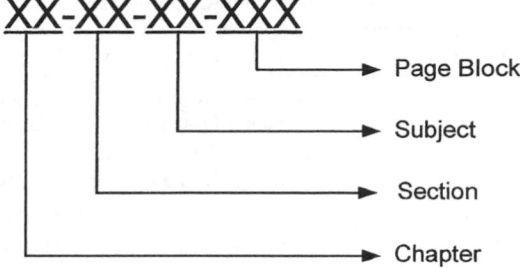

Example:

52	Doors
52-11	Passenger Doors
52-11-02	Passenger Door Handle
52-11-02-401	R/I Procedure for Pax Door Handles

Figure 5-1 ATA format for maintenance manuals. (*Source: Air Transport Association of America (ATA); iSpec 2200. Reprinted with permission.*)

equipment is ATA Chapter 23 and so forth. Table 5-4 shows the chapter assignments.[*]

The ATA codes are further broken down into three sets of two-digit numbers followed by a three-digit number. This identifies the chapter, subject, section, and page block, respectively. Figure 5-1 shows the structure of the number. The first two digits (ATA Chapter) are the same for all manufacturers and are used throughout the maintenance manual system. The second (section) and third (subject) groups may vary from one manufacturer to another and from one model aircraft to another of the same manufacturer because of differences in the structure of the systems to which they apply.

The last group of digits (page block) is the same for all maintenance manuals. The page blocks refer to specific types of information contained in the airplane maintenance manual. For example, pages 001–099 are reserved for the description and operation of the chapter's systems. Pages 301–399 contain removal/installation procedures for the various components within the system or chapter (see Table 5-5 for a list of page blocks).

The advantage of this system is quite apparent to a line maintenance mechanic who works on a Boeing 757, then a Douglas MD-80, an Airbus A320, and then a Lockheed L-1011 in the course of a single day. No matter what the aircraft, if a write-up concerns a hydraulic system component, the mechanic knows that any maintenance manual information he or she needs will be found in ATA Chapter 29. If there is a discrepancy in the aircraft landing lights, help will be found in ATA Chapter 33 regardless of the aircraft. The following paragraphs discuss each page block of the AMM.

---

[*] Air Transport Association of America, ATA; iSpec 2200.

TABLE 5-5   Airplane Maintenance Manual Page Block Assignments

Block	Title	Description
001–099	Description and operation	Identifies the various operational modes of the system and describes how the system and its essential components work
101–199	Fault isolation	Fault trees used to perform fault isolation for various problems occurring within a system
201–299	Maintenance practices	An R/I procedure followed by a BITE test, a functional test, an adjustment procedure, or servicing instructions
301–399	Servicing	All servicing tasks: check, fill and replacement of oil, hydraulic fluid, water, fuel, etc.
401–499	Removal/installation	Detailed, step-by-step instructions on how to remove a line replaceable unit (LRU) and replace it with a like item
501–599	Adjustment/test	Procedures for making adjustments or performing tests to the systems whenever a component or system has just been replaced or after normal maintenance when such adjustments or tests are required
601–699	Inspection/check	Zonal inspections of aircraft
701–799	Cleaning/painting	Procedures for cleaning and painting of the aircraft
801–899	Approved repairs	Repairs to structure and aircraft skin approved by FAA for airline maintenance organization incorporation

SOURCE: Air Transport Association (ATA); iSpec 2200. Reprinted with permission.

Description and operation (pages 001–099)

The description and operation (D&O) page block tells what the system does, identifies the various operational modes, and describes in detail how the system and its essential components work. Mechanics and technicians often consider this part of the manual too detailed for their needs on the line and in the hangar, but the information provided here is necessary for serious troubleshooting. Maintenance personnel need to understand the theory of operation and the operating modes of the system in order to effectively determine what is wrong with a deviant system. The engineering staff needs this data in order to identify changes or improvements in the maintenance program as well as to assist maintenance in solving the more difficult problems.

Fault isolation (pages 101–199)

This page block includes fault trees used to perform fault isolation for various problems occurring in a system. Contrary to popular belief, these fault trees will not find all the problems which might develop within a given system throughout its lifetime. These procedures were written to find specific faults based on flight deck effects; i.e., lights, messages, warnings, etc. that are available to the flight crew during the flight. These troubleshooting procedures were not necessarily written to find every fault that could ever exist in a given system. Many procedures have been modified over the years, due to faults occurring in the field that were not conceived of when the manual was originally produced. But for complex equipment it is often quite difficult to write a step-by-step procedure or fault tree to find every possible fault the system could experience. If that were possible, the resulting fault tree would be too long and the procedure too complicated to be useful. (That is why we have included an appendix on troubleshooting techniques in this book.)

Maintenance practices (pages 201–299)

The maintenance practices block is used whenever two or more actions must take place to complete the maintenance activity. Usually a 200 page block procedure will be an R/I procedure followed by a BITE test, a functional test, or an adjustment procedure or even servicing instructions. If the auxiliary procedure is simple, it is included in the 200 page block along with the main procedure for convenience. If it is too long or too complex to repeat, the main procedure will reference the appropriate auxiliary procedure by chapter, section, subject, and page block.

Servicing (pages 301–399)

The 300 page block includes all servicing tasks: fill and replacement of oil, hydraulic fluid, water, and fuel; lubrication actions; and the handling of waste, etc. These procedures include step-by-step instructions as well as a list of required materials and their specifications where applicable.

Removal/installation (pages 401–499)

Removal/installation (R/I) procedures are written to provide detailed, step-by-step instructions on how to remove a line replaceable unit (LRU) and replace it with another like item. With simple installations, such instructions are not necessary to a mechanic or technician who is worth the title. But other equipments require a specific sequence of steps to prepare for removal and then to remove the components. In many instances, certain conditions must be met prior to removal such as pulling circuit breakers, disconnecting power, hydraulics, etc. These conditions are addressed in the procedure. The installation requires an equally meticulous series of steps. In some cases, additional procedures, such as ground tests, must be performed after installation. These are identified and referenced in the R/I procedure but are covered in the other page blocks.

Adjustment/test (pages 501–599)

The 500 page block contains procedures for making adjustments to the systems whenever a component or system has just been replaced (by an R/I) or during normal maintenance (scheduled or unscheduled) when such adjustments are required. This page block also contains the operational test procedures used to check out a system without test equipment. This is a relatively simple check to verify proper operation using only what is available in the aircraft. The 500 page block also contains the functional test procedures which are used for more detailed system checkout. These tests usually require additional test equipment and/or tools and may involve the measurement of certain parameters of the system.

Inspection/check (pages 601–699)

The 600 page block covers the zonal inspection activities. Each identified zone of the aircraft is inspected for various discrepancies.

Cleaning/painting (pages 701–799)

The 700 page block contains procedures for washing, cleaning, and painting the aircraft. It includes specifications for materials to be used.

Approved repairs (pages 801–899)

The 800 page block identifies repairs to structure and aircraft skin that have been approved by the FAA for operator accomplishment.

A Closer Look at the TPPM

The purpose of the TPPM is to identify all aspects of the maintenance and engineering organization. This would include (a) the identification of key personnel, descriptions of their job functions and their qualifications; (b) a definition of the operator's philosophy and goals; (c) layout drawings and maps of the maintenance facilities including shops, hangars, ramps, and other significant buildings and areas related to maintenance activities; (d) specific items in accordance with FAA regulations as well as items, at the discretion of the operator, which describe, in detail, how specific maintenance, inspection, and testing activities will be accomplished.

The TPPM is a controlled document and therefore should be issued in limited distribution only to those units within the airline that need the information. Some airlines provide full copies to all M&E units while others provide only those portions of the manual that apply to that organization. For example, information relating to specific flight line operations need not be available to hangar or shop personnel. Likewise, information concerning engineering responsibilities need not be distributed to the flight line or to outstations unless the information is directly related to those activities. The entire document, however, should be available in the central maintenance library (see Chap. 10).

The TPPM should contain a list of effective pages (LEP), the revision number or letter identification, and revision dates. A list of terms and acronyms used in

TABLE 5-6   Technical Policies and Procedures Manual (TPPM)

General
    Manual control system
    Organization of the TPPM
    Administration
        Organizational chart
        Key personnel
    Operations specifications
    Maps of key locations
    Listing of approved manuals
    Glossary of terms
Quality assurance and control
    Organization
    Liaison with regulatory authority
    Inspection methods and standards
    Airworthiness release
    Required inspection items (RIIs)
    Special inspections
    Parts and material inspections
    Calibration of tools and test equipment
    Continuing analysis and surveillance program
    Quality assurance audits
    Reliability analysis program
    Short-term time escalation program
    Test, ferry and special flights
    M&E record keeping system
Engineering
    Organization
    Airworthiness directives
    Service bulletins/service letters
    Engineering orders
    Fleet campaigns
    Minimum equipment lists (MEL)
        Development
    Configuration deviation lists (CDL)
        Development
    Maintenance program development
    Weight and balance control program
    Publications/technical library[*]
Production planning and control
    Organization
    Airplane routing[†]
    Production forecasting
    Task card development
    Maintenance planning
    Manpower planning
    Material planning
    Facility planning
    Production scheduling and control
        On-airplane
    Production scheduling and control
        Shops
    Performance measurement
    Budgeting and cost control

(Continued)

TABLE 5-6   Technical Policies and Procedures Manual (TPPM) (*Continued*)

Airplane maintenance
  Organization
  Approved maintenance arrangements
  Contractual arrangements for maintenance
  Airplane logbooks
  Airworthiness release
  Nonroutine maintenance
  MEL, DDG, and CDL
    Usage
  Deferred maintenance
    Authorizations
    Procedures
  Repeat mechanical discrepancy system
  Parts robbing
  Maintenance control center (MCC)
  Standard maintenance practices
Shop repair and overhaul
  Organization
  Contractual arrangements
  Maintenance release
  Component repair/overhaul control
  Standard shop practices
  Shop records
Tools, equipment and facilities
  Organization
  Motorized equipment
  Fuel storage and handling
  Facility maintenance
  Tools and test equipment
Maintenance and inspector training
  Organization
  General policy
  Personnel licensing
  Basic training requirements
  Training categories and courses
  Initial training
  Recurrent training
  Contractor training
  Training records
Materiel management
  Organization
  Stock numbering system[‡]
  Serviceability of aircraft parts
  Shipping and receiving
  Rotable/repairable parts tracking system
  Storage of parts and supplies
  Satellite stores
  Purchasing
  Inventory control
  Parts pooling/parts borrowing
  Parts loan control
  Warranty claims control
  Outside repair of rotable/repairable items

(Continued)

TABLE 5-6   Technical Policies and Procedures
Manual (TPPM) (*Continued*)

Safety program
  Organization
  Policy
  Safety procedures
  Accident/incident reporting
Maintenance forms
  Policy
  Responsibility
  Preparation and distribution instructions
  Samples and usage instructions

---

* If library is part of engineering. Otherwise it would
be listed separately.
  † This may be a joint effort with flight operations.
  ‡ Some airlines assign their own stock numbers for all
parts and supplies in order to standardize the number
format.

the document should also be included. The manual must make provisions for distribution to maintenance and ground personnel. If the manual is in more than one volume, the contents of all volumes should be listed in each volume.

These guidelines were based on the information contained in the FAA Airworthiness Inspector's Handbook, which defines the minimum contents of the manual. Consideration should be given, however, to inclusion of additional internal policies and procedures that provide complete instructions to maintenance and engineering personnel on the performance of their duties and responsibilities.

This manual is an administrative tool used to control and direct the activities of maintenance personnel. It should define all aspects of the maintenance operation. The manual should include detailed instructions or specific references for accomplishing inspection and maintenance functions. It should also include forms, instructions, and references for recurring, nonroutine requirements such as engine changes, and abnormal occurrences such as hard landings, lightning strikes, bird strikes, etc.

The manual should enable the operator's maintenance and servicing personnel to assure airworthiness of the airplanes. The complexity of the manual varies with the complexity of the operation. The manual must describe areas of application for manufacturer's technical manuals. Since this manual is the bible of the unit, it should also be used extensively in the maintenance training activities of the airline. Table 5-6 shows the outline of the TPPM for a typical midsized airline. Other airlines may be organized differently and thus would have a different manual layout.

Chapter

6

Requirements for a Maintenance Program

Objectives of a Maintenance Program

In Chap. 3 we talked about the five objectives of a maintenance program. In this chapter, we will begin to outline a maintenance program that will address these five objectives. There are certain regulatory requirements that each airline must adhere to and there are certain additional activities that an airline needs to have in place to carry out these maintenance program requirements. We will discuss the FAA requirements first; discussion of the additional requirements will follow. These will then be combined, in Chap. 7, into a workable maintenance and engineering organizational chart.

Aviation Maintenance Program Outlined (AC 120-16D)

The Federal Aviation Administration (FAA) requires each commercial airline to have an operations specifications (Ops Specs) to identify how they will operate as a public transport. The Ops Specs must contain a description of the airline's operations and maintenance programs. On the maintenance side, general requirements are identified in FAA Advisory Circular, AC 120-16D, entitled "Air Carrier Maintenance Programs." The essential elements or programs it identifies are listed below. We will discuss each in detail later.

1. Airworthiness responsibility
2. Maintenance manual
3. Maintenance organization
4. Maintenance schedule
5. Maintenance record keeping system

6. Accomplishment and approval of maintenance and alterations

7. Contract maintenance

8. Continuing analysis and surveillance

9. Personnel training

10. Hazardous materials and dangerous goods

Federal Aviation Regulation (FAR) 121.373 requires each operator to have a "continuing analysis and surveillance" effort in place to ensure that the airline's maintenance and inspection programs are effective. In the past, this requirement, by all reasonable interpretation, established an internal audit program, usually called quality assurance or QA for short, and a reliability program, which is similar to the condition monitoring process discussed earlier in Chap. 2. Together, they constituted a continuing analysis and surveillance program (CASP) to satisfy the FAR requirement. The recent revision to AC 120-16D, however, incorporated a continuing analysis and surveillance system (CASS) as part of the basic maintenance program. Other important FAA requirements are related to record keeping and are outlined in FAR 121.380 (maintenance recording requirements), FAR 121.380a (transfer of maintenance records), FAR 43.2 (records of overhaul and rebuilding), and FARs 43.9 and 43.11 (content, form, and disposition of records …). These have also been incorporated into the revised advisory circular. These 10 items from AC 120-16D will be discussed individually below.

Airworthiness responsibility

Under FAA regulation, an air carrier or operator is responsible for all maintenance and alteration on that airline's aircraft. The airline must have operations specifications for each model aircraft flown and must adhere to the FAA approved maintenance program the Ops Specs identifies. This program can be modified if the airline can show through data and records that a change is warranted. The FAA must approve the changes. The airline must also follow its own policies and procedures as well as those of the regulatory authority in carrying out the maintenance and inspection program. In certain instances, an airline may have another carrier or third party maintenance organization do some or even all of its maintenance under contract. However, the operating airline is responsible for ensuring that any work done for them by these outside contractors is done to the airline's own maintenance schedule, standards, and requirements, and in accordance with the airline's regulatory authority requirements regardless of those requirements governing the contracted organization. In short, the airline (i.e., the operating certificate holder) is responsible for maintaining its own aircraft in an airworthy condition regardless of who actually performs the work.

Maintenance manual

The airframe manufacturers and the vendors of various equipments installed on the aircraft, or used in maintenance efforts, provide maintenance manuals on the equipment. The maintenance manual required by AC 120-16D, however, is really a system of manuals and an expansion of the manufacturers' manuals. While these manuals identify specifics of the equipment to be maintained and offer detailed procedures for such accomplishment, the maintenance manual discussed here involves other areas of concern such as the management and administration of maintenance; the procedures for work performance; and procedures for inspection, audit, and analysis of the maintenance effort. In short, this maintenance manual is the primary, all-inclusive, expression of how maintenance will be conducted and how the program will be monitored and improved. We discussed manuals in Chap. 5. The TPPM (GMM or MOE) written by the airline should meet this requirement.

Maintenance organization

The FAA states that an airline must have a maintenance organization "that is able to perform, supervise, manage, and amend your program, manage and guide your maintenance personnel, and provide the direction necessary to achieve your maintenance program objectives."[*] The essential elements of this organization as discussed in the AC are summarized as follows:

1. An organization that is capable of doing the required work
2. A director of maintenance (or similar title) responsible for the overall activity—must be an FAA licensed mechanic
3. For part 121 operators, a chief inspector (or similar title)
4. An organization or process to develop and upgrade a maintenance manual that describes all aspects of the maintenance program
5. Oversight and supervision activities to ensure that maintenance is accomplished in accordance with the airline's manual
6. An inspection function for required inspection items (RIIs)[†] that is separate from other routine inspection and maintenance functions
7. Competent personnel and adequate facilities available for the maintenance to be performed
8. Procedures to ensure that each aircraft released for service after maintenance is airworthy and properly maintained
9. Efforts to ensure that the maintenance program remains effective as conditions change
10. Management personnel who are qualified and have sufficient experience and expertise to effectively organize, manage, and control the maintenance program

---

[*] AC 120-16D, paragraph 400, page 7.

[†] These required inspection items are defined in a later section of this chapter: "Accomplishment and Approval of Maintenance and Alterations."

Maintenance schedule

The FAA requires an airline to have a maintenance schedule which identifies what maintenance will be done, how it will be done, and when or how often it will be done. This maintenance program comes from data supplied by the airframe manufacturer in various documents delivered with the aircraft. The basic maintenance program of scheduled tasks is developed by the airframe manufacturer and identified in the Maintenance Review Board (MRB) report, an FAA approved document. Additional information and tasks related to maintenance may also be provided in other manufacturer documents such as the maintenance planning data (MPD) document (Airbus and Boeing) and the on aircraft maintenance program (OAMP, McDonnell-Douglas). Tasks are divided into groups based on the suggested interval—flight hours, flight cycles, or calendar time. Checks may be done daily, every flight, or they may be identified for specific periods of operation such as every 200 flight hours, every 3000 flight hours, every 100 cycles, etc.

These manufacturer's documents, however, are only guidelines. Each operator is different: airplane configuration, operational and environmental conditions, even the quality and extent of operations and maintenance differ from one airline to another. For these reasons, the maintenance program requirements and the schedule at which tasks must be performed will vary from airline to airline. Therefore, it is an airline responsibility to adjust the initial MRB schedules to comply with the individual airline needs. These work packages and their adjustment were discussed in Chap. 2.

Maintenance record keeping

Commercial aircraft are delivered to the operator with a U.S. standard airworthiness certificate showing that the aircraft was built to the type certificate standards and is in an airworthy condition at delivery. It is the airline's responsibility to keep that aircraft in an airworthy condition. To ensure that this is accomplished, the FAA requires the operator to keep accurate records of maintenance and alteration activities. Failure to make and keep accurate records can subject the operator to substantial fines or imprisonment. Two types of records are required: summary information and airworthiness status information.

Other records, in various forms, must also be kept to conduct a successful program. One of these is the maintenance logbook. This book is maintained in the aircraft and includes flight information relative to each leg of the flight and includes flight times, fuel and oil uplift, crew data, etc. It also provides a place for the flight crews to identify any maintenance related problems they encounter during flight. The form includes space for the mechanic to identify corrective action taken and to release the aircraft for service.

Other records must be maintained in the form of reports for certain types of maintenance problems. These would include the mechanical reliability report (MRR), the mechanical interruption summary (MIS), and reports of major alterations and major repairs.

Accomplishment and approval of maintenance and alterations

The airline maintenance program must include instructions for conducting maintenance on the aircraft as well as specific maintenance for engines, propellers, parts, and appliances. This will include scheduled and unscheduled maintenance and will involve both on-aircraft and off-aircraft (i.e., in shop) maintenance activities. The airline must also address aging aircraft and corrosion problems. Certain components and systems on the aircraft must be designated as RIIs. These are defined by the FAA as "those items which could result in unsafe operation of the aircraft if maintenance is not performed correctly or if improper parts are used."[*] These RIIs appear in all elements of the operator's maintenance program and receive the same consideration regardless of when and where they occur. The FAA does not specify what should be on the operator's RII list but it does require the airline to identify its own, unique items and identify, in writing, the names of mechanics qualified and authorized to perform those inspections.

Contract maintenance

Although an airline has responsibility for all maintenance on its aircraft, it does not always perform all of the maintenance itself. Very often, some or all of the maintenance may be performed under contract with some other airline or some third party maintenance organization. Contract maintenance could be done on a regular basis, as is most often the case, but there are instances when the aircraft is at some base where the airline has no maintenance activities of its own and has no permanent contractor. In these cases, the airline will enter a temporary contract agreement with a repair organization for this one-time activity.

The maintenance program of the airline must include procedures for making these arrangements to ensure that the work is done properly, according to the operator's own program and procedures, and that the maintenance is properly signed off and recorded. This means that your airline is responsible for providing these outside maintenance units with proper training on your procedures and for assuring that these outside maintenance people have the personnel, skills, and facilities to accommodate the work required. For long-term contracts, the airline would perform an audit of the prospective organization. On short-notice actions this verification of capability may be more difficult to achieve but it must be accomplished.

Continuing analysis and surveillance system

In Federal Aviation Regulation 121.373, Continuing Analysis and Surveillance, the FAA indicates the need for monitoring the airline activities to ensure that the

---

[*] Federal Aviation Regulation 121.371.

maintenance and inspection programs outlined in the Ops Specs are effective. Many operators interpreted this to mean the establishment of a quality assurance program and a reliability program. The FAA has recently produced Advisory Circular 120-79 to address the subject. It is summarized in AC 120-16D as part of the suggested airline maintenance program.

Essentially, CASS is a program to detect and correct deficiencies in maintenance program effectiveness and performance. It looks at possible problem areas, determines the corrective action required, and tracks the activity afterward to determine the effectiveness of the correction. This is accomplished through data collection and analysis and through monitoring of all activities in the maintenance function of the airline, its suppliers, and its contractors.

Personnel training

The FARs are rather brief in stating the training requirements for aviation maintenance. Part 121 of the FARs states, in part, that airlines should "have a training program to ensure that each person (including inspection personnel) who determines the adequacy of work done is fully informed about procedures and techniques and new equipment in use and is competent to perform his duties."[*] This is admittedly brief and general, but AC 120-16D provides more light on the subject. Part 147 of the FARs discusses the requirements for Aviation Maintenance Technician Schools in which one can earn an airframe and power plant (A&P) license, but this license does not fully qualify one to work on the aircraft of a particular airline. It merely means that the person having the license is qualified for the job of maintenance mechanic. In order to be qualified to do the airline's work, a mechanic must receive orientation training on the airline, its policies, its procedures, and its equipment configuration. He or she must be trained at the airline to work on the carrier's specific equipment or the airline must validate the mechanic's skills using the appropriate testing methods. This airline training requirement also implies that any changes to equipment, procedures, regulations, etc. must be addressed by the airline training organization to ensure that the mechanic is up to date in all aspects of the job.

Hazardous materials and dangerous goods

Some aircraft components and some of the consumable goods used on aircraft are considered hazardous or dangerous to humans, to the environment, or to aircraft components. This includes caustic substances dangerous to eyes, skin, and lungs as well as to metal, fabric, and other materials. Radioactive substances, flammable materials, even light and sound can have adverse effects on people and things. Safety issues including heavy and unstable loads, set up and use of scaffolding and stands, working in high places, even fatigue and other human conditions fall into this area of concern. The airline is required to identify these and similar items and

---

[*] Federal Aviation Regulation 121.375.

conditions and to provide airline employees with the necessary equipment and training on protection, storage, handling, etc. of these situations. The regulations which cover these hazardous and dangerous items are those of the Department of Labor's (DOL) Occupational Safety and Health Administration (OSHA).

Summary of FAA Requirements

The objectives of an airline maintenance program were stated in Chap. 3 as follows:

1. To ensure the realization of the inherent safety and reliability levels of the equipment
2. To restore safety and reliability to their inherent levels when deterioration has occurred
3. To obtain the information necessary for adjustment and optimization of the maintenance program when these inherent levels are not met
4. To obtain the information necessary for design improvement of those items whose inherent reliability proves inadequate
5. To accomplish these objectives at a minimum total cost, including the cost of maintenance and the cost of residual failures

To meet these objectives, an organization must perform certain scheduled maintenance tasks (objective 1) to maintain the equipment capability. Unscheduled tasks are done whenever the equipment has deteriorated below acceptable standards or has completely failed (objective 2). Objective 3 requires that the operator have some sort of data collection program in place to monitor reliability levels of the equipment and investigate problem areas to effect maintenance program improvement when applicable. Objective 3 can also address deficiencies in the management and administrative aspects of the maintenance program. Objective 4 requires that the operator initiate action to effect redesign if reliability standards cannot be met and this deficiency is not attributed to the operator's maintenance program. Objective 5 indicates that the maintenance program should be a direct asset to the organization in that the operator does not waste time, money, or manpower performing unnecessary or ineffective maintenance but performs only that maintenance which is necessary and performs it in a timely manner.

To accomplish the above objectives, the programs and processes required by the FAA as described above must be put into place. An effective maintenance program is developed for the equipment and systems based on the best knowledge and ability of the manufacturers' and the industry's representatives. This maintenance program is then employed by the operator in an effort to maintain the equipment in top operating condition. Through the collection and analysis of performance data during actual operation, and through monitoring the effects of maintenance within the operator's own environment, the maintenance program can be tweaked and adjusted, as necessary, to optimize the entire set of processes. This results in an optimized maintenance program that not only satisfies objective 5 but also allows the operator to meet objectives 1, 2, 3, and 4.

Additional Maintenance Program Requirements

In addition to the maintenance program elements described in the previous sections, there are a number of other activities needed to carry out an effective maintenance and engineering program. The basic structure of the organization discussed here may not be adequate for all maintenance organizations. Some organizations may need to expand or combine activities, out of necessity, as dictated by the size of the specific operation. The important thing to remember is that, regardless of the organizational arrangement, these functions are necessary to carry out an effective and efficient maintenance and engineering program. These additional activities and their implementing organizations are generally called engineering, materiel, planning, maintenance control, training, computing, and publications. We will discuss each of these in subsequent sections.

Engineering

The primary purpose of the engineering section of the maintenance organization is to establish the initial maintenance program from the manufacturer's maintenance manual and other documents and to continually upgrade the program over time. Engineering will also provide technical assistance in troubleshooting equipment problems; develop workable maintenance processes and procedures when required; review manufacturer's service bulletins and other maintenance tips, changes or suggestions; and provide engineering expertise to the company or its hired consultants in designing and modifying the maintenance facilities (i.e., hangars, shop, ramps, etc.).

Materiel

The function of the materiel section is to provide the maintenance organization with parts and supplies necessary to carry out the maintenance activities. This would include the purchase and warehousing of the necessary spare parts, supplies, and tools for the maintenance activities; issuance of parts to mechanics as needed; handling of warranty claims on parts, equipment and tools; and passing repairable components to the appropriate workshop or vendor for repair.

Planning

The planning section is responsible for planning all of the scheduled maintenance activities including the manpower, facilities, and supplies needed for these activities. Planning also collects data on the time, manpower and facilities actually used in the performance of the maintenance to accurately readjust these requirements for use with subsequent maintenance planning activities.

Maintenance control center

The maintenance control center (MCC), sometimes called the maintenance operations control center (MOCC), is the nerve center of the line maintenance organization; it is responsible for keeping track of all vehicles in operation. Vehicle location, maintenance and servicing needs, and other requirements are monitored by MCC during the operational phase of activity via telephone, radio, facsimile, and any other available means of communication. The MCC keeps track of the vehicles and coordinates with key units throughout the operations, maintenance, and engineering activities so that maintenance, when needed, can be coordinated and expedited to minimize delays and down time. The MCC locates and dispatches the necessary personnel within the company who can provide whatever maintenance, troubleshooting, or parts assistance that is needed to support the operational phase of the activity. Maintenance crews at outstations can coordinate maintenance actions, the borrowing or buying of parts locally, and even the contracting of temporary third party maintenance personnel through the MCC at the home base.

Training

Maintenance training is an ongoing process. Although maintenance mechanics receive initial training through certain formal training schools to qualify for the job, continual training is required to keep them current, to refresh their skills when necessary, and to develop new skills and learn new processes and procedures as these are developed. The training section can be part of the maintenance and engineering organization or it can be part of the airline's overall training program that also covers the nonmaintenance training requirements. If a centralized training unit is used, maintenance and engineering should appoint one of their own managers as the training focal point so that M&E needs are met. The training section keeps records of the training received by all personnel. The training section is also responsible for training engineers, supervisors, managers, and inspectors, as required, so that they can carry out their respective duties within the company's maintenance and engineering operation.

Computing

The computing section provides the equipment, the software, the training, and the support for all computing activities within the maintenance and engineering organization. In some airlines this section may be included within the company's computer organization. It is recommended, however, that computer support for maintenance have dedicated personnel and that they work closely with, if not directly for, the maintenance and engineering organization. Various computer programs are available for maintenance activities, which include modules for data collection on malfunctions; for parts tracking and control; for collecting and manipulating reliability data, such as failure rates, removal rates, and time limitations for parts, etc.; for tracking of serial numbered parts; and for numerous other traceable information needs for monitoring maintenance activities. All maintenance activities need to be coordinated and tracked and the maintenance computer systems should be under the control of people who know maintenance as well as computers.

Publications

The publication section (or technical library) of the maintenance and engineering organization is responsible for keeping all technical publications up to date, whether they are on paper, microfilm, or electronic media. The publications section receives all publications and is responsible for distributing the documents or revisions (partial or complete) to the appropriate work centers. The work center personnel are responsible for inserting changes and disposing of obsolete pages, but technical publications personnel should spot check the work centers to see that this is being done. During the yearly audit of each unit, QA will check to see that all documents are up to date (see Chap. 17).

Summary

This section has discussed, in general terms, the kinds of activities and organizations needed to support the maintenance function. A suggested M&E organizational structure will be discussed in detail in the next chapter, "The Maintenance and Engineering Organization."

The Maintenance and Engineering Organization

Organization of Maintenance and Engineering

The structure for an effective maintenance and engineering organization will vary with the size and type of organization. It may also vary with the management philosophy of the company. But one thing must be kept in mind: the organizational structure must allow the company to meet its goals and objectives and each unit within the company must be endowed with sufficient personnel and authority to carry out those objectives and meet those goals.

The following structure was determined, from experience and observation, to be the most efficient and effective one for a mid-sized commercial airline. For application to large or small airlines, this structure will have to be modified; but all of the functions identified here will have to exist separately or in combination to accomplish all of the functions and activities identified in Chap. 6 as essential for effective operation.

Organizational Structure

The basic organizational structure for our mid-sized airline is shown in Fig. 7-1. There are three basic concepts underlying the structure we have defined. Two of these come from traditional management thinking. These are the concepts of span of control and the grouping of similar functions. The third concept is somewhat unique to aviation: the separation of production activities (maintenance and engineering) from the oversight functions of inspection, control, and monitoring (quality assurance, quality control, reliability and safety).

Span of control

The span of control concept may be considered passé to some, but it is still a useful concept. This concept states that a supervisor or manager can effectively

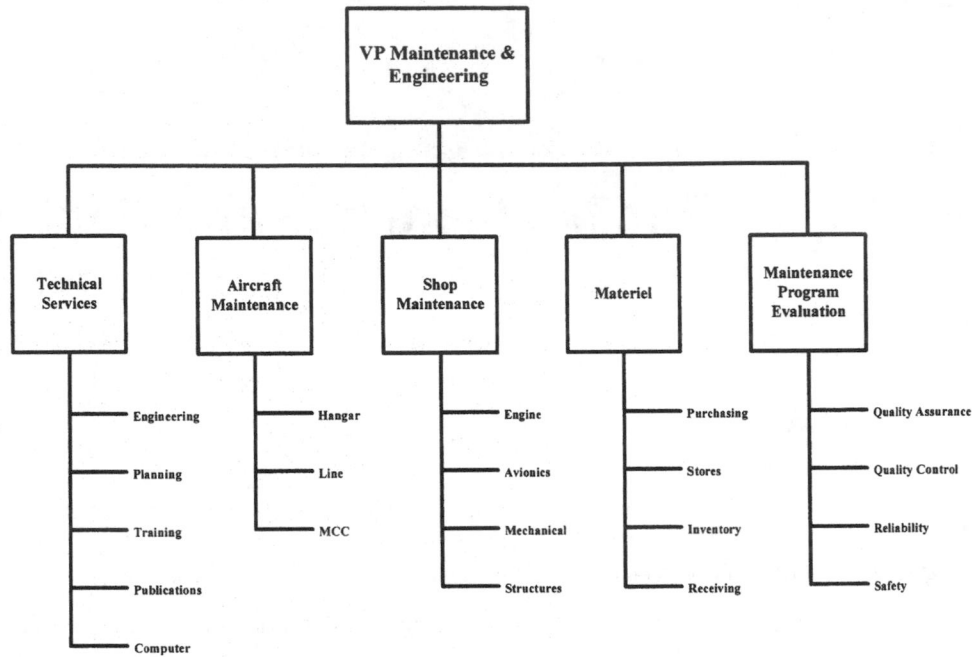

Figure 7-1 Typical maintenance and engineering organization.

supervise or control three to seven people. Any less than three would be ineffective use of time and manpower and any more than seven would spread the boss too thin. In the organizational structure shown in Fig. 7-1, we have adhered to this concept. The VP of maintenance and engineering supervises five directors. Each director has the necessary number of managers under him or her to carry out the prescribed functions of the directorate. We find that by limiting the number of people that a manager has to supervise, the organization's work is divided into pieces that are more easily managed without losing the people-to-people contact that is so necessary for a happy and efficient work force.

At the lower levels of the organization, where the actual maintenance work is performed by workers with many different skills, the span of control is usually not so narrow. A line or hangar maintenance supervisor may have as many as 20 or 30 of these specialists to supervise. But at the upper management levels, we like to keep the span of control at the lower number. This is not to say that a wider span cannot be utilized, however. All management activities must be organized to work with the available resources and within the current management's capabilities and philosophy.

Grouping of similar functions

The second basic concept of the organizational philosophy we are using is the grouping of similar functions under one director, manager, or supervisor. What this comes down to is that all maintenance activities (line, hangar, and MCC) are under one manager. All maintenance overhaul shop functions (electrical and electronics shops, mechanical shops, hydraulics, etc.) are likewise grouped. All inspection activities—whether it is inspecting the company's workers, inspecting parts, or inspecting the suppliers of parts—are grouped into one organization (maintenance program evaluation functions). Those handling the purchase of supplies, those performing engineering work, and those doing the planning are also grouped accordingly so that the managers and directors can maintain proper surveillance and control over areas in which they have expertise.

Separation of production and oversight functions

A third concept that is applied here may be unique to the maintenance organization. Under the FAA philosophy, an airline receives certification to operate as a commercial air transport company and that authorization is, for all practical purposes, permanent. Some foreign airlines must be recertified by their regulatory authority annually. Under the FAA rules, for an airline to be certificated, it must have certain programs in place including a self-monitoring function to ensure that it is performing according to the rules (its own rules as well as those of the regulatory authority). This alleviates the FAA from having to recertify each airline every year. This requirement for self-monitoring is usually in the form of quality assurance (QA), quality control (QC), reliability, and safety programs. Combined, these functions constitute the core of the CASS requirement mentioned in Chap. 6.[*] It is recommended, and generally practiced, that these self-monitoring functions operate separately from the maintenance and engineering functions they are monitoring to prevent any conflict of interest problems. This separation is built into the organizational structure shown in Fig. 7-1 and is discussed below by selective grouping.

The M&E Organizational Chart

Figure 7-1 is the basic organizational chart for the maintenance and engineering organization of our "typical" mid-sized airline. We will briefly discuss each layer and each function. The structure starts with the VP level and continues downward with designations Director, Manager, and Supervisor as appropriate. Your organization may have other titles that their operatives prefer to use but the structure should be similar to Fig. 7-1.

General Groupings

Vice president of maintenance and engineering

The head of the entire maintenance and engineering function within the airline should be at a relatively high level of the airline's structure. He or she should be directly under the head of the airline or under the head of the company's

---

[*] See also FAA AC 120-79, Continuing Analysis and Surveillance System (CASS).

operational activity (President, Chief Operating Officer, or whatever title is used). The VP of M&E position should also be at the same level as the head of flight operations (VP Flight Ops or whatever he or she is called). Flight operations and maintenance are considered to be two sides of the same coin; they complement each other and carry equal weight.

The flight operations department is responsible for conducting the air transportation operations; i.e., the flying. Maintenance and engineering, on the other hand, is responsible for delivering airworthy vehicles to the operations department to meet the flight schedule. The M&E department is responsible for conducting all scheduled maintenance, modification, etc. on the vehicles within the specified limits of the maintenance schedule and still meet the operations department's flight schedule. Without maintenance, flight operations would be quite limited in their activities; without flight operations, maintenance wouldn't have much purpose in maintaining the equipment. They need each other and the airline needs both.

Directors of major functions

The five major functions shown in Fig. 7-1 are, in the order addressed in this book, technical services (which includes engineering, planning, training, technical publications, and computing); aircraft maintenance (flight line, hangar, outstations, and the maintenance control center); overhaul shops (for off-aircraft maintenance, repair, and overhaul); materiel services (responsible for ordering and maintaining supplies, handling warranties, and moving repairable and consumable parts through the system); and maintenance program evaluation (the monitoring activity for the organization, its workers and its suppliers). As you can see, there is more here than just maintenance and engineering. We will discuss each of these in more detail later.

Managers and supervisors

Within each directorate, there are several managers. Each of these managers has a specialized area of responsibility within the overall scope of the directorate's function. Specific activities within each manager's area of responsibility require staffs of specialists with supervision by knowledgeable people. In some large organizations, the supervisor may need additional separation of activities or duties and appoint "leads" or "straw bosses" to decrease his span of control to a workable size. However, for most operators, the span of control can be much wider at this level.

Manager Level Functions—Technical Services Directorate

The technical services directorate contains numerous activities and services that support the maintenance and inspection functions. In the typical setup of Fig. 7-1, we have identified various activities for each directorate. Each activity is under the direction of a manager. There may be further echelons of management such as supervisors and leads as necessary.

Engineering

The manager of engineering is responsible for all engineering functions within the M&E organization. This includes (a) the development of the initial maintenance program (tasks, intervals, schedules, blocking, etc.); (b) the evaluation of service bulletins (SBs) and service letters (SLs) for possible inclusion into the airline's equipment; (c) oversight of the incorporation of those SBs and SLs that they deem beneficial; (d) overseeing the incorporation of airworthiness directives (ADs), the modifications that are required by the regulatory authority; (e) the evaluation of maintenance problems determined by the reliability program and for problems (if any) resulting from the maintenance checks performed by maintenance; and (f) for establishing the policies and procedures for the M&E organization. The engineering department employs a cadre of engineering specialists, usually enough to cover, with a high degree of expertise, any and all specialties within the aircraft's technical realm: power plant, structures, avionics, aircraft performance, and systems (hydraulic, pneumatic, etc.). These positions are at the supervisor level with several engineers in each group with their own specialties, if required.

The engineering department is also involved in the planning of facilities (new hangars, maintenance shops, storage facilities, buildings, etc.) for the airline, which are to be used by the M&E organization. Although engineering usually will not actually do the design and engineering work, they will work with the engineering consulting firm or contractor that has responsibility for the project to ensure that the final result meets the airline's requirements.

Production planning and control

The manager of production planning and control (PP&C) is responsible for maintenance scheduling and planning. This function must plan and schedule the manpower, parts, facilities, tools, and any special assistance required for all maintenance or modification activities. Included in the functions of PP&C are the following: (a) all planning activities related to maintenance and engineering (short, medium, and long term); (b) the establishment of standards for man-hours, materiel, facilities, tools, and equipment; (c) work scheduling; (d) control of hangars; (e) on-airplane maintenance; and (f) monitoring of work progress in the support shops.

Training

The manager of technical training is responsible for curriculum, course development, administration, and training records for all formal training attended by the M&E unit's employees. The organization coordinates any training required outside the unit (vendor training) and coordinates with line and hangar maintenance personnel for the development of on-the-job training and remedial or one-time training activities. The training section must be able to establish new and special training courses to meet the needs of the airline. These course requirements are often the result of problem investigation by reliability, incorporation of new equipment or modifications, or the addition of aircraft types to the fleet.

Technical publications

The manager of technical publications is responsible for all technical publications used by the M&E organization. Technical publications (or Tech Pubs) keeps a current list of all documents received from manufacturers and vendors as well as those produced in-house by the airline. Also on record are the number of copies, in paper, microfilm, or compact disc (CD) format, that each work center should receive. The Tech Pubs organization is also responsible for ensuring that appropriate documents and revisions are distributed to these various work centers. Work centers are responsible for keeping their own documents current, but Tech Pubs usually conducts periodic checks to see that this is being done. Tech Pubs is also responsible for maintaining the main technical library and any satellite libraries within the airline's system, including those at outstations.

Computing services

The manager of computing services is responsible for the definition of the M&E organization's computing requirements: (*a*) selection of software and hardware to be used, with usage information and requirements inputs from the individual units; (*b*) training of maintenance, inspection, and management personnel on computer usage; and (*c*) provide continuing support to the using organizations.

Manager Level Functions—Aircraft Maintenance Directorate

The aircraft maintenance directorate has responsibility for the major aircraft maintenance activities: maintenance on the flight line and maintenance performed in the hangar. Three managers report to the director of airplane maintenance: one for each of these activities and one for MCC. For airlines with different model aircraft or with two or more maintenance bases, the number of aircraft maintenance managers may be increased as necessary for the scope of the operation.

Hangar maintenance

The manager of hangar maintenance is responsible for compliance with the airline's policies and procedures relative to all work done on the aircraft in the hangar, such as modifications, engine changes, "C" checks (and higher), corrosion control, painting, etc. The hangar maintenance function also includes various support shops (welding, seat and interior fabric, composites, etc.) as well as ground support equipment.

Line maintenance

The manager of line maintenance is responsible for compliance with the airline's policies and procedures relative to the work done on the aircraft on the flight line while the aircraft is in service. Such activities include turnaround maintenance and servicing, daily checks, short interval checks (less than "A" check interval), and "A" checks. Sometimes, simple modifications can be done by line maintenance in order to avoid unnecessary use of the hangar. Line maintenance may also be utilized to perform line maintenance activities for other airlines under contract.

Maintenance control center

The function known as the maintenance control center (MCC) keeps track of all aircraft in flight and at outstations. All maintenance needs of these vehicles are coordinated through the MCC. The MCC also coordinates downtime and schedule changes with the flight department. Some airlines might have a supervisor of line stations to coordinate outstation activities but he or she is often part of the home base MCC operation.

Manager Level Functions—Overhaul Shops Directorate

The overhaul shops directorate consists of those maintenance shops that perform maintenance on items removed from the aircraft. These shops include engine shop(s), electrical shop, electronics (or avionics) shop, and various mechanical shops. These may be separate shops or some may be combined for convenience, depending on the operation. Some of these shops may also perform contract work for other airlines.

Engine shops

The manager of the engine overhaul shops is responsible for all maintenance and repair done on the organization's engines and *auxiliary power units* (APUs). If more than one type engine is used, there may be a separate engine shop for each type performing the work, but these would usually be under one senior manager with a supervisor for each engine type. The engine build up activities would generally come under the engine shop manager.

Electrical and electronics (avionics) shops

The manager of electrical/electronics shops is responsible for all off-aircraft maintenance of electrical and electronics components and systems. There are a variety of components and systems in this field with wide variations in the equipment and in the skills needed to address them. There may be several shops (radio, navigation, communications, computers, electric motor–driven components, etc.) with separate supervisors. Shops are combined at times, however, to optimize manpower and space and to reduce test equipment inventories.

Mechanical component shops

The manager of mechanical component shops has responsibilities similar to those of the manager of avionics shops. The only difference, of course, is that these shops would address mechanical components: actuators, hydraulic systems and components, aircraft surfaces (flaps, slats, spoilers), fuel systems, oxygen, pneumatics, etc.

Structures

The structures shop is responsible for maintenance and repair of all aircraft structural components. This includes composite material as well as sheet metal and other structural elements.

Manager Level Functions—Materiel Directorate

The materiel directorate is responsible for the handling of all parts and supplies for the M&E organization: (*a*) purchasing; (*b*) stocking and distribution (stores); (*c*) inventory control; and (*d*) shipping and receiving of parts and supplies used by the M&E organization. This includes not only the parts and supplies used in the maintenance, servicing, and engineering of the aircraft but also the supplies used for the administration and management of M&E (i.e., office supplies, uniforms, etc.).

Purchasing

The manager of purchasing is responsible for buying parts and supplies and tracking these orders through the system. This begins with the initial issue of parts when a new aircraft is added to the fleet and a continual replenishment of those parts based on usage. The purchasing unit is also responsible for handling warranty claims and contract repairs.

Stores

The manager of stores takes responsibility for the storage, handling, and distribution of parts and supplies used by the maintenance personnel in line, hangar, and shop maintenance activities. Stores areas, or parts issue points, are placed near the various work centers to allow mechanics quick access to parts and supplies and minimize time spent in obtaining those parts and supplies.

Inventory control

The manager of inventory control is responsible for ensuring that the parts and supplies on hand are sufficient for the normal, expected usage rate without tying up excessive funds in nonmoving items and without running out of stock too soon or too often for commonly used items.

Shipping and receiving

Manager of shipping and receiving is responsible for packing, waybill preparation, insurance, customs, etc. for outgoing materials as well as customs clearance, unpacking, receiving inspection, tagging, etc. for incoming materials. This includes all parts being shipped into and out of the airline.

Manager Level Functions—Maintenance Program Evaluation Directorate

The maintenance program evaluation (MPE) directorate is an organization tasked with the job of monitoring the maintenance and engineering organization. The MPE unit will be responsible for the CASS activities. The unit's functions include quality assurance, quality control, reliability, and safety.

Quality assurance

The manager of quality assurance is responsible for assuring that all units of M&E adhere to the company policies and procedures as well as FAA requirements. The manager of QA sets the standards for the M&E operation and the QA auditors ensure compliance to those standards through yearly audits. Quality assurance is also responsible for auditing outside suppliers and contractors for compliance with the company's, as well as the regulatory authority's, rules and regulations.

Quality control

The manager of quality control is responsible for conducting routine inspections of maintenance and repair work, certifying maintenance and inspection personnel, and management of the required inspection items (RIIs) program. This latter function involves the identification of RIIs and the certification of specific personnel authorized to inspect and accept the work. The QC organization is also responsible for the calibration of maintenance tools and test equipment and performs or oversees the nondestructive testing and inspection (NDT/NDI) procedures.

Reliability

The manager of reliability is responsible for conducting the organization's reliability program and ensuring that any problem areas are promptly addressed. This responsibility includes data collection and analysis, identification of possible problem areas (which are then addressed in detail by engineering), and publication of the monthly reliability report.

Safety

The safety organization is responsible for developing, implementing, and administering the safety and health related activities within the M&E organization. The safety manager is also responsible for handling all reports and claims regarding M&E safety issues.

Summary of Management Levels

For all of the above organizations, the respective directors, managers, and supervisors are also responsible for the more mundane activities that are necessary for any smoothly operating organization. Those activities include the handling of administrative and personnel duties; the budgeting and planning requirements for their respective organizations (both long and short term); and the necessary interactions with some or all of the other organizations, including those outside of M&E, through a plethora of meetings, letters, documents, memos, bull sessions, and chance meetings in the hallway.

Organizational Structure and the TPPM

The maintenance management organization discussed here is based on the conventional approach where we group similar activities and provide a structure within which all can work. It does not, however, subscribe to the "chain of command" philosophy where each hierarchical level has dominion over the lower tiers. Rather it is meant to encourage the more modern approach of "cross-functional coordination."

This maintenance management structure can be classified as a system (see Appendix A). Figure 7-1 represents a collection of structural and procedural components designed to work together efficiently to perform the maintenance management function. As with any system, the theoretical design may differ from what we actually attain when the plan is implemented in the real world. That is, even management systems contain some entropy, some imperfection, both natural and man-made (see Chap. 1). Thus, it is important to understand management's dual role in setting up and running an organization. Management personnel have responsibilities similar to those of systems engineers: they must develop a workable system and they must strive for a minimum amount of imperfection (entropy) within that system. Management personnel also have responsibilities similar to those of system mechanics: their ongoing job is to combat the natural increase in entropy that their system will doubtless undergo over time.

A manager is, in a sense, similar to an airplane pilot. In the early days of flying, it was a vigorous effort for the pilot to fly the aircraft. In the Wright brothers' first airplane, the operator laid down on his stomach and operated the necessary controls with his hands, his feet, and his hips. Later models allowed him to sit upright. For many years the pilot flew the airplane by "feel." The vehicle was an extension of the pilot; the pilot and his or her aircraft were one unit; they flew together. In today's modern aircraft, the pilot has the benefit of various communication, navigation, and control systems which almost fly the airplane unassisted. The pilot, then, after setting everything in working order, "sits back and manages the flight."

This does not mean that a pilot is less important and no longer needs rigorous training. On the contrary, he or she must know as much as—actually more than—any earlier pilot had to know. When something goes wrong, or does not go as well as planned, the pilot must know instantly what to do, how to take over from the automatic systems and fly the aircraft manually.

Management of maintenance and other technical activities is a similar effort for those managers confined to the ground. In our typical management structure, we have identified the organization necessary to carry out the M&E functions. Management has determined this structure based on the rules stated earlier: grouping of like functions, span of control, and separation of monitors from those monitored. Further establishment of M&E operations is spelled out in detail in the airline technical policies and procedures manual (TPPM) which is meticulously developed by management at the beginning of operations to insure smooth, cross-functional coordination among the M&E units, and to accomplish the stated goals and objectives of the organization. Once the M&E organization and its operational policies and procedures are established, and the hired personnel are trained on those elements, management can then "sit back and manage the operation."

Variations from the Typical Organization

It is obvious that the above organizational structure will not work for all commercial operators. Airlines smaller than our "typical" airline as well as those which are much larger, cannot operate efficiently under this arrangement. There must be variations in this structure to accommodate the differences. These are discussed next.

Small airlines

Small airlines may not be able to organize in the manner shown in Fig. 7-1 for two reasons. One, they may not have enough personnel to populate all these positions; and two, they may not have enough work to keep all, or some, of these people occupied full time. It is obvious, then, that the management structure must be altered. This can be done in several ways.

First of all, we must state that all of the activities identified in the typical organizational chart must be addressed to some extent in any airline. All of these functions are necessary for efficient operation. However, due to size and personnel limitations, one individual or one section may be asked to perform more than one of these functions. For example, quality control functions might be assigned to personnel in the work centers. Mechanics and technicians would perform the inspection work as needed as an adjunct to their regular duties in maintenance. These QC inspectors, however, would be supervised by the quality assurance organization (or QA person) regarding these inspection activities. More on this will be discussed in Chaps. 17 and 18.

Reliability and engineering functions might be combined in smaller airlines, also. Technical publications, training, and even production planning and control may be combined with engineering to utilize available skills. Line and hangar maintenance functions may be separate organizations but utilize many of the same personnel. The two functions may also be combined as one maintenance organization.

Large airlines

For the larger airlines, especially those with more than one maintenance base, an organizational structure different from Fig. 7-1 will be necessary. There will be a need for a hangar maintenance organization at each base where that type of work is done. For instance, MNO airlines may do hangar maintenance on their 757s at Denver and on their A310s at Kansas City. One hangar maintenance organization at the home base (wherever that may be) would not be adequate. It may be necessary, though, to have a corporate level manager responsible for both units as well as separate managers at each site. The same would apply to production planning and control and certain support shops for this arrangement. Again, it should be emphasized that it is important to have the functions listed in our typical structure addressed no matter how the airline is actually organized.

Full versus Partial organizational structure

It should also be pointed out that this "typical" airline structure is not adequate for an airline that does not, itself, perform all the functions listed in Fig. 7-1. Many small airlines, and some larger ones, do not do their own hangar maintenance and, therefore, do not need the hangar maintenance organization. The same is true for those airlines that outsource their shop maintenance in one or more areas (avionics, hydraulics, etc.). But even if certain functions are not performed by the airline itself, these functions must be accomplished to properly maintain the equipment. The airline must designate someone in the M&E organization to be responsible for these functions, to see to their completion and to coordinate these actions with other airline activities. These and other variations will be discussed in the appropriate chapters later in the book.

Technical Services

The technical services directorate is responsible for providing technical assistance and support to all M&E activities. Part II begins with Chap. 8, Engineering. This is the main group in technical services and sometimes, in small airlines at least, will include some or all of the other support functions. The main job of engineering is to establish the maintenance program and subsequent schedules and to provide engineering expertise and technical assistance to all other units within M&E.

Production planning and control (PP&C), discussed in Chap. 9, is the primary force in driving the day-to-day work activities of maintenance. This unit is responsible for planning and scheduling all maintenance activities at the airline. The other functions of technical services are Technical Publications, Chap. 10, which is responsible for document currency and distribution; Technical Training, Chap. 11, responsible for all training activities in M&E including maintenance, management, inspection, and auditing personnel; and Computer Support, Chap. 12, responsible for the main M&E computing system development and upkeep including the training of M&E personnel in computer operation and use. Figure II-1 shows the organizational chart of the technical services units.

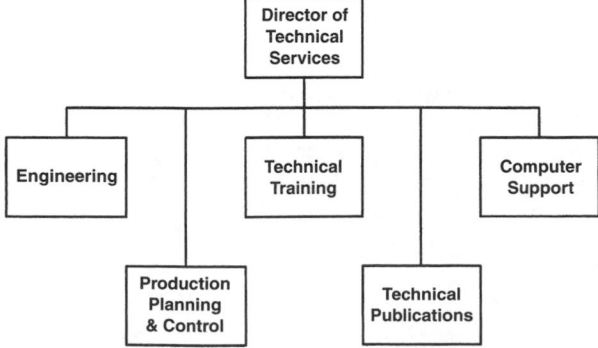

Figure II-1 Organizational chart for technical services.

Engineering

Introduction

There is discussion in the aviation industry about whether or not an airline needs an engineering component. In former times, airlines were instrumental in determining what they wanted in terms of aircraft size, range, and operating systems. The airlines would establish specifications and present these to the various airframe manufacturers who would then compete for the contract and ultimately produce the final product. In recent years, however, the general trend has been to leave the design and development of new aircraft to the airframe and engine manufacturers. The airlines' only stipulation is, essentially, "build something we can use effectively and something we can afford."

With this latter approach, many airlines considerably reduced the size of their engineering staffs and some eliminated them altogether. But there are other things to consider before closing the engineering office at an airline. Although the airline is not involved with design of new aircraft, other than defining basic requirements, there are still reasons for hiring people with engineering skills and background. These reasons are the subject of this chapter.

Engineering is defined by the Engineers' Council for Professional Development as the "profession in which a knowledge of the mathematical and natural sciences gained by study, experience, and practice is applied with judgment to develop ways to utilize economically the materials and forces of nature for the benefit of mankind." The *Encyclopedia Americana* says "Engineers, unlike scientists, work toward the solution of specific practical problems." The *Encyclopedia Britannica* adds: "All engineers must have a positive interest in the translation of the theoretical into the practical." In other words, an engineer is one who applies mathematics and scientific principles to the effort of resolving practical problems.

Engineers are usually identified by some specialty: civil, mechanical, electrical, aeronautical, transportation, nuclear, to name a few. None of these specialties apply directly to aviation except aeronautical and these aero engineers would normally be involved with design and development of air and space systems and equipment which, as we have said, the airline no longer does. All the other engineering disciplines listed above have specialties which may be applicable to some aspect of an airline operation but we cannot afford to hire them all. We would not have enough work to keep them all busy and they are not often capable of working in each other's area. What we do need in a typical airline maintenance organization are people trained as "maintenance engineers."

In Chap. 3, we defined *maintenance* as "the process of ensuring that a system continually performs its intended function at its designed-in level of reliability and safety." Maintenance engineers, then, are those degreed engineers who have knowledge, experience, and training in the field of aviation maintenance. That is, they need to know basic engineering as well as the technical details of the equipment used in aviation and the maintenance and operation of that equipment. Maintenance engineers at the manufacturer's plant develop maintenance programs from the MSG-3 activity (Chap. 2) and produce the various maintenance documents (Chap. 5). At the airline, maintenance engineers are responsible for applying the manufacturer's program and adjusting it, when necessary, to the real world situation. Most colleges and universities, however, do not have courses in maintenance engineering. Those who pursue this profession are very often experienced mechanics with interest in the engineering area or they are engineers with an interest in the aviation maintenance field.

The engineering department of an airline can vary widely; they perform many functions for the airline as a whole and specifically for the M&E organization. In some airlines, engineering is a corporate unit separate from the M&E operations and in others it is part of M&E. The size of the airline often determines which is most desirable. In those airlines where engineering is outside the M&E organization, their function is usually oriented toward major engineering type activities such as the development and support of buildings and other facilities; major aircraft modification design; and detailed engineering studies of maintenance problems as well as other airline technical problems.

In most airlines, however, engineering is an integral part of the maintenance and engineering organization and their main function is to support maintenance. The engineering section is also responsible for developing the maintenance program at the airline, for providing analytical assistance to the maintenance organization, and for providing troubleshooting assistance to line, hangar, and shop maintenance personnel on difficult problems.

Makeup of Engineering

The airline engineering department is made up of the more experienced people of the maintenance organization. They must be knowledgeable of the total maintenance operation as well as the airline and regulatory requirements. Ideally, an airline would have both degreed engineers and senior licensed mechanics in the engineering department. There would be engineering staff for each type of equipment: avionics, electrical, hydraulic, pneumatic, power plant (engines and APU), structures, and mechanical systems. Avionics may even be divided into communications and navigation systems; and mechanical systems into flight controls, hydraulics, etc. Some airlines may have different groups of engineers for each model of airplane and/or engine.

This distribution of specialties is determined, for the most part, by the size of the airline, however. For very small operators, there may be only one or two people in engineering. These are usually senior mechanics but they are required to provide the same assistance discussed above on all types of equipment. The larger the airline, the larger and more diverse the engineering department will be.

Mechanics and Engineers

Some airlines have engineering departments made up entirely of mechanics, while others have departments made up entirely of degreed engineers. Neither of these schemes is entirely satisfactory for our purposes. Although the mechanics are fully versed in the details of the systems and components in service, are experienced in the governing rules and regulations, and understand the idiosyncrasies of their fleet, they often do not have the same analytical discipline and other training of engineers. On the other hand, graduates of engineering colleges, more often than not, lack a suitable understanding of airplanes, aircraft engines, and the multitude of systems and components needed to provide airworthy vehicles for air transportation. The engineering curricula provide no training in maintenance and very little about other engineering disciplines.

Engineers and mechanics are trained differently and each approaches problems in different ways. While the mechanic's approach is somewhat "reactive," the engineer's approach is more "proactive." But, it takes both disciplines to run an effective engineering operation at an airline. Let's look briefly at each.

Mechanics

Mechanics and technicians study the practical aspects of aviation systems and equipment. They may specialize in avionics systems (electrical, electronic, communication, computer) or mechanical systems (hydraulics, pneumatics, flight controls, structures). This is the case particularly if they work in shop or hangar maintenance or for a third party organization doing maintenance or overhaul. If the mechanic works on the flight line, preparing aircraft for flight or servicing and maintaining aircraft in transit, he or she may be required to address all systems—a "Jack or Jill of all trades" you might say.

In either case, the mechanic is trained to address each system or unit with an understanding of how it is supposed to work and how it is supposed to be operated. When there is a discrepancy, the mechanic follows standard procedures for troubleshooting, fault isolation, and repair. Procedures for removal and installation, as well as for testing the installed unit, are all standardized.

An experienced mechanic also knows what kinds of things can go wrong (in operation as well as in installation and testing) that require more detailed analysis for determination of the problem. This last skill only comes with experience; it can be taught only in a cursory manner (see Appendix C). But, no matter how well trained a mechanic may be and no matter how much experience he or she might gain, often there are problems that cannot be resolved with these standard approaches. The neophyte mechanic may conclude that these problems cannot be solved. The more experienced one will realize the need to "dig deeper" into the problem. If this fails to produce a solution, it may be necessary to call upon the engineering staff for help (assuming they are properly qualified).

Engineers

In this book, we use the term *engineer* to identify those who have academic degrees in some engineering field. These people are trained differently than mechanics. Engineers are trained in the basics of science and engineering (mathematics, chemistry, physics, etc.); in the techniques of inductive and deductive reasoning; as well as in the areas of statistical analysis, problem solving, and systems engineering. Engineers also specialize in one particular engineering discipline—civil, electrical, mechanical, aeronautical, structural. Seldom do engineers spread themselves over the gamut of aviation disciplines. But this is not to say that they are not capable of assisting the mechanics in problem solving.

The engineer should be able to pick up a problem where the mechanic leaves off. If all the common and usually effective procedures applied by the mechanic did not work, then the engineer (or any first class mechanic for that matter) must begin by looking at the problem from a new angle. This requires that the engineer understand more than the basics of system operation. He or she must also understand the kinds of things that can go wrong and the kinds of things that can be influenced by outside forces not accounted for in the standard maintenance procedures. The engineer must be able to develop new and innovative procedures for studying and analyzing problems and must understand the "big picture" to effectively come to an appropriate answer. This is what engineers are supposed to do. Engineers are basically "problem solvers."

Appendix C provides information on basic troubleshooting techniques that apply to both mechanics and engineers. Appendix D provides some insight to the engineer's approach to problem solving. Although this appendix relates primarily to reliability alerts (see Chap. 19), the approach can apply to any problem to be solved.

One important thing to realize, however, is that for all the engineer knows about engineering, about problem solving, and about systems and their interactions, he or she must also know the airplanes, the engines, and the associated systems on those airplanes to effectively apply this knowledge to the solution of real airplane problems. It takes both disciplines—engineering and maintenance—as well as both types of experts—engineers and mechanics—to make an effective and efficient maintenance and engineering organization run smoothly.

Engineering Department Functions

The engineering department provides preparation, study, and analysis of various aspects of the maintenance operation. They evaluate maintenance requirements and establish the maintenance program for the airline. They also evaluate suggested modifications of aircraft systems for possible incorporation into the fleet and provide technical assistance to maintenance. Engineering prepares the units for handling new equipment and facilities and provides assistance, where needed, in all other aspects of maintenance. These functions are discussed below.

Development of the maintenance program

Each airplane model has an initial maintenance program developed by the Industry Working Groups and defined in the manufacturer supplied documentation. This is a suggested maintenance program for new operators and new equipment. Once in the field, operators can adjust the program to suit their own needs and operational environment (see Chaps. 2 and 19).

This initial maintenance program is a generalized program and must be tailored to the individual operator from the very beginning. The manufacturer produces the FAA approved MRB report and a maintenance planning document (see Chap. 2). It is the responsibility of the engineering department at the airline to package these tasks into workable units based on such factors as time, space, personnel, fleet schedules, and overall airline capabilities. For some airlines, the designated letter checks (A, B, C, and D) are sufficient. The fleet is large enough for the airline to schedule people and facilities for continuing checks (for example, one airplane per week or per month). In small airlines, there are not enough airplanes to allow this continued scheduling of "C" checks. Due to the higher manpower requirements for the "C" check, it is necessary for the small airline to adjust the schedule to smooth out the work.

For most operators, the "A" check is done monthly. The "C" check comes about yearly (every 12 to 18 months for newer models) and requires a concentration of manpower for the 3 to 7 days required to perform it. For the small airline, manning this "once a year" effort is not feasible. To remedy the matter, the "C" check is divided into parts, called phases, and each part is conducted separately. For example, a "C" check could be divided into four phases (C1, C2, C3, and C4) each one carried out every 3 months until the entire "C" check is performed. An airline may divide the "C" check into 12 packages and perform one package a month along with each scheduled "A" check. In either case, the manpower utilization is more constant throughout the year, the checks are done within the prescribed time limit, and the airline workload is stabilized.

The responsibility for selecting the tasks to be done, for packaging the tasks into workable check packages, and ensuring that all task limits are met (time, cycles, etc.) lies with the engineering department. Actual scheduling of the checks for individual aircraft is a function of the production planning and control department (see Chap. 9).

The tasks performed by maintenance at any of these checks can be quite detailed. To ensure that they are carried out correctly, task cards are issued to the mechanics. Many airlines use task cards produced by the airplane manufacturers and some write their own cards. Still others develop a combination of the two. Whichever method is used, it is the responsibility of engineering to develop these task cards, assemble them into appropriate packages, and ensure that they are current and effective.

Develop technical policies and procedures manual for M&E

This document contains all the necessary information to describe the M&E organization and its responsibilities. It identifies the organizational structure, provides information on duties and responsibilities of key personnel and key organizations and provides a series of maps and layouts of the airline's facilities. It also gives detailed descriptions of how work is to be carried out, who is to perform the work and how it will be managed, inspected, and released (if applicable). Engineering is responsible for developing this document with inputs from the other M&E units.

The FAA defines the minimum requirements for the manual in FAR 121.369 but consideration should be given to additional policies and procedures that provide complete instructions to maintenance and engineering personnel for the conduct of their work. The manual can be a single document in loose leaf form, it can be a series of separate documents, or it can be a multiple volume set. Chapter 5 gives an outline of a typical TPPM.

Evaluate changes in the maintenance program

From time to time there will be problems with the effectiveness of the maintenance program. Individual tasks may be ineffective or less than adequate. Some MRB tasks eliminated from the original program may, in retrospect, need to be reinstated. In some cases it may be necessary or desirable to shorten or extend the intervals between repetitive tasks to improve the overall performance or reduce in-service failures of a system or component. This adjustment of the maintenance program is the job of the engineering staff. Data collection by the reliability organization and analysis of the problem by engineering are necessary to carry out this function.

Evaluate changes in aircraft or system configuration

From time to time, the airplane, engine, and component manufacturers develop modifications and improvements for their respective systems, which are intended to improve operations, reliability, and/or maintenance processes. These are issued as service bulletins (SBs) or service letters (SLs). If a safety or airworthiness issue is involved, the modification may be issued by the FAA as an airworthiness directive (AD).

Since service bulletins and service letters are not FAA requirements, the airline has the option to incorporate or ignore the modification. Many airlines will incorporate these suggestions on faith; others will ignore them. For most operators however, the airline's engineering department will evaluate the feasibility of incorporation. They will look at the cost of incorporation and the benefits in terms of reduced maintenance, improved performance, or passenger convenience (or any combination of these) and, based on this cost-benefit analysis, make the decision to incorporate or not to incorporate.

Airworthiness directives are mandatory, so there is no need for engineering to evaluate the change. Engineering will, however, be required to provide the necessary information needed by maintenance to accomplish the modification regardless of whether it is an AD, SB, or SL. This will be accomplished by issuing a detailed instruction produced in the form of an engineering order (EO) which is discussed below.

Evaluation of new aircraft added to the fleet

One of the primary functions of engineering is to evaluate new equipment for the airline. When the business people of the airline decide to expand the operation, one of the first questions to resolve is "What airplane/engine combination should we buy?" Part of this decision is based on the routes to be flown, the destination cities, the expected market share and, of course, the cost of the equipment versus the revenue expected. These are operations and business decisions based on market conditions and airline goals and objectives.

Another important part of the decision, however, is "What is the best equipment to buy from the maintenance and engineering standpoint?" The two decisions—business and technical—must be reconciled to the satisfaction of the overall airline goals. At this point, for the sake of the present course of study, we will skip the business decision and concentrate on the technical decision.

Let us assume that the choice is to be made between two new models—both are two engine airplanes, the Boeing 767 and the Airbus A330. There are a number of questions to be answered in regard to maintenance.

1. What engines are available for these models? Are they the same or similar to engines in the airline's current fleet? This is important because there may be a need for additional maintenance and test facilities for these new engines. The cost and the feasibility of this is very important. Training needs for engine mechanics and additional staffing (if any is required) are also to be considered.

2. What is the range of these airplanes? Will the airline need to position their own line personnel at outstations or arrange for contract personnel at the site to support maintenance or turnaround on these new models? Can existing outstation personnel handle these new airplanes? Can they do so with or without additional training? Or with minimal upgrade training?

3. What new technology is included in these new models? Are the skills of the current maintenance and engineering staff sufficient to maintain these airplanes or will they require additional training? Additional manpower? Will this involve extensive training or "differences training" only?

4. Based on current knowledge of the maintenance programs for these two airplane models, will the scheduled checks be compatible with current schedules (i.e., check cycles) for the existing fleet? What changes will have to be made (if any) to existing maintenance activities (hangar space, production planning, flight line, MCC) to accommodate the new model?

5. Will additional ground support equipment (GSE) be needed for these new airplanes? If so, what equipment?

6. Will the existing hangars be suitable for these airplanes? Will they need to be modified or will a new hangar be required? This may require interface with outside builders or contractors.

7. What will be the increased need for parts and parts storage at the home base and at outstations to support the new airplanes? This could involve a considerable amount of financial investment for parts not common to the existing fleet.

8. What is the industry experience on these two models relative to maintenance support (i.e., parts availability, parts delivery, failure rates, removal rates, amount of maintenance required)?

These and other questions must be considered by the engineering department, with inputs from other units within M&E, prior to the decision as to which airplane should be purchased. This preliminary analysis must include information on costs as well as training requirements and time frames for upgrade of facilities and personnel. Once the decision is made on which airplane and engine to buy, the engineering department must then develop more detailed estimates and devise implementation plans for all aspects of the integration of the new model into the maintenance plan. These efforts must also include data on the number of airplanes to be purchased and the time schedule for delivery.

Evaluation of used aircraft to be added to the fleet

If the airline is contemplating the purchase or lease of used airplanes from another airline or leasing organization, other items must be considered in addition to the above items relating to equipment differences from the existing fleet. These items would include such information as the current configuration of the airplane, including engine type; the maintenance program and check schedule that the current operator is using; status of modifications (ADs and SBs). Are these requirements the same as, similar to, or different from your airline's current equipment? How will this affect training, maintenance support, materiel support, outstation activities, etc.? If airplanes are to be leased, what modification and configuration standards must be met by the operator; by the lessor? What configuration should the airplane be in at termination of the lease?

Note: There have been cases where an airplane in ETOPS[*] configuration was leased to an operator who did not fly the airplane in ETOPS service and, therefore, did not keep up with the newer ETOPS modifications. When the airplane was returned at the end of the lease, the airline discovered that they were responsible for returning the airplane to ETOPS configuration at their own expense.

The condition of the aircraft at termination of the lease and return to the lessor should be clearly stated and understood at the signing of said lease. What condition (state of ADs, SBs, configuration) as well as who is responsible for making the required adjustments—lessor or lessee—must be clearly stated at the outset.

Evaluation of new ground support equipment

On a smaller scale, the engineering department will also be called upon to evaluate the need for new equipment in support of aircraft added to the fleet. This would include tools, test equipment, stands, electric and pneumatic carts, heaters, tow bars, tractors, etc. Some existing equipment may or may not be usable with the new airplane models (purchased or leased). In some cases, the GSE, though usable, may not be available in sufficient quantity to serve the increased fleet size. Additional purchase would be necessary in such cases.

Development of new facilities for M&E

At times, it is necessary for the airline to build new facilities or expand existing ones to support new equipment, airline expansion, or modernization efforts. This would include projects such as hangars, engine test facilities, component shops, storage facilities for various types of equipment, and storage for special parts. The engineering department will not (usually) be involved in the design and construction of these new facilities. That will be contracted out to more appropriate companies. Engineering will, however, have a considerable input into the design in terms of requirements. A hangar, a workshop, or any other facility must be designed for the express use of the airline and the M&E organizations that will occupy it. Therefore, the engineering department will act as liaison between the users and the designers and builders to ensure that the finished product is acceptable.

Issuance of engineering orders

Any work performed by maintenance in the form of standard checks—daily, 48-hour, transit, "A" check, "C" check—is done on "standing orders" from the VP of maintenance and engineering as identified in the maintenance section of the

---

[*] ETOPS (extended range operations with two-engine airplanes) is discussed in Appendix E.

Ops Specs. Any work not included in these standard checks must be assigned by engineering order. Some airlines may call this document by another name, such as work order, technical order, or engineering authorization (EA). This EO is developed by engineering, with inputs from appropriate work centers, to define the scope of the job and schedule the work. Work performed as a result of SBs, SLs, ADs, and all work resulting from evaluation of problems defined by reliability investigations or QC reports, will be issued on an engineering order. All work centers involved in the particular project will be defined on the EO: maintenance (line, hangar, or shop as appropriate); material (for parts, supplies, tools); quality control (inspection of work if required); training (remedial, upgrade, or new course). Engineering releases the EO after all involved organizations (maintenance, materiel, planning, etc.) have agreed to its contents. Engineering then tracks the work progress and closes the EO when all has been completed. In certain instances, airline modifications are made to the fleet, either by directive or through the airline's own initiative. These "fleet campaigns" are also controlled by EOs. These EOs cannot be closed out until the entire fleet has been worked. The preparation of an EO is discussed at the end of the chapter.

Provide assistance in troubleshooting difficult problems

The day-to-day problems that mechanics run into on the line, in the hangar, and in the shops, are often routine and call for well-defined responses. At times, the problems are more elusive and the mechanic must apply his or her troubleshooting skills to resolve the problem. When the problem eludes the mechanic's expertise, assistance is available from engineering to get to the bottom of the problem. This assistance can be given to line, hangar, and shop people as well as vendors handling warranty claims or working on contract. Parts suppliers who perform repairs on rotable units and contractors doing third party maintenance may also require engineering's assistance. It should be noted that this is not the primary responsibility of engineering and should be used only in difficult circumstances. Engineering is not a substitute or replacement for maintenance.

Other engineering functions

Engineering can also provide expertise to training, materiel, the technical library, or any other M&E organization needing technical help. They are considered the technical experts of the organization and are available to lend technical assistance to anyone in the airline needing such assistance.

Engineering Order Preparation

Engineering initiates an engineering order for any work not included in the standard maintenance program plans as established by the Ops Specs. However, the need for an EO can be generated from various sources. Its implementation can also take various paths depending on the type and complexity of the work involved. For example, EOs related to maintenance modifications and other directives (ADs, SBs, SLs, etc.) will be scheduled by the planning organization (PP&C). Other problems may necessitate changes in the maintenance program (intervals, tasks, etc.); change in processes; parts procurement activities; or may require training (refresher or upgrade; classroom or on the job). In these cases, the EO might be issued directly to the M&E unit or units involved. The following eight steps generalize the process.

1. A decision is made to do work based on one of the following: reliability program alert; work force requirement (QA, QC, maintenance manager, or mechanic); an AD, SB, SL, or fleet campaign.

2. Engineering analyzes the work requirements (problem and solution): troubleshoot or investigate the problem to determine scope and needs; analyze AD, SB, SL, etc. if applicable for time, manpower, etc. requirements.

3. Determine the approach to follow: incorporate work into PP&C check or other scheduled or unscheduled maintenance activity; schedule other corrective action as necessary; issue EO as required.

4. Identify the needs for schedule and performance of the work: engineering studies, plans, etc.; the need for special skills if any (in-house or contract); the need for parts and supplies (on hand or order, consider lead time for delivery); determine need and availability for special tools and/or test equipment needed.

5. Identify work required: manpower (maintenance, engineering, contract, etc.); facilities (hangar space, GSE, etc.); time requirements for work to be done.

6. Call a coordinating meeting to finalize EO (if necessary): all organizations involved in the work; coordinate and resolve difficulties.

7. Issue engineering order: PP&C will plan work and monitor execution; or EO may go directly to materiel, training, etc. as necessary.

8. Engineering closes EO when all work is completed: notification comes from each work center involved in the particular EO; for fleet campaigns, ADs, etc. involving entire fleets, EO remains open, PP&C schedules each aircraft for incorporation; engineering closes EO when fleet is complete.

Production Planning and Control

Introduction

Production planning and control (PP&C) is one of the key organizations within M&E. It is the heart of the maintenance organization. Although the title of this activity is fairly common throughout the airline industry, the activities actually performed sometimes fall short of the ideal notion of what PP&C should be. The PP&C organization is primarily responsible for planning and scheduling all aircraft maintenance activity within the airline.

The title of PP&C is a bit misleading. It implies two functions: planning and control. Actually PP&C has three primary functions: forecasting, planning, and control. Forecasting activities include the estimated maintenance workload for the long term and the short term based on the existing fleet and business plans and on any known changes in these for the forecast period. Planning involves the scheduling of upcoming maintenance and includes the planning and scheduling of all manpower, parts, facilities, and time frame requirements for such maintenance: less than "A" check items, daily checks, 48-hour checks, transit checks, and letter checks (A, B, C, etc.). These plans would include incorporation of SBs, SLs, and ADs as well as other modifications deemed necessary by the airline. This plan is somewhat idealized, however. During the actual performance of maintenance, many things occur that require alteration of the plan. The control function allows adjustment of the plan and keeps (or attempts to keep) the check on schedule. There are several methods of adjusting the plan including deferral of maintenance to a later check, addition of personnel to complete the work, or outsourcing the work to a contractor. Feedback from a check allows PP&C to adjust the planning effort for future checks.

There is an old saying that captures the gist of PP&C: "Plan your work and work your plan." The production planning aspect of PP&C does the planning. This is the first step in accomplishing the work at hand and must always precede action. Without planning, action would be impulsive and produce unpredictable results.

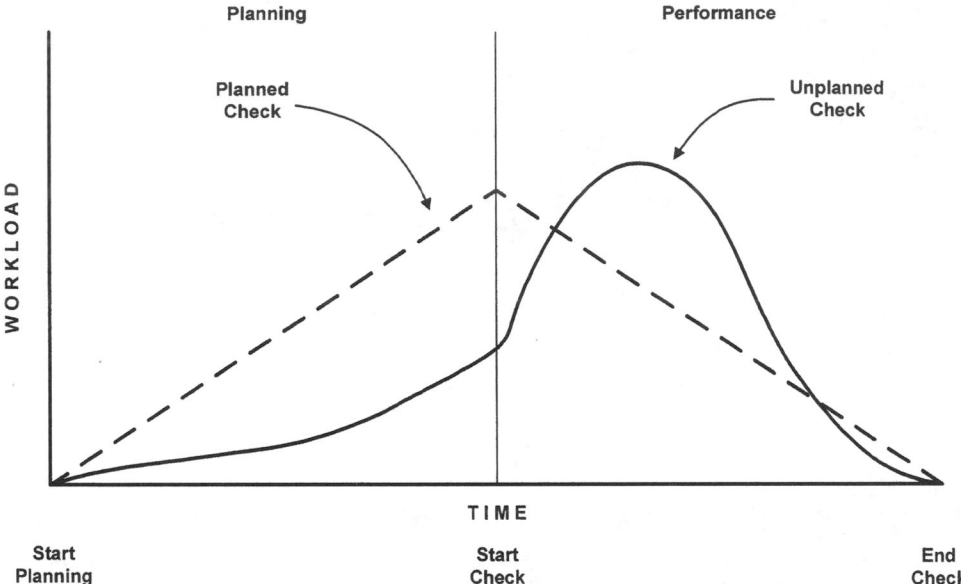

Figure 9-1   The importance of planning. (*Source: From a similar drawing in John Revere:* The Management of Aircraft Maintenance, *3rd ed., Keogh Management Services, Edina, MN. Reprinted with permission.*)

The production control aspect of PP&C "works the plan." The control phase begins with a meeting of all involved work units before the plan is finalized. Control efforts continue during the performance of the work and immediately following it. This ensures compliance with the plan as closely as possible and takes action where necessary to adjust the plan as indicated by deviations and circumstances that invariably occur during real-world activities.

Figure 9-1[*] shows how work is expended on a typical project with and without proper planning. The preliminary planning consists of the development of the maintenance program and its schedule established by the engineering section as well as the individual check planning efforts of PP&C. Once the check has begun, the work progresses smoothly. This proper approach is shown by the dashed line. Without the preliminary planning of PP&C, the implementation effort, as shown by the solid line, swells as the work progresses, mostly due to unexpected events and delays.

To illustrate this, take the example of the first "C" check performed by a new operator on a two-engine jet. Normally, this check would take 4 or 5 days depending on shift schedules. A certain (nameless) airline approached the task in the following manner. One week before the check was due, the management took

---

[*] This chart is a variation of a similar chart in John J. Revere, PMP: *The Management of Aircraft Maintenance*, 3rd ed.; Keogh Management Services, Edina, MN, 1995.

the MPD document for the airplane from the shelf to see what was required for the "C" check. They discovered that, without adequate preplanning, they were unable to complete the check in 5 days. Instead, it took them 4 weeks to perform the check. They learned a valuable lesson that day: "Plan your work and then work your plan."

The goals of PP&C are (a) to maximize the M&E contribution to the airline; (b) to plan and organize work prior to execution; and (c) to adjust plans and schedules to meet changing requirements. We will discuss forecasting, planning, and control in turn. Then we will consider the advantages and disadvantages of the various organizational schemes for PP&C.

Forecasting

Forecasting is concerned with the future workload of the M&E organization. It must take into account the routine maintenance requirements as well as all planned changes in the future operations relative to maintenance. Any changes in fleet size and make up, changes in route structure, and changes in facilities, manpower, and skill requirements must be tracked. Future plans must also accommodate aging and replacement of equipment, adding new equipment, and the planned incorporation of ADs and SBs. Activities throughout M&E will change as these assets and requirements change. The forecast function ensures that M&E is up to date on these changes and is ready to adjust their processes and procedures accordingly.

Forecasts are usually made for the long and short term but often an intermediate term forecast is also made. The long term forecast would be for 5 to 10 years. The changes that are planned by the airline in the long term will affect maintenance and engineering activities. These changes will impact scheduling, budgeting, training, manpower, and facilities within M&E. Adjustments must be made in all of these areas for M&E to meet its goals and objectives, so plans must be made in advance to accommodate the growing (or shrinking) airline. This long-term forecast is somewhat general in nature and is subject to revision on a yearly basis.

Short-term forecasts are more detailed and usually cover 1 to 2 years. These forecasts contain more definitive plans with attention to actual manpower and budget numbers. Schedules for checks and known modifications are finalized in the short-term plans.

Larger airlines may also develop intermediate forecasts for periods of 2 to 5 years. Thus, the three forecasts provide a continuous plan for M&E to follow in an effort to keep up with the changes in the operational climate and be ready to change the M&E activities accordingly.

Production Planning

While forecasting is long range and general, planning deals with the day-to-day activities of M&E. The goal of M&E is to deliver airworthy vehicles to the flight department in time to meet the flight schedule, with all maintenance activities completed or properly deferred. In business terms this is what we "produce"—airworthy vehicles with all maintenance properly addressed. Thus, the activities of line, hangar, and shop maintenance constitute the production aspect of M&E. Production planning, then, is the planning of that work with the stated goals in mind.

Engineering has developed the maintenance plan from the MRB or Ops Specs document and divided the work into the appropriate work packages, identifying the tasks to be done, the intervals at which they will be done, and the manpower requirements for each task. The check package schedule for a typical mid-sized airline is depicted in Table 9-1. Planning must now take this engineering package and plan, schedule, and adjust the work for each check and for each aircraft, adding any additional tasks as necessary. Estimated man-hours are shown in Table 9-2 for our mid-sized airline.

Production planning involves the planning of all maintenance activities: daily, 48-hour, and transit checks; letter checks; and modifications due to airworthiness directives, service bulletins, service letters, and engineering orders. It also involves the planning and scheduling of all aspects of these checks including manpower, parts, supplies, and facilities. Coordination with flight operations and with ground handling and support activities is also included in the planning effort.

The daily, 48-hour, and transit checks are usually standardized and require little or no effort on the part of PP&C other than scheduling. The appropriate work packages are developed by engineering and issued as necessary for the required checks. Line maintenance is usually responsible for these checks and the routine tasks are administered by the maintenance control center. The PP&C unit merely monitors this activity. Additional tasks, whose intervals are less than the "A" check, are usually added to these checks or performed concurrently by a separate work crew. Occasionally, SBs and other modifications, if simple and involving small amounts of time, will be included (by EO) in the line checks. This planning and scheduling would be done by PP&C with cooperation from MCC and line maintenance for implementation.

All "A" checks and higher are planned, scheduled, and coordinated by PP&C and their content varies from check to check. These activities are more involved than the 48-hour and transit checks so the planning is started well in advance of the actual check. For "A" checks, planning begins 1 to 2 weeks prior to the scheduled check. For "C" checks, the planning begins about 4 weeks in advance. In certain cases, such as the incorporation of SBs or ADs, the lead time on parts availability may require that the planning for those items be started even earlier. We will discuss these items as they arise. We will first look at the planning of the tasks scheduled at intervals less than the "A" check and say a word about multiple checks before addressing the "A" and "C" checks themselves.

Maintenance tasks at less than "A" check interval

Certain maintenance items in the MRB report are designated for time and cycles that are less than the "A" check cycle. The PP&C unit is responsible for issuing weekly, biweekly, or daily schedules for these items to the line maintenance

TABLE 9-1 Aircraft Maintenance Check Schedule (Typical A/L Example)

	747-400	747-200/300	DC-10-30	A300B4	F50
Transit check	At each stop whenever aircraft is in transit				
Daily check	Before first flight or whenever aircraft is on ground more than 4 hours				
"A" check	Every 600 FH	Every 500 FH or 7 Weeks	In 3 parts A1, A2, A3 465 FH or 9 weeks	In 4 parts A1, A2, A3, A4 Every 385 FH or 11 weeks	Every 650 FH or 4 months
"B" check	In 2 parts B1, B2 Every 1200 FH	In 2 parts B1, B2 Every 1000 FH	None	None	Every 1300 FH or 8 months
"C" check	In 2 parts C1, C2 Every 5000 FH or 18 months	Every 4650 FH or 24 months	In 2 parts C1, C2 Every 4500 FH or 20 months	In 2 parts C1, C2 Every 3000 FH or 18 months	In 2 parts C1, C2 Every 4000 FH or 25 months
"D/HMV" check	First check done between 25K & 27.5K FH Subsequent every 25K FH or 6 years	First check at 25K FH or 6 years Subsequent every 20K FH or 5 years	Every 20K FH or 6 years	Every 12K FH or 4 years	In 2 parts H1, H2 Every 12K FH or 6 years

FH: flight hours; HMV: heavy maintenance visit.

NOTE: Some maintenance planning documents from the manufacturer do not have specified "B" checks. Airlines, however, can identify their own checks or identify existing checks by any name or letter they choose.

The schedule above was taken from an international airline with a fleet of 30–40 A/C. It has been modified slightly for illustration.

When FH and calendar times are both given, the check will be performed at whichever comes first.

Where checks are split into parts, e.g., 'B1, B2 every 1000 FH,' B1 will be done at 1000 FH and B2 at 2000 FH. This pattern is repeated so that each part is done at 2000 FH intervals.

TABLE 9-2 Average Check Package Man-hours (Example)

A/C type	Check type	Routine	Variable routine	Nonroutine	Total
747-400	A	100	–	–	100
	B	300	300	600	1,200
	C	900	810	1,710	3,420
	D (HMV)	4000	20,000	36,000	60,000
747-200/300	A	300	150	450	900
DC-10-30	A	410	369	467	1,246
	C	1800	1,260	2,142	5,202
	HMV				65,000
A300B4	A	550	220	539	1,309
	C	1600	1,120	2,176	4,896
	D (HMV)				
F50	A	71	71	142	284
	B	300	90	234	624
	C	930	465	1,116	2,511
	D (HMV)	2119	1,060	2,861	6,039

Some checks are not done by the airline. The checks are either contracted out or the airplanes are leased and the owner does the checks. Also, aircraft may be fairly new and no D or HMV checks are due at this time.

Times required will vary from check to check depending on many factors as discussed in the text.

organization for timely accomplishment. These tasks can be scheduled at specific times on overnight checks; at certain turnaround times, if time permits; or included in "A" checks if time permits. These items can be accomplished by line maintenance personnel assigned to meet aircraft on normal turnaround or they can be assigned to a special crew of line maintenance people who are separate from the turnaround crew. The method is up to the airline and is usually determined by local conditions and manpower availability. Regardless of how these tasks are accomplished, it is PP&C's responsibility to schedule them and follow up on them in order to ensure that they are completed within the scheduled interval.

There is one problem that airlines sometimes get into concerning these less than "A" check tasks. That is to defer these tasks day after day, due to pressing work by the turnaround crew. If these tasks are habitually put off to a more convenient time, the deadline for completion gets nearer and nearer. Finally, the airline has to take the aircraft out of service for several hours in order to complete the maintenance so as not to exceed the FAA time limits. Such delays can be costly.

Multiple checks

You will recall from Chap. 2, that some MRB items are done at intervals that place them on every other, every third, etc. check. This is true for "A" checks as well as "C" checks. What this means is that each "A" check or "C" check performed, depending on where the aircraft is in the maintenance cycle, will have a different set of tasks to perform and thus will require different amounts of time,

TABLE 9-3 Typical Aircraft "A" Check* and "C" Check[†] Schedule

Check	300	600	900	1200	1500	1800	2100	2400	2700	3000	3300
1A	X	X	X	X	X	X	X	X	X	X	X
2A		X		X		X		X		X	
3A			X			X			X		
4A				X				X			
5A					X					X	
C										X	

*"A" check = 300 hours.
[†]"C" check = 3000 hours

manpower, etc. This is just one more of PP&C's responsibilities: to ensure that parts and supplies, manpower, facilities, and time are available for this variance in the check schedule. Table 9-3 shows a typical pattern for multiple "A" checks. These cycles are carried out until changed by FAA approval.

It should also be noted that every "C" check includes all the "A" check items required by the table. In some instances, this means that task cards may need to be combined. For instance, an "A" check may require an operational test of a system while the "C" check will require a functional test of the same system. The maintenance manual (and subsequently the task cards) would give complete test instructions for each individual test. Doing both, however, may involve a duplication of certain unnecessary steps. These task cards, then, must be modified by engineering or by standing orders given to avoid the unnecessary action. The "C" check items can also be originally scheduled for longer intervals designated as 2C (every second), 3C (every third), and so forth. A chart similar to Table 9-3 can be drawn for multiple "C" checks to aid planners.

Phased checks

Phased checks are different from multiple checks and therefore have a different (but not too different) numbering scheme. An "A" check may be split into two phases, each one performed on successive nights to minimize maintenance crew needs and down time. The right side of the aircraft might be done on the first phase, called an "A1" check and the left side on the second phase, the "A2" check. A "C" check may be broken down into four parts (C1, C2, C3, and C4) and performed every 3 months or so, depending on the full "C" check cycle. This check could also be divided into 12 parts, one done each month (C1, C2, ... C12).

"A" check planning

"A" checks are usually routine. The tasks required are defined by engineering using the MRB or Ops Specs document. The time, manpower, and parts and supplies needed are generally fixed (see Chap. 2 for discussion of adjustment of MRB task time estimates). There are variations, however, that must be addressed. When there is a write-up in the aircraft maintenance log that cannot be addressed at turnaround or on daily or over-night checks, it may be deferred until a later time. The deferral may be a result of a lack of parts, a temporary lack of skilled labor, or lack of sufficient time required (at the time of occurrence) to effect resolution. In these cases, the deferred maintenance is scheduled by PP&C for the next "A" check. The necessary parts, supplies, and personnel should be available at that time.

Performance of an "A" check may also include, because of time and parts constraints, some "less than "A" check" items (100 hours, 250 cycles, etc.). These may be near the time or cycle interval and so are placed with the "A" check for convenience. If there are SBs or SLs that do not require extensive time or parts to complete, these may also be scheduled for the "A" check.

Thus, even though an "A" check is relatively simple and straight forward, there is still some planning required. Since PP&C is responsible for that planning and scheduling, they will develop the work package and send it to the applicable work centers for review a few days before the scheduled date of the check. This allows adjustment for changes in circumstances. (This is the beginning of the "control" portion of PP&C.)

The "B" checks, if they are used, are often similar to "A" checks but involve different tasks, usually at intervals which fall between consecutive "A" checks. The planning for these is essentially the same as for "A" checks.

"C" check planning

The "C" check is usually done about once a year (12 to 18 months on the newer model aircraft), depending on the airline flight schedule. The planning effort is more detailed and more elaborate than for the "A" check. Normally, a "C" check will take 4 to 7 days to complete, depending upon the model and the circumstances. The number of shifts worked, the availability of manpower and parts, and the skill requirements for the work will affect the length of time involved. The check will consist of three categories of tasks: routine, variable routine, and nonroutine.

Routine tasks are those tasks identified in the MRB document. These are items that must be performed at the specified interval. Since some of these items are performed every "C" check and others are performed every second, third, or fourth check (2C, 3C, or 4C), the amount of time required to perform each scheduled check will vary from check to check. This scheduling and variation in time requirements are PP&C's concern.

Variable routine tasks are those tasks which vary from one check to another and from one aircraft to another. These tasks include incorporation of service bulletins and airworthiness directives, as well as fleet campaigns, items deferred from previous maintenance checks and any other one-time maintenance actions required for a particular aircraft. The time required to accomplish these tasks is generally fixed so these items are similar to the routine tasks for planning purposes.

Nonroutine tasks are those work items that are generated by the accomplishment of other, routine tasks. For example, if a routine task says to inspect the wheel-well area for hydraulic leaks, the task will take a certain amount of time (scheduled). If a leak is discovered, however, it must be addressed. This constitutes the production of a nonroutine maintenance task and subsequently a nonroutine task card. Since the number of nonroutines can only be estimated and the amount of time required to complete the nonroutine item varies with many factors, it becomes an interesting task for PP&C to properly estimate the time needed to complete these nonroutine items and the entire check.

Below is a list of items that might be included in a "C" check. Not all of these would be included each time, however.

1. "C" check items from the approved maintenance program (routine)

2. Deferred maintenance from line or other check packages (variable routine)

3. Incorporation of SBs, SLs, ADs (variable routine)

4. Incorporation of airline mods and fleet campaigns (variable routine)

5. Cleaning, painting of aircraft (variable routine)

6. Work generated by inspections and routine items (nonroutine).

It is the job of PP&C to collect and schedule these items using accurate estimates of the time required for routine and variable routine items and predicting a reasonable amount of time for nonroutines and other delays. Once the package is set and the time estimated, PP&C must arrange for and schedule all the necessary elements for proper execution of the package. That would include the following:

1. Locate and secure hangar space for the duration of the check

2. Obtain a release of the airplane from operations for maintenance purposes (this may be accomplished by MCC)

3. Arrange for and schedule the washing of the aircraft

4. Secure tow vehicles and manpower needed to move the airplane to the wash rack and then into the hangar

5. Ensure all parts and supplies needed to carry out the check will be on hand

6. Ensure delivery of those parts and supplies to the hangar at the time needed

7. Identify manpower and skills needed for the check

Table 9-4 shows our typical airline's estimate for the man-hours planned for a "C" check on the Airbus A300B4.

As with the "A" check, the "C" check package must be developed and distributed to the applicable work centers prior to the start of the activity. The package would be sent out 1 to 2 weeks before the scheduled date of the check. A meeting of all involved units will then be held to discuss and finalize this into a workable

TABLE 9-4 Summary of Aircraft Check Package Man-hours (Example B1 Check for A330 aircraft)

Work type	AF	ENG	ELEC	INST	RADIO	AIM	LUB	UTIL	TOTAL	%	NDT	ASM	PS/FG	Total	All Wk Ctrs	Grand Total
Routine*	71	28	19	3	3	62	7	115	308	37.71						308
Variable routine†																
SIP	18	18	2		14		15		67	7.99						67
SSI																
Component change	3					6			9	·1.07						9
Eng change																
APU change																
LDG change																
SI	33	48	6	9	9	6			111	13.23	5			5		116
Modifications	23	7	32			2			64	7.63		15		15		79
EN	10	15		2					27	3.22	5			5		32
MARF																
Other	20	11	5	6	10	1	10	8	71	8.46						71
Nonroutine‡	51	25	17	3	3	46	2	35	182	21.69		14	12	26		208
Total	229	152	81	23	39	123	34	158	839	100	10	29	12	51		890
Man-hours available																
Variance																

*Tasks from the MRB or Ops Specs.
†Routine items that vary with aircraft, check, and other planning decisions.
‡Tasks generated from other tasks.

plan. This will allow for any last minute changes needed because of circumstances that PP&C was unaware of at the time of plan origination. Such circumstances would be as follows: certain items may need more time to complete than has been scheduled; recently deferred items may have priority; required parts not received; or manpower may not be available due to illness, vacations, etc. The check package would be adjusted as necessary. In rare cases, the time for the check might be extended one day or one shift as needed. This, of course, would have to be coordinated with operations and the business office to accommodate rescheduling the aircraft for service.

The final effort of PP&C will be to produce the check package, from the computer data base (or by hand) and issue work cards for use by mechanics and quality inspectors during the check. On the date scheduled, the aircraft will be washed and rolled into the hangar and the check begins. (How this check is carried out is detailed in Chap.14.)

Production Control

The plan produced by PP&C allows a certain amount of time for the performance work based on past knowledge of the work to be done and also based on the assumption that parts, supplies, manpower, and facilities will be available when needed. The plan also assumes that there is no variation in the flow of work activity. The PP&C planners can only estimate the amount of time required for nonroutine items and this can be less than accurate. Take, for instance, a routine task that says "check the hydraulic line for leaks." If there are no leaks, the inspection task should take a specific amount of time, but since there is no way for the planner to determine if there will be leaks or to know the extent of any leak(s) found, there is no way for him or her to accurately estimate the time required to perform the nonroutine task of repairing the leaks. But it still must be estimated and scheduled.

However, through feedback from similar tasks on previous checks the planner can get some idea of what might be expected. It is important, then, for those doing the work and controlling the check to provide information back to planning to help them to make more accurate estimates for the next check planning effort. Often this can be adjusted during the planning meeting mentioned above.

A routine task of removing and replacing a hard time item may take 2 hours under normal circumstances. On one particular occasion, suppose a bolt is sheared off during the installation. This will require additional work in extracting the broken bolt. The tools to do this may not be readily available at the site and the process of removing the bolt and redressing the threads may take a considerable amount of time. There probably would be an inspection or investigation to determine why this occurred (improper use of tools by mechanic, weakened part, out-of-calibration torque wrench). The time elapsed may be significant and it may, due to the location of the activity, cause another mechanic delay in working another task within that same area.

All of this is "business as usual" in the real world of maintenance. It is important, then, for maintenance to keep track of the time spent on each task. Although mechanics, and their unions, don't like the idea of being timed, it is important for scheduling and planning purposes to know how long a given job should take, the kinds of things that might go wrong when performing that job, and the time required to rectify the problems that do occur. It should be understood by management and mechanics alike, that some people will take longer than others to do a job and that the same person will take longer on some days than on other days. This is not unusual, this is a fact of life—so tracking the time to do a task is not to be used for disciplinary purposes; it is to be used only for practical planning purposes. Managers, engineers, and mechanics all have need, from time to time, to adjust the plan's schedule for numerous good reasons, and this must be respected and planned for.

Feedback for Planning

An airplane makes no money on the ground; taking all the time you need for maintenance is not usually an option. It is important, therefore, for maintenance and planners to know how much time is needed to perform the tasks and the overall checks so that planning can be done accurately and the check can be completed within a reasonable amount of time.

The original plan for a letter check is developed on the best information at hand. The plan is then reviewed by all the work centers involved to head off any obvious problems. But when the time comes to work the plan, other factors come into play that require changes to be made. It is very important that these changes get back to the PP&C planners so that the next planning effort can take these things into account.

What the planners need to know to adjust future plans are the following:

1. The amount of time required to perform each task

2. The amount of time lost in waiting for delivery of parts and supplies

3. The down time for unusual circumstances

4. The additional time required for nonroutine findings

5. The variation in manpower availability

6. Lost time due to parts robbing from other jobs (or from the aircraft in check)

This information is used in many ways. Scheduling of tasks can be more accurate if the actual time requirements are known instead of the estimated or calculated time requirements from the maintenance planning data. If time is being lost because parts or supplies are not at the work place when needed, arrangements must be made for more timely delivery for the next scheduled check. And if there is going to be a change in available personnel (due to vacations, etc.) for the next check, this may also have an effect on the accomplishment of the work and should be included in the plan.

Parts robbing at airlines is an age-old problem. Those working on the flight line have an obligation to return aircraft to service as quickly as possible. If parts are required to do that and the parts are not available in stock, the most likely source would be any airplane that is not currently scheduled for flight. That makes the one setting in the hangar for "C" check a prime source. Presumably, the part can be ordered and, hopefully, arrive before the "C" check is done. Unfortunately, for those doing the "C" check, this often requires the same work to be done twice and the result is more time than necessary taken to finish the check.

Although parts robbing has a detrimental effect on the scheduled check, it is not just a problem for planning. It is really a problem for the whole M&E organization. One that should be resolved by someone other than (higher than) PP&C. Its effect, however, until resolved, still must be included in check planning efforts. Parts robbing is discussed further in Chap. 14.

Organization of PP&C

This planning work can be done by a centralized or decentralized PP&C group. In the centralized group, all functions—forecasting, planning, and control—are done in the organization with liaison to the work centers during actual performance of work. In a partially decentralized organization, the forecasting and planning would be done by PP&C and the control would be done by personnel in the hangar or other work centers. There must be feedback and coordination between the two factions, however, for PP&C to develop usable plans in the future.

In some airlines, the PP&C function is entirely decentralized. That is, all the planning and the control is done by each work center. The problem encountered in this arrangement is that there may be little or no coordination among the work centers. If the airline structure and size is such that the planning has to be done by the individual work centers instead of an overall group, there must still be some coordination and control at the M&E organizational level. Usually, however, the totally decentralized approach is not recommended.

10

Technical Publications

Introduction

In Chap. 5, we discussed the numerous documents needed to address the maintenance activities of a modern commercial airline. It should be immediately apparent that producing, distributing, and updating these documents is a considerable task. For that reason, we have established the technical publications department within the technical services directorate of our typical midsized airline. In the smaller airlines, for reasons we have discussed before, a different arrangement may be more effective. In these small airlines, the technical publications unit could be part of the engineering organization or possibly quality assurance. Larger airlines may require an expanded publications unit. In any case, the functions and requirements discussed in this chapter will apply to all airlines no matter how they are organized.

Functions of Technical Publications

The technical publications organization essentially has three functions: (*a*) to receive and distribute, within the airline, all those publications issued by outside sources; (*b*) to print and distribute the publications generated by the various organizations within the airline; and (*c*) to establish and maintain a complete, up-to-date library system for all such documents as needed for the operation of M&E.

Outside sources of documents would include airframe and engine manufacturers, vendors and manufacturers of equipment installed on the aircraft, and manufacturers of special tools and test equipment used in the maintenance effort. These documents may consist of initial issue of maintenance manuals and other such documents as well as any periodic or occasional revisions to those manuals. This would also include service letters (SLs), service bulletins (SBs), or maintenance tips issued by these manufacturers or vendors. Federal Aviation

Regulations (FARs), airworthiness directives (ADs), advisory circulars (ACs), and other official publications from the airline's regulatory authority would also be included here.

Internal airline documents consist of the airline technical policies and procedures manual (TPPM), the reliability program manual, and any other maintenance and inspection documents generated by the airline itself (see Chap. 5 for a detailed list). Many of the documents produced by other M&E units, such as engineering, QA, etc., may be created by the unit having primary responsibility but will usually be reproduced and distributed by technical publications simply because the process and facility for doing so is already in place. This could include such documents as monthly reliability reports, engineering orders, work packages for line or hangar maintenance checks, tool and equipment calibration schedules, and other such documents.

Airline Libraries

The primary reason for having a technical publications organization is to ensure that all applicable publications related to the airline operation are available to the users and are up to date with the latest changes. The most common way to accomplish this is to establish a main library for the M&E organization. If the M&E organization is of any appreciable size, the location of a single library would be inconvenient for many users and the number of copies of each document might be limited. For that reason, the technical publications organization at most airlines maintains, in addition to the main library, one or more satellite libraries strategically located to minimize travel times to access the information needed. While the main M&E library will contain all publications related to maintenance, engineering, and inspection activities, the documents on hand at any satellite library will usually be limited to copies of only those documents relating to the particular function served. Each library—main and satellite—should contain the necessary tables, chairs, shelves, microfilm readers and printers, computer terminals, and copy machines as needed to serve the users and the document formats (paper, microfilm, electronic) which will be available there. Table 10-1 is a list of some of the possible locations of satellite libraries.

TABLE 10-1   Satellite Libraries

Maintenance control center (flight line)
Line stations (1 or more)
Hangar dock
Overhaul shops in hangar
Engineering
Maintenance training
Production planning
Quality assurance
Reliability (may be colocated with engineering or QA)
Materiel

Control of Publications

Maintenance related documents are classified as either "uncontrolled" or "controlled" documents. Uncontrolled documents are issued for general information only and are not used to certify airworthiness. They do not require any of the tracking system requirements discussed below for controlled documents.

Controlled documents are those documents that are used to certify airworthiness of the aircraft, engines, and components. Each controlled document will contain a list of effective pages (LEP) and a record of revisions to the document identifying the revision number or letter and the date of that revision. The LEP will also reflect the active page numbers of the latest revision. Table 10-2 is a typical list of controlled documents.

One master copy of each controlled document will be kept on file in the main technical library of the M&E organization either in paper or microfilm format. Each copy of a controlled document (including the master) will be issued a library number; e.g., "Copy 6 of 14" in addition to any document number. The library staff will maintain records of each distributed document by document name, document number, library number, the name of the department to which it is issued, and the name of the person responsible for documents within that organization.

Manufacturer's documents usually have standard revision cycles (e.g., 3 months, 4 months, yearly), but some are revised on an "as needed" basis. Regulatory authorities also have some regular and some irregular revision cycles for their publications. While the airline can set revision cycles of its internal documents as it chooses, it is often necessary to make revisions to these internal documents in accordance with the changes made by the other documents (manufacturers, FAA, etc.); therefore local revision cycles would be in line with these changes.

It is the airline's responsibility to address these changes as quickly as possible. The technical publications organization has the responsibility of issuing revisions—whether separate pages or whole documents—to the appropriate work centers as soon as they are received. For this reason, they need to determine how many copies are needed and in what format (paper, microfilm, electronic) so that this distribution can be done efficiently without the need for making or ordering additional copies. This information can be kept on paper, 3×5-in file cards, or on the computer system.

TABLE 10-2   Controlled Documents Listing

Operations specifications
Technical policies and procedures manual[*]
Manufacturer and vendor manuals (see Table 5-1)
Regulatory authority documents (see Table 5-2)
Applicable airworthiness directives
Applicable aircraft type data sheets
Applicable aircraft supplemental type certificate

[*]If the airline chooses to publish the inspection and reliability program manuals separately from the TPPM, they will also be controlled documents.

Document Distribution

Technical publications will package documents and revisions and send them to the using organizations by the most appropriate means (e.g., hand carried, sent through company mail, shipped on company airplanes, or sent by commercial courier service). This package should be accompanied by a letter or other form from technical publications identifying the material being sent by document number, copy number, and revision date. It should also identify to whom it was sent and the date it was sent. There should also be a space for the recipient to sign (or initial) to verify receipt. The person receiving the documents will check the package for content and applicability and return the signed acknowledgement to Tech Pubs. Verification is returned to the technical publications office by the most convenient means.

This process ensures that these documents have, in fact, been controlled up to the point of delivery and receipt. It is the receiving unit's responsibility to actually make the changes to their documents and to ensure that they are kept up to date at all times. Whether or not this is done can be checked periodically by the technical publications staff, quality control inspectors, or even maintenance management. It will most certainly be an item of concern on the quality assurance or regulatory authority audits.

Introduction

An airline is responsible for the proper training of all its personnel. This includes flight crews, cabin crews, ground handling crews, maintenance mechanics and technicians, inspectors, auditors, managers, computer operators, and administrative personnel. A significant portion of their training—especially for flight crews, cabin crews, and maintenance personnel—is usually accomplished prior to hiring into the airline. This involves formal, specialized training sanctioned by the FAA and the issuance of an FAA license for the particular specialty.

To be eligible for a mechanics license (FAR 65.71) a person must (*a*) be at least 18 years of age; (*b*) be able to read, write, speak, and understand the English language; (*c*) have passed all the prescribed tests within a 24-month period; and (*d*) comply with the FAR requirements that apply to the rating he or she seeks. These items qualify him or her for the airframe and power plant (A&P) license. However, having an A&P license does not mean that a mechanic or aviation maintenance technician (AMT) is capable of working on specific equipment or systems at a certain airline. The A&P license signifies that the mechanic or AMT has completed the basic training for aviation maintenance but he or she must be trained to perform maintenance and servicing activities on the airline's specific equipment; and that training must be documented. In case of an aviation accident or incident, the investigator often asks "Was the mechanic properly trained?" The answer given must be backed up by documentation showing not only the extent of the training but also when and where it was done. Currency is very important. FAR 121.375 specifies the general requirements; various other FARs provide details on training requirements.

The subject and extent of training required after the employee receives his or her A&P license and is hired by the airline varies throughout the industry and that variation is based on many things. This chapter will discuss the various types of training requirements an airline must meet.

The airline, having selected those people with proper training and experience as fit their needs, will then place these new hires in orientation classes in order to train them on the airline's specific policies, procedures, paperwork, and equipment. Over time, it will be necessary to provide additional training to various personnel either at the airline or at some outside facility such as a manufacturer's or a vendor's plant, at another airline, or at special training schools. The training received by each employee must be recorded in his or her training records (or personnel file) and any licenses affected by the training must be monitored and updated accordingly.

Organization

Since all airline personnel require training of one sort or another, it is necessary to have a training organization to address these needs. This organization can take on various forms. There can be an airline training organization or school at corporate level that is responsible for the training of all airline personnel or there can be separate organizations responsible for maintenance training, flight crew training, cabin crew training, and management and administrative personnel training as necessary.

There are numerous arguments for and against any of these arrangements and much depends upon the size of the airline, its actual requirements for training, and the airlines own management structure and philosophy. In this book, however, we endorse the concept of a separate training organization for all of maintenance and engineering. For midsized and larger airlines, this is more efficient. For large airlines with a high turnover of personnel, or airlines undergoing a change of fleet size or makeup, there will be a considerable amount of training activity. The same might be said for airlines with new, inexperienced maintenance crews. It is the technical training organization's responsibility to provide the training required either through existing airline courses or by arranging any new or one-time courses to accommodate the needs. Instructors would be either full-time training instructors or specialists drawn from other M&E organizations (e.g., engineering, maintenance, QA, QC, safety, planning, etc.).

For airlines whose personnel are fully trained and experienced and those without significant fleet or personnel changes, the requirement for ongoing training is minimal and a full-time M&E training organization may not be necessary. However, it is necessary for the M&E organization of such an airline to have a training coordinator in place to properly address any training needs that may arise through quality audits, the reliability program, the hiring of new personnel, or the access of new equipment.

It is this training coordinator's responsibility to monitor licenses and additional training requirements of mechanics, technicians, auditors, and inspectors, as determined by QA, QC, reliability, or maintenance management, and to arrange for that training as necessary. This training can be done by airline personnel (if qualified) working in M&E, by the airline training organization (if one exists), or by any appropriate outside source.

This training coordinator could be a maintenance supervisor or engineer within M&E (maintenance, QA, QC, engineering, etc.). In this case, the training coordinator is a part-time job added to his or her primary duties. However, because of the requirement for QA to maintain standards, the training coordinator must answer to QA in the performance of his or her training duties.

Training for Aviation Maintenance

For maintenance people, there are several different kinds of training activities that are required from time to time: (*a*) formal training; (*b*) organizational training; (*c*) manufacturer's training; (*d*) quality training; (*e*) on-the-job training; (*f*) upgrade training; and (*g*) refresher training. Each of these is discussed below.

Formal training

This training is usually accomplished before the mechanic is hired. A&P mechanics and technicians can come from FAA approved A&P schools, from technical/trade schools with appropriate aviation curricula, or from the U.S. military services. The FAA approved schools usually graduate students with the appropriate license (airframe/power plant or avionics). The other two sources of training require that the applicant arrange with the FAA to take the necessary tests for attaining the desired license. Some airlines have a special program where they hire mechanic trainees out of high school or other equivalent curricula and train them as aircraft mechanics either at their airline, at contractor airlines, or at special schools that are approved by the regulatory authority. They are airline employees while they study.

Organizational training

This training is developed and conducted by the airline organization itself and covers the airline's basic policies and procedures, paper work, and specific aviation systems and equipment in use at the airline. These curricula could include full courses for a particular airframe and its systems or could involve only the differences between the airline's equipment and that for which the mechanic has current experience. All training courses should address the safety and human factors issues as applicable.

Manufacturer or vendor training

Airframe, engine, and aircraft equipment manufacturers often offer specialized training on their products or on special activities related to their products either at their facilities or at the airline. The airline training organization makes all arrangements and monitors the activity.

Quality training

Quality assurance auditors require training in auditing procedures and techniques as well as refresher training on regulations and airline policies; quality control inspectors need to be trained on inspection techniques and on tool and equipment calibration. Mechanics authorized to perform required inspection items (RIIs) must receive special training from the airline or an outside organization in inspection techniques and other details of the units for which they will be responsible.

On-the-job training (OJT)

On-the-job training involves special procedures that cannot be covered completely or effectively in classroom sessions and those that can only be accomplished by hands-on experience on the job. In some specialties, OJT might be the only training required. For certified mechanics, OJT may be used exclusively in upgrade or refresher training (see below) or in conjunction with classroom work. This "hands-on training" is usually done by the work center but will be coordinated with the training section that will update the employee's training records.

Upgrade training

This kind of training is required when new equipment is incorporated in the unit's vehicles or fleet or when new procedures are implemented in the maintenance activity. Other upgrade training classes may be conducted (on- or off-site) to permit mechanics to upgrade their licenses or their work status.

Refresher training

This training is required whenever it is noted that a mechanic or technician is "rusty" and needs to review or reverify certain skills. This may occur because the mechanic has had extended periods of time where he or she was not exposed to the equipment or maintenance activities.

These latter two types of training, upgrade and refresher training, are usually developed by the organization, and are done on an "as necessary" basis.

Maintenance Resources Management

Considerable interest has developed in recent years in the subject of human factors in maintenance (HMF). Appendix B of this book discusses human factors. The training organization is tasked with the responsibility of developing a basic course in human factors (HF) and in incorporating HF into other training courses as applicable. The FAA has issued Advisory Circular AC 120-72, maintenance resource management (MRM) training to outline the requirements for this type of training. Appendix 1 of AC 120-72 outlines a typical program; paragraph 11 of the document (pages 21–29) provides guidelines for developing such a course. These guidelines can also be used, with some modification, to develop other M&E courses.

Airframe Manufacturer's Training Courses

Whenever an airline buys one or more aircraft from the airframe manufacturer (Boeing, Lockheed, Airbus, etc.) they usually get, as part of the purchase price, a certain number of training slots for the manufacturer's training classes on that model. This would include courses on the airframe, power plant, and avionics equipment installed. Who attends these classes for the airline differs from operator to operator and is often dependent on airline size and management. For small airlines, the mechanics who will be working on the aircraft systems while in service or their supervisors will attend these classes. Very often, both will attend. In larger airlines, some or all of these training slots may be given to the maintenance instructors of the airline's training organization. The choice, of course, is at the airline's discretion. If airline training instructors attend, they will return with the responsibility of creating the airline's version of the course and presenting the material to the airline's mechanics.

In cases where the new equipment is only partially different from equipment currently in use—a 767-300, for instance, going to an airline that already flies 767-200s—only the differences between the two models need be taught to the airline personnel. This airline may already have a 767-200 course established and mechanics will need only to be taught the differences in the 767-300. Meanwhile, the airline's existing course can be modified to include the differences and subsequent trainees at the airline can get training on either or both as necessary.

On many occasions manufacturers will offer special courses on specific equipment at their plant or at the airline's location. Engine condition monitoring (ECM) courses are offered by all engine manufacturers to train airline people on the use of their special computer programs that monitor engine health. Since only a few people at each airline need this training, there is usually no on-site training. Mechanics, managers, inspectors, or instructors from several airlines may be trained in a single class at the engine manufacturer's facility or some other convenient place.

Airframe, engine, and equipment manufacturers may provide a variety of "one-time" programs at the airline venue. This might include training on such topics as extended range operations with two engine airplanes (ETOPS); corrosion protection and control program (CPCP); maintenance error detection aids (MEDA); nondestructive test and inspection techniques (NDT/NDI); aviation safety; reliability programs; and the like. Although these courses are presented by outside sources, the airline training office is involved, since they must provide classroom space and other assistance as necessary and they must update the training records of those in attendance.

Other Airline Training Courses

Other courses presented by the training organization are often "one-time" courses implemented to address some detected deficiency within the M&E operation. The QA auditors or QC inspectors may determine that some procedure needs to be improved or is not being performed correctly by one or more mechanics. It may also be noted that certain mechanics are weak in certain areas. In such cases as these, it may be necessary to set up special refresher training classes to accommodate the problem. These could be classroom, laboratory, or on-the-job training sessions, or some combination of these as necessary. In an airline with an M&E training organization, this would be handled by the available instructors or by a qualified mechanic, manager, engineer, or inspector from within M&E. If an M&E training organization does not exist, the training coordinator must arrange such training with any other sources available. If the M&E training organization does exist but is incapable of performing this particular training (for whatever the reason), arrangements should be made by the training organization for outside assistance.

Note: It should be understood that training deficiencies among certificated mechanics and technicians can jeopardize their certification and the airline's operations certificate. It should also be understood, however, that not all personnel are perfect. The airline management must always be alert to any training needs and must ensure that qualified personnel are employed in performing and certifying all maintenance work that is accomplished.

There are additional training requirements at an airline that may be necessary from time to time and they may or may not be available in-house. Nevertheless, the training department will be responsible for arranging for the accomplishment of the training. This would include the specialized training required for quality assurance auditors, quality control inspectors, RII inspectors, NDT/NDI procedures, engine operations (run-up, boroscope inspection, etc.), taxiing, and towing of aircraft. The training organization is required to respond to airline needs by either conducting these classes themselves or by coordinating with other qualified training units.

It should be noted here that any requirement for training of M&E personnel, whether it can be done by the airline staff or not, is the primary responsibility of the training coordinator, the M&E training organization, or the airline training school—whichever is extant at the airline in question. The important thing to remember is that the M&E organization must maintain some sense of control over the training of its own personnel regardless of the airline's organizational structure or management philosophy and must keep adequate records of such training that affects the certification and capabilities of the mechanics and the airline.

12

Computer Support

What Is a Computer?

To some people, the computer is little more than a toy. Games and other pastimes are available in such variety and number that special stores are dedicated to the exclusive sale of these products. Almost every desktop computer sold includes certain games with the basic software. To other people, however, the computer is a tool. It does work by extending or amplifying the power, dexterity, and skill of its user. It comes in a wide variety of forms, from simple but specialized processors in toasters and other household appliances, to massive mainframe processing and storage units that take up whole floors of buildings in corporate, government, or military organizations. Traffic signal systems on our city streets are controlled by computer; personnel and payroll records are processed by computer; even your grades for college classes are kept on computer.

In our humble profession of aviation maintenance, the computer is used for numerous day-to-day activities such as communications (letters, memos, messages, e-mails); filing (flight, maintenance, and materiel data); and a myriad of data processing, graphic, and report writing activities. But generally, people have a rather unclear notion of just what a computer—or a computer system—is capable or not capable of doing. This should be clarified at the outset.

First of all, a computer cannot do anything of its own volition, for it is not human; it has no capability of voluntary action. The computer is limited by whatever hardware and software capabilities have been given to it by its designers and programmers. Secondly, the computer can only do what it has been designed to do within the limits of that design (hardware and software). All input data will be processed the same way according to the computer instructions written into the software and, except in certain cases where steps are written to detect some (but not all) errors in the input data, the computer cannot determine the validity of the input or the results.

Two things, then, are very important: (*a*) the computer user must understand what this tool is to be used for and must use it within those limits and (*b*) developers of computer hardware and software must be cognizant of the users' wants, needs, and capabilities so they can design a system that is usable. Appendixes A and B talk about systems engineering and human factors, respectively. In these articles, we emphasize the need to consider the human user during the design phase of any complex system. The design of a computer system is just one place where this concept is of great importance.

No matter how brilliant the designers of the hardware and software are, their systems are not acceptable unless we, the users, can use them to do our job, and we should not have to know the computer designer or programmer's job skills to do so. The computer people must build the system that we can use to do the job we want to do, and in the manner that we want it done.

In this book, we will talk about computer systems in the context of Appendixes A and B. That is, the system will consist of hardware, software, input and output peripherals, interfaces, and users and operators.

Airline Uses of Computers

An airline's need for a computer (as anyone else's need) is dynamic—always changing. The more we attain in computer capability the more we want: more memory, more speed, more flexibility, more everything. As we grow in computer usage skills we see more and more that we want to do with this marvelous tool. Even the small airline has a considerable need for the talents of a good computer system. Large airlines such as United, Delta, or British could not operate efficiently without computers. Perhaps they could not operate at all. In the following paragraphs we will show just a few of maintenance and engineering's use for the computer.

Maintenance tasks

All tasks listed in the MRB report selected by the airline engineering section and any additional tasks identified by them would be entered into the computer by engineering. Each item of the letter checks will be identified by its check and interval including those tasks designated as multiple checks; i.e., 1A, 2A, 3A, 1C, 2C, 4C, and so forth. These data would then be accessible by production planning and control for the purpose of generating the work package for the individual check performed by line or hangar maintenance.

These check packages would include task cards for the particular check to be done. For example, if B757, tail number 318, is due for its fourth "A" check, the check package developed by PP&C would include those tasks identified as 1A, 2A, and 4A in the maintenance program (see Table 9-3, Chap. 9) and any tasks deferred by line maintenance, as well as any ADs, SBs, or other tests or modifications that have been identified to be accomplished during this check period. Another aircraft, say a B757, tail number 319, may be newer and will be undergoing its third "A" check after 318 leaves the hangar. For this check, PP&C will select tasks from the computer identified as 1A and 3A to create the check package.

The PP&C organization needs the capability of extracting these data from the computer and generating standardized task cards for all work required. In addition, any nonroutine work generated as a result of routine inspections or functional tests, as well as that generated by QC inspectors, would also require task cards to be generated by the computer to complete the package.

When all the work is done and the aircraft is released from check by QC, the results are summarized and recorded in the computer for future reference. Thus, reliability, engineering, maintenance, or anyone in need of the data can access the computer for the information. Such uses for the information would be to aid in troubleshooting future problems, collect statistics for reliability reports, provide justification for interval escalation, or a number of other useful purposes.

The PP&C unit also needs to regularly scan the computer's maintenance task database to determine all upcoming tasks whose intervals are less than the "A" check interval so that they may be properly scheduled prior to their maximum time or cycle limits.

Aircraft and engine data

Each aircraft in service accrues flight time and flight cycles. These data, recorded in the computer by flight operations or line maintenance, are useful to numerous organizations and for many purposes. Maintenance needs the data to determine when maintenance tasks and checks are due. Materiel needs to know how many hours and/or cycles have accrued for certain serial-numbered and time-limited parts. Materiel also needs to know the location of such parts; i.e., on which aircraft, in the shop, on the shelf, in transit to or from maintenance. And the computer program must be able to tally time and/or cycles on these parts as they are moved from one place to another.

Materiel

One of the largest and most important uses of the computer is to identify, locate, and process thousands of parts and supplies needed for M&E activities. Besides identifying each part by part number and vendor, materiel needs to know how many parts are on hand, where they are located, whether or not they are repairable or under warranty, what the "normal" usage rate is, when to reorder (this involves the lead time to receive the parts), and where a repairable part is at any given time (aircraft, shop, vendor, or stores).

The uses an airline has for a computing system are legion. Organizations such as QA, QC, reliability, and training all have their own needs and much of the data are shared. Some units provide inputs to the computer for others to utilize in various forms. We will leave it as an exercise for the student to determine computer requirements and to identify what inputs and outputs would be needed to accommodate these requirements for your own airline. This is something an

TABLE 12-1   Computer Software Modules (Examples)

Airplane maintenance module
Time recording module
Component maintenance module
Modification management module
Data analysis and monitoring module
Shop planning module
Materiel management module
Aircraft performance module
Additional modules for business activities (ticketing, scheduling, etc.)

airline would have to do anyway and is discussed further in a later section of this chapter.

Computer Program Modules

The software needed to accomplish the M&E requirements can be quite complex. If an airline is going to go from manual operation to computerized operation, it could be a rather extensive project to install the system and train everyone on its proper use. To ease the problem, most software packages are produced in modular form. This allows a user to implement one or a few modules at a time. Table 12-1 shows a list of computer modules available from various software developers. Each has its own input requirements but each provider's software system is designed to be compatible with all its own modules. You cannot usually mix modules from different software packages.

It is usually recommended that an airline begin with the materiel module. Getting parts and supplies processing taken care of first is a major accomplishment. Engineering and maintenance modules might come next. The engineering module would get the maintenance tasks and program schedules organized. The maintenance module would allow the aircraft maintenance logbook information to be entered (usually by MCC) on a regular basis. These data could then be utilized by maintenance crews for troubleshooting subsequent problems and by reliability for their data collection and analysis activities for the monthly reliability report. This report, of course, would access additional information from the computer such as flight time and cycles flown for the month, number and types of aircraft in service as well as those out of service (see Chap. 19).

Selecting a Computer System

There is a right way and a wrong way to select a computer system for airline maintenance or any other application for that matter. The mistake often made by airlines is to spend a considerable sum of money for a mainframe computer, with standard peripherals, and then try to make it work for their operation. A more "modern" manager may buy a truckload of PCs with the intention of networking them together into a "system." In either case, this can be somewhat limiting at the outset and can cost a lot to modify it to work as you really need it to work.

The most effective approach is quite opposite to the method described above. Basically, the sensible approach is to determine what you want the computer to do, find out what software is available to do it, and then determine the platform needed to run the software. Although there may be some interaction among these three simple steps, the result will be more satisfying than the naive approach discussed above. Let us look at the three steps.

Step one

Step one is actually a two-part process. The first part in this process requires that you determine what you want the computer to do. What outputs do you want in terms of raw data, reports, charts, and graphs? What calculations and data manipulation capabilities do you want to have available? The second part of the first step is to determine what input data you need to meet these output and processing requirements. Who will input these data (what organization)? How will it be input (keyboard, scanner, download)? What format should be used for input? What data can be shared with other M&E units? Other airline units? These inputs and outputs will dictate to some extent what peripheral devices will be needed to support your needs: keyboards, terminals, scanners, printers, etc. There may also be a need to accommodate interface with other computers within the airline.

Step two

The second step in the simplified process is to determine the software that you will need to meet your computing requirements. This not only includes the handling of input and output data but also the processing, calculating, and other data manipulations needed to accomplish your needs. In planning your computer system, you should also consider future needs so that the capability to add, delete, or change processes, reports, etc. will be available to you.

There are several choices in the approach to software selection and each has its own merits. First, there is off-the-shelf software—fixed packages that do basic operations, produce standard reports, etc., in accordance with someone's idea of just what you need to get started. This might be affordable but will also become more and more limited as your needs and interests develop. Some software developers offer customizing of their software for an additional price. This may be more acceptable but can still be limiting as your airline and its needs grow. Flexibility and growth potential are very important in software selection.

A second alternative is to have the software developed specifically for your organization. This will, no doubt, be more expensive than the previous option but it will also be more satisfactory to your operation. This option will also require that you work closely with the developer concerning your wants and needs.

A third option, open to those who have the skills available, is to write your own software to ensure that you get exactly what you want and need at a reasonable price.

TABLE 12-2   Buying a New Computer System

Step 1.1—What do I want the computer to do?

Outputs	Raw data, reports, charts, graphs, manipulations, calculations
Shared data	Data used by other airline and M&E units
Flexibility	Adding, deleting, changing needs

Step 1.2—How do I get that desired output?

Inputs	What information, who inputs, how input, what format
Software	Processing, calculation, chart, graph, report requirements

Step 2—What software will accommodate the inputs, outputs, and processing requirements?

Off the shelf	Prepackaged; may be limited
Off the shelf	Tailored to my needs; more flexible
Custom SW	Software written for my airline; more flexible
Custom SW	Software written by my airline; most flexible

Step 3—What platform is required to run the selected software?

Main frame
Mini computer
Microcomputer (desktop)
Combination

There are many large airlines that have done this quite successfully. Some of them offer their creations for sale to other airlines. As with any good software package, these are written so that they can be easily customized and modified for future needs.

Step three

The third and last step in our simplified process is to select the hardware needed to run the selected software and to accommodate the desired input and output requirements. This could be a mainframe computer system, a mini computer, or a group of networked desktop computers. With today's capabilities, a single desktop (or laptop) computer might be sufficient for an air taxi service with only one airplane. This three-step process is summarized in Table 12-2.

Chances are that an airline would want a mainframe (for storage capacity and major sorting and processing functions) accessed by smart terminals or desktop computers, used as smart terminals, for data input and output. In the latter case, the desktop could be used for other activities aside from the main computing effort; e.g., correspondence, unit-specific activities, or games.

Maintenance and Materiel Support

In earlier chapters, we discussed two types of maintenance: scheduled and unscheduled. The working maintenance organization, however, is not divided in that manner. For operational reasons, maintenance activities are divided into the categories of on-aircraft maintenance and off-aircraft maintenance. On-aircraft maintenance is further divided into line and hangar maintenance activities. The unique feature of on-aircraft maintenance is that the effort is performed at or on the aircraft. Components and systems are troubleshot, repaired, and tested in the airplane and faulty units are removed and replaced with functional units. The aircraft is then returned to service. The units removed are either discarded or sent to the appropriate shop for repair. This shop activity constitutes the bulk of the off-aircraft maintenance activity.

In support of both on- and off-aircraft maintenance activities is the requirement for parts and supplies, which are handled by the materiel section, and the need for (in certain cases) special tools and equipment, which is handled by the tool sheds that may be located in several places (line and hangar) for convenience. There is also a requirement for stands, power units, heaters, and various other equipments designated as ground support equipment, or GSE. Although line and hangar people often share some of this equipment, it is usually handled by a single GSE organization. This GSE organization is also responsible for maintenance and servicing of this ground support equipment.

Chapter 13 will discuss the on-aircraft maintenance activities for all aircraft in scheduled service. Chapter 14 will discuss hangar maintenance, which is also on-aircraft maintenance, as well as the tool sheds and GSE. Off-aircraft maintenance will be discussed in Chap. 15, and materiel support will be covered in Chap. 16. Figure III-1 shows these organizations.

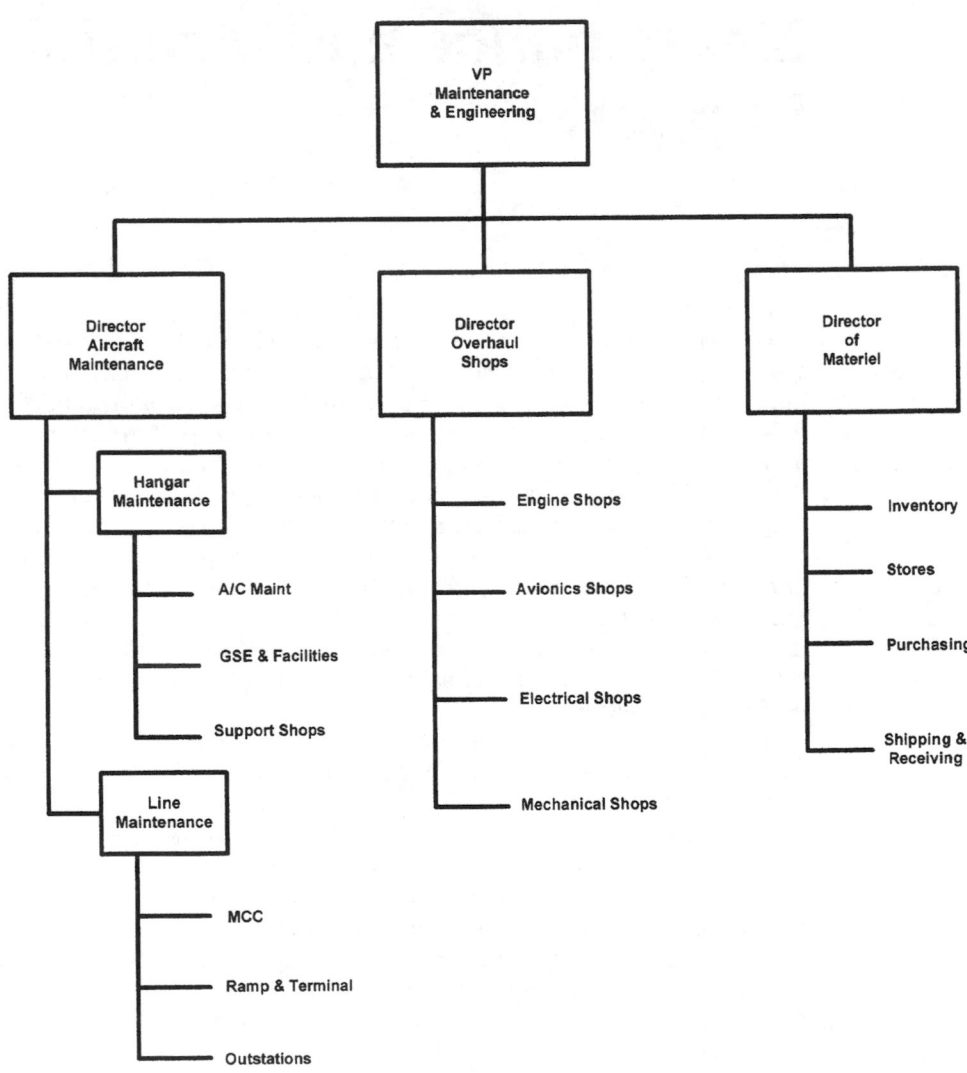

Figure III-1   Organizational chart for maintenance and materiel

13

Line Maintenance (on-Aircraft)

Makeup of Line Maintenance

Depending on the size of the airline, the line maintenance organization may take on different structures. But in our typical midsized airline, organized according to the chart in Fig. III-1, we have a maintenance control center (MCC), to coordinate all maintenance activity on the flight line at the home station and at all outstations where the operator's aircraft will land; a supervisor of ramp and terminal maintenance, to manage the local, home base activities; and a supervisor of outstations to coordinate all maintenance activities at other stations, whether or not those stations are manned by the airline. In some cases, the latter function is handled by the MCC and the outstation supervisor will be part of that center.

The kind of work done by line maintenance is any maintenance that can be done on the aircraft in service without taking them out of service; i.e., without removing them from the flight schedule. This includes everything from daily, 48-hour, and transit checks; the less than "A" check items; and, in most airlines, the "A" checks themselves as described in Chap. 2. If an airline has "B" checks (at intervals between "A" and "C" checks), these are usually done by line maintenance also.

The crews used for line maintenance, again determined by the size of the organization, may consist of a single crew to perform all of the items mentioned above or they may be separate crews for certain tasks. For example, one crew might be assigned exclusively to transit checks to handle all servicing and all logbook discrepancies of scheduled aircraft. Daily and 48-hour checks, usually performed first thing in the morning or overnight, may be handled by this crew or another dedicated crew.

The less than "A" check items may be handled by a separate crew on the third shift (overnight) or by the transit crew after the turnaround maintenance is done (if time permits). This arrangement often requires the less than "A" check tasks to be scheduled several days in advance. Due to the more pressing work of turnaround, these added tasks are often slipped from 1 day to the next until the deadline is reached. At this time, it is often necessary to take the airplane out of service long enough to complete the items within the prescribed interval. This arrangement is not recommended.

In many airlines, these less than "A" check interval tasks are added to other task schedules such as the daily check or an overnight. All of this work is defined by engineering and scheduled by production planning and control (see Chaps. 8 and 9, respectively) and is administered by the maintenance control center.

Functions that Control Maintenance

There are two organizations in M&E responsible for controlling maintenance activities and these are shown in Fig. 13-1. We have already discussed the primary control function, production planning and control, in Chap. 9. This group requires input from various sources identified on the left of Fig. 13-1. Any maintenance that is identified in the airline's maintenance program, plus any additional requirements for modification, upgrade, or maintenance deferred from earlier checks, are controlled (scheduled) by PP&C. This maintenance is directed

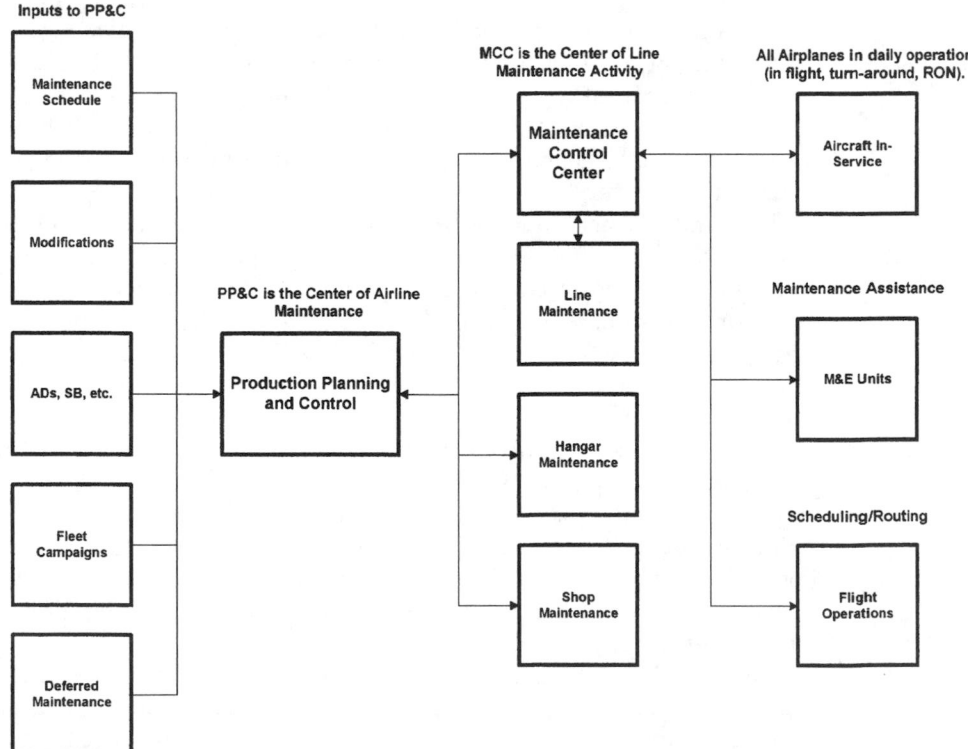

Figure 13-1   Functions controlling maintenance.

toward the hangar, the shops, and the flight line as necessary. The PP&C organization interfaces with line maintenance through the second controlling activity, the maintenance control center.

The MCC coordinates all maintenance activity—scheduled or unscheduled—for the aircraft in service with the applicable M&E organization and with the flight operations. Note the double-headed arrows in Fig. 13-1. These indicate a two-way communication. The MCC must deal with all aircraft in the flight schedule, regardless of where they are in the route structure, and must coordinate all maintenance activity whether it is done by the airline or a third party. The MCC also coordinates the contracting of maintenance at units where no previous maintenance agreement exists. The MCC also coordinates with any of the airline's M&E units for support of in-service aircraft discrepancies and the rescheduling of maintenance actions; and with the flight operations organization regarding down times, flight delays, and cancellations.

If maintenance is required by an aircraft in service and such support is not available at the aircraft's current location, maintenance may be deferred—all other requirements being met. This deferral will be handled by the MCC and they will schedule the work for another outstation or the home base wherever the appropriate time, facilities, and manpower exist. If the maintenance must be deferred to a major check ("A" check or higher) then MCC would coordinate that action with PP&C who will then schedule the work for an appropriate down time and ensure that parts, supplies, etc. will be available for that check. These deferrals, of course, must be in accordance with MEL and CDL requirements.

Maintenance Control Center Responsibilities

This is the heart of line maintenance. Regardless of how large or small an airline is, the MCC function must be established and must be in control. Their purpose is manyfold: (a) to ensure that daily checks are completed prior to the first flight of the day for each aircraft; (b) to perform transit or turnaround maintenance on all transit aircraft; (c) to coordinate servicing of these aircraft (food, water, waste, fuel, etc.); (d) to troubleshoot maintenance problems and schedule repairs (if possible) in the allotted turnaround time or defer that maintenance until a more appropriate time; (e) to coordinate with materiel, engineering, inspection, planning, and any other M&E organization as necessary for assistance in resolving maintenance problems; (f) coordinate with flight operations for the maintenance, or deferral of maintenance, whenever the schedule may be impacted; (g) track all aircraft during flight to determine their location, maintenance requirements, and status; (h) coordinate maintenance at outstations with other airlines or third party contractors as necessary; and (i) collect and forward logbook pages, QC write-ups, mechanical reliability reports, and any other reports (IFSDs, bird strikes, etc.) required by the airline or the FAA for aircraft in service.

Needless to say, the personnel in MCC have quite a large job to perform. To do this, they need the right facilities to aid them in the performance of the job.

First, they need a centrally located room near the main flight line operations where they can have close contact with all of the activity.

Secondly, the MCC should have sufficient tally boards or computer displays of all aircraft (by aircraft type and tail number) to identify flight schedules, flight durations, current location of aircraft, and maintenance needs, if any. These boards should also display the status of that maintenance and the due date of the next scheduled maintenance checks (A, B, C, etc.). If these checks are performed only at certain bases, it is MCC's responsibility to coordinate with flight operations and scheduling to see to it that the aircraft is in the proper place for that check when it comes due. The MCC should be "on top" of everything that is happening to all aircraft in service.

Thirdly, the MCC must have sufficient communications devices to carry out all the requirements stated above. That means telephones for internal and external conversations with anyone related to a given problem; radios for communications with aircraft; hand-held radios (or cell phones) for communication with maintenance crews on the line and in the field not accessible by other communications devices; and teletype, facsimile machines, and/or computer terminals for the transfer of data and forms between the various units.

To carry out many of the tasks assigned to it, the MCC must have access to maintenance manuals and other technical documents. The fourth requirement for MCC, then, is to have within the facility an extensive technical library (see Chap. 10). Since MCC is first to be notified of any maintenance problems, they are the first line of defense and are the ones responsible for effecting a speedy solution. They must coordinate with other M&E units to reach that successful completion. The MCC is in charge and is responsible for returning the aircraft to service.

And finally, MCC must have sufficient, qualified staff to carry out these activities and the ability to manage quick and accurate responses to any and all problems relating to maintenance of in-service aircraft. All MCC staff should be licensed mechanics. The MCC plays a very significant role in the effort to meet the goals and objectives of the maintenance and engineering organization as well as those of the airline.

One special function of the MCC is in support of the airline's reliability program. The MCC is responsible for identifying and reporting all delays and cancellations of aircraft. Since line maintenance and their procedures are integral to these delays, MCC will be a key player in the investigation and the solution to the problem. In addition, the MCC is responsible for investigating and resolving one of the unique reliability problems at an airline: repeat discrepancies. *Repeat discrepancies* are normally defined as problems or write-ups that occur more than three times in 5 days. For some airlines they specify four events in 7 days. This rate is usually specified in the airline's Ops Specs. If not, it should be clearly stated in the airline's reliability program document (see Chap. 19).

If a problem recurs often in a short period of time, there must be something wrong. It could be a procedure, a mechanic, the operational conditions (maintenance or nonmaintenance), environmental conditions, or bad parts. Whatever the reason, MCC does an immediate investigation to determine the problem and to effect a correction or solution. This is an effort to get on top of a problem without waiting until reliability data shows something wrong; it is an effort to resolve the problem before it gets any bigger. In all likelihood, a repeat discrepancy will not even show up in the reliability data. If the problem appears and is addressed quickly, it will not recur in sufficient numbers to result in a reliability alert; however, if not addressed immediately, the opposite may result (see Chap. 19).

Line Maintenance Operation—General

Figure 13-2 shows the typical flight line activities for a given flight.

An aircraft may or may not experience any faults or discrepancies during the flight. When the aircraft arrives at the gate, normal services (fuel, food, etc.) will be provided as well as the exchange of passengers, their baggage, and any cargo. If a failure or discrepancy did occur in flight, there are two possible scenarios. Normally the problem is written up in the aircraft maintenance logbook and addressed by the ground crew upon flight arrival. Maintenance actions would be as indicated by the center column blocks of Fig. 13-2. To minimize delay on

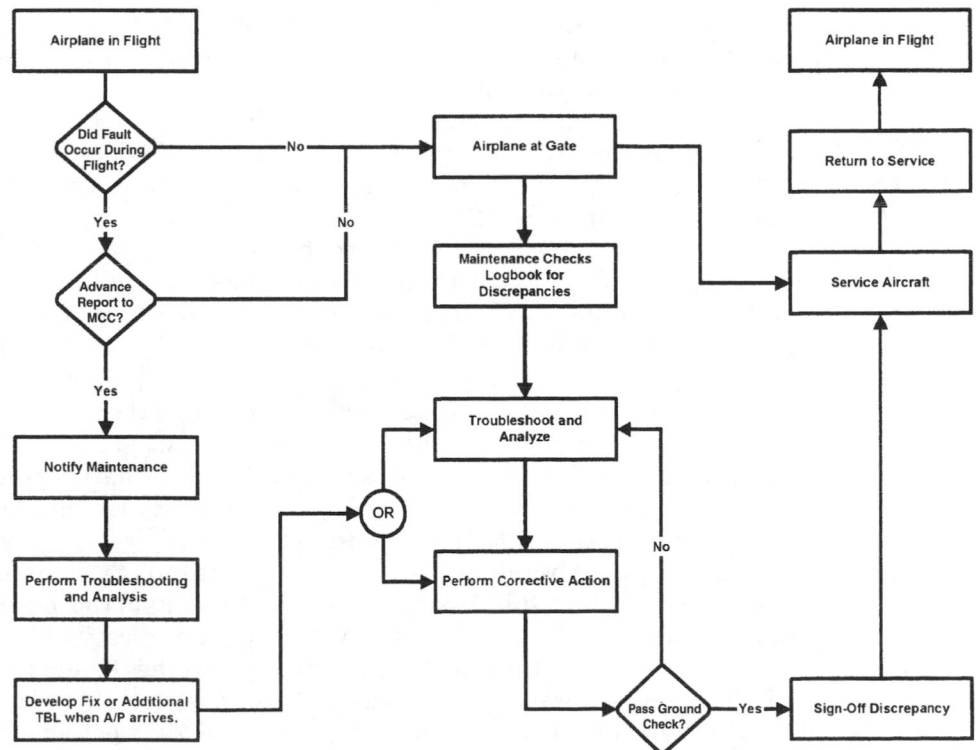

Figure 13-2   Line maintenance operations—turnaround.

the ground, however, it is recommended that advance warning be given to the maintenance personnel by the flight crew through flight operations and the MCC. This allows maintenance to spend time before the aircraft arrives to review past records and troubleshoot the problem. Thus, the actions shown in the left hand column of Fig. 13-2 are employed. In many cases, the maintenance crew can meet the aircraft with a solution in hand thus minimizing maintenance downtime and delays. This may be accomplished by a separate team or the same team that handles any other logbook items. Note that both sign-off of all discrepancies (or deferrals) and servicing of the aircraft must be completed prior to returning the aircraft to flight service.

Aircraft Logbook

The flight crew maintains a logbook in each aircraft and enters specific information related to each flight leg. This log contains basic information such as names of flight crew personnel; flight number, route, and flight times (arrival and departure as well as total flight hours and cycles). It also contains a section designed to allow the crew to write any discrepancies encountered during the flight. Once the aircraft has landed and arrived at the gate, maintenance personnel will address the problems, either by fixing the problem or deferring it to another time. Once such action has been completed, maintenance personnel enter the appropriate information in an adjacent block to the write-up. The aircraft is then released for service.

The logbook usually has a separate section in the back for maintenance crews to list any deferred maintenance actions so that the flight crew can be aware of current status of the aircraft. This log identifies the date repair is to be accomplished per the airline's MEL (see Chap. 1).

The aircraft logbook pages will be collected at the end of each flight day by MCC. For aircraft that do not return to the home base daily, the logbook pages can be faxed to the MCC. Actual pages will be submitted upon the aircraft's return. Information from the log will be entered into the M&E computer system concerning flight time and cycles; maintenance write-ups and the actions taken will also be entered. The ATA chapter designations and the airline's action taken codes entered by maintenance personnel will be checked by MCC for accuracy before entering such data into the computer. The information entered into the computer will be used by M&E, QA, QC, and reliability for various actions and future reference. After MCC has processed the logbook information, the log will be returned to the aircraft and be ready for the next day's flight activities.

Some modern aircraft have supplanted (or augmented) the logbook with electronic means. The ACARS system (ARINC Communications and Reporting System) is used to automatically transmit data to the airline's home station. This, however, requires expensive equipment in the aircraft and on the ground. For that reason, some airlines do not use ACARS. It is possible with ACARS, however, for the crew to transmit logbook reports to the MCC by radio prior to landing, thus facilitating maintenance actions.

Ramp and Terminal Operations

Transiting aircraft are the subject of a lot of attention at any airport, and that attention is usually concentrated in a short (often 30-minute) time span called the *turnaround*. During this turnaround, flight handling, servicing, and maintenance chores must be accomplished. Although not all of the following would be required at every turnaround, the list below provides an overview of what must be done.

Flight handling

The main purpose of flight handling is to move passengers, their baggage, and/or any carried cargo off and onto the aircraft as necessary. This begins with parking the aircraft at the gate and positioning the air stairs or the gateway ramp and opening the aircraft doors. This is a joint effort involving maintenance, ground handling crews, the flight and cabin crews, airline terminal personnel, and the FAA tower people responsible for ground control. Watching this activity from the passenger lounge, one sees a well-coordinated ballet of workers and machines.

The baggage and cargo loading equipment and crews form a second wave of activity followed by servicing and maintenance activities. Servicing consists of refueling, adding potable water, and all the food and beverages for the next flight as well as removing the trash and other waste materials of the previous one.

In the meantime (it is difficult to separate one activity from another from your vantage point in the passenger lounge), the maintenance crew has entered the airplane, checked the logbooks and, if possible, talked to the crew about any problems they may be having with the equipment. Maintenance will check out and troubleshoot the problems and initiate repairs. In some cases (recommended whenever possible), advance warning of problems has allowed maintenance to troubleshoot a problem ("on paper") prior to aircraft arrival, using the fault isolation manual (FIM) and the airplane maintenance manual (AMM), and they can meet the airplane with a possible solution already in hand. If maintenance is completed, it is so noted in the logbook. If not, it is deferred according to predetermined procedures and that action is noted in the logbook. The flight crew is also notified of this condition prior to the next flight.

These deferrals must be handled in accordance with MEL requirements (see Chap.1) and with the pilot in command (PIC) who has final say on whether or not to dispatch the aircraft in such condition. If the deferral is not allowed, maintenance must effect repairs at once and, in some cases, take responsibility for a flight delay or cancellation (see Chap. 19). If a delay or cancellation does occur, MCC must coordinate with flight operations and with the airline's terminal personnel to handle the passengers and, if required, their baggage.

So, you see, although maintenance is our main concern in this book, line maintenance is only a part of the activity on the line at any aircraft turnaround. Their efforts are extremely important and must be completed within a matrix of activity and within a narrow window of opportunity. But transit maintenance is not all the line maintenance organization has to do. In some airlines, their line maintenance crews also perform some or all of the above functions under contract for other airlines landing at this station that do not have their own maintenance people assigned. This contract work is coordinated through the MCC.

Other Line Maintenance Activities

After the excitement, fervor, and expedience of the turnaround effort has subsided, the line maintenance organization attends to numerous other tasks. One of these is the performance of the daily or 48-hour check (see Chap. 2) on all assigned aircraft. These checks are usually done before the first flight each day (overnight or morning). The daily or 48-hour check consists of specific items outlined in the maintenance program identified in the unit's Ops Specs. The airline may add other items as necessary. Table 13-1 shows a typical 48-hour check for a twin-engine jet; Table 13-2 is a typical transit check for the same airplane. These will differ somewhat for passenger and cargo aircraft and for an airline's specific equipment.

In addition to the daily and 48-hour checks, those items in the maintenance program that are scheduled at times less than the "A" check interval are performed by line maintenance personnel either during the turnaround (if time permits) or whenever the aircraft is on the ground for a sufficient amount of time, such as overnight or wide gaps in the daily flight schedule. This down time is also utilized by production planning and control (see Chap. 9) for scheduling the "A" check itself. Usually, this check can be done overnight with sufficient crew or it can be split into two phases and performed on consecutive nights by a smaller crew (left side of aircraft one night, right side the next).

The line maintenance crews may also be required to perform special inspections or even simple modifications to or inspections of equipment during the turnaround or overnight periods as time and conditions permit. These mods or inspections may be suggested by manufacturers, dictated by regulatory authorities, or imposed by the airline QA/QC units. They may be required on a single aircraft

TABLE 13-1   Typical 48-Hour Check (Twin-Engine Jet)

- Check brakes for condition
- Check oil levels for IDGs and APU
- Check main and nose landing gear tires for wear
- Check main and nose landing gear tires for inflation pressure
- Check main and nose landing gear assemblies for condition
- Check tail skid shock popup indicator
- Operational check of standby power
- Test engine, APU, cargo squibs on squib test panel
- Test escape slide squib on test panel (passenger aircraft)
- Apply brakes and check landing gear brakes for engagement and wear
- Operational check of interior emergency lights
- Operational check of fire/overheat systems
- Operational check of TCAS (if installed)
- Visually check cargo door seals for condition (ETOPS)

TABLE 13-2   Typical Transit Check (Twin-Engine Jet)

- Service engine oil as required
- Check RAM air inlet/exhaust doors and cabin pressure outflow valve for condition and obstructions

- Check positive pressure relief valves for indication that valves have opened
- Check all movable flight control surfaces for condition, obstructions, and locks
- Make sure that the fueling station door is closed
- Check nose and main landing gear tires and wheels for obvious damage
- Check navigation and communication antennas for condition
- Check static ports, TAT probe, pitot static probes, and AOA vanes for condition
- Check crew oxygen discharge disc for presence
- Check drain mast areas and drains for leakage of fuel and/or hydraulic fluid
- Check vertical fin and rudder, horizontal stabilizers and elevators for obvious damage, evidence of fluid leakage and missing or damaged static dischargers

- Check lower wing surfaces and wing tips for obvious damage and fuel leakage
- Check engine cowlings for obvious damage; check that blowout door is not open and latches are secure; check for signs of fluid leakage

- Check inlet cowl, fan rotor spinner and fan rotor blades (both engines)

---

or the entire fleet. If the checks are simple or involve short time expenditure, line maintenance crews are capable of carrying out the tasks. However, if the time requirements are longer, these tasks can be allotted to a longer maintenance visit such as the daily, 48-hour, or an overnight; or if the task requires opening of panels, tear down or removal of components, or other extensive maintenance activities, the tasks might be relegated to hangar or shop maintenance (see Chaps. 14 and 15).

Line Station Activities

Two terms have been used, somewhat interchangeably, in reference to maintenance activities at stations that are not the home base of the airline. These terms are *line station* and *outstation*. These terms are usually considered synonymous. For the most part, line station activity is a smaller version of the home station activity. The same type of activities take place relative to transiting aircraft. However, the line station may have limited personnel and skills; limited availability of parts and supplies; and limited facilities (stands, hangar space, GSE) for the performance of maintenance.

One of the consequences of this arrangement is that a greater number of deferred maintenance actions will be taken at line stations than at the home base. In some cases, the repair can be done at the next stop, at some other stop along the route, or deferred until arrival at the home base. These deferral actions must be coordinated with MCC.

The airline's MCC at the home base must provide or arrange for the parts, supplies, and maintenance personnel required for the resolution of any problems that occur when there are limitations in any of these areas at that station. This is also true for stations where the airline has no permanent activity. Crews and supplies must be obtained on site from other airlines or flown to the site by the operator. As a last resort, the aircraft may have to be flown home or ferried to another suitable site for repairs. Of course, arrangements for disposition of the passengers must also be made with the business office and flight operations. In all of these situations, the MCC is responsible for making all the arrangements and for coordinating with all parties concerned.

Other concerns at outstations include the contracting of maintenance personnel on site for effecting repairs and for servicing the aircraft. Unless the airline has made previous contractual arrangements with the station, arrangements for maintenance are handled by the MCC. At some airlines, however, the pilot in command has the authority to contract for any services needed but this must also be coordinated with MCC. No matter how the problem is handled, it should be spelled out in the airline's TPPM and all activity should be reported through the airline's MCC for coordination and execution within the airline.

Maintenance Crew Skill Requirements

It is often thought that, because of the simple nature of the work—turnaround maintenance and servicing—the line maintenance unit can be manned by the newer, less experienced personnel. Nothing could be further from the truth. The work done by line maintenance covers a broad scope of activity. While the shops and hangar can employ specialists who work essentially on one or a few items repeatedly, line personnel need to know the entire aircraft: all of its systems and their interactions. Line mechanics have to deal with a different problem, often on a different type of aircraft, each time they are called upon to meet an incoming flight.

The crews assigned to line maintenance must be well qualified in their profession. They should be certified mechanics approved by the regulatory authority and the airline to work on airframe, power plant, and aircraft systems, and they must be certified to sign off maintenance tasks and authorize an aircraft to "return to service." The line maintenance crew may also include unlicensed helpers and trainee personnel, but they must work under the supervision of qualified personnel. Dedicated QC inspectors may be assigned to the line crews (larger airlines) or line maintenance personnel can be appointed as designated inspectors to address the quality issues as they arise (see Chap. 18). The QC inspectors of either type can also be part of the MCC staff depending on requirements and size of the operation.

The skills required by the line maintenance crews are just as broad-based as the work effort. Crews must be familiar with all aircraft types within the airline's fleet. They must be familiar with applicable FAA rules and regulations as well as the airline's policies and procedures that relate to the line maintenance activities. Although these line crews will ordinarily be supervised and supported by MCC, there are times (overnight) when the line crew is performing the duties of MCC in addition to their normal duties.

General maintenance skills and techniques are a must, but the line maintenance crews must also know what specialists, if any, will be needed to complete a particular job if they cannot handle it themselves. Much of this effort, of course, would be handled by the line maintenance supervisor or by MCC. But keep in mind that in small airlines, these may all fuse together into one crew—or into one or two people. Since the line maintenance crew is responsible for whatever arises, they need to have the necessary skills to perform scheduled and unscheduled maintenance, to troubleshoot the problems, to perform required inspections (RIIs) and conditional inspections (hard landings, bird strikes, etc.), and to do all the required paperwork.

The paperwork includes logbook handling (pilot reports, or PIREPS); task card handling ("A" check and below); engineering orders (see Chap. 8); repeat items (with MCC); incoming and outgoing deferred maintenance items (DMIs); and any other reports or MCC actions that may occur.

The makeup of the line crews, the number of shifts, shift length, and scheduling of personnel, is dependent on several factors: the size of the airline, the flight schedule, types of aircraft flown (different types often require different skills), and type and amount of work performed. Each airline must decide the most appropriate approach to meet their own needs.

One last point of line maintenance activity must be stressed. If any maintenance work is being done that requires it to be spread across two (or more) shifts, there must be procedures written on the manner in which job information is transferred from one work crew to the next to ensure proper completion of the work. Some airlines accomplish this by requiring the original crew to continue past their normal duty hours until the job is completed. Thus, no changeover procedures are required. Other airlines, however, prefer to pass the job (maintenance as well as inspection and paperwork) to the crew on the next shift. Whichever way it is done, the procedures for the transfer of work and inspection activities must be spelled out in the TPPM (see Chap. 5).

Morning Meeting

One of the most important activities of the M&E operation is the morning meeting. This is held first thing each morning and addresses the current maintenance status: (*a*) the day's flight schedule; (*b*) the maintenance status of each aircraft in service; (*c*) specific needs of maintenance; and (*d*) any significant problems or changes which may affect the day's flight and work schedules. This meeting may also discuss (or there may be a separate meeting) upcoming hangar and shop maintenance activities and problems. The purpose of these meetings is for M&E managers and supervisors to keep abreast of everything that is going on in the maintenance area and to quickly address any problems that may arise.

Hangar Maintenance (on-Aircraft)

Introduction

Hangar maintenance, whether or not the airline actually has a hangar for such activity, refers to that maintenance which is done on out-of-service aircraft. This includes any major maintenance or modification on aircraft that have been temporarily removed from the flight schedule, usually for that express purpose. The types of activities addressed in hangar maintenance are (*a*) scheduled checks above the "A" check (i.e., C, D, heavy maintenance visit, etc.); (*b*) modifications of aircraft or aircraft systems by service bulletin, airworthiness directive, or engineering order; (*c*) fleet campaigns; (*d*) special inspections required by the airline, the FAA, or other operational conditions; (*e*) painting of aircraft; and (*f*) aircraft interior modifications.

Any hangar visit can include various combinations of the above listed activities in order to achieve maintenance objectives and to minimize maintenance downtime. Scheduling of these activities is done by the production planning and control organization with coordination of all involved units. This planning process was discussed in Chap. 9.

Washing of the aircraft can be done outside on the ramp or in special apron areas but painting of aircraft should be done inside a dedicated paint hangar if possible. The main hangar (the only hangar for some airlines) is usually dedicated to maintenance. This facility must, first of all, be large enough, with hangar doors closed, to house the largest aircraft in the airline's fleet that will be serviced. This hangar should include height for the vertical tail section as well as space around the aircraft to place stands and other work units necessary for accomplishment of the maintenance work. On occasion, airlines are required to work on aircraft with the vertical tail section sticking out of the hangar with hangar doors not fully closed. This is usually acceptable to the alternative of modifying the hangar or building a new one.

The hangar building itself also provides space for numerous support shops, overhaul shops (see Chap. 15) and ground support equipment (GSE) as well as office space for the hangar maintenance staff. A dock area should be provided to serve as the control center of the hangar maintenance check in progress. This includes the space where work cards are kept for the purpose of assigning work and signing off the various job tasks. This area is also the central point for supervisory and inspection personnel. This dock area is to hangar maintenance what the MCC is to the line maintenance: the center of activity and control. The parts and supplies needed for the maintenance being performed in the hangar should be stored in a dedicated area as near the aircraft as possible. Separate space should be provided for items removed from the aircraft and for new items to be installed. All items should be properly tagged.

For airlines with mixed fleets, there may be more than one hangar—a separate facility for each type of aircraft or each size (two- vs. four-engine, wide body vs. narrow body, etc.) In some cases, an airline can fit two aircraft (same or different) in one hangar and accommodate simultaneous maintenance on both. Hangar layout floor maps for multiple aircraft usage should be identified in the airline's TPPM. Separate hangar docks as well as separate maintenance crews are often utilized for these mixed fleet operations.

Large and small airlines may have different hangar capabilities and needs from those mentioned above but the operation is essentially the same: (a) hangar space must be adequate for the work performed and (b) hangar maintenance must be planned, scheduled, and controlled to ensure that required work is accomplished and is completed on time. A typical hangar visit, a "C" check, will be discussed at the end of the chapter.

Organization of Hangar Maintenance

Hangar maintenance is a manager level position under the director of airplane maintenance. Under this manager of hangar maintenance in a typical organizational structure are three supervisory positions: aircraft maintenance, GSE and facilities, and support shops. The supervisor of aircraft maintenance is responsible for all the hangar maintenance activities. He or she controls the flow of aircraft into and out of the check as well as the maintenance crews working the checks, and coordinates with overhaul and support shops, materiel, production planning and control, flight line maintenance, and flight operations organizations regarding the aircraft in the hangar. The supervisor of GSE and facilities is responsible for all ground support equipment used to support hangar as well as flight line maintenance activity as well as the buildings and facilities used by maintenance. The supervisor of support shops is responsible for all support activities for aircraft service and maintenance that is not designated as overhaul shops. These support shops include those in support of welding; composite materials; sheet metal; upholstery, seats and interiors; etc. The following sections of this chapter will discuss the hangar maintenance, support shops, and GSE. Overhaul shops will be discussed in Chap. 15.

Problem Areas in Hangar Maintenance

There are several areas within the hangar maintenance activity that, at times, may cause some problems. These are discussed below to prepare the reader for the real world of maintenance.

Nonroutine items

The basic maintenance checks have task requirements for various inspections, functional checks, and operational checks of aircraft equipment. These are called routine maintenance items and require a fixed amount of time to be carried out. The time requirements are identified in the MPD/OAMP and are the estimated times required for conducting the job assuming that all parts and supplies, all tools and equipment, and all required personnel are available and at the aircraft. It also assumes that the job will go smoothly, without delay or interruption, and that mechanics know exactly what to do and how to do it. Airlines usually multiply the estimated time by two or three (more for older aircraft) in order to be more realistic. This is usually done by engineering when the maintenance program is developed or by PP&C when the planning is done.

If that were all that had to be done, most checks would be straightforward activities requiring a fixed amount of time. However, many of the routine tasks will reveal problems that must be addressed. The requirements in skill, parts, supplies, and time can vary considerably depending on the nature of the discrepancy found. These are called nonroutine items and, by their nature, can extend the down time needed to accomplish the hangar check. It is the responsibility of PP&C to adequately estimate the time required for these nonroutine items and it is an ongoing effort of the maintenance crew management to ensure that these nonroutine items do not cause any undue delay in bringing the aircraft out of the scheduled check on time. While no mechanic likes to be timed for his or her work, it is important for planning purposes to know how long it takes (on average) to perform these nonroutine jobs so that proper planning can be done. It is a skill that is learned over a period of several check cycles.

Parts availability

One activity that affects maintenance down time is the time mechanics spend "chasing parts." Again, it is a function of PP&C to determine what parts and supplies will be needed for routine and nonroutine work, as well as for items deferred from other maintenance checks and those parts required by service bulletins, airworthiness directives, and any other work to be incorporated in the scheduled check. Materiel (Chap. 16) is responsible for the delivery of parts and supplies to the hangar just-in-time (JIT) for maintenance to use them. The hangar management, in turn, must provide a parts staging area in the hangar near the aircraft dock for these parts and supplies to be delivered and stored. This area must be accessible to the work force and at the same time protected from parts robbing or pilferage. This area should also provide space for mechanics to drop off any parts removed from the aircraft that are to be repaired or discarded, so that materiel may properly process them. It is the responsibility of maintenance to insure that these items are properly tagged. The establishment of this parts staging area and the delivery of parts when needed allows maintenance people to exert their time and effort on the job they were hired to do—maintenance—rather than spend it traipsing around the airport gathering the parts and supplies they need.

The saga of parts robbing

Parts robbing, or cannibalization as it was once called, is a necessary evil in aviation maintenance. We are primarily against the process but understand its necessity at times. This is particularly true if you want to meet the goals we have established for airline maintenance program: To deliver airworthy vehicles to the flight department in time to meet the flight schedule and to deliver them with all required maintenance completed. Returning an airplane to service quickly by line mechanics is an admirable effort but robbing parts from another aircraft in order to do so often results in the delay of that second aircraft being returned to service. A typical scenario goes something like this.

Aircraft tail number (TN) 317 is in transit (30-minute turnaround) and requires a part that is not available in stores. To avoid delay or cancellation of TN 317's scheduled flight, the needed part is taken from TN 324, which is in the hangar undergoing "C" check. Thus, TN 317 is returned to service (without incurring a delay) and flight operations, line maintenance, the airline business office, and the passengers are all happy. But what about hangar maintenance? Two problems come to mind.

First, if hangar maintenance has done the necessary maintenance (routine, nonroutine, modification, etc.) on the system from which the subject part was robbed, this work will have to be repeated, in whole or in part, possibly causing delay in the "C" check. The second problem involves ordering the required part for replacement on TN 324. Did line maintenance order the part? Did hangar maintenance order it? Does anyone know? Meanwhile, hangar work goes on and TN 324 is ready to come out of "C" check except that the robbed part has not arrived. (Was it ever ordered?) In respect to our goals, then, the part must be robbed from another aircraft, say TN 347, which is due in for "C" check the day after TN 324, rolls out. Thus, the part is installed and TN 324 comes out of check and is returned to service on time. The question now is whether or not the part has been ordered to restore TN 347 by the end of its hangar stay. This robbing sequence could presumably go on aircraft after aircraft without ever actually ordering the part (if you have sufficient number of aircraft available) but, sooner or later, the delays and extra work will begin to add up and airlines with small fleets will soon run out of aircraft to rob from.

The following rules regarding parts robbing should be established in the airline's TPPM: (*a*) the policy of parts robbing should be discouraged unless absolutely necessary; (*b*) parts must be ordered through materiel even if the required part is available from another aircraft; (*c*) parts robbing should only be done with the consent of the management responsible for both aircraft involved (i.e., the aircraft robbed and the aircraft receiving the robbed part); and (*d*) approval for such parts robbing should be given only by the director of airplane maintenance or his or her designate once it has been determined that all other requirements have been attended to.

In the above illustration, the two managers involved in the robbing action were the managers of line and hangar maintenance. In some cases however, this robbing activity could be between two aircraft on the line or two aircraft in the hangar. The appropriate personnel to consent to the activity would include the duty supervisor or crew chiefs, on the line, or dock manager(s), in the hangar, with final approval given by their management. The intent here is to see to it that the aircraft are returned to service promptly, that the required part is on order, and that all M&E units concerned are aware of the situation and its status. It is in keeping with the fifth objective of maintenance to avoid unnecessary repetition of work. If it is necessary to increase the stock level of the subject part in order to avoid parts robbing, this can be determined and addressed early in the process thus avoiding similar problems in the future.

Maintenance Support Shops

These shops differ from those discussed in Chap. 15. While employees in these support shops require special skills and training for the work they do, they do not require FAA licenses as those who work in the overhaul shops are required to have. Support shop work, while in support of all aircraft, can be done on or off the aircraft; but since it is usually extensive in nature, it is normally done while the aircraft is out of service. Thus, support shops normally are part of the hangar maintenance function.

Hangar support shops consist of various specialties. They perform work to refurbish or repair aircraft panels, surfaces, and cowlings made of sheet metal and composite materials. There will also be a fabrics and interiors shop for the repair and refurbishment of aircraft interiors. Aircraft seats, both passenger and crew, will be removed, installed, and repaired by a seat shop which may be part of or separate from the interiors shop. Other shops associated with the hangar activity would be those doing work in welding (gas, electric, and heliarc).

The work performed by these shops is not directly a part of the scheduled maintenance program and is not specified in the MRB document or the airline's Ops Specs as routine or nonroutine maintenance but work will be required on the various components mentioned above from time to time either by nonroutine work card or by SB, AD, or EO. Additional work for these shops may come from the GSE and facilities requirements whenever such special skills are needed to repair these units. Airlines may also perform work in these support shops for other airlines or fixed base operators.

Ground Support Equipment

Modern commercial aircraft require a considerable amount of tools and equipment to support the maintenance and operations activities. In addition to the tools and test sets used by mechanics and technicians for normal maintenance,

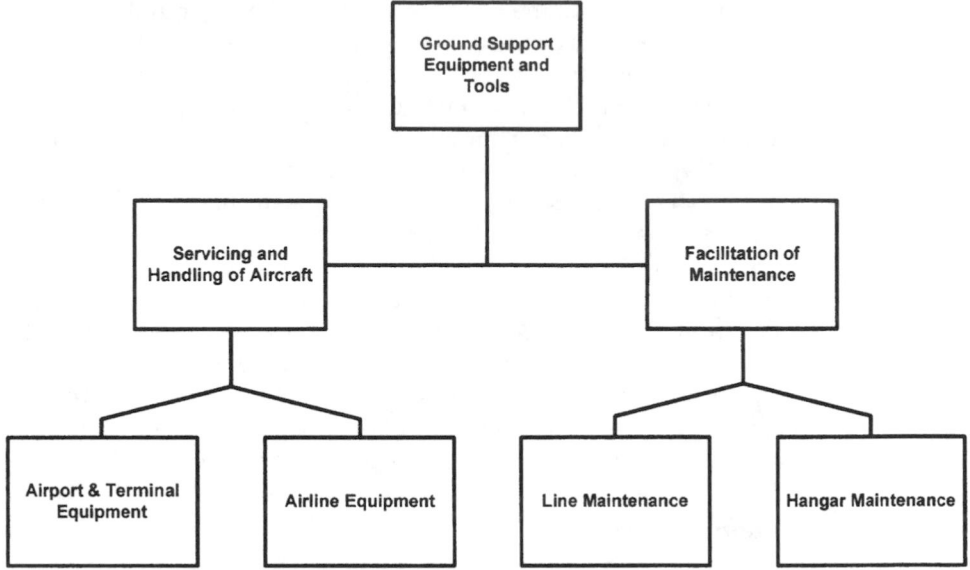

Figure 14-1 Ground support equipment categories.

there is a vast array of equipment that comes under the special heading of ground support equipment. There are also special tools and jigs for maintenance activities that are designed for one type of aircraft only; other special tools and jigs are usable on several types of aircraft.

Ground support equipment is defined as "that equipment required to support the operation and maintenance of the aircraft and all its airborne equipment."[*] This GSE includes an extensive variety of equipment ranging from simple jacks and stands to million dollar towbarless towing vehicles. For the sake of discussion, we can divide GSE into two broad categories: (*a*) equipment to support the servicing and handling of operational aircraft while engaged in flight turnaround and ground movement activities; and (*b*) equipment used to facilitate maintenance whether at turnaround or during scheduled or unscheduled downtime.

The first category, servicing and handling equipment, can be further divided into GSE that is owned and operated by the airport authority or terminal operator and that owned by the airline itself. The second category, maintenance equipment, includes equipment that may be used on the flight line, in the hangar, or shared by both activities. This breakdown is shown in Fig. 14-1. Table 14-1 is a list of typical ground support equipment used for handling, servicing, and maintaining aircraft. The table identifies typical ownership and usage of the GSE.[†]

---

[*] Air Transport Association of America (ATA); *Common Support Data Dictionary* (CSDD); revision 2001.1.

[†] This discussion, as well as Fig. 14-1 and Table 14-1, are based on the assumption that all maintenance is done by the airline. If any maintenance is outsourced to a third party, some of the GSE listed may belong to that third party organization.

TABLE 14-1   List of Ground Support Equipment (GSE) Items

Name of GSE item	Airport owned	Airline owned	Usage (L, H, B)*	Handling & servicing	Maintenance
Air start units	X	L	X		
APU cradles	X	B		X	
Axle jacks	X	B		X	
Baggage carts	X	L	X		
Baggage loaders (at A/C)		X	L	X	
Battery charging equipment		X	B		X
Boarding wheelchairs		X	L	X	
Cargo container/pallet handling		X	L	X	
Cargo trailers	X	L	X		
Communications equipment		X	B	X	X
Deicing equipment (motorized & stationary)	X		L	X	
Diesel powered ground power units		X	B	X	X
Fixed jacks	X	B		X	
Hydraulic oil fill carts & couplings		X	B		X
Hydraulic test carts		X	B		X
Lavatory service components		X	B	X	
Lifting equipment: cranes & platforms		X	B		X
Nitrogen servicing equipment		X	B		X
Oxygen servicing equipment		X	B		X
Passenger loading bridges	X		L	X	
Passenger loading stairs (powered & unpowered)	X	X	L	X	
Pneumatic air start units, couplings & accessories		X	B	X	X
Potable water service components		X	B	X	
Power supplies: 28 vdc & 400 Hertz		X	B	X	X
Recovery jacks	X	L		X	
Refueling trucks X	X	L	X		
Snow removal equipment (ramp & runway)	X		L	X	
Specialized maintenance tools		X	B		X
Stands and scaffolding (many variations)		X	B	X	X
Thrust reverser dollies		X	B		X
Towbarless A/C handling tractors	X	X	L	X	X
Towbars	X	L	X	X	
Towing tractors (gas, diesel, electric)	X	X	B	X	X
Variable jacks	X	B		X	
Weigh systems	X	L		X	
Wheel and tire build-up fixtures		X	B		X
Wheel and tire dollies		X	B		X
Wheel chocks	X	B	X	X	

*L: line; H: hangar; B: both line and hangar.

To maximize in-service reliability and profitability, operators must procure GSE and tooling appropriate for their aircraft when a new model is being incorporated into the fleet. Tugs, tows, towbars, and other special tools and fixtures are sometimes mated to specific aircraft models. Other GSE and tooling can be used on more than one type aircraft. The GSE and facilities organization must work with engineering at the outset, whenever the purchase or lease of new aircraft is considered, to determine what existing equipment and tools (if any) can be used with the new model and to determine what additional equipment and tools must be ordered specifically for the new model. This activity should be done at least 9 to 12 months prior to delivery of the first aircraft so that these tools and equipment will be available when the aircraft arrives.

Selection of GSE and tooling is related to a number of variables: (*a*) the type and level of maintenance to be performed by the airline; (*b*) the number of line stations to be supported (multiple units may be required); (*c*) the number of ramp operations to be accommodated (individual or simultaneous use requirements); (*d*) the extent of overhaul work to be done by the operator; and (*e*) coordination with other units for borrowed equipment or contract work to be done (by or for your airline).

Because of the complexity and variety of this equipment it is usually handled by a separate maintenance activity within the airline. For small to midsized airlines, the GSE is handled by a group attached to the hangar maintenance organization (see Fig. III-1) and often housed in the same hangar as other overhaul and support shops. In larger airlines, GSE may have a separate manager or director under M&E and housed in its own hangar. Either way it may be organized, its job is to support maintenance both on the flight line and in the hangar.

Because of the size and quantity of ground support equipment, it is often stored outside the hangar in a designated area on the ramp near the operator's facilities. Some smaller equipment would be stored in the hangar. Special tools and fixtures may be stored in the hangar tool shed.

The GSE and facilities group in our typical midsized airline is also responsible for general maintenance and upkeep of all GSE as well as the general maintenance and upkeep of all buildings and facilities used by the M&E organization.

Hangar Maintenance Activity—A Typical "C" Check

The content of a "C" check will vary from one airline to another, from one aircraft to another, even from one check to another for the same aircraft or type. The discussion that follows is typical and, for convenience, is divided into several stages, which, in reality, may overlap or even fuse together. For this illustration, we will break the typical check into five sections: (1) preparation; (2) preliminary activities; (3) conduct of the check; (4) completion and sign-off; and (5) return to service.

Preparation for "C" check

We have already discussed the preliminary activities of engineering (Chap. 8), production planning and control (Chap. 9), and the M&E planning meeting (also Chap. 9) so these will not be repeated here. To begin the actual check, the hangar maintenance organization must prepare for receipt of the aircraft and for the logistics and management of the check. The hangar is cleaned; space is cleared for the aircraft; stands, scaffolding, and other equipment needed are brought into the hangar for immediate use or made available for later use.

The parts storage area is stocked with parts and supplies needed for the work to be performed. This, of course, is an ongoing process throughout the check. The parts and supplies will be delivered "as needed" or just-in-time.

In the dock area, where administration and management of the check takes place, a large wall rack with pockets is populated with all routine task cards as required by the maintenance program and the particular check to be performed. There is a row for the cards of each work center (avionics, hydraulics, etc.) and two marked-off areas to separate the completed cards from those still to be worked. Work crews are available or on standby waiting for the arrival of the aircraft.

Preliminary "C" check activities

The first order of business, usually, is to wash the aircraft. The vehicle is towed by ground crews, with appropriate "wing walkers" and communications gear for safety, to the wash rack area for a thorough cleaning. After washing is done, the aircraft is towed to the hangar where it is parked and chocked; now the work begins. Panels and cowlings are opened and visual inspections are conducted. Any discrepancies found at this time will require nonroutine work cards. These cards are generated by QC and are placed in the card rack for later accomplishment with other work cards. Next, or in conjunction with the inspections, the stands and scaffolding (as needed) will be placed around the aircraft to allow access to work areas during the check. Any ground power, pneumatic, or hydraulic carts, as well as any special tools and test equipment needed for the scheduled tasks, will also be put into place.

Conduction of the "C" check

Mechanics are assigned to tasks according to the check schedule produced by PP&C in an efficient manner. The work to be done in any given area by more than one work center is scheduled in sequence to avoid congestion in the work area and to minimize the opening and closing of panels, cowlings, etc. Any nonroutine items generated during normal work will be written on nonroutine cards and worked or scheduled for work at a later time. Most units produce a PERT chart or some other form of visual aid showing the planned work schedule. This chart is updated, or annotated, as necessary during the check to accommodate the nonroutine work or any other delays or schedule adjustments that may be encountered.

Requests for additional parts and/or supplies not in the original plan, or for parts and supplies not yet delivered to the work site, will be relayed to materiel by the dock staff. Materiel will deliver these items to the parts staging area to eliminate parts chasing by mechanics.

Quality control inspectors will reinspect any items previously rejected and approve the work (buyback, see Chap. 18). Any delays in the check schedule, especially those affecting return to service, will be coordinated with MCC and flight operations by the dock manager. If all goes well, the "C" check will be completed on time and the aircraft will come out of check "clean," i.e., all required tasks completed with no deferred maintenance items.

Completion and sign-off of the "C" check

Although the maintenance work is the key part of the effort, the check is not really complete until it has been assured that all task cards—routine and non-routine—have been completed, signed off and, where required, inspected, stamped, and approved by quality control. That includes all rejected work and the subsequent rework and buyback actions. The person responsible for this activity is the senior QC inspector assigned to the check. He or she must review every work card for mechanics' signatures or initials as required indicating accomplishment and completion of the task and for QC stamps (and initials) for any work where QC inspection is required. Any discrepancies noted at this time must be corrected even if it requires further work and inspection. When all work cards have been completed, signed off, and accepted, QC signs off the check as complete and releases the aircraft out of check, ready for service.

Return to service

Once QC has signed off the check, the dock manager notifies MCC and flight operations of the availability of the aircraft. The aircraft is then towed from the hangar to the ramp by maintenance and Flight Ops returns the aircraft to the active flight schedule. Ground crews service the vehicle (fuel, food, etc.) and cabin crews ready the aircraft for passengers.

Meanwhile ...

Once the check is completed and the aircraft has been moved out of the hangar, there is a requirement for a clean-up effort in the hangar and the dock area. First, all completed task cards must be collected and sent to other M&E units (PP&C, engineering, and reliability as required) for analysis and recording of significant items. This will aid PP&C in planning future checks and will permit engineering and reliability to tally the information on check findings to aid in future problem investigations and for possible adjustment (escalation) of task or check intervals. Any unused, repairable, or discarded items remaining in the parts staging area will be removed by materiel and processed as necessary. Hangar and dock areas will be cleaned and put in order for the next activity when the whole process is repeated for the next aircraft, which may be the same model with similar check requirements, or a different model aircraft with completely different requirements. The size of the airline and its fleet makeup will vary hangar activities for specific checks, but the process is essentially the same for all of them.

15

Maintenance Overhaul Shops (off-Aircraft)

Organization of Overhaul Shops

The director of overhaul shops is responsible for overall management and administration of maintenance for those components and equipments that are required to be removed from the aircraft for the purpose of maintenance. This maintenance can be anything from simple cleaning and adjustment up to and including complete overhaul as necessary.

Shop maintenance is usually done on an out-of-service basis; that is, the equipment is removed from the aircraft and replaced with serviceable units by line or hangar maintenance personnel. The removed unit, properly tagged as to maintenance status, is then sent to materiel where it is either discarded according to standard maintenance procedures or routed to the appropriate shop for repair. This would include the airline's shops or those of a contractor. Units under warranty would be sent to the manufacturer or to a designated warranty repair facility by materiel. Upon completion of such repair the unit is returned to materiel with a serviceable tag where it will be returned to the stores for future issue. On certain occasions, determined by the airline and the circumstances, a unit may be removed from an aircraft by line or hangar maintenance personnel, sent to the appropriate shop for repair, and returned to the aircraft for reinstallation.

Types of Shops

There are two types of shop maintenance activities in an airline maintenance organization. The functions and relationship to other organizations differ somewhat. There are support shops, which include such special skills and activities as welding, sheet metal, composite materials, aircraft interiors, etc. These shops are usually part of the hangar maintenance organization. The work they do is primarily in support of out-of-service aircraft, although some support is given to line maintenance as needed (see Chap. 14 for discussion of these shops).

The other type of maintenance shops at an airline, the overhaul shops, involve support for the specialized equipment on the aircraft such as engines; avionics, hydraulic, and pneumatic systems; structures; etc. The work performed in these shops is on equipment that has been removed from the aircraft during line or hangar maintenance operations. The organizational chart (Fig. 7-1) of our typical midsized airline shows these shops in general terms but any number of variations is possible depending upon the size of the fleet, the availability of qualified personnel, and the amount of shop work to be handled by the airline.

Engine shops

The engine shop is the largest shop in terms of space requirements. Besides a shop area for working on small parts (bench work) and the office area required for management and administration, the engine shop also needs an area for engine buildup (EBU) activities. This is where certain components are added to a basic engine to configure it for a given model aircraft or for a specific position on the airplane (i.e., right, left, or center; or wing position 1, 2, 3, or 4). This effort requires a suitable engine stand for holding the engine while the EBU process is underway. The EBU activity, done off-aircraft, minimizes the time required for an engine change and results in shorter down time for the aircraft. This is known as the quick engine change, or QEC, process.

The engine shop also requires an engine run-up area situated away from the main facilities (for noise reasons, mainly) to allow ground testing of engines mounted on the aircraft before or after maintenance. A large sound barrier (baffle) structure is part of this engine run-up area. For airlines with mixed fleets, there may be separate engine shops for different models; however, some facilities may be combined.

Avionics shops

Avionics is a term that refers to a wide assortment of systems used in aviation that include both electrical and electronics systems. The group of avionics shops can take on a variety of configurations depending on many factors. There may be a separate electrical shop that addresses electrical system components only, such as motors, generators, power distribution systems, power busses, etc. A separate battery shop may be established for the repair, storage, and charging of aircraft batteries. Electronics systems, which include radios, navigation systems, computers, control units of all types, etc., will be handled by various specialty shops in large airlines but may be combined into a single avionics shop for smaller operators.

Instruments, both conventional electromechanical instruments as well as electronic or "glass cockpit" displays, will be handled by the appropriately skilled technicians in either a single instrument shop or in separate shops for each of the two types mentioned. Conventional instruments would be flap position indicators, aircraft attitude indicators, magnetic compass, and any other galvanometer type instruments. The glass cockpit instruments, more correctly referred to as "displays," include CRT versions of the above instruments. In the modern airliners, the same display units can sometimes be used for an attitude display indicator (ADI) as well as the horizontal situation indicator (HSI) which shows a map of the flight plan with waypoints and other information. Other displays may use liquid crystal display (LCD) panels. These electronic displays are more the domain of the electronics shop rather than the instruments shop, however.

Mechanical shops

Mechanical component shops can also be separate or combined depending upon airline size and requirements. These shops would include hydraulics systems and components, pneumatics systems and components (heat, air), oxygen systems, flight control surfaces, etc. The wheel, tire, and brake shop has the responsibility for various actions relating to the aircraft: (*a*) the repair, assembly and, disassembly of aircraft wheels; (*b*) the repair, servicing, and retreading of aircraft tires; and (*c*) adjustment and replacement of aircraft brakes. Again, these activities may be performed in one or several shops depending on the amount of work and the complexity of the fleet.

Outsourcing of shop maintenance work

As with line and hangar maintenance, some or all of the shop maintenance at a given airline can be outsourced to other airlines or to third party maintenance organizations. In the case of partial outsourcing, the director of overhaul shops is responsible for coordinating these activities into the overall airline maintenance plan. If all shop maintenance is done by outside contractors, the overhaul shops directorate would not exist at the airline. However, to insure that work is done within the airline's schedule and maintenance plan, someone in the aircraft maintenance directorate of the M&E organization must be designated as overhaul shop maintenance coordinator. Quality assurance will identify the standards to which these outside contractors must abide (see Chap. 17).

Operation of Overhaul Shops

Work on a flight line is hectic, at times, subject to flight schedules, maintenance emergencies, foul weather, and the ever-irritating "time limitations." Hangar work may be less hectic with more time to accomplish each job, but there is still a time limitation and other pressures. In shop maintenance, however, the pressures of time and schedule are somewhat lessened by the nature of the shop operation.

Items come in for servicing, repair, or overhaul and are addressed, usually by specialists in the type of equipment or system involved. Some of the basic troubleshooting has already been done to indicate such-and-such a unit is bad and has to be replaced. This done, the mechanic turns the errant item into materiel and draws a good one for installation. Materiel, then, sends the properly tagged incoming unit to the appropriate shop. The shop mechanic or technician then uses his or her standard bench check procedures to determine the problem, make the necessary repairs, and perform some check to ensure that the job has been successful. Once maintenance is completed, the proper paperwork filled out and attached and the serviceable unit is sent back to materiel for placement in stores for reissue when needed.

Each maintenance shop will have a work area, a storage area with adequate separation of serviceable, unserviceable, and discarded units. Usually they will have a spare parts area, maintained by materiel, for the small parts needed for the work. Again, proximity of these areas to the work area minimizes the time a mechanic spends in "parts chasing." Of course, each shop will be equipped with the necessary tools, work benches, test stands, and test equipment for the type of equipment to be worked on. Appropriate safety equipment for the work performed and hazardous materials handled (if any) should be readily available and accessible to the employees. Suitable office space will be provided for administrative and management functions.

The overhaul shops generally work a standard shift, with or without overtime; night shift and weekend work depends on the airline and its workload. The pace may be slower than on the line or in the hangar, but short turnaround for maintenance (mean time to repair, MTTR) is still important. The number of items held in stock (see Chap. 16) is based not only on the failure rate for your fleet, but also on the amount of time it takes to pass the repairable item through maintenance. The sequence goes like this: (*a*) remove unit from the aircraft; (*b*) turn the unit in to materiel for replacement; (*c*) route unit to the repair facility (in-house or third party); (*d*) return serviceable unit to stores for reissue.

Shop Data Collection

The airline's maintenance reliability program, discussed in detail in Chap. 19, involves many data collection tasks throughout the M&E activity. One very important source of such data is the overhaul shops. While flight line and hangar reports provide information on systems and components, the shop data provide useful information on internal components of equipment and subsystems that contribute to the on-aircraft failures and write-ups. These shop data collection efforts are submitted through shop tear-down reports, that identify servicing, repair, and overhaul actions taken as well as on the parts and supplies used in that maintenance work. These components are then tracked by reliability to determine if there is an unnecessarily high failure rate that should be of concern to the airline or the equipment manufacturer.

Materiel Support

Organization and Function of Materiel

Materiel is one of the key units within an airline's maintenance and engineering organization. It is the one that spends the most money and is, therefore, under scrutiny by the airline's higher management as well as the M&E management. The high-level concern for operating costs is at the root of one rather prominent controversy in the M&E area. That controversy is "who should have control of materiel: maintenance or finance?"

Our recommendation, and one that has proven to be quite successful in a great many airlines throughout the world, both large and small, is that materiel should be part of the M&E organization. If finance, accounting, or any other unit outside maintenance is in control, there is a fear that the lack of (or at least a lessened) knowledge of maintenance and its idiosyncrasies could result in poor decisions—such things as how much to spend; what parts to buy and how much to stock; determining what constitutes a suitable substitute part; and so forth—that affect the quality of maintenance.

The other side of the argument is that maintenance would not have full understanding about budgets and costs and would spend too much money on parts or have too many assets tied up in "rainy day" stock levels. Unfortunately, both situations are possible and both situations do exist in today's airlines, both foreign and domestic. And the discussion goes on without resolution. What we need to emphasize here, however, is that both of these extremes should be avoided.

People in the performing arts (symphonies, ballet companies, acting groups, etc.) have an adage that they give as a guideline to their boards of directors: "Artistic decisions should not be made by nonartistic people." In other words, the board's job is to take care of the business end, not the artistic end, of the activity. We need only modify this slightly for aviation: "Technical decisions should not be made by nontechnical people." This is the philosophy behind the need for management with technical background in the M&E field that we discussed in

Chap. 7. Mechanics, engineers, and technical management in M&E are aware of the changing requirements of aging equipment and the increasing need for spare parts with age. These working experts are also aware, from experience, of what constitutes a reasonable substitute for a given part and what does not, even though the specifications for both units are within limits. The past experiences of these people are more conducive to addressing the goals of M&E than the experience of the finance and administration people.

Our recommendation, then, is that the materiel support effort be an integral part of the maintenance and engineering organization with oversight by accounting and finance for expenditures. With that said, we move on to the functions of materiel. Briefly, these are (a) to provide parts and supplies for all aspects of the M&E operation; (b) to maintain adequate supplies of these items on hand and in convenient locations for quick access by maintenance; and (c) to provide adequate support to the maintenance organization within reasonable budget constraints.

The Materiel Directorate

As shown in the organizational chart of an ideal midsized airline (Fig. 7-1), a portion of which is reproduced as Fig. III-1, the materiel directorate has four management positions: inventory control, stores, purchasing, and shipping and receiving.

Inventory control

Inventory control is responsible for ensuring that all the necessary parts and supplies are on hand and available at selected locations throughout M&E. Its purpose is to support all maintenance activities by maintaining proper stock levels in stores and by initiating reorders at appropriate times. They are also responsible for adjusting the stock levels as changes in usage and fleet makeup dictate.

Stores

Stores is responsible for issuing parts to and exchanging parts with the mechanics. Stores is also responsible for delivering parts to the work centers as necessary, and ensuring that parts and supplies that require special storage and handling are properly managed. Stores also routes repairable units to the appropriate maintenance shop.

Purchasing

Purchasing is responsible for the procurement of all parts and supplies used by M&E. They deal mainly with suppliers and manufacturers attending to such things as specifications, costs, delivery, etc. Essentially, purchasing has primary budget control in materiel and works closely with finance on expenditures and budget matters.

Shipping and receiving

Shipping and receiving will handle all packing and unpacking of parts and supplies being shipped into and out of the airline. This unit will also maintain QC capabilities to handle any inspections that might be needed relative to the shipment or receipt of goods.

How the materiel unit is organized, of course, depends on the size of the airline, the availability of qualified personnel, and the management and administrative philosophies of the airline. Some activities above may be combined for convenience. In the sections that follow, we will discuss the various functions the materiel organization must perform without further discussion of how the unit should be organized.

M&E Support Functions of Materiel

These support functions can be stated briefly as (*a*) ordering; (*b*) storing; (*c*) issuing; (*d*) controlling; and (*e*) handling of parts and supplies. The first four involve mainly parts and supplies while the last (handling) involves the movement of parts between the various facilities concerned. We will address these items separately.

Parts ordering

Ordering of parts includes the initial provisioning when new equipment and systems become part of the fleet. It also includes reordering whenever supplies on hand drop below a certain level (more on this later). The initial provisioning is established at the outset by a recommended spare parts list prepared by the airframe manufacturer. This list is based on the manufacturer's recommendations and on fleet-wide experience of those airlines already using the equipment in similar operations.

Based on initial provisioning and on the airline's ongoing experience after entering service with the model, changes in the stock levels and quantities held will be inevitable. The components on hand and the quantity needed for day-to-day operation is determined by a number of variables and these will differ from one operation to the next. The flight schedule—number of hours and cycles flown, stage length, flight environment—as well as the number of aircraft in the fleet, affect the usage rate of components and thus the number of parts needed in stock to support the maintenance and operations. The location of where maintenance is done may also affect stock levels in that extra parts and supplies may be needed at several line stations to facilitate maintenance.

Also, the quality of maintenance—the abilities and skills of the maintenance staff—may also affect the need for spare parts and assemblies. A continual perusal of stock usage by the materiel section is necessary to optimize the stock levels on hand. This usage rate, of course, affects the frequency at which parts are purchased; that is, the reorder point. This requires the establishment of usage rate and reorder point data for all parts and supplies used. For repairable items, the lead time for repair action (i.e., the time required to send the item to the maintenance shop, repair it, and return it to stores for reissue) could affect both the required stock levels and the reorder point since available stock would be subject to use in other aircraft maintenance actions during this repair cycle.

And finally, the effect of quantity discounts from certain suppliers on specific items may determine a more economical reorder point for those items. This, however, must be reconciled with the costs of storage of the additional materiel purchased.

Parts storage

Storing of parts is the next materiel function to consider. There are two concepts here: (*a*) putting every part where it can readily be located and issued when needed; and (*b*) storing certain parts under specified conditions. The latter category includes proper storage of fuels, lubricants, paints, oils, and other flammable or perishable items. Oxygen bottles and the tools used on oxygen systems require special handling and storage. All of this proper storage is a materiel function.

The basic or standard storage arrangement is the traditional array of storage shelves or bins, marked by a coordinate system so that every part has a location and each location is easily found. This, most often, is a "row-shelf-bin" locator grid of the operator's choosing. For example, part number 1234-5678-C could be located in D-2-14; that is, row D, shelf 2, bin number 14. Here the rows of shelves are lettered: "A, B, C ...." The shelves, numbered from top to bottom, are "1, 2, 3 ...." And finally, each bin (on each shelf) is numbered consecutively from left to right: "1, 2, 3 ...." Any similar system can be used.

This location system might be further stratified by aircraft model. While many components, subassemblies and units may be used on several model aircraft, many are unique to one model. Most airlines with mixed fleets have separate parts bins for each model to allow separate cost information to be kept by model. Any need to issue a part from one model's stores for use on another model will be handled through the paperwork process by materiel personnel. This would include computer records to show availability and location of parts.

Additional storage facilities would be necessary for specific operations. To facilitate maintenance and minimize the time required by maintenance for parts chasing, for example, spare parts could be available at line stations to support limited maintenance in addition to the normal turnaround maintenance. Special storage shelves and bins should be available to line maintenance for daily, 48-hour, transit, or "A" checks whenever parts and supplies are needed for these actions. Likewise, storage bins and shelves should be established in the hangar to accommodate those parts and supplies used for "C" checks and other hangar activities (more on this in Delivery of Parts below).

Parts issue

Issuing parts to mechanics is another major function of materiel. Items such as bolts, nuts, and other common hardware are better stored in open, accessible bins near the work location so that the mechanics have easy access. For other items, such as black boxes, assemblies, and other major items, it is better for all concerned to have "parts windows" or other facilities where materiel personnel can issue parts to mechanics, as needed, and attend to the proper handling of the parts tags and other important paper and computer work.

Some of these parts, of course, are repairable and the mechanic is required to "give one to get one." This exchange is handled by the materiel control clerk who also ensures that the maintenance tags on both units are properly filled out (by the mechanic) and that the unit turned in is routed to the appropriate repair facility for rework. For those items that are not repairable, materiel is responsible for discard of the unit.

This parts issue window should be as close to the work center as possible to minimize parts chasing time for mechanics. In some airlines, the necessary parts can be ordered through a computer terminal at the work site and delivered to the mechanic by materiel (see Controlling Parts later). No matter what method of issue is used, it is the responsibility of materiel to update the computer "quantity on hand" information each time a part is drawn or exchanged. In the case of repairable parts, materiel (through the computer) must also keep track of where the part is at all times (shop, stores, in transit, on aircraft).

Another useful service offered by materiel is the buildup of kits for certain maintenance actions. To remove and replace some items, certain hardware is needed in addition to the primary unit and its accessories. Very often removed hardware, "O" rings, gaskets, and the like, are not reusable. For certain SB or AD actions, additional components (harnesses, brackets, hardware) are needed for completion. It is a boon to maintenance when materiel can develop kits of all these necessary parts and issue them together as a package. These kits can be developed with the assistance of maintenance or engineering personnel. Very often, SB and AD modifications are available to the airline in kit form supplied by the airframe manufacturer or component vendor.

Some airlines aid their line station maintenance activities by maintaining "fly-away kits" (FAKs) on board the aircraft. These kits contain items that might likely be needed for turnaround maintenance and servicing at stations where maintenance crews are available but such supplies are not. Items such as tires, engine oil, and other common components may be included.

The purpose of the FAK is to provide these items when needed but the extra weight on board the aircraft may be a limiting factor on how much is carried. The units carried in the FAK should be based on past experience of that aircraft on that route and update of the contents of the kit should be reconsidered every 6 months or so to eliminate carrying unnecessary components and leaving out those often needed. This is something that needs to be monitored by materiel. In addition to monitoring the content of the FAK, materiel must replace the used items to ensure completeness of the kit. The responsibility for the items in the FAK belongs to maintenance. Whenever a part is taken from the FAK, materiel should be notified for replacement. If the unit is repairable, it must be processed accordingly and not returned to the FAK in unserviceable condition. There should be a log associated with the FAK to identify content and usage.

Some airlines use FAKs and some do not. It is a matter of individual preference. Often, however, airlines flying ETOPS will use FAKs to facilitate maintenance activities to avoid downgrading an ETOPS flight to a lesser diversion time (180 to 120 minutes) or to a non-ETOPS flight. Such downgrades usually mean longer flight lengths and subsequently generate problems with flight connections for the passengers. The FAK becomes quite important in these situations.

Parts control

Controlling parts covers a variety of activities. We have already mentioned identification of storage locations for all parts and the need for tracking certain components such as repairables through their processing. We have also mentioned the need for materiel to deliver parts and supplies to maintenance work centers to minimize or eliminate the time spent by maintenance personnel in parts chasing. Additional personnel in materiel for this purpose are a great help to the maintenance effort.

It is also necessary to track flight hours, flight cycles, calendar time, and location of parts that are designated as "time-limited" parts. These are serial-numbered parts that require removal from service before a specified interval has elapsed. These parts accrue time or cycles only while in service. Therefore, the aircraft on which they are mounted must be known and its time and/or cycles must be tallied against the part. If the component is removed before its time limit is reached, it can be repaired, restored, or completely overhauled as necessary with or without zeroing out the time (details on zeroing out time-limited items are discussed in Chap. 18). If the item is placed in stores for reuse on another aircraft after this action has been completed, its time and cycle tally will begin again (at the previous level or at zero) as soon as it is reinstalled on an aircraft. Materiel, through the computer system, will be responsible for tracking time-limited parts.

This controlling of parts going to and from internal maintenance organizations, vendors, or outside repair contractors and warranty holders is the primary control function of materiel, but there is an additional control requirement. Parts are occasionally removed from larger assemblies (officially authorized or not) to facilitate line or hangar maintenance efforts and to quickly return an operating aircraft to service. While this expedites the maintenance and minimizes the effect on flight schedules, the negative side is an adverse effect on maintenance and materiel costs and efforts later on.

This cannibalization renders the major assembly (the one robbed) unusable or requiring maintenance. If materiel authorizes this cannibalization to expedite line or hangar maintenance, it must initiate reorder and subsequent repair of the robbed unit. If such cannibalization is not authorized by materiel, then maintenance is responsible for the robbing and thus for the reordering and subsequent maintenance action on the robbed assembly.

One of the parts control processes employed by many airlines is the "parts quarantine" area. This area is used to separate parts removed from aircraft until it can be determined if repair is necessary or if a unit can be returned to stores for reissue. If the replacement part fixes the problem, it is assumed that the part in quarantine is in need of repair and materiel routes it to the appropriate repair facility. If the replacement unit does not resolve the problem, then the one in quarantine is assumed to be okay and is returned to stores. This is not always the best approach, however. Some airlines will return the quarantined part to the shop for checkout before returning it to stores to ensure serviceability.

This quarantine activity is an integral part of troubleshooting and should be monitored by QA and reliability to determine if the troubleshooting skills of maintenance personnel are in question. See the "no fault found" (NFF) process discussed in Appendix C.

Parts handling

Handling of parts and supplies is sometimes referred to as "shipping and receiving." However, this latter term does not tell the whole story. Handling begins with receipt of parts and supplies and involves, in some cases, an incoming inspection by quality control to insure that the part is the correct one: part number, serial number if applicable, modification status, serviceability, expiration date (if applicable), and so forth. Physical condition is also examined. This can be done by QC or by someone in materiel designated by QC to perform such inspections (see Chap. 18). After receipt and incoming inspection, the parts are distributed to the proper place—stores, hangar, line, shops, etc.—and computer records are updated accordingly.

During day-to-day operations, materiel is issuing parts to mechanics and, in some cases, accepting an exchange part. This exchange requires that materiel, upon checking for proper tagging by the mechanic, route the part to the appropriate shop, vendor, or contractor for repairs. Upon return of the repaired part, materiel will check the tag for correctness, update the computer record, and route the part to stores.

One function that comes under this topic of handling of parts, a rather important financial consideration that airlines sometimes overlook, is the handling of warranty repairs. It is a fact that many aircraft components are expensive and that maintenance costs are also high. It is very important, then, for an airline to take advantage of any warranty claims it may have to avoid unnecessary costs (see objective 5 in Chap. 3).

Whenever a part is turned in to materiel in exchange for a serviceable one, materiel's first responsibility is to check the warranty status of the incoming part. If it is still under warranty, it is processed and shipped to the warranty holder (or designated repair facility) for repairs. If the part is no longer covered by warranty, then it will be sent to the appropriate in-house or third-party facility for repair.

If parts are shipped out for warranty repair, they sometimes incur longer lead times before being returned to stores. In this case, the airline has two options. The usual one is to increase the stock level or reorder point in order to accommodate this extension. In some cases, however, airlines that have the capability to do the repair work, enter into a contract with the warranty holder to perform the repair work themselves. This not only reduces the processing time but it also provides the airline with additional revenue for the contract work.

Other Materiel Functions

The five functions discussed above—ordering, storing, issuing, controlling, and handling—are basic to the materiel function and deal directly with maintenance. There are two additional functions that operate more or less in the background of the day-to-day maintenance support activity. These are the functions of stock level adjustments and budgeting efforts.

Stock level adjustments

The initial provisioning of an airline is similar to the initial maintenance program developed for a new aircraft and a new operator (see Chap. 2). Experience of the operator will indicate the need to change this "starting point" over time. The parts required, the quantity needed in stock, and the reorder points will be determined by the actual maintenance activity and this will vary from airline to airline as well as from route to route within an airline. It could also vary with the seasons and with the quality of maintenance available. None of these variants can be totally controlled by management but they must be monitored regularly and appropriately addressed. Therefore, it is necessary to have a continual surveillance of parts usage and adjustments need to be made as necessary. This is a joint effort of the maintenance and materiel sections and is commensurate with the cost control and budgeting activities.

Budgeting efforts

The modern approach to management requires each and every manager to be cognizant of the cost requirements of the organization that he or she commands. If M&E wants full control of materiel as we suggested in the beginning of this chapter, then M&E must take full responsibility for the costs incurred and the budgeting of the whole activity. This is primarily the responsibility of the director of materiel, but he or she will (undoubtedly) delegate to each manager the responsibility for his or her own activities. Of course, in the final analysis, accounting and finance at corporate level will maintain oversight of the effort and make the final determination as to budget allocations. After all, accounting and finance also has a boss—the CEO of the airline.

One of the major problems in establishing stock levels is the cost of the items stocked. Some airlines overstock to hedge against running out of an item when it is sorely needed. The result of this overstocking may be to minimize maintenance down time and subsequent delays and cancellations, but the penalty is having too much money tied up in supplies that are not used, not needed, or in some cases, become out of date or obsolete while sitting on the shelf.

The other extreme embraced by some airlines is to invest very little in spare parts, thus minimizing the amount of money needed to start up and run the airline. The downside here is that the maintenance downtime as well as the delays and cancellations tend to increase to the detriment of the flight schedule, passenger satisfaction, and even the quality of maintenance.

Like so many things in the airline industry, budgeting and stock levels both become precarious juggling acts that require skill, dexterity, and perhaps a little luck to carry them off.

IV

Oversight Functions

In Chap. 6, we discussed the CASS requirement of FAA AC 120-16D. The FAA Advisory Circular AC 120-79 provides further details on CASS including various ways to organize the function. In this book, we address the CASS requirement through four oversight organizations. Each function encompasses specific areas of interest that assist the director of maintenance program evaluation (MPE) in these oversight efforts (Fig. IV-1). These units are called (in our structure) quality assurance, quality control, reliability, and safety and are each addressed in a separate chapter (Chaps. 17 through 20).

Quality assurance (QA) is the organization responsible for carrying out certain administrative actions for the director of MPE and for conducting annual audits of all M&E organizations, including those outside the airline that provide work or other assistance to the airline. Quality control (QC) looks specifically at maintenance practices and the actual conduct of the maintenance work. They are also responsible for special inspections and the calibration of tools and test equipment. The reliability organization has the responsibility of monitoring failure rates, removals, etc. of aircraft systems and components to measure the effectiveness of the overall maintenance program. If any deficiencies are noted, reliability turns the problem over to engineering for investigation and development of an adequate solution. The remaining oversight function is safety. The safety organization looks specifically at the health and safety issues involved in the M&E activities. This means establishing the health and safety program and overseeing its implementation.

Each chapter in Part IV is written to discuss a particular oversight function independently. The airline's CASS, however, should integrate the activities on all the oversight units to fully monitor the airline maintenance and inspection program. An airline with an FAA approved reliability program will usually have a board established to address problems uncovered during these activities. This board, made

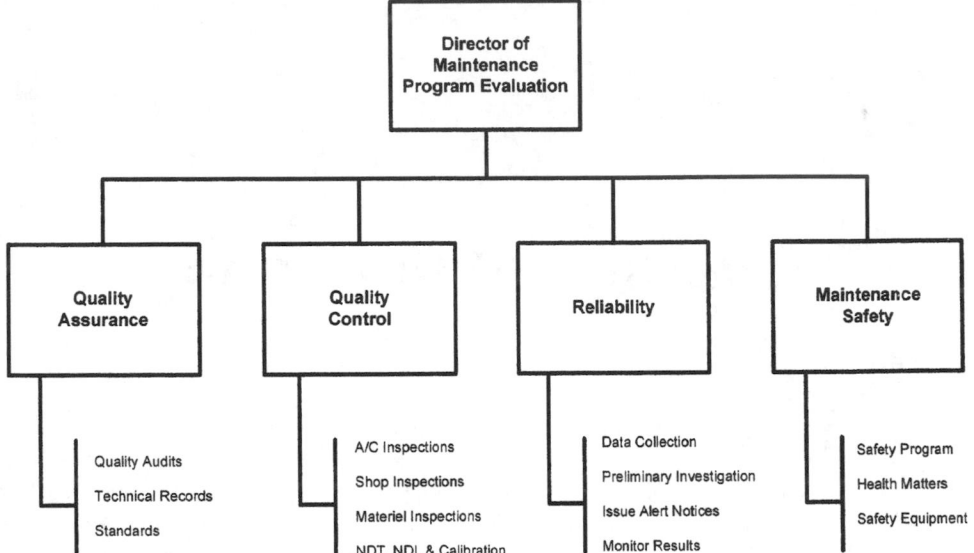

Figure IV-1   Organizational chart for maintenance program evaluation.

up of representatives of all the M&E units, reviews the program as well as the problem analysis and solution for problems detected through the reliability program and is usually called the reliability control board (RCB).

To address and subsequently resolve any problems or issues related to findings of any of the other oversight activities, the airline should establish a maintenance program review board (MPRB). This board replaces the RCB mentioned above. Since the oversight functions vary in scope, the actions of the MPRB will also vary. For example, write-ups resulting from the QA audits will primarily be infractions of the airline or FAA rules and regulations and thus corrective action will be to bring the unit into compliance. If, on occasion, the QA write-up requires a change in rules or procedures, the MPRB will be enlisted to discuss the matter and determine the necessary approach. If FAA regulations are involved, the director of MPE will coordinate MPRB action with the FAA. For QC, reliability, and safety issues, the analysis and corrective action will vary with the type of problem and the units involved. Likewise, the MPRB involvement will vary.

The MPRB is defined in Chap. 19, since its major efforts will be with reliability issues.

17

Quality Assurance

Requirement for Quality Assurance (QA)

For each type of aircraft flown, the airline must generate the operations specifications (Ops Specs) that establish, among other things, the maintenance and inspection programs to be used to keep the aircraft in an airworthy condition. This is referred to as the continuous airworthiness maintenance program or CAMP and is defined in the operator's Ops Specs. The Ops Specs is approved by the FAA, but it is not enough to ensure that such programs are effective. Federal Aviation Regulation (FAR) 121.373 (Continuing Analysis and Surveillance) provides an additional requirement. Paragraph (a) of 121.373 reads as follows:

> Each certificate holder shall establish and maintain a system for the continuing analysis and surveillance of the performance and effectiveness of its inspection program and the program covering other maintenance, preventive maintenance, and alterations and for the correction of any deficiency in those programs, regardless of whether those programs are carried out by the certificate holder or another person.

What this means is that, although the airline has an FAA approved maintenance and inspection program in place, they must monitor these programs to determine their effectiveness and implement appropriate corrective action whenever any portion of such programs proves to be ineffective. This requirement of the operating airline covers not only the work they perform themselves but also any work performed for them by third-party organizations including other airlines. This review of the airline maintenance and inspection programs is further addressed in FAA Advisory Circular AC 120-79.

In this chapter we will discuss quality assurance activities only. Other CASS requirements are discussed in subsequent chapters. The functions of QA are (*a*) the administration and management of QA and CASS activities; (*b*) the conduction of QA audits of all M&E organizations; (*c*) the maintenance of technical records; and (*d*) liaison with the regulatory authority for all M&E functions.

Quality Audits

In support of the FAR 121.373 requirements (i.e., CASS), a quality audit should be performed on each and every unit within the M&E organization. Generally, this would be done on a yearly basis but other schedules (more or less often) may be appropriate for certain areas. This audit should be a detailed, fact-finding effort designed to look at all aspects of the operation, determine any discrepancies, and establish a corrective action with a finite time for correction of each such discrepancy. This means the auditor, or audit team if one is required, will look at administrative and supervisory aspects of the operation being audited as well as the performance of work. In relation to work performance, they will look at (a) the adequacy of tools, test equipment, and facilities; (b) the competency of assigned personnel (licenses, training, skills, and skill levels, etc.); (c) shop and office orderliness; and (d) the use and handling of tools, parts, supplies, and paperwork. The following is a sample, but not exhaustive, list of airline activities that should be audited.

1. Processes and procedures related to line, hangar, and shop maintenance: logbooks; completed checks; conduct of transit, daily, and 48-hour maintenance checks; handling of deferred maintenance; fueling activities; quality control inspections; procedures related to work transfer at shift change; and procurement of parts and supplies.

2. Processes and procedures related to materiel: receiving, storing, labeling, and handling of parts and supplies, including high-value, time-limited, and flammable items; tracking of time limited parts; processing of warranty claims; establishment and replenishing of fly-away kits; hangar, line, and outstation parts allocations.

3. Processes and procedures related to engineering: development of maintenance program; investigation of problem areas; establishment of policies and procedures; procedures for the evaluation of service bulletins, service letters, and airworthiness directives.

4. Processes and procedures related to training of maintenance and inspection personnel in the use of computing systems, manuals, documentation, technical libraries, and safety equipment.

Table 17-1 shows the units of M&E and various areas of interest to those performing the quality audits.

These quality audits should be performed on each M&E organization by the supervisor of quality audits and his or her staff once per year. A schedule should be prepared in advance of each calendar year showing approximate dates and subject of each audit. This is not an attempt to "catch" someone doing wrong. The purpose is to review current operations and ensure that deficiencies are corrected. However, spot checks or surprise audits could be implemented if the situation

TABLE 17-1 Quality Audits

Audit Subjects	Hangar	Line	Shops	Contractors	Vendors	Fuel	Tech. Lib.	Logbooks	Checks	Materiel	Tools & Eq	Deferrals	Oxygen	Training	Safety
1. Adequacy & Upkeep of Facilities	x	x	x	x		x				x	x		x	x	
2. Adequacy and Serviceability of GSE	x	x													
3. Serviceability & Calibration: Tools & Test Eq.	x	x	x	x							x				
4. Use of Technical Manuals	x	x	x	x											
5. Availability of Skilled & Qualified Personnel	x	x	x	x					x					x	
6. Paperwork Handling	x	x	x	x	x				x						
7. Required Inspection Items Handling	x	x	x	x											
8. Personnel Records	x	x	x												
9. Parts: Availability, Handling, Control	x	x	x	x						x					
10. Fuel & Oil: Dispensing & Storage	x	x				x									
11. Deicing Chemicals: Dispersing & Storage	x	x													
12. Compliance with Airline Requirements				x	x										
13. Capabilities				x											
14. Cleanliness & Quality of Fuel						x									
15. Periodic Test & Inspection of Fuel Facilities						x									
16. Fuel Handling Equipment		x				x									
17. Fueling Procedures						x									
18. Revision Status of Manuals		x					x								
19. Distribution Procedures for Manuals							x								
20. Proper Revision Sign Off	x	x					x								
21. Currency & Completeness of Manuals	x	x		x			x								
22. Completeness of Logbooks								x							
23. Proper Sign Off of Discrepancies								x	x						
24. Transfer of Data to Tracking System								x							
25. Handling of Deferred Maintenance	x	x						x							
26. Improper Maintenance Write-ups in Logbook	x	x						x							
27. Completeness of Check Packages									x						
28. Inspection Stamp Usage	x	x							x						

(Continued)

TABLE 17-1 Quality Audits (Continued)

Audit Subjects	Hangar	Line	Shops	Contractors	Vendors	Fuel	Tech. Lib.	Logbooks	Checks	Materiel	Tools & Eq	Deferrals	Oxygen	Training	Safety
29. Airplanes Identified									x						
30. Handling Items Deferred out of Check									x						
31. Receiving Inspections										x					
32. Serviceable Tag Sign Off			x							x					
33. Shop Finding Reports				x	x					x					
34. Quarantine Areas										x					
35. Shelf Life Control (Stores)										x					
36. Separation of Serviceable from Unserviceable										x					
37. Currency of Calibration Stickers											x				
38. Re-Calibration Control System											x				
39. Traceability of Standards (NIST)											x				
40. Reporting & Rectification of Deferred Items	x	x										x			
41. Reasons for Deferrals												x			
42. Proper Control of Deferrals												x			
43. Cleanliness of Tools, Work Areas, Parts													x		
44. Proper Storage of Oxygen Bottles													x		
45. Quality of Oxygen													x		
46. Availability of Safety Equipment	x	x	x												x
47. Safety Training	x	x	x											x	x
48. Accident/Incident Reporting	x	x	x												x
49. Identification of 'No Smoking' Areas	x	x	x			x									x
50. Hazardous Materials Labeling & Handling	x	x	x												x
51. Training Course Syllabus														x	
52. Maintenance of Training Records														x	
53. Processing Warranty Claims										x					

calls for it.[*] It is important that each aspect of the M&E operation be audited yearly to ensure compliance with regulatory and airline requirements. It is equally important that these audits be taken seriously. Any discrepancies must be addressed and corrective action implemented in a timely manner.

Audits should be standardized. Although specific areas of investigation would vary from one audit to another, as can be seen in Table 17-1, there are certain items that are common to many organizations. Standard forms should be developed with specific areas of interest noted for each unit audited.

The supervisor of quality audits is also responsible for auditing all outside organizations that have dealings with M&E. This includes parts suppliers, parts pools, third-party maintenance organizations, and other contractors. This is not just a cursory approval of an organization that has already received approval by its own regulatory authority or that airline's QA department. The quality audits performed by your airline must ensure that the work performed by these contractors is in compliance with your airline and your regulatory requirements, no matter how similar or different they may be from the contractor's. Remember, FAR 121.373 says that an airline is responsible for monitoring all maintenance on its aircraft regardless of who performs that maintenance.

Certain other types of audits can be performed either on a yearly or on an as necessary basis. These are audits of certain processes, procedures, or functions, which may span two or more organizations or activities within M&E. Each organization involved would be audited for their part in the larger process, procedure, or function without a full audit of their organization (unless that is deemed necessary due to these or other findings). These audits include the following:

1. *Ramp operations.* All line maintenance and support functions related to activities in the airport ramp and gate areas. This would include parking, taxiing, refueling, aircraft servicing, loading and unloading (passengers, cargo, etc.), and turnaround maintenance. Such an audit might be performed in conjunction with a problem concerning delays and cancellations or with terminal operations in general.

2. *Airplane tire pressures.* The process for checking and adjusting tire pressures (inspection techniques, use of nitrogen, etc.) throughout the fleet might be audited. This would include all model aircraft, all stations where such work is likely to be done, and the crews involved.

3. *Shop records.* Although this subject would normally be part of a standard audit for any unit where records are kept, situations may arise that require an audit of the record keeping process airline-wide. New procedures, new computer processes, reliability program findings, for example, could necessitate such an audit.

---

[*]Most airlines find the scheduled audits to be quite a sufficient workload for the QA Audits section. Spot checks are used only in special cases.

4. *Required inspection items (RIIs).*   Again, this would be included in the standard audit each time any unit involved with RIIs is audited. But it may be necessary to check the RII process itself, as well as to review the authorization of those mechanics performing RIIs.

5. *AD and SB compliance.*   All ADs are required to be implemented within some specified time limit and often apply to specific aircraft (by tail number, model, or dash number, etc.). Service bulletins, although optional, must be reviewed for proper compliance if incorporated. Sometimes an AD is generated for an already released SB. Even if the airline rejected the SB (for whatever reason) as an AD it must be incorporated. This audit would look at engineering for the handling of ADs and SBs and the subsequent generation of EOs and other work orders; it will also look at appropriate units involved in the incorporation of these modifications (maintenance, materiel, training, etc.).

6. *Major repairs and alterations.*   These audits are usually performed to ensure compliance with requirements whenever major aircraft repairs or alterations are done. These modifications would be performed on a fleet of aircraft but the audit would normally be done only once.

7. *Safety equipment.*   Availability and accessibility of safety equipment in the various work centers may be part of the center's normal audit but a special audit of all safety equipment may be desirable at times. This may include an audit of the safety organization itself.

8. *Safety training.*   Training in the location and use of safety items and the proper employment of safety measures is also done in conjunction with work center audits but, again, a special audit of the entire safety program may be in order.

9. *Accident/incident reporting.*   These processes and procedures would be addressed in an audit of safety organization but an audit may be necessary of the total program, including other work centers.

10. *Fire protection/prevention.*   All systems, equipment, and procedures related to fire protection and fire prevention may be the subject of a one-time audit.

11. *Hazardous materials handling.*   The proper handling of these materials requires training of personnel who have contact with such materials. The overall program, spanning several work centers, may be audited.

ISO 9000 Quality Standard

There has been much interest lately in quality: quality of workmanship, quality of service, quality of life. Most of industry throughout the world is adopting the international standard of quality, known as ISO 9000 (ISO, International Standards Organization). This standard establishes the requirement for a

TABLE 17-2 ISO 9000 Requirements for Quality Organizations

ISO 9000 requirement	9001	9002	9003	Maintenance
1. Management responsibility	X	X	X	X
2. Documented quality system	X	X	X	X
3. Review of customer contracts	X	X		
4. Implement process controls	X			X
5. Document control	X	X	X	X
6. Purchasing control	X	X		X
7. Supplier controls	X	X		X
8. Product traceability	X	X	X	X
9. Documented processes	X	X		X
10. Inspection and testing	X	X	X	X
11. Calibration of tools and test equipment	X	X	X	X
12. Inspection and test of products	X	X	X	X
13. Control of nonconforming products	X	X	X	
14. Document corrective action	X	X		X
15. Protect parts, etc. from damage, theft, etc.	X	X	X	
16. Quality records required	X	X	X	X
17. Internal quality audits	X	X		X
18. Document training	X	X	X	X
19. Track servicing	X			X
20. Use statistical techniques to track quality	X	X	X	X

SOURCE: Adapted from Levitt, Joel: *The Handbook of Maintenance Management*; Industrial Press, Inc., New York, 1997, Chap. 18. Reprinted with permission.

quality system in organizations performing design and/or manufacturing or providing technical service to others. It identifies three types of organizations, with the ISO 9000 specification tailored to each one. The following information comes from *The Handbook of Maintenance Management* by Joel Levitt.[*]

ISO 9001 is for facilities that design/develop, produce, install, and service products or provide services to customers who specify how the product or service is to perform.

ISO 9002 is for facilities that provide goods or services to the customer's design specifications.

ISO 9003 is for those doing final inspection and testing.

Each facility must be certified to the applicable ISO 900X program based on the type of work performed. Maintenance (aircraft or other) is not specifically addressed in any of these ISO standards but many aviation regulatory authorities outside the United States require commercial airline operators to develop a quality standard using ISO 9000. Table 17-2 outlines the requirements for each type of ISO 9000 organization. The far right column (added by this author) identifies those items that would relate to aviation maintenance.

---

[*]Levitt, Joel: *The Handbook of Maintenance Management*; Industrial Press, Inc., New York, 1997, Chap. 18. Reprinted with permission.

Technical Records

In Chap. 6, we identified the FAA requirement for an operator to maintain certain records on the status of the operating aircraft. This requirement is to ensure that aircraft are maintained in airworthy condition and in accordance with certification requirements. These records allow FAA or other regulatory authorities to see that this is being done. It shows the current status of the aircraft and that the status is up to date. It also allows a new operator, if the aircraft is sold, leased, or returned to a lessor, to know the exact status of the aircraft with respect to ADs, SBs, and other modifications and major repairs. It also lets the new operator know what the maintenance schedule is for that aircraft and where it stands in the progression of letter checks at the time of transfer; i.e., how long until the next "A" check or "C" check and what multiple checks (3A, 4C, etc.) might be due.

There are four classifications of records an operator must keep: continuous, routine, repetitive, and permanent.

Continuous records, listed in Table 17-3, are continuously updated to reflect the status of the airline's operation at any point in time. Routine records, in Table 17-4, are usually maintained for a period of 15 months. Some routine records may be transferred to permanent status as noted in the table.

Repetitive records, shown in Table 17-5, identify all work that is repeated at regular intervals such as daily, transit, and letter checks. Normally, the letter

TABLE 17-3   Continuous Records

General records (aircraft, engines, components, appliances)
Time in service records
  Time limits
  Time since last overhaul
  Time since last inspection
Life limited parts
  Operating limits
  Accumulated hours and cycles
  Modifications per SB and/or AD
  Product improvement by manufacturer or operator
AD status
  List of applicable ADs
  Date and time in service
  Methods of compliance (AD, SB, EO, etc.)
  Time to next action for recurring ADs

Aircraft records
Current inspection status
  Time in service since last inspection
  Routine tasks performed during last inspection
  Nonroutine tasks performed during last inspection

Component records
Overhaul list (FAR 121.380)
  Time since last overhaul
  Time remaining to next overhaul
Component history cards

TABLE 17-4   Routine Records

General records (aircraft, engines, components, appliances)
Fleet campaigns (may be transferred to permanent)
Completed checklists
  Maintenance ferry checklist
  Engine-out ferry checklist
  Test flight checklist

Aircraft records
Logbooks
  Flight logbook
  Maintenance logbook
  Cabin logbook

Engine and APU records
Logbooks

Maintenance training records

TABLE 17-5   Repetitive Records

Aircraft records
Maintenance/inspection checks (daily, 48-hour, transit, letter checks)
  Signed off routine task cards
  Signed off nonroutine task cards
  Package closeout records
Maintenance/inspection checks (4C, D, structural—all aircraft)
  Signed off routine task cards (may be transferred to permanent)
  Signed off nonroutine task cards (may be transferred to permanent)
  Package closeout records
Weight and balance

Engine and APU records
Overhaul, check, and hot section inspections

TABLE 17-6   Permanent Records

General records (aircraft, engines, components, appliances)
AD compliance records
  Signed paperwork (task cards, EOs, etc.)
SB/SL compliance records
  Signed paperwork (task cards, EOs, etc.)
Major repairs/alterations records
  Accident reports
  Repair authorizations, sketches, drawings
  SBs, STCs, modifications, EOs
  Weight/CG change reports
  Test flight reports
FAA form 337 (major repairs and alterations)

check records are kept only until completion of the next check. However, information from these checks would be needed for justification of interval adjustment (see Chap. 2). In such cases, the check package data remains on file or the significant items from each check, each aircraft, are summarized and filed for future use and the original check package paper is destroyed.

Permanent records, listed in Table 17-6, identify permanent changes to the configuration of the aircraft, engines, components, and appliances and are retained permanently. If the aircraft is sold, leased, or returned to a lessor, the permanent records must be transferred to the next operator with the aircraft.

Other Functions of QA

The portion of QA that handles records may also be responsible for monitoring the currency of mechanics' licenses and inspectors' qualifications and authorizations (RIIs and conditional inspections). This group would also have administrative control over the development and modification of the TPPM and other documents requiring approval from the director of MPE.

Quality Control

Introduction

The inspection function of an airline M&E organization is part of the basic maintenance program established by the Ops Specs as discussed in Chap. 6. It consists, in part, of inspections performed by the mechanics during routine maintenance work: general visual inspections, detailed inspections as well as the obvious checking and rechecking of one's own work. Some maintenance actions require a "second pair of eyes" to perform an inspection to ensure that the work was performed correctly or to double-check the work. This includes the required inspection items (RIIs) and also includes oversight checking of newly hired or newly trained personnel to ensure they are performing up to standards. Still another type of inspection, the conditional inspection, is required for special events such as bird strikes, hard landings, lightning strikes, flights through heavy turbulence, or the accidental dragging of wing tips or engine pods upon landing or taxiing. For these special events, the inspection must be detailed enough to detect possible structural damage and may require special nondestructive techniques for test and inspection (NDT/NDI). For a mechanic to carry out RIIs or conduct conditional inspections, he or she must be properly trained, qualified, and approved to do said inspections by quality assurance as per FAR 121.371.

Quality Control Organization

To carry out all of these inspection requirements, it is necessary to establish a quality control function within the M&E organization. This function can take various forms. In the typical midsized airline, we have included the quality control function within the MPE directorate. This is assuming that the organization is large enough to employ full-time QC inspectors. In smaller organizations, however, the QC inspectors may, by necessity, be located in the work centers. Very often, however, an airline will have both types of inspectors. Full-time inspectors are called "dedicated inspectors" while the part-time inspectors are called "delegated inspectors" (sometimes called "designated inspectors"). In either case, someone in the MPE organization should have oversight of all QC inspectors. This oversight function is usually given to QA if there is no QC department.

A *dedicated inspector* may be an experienced mechanic, technician, or engineer, must hold a valid A&P license, and must be trained on general inspection techniques as well as on the special techniques required for the specific areas to which he or she is assigned to inspect. A QC inspector must be approved by the QA organization to conduct such inspections.

A *delegated (or designated) inspector* may be a mechanic or supervisor in a specific work center who is qualified to perform certain inspections. He or she is often limited to perform inspections only in specific areas simply because there is no other expert in the airline qualified to do such inspection or there is not enough of such work to assign anyone to the inspection work full-time. In other instances, where workload is insufficient for full-time inspectors, the delegated inspector may be required to perform all QC inspection within a given work center. To maintain the separation of inspectors from the inspected, however, it is considered that during the inspection activities, the delegated inspector is working for QC (or QA) not for the work center.

Internally, QC is divided into four functions, each under its own supervisor. Size of the airline and management preference may suggest other arrangements, but in our typical midsized airline, we have supervisors for aircraft inspections, shop inspections, materiel inspections, and testing and calibration.

The supervisor of aircraft inspections would oversee all QC inspectors, dedicated or delegated, who are responsible for the inspections performed on the aircraft whether in the hangar or on the line. The supervisor of shop inspections has the same responsibilities for those inspections performed in all support and overhaul shops for off-aircraft maintenance. The materiel inspections supervisor is responsible for all inspections required on incoming and outgoing components handled by materiel.

The fourth position on the QC organizational chart is responsible for supervision of all nondestructive test and inspections (NDT/NDI) and for the calibration of tools and test equipment used throughout M&E. This includes electronics test equipment used on the line, in the hangar, and in the shops as well as special tools, such as torque wrenches, which require regular check for calibration accuracy. The QC unit is responsible for seeing that all such tools and equipment have valid calibration stickers showing the last calibration date or the date the next calibration is due; i.e., expiration of the current calibration. Quality control is also responsible for sending such equipment to the appropriate calibration laboratory, which may be run by the airline or by a third party.

FAA and JAA Differences

The above discussion covers the approach to QC relative to the U.S. standards. In Europe, airlines under the Joint Aviation Authorities (JAA) have a different set up. Under JAA rules there is no quality control organization, only quality assurance. However, all aspects of the QC function discussed above still exist under JAA but are controlled differently. The JAA is not a regulatory authority.[*] It is an advisory group with the purpose of standardizing aviation regulations throughout Europe. In all cases, the regulatory authority of the airline's own country has the final say in what the airline should do.[†]

The certified and trained mechanic is considered qualified enough to inspect his own work to assure that it has been done properly. If the mechanic is properly trained and is a conscientious worker, this is to be expected. These mechanics, however, must be properly trained in the inspection techniques and must be approved by the QA department to do the inspection. For those inspections (safety or airworthiness related, for example) that require a second pair of eyes, the second person, under JAA rules, must also be properly trained and approved by QA. For the conditional inspection items mentioned above where structural damage might be involved, the inspector or mechanic performing such inspections must also be trained in the proper techniques (i.e., NDT/NDI) for the given inspection and be approved by QA to perform these conditional inspections.

Under JAA rules, where there is no QC, the mechanic does not have "free run" of the situation. The key words used above are "properly trained and approved by QA." This is true for FAA or JAA. In other words, the requirements are the same under both FAA and JAA jurisdictions, only the terminology and the titles used are different.

QC Inspector Qualifications

Anyone working as a quality control inspector, whether dedicated or delegated, must possess certain qualifications. The basic qualification for all inspectors is to have a valid mechanic's license and at least 2 years work experience under that license. This implies formal training in the systems and equipment to be inspected. He or she should also have a thorough knowledge of airline and regulatory rules and procedures and should have completed a QC inspector course conducted by the airline or other qualified organization.

The inspector's course should cover the duties and responsibilities of QC inspectors and instructions in inspection procedures and techniques. The course should include instruction on corrosion, its detection, and its control. Nondestructive test and inspection techniques should be addressed to the extent that the individual inspector requires for his or her duties. The course should also include a review of regulatory and airline procedures related to the inspector's specialty.

Once trained and approved for QC inspection, the mechanic is required to maintain proficiency in the inspection methods used, the specifications of the

---

[*] The European Union (EU) is in the process of establishing the European Aviation Safety Agency (EASA) to regulate aviation in the EU.

[†] Joint Aviation Agency Regulation JAR OPS 1.

equipment involved, the methods and procedures for determining quality, and the proper use of inspection aids, tools, and applicable NDT/NDI techniques.

The airline must keep a record of those personnel who are authorized as QC inspectors. Their status, dedicated or delegated, as well as the items they are qualified and authorized to inspect must be recorded and made available to regulatory personnel.

Basic Inspection Policies

The airline should establish the basic inspection policies for all dedicated and delegated inspectors to abide by. The policies most generally accepted by the industry address the following areas: (*a*) use of an inspector's stamp for official acceptance of work; (*b*) the continuity of inspection across shift boundaries; (*c*) the countermand of inspector's decisions; (*d*) reinspection of rejected work (buyback); and (*e*) the inspection of one's own work. Each of these is discussed below.

Inspection stamp

All authorized QC inspectors are issued an inspector's stamp. These stamps are numbered and controlled and each inspector is responsible for the security of his or her own stamp. When work is done by a mechanic, it is signed off by the mechanic on the appropriate work card or other official paperwork. If a specific task requires QC inspection, the inspector, after reviewing and accepting the work, will approve it by stamping and initialing the work card or task card. The stamp must be surrendered to QA whenever the inspector leaves the company or is no longer in the inspection unit.

Continuity of inspection

Whenever work spans more than one shift, the airline is required to have procedures in place (in the TPPM) to ensure that complete information and status of the work progress is passed on to the next shift. This policy must also include the transfer of inspection authority to the next shift of inspectors. In some airlines, the original work crew remains on the job until the work is completed, even if overtime is involved. In other airlines, crews work 10- to 12-hour shifts, which covers most jobs. But inspectors, often considered as management level, may work only 8-hour shifts. Whatever the shift schedule, the airline procedures must specifically identify how continuity will be maintained to ensure correctness of the work and of the inspection efforts.

Countermand of inspector's decisions

A QC inspector's decision to accept or reject a job, or ask for a rework, cannot be countermanded or overridden by the mechanic or by the mechanic's management. When a delegated QC inspector in any shop or work center is performing an inspection, his or her decisions cannot be overridden by his or her own work center supervisor since the inspection is done under QC management. The only ones who can override an inspector's decision are the manager of QC, the director of MPE, or the VP of M&E. Where the QC inspectors are directly under QA authority, the director or manager of QA has override authority. In any case where an inspector's decision has been overridden, the responsibility for the action falls upon the airline and not on the inspector or the mechanic.

Buyback policy

Any discrepancy written up by QC during a check (A, C, etc.) or in any spot check and any work rejected by QC during their acceptance inspection, must be reinspected by QC after the rework has been accomplished to gain final approval. This final inspection and approval is called "buyback." For "B" checks and lower, if no QC inspector is available, the supervisor of the mechanic performing the work has buyback authority.

Inspection of one's own work

Neither a mechanic nor an inspector can inspect and approve his or her own work where two signatures are required. It is an accepted fact that a mechanic who is qualified and conscientious will be able to "self-inspect" his or her own work to ensure that it has been done correctly. However, if the work requires a second pair of eyes or a second signature, the second person cannot be the same as the first.

Completion of work

Each work package has a list of tasks that must be completed for the check to be complete. Most tasks require only the mechanic's sign-off to indicate completion. Some tasks require a QC inspector to inspect, approve, and sign off the task also. In addition to this, the senior QC inspector assigned to the check has the responsibility of checking to see that all tasks have been completed successfully and signed off properly. This involves checking each task card for completion and sign-off, ensuring that all rejected work has been reworked and accepted, and verifying that any QC write-ups generated during the check have been addressed. Any tasks not completed for whatever reason, must be properly deferred. Normally, an airline wants an aircraft to come out of an "A" or "C" check "clean"; i.e., no deferrals, but this is not always possible. Once all the work has been completed and signed off (or deferred), the QC inspector accepts the work package as complete, signs it off, and releases the aircraft out of check.

Other QC Activities

In addition to the inspection activities mentioned above, the QC organization also has responsibility for special nondestructive test and inspection techniques, the calibration of certain tools and test equipment used in maintenance, and a number of special reports to the regulatory authority concerning maintenance problems. We will discuss each of these in turn.

Nondestructive test and inspection

There are a number of special test and inspection activities used in maintenance that require the partial or complete disassembly of components and some that require other means that render the tested unit unserviceable. Although the first type can be tolerated, the second cannot. To avoid the disassembly or destruction of components, several methods of test and inspection have been developed to provide a look at or into certain component and system conditions without permanently destroying the parts. These are called, for obvious reasons, nondestructive test or nondestructive inspection techniques.

The NDT/NDI techniques used in aircraft maintenance include the use of x-rays, ultrasound, dyes, magnetic particle detectors, and boroscopes. Each is unique and each has its particular applications. The QC organization is responsible for conducting these tests and inspections or, in some cases, training the mechanics in the use of these techniques. Table 18-1 lists these NDT/NDI techniques and their applicability.

Calibration of tools and test equipment

Certain measuring tools and test equipment used in maintenance require calibration on a periodic basis. The standards used in the United States are those of the National Institute of Standards and Technology (NIST). The airline must provide for the calibration of tools and test equipment with on-site standards, which can be traced back to the NIST. Maintenance requirements are to use only those tools and test units that have been calibrated and certified as serviceable. Responsibility for this lies with QC although a dedicated laboratory facility

TABLE 18-1   NDT/NDI Techniques

X-ray	To view internal conditions of certain materials to indicate internal holes, cracks, or other problems.
Ultrasonic	Similar to x-rays but uses high-frequency sound waves. Internal aberrations will conduct the sound differently and thus generate different patterns on the monitor.
Eddy current	Eddy currents set up in various materials exhibit certain patterns. Internal cracks in materials would alter the pattern and thus show areas of weakness.
Dye penetrant	Special dyes are introduced into various flow systems. Leaks in the tubing, gaskets, connectors, etc. will be identified by leakage of the dye at the errant point.
Magnetic particle	Chip detectors strategically placed in engines to detect metal particles in the oil indicating engine wear.
Boroscope	To view the internal condition of the jet engine rotor blades, a special video probe is inserted into an access hole in the engine. The internal section of the engine then can be viewed on an external monitor while the engine fan is rotated to view all blades. *Caution*: The probe must be removed and the access hole secured before running the engine.

is usually established, with specially qualified metrological technicians employed, to accomplish the work.

Properly calibrated tools and test equipment will carry calibration stickers that will identify either the date of last calibration or the date calibration is due. The stickers should also include the initials and stamp of the approving laboratory. Mechanics should use only tools and test equipment that have valid calibration stickers. Compliance will be monitored by QC and QA.

A valid calibration sticker, however, does not guarantee that the tool or test unit is still within calibrated limits. These units malfunction occasionally and a good mechanic should be able to detect such problems. The TPPM should spell out procedures for mechanics and technicians to use in reporting an out-of-calibration tool or instrument to QC. The processing to and from the calibration lab can be through QC or materiel.

Special reports to the regulatory authority

A mechanical reliability report (MRR)[*] is submitted whenever any malfunction or defect shown in Table 18-2 occurs. The MCC notifies QC whenever an incident occurs and QC prepares a report to the FAA. Such reports are usually submitted covering a 24-hour period (9:00 AM Monday to 9:00 AM Tuesday, for example) to the certificate-holding office of the airline. The report consists of type and identification number of the aircraft; the airline name; and the date, flight number, and flight stage when the incident occurred. The report would also include the nature of the incident, emergency procedures involved (if any), apparent cause, equipment affected, disposition, and a brief narration of any other pertinent information related to the incident. Information not available at the time of the original submission must be provided to the FAA in a follow-up report when the information becomes available.

A mechanical interruption summary (MIS) will be submitted to FAA for every flight interruption, unscheduled change of aircraft routing, or any unscheduled stop or diversion caused by mechanical difficulties (known or suspected) that do not fall in the MRR categories of Table 18-2. The MIS report is also the responsibility of QC with information supplied by the MCC.

Required inspection items

Mechanics throughout the M&E organization may be involved with RIIs but it is a QC responsibility to see that the program is properly administered. The FAA defines an RII as "any item which, if performed improperly or improper parts are used, could endanger the safe operation of the aircraft."[†] This would include such tasks as the following:

---

[*] Federal Aviation Regulation 121.703.

[†] Federal Aviation Regulation 121.369

TABLE 18-2 Mechanical Reliability Reports*

A fire or fires during flight
Whether or not the related fire warning system functioned properly
If not protected by a fire warning system

False fire warning

Engine exhaust system that causes damage during flight to
Engine
Adjacent structure
Equipment
Components

Aircraft component that causes accumulation or circulation in crew/passenger cabin of
Smoke
Vapor
Toxic fumes

Engine shutdown due to
Flameout
Foreign object ingestion
Icing

Engine shutdown when external damage to engine or airplane occurs

Shutdown of more than one engine

Fuel or fuel dumping system that
Causes leakage during flight
Affects fuel flow

Landing gear operation during flight
Extension or retraction
Opening or closing of landing gear doors

Braking system components resulting in loss of braking force when A/C is on the ground

Failure of all inertial navigation systems in flight

Any A/C components or systems that cause the crew to take emergency action
Cabin decompression in flight
Evacuation on the ground

Any failure, malfunction, or defect which occurs or is detected at any time if the airline determines that it has or may endanger the safe operation of the aircraft.

---

*Summarized from the general maintenance manual of a now defunct U.S.-based midsized airline. Also see Federal Aviation Regulation 121.703.

1. Installation, rigging, or adjustment of flight controls

2. Installation and repair of major structural components

3. Installation of engines

4. Overhaul, calibration, or rigging of components such as engines, transmissions, gear boxes, and navigation equipment

In the case of an RII, the mechanic performing the work must sign off the task when completed. Then a second pair of eyes must review the work and sign off also.

This second pair of eyes should be a mechanic who has been approved by QA to perform such inspections.

The FAA does not specify what items should be identified as RIIs but does require the airline to evaluate their own work program and identify the RIIs applicable to their operation. In addition to identifying RIIs, the airline must also specify who in their organization or any other contract organization is qualified and authorized to perform these inspections. FAR 121.371 is quite specific:

> (a) No person may use any person to perform required inspections unless the person performing the inspection is appropriately certificated, properly trained, qualified, and authorized to do so.
>
> (b) No person may allow any person to perform a required inspection unless, at that time, the person performing that inspection is under the supervision and control of an inspection unit.
>
> (c) No person may perform a required inspection if he or she performed the item of work required to be inspected.
>
> (d) Each certificate holder shall maintain, or shall determine that each person with whom it arranges to perform its required inspections maintains, a current listing of persons who have been trained, qualified, and authorized to conduct required inspections. The persons must be identified by name, occupational title, and the inspections that they are authorized to perform. The certificate holder (or person with whom it arranges to perform its required inspections) shall give written information to each person so authorized describing the extent of his responsibilities, authorities, and inspectional limitations. The list shall be made available for inspection by the Administrator upon request.[*]

---

[*] Federal Aviation Regulation 121.371.

Introduction

Reliability is a word with many meanings and connotations. In this book we have been in the habit of defining words that have special meaning to aviation, to maintenance, and to engineering. In the case of reliability, we must first discuss one important difference in the application of this term.

There are two main approaches to the concept of reliability in the aviation industry. One looks essentially at the whole airline operation or the M&E operation within the whole and the other looks at the maintenance program in particular. There is nothing wrong with either of these approaches but they differ somewhat and that difference must be understood.

The first approach is to look at the overall airline reliability. This is measured essentially by dispatch reliability; that is, by how often the airline achieves an on-time departure[*] of its scheduled flights. Airlines using this approach track delays. Reasons for the delay are categorized as maintenance, flight operations, air traffic control (ATC), etc. and are logged accordingly. The M&E organization is concerned only with those delays caused by maintenance.

Very often, airlines using this approach to reliability overlook any maintenance problems (personnel or equipment related) that do not cause delays and track and investigate only those problems that do cause delays. This is only partially effective in establishing a good maintenance program.

The second approach (which we should actually call the primary approach) is to consider reliability as a program specifically designed to address the problems of maintenance—whether or not they cause delays—and provide analysis of and corrective actions for those items to improve the overall reliability of the equipment. This contributes to the dispatch reliability as well as to the overall operation.

---

[*] On-time departure means that the aircraft has been "pushed back" from the gate within 15 minutes of the scheduled departure time.

We are not going to overlook the dispatch reliability, however. This is a distinct part of the reliability program we discuss in the following pages. But we must make the distinction and understand the difference. We must also realize that not all delays are caused by maintenance or equipment even though maintenance is the center of attention during such a delay. Nor can we only investigate equipment, maintenance procedures, or personnel for those discrepancies that have caused a delay. As you will see through later discussions, dispatch reliability is a subset of overall reliability.

Types of Reliability

The term reliability can be used in various respects. You can talk about overall reliability of an airline activity, the reliability of a component or system, or even the reliability of a process, function, or person. Here, however, we will discuss reliability in reference to the maintenance program specifically.

There are four types of reliability one can talk about related to the maintenance activity. They are (*a*) statistical reliability, (*b*) historical reliability, (*c*) event-oriented reliability, and (*d*) dispatch reliability. Although dispatch reliability is a special case of event-oriented reliability, we will discuss it separately due to its significance.

Statistical reliability

Statistical reliability is based upon collection and analysis of failure, removal, and repair rates of systems or components. From this point on, we will refer to these various types of maintenance actions as "events." Event rates are calculated on the basis of events per 1000 flight hours or events per 100 flight cycles. This normalizes the parameter for the purpose of analysis. Other rates may be used as appropriate.

Many airlines use statistical analysis but some often give the statistics more credence than they deserve. For one example, airlines with 10 or more aircraft tend to use the statistical approach, but most teachers and books on statistics tell us that for any data set with less than about 30 data points the statistical calculations are not very significant. Another case of improper use of statistics was given as an example presented in an aviation industry seminar on reliability. The airline representative used this as an example of why his airline was going to stop using statistical reliability. Here is his example.

> We use weather radar only two months of the year. When we calculate the mean value of failure rates and the alert level in the conventional manner [discussed in detail later in this chapter] we find that we are always on alert. This, of course, is not true.

The gentleman was correct in defining an error in this method, and he was correct in determining that—at least in this one case—statistics was not a valid approach. Figure 19-1 shows why.

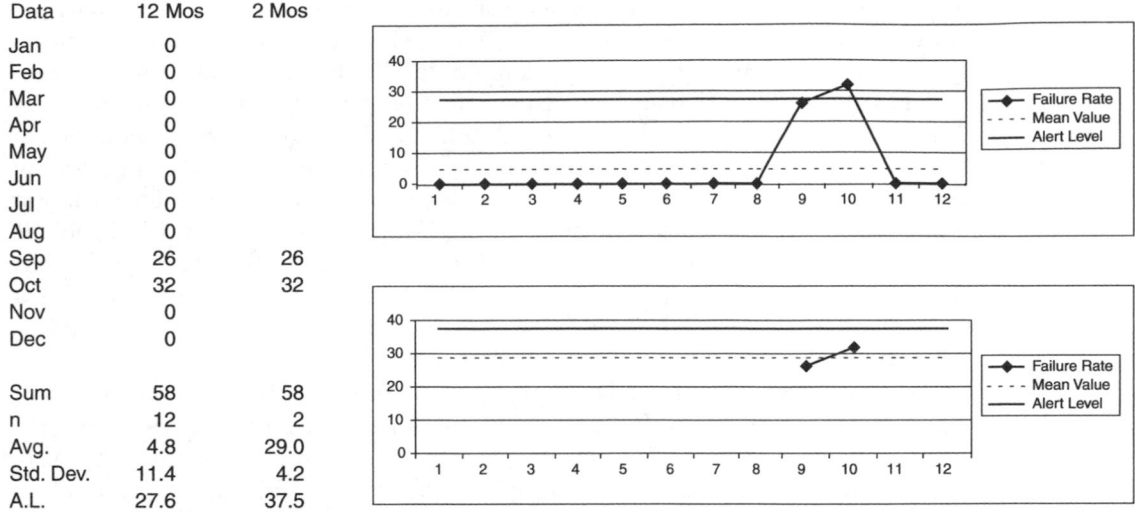

Data	12 Mos	2 Mos
Jan	0	
Feb	0	
Mar	0	
Apr	0	
May	0	
Jun	0	
Jul	0	
Aug	0	
Sep	26	26
Oct	32	32
Nov	0	
Dec	0	
Sum	58	58
n	12	2
Avg.	4.8	29.0
Std. Dev.	11.4	4.2
A.L.	27.6	37.5

Figure 19-1   Comparison of alert level calculation methods.

The top curve in Fig. 19-1 shows the two data points for data collected when the equipment was in service. It also shows 10 zero data points for those months when the equipment was not used and no data were collected (12-month column). These zeros are not valid statistical data points. They do not represent zero failures; they represent "no data" and therefore should not be used in the calculation. Using these data, however, has generated a mean value (lower, dashed line) of 4.8 and an alert level at two standard deviations above the mean (upper, solid line) of 27.6.

One thing to understand about mathematics is that the formulas will work, will produce numerical answers, whether or not the input data are correct. Garbage in, garbage out. The point is, you only have two valid data points here shown in the bottom curve of Fig. 19-1 (2-month data). The only meaningful statistic here is the average of the two numbers, 29 (dashed line). One can calculate a standard deviation (SD) here using the appropriate formula or a calculator, but the parameter has no meaning for just two data points. The alert level set by using this calculation is 37.5 (solid line). For this particular example, statistical reliability is not useable, but historical reliability is quite useful. We will discuss that subject in the next section.

Historical reliability

Historical reliability is simply a comparison of current event rates with those of past experience. In the example of Fig. 19-1, the data collected show fleet failures of 26 and 32 for the 2 months the equipment was in service. Is that good or bad? Statistics will not tell you but history will. Look at last year's data for the same equipment, same time period. Use the previous year's data also, if available. If current rates compare favorably with past experience, then everything is okay; if there is a significant difference in the data from one year to the next that would be an indication of a possible problem. And that is what a reliability program is all about: detecting and subsequently resolving problems.

Historical reliability can be used in other instances, also. The most common one is when new equipment is being introduced (components, systems, engines, aircraft) and there is no previous data available on event rates, no information on what sort of rates to expect. What is "normal" and what constitutes "a problem" for this equipment? In historical reliability we merely collect the appropriate data and literally "watch what happens." When sufficient data are collected to determine the "norms," the equipment can be added to the statistical reliability program.

Historical reliability can also be used by airlines wishing to establish a statistically based program. Data on event rates kept for 2 or 3 years can be tallied or plotted graphically and analyzed to determine what the normal or acceptable rates would be (assuming no significant problems were incurred). Guidelines can then be established for use during the next year. This will be covered in more detail in the reliability program section below.

Event-oriented reliability

Event-oriented reliability is concerned with one-time events such as bird strikes, hard landings, in-flight shutdowns, lightning strikes, or other accidents or incidents. These are events that do not occur on a regular basis and therefore produce no useable statistical or historical data. Nevertheless, they do occur from time to time, and each occurrence must be investigated to determine the cause and to prevent or reduce the possibility of recurrence of the problem. In ETOPS operations,[*] certain events that relate to successful conduct of ETOPS flights are designated by the FAA as actions to be tracked by an "event-oriented reliability program" in addition to any statistical or historical reliability program.

Dispatch reliability

Dispatch reliability is a measure of the overall effectiveness of the airline operation with respect to on-time departure. It receives considerable attention from regulatory authorities as well as from airlines and passengers, but it is really just a special form of the event-oriented reliability approach. It is a simple calculation based on 100 flights. This makes it convenient to relate dispatch rate in percent. An example of the dispatch rate calculation follows.

If eight delays and cancellations are experienced in 200 flights, that would mean that there were four delays per 100 flights, or a 4 percent delay rate. A 4 percent delay rate would translate to a 96 percent dispatch rate (100 percent − 4 percent

---

[*] Requirements for extended range operations with two-engine airplanes (ETOPS) are outlined in FAA Advisory Circular AC 120-42A, and also discussed in Appendix E of this book.

delayed = 96 percent dispatched on time). In other words, the airline dispatched 96 percent of its flights on time.

The use of dispatch reliability at the airlines is, at times, misinterpreted. The passengers are concerned with timely dispatch for obvious reasons. To respond to FAA pressures on dispatch rate, airlines often overreact. Some airline maintenance reliability programs track only dispatch reliability; that is, they only track and investigate problems that resulted in a delay or a cancellation of a flight. But this is only part of an effective program and dispatch reliability involves more than just maintenance. An example will bear this out.

The aircraft pilot in command is 2 hours from his arrival station when he experiences a problem with the rudder controls. He writes up the problem in the aircraft logbook and reports it by radio to the flight following unit at the base. Upon arrival at the base, the maintenance crew meets the plane and checks the log for discrepancies. They find the rudder control write-up and begin troubleshooting and repair actions. The repair takes a little longer than the scheduled turnaround time and, therefore, causes a delay. Since maintenance is at work and the rudder is the problem, the delay is charged to maintenance and the rudder system would be investigated for the cause of the delay.

This is an improper response. Did maintenance cause the delay? Did the rudder equipment cause the delay? Or was the delay caused by poor airline procedures? To put it another way: could a change of airline procedures eliminate the delay? Let us consider the events as they happened and how we might change them for the better.

If the pilot and the flight operations organization knew about the problem 2 hours before landing, why wasn't maintenance informed at the same time? If they had been informed, they could have spent the time prior to landing in studying the problem and performing some troubleshooting analysis. It is quite possible, then, that when the airplane landed, maintenance could have met it with a fix in hand. Thus, this delay could have been prevented by procedural changes. The procedure should be changed to avoid such delays in the future.

While the maintenance organization and the airline could benefit from this advance warning of problems, it will not always eliminate delays. The important thing to remember is that if a delay is caused by procedure, it should be attributed to procedure and it should be avoided in the future by altering the procedure. That is what a reliability program is about: detecting where the problems are and correcting them, regardless of who or what is to blame.

Another fallacy in overemphasizing dispatch delay is that some airlines will investigate each delay (as they should) but if an equipment problem is involved, the investigation may or may not take into account other similar failures that did not cause delays. For example, if you had 12 write-ups of rudder problems during the month and only one of these caused a delay, you actually have two problems to investigate: (a) the delay, which could be caused by problems other than the rudder equipment and (b) the 12 rudder write-ups that may, in fact, be related to an underlying maintenance problem. One must understand that dispatch delay constitutes one problem and the rudder system malfunction constitutes another. They may indeed overlap but they are two different problems. The delay is an event-oriented reliability problem that must be investigated on its own; the 12 rudder problems (if this constitutes a high failure rate) should be addressed by the statistical (or historical) reliability program. The investigation of the dispatch delays should look at the whole operation. Equipment problems—whether or not they caused delays—should be investigated separately.

A Definition of Reliability

Reliability can be defined as "the probability that an item will perform a required function, under specified conditions without failure, for a specified amount of time."[*] Reliability can also be thought of as dependability or stability. A system or component is "reliable" if it can be counted upon to perform in a dependable manner.

A Reliability Program

A reliability program for our purposes is, essentially, a set of rules and practices for managing and controlling a maintenance program. The main function of a reliability program is to monitor the performance of the vehicles and their associated equipment and call attention to any need for corrective action. The program has two additional functions: (*a*) to monitor the effectiveness of those corrective actions and (*b*) to provide data to justify adjusting the maintenance intervals or maintenance program procedures whenever those actions are appropriate.

Elements of a Reliability Program

A good reliability program consists of seven basic elements as well as a number of procedures and administrative functions. The basic elements (discussed in detail below) are (*a*) data collection; (*b*) problem area alerting, (*c*) data display; (*d*) data analysis; (*e*) corrective actions; (*f*) follow-up analysis; and (*g*) a monthly report. We will look at each of these seven program elements in more detail.

Data collection

We will list 10 data types that can be collected although they may not necessarily be collected by all airlines. Other items may be added at the airline's discretion. The data collection process gives the reliability department the information needed to observe the effectiveness of the maintenance program. Those items that are doing well might be eliminated from the program simply because the data show that there are no problems. On the other hand, items not

---

[*] Air Transport Association of America (ATA); *Common Support Data Dictionary* (CSDD), revision 2001.1.

being tracked may need to be added to the program because there are serious problems related to those systems. Basically, you collect the data needed to stay on top of your operation. The data types normally collected are as follows:

1. Flight time and cycles for each aircraft
2. Cancellations and delays over 15 minutes
3. Unscheduled component removals
4. Unscheduled engine removals
5. In-flight shutdowns of engines
6. Pilot reports or logbook write-ups
7. Cabin logbook write-ups
8. Component failures (shop maintenance)
9. Maintenance check package findings
10. Critical failures

We will discuss each of these in detail below.

Flight time and flight cycles. Most reliability calculations are "rates" and are based on flight hours or flight cycles; e.g., 0.76 failures per 1000 flight hours or 0.15 removals per 100 flight cycles.

Cancellations and delays over 15 minutes. Some operators collect data on all such events but maintenance is concerned primarily with those that are maintenance related. The 15-minute time frame is used because that amount of time can usually be made up in flight. Longer delays may cause schedule interruptions or missed connections, thus the need for rebookings. This parameter is usually converted to a "dispatch rate" for the airline as discussed above.

Unscheduled component removals. This is the unscheduled maintenance mentioned earlier and is definitely a concern of the reliability program. The rate at which aircraft components are removed may vary widely depending on the equipment or system involved. If the rate is not acceptable, an investigation should be made and some sort of corrective action must be taken. Components that are removed and replaced on schedule—e.g., HT items and certain OC items—are not included here but these data may be collected to aid in justifying a change in the HT or OC interval schedule.

Unscheduled removals of engines. This is the same as component removals but obviously an engine removal constitutes a considerable amount of time and manpower; therefore, these data are tallied separately.

In-flight shutdown (IFSD) of engines. This malfunction is probably one of the most serious in aviation, particularly if the airplane only has two engines (or one). The FAA requires a report of IFSD within 72 hours.[*] The report must include the

---

[*] See Federal Aviation Regulation 121.703, Mechanical Reliability Report.

cause and the corrective action. The ETOPS operators are required to track IFSDs and respond to excessive rates as part of their authorization to fly ETOPS. However, non-ETOPS operators also have to report shutdowns and should also be tracking and responding to high rates through the reliability program.

Pilot reports or logbook write-ups. These are malfunctions or degradations in airplane systems noted by the flight crew during flight. Tracking is usually by ATA Chapter numbers using two, four, or six digits. This allows pinpointing of the problems to the system, subsystem, or component level as desired. Experience will dictate what levels to track for specific equipment.

Cabin logbook write-ups. These discrepancies may not be as serious as those the flight crew deals with but passenger comfort and the ability of the cabin crew to perform their duties may be affected. These items are written up by the cabin crew sometimes in a separate cabin log and transferred to the flight log or they are entered directly into the flight crew logbook (maintenance log).

Component failures. Any problems found during shop maintenance visits are tallied for the reliability program. This refers to major components within the black boxes (avionics) or parts and components within mechanical systems.

Maintenance check package findings. Systems or components found to be in need of repair or adjustment during normal scheduled maintenance checks (non-routine items) are tracked by the reliability program.

Critical failures. Failures involving a loss of function or secondary damage that could have a direct adverse effect on operating safety.

Problem detection—an alerting system

The data collection system allows the operator to compare present performance with past performance in order to judge the effectiveness of maintenance and the maintenance program. An alerting system should be in place to quickly identify those areas where the performance is significantly different from the normal. These are items that might need to be investigated for possible problems. Standards for event rates are set according to analysis of past performances and deviations from these standards.

This alert level is based on a statistical analysis of the event rates of the previous year, offset by 3 months. The mean value of the failure rates and the standard deviation from the mean are calculated and an alert level is set at one to three standard deviations above that mean rate (more on setting and adjusting alert levels later). This value, the upper control limit or UCL, is commonly referred to as the alert level. However, there is an additional calculation that can be made to smooth the curve and help eliminate "false alerts." This is the 3-month rolling average, or trend line. The position of these two lines (the monthly rate and the 3-month average) relative to the UCL is used to determine alert status.

Setting and adjusting alert levels

It is recommended that alert levels be recalculated yearly. The data used to determine alert level are the event rates for the previous year offset by 3 months. The reason for this will be explained shortly.

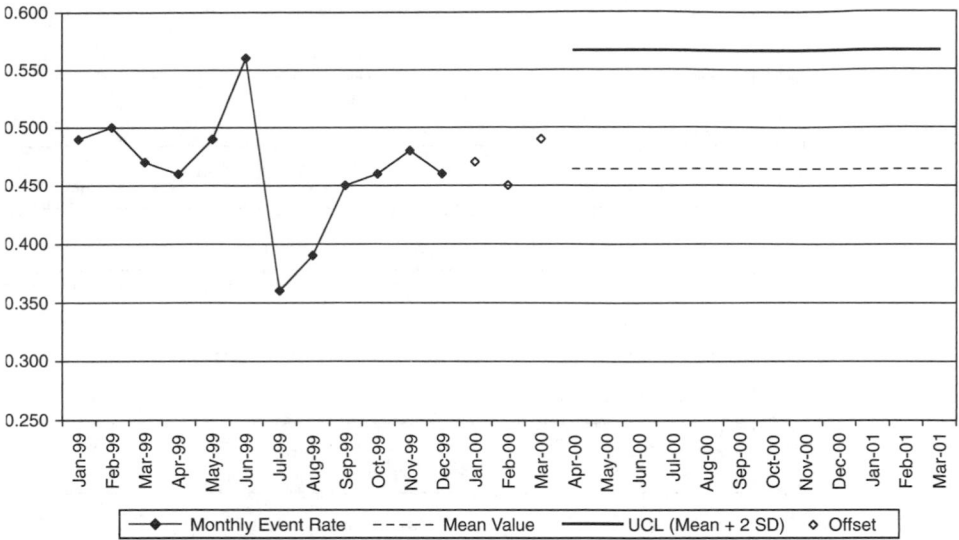

Figure 19-2 Calculation of new alert levels.

Figure 19-2 shows the data used and the results in graphic form. In this example, we are establishing a new alert level for the year April 2000 through March 2001. This level is represented in Fig. 19-2 as the upper straight line. These data were obtained using the actual event rates for January 1999 through December 1999 shown on the left of the figure. The three data points between (shown as diamonds for January to March 2000 in Fig. 19-2) will be used in calculating a 3-month rolling average to be used during the collection of new data. This will be discussed later.

Basic statistics are used for the calculations. From the original data (January–December 1999) we calculate the mean and the standard deviation of these data points. The mean is used as a baseline for the new data and is shown as the dashed line on the right side of Fig. 19-2. The solid line on the right of Fig. 19-2 is the alert level that we have chosen for these data and is equal to the calculated mean plus two standard deviations. Event rates for the new year, then, will be plotted and measured relative to these guidelines.

Reading alert status

The data shown in Fig. 19-3 show 1 year of event rates (solid jagged line with triangles) along with the mean value (bottom straight line) and the alert level (upper straight line). As you can see, the event rate swings above the alert level several times through the year (February, June, October, and December). Of course, it is easy to see the pattern as we look at the year's events. But in reality, you will only see 1 month at a time and the preceding months. Information on what is going to happen the next month is not available to you.

When the event rate goes above the alert level (as in February), it is not necessarily a serious matter. But if the rate stays above the alert level for 2 months

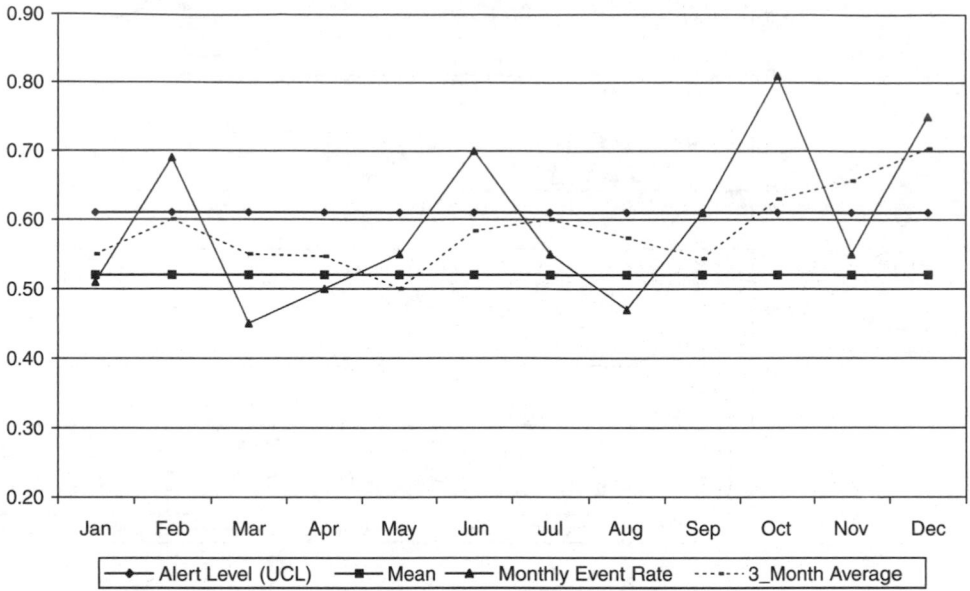

Figure 19-3 Reading alert status.

in succession, then it may warrant an investigation. The preliminary investigation may indicate a seasonal variation or some other one-time cause, or it may suggest the need for a more detailed investigation. More often than not, it can be taken for what it was intended to be—an "alert" to a possible problem. The response would be to wait and see what happens next month. In Fig. 19-3, the data show that, in the following month (March) the rate went below the line, thus, no real problem exists. In other words, when the event rate penetrates the alert level, it is not an indication of a problem; it is merely an "alert" to the possibility of a problem. Reacting too quickly usually results in unnecessary time and effort spent in investigation. This is what we call a "false alert."

If experience shows that the event rate for a given item varies widely from month to month above and below the UCL as in Fig. 19-3—and this is common for some equipment—many operators use a 3-month rolling average. This is shown as the dashed line in Fig. 19-3. For the first month of the new data year, the 3-month average is determined by using the offset data points in Fig. 19-2. (Actually, only 2 months offset is needed but we like to keep things on a quarterly basis.) The purpose for the offset is to ensure that the plotted data for the new year do not contain any data points that were used to determine the mean and alert levels we use for comparison.

While the event rate swings above and below the alert level, the 3-month rolling average (dashed line) stays below it—until October. This condition—event rate and 3-month average above the UCL—indicates a need to watch the activity more closely. In this example, the event rate went back down below the

UCL in November but the 3-month average stayed above the alert level. This is an indication that the problem should be investigated.

Setting alert levels

These upper control limits or alert levels, and the mathematics that produced them are not magical by any means. They will not tell you when you have a definite problem nor will they tell you where or what to investigate. What they will do is provide you with intelligent guidelines for making your own decisions about how to proceed. But the whole process begins with your intellect and your ability to set these alert levels to an effective level.

Earlier in this chapter we talked about an airline that was rejecting statistical reliability and gave an example of why. Another of the reasons the gentleman gave for this decision was that "we know we have problems with engines, but engines are never on alert." If you use the UCL concept to alert you to possible problems and you do not get an alert indication when you know you have problems, then it should not take much thought to make you realize that your chosen alert level is wrong. This alert level is a very important parameter and it must be set to a useable level, a level that will indicate to you that a problem exists or may be developing. If not set properly, the alert level is useless. And that is not the fault of statistics.

This use of an alert level is designed to tell you when you have (or may have) a problem developing that requires investigation. But you have to know what conditions constitute a possible problem and set the alert level accordingly. You have to know your equipment and its failure patterns to determine when you should proceed with an investigation and when to refrain from investigating. You have to recognize "false alerts." You also have to know whether or not the event rate data points for a particular item are widely or narrowly distributed; that is, if it has a large or small standard deviation. This knowledge is vital to setting useable alert levels.

Many airlines erroneously set all alert levels at two standard deviations above the mean. Unfortunately, this is not a good practice. It is a good place to start but there must be an adjustment in some cases to provide the most useable data and to avoid false alerts.

As we discussed in Chap. 1, not everything fails at the same rate or in the same pattern. Event rates tracked by a reliability program can be quite erratic, as the data in Fig. 19-3 show. For other rates, the numbers can be more stable. This characteristic of the data is depicted by the statistical parameter of standard deviation—the measure of the distribution of data points around the mean. A large standard deviation means wide distribution, a large variation in point values. A small standard deviation means that the points are closer together.

Figure 19-4 shows the difference between two data sets. The data points in (A) are widely scattered or distributed about the mean while those in (B) are all very close together around the mean. Note that the averages of these two data sets are

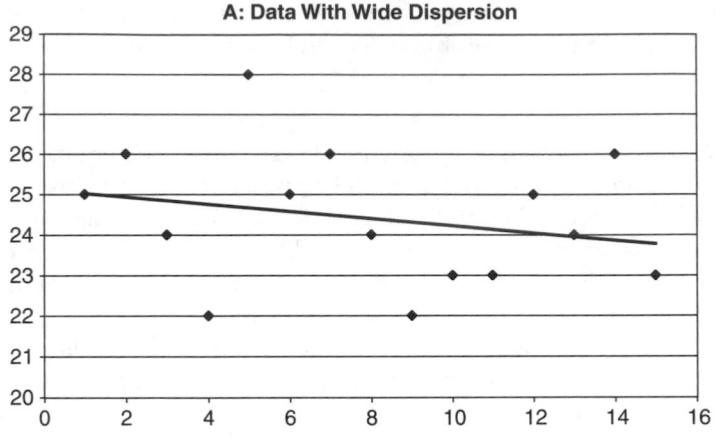

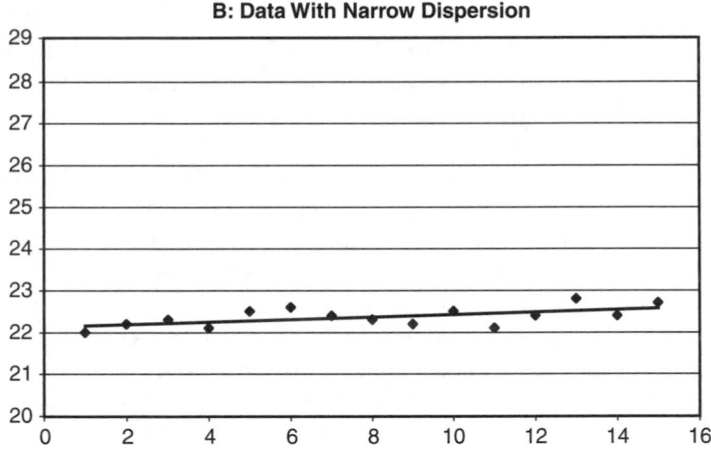

Figure 19-4   Dispersion of data points.

nearly equal but the standard deviations are quite different. Figure 19-5 shows the bell-shaped distribution curve. One, two, and three standard deviations in each case are shown on the graph. You can see here that, at one SD only 68 percent of the valid failure rates are included. At two standard deviations above the mean, you still have not included all the points in the distribution. In fact, two standard deviations above and below the mean encompass only 95.5 percent of the points under the curve; i.e., just over 95 percent of the valid failure rates. This is why we do not consider an event rate in this range a definite problem. If it remains above this level in the following month it may suggest a possible problem. On the other hand, if the event rate data you are working with had a small standard deviation, it would be difficult to distinguish between two and three SDs. In this case, the alert level should be set at three SDs.

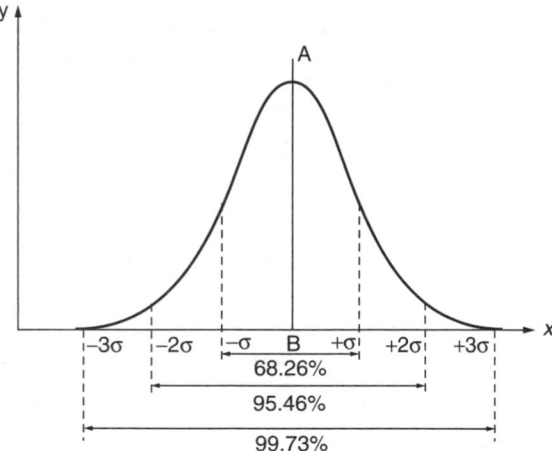

Figure 19-5 Standard bell-shaped curve. (*Source: The Standard Handbook for Aeronautical and Astronautical Engineers*, New York, NY: McGraw-Hill, 2003.)

This alert level system can be overdone at times. The statistics used are not exact. We are assuming that the event rates will always have a distribution depicted by the bell-shaped curve. We assume that our data are always accurate and that our calculations are always correct. But this may not be true. These alert levels are merely guidelines to identifying what should be investigated and what can be tolerated. Use of the alert level is not rocket science but it helps ease the workload in organizations with large fleets and small reliability staffs. Some airlines, using only event rates, will investigate perhaps the 10 highest rates; but this does not always include the most important or the most significant equipment problems. The alert level approach allows you to prioritize these problems and work the most important ones first.

Data display

Several methods for displaying data are utilized by the reliability department to study and analyze the data they collect. Most operators have personal computers available so that data can easily be displayed in tabular and graphical forms. The data are presented as events per 100 or 1000 flight hours or flight cycles. Some, such as delays and cancellations, are presented as events per 100 departures. The value of 100 allows easy translation of the rate into a percentage.

Tabular data allow the operator to compare event rates with other data on the same sheet. It also allows the comparison of quarterly or yearly data (see Table 19-1). Graphs, on the other hand, allow the operator to view the month-to-month performance and note, more readily, those items that show increasing rates and appear to be heading for alert status (see Fig. 19-3). This is a great help in analysis. Some of the data collected may be compared on a monthly basis, by event, or by sampling.

TABLE 19-1   Pilot Reports per 100 Landings (by ATA Chapter)

ATA Chapter	System	PIREPS	June-99	July-99	August-99	Three-month average	UCL	Mean	Alert status
21	Air conditioning	114	3.65	3.77	3.80	3.74	3.75	2.70	YE
22	Auto flight	43	1.80	1.48	1.45	1.58	1.39	1.21	WA
23	Communications	69	3.44	2.75	2.33	2.84	2.80	2.30	CL
24	Electrical power	29	1.15	0.87	0.98	1.00	0.94	0.60	AL
25	Equip/furnishings	104	4.17	3.69	3.52	3.79	5.43	4.38	
26	Fire protection	30	1.80	1.30	1.01	1.37	2.19	1.14	
27	Flight controls	48	0.99	3.07	1.62	1.89	1.94	1.26	
28	Fuel	36	0.65	1.16	1.22	1.01	2.32	1.27	
29	Hydraulic power	17	0.73	0.43	0.57	0.58	1.58	0.82	
30	Ice & rain protection	12	0.61	0.65	0.41	0.56	0.72	0.56	
31	Instruments	49	1.76	1.48	1.66	1.63	2.46	1.66	
32	Landing gear	67	2.41	2.06	2.27	2.25	2.72	1.76	
33	Lights	72	3.48	3.15	2.43	3.02	3.32	2.42	
34	Navigation	114	4.81	6.62	3.85	5.09	5.58	4.70	
35	Oxygen	19	0.31	0.67	0.64	0.54	0.41	0.23	YE
36	Pneumatics	25	1.11	0.80	0.85	0.92	1.19	0.77	
38	Water & waste	16	0.42	0.36	0.54	0.44	1.10	0.56	
49	Aux. power	42	1.41	1.48	1.42	1.44	1.63	1.38	
51	Structures	0	0.00	0.00	0.00	0.00	0.16	0.09	
52	Doors	31	1.41	1.05	1.05	1.17	1.62	0.92	
53	Fuselage	0	0.00	0.00	0.00	0.00	0.33	0.02	
54	Nacelles & pylons	1	0.00	0.00	0.08	0.03	0.22	0.10	
55	Stabilizers	0	0.00	0.00	0.00	0.00	0.16	0.09	
56	Windows	0	0.00	0.04	0.00	0.01	0.09	0.06	
57	Wings	0	0.00	0.00	0.00	0.00	0.33	0.15	
71	Power plant	11	0.65	0.54	0.37	0.52	1.30	0.91	
72	Engine	4	0.31	0.29	0.14	0.25	0.47	0.22	
73	Fuel & controls	17	0.96	0.47	0.57	0.67	0.84	0.61	
74	Ignition	11	0.08	0.40	0.37	0.28	0.46	0.30	
75	Air	53	1.52	1.63	1.79	1.65	1.11	0.66	RA
76	Engine control	3	0.23	0.14	0.10	0.16	0.33	0.15	
77	Engine indicating	22	0.53	0.76	0.74	0.68	0.96	0.68	
78	Exhaust	3	0.50	0.43	0.10	0.34	0.90	0.64	
79	Oil	5	0.19	0.22	0.17	0.19	0.83	0.48	
80	Starting	3	0.27	0.29	0.10	0.22	0.28	0.17	CL
	Total	1070							

NOTE: Alert status codes: CL = clear from alert; YE = yellow alert; AL = red alert; RA = remains in alert; WA = watch.

Table 19-1 is a listing of pilot reports (PIREPS) or maintenance logbook entries recorded by a typical airline for 1 month of operation for a fleet of aircraft. The numbers are examples only and do not represent any particular operator, aircraft, or fleet size. For these data, a tally is kept by ATA Chapter and event rates are calculated as PIREPS per 100 landings. The chart shows data for the current month (August'99) and the two previous months along with the 3-month rolling average. The alert level or UCL and the mean value of event rate, calculated as discussed in the text, are also included. Seven of these ATA chapters have alert indications noted in the last column.

Chapter 21 has had an event rate above the UCL for 2 months running (July, August); therefore, this represents a yellow alert (YE). Depending on the severity of the problem, this may or may not require an immediate investigation. Chapter 24, however, is different. For July, the event rate was high, 1.15. If this were the first time for such a rate, it would have been listed in the report for that month as a watch (WA). The rate went down in July but has gone up again in August. In the current report, then, it is a full alert condition. It is not only above the alert level, it has been above 2 of the 3 months, and it appears somewhat erratic. It is left as an exercise for the student to analyze the other alert status items. What about ATA Chapter 38?

Data analysis

Whenever an item goes into alert status, the reliability department does a preliminary analysis to determine if the alert is valid. If it is valid, a notice of the on-alert condition is sent to engineering for a more detailed analysis. The engineering department is made up of experienced people who know maintenance and engineering. Their job relative to these alerts is to troubleshoot the problem, determine the required action that will correct the problem and issue an engineering order (EO) or other official paperwork that will put this solution in place.

At first, this may seem like a job for maintenance. After all, troubleshooting and corrective action is their job. But we must stick with our basic philosophy from Chap. 7 of separating the inspectors from the inspected. Engineering can provide an analysis of the problem that is free from any unit bias and be free to look at all possibilities. A unit looking into its own processes, procedures, and personnel may not be so objective. The engineering department should provide analysis and corrective action recommendations to the Airline Maintenance Program Review Board (discussed later) for approval and initiation.

Note: Appendix C discusses the troubleshooting process that applies to engineers as well as mechanics; and Appendix D outlines additional procedures for reliability and engineering alert analysis efforts.

Corrective action

Corrective actions can vary from one-time efforts correcting a deficiency in a procedure to retraining of mechanics to changes in the basic maintenance program. The investigation of these alert conditions commonly results in one or more of the following actions: (a) modifications of equipment; (b) change in or correction to line, hangar, or shop processes or practices; (c) disposal of defective parts (or their suppliers); (d) training of mechanics (refresher or upgrade); (e) addition of maintenance tasks to the program; or (f) decreases in maintenance intervals for certain tasks. Engineering then produces an engineering order for implementation of whatever action is applicable. Engineering also tracks the progress of the order and offers assistance as needed. Completion of the corrective action is noted in the monthly reliability report (discussed later).

Continual monitoring by reliability determines the effectiveness of the selected corrective action.

Corrective actions should be completed within 1 month of issuance of the EO. Completion may be deferred if circumstances warrant, but action should be completed as soon as possible to make the program effective. Normally, the Maintenance Program Review Board (MPRB) will require justification in writing for extensions of this period; the deferral, and the reason for deferral, will be noted in the monthly report.

Follow-up analysis

The reliability department should follow up on all actions taken relative to on-alert items to verify that the corrective action taken was indeed effective. This should be reflected in decreased event rates. If the event rate does not improve after action has been taken, the alert is reissued and the investigation and corrective action process is repeated with engineering taking a different approach to the problem. If the corrective action involves lengthy modifications to numerous vehicles, the reduction in the event rate may not be noticeable for some time. In these cases, it is important to continue monitoring the progress of the corrective action in the monthly report along with the ongoing event rate until corrective action is completed on all vehicles. Then follow-up observation is employed to judge the effectiveness (wisdom) of the action. If no significant change is noted in the rates within a reasonable time after a portion of the fleet has been completed, the problem and the corrective action should be reanalyzed.

Data reporting

A reliability report is issued monthly. Some organizations issue quarterly and yearly reports in summary format. The most useful report, however, is the monthly. This report should not contain an excessive amount of data and graphs without a good explanation of what this information means to the airline and to the reader of the report. The report should concentrate on the items that have just gone on alert, those items under investigation, and those items that are in or have completed the corrective action process. The progress of any items that are still being analyzed or implemented will also be noted in the report, showing status of the action and percent of fleet completed if applicable. These items should remain in the monthly report until all action has been completed and the reliability data show positive results.

Other information, such as a list of alert levels (by ATA Chapter or by item) and general information on fleet reliability will also be included in the monthly report. Items such as dispatch rates, reasons for delays and/or cancellations, flight hours and cycles flown and any significant changes in the operation that affect the maintenance activity would also be included. The report should be organized by fleet; that is, each airplane model would be addressed in a separate section of the report.

The monthly reliability report is not just a collection of graphs, tables, and numbers designed to dazzle higher-level management. Nor is it a document left on the doorstep of others, such as QA or the FAA, to see if they can detect any problems you might have. This monthly report is a working tool for maintenance management. Besides providing operating statistics such as the number of aircraft in operation, the number of hours flown, and so forth, it also provides management with a picture of what problems are encountered (if any) and what is being done about those problems. It also tracks the progress and effectiveness of the corrective action. The responsibility for writing the report rests with the reliability department, not engineering.

Other Functions of the Reliability Program

Investigation of the alert items by engineering often results in the need to change the maintenance program. This can mean (a) changes in specific tasks; (b) adjustments in the interval at which maintenance tasks are performed; or (c) changes in the maintenance processes (HT, OC, and CM) to which components are assigned. A change in the task may mean rewriting maintenance and/or test procedures or in implementing new, more effective procedures.

Adjustments in the maintenance interval may be a solution to a given problem. A maintenance action currently performed at, say a monthly interval, should, in fact, be done weekly or even daily to reduce the event rate. The reliability program should provide the rules and processes used to adjust these intervals. The Maintenance Program Review Board must approve these changes and, in certain instances, the regulatory authority must also approve. Generally, though, the change to a greater frequency (shorter interval) is not difficult. One should keep in mind, however, that this means higher cost of maintenance due to the increase in maintenance activity. This cost must be offset by the reduction in the event rate that generated the change and a reduction in the maintenance requirements resulting from the change. The economics of this change is one of the concerns engineering must address during the investigation of the alert condition. The cost of the change may or may not be offset by the gain in reliability or performance (see objective 5 in Chap. 3).

Administration and Management
of the Reliability Program

On the administration and management side, a reliability program will include written procedures for changing maintenance program tasks as well as processes and procedures for changing maintenance intervals (increasing or decreasing them). Identification, calculation, establishment, and adjustment of alert levels and the determination of what data to track are basic functions of the reliability section. Collecting data is the responsibility of various M&E organizations such as line maintenance (flight hours and cycles, logbook reports, etc.); overhaul shops (component removals); hangar (check packages); materiel (parts usage).

Some airlines use a central data collection unit for this, located in M&E administration, or some other unit such as engineering or reliability. Other airlines have provisions for the source units to provide data to the reliability department on paper or through the airline computer system. In either case, reliability is responsible for collecting, collating, and displaying these data and performing the preliminary analysis to determine alert status.

Maintenance program review board

The solution of reliability problems is not the exclusive domain of the reliability section or the engineering section; it is a maintenance and engineering organization-wide function. This group approach ensures that all aspects of the problem have been addressed by those who are most familiar with the situation. Therefore, oversight of the program is assigned to a Maintenance Program Review Board that is made up of key personnel in M&E. Based on the typical organization of Chap. 7, the MPRB would consist of the following personnel:

1. Director of MPE as chairman

2. Permanent members
    a. Director of technical services
    b. Director of airplane maintenance
    c. Director of overhaul shops
    d. Manager of quality assurance
    e. Manager of quality control
    f. Manager of engineering
    g. Manager of reliability
3. Adjunct members are representatives of affected M&E departments
    a. Engineering supervisors (by ATA Chapter or specialty)
    b. Airplane maintenance (line, hangar)
    c. Overhaul shops (avionics, hydraulics, etc.)
    d. Production planning and control
    e. Materiel
    f. Training

The head of MPE is the one who deals directly with the regulatory authority, so as chairman of the Maintenance Program Review Board, he or she would coordinate any recommended changes requiring regulatory approval.

The MPRB meets monthly to discuss the overall status of the maintenance reliability and to discuss all items that are on alert. The permanent members, or their designated assistants, attend every meeting; the advisory members attend those meetings where items that relate to their activities will be discussed. Items coming into alert status for the recent month are discussed first to determine if a detailed investigation by engineering is needed. Possible problems and solutions may be offered. If engineering is engaged in or has completed investigation of certain problems, these will be discussed with the MPRB members. Items that are currently in work are then discussed to track and analyze their status and to evaluate the effectiveness of the corrective action. If any ongoing corrective actions involve long-term implementation, such as modifications to the fleet that must be done at the "C" check interval, the progress and effectiveness of the corrective action should be studied to determine (if possible) whether or not the chosen action appears to be effective. If not, a new approach would be discussed and subsequently implemented by a revision to the original engineering order.

Other activities of the MPRB include the establishment of alert levels and the adjustment of these levels as necessary for effective management of problems. The rules governing the reliability program are developed with approval by the MPRB. Rules relating to the change of maintenance intervals, alert levels, and all other actions addressed by the program must be approved by the MPRB. The corrective actions and the subsequent EOs developed by the engineering department are also approved by the MPRB before they are issued.

Reliability program document

We are a nation of document producers. For everything we do, we have to write down procedures for future reference. Therefore, every aspect of the reliability program described above must be documented in an official document signed by the Maintenance Program Review Board chairman and approved by the regulatory authority. This document includes a detailed discussion of the data collection, problem investigation, corrective action implementation, and follow-up actions discussed above. It also includes an explanation of the methods used to determine alert levels; the rules relative to changing maintenance processes (HT, OC, CM) or MPD task intervals; when to initiate an investigation; definition of the MPRB activities and responsibilities; and the monthly report format. The document would also include such administrative elements as responsibility for the document, revision status, a distribution list, and approval signatures.

Once the reliability program is defined and accepted by the airline (MPRB and QA), it is submitted to the FAA for approval. When this has been done, the airline is free to proceed. Changes in intervals, maintenance processes, alert levels can then be made without further FAA approval. This is part of the "self-policing" philosophy FAA has regarding airline operation.

The reliability program document is a controlled document and thus contains a revision status sheet, a list of effective pages, and a limited distribution within the airline. It is usually a separate document but can be included as part of the TPPM (see Chap. 5).

FAA interaction

It is customary, in the United States, to invite the FAA to sit in on the MPRB meetings as a nonvoting member. (They have, in a sense, their own voting power.) Since each U.S. airline has a principal maintenance inspector (PMI) assigned and usually on site, it is convenient for the FAA to attend these meetings. Airlines outside the United States that do not have the on site representative at each airline may not find it as easy to comply. But the invitation should be extended nevertheless. This lets the regulatory authority know that the airline is attending to its maintenance problems in an orderly and systematic manner and gives the regulatory people an opportunity to provide any assistance that may be required.

20

Maintenance Safety

Industrial Safety

The Code of Federal Regulations, Title 29, Part 1910, deals with industrial safety (29 CFR 1910). Its title is "Occupational Safety and Health Standards" and is part of the U.S. Government regulations for the Department of Labor (DOL). The agency within DOL responsible for enforcing these regulations is the Occupational Safety and Health Administration (OSHA). Aviation is not addressed specifically in these OSHA regulations but all aspects of the aviation maintenance activity (as well as flight operations, office, and terminal activities) are covered. Table 20-1 lists the subparts of Part 1910 as of January 2003. It is up to the aviation industry itself to ferret out those parts and subparts of 29 CFR 1910 that apply to aviation matters and materials and to tailor the requirements directly to those airline activities.

Safety Regulations

The federal hazard communications (FHC) standard, 29 CFR 1910.1200, requires that management provide information about chemical hazards in the work force to all employees. This becomes part of the airline's safety program through the distribution of maintenance safety data sheets (MSDS). These data sheets are generated by the chemical manufacturer and identify the hazards, precautions, and first aid instructions relative to the chemical's use. The airline safety managers must make the appropriate MSDSs available to anyone who may use or come in contact with the chemical. The airline may add any additional information to the MSDS as necessary to clarify the use of the chemical as well as provide information on reporting incidents and hazards. The manufacturer's MSDS is general and deals with the chemical; the airline additions to the MSDS address specific airline concerns and procedures.

TABLE 20-1   Occupational Safety and Health Standards

Subpart	Title
A	General
B	Adoption and extension of established federal standards
D	Walking–working surfaces
E	Means of egress
F	Powered platforms, man-lifts, and vehicle-mounted work platforms
G	Occupational health and environmental control (ventilation, noise, nonionizing radiation)
H	Hazardous materials
I	Personal protective equipment
J	General environmental controls (sanitation, lockout/tagout, marking of hazards)
K	Medical and first aid
L	Fire protection
M	Compressed gas and compressed air equipment
N	Materials handling and storage
O	Machinery and machine guarding
P	Hand and portable power tools and other hand-held equipment
Q	Welding, cutting, and brazing
R	Special industries (pulp, paper, textiles, etc.)
S	Electrical
T	Commercial diving operations

Physical hazards, such as noise, ionizing radiation, nonionizing radiation, and temperature extremes, for example, are governed by other parts of 29 CFR 1910 and should also be addressed in the airline's safety program. This program would provide for the availability, training, and use of protective equipment, safety measures, and safety processes.

Posture, force, vibration, and mechanical stress are common hazards workers are subject to in all work areas. The amount and type of exposure, of course, varies with the work being done. The airline safety program should address each work center's specific needs.

Viruses, bacteria, fungi, and other substances that can cause disease are included in the regulations. These biological hazards come under the health classification and also vary depending upon the kind of work being done and other work environment conditions.

Many of these safety and health requirements are already addressed in aviation industry documents and regulations. Airframe manufacturer's maintenance manuals, for example, usually cover safety features related to the performance of maintenance such as the use of safety harnesses, use of protective clothing and equipment, the proper handling of hazardous materials, and the lockout and tagging of certain electrical and mechanical equipment to avoid inadvertent operation or subsequent accidents while people are working on or near such systems. The airline's operations specifications may identify other safety requirements. The TPPM, of course, should contain a summary of the entire maintenance safety program and the safety manager should monitor all aspects of the program to ensure compliance with the OSHA requirements. This compliance, of course, is part of the QA audit responsibilities, but due to the special nature, safety is established as a separate function to monitor these activities.

Maintenance Safety Program

FAR 119.65 identifies, but does not define, the basic positions required to operate an airline. Although certain positions are deemed necessary, the certificate holder will determine actual titles as well as the level of the office within the structure. Paragraph (d) of 119.65 says that the certificate holder will define the "duties, responsibilities, and authority"[*] for all positions in the organization. The person in charge of safety is responsible for the overall safety program at the airline. There may be separate safety program managers for flight operations, maintenance, and the other administrative and managerial functions of the airline. One may be coordinator of the others but the individuals will have responsibilities in their own work areas. In our typical, midsized airline (see Fig. 7-1) we have identified the maintenance safety program within the MPE directorate with the other maintenance oversight functions.

The maintenance safety program manager has the following primary responsibilities:

1. Identify and assess all health and safety hazards within the various M&E work areas

2. Determine protective measures needed for hazardous conditions and ensure that protective clothing and equipment are available to the workers as necessary

3. Make information available to workers handling hazardous chemicals, on the hazards and handling procedures involved with those chemicals, including any data supplied by the manufacturer, and any additional information deemed necessary for the airline activities

4. Provide training on the identification of hazards, on the location and use of safety equipment, and on first aid and reporting procedures involved

5. Establish and document the safety program in the technical policies and procedures manual (TPPM).

General Responsibilities for Safety

Safety, as has been said by so many others, is everyone's job. Certain responsibilities for safety, however, are assigned to the company itself; other responsibilities are assigned to the safety manager (coordinator, director, or whatever his or her title), to the individual supervisors, and to the employees. Each of these is discussed in turn.

---

[*]Federal Aviation Regulation 119.65.

Company responsibilities

The airline is required to provide safe and sanitary working conditions in all its facilities. This will include adequately stocked and continually updated first aid kits in all hangars and work centers; eye wash and shower facilities in areas where acids and other caustic or irritant materials are used; and fire extinguishers, both chemical and CO_2 types as applicable, in easily accessible locations throughout the M&E work areas. Fire extinguishers should be checked regularly to ensure viability and tagged to indicate the date of such inspection. Appropriate protective clothing should be available to employees who are required to work with acids and corrosive materials destructive to normal clothing. Safety glasses or goggles, earplugs, and protective shields should also be available and accessible. The company is also responsible for providing the necessary training on the use and location of these safety items and the establishment, in the technical policies and procedures manual, of requirements for the use of safety equipment and the applicable procedures for such use.

To protect equipment and personnel, the airline must also provide for adequate grounding of aircraft and adequate fire extinguishing capabilities on the flight line and in the hangar, including automatic deluge systems for the hangar. Procedures for moving people and aircraft out of burning hangars and buildings are also required.

Safety manager responsibilities

The safety coordinator is manager and administrator of the safety program. He or she is responsible for establishing the safety rules and procedures; for auditing the M&E facilities, along with QA, for adherence to safety policy; for developing improvements in the safety program; and for maintaining records and filing claims relative to accidents and incidents involving M&E personnel and equipment. The filing of accident and incident claims may be an airline administrative function (personnel, legal, etc.) but the M&E safety coordinator will be directly involved with claims from the M&E areas.

Supervisor responsibilities

Each work center supervisor is responsible for the safety of his or her facilities and personnel, beginning with clean, well-kept offices, shops, and other work areas. The supervisor must enforce all safety rules and provide instructions and interpretations of rules, regulations, and methods for preventing accidents or incidents within his or her work area.

Employee responsibilities

Each employee, licensed mechanic, or unlicensed helper; each worker, supervisor, or manager, is responsible for compliance with all airline safety rules and practices and will report deficiencies when noted. The employee is also responsible for proper use of tools and equipment and the proper operation of machinery.

General Safety Rules

There are several special areas of concern for any airline maintenance safety program that require further discussion. These are smoking regulations, fire prevention, fire protection, storage and handling of hazardous materials, fall safety and protection, and hangar deluge systems.

Smoking regulations

The term *smoking materials* refers to cigars, cigarettes, pipes, and other flammable materials such as matches and lighters. The safety coordinator should designate "No Smoking" areas and the regulations must be enforced. Typical no smoking areas include the following: (*a*) inside aircraft at any time; (*b*) within 50 feet of an aircraft parked on the ramp; (*c*) within 50 feet of any refueling activity or refueling equipment; (*d*) within 50 feet of oil, solvent, or paint storage areas; (*e*) inside hangars, except in offices, washrooms, and other areas designated for smoking; and (*f*) any location of the airport designated as no smoking by the airport authority.

Other requirements for fire safety relative to smoking materials also apply. Personnel should refrain from smoking after being subjected to fuel spills or other flammable materials or vapors. This applies to other personnel who may encounter those involved in such spills. The restriction applies until the spilled material has been cleaned up and the vapors eliminated.

Lighted smoking materials should not be carried from one designated smoking area to another through nonsmoking areas. Smoking materials should be extinguished only in suitable ashtrays or other fireproof containers and not on floors, in trashcans, or in other unsuitable receptacles.

Fire prevention

Smoking materials are not the only sources of ignition for fires. Electrostatic discharge can also provide the spark needed for ignition of flammable vapors and other substances. For that reason, all aircraft should be properly grounded while they are in the hangar or on the ramp, especially during refueling and defueling operations. Other materials susceptible to combustion include rags and paper. Combustible rags must be stored in National Fire Protection Association (NFPA) approved, closed containers and paper and other combustible trash must be stored in suitable trashcans. Other items, such as volatile cleaning fluids with a low flash point, along with oils and paints, must also be properly stored and handled. When these items are present, the no smoking rules will apply and adequate ventilation will be required.

The supervisor of any work center where these volatile materials are used must ensure that the products are stored properly and in quantities commensurate with reasonable needs. Use of these and other volatile materials will not be carried out in any room where there are open flames, operating electrical equipment, welding operations (arc or acetylene), or grinding activities.

Flammable materials, such as paints, dopes, and varnishes must be kept in NFPA approved, closed containers away from excessive heat or other sources of ignition. Bulk supplies of these must be stored in a separate building at a location remote from the maintenance activity. If it becomes necessary to perform welding activities on aircraft, the management must determine proper procedures and arrange for standby fire fighters and equipment during the exercise.

Hangar deluge systems

Airplane hangars are complex and expensive structures, and they often contain one or more aircraft, which are considerably more expensive than the building itself. The multitude of other equipment in the hangar, and the fact that aircraft may be jacked up, surrounded by scaffolding and maintenance stands, or in some other condition detrimental to moving them readily, make it imperative that these hangars be equipped with sufficient fire suppression equipment to protect the airline's investment.

There will be fire extinguishers positioned around the aircraft and hangar work areas (both CO_2 and foam as required) and all fire and safety regulations will be enforced. But there is one more very important system required to protect the 50-to 150-million dollar aircraft. This equipment, installed in numerous hangars around the world, is known as the *hangar deluge system*. These are elaborate systems with tanks of fire retardant chemicals buried in the ground or beneath the hangar floor, connected with a plumbing system that essentially mixes the retardant with water to create the foam and dispenses it throughout the hangar. The system usually has a control room in, or adjacent to, the hangar where operators can operate the system and direct the firefighting equipment (movable, adjustable nozzles) to specific areas; or the system can be automatic, covering the entire hangar.

The order of activity is to evacuate personnel from the hangar and release the fire suppressant. The time it would take to move an aircraft out, if it were in a condition to allow such movement, would very often be more time than one would have.

Fall prevention and protection

The OSHA regulations concerning fall protection and prevention refer to work surfaces, scaffolding, and other high and precarious places such as building construction sites, but not specifically the wings and fuselages of airplanes where maintenance people have to go occasionally. However, the same philosophy exists. Dangerous areas must be identified and should have specific equipment and procedures in place to protect anyone involved in working these areas.

Aircraft do not have nice, flat surfaces as afforded by buildings and scaffolding. And, although OSHA rules for such structures (rails, safety belts, and harnesses) do apply, the rounded surfaces of the airplane present additional problems. For one thing, aircraft surfaces are not always safe to walk on at all and are so noted with large, black letters: "NO STEP." The curved surfaces, and the fact that there is usually no structure to grab hold of to retard your fall, makes aircraft walking even more dangerous than other high places. The OSHA rules specify that a worker should not have a distance greater than 4 feet in which to fall. Anything greater requires safety gear in the form of rails, belts, or harnesses or some combination of these. The top of a 747 fuselage is 32 feet 2 inches from the tarmac—approximately three stories high.

Accident and Injury Reporting

Each incident involving airline personnel that results in damage to facilities and/or equipment or in injury to personnel must be reported to the safety manager regardless of whether the personnel, equipment, or facilities is owned by the airline or some other unit. An initial report will be made immediately after the accident or incident occurs using telephone, telex, fax, radio, or any other means of communication available. This report should be made directly to the safety office if the event occurred on the home base or through the MCC if it occurred at an outstation. Within 24 hours of the event, the work center supervisor where the accident or incident occurred will send a completed accident report or personnel injury report, as applicable, to the safety office. Forms for such reports should be developed by the safety office and made available to all airline work centers. Samples of these forms and the instructions for proper completion and submission of the forms should be included in the safety program section of the technical policies and procedures manual.

The safety office will create a log of all accident and incident activities involving airline personnel whether at the home station, at outstations, or at contractor facilities. The PP&C organization will issue a work order number for the tracking of each accident or incident through the process of investigation, repair, insurance claims, or any other process required. The work order will also serve to collect time and cost data relative to the accident or incident.

Part

V

Appendixes

The material in the following appendixes is provided to enhance the other chapters in the book. Systems Engineering, Appendix A, normally a design engineering activity, is extended here to include the entire life span of the equipment. Understanding systems is important to understanding aircraft and maintenance problems. Both engineers and maintenance personnel can benefit from this approach.

Human factors in maintenance has received a lot of emphasis in recent years. Appendix B of this book provides a brief history of the field and an overview of human factors activities in aviation maintenance. It also discusses the need to include human factors in the systems engineering concept.

Troubleshooting is often poorly taught in tech schools and sometimes it is omitted all together. Appendix C, "The Art and Science of Troubleshooting," is provided here as a guideline to assist M&E in developing better techniques for solving problems in line, hangar, and shop maintenance as well as in engineering.

Appendix D, "Investigation of Reliability Alerts," is about the process of analyzing reliability alert conditions and resolving maintenance problems. It is primarily for use by reliability and by engineering. This process is both an application of and extension of the troubleshooting process discussed in Appendix C.

Appendix E is a brief discussion of the extended range operations with two-engine aircraft (ETOPS).

Appendix F is a glossary of commonly used terms.

Systems Engineering

Introduction

Ordinarily, when we speak of systems or systems engineering we think of electrical, mechanical or hydraulic systems or systems which combine some or all of these disciplines. We usually think of weapons systems, communications systems, and other collections of many parts, components, and disciplines. But there are other types of systems: governmental systems (democracy, oligarchy, dictatorship, etc.), operational systems (checklists, procedures, etc.), and maintenance systems (groups of scheduled tasks, procedures for unscheduled maintenance, etc.). Even paperwork can be considered a system; for example, a series of forms one fills out for a job or for a government or commercial contract. A system, then, can be more than mechanical or electrical parts. A system is a set of elements of one sort or another that, together, perform some function or allow some desired result. Any organized set of components, procedures, actions—mechanical, electrical, mental, physical, procedural, conceptual—that are organized to produce some intended result can be classified as a system. A system is an instrument of accomplishment.

This system concept can be applied before, during, or after the fact. By that we mean system concepts can be applied prior to the creation of some entity (design work); during the process of design and development (step-by-step procedures through a process); or after the fact (analysis of results, maintenance, or operation of the system).

Systematic versus Systems Approach

There are two terms that are used, often interchangeably, which are not quite the same. Those terms are the *systematic approach* and the *systems approach*. The term *systematic approach* usually refers to a step-by-step process, an essentially linear process or procedure where one accomplishes some goal by performing one step at a time, in sequence, until the desired result or goal is achieved. An example would be a flight crew's checklist or a maintenance procedure for testing a unit or for removing and replacing a component. The systematic approach is a deliberate step-by-step process performed the same way every time. It is methodical; it is systematic.

The *systems approach*, as used in this book, is somewhat different. A system can be simple in construction and involve a series of steps or processes performed one at a time or in a continuous flow. But most systems are a bit more complex. Perhaps there are numerous elements performing simultaneously, in consonance with or, in some instances, in opposition to one another, such as feedback loops (electrical) or dampers (mechanical). There can be various inputs and outputs exchanged by various elements of the system all controlled by numerous internal and external events. This is truly a multidimensional process—quite different from a simple, linear one.

The systems approach to any problem or system involves the ability to see all of these interacting elements in relation to one another and to understand the overall outcome of their activity. The systems approach is the process of looking at, understanding, and reacting to all aspects of the complex system individually and collectively. While all the parts must function as intended by the designers, the conglomerate of all these interacting parts must also function together as the system was intended. The systems approach, then, is the process of seeing and understanding all aspects of the system at once and how they interact to achieve the desired goal. And this is true whether you are designing a system, using a system, maintaining a system, or teaching the system's attributes to someone else. You may use the systematic approach at certain times during the process but the systems approach requires simultaneous knowledge and understanding of all processes and elements within the system. In Appendix C, we illustrate how one sometimes needs to use a systematic approach on one section, function, or aspect of a system while trying to pinpoint a problem, but the overall process of fault location must also consider the system and its function as a whole. Thus, although the systems and the systematic approaches are significantly different, they are not necessarily mutually exclusive.

Systems Engineering

Systems engineering is a term used to describe the work of engineers and designers who address the "total systems aspect" at the design level of systems. The systems engineer is concerned with the system as a whole. He or she is tasked with ensuring that all interrelated components of a system interface properly and that all elements within the system ultimately function to provide the overall intent of the original system concept. The systems engineer is responsible for the "big picture" design aspects, for compatibility of interconnecting components (interface control), and for the overall system performance.

Definitions

To understand systems more thoroughly, we must first define a few terms: system, system boundaries, system elements (internal and external), and system interfaces. These are addressed below in turn.

System

Each engineering discipline has its own definition of a system. The *Systems Engineering Handbook*, by Robert E. Machol[*] lists six definitions of a system from various sources. Some of them are fairly concise; some are quite wordy. One of the definitions given involves mathematical equations. Other sources list additional, but similar, definitions.[†,‡,§] When scrutinized, however, all of these definitions are essentially identical. We can generalize them by stating, "A system is a collection of components working together to perform a certain function."

This, however, is not an adequate definition. In Fig. A-1,[¶] Rube Goldberg's "system" satisfies the definition but it is hardly an efficient method of performing the intended function. It isn't repeatable; it may not even work at all. In other words, it is a bad design. Some additional engineering must be done to Mr. Goldberg's system to solve the problem more efficiently. Two important concepts, design and efficiency, are missing from the basic definition stated above. We need to add these words to the definition so we can avoid imperfect systems.

> A *system* is a collection of components designed to work together to efficiently perform a certain function.

These two added words are the most important parts of the definition. No system is a good system unless it does its designed function efficiently. And no system can do that if it is composed of a collection of parts that were selected without regard to the interaction of those parts with one another. We will see later that the successful interface between individual components of a system is a very important part of systems engineering.

---

[*]Machol, Robert E. (ed.): *System Engineering Handbook*, McGraw-Hill, New York, NY, 1965.

[†]Skolnik, Merril I.: *Introduction to Radar Systems*, Chap. 13, Systems Engineering and Design, McGraw-Hill, New York, NY, 1965.

[‡]Meredith, Dale D., et al: *Design and Planning of Engineering Systems*, Prentice-Hall, Englewood Cliffs, NJ, 1973, p. 6.

[§]Fink, Donald G., editor-in-chief: *Electronics Engineers' Handbook*, Section 5, Systems Engineering, McGraw-Hill, New York, NY, 1975, p. 5-2.

[¶]Wolfe, Maynard Frank: *Rube Goldberg Inventions*, Simon & Schuster, New York, 2000, p. 122. Reprinted with permission.

Figure A-1   A Rube Goldberg system. (*Source: Rube Goldberg is the ® and © of Rube Goldberg, Inc.*)

System levels

Any system can have associated parts, which can be called subsystems. These subsystems are systems in their own right and these systems, too, can have subsystems. Everything from the atom to the universe (not inclusive) is a subsystem of some other system and every thing from the atom to the universe (inclusive) is made up of subsystems. This "onion structure" defines the complexity of the world of systems engineering. To simplify matters, we need to define the limits of what we wish to study or build. This is done by identifying system boundaries.

System boundaries

The limits of consideration for a study, analysis, observation, or usage of a collection of components will identify the system boundaries. These boundaries vary with the extent of the study or with the degree or scope of consideration. For example, to an avionics engineer, a system may consist of the components that make up the spoiler control system on an airplane. A circuit designer might consider a single printed circuit board (PCB) in the spoiler control module as his or her system. To an aeronautical engineer, however, this spoiler control system would be just one component of the airplane flight controls system.

System element

Any component that can be assigned a function or an attribute within the context of the defined system is referred to as an element of the system. System elements can be internal or external depending on how the system boundaries are defined. We also use the terms *component* and *subsystem* interchangeably with the term *element*.

Internal elements

Internal elements are those elements that are within the defined boundaries of the system. They are the components or parts with which the system designer, user, operator, or maintainer is most concerned. These elements are what make the "black box" or system work, provided the inputs are available and correct.

External elements

Elements outside the defined boundaries of the system that have a direct or indirect relationship with system operation are called external elements. These elements may or may not be controllable. External elements consist, mainly, of system inputs and outputs. This would include operator or user inputs or signals, voltages, etc. from other interfacing systems. Electromagnetic interference (EMI) and weather might also be external elements of some systems.

System interface

An interface exists whenever two systems or two elements of a system connect or interact. This interaction can be direct or indirect; it can be electrical or mechanical; it can be through sensory devices or transmission devices. One interface we will consider in Appendix B is the interface between the human being and the defined system.

System Interface Control

One of the primary functions of the systems engineer at the design level is to ensure that, wherever two systems or system elements interact, this interface is designed for optimum performance. This is called interface control. With very complex systems, and in systems where various elements and subsystems are designed and built by different organizations, these interfaces must be precisely defined with specifications and tolerances, in a systems interface specification. This will ensure that all designers concerned will be working to the same set of specifications and that the system which results when these elements are connected together will "efficiently perform" the intended function.

Interface control, then, is the process of ensuring that all elements of the system efficiently and effectively interact with all other related elements. Mechanical or physical parts that have to engage; electrical or digital signals that are exchanged; data transmission modes and media required for communication; and many other elements, all have to be "designed" to interface properly.

Here is one fairly obvious example: One element of a system requires 28 volts direct current (dc) power input. Another element in the same system requires 115 volts alternating current (ac) at 400 Hertz. A computer chip, used in one of the unit's circuit boards, requires a regulated ±5 volts dc. The power supply designer, who may work for a different department or even a different company, must provide a power supply unit (i.e., a subsystem) that will deliver all these voltages to the main system. Other specifications, such as voltage regulation and current limiting parameters may also be specified by the system designer. Cables and connectors from the power supply must be compatible with all the interfacing units and care must be taken so that the cables supplying power to these units cannot inadvertently be crossed, delivering the wrong power to the unit. Possible signal loss or deterioration due to cable length must also be considered.

System Optimization

System optimization is another important concept in systems engineering. Optimizing one element or interface of a system will not necessarily optimize the entire system. When all elements of a system are optimized according to their respective designs and the corresponding state of the art in that discipline, they may no longer be compatible with regard to interface control. Here are some examples. One sophisticated electronic element may be too sensitive to variations in the inputs from some interfacing elements (signals or power inputs). A mechanical element (e.g., a metal clamp) may be made of a highly durable material to withstand extreme heat and vibration in the area where it will be used (on a jet engine, for example). But this clamp may be too hard for the delicate insulation of the fire sensing wire it is required to hold in place. As a result, the insulation could wear away, under the extreme vibration it endures, and eventually cause a short circuit and a false fire warning indication.[*]

There are a number of examples like the one concerning the clamps that are discovered during the operation of a system. While not all possible malfunctions or system imperfections can be predicted prior to or during the design phase of the system, the next similar system developed can have the benefit of these "lessons learned."

System optimization is the process of ensuring that all elements and all interfaces work together in such a way as to provide the best overall performance of the total system. System optimization includes not only operational performance but also system reliability, maintainability, and economic factors related to operation and maintenance.

An Example of a System—The "Onion Layered" Structure

Let us talk about the component at the center of our interest in this book, the commercial aircraft. These systems (airplanes) are a part of the commercial aviation system that is, in turn, part of the air transportation system. Air transportation is a part of the total national transportation system, which consists of air, land, sea, pipeline, and rail systems.

If we consider the airplane our system of interest, we can consider any of its hundreds of subsystems—flight controls, for example. Flight controls can be

---

[*] This situation actually occurred on a modern jet airliner engine.

divided into two broad categories: primary flight controls (ailerons, elevators, rudders) and secondary flight controls (flaps, slats, spoilers, trim tabs). Any one of these systems or subsystems can be further divided into components categorized as electrical, mechanical, or hydraulic and each of these could be designated a subsystem or even a sub-sub-system of the chosen system.

An electronics control unit for a flight control system may include one or more black boxes (and they aren't always black); each box will contain subsystems and components such as transformers, terminal strips, printed circuit boards and so forth. The PCBs will consist of circuits (hard wired or integrated) that consist of other components such as resistors, capacitors, and the like. We can take this "onion-layer structure," as it is sometimes called, all the way down to the level of the atom if we wish. Those responsible for the development of integrated circuits (ICs) and other solid-state devices might be very much interested in that "system."

As you can see from this discussion and from Table A-1, the use of the system/subsystem terminology could get quite unwieldy after three or four layers. So, to avoid confusion, we will address any level in this hierarchy as a "system" and its components or constituent parts as "subsystems." The standard terminology, then, will be this: a system is the set of components we are concerned with and this system is identified by the boundaries we set. Then we can speak of any additional components or elements as being "internal" or "external" to our specified system.

But a system is not just components. A system will include people (users, operators, maintainers) as well as processes and/or procedures for the system's use, operation, or maintenance. A system may require inputs from electrical, mechanical, and/or hydraulic systems or components as well as inputs from a user, an operator, or a maintenance technician. A system will undoubtedly provide outputs in various forms (electrical signals and waveforms, mechanical motion, instrument displays, computer data) to be used by humans, by other systems, or by both.

How deep one goes into this layered world is dependant on one's interest in the system. Let us take a printed circuit board, for example, whose purpose is

TABLE A-1　Systems and Subsystems

Transportation system
Air transportation
Commercial aviation
Airplane
Flight controls
Primary and secondary flight controls
Electrical, mechanical, hydraulic components
Black box units, mechanical units
PC boards, transformers, etc.
Circuits
Components
Molecular structure

to provide an analog voltage to a flight deck display showing the angle of flap extension on the airplane wing. For the line mechanic who is addressing a flap system write-up, the area of interest would be the black box containing the errant PC board. This "black box" is a unit that can easily be removed and replaced so as to return the airplane to service. The technician in the avionics shop, however, would have a keen interest in the PC board and its effect on the operation of the system; i.e., the flap angle indicator. Those mechanics and engineers interested in any higher-level system in the chain would not be as interested in the PC board details. Likewise, only those building the PC board or its integrated circuits would have any interest in the physical and atomic properties of the components on the IC.

Summary

It is conventional, in design engineering, to apply the systems engineering concepts at the outset of new system development. This effort ensures that each component or subsystem is designed for compatibility with the rest of the system to guarantee that system goals and objectives will be met regardless of who builds the component or subsystem. Although the users of these systems will not (usually) be involved with the design or redesign of the systems, the knowledge of systems concepts and systems engineering techniques are important in understanding the system and its operation. Knowledge of systems is also useful in the maintenance and troubleshooting of these systems. This should be kept in mind as you read and study the main chapters in this book.

Human Factors in Maintenance

Background

In the early 1980s, the aviation industry implemented crew resource management (CRM) as an effort to detect and correct human errors made by flight crews. The action was successful and is continuing. In the 1990s, it was determined that the same approach should be used to identify and correct errors in maintenance activities that contributed to aircraft accidents and incidents. This activity—human factors in maintenance (HFM)—has developed into the maintenance resource management (MRM) program. The FAA addresses this activity in Advisory Circular AC 120-72.[*]

While many people assume that human factors in maintenance refers to the actions of mechanics, the MRM program admits to several major areas where maintenance errors can occur. These areas are (*a*) equipment design and manufacture; (*b*) manufacturers' documentation and procedure writing; (*c*) airline procedures and work areas; and (*d*) mechanic training and performance.

The airframe and equipment manufacturers have implemented HF programs to improve design such that maintenance can be performed more easily and reduce the number of possible errors that can be made. Improvements in maintenance manuals and other documents are also under manufacturer's scrutiny and certain academics are looking into the problem of human error. But the airlines also have a responsibility to monitor the processes and procedures they employ and to modify those with respect to human error reduction. The training organization should modify courses to accommodate any changes necessary to meet the HF aspect and is also required to develop and implement an HFM course. The AC mentioned above provides guidelines on establishing such a course.

---

[*] Federal Aviation Administration: AC 120-72, Maintenance Resource Management Training, September 28, 2000.

In this appendix, we will first discuss human factors as a part of systems engineering (see Appendix A); then we will address some of the other activities in HFM.

Basic Definitions

Human factors is defined in the *Handbook of Aeronautical and Astronautical Engineering* as follows:

> Ergonomics [*Human factors*] is the scientific discipline concerned with the understanding of the interactions among humans and other elements of a system, and the profession that applies theory principles, data and methods to design in order to optimize human well-being and overall system performance. ...[*]

Another popular definition is rather brief but captures the essence of *human factors*.

> In capsule form, the nub of human factors can be considered as the process of designing for human use.[†]

In the past, human factors has usually referred to physical characteristics of people such as size, strength, physical dexterity, and visual acuity. But there are other human attributes that affect a system's performance and the human's ability to use or maintain the system. Such human characteristics as a lack of knowledge or understanding of how the system works can lead to improper use or to inadequate troubleshooting or improper maintenance. Human forgetfulness or even a person's attitude can affect how well the system works, or how that person interfaces with the system. The human attributes of those people who interface with systems in any way can have an effect on how well the system performs through their ability or lack of ability. Design people may not understand the needs of maintenance, trainers may not be able to communicate the correct information to others, and operators may use the system improperly.

Human Factors and Systems Engineering

In Appendix A of this book, we discussed systems engineering. We discussed systems boundaries, system elements, and the interfaces relative to the interaction of these systems, subsystems, and components. Here, we take up the notion that the human being—the user, operator, or mechanic, as well as all others (writers, designers, teachers, etc.) who interface with the system—must be considered as elements of the system. Likewise, these elements and interfaces must be addressed during the design stage of the system.

---

[*]Kesterson, Bryan P., William L. Rankin, Steven L. Sogg: Maintenance Human Factors, Section 18, Part 8, *The Handbook of Aeronautical and Astronautical Engineers*, McGraw-Hill, New York, NY, 2001.

[†]McCormick, Ernest J.: *Human Factors in Engineering and Design*, 4th ed., McGraw-Hill, New York, NY, 1976, p. 4.

The human interaction with systems makes it imperative that the users, operators, and maintenance people be considered during the design, development, and operational phases of the system's life. During design and development, the human requirements and interactions must be known or anticipated at all levels of the system. This includes not just the equipment but also the manuals and the training program for that equipment. During the operational phase, feedback from the field will dictate changes necessary for system improvement relative to the operator, user, or mechanic in terms of local procedures as well as manufacturer's procedures, training, and design efforts. Lessons learned during this operational period relative to human interaction with the system can be used to advantage by the manufacturers in the development of new systems or modification of existing ones.

Traditionally, the systems engineer needs to be familiar with a variety of engineering disciplines to perform his or her job successfully. Adding human factors to the toolbox means adding one more discipline: human factors engineering. This involves not just the understanding of human characteristics but also how these characteristics relate to the overall operation of the system. It requires the systems engineer to understand the effects these humans can have on the system operation whether the necessary interaction exists or not, whether the response is correct or incorrect, and even if the response or interaction is absent when it is required. It is necessary for the systems engineer to address these effects as part of the basic system design. The effects of human presence are as real as the presence of voltages and mechanical linkages. The human being is an element of the system. When all the elements are working properly, the system will work properly.

Goals of the System versus Goals of the User

Elwyn Edwards[*] states that the effectiveness of a system is measured by the extent to which the system goals are achieved. McCormick[†] also mentions the functional effectiveness of the system as one of the goals of design. In this appendix, we integrate the philosophy of systems engineering, discussed in Appendix A, with the philosophy of human factors. In doing that, we consider the significant goals to be not the goals of the system but rather the goals that the user of the system expects to achieve by employing the system.

We can no longer design for the sake of the system or for the sake of technology. This new philosophy requires that we now design for the system application. A system, whether a simple tape player or an exotic mode of transportation, is just a tool. It is a tool used by people to accomplish some personal or work-related goal. To make that tool "user friendly" we must design it to be usable by

---

[*] Wiener, Earl L., David C. Nagel (eds.): *Human Factors in Aviation*, Academic Press, Harcourt Brace Jovanovich, no date. From the introduction by Elwyn Edwards.

[†] McCormack, *Human Factors in Engineering and Design*.

human beings. That means that the system not only has to perform some function efficiently but it has to perform that function in the manner that the system user wants it performed.

A system that achieves the design goals of a collection of mechanical and electrical parts may represent engineering perfection, but if the device cannot be used by people for some human purpose, it is just a collection of mechanical and electrical parts; just another "contraption."

Designing for the Human Interface

Whether we are talking about electrical or mechanical systems, about processes or procedures to be carried out, or about forms we need to complete during maintenance, the interface between these systems and the human users must be addressed as any other system interface; and the system optimization efforts we spoke of in Appendix A must be applied to make the total system—including the user—work efficiently. The main difference, however, is that these humans, unlike the other system elements, cannot be redesigned during the optimization process for the improvement of the total system operation. Therefore, the designers of these systems must adhere to several basic rules. The first of these is to design the system to be compatible with human abilities, capabilities, needs, and strengths. The second is to design these systems around human failings and deficiencies so as to avoid possible human error.

The third rule is especially important in developing good, usable systems. For any problem or condition that cannot be accommodated by the first two rules above or one that is limited due to various constraints, such as design limits, trade-offs, or budget requirements as discussed in Chap. 1 of this book, the designers must provide the users, operators, and mechanics—as well as other human elements involved—with sufficient education and training on the system to resolve any human factors–related problems that could arise from improper understanding of the design. These basic design rules for human interface with systems are summarized in Table B-1.

Human Factors in Maintenance

In Appendix A, we extended the definition of systems to include more than just the electromechanical components we normally consider. A "system" can also be a checklist, a procedure, or a form to be filled out. Maintenance, of course, deals

---

TABLE B-1   Human Factors Design Guidelines

1. Design the system to be compatible with human abilities, capabilities, needs, and strengths.
2. Design the system to compensate for human failings and deficiencies to avoid human errors.
3. Provide the human elements of the system with sufficient education and training to resolve any human factors related problems that could not be alleviated by application of the first two rules above.

with all of these kinds of systems and the human element is just as important in each of these. How maintenance people perform is only part of the problem; the facilities in which they work, the equipment they encounter, the forms, processes and procedures they use, are all subject to human actions and therefore to human error. And the errors are not always due to the mechanic. There are several areas in maintenance that contribute to the errors made by the users, operators, or mechanics.

Human Factors Responsibilities

Human factors efforts are usually divided into three basic categories of activity: (*a*) aircraft and component design, (*b*) maintenance product design, and (*c*) maintenance program applications.[*] Each of these is discussed below.

Aircraft and component design

The responsibility for this category rests with the manufacturers of airframes, engines, and installed equipment. It deals with the task of designing for maintainability. This concerns the design of equipment that can be worked on for service, inspection, adjustment, and removal/installation (R/I) efforts. These design efforts must ensure that there is sufficient workspace to do the work required and that there is also enough space to use the tools and test equipment that may be needed. The manufacturer's responsibility also includes consideration of the weight and handling characteristics of the unit undergoing maintenance. Equipment parameters must be within the physical limits of the workers required for the particular task. If this cannot be accommodated, special handling equipment must be developed to permit proper handling and to protect both the equipment and the workers from harm. Design effort should also take into account the number and skills of the workers required for a given task to be completed with reasonable manning requirements.

Whenever computer diagnosis is utilized, using built-in test equipment (BITE) or other external systems, the equipment, processes, menus, and other task or information selection methods must be designed for the mechanic's ease of use and understanding; that is, it should be "user friendly." Results from such activities must be understandable and usable by the mechanic.

Maintenance product design

Maintenance personnel require auxiliary equipment and written material to perform the required maintenance on aircraft systems. Ground support equipment (GSE), special tools and test equipment, and various forms of documentation must be designed with the mechanics' capabilities and limitations in mind and these products must be made available to the mechanics. Mechanics must be able to use

---

[*] Kesterson, Rankin, and Sogg: *Maintenance Human Factors*.

the GSE and tools effectively, so the design requirements discussed above for airframes, engines, and installed equipment must apply to these elements also.

Documentation, whether written by the manufacturer, the regulators, or the airline, must be clear, understandable, and accurate (i.e., technically correct) for the mechanic to effectively utilize the information. This written information must also be accessible to the mechanics on the line, in the hangar, and in the shops, as necessary. It must also be available to the training organization. The user-friendly approach is also required for all these maintenance products.

Maintenance program applications

The basic maintenance program developed by the MSG process is based on the needs of the equipment (i.e., design goals, safety, and reliability) and on the regulatory requirements (safety, airworthiness, etc.). When the airline receives the aircraft and its initial maintenance program, that program is usually tailored to the specific airline operation. This adjustment of tasks and task intervals must also include human factors considerations. That is, the adjustment of the program must be in line with the human capabilities and requirements concerning work schedules, endurance, and skill makeup of the work crew to avoid over work, fatigue, etc. The appropriate GSE, tools, and test equipment must be provided to do the work and the work force must be properly trained on all aspects of the job: the actual maintenance work to be performed; the use of GSE, tools, and test equipment; the use of built-in or external computer diagnostic equipment; and the basic human factors aspects of the job. These actions are the responsibility of the airline itself.

Safety

Chapter 20 of this book discusses the safety and health issues related to maintenance. It does not take much deep thought to realize that safety is also a human factors issue. Although the two fields relate to different aspects of the maintenance activity, they are not mutually exclusive.

Summary

The manufacturers of airframes, engines, and installed equipment are doing their part to reduce the chances of human error in maintenance, but they require inputs from airline operators and third-party maintenance organizations. Research from the academic community (behavior scientists, etc.) is also necessary to advance the state of the art. Meanwhile, the airline operators and other maintenance facilities are responsible for the actions of their mechanics and the materials with which they work. In human factors, as well as in safety, the work force at all levels must be constantly aware of problems and be ready to effect solutions. Human factors is a way of life.

C

The Art and Science of Troubleshooting

Introduction

One of the most common misconceptions about troubleshooting is that it is basically a series of wild-assed guesses (WAGs) or, at best, a series of scientific WAGs (SWAGs). This is not the case if you know what you are doing; it is of little help if you do not. And then there are those who claim that you cannot "teach" troubleshooting. This author disagrees with that notion. It is possible that some people cannot teach the subject due to a lack of knowledge or skill and it may also be possible that some people cannot learn the technique for some reason or another. But experience has shown that the art and the science—and it is a combination of the two—can be taught. That is, it can be taught up to a point. Since there is some skill involved in troubleshooting (i.e., the art), what one learns about it must come from within. However, there are some basic concepts to be applied in troubleshooting (i.e., the science) that can be taught.

This appendix will attempt to show you the systematic approach to troubleshooting, the aspects that can be taught. It will address both the art and the science of troubleshooting.

As electronic and mechanical equipment gets more and more complex, the job of the technician or mechanic gets more and more frustrating. Today's "new generation" jet airplanes constitute the most intricate and complex systems ever engineered by human effort. In the past, each piece of equipment or each system required its own specialist to maintain and repair it to optimum condition. Troubleshooting consisted of checking out the system to determine if it was at fault and querying the user to determine if it was properly operated.

Today, with electronic control of mechanical systems, redundant systems, computer fault recording, and cross-feeding of data between and among systems for logical decision making, the technician or mechanic requires not only a broader knowledge of his or her own equipment but also knowledge of those systems with which that equipment interfaces. Inputs from air/ground relays, gear-down sensors, air data computers, and from numerous other systems and sensors, blur or even erase the dividing lines between individual systems and components. Now, the repairman needs to know the entire airplane to effectively isolate the problems indicated by crew write-ups, fault balls, computer fault messages, flight deck lights, and other "things that go bump in the flight."[*] The mechanic needs to understand the systems approach.

While airplane manufacturers provide fault isolation manuals to the mechanic that include systematic fault trees for the isolation of problems, this effort is neither complete nor entirely satisfactory. These fault location procedures were usually written to find specific faults; they do not necessarily allow you to find all the faults that might occur within the system addressed by that fault tree. It is up to the mechanic or technician to provide the additional procedures or make modifications to existing procedures to find these other problems. These procedures constitute part of the science of troubleshooting, and it is an incomplete science at that.

The art of troubleshooting, which is just as important as the science, can only be learned by continued effort in studying and repairing the equipment. This art involves the ability to think a problem through and to apply all you know about the problem, the equipment, and the nature of failure so that you can fathom the most difficult and perplexing of problems. This appendix will, first, identify the basic steps in the troubleshooting process and will, then, discuss the process by which one learns the art of troubleshooting.

Three Levels of Troubleshooting

You can divide maintenance problems into three general categories: (*a*) problems with components or systems (i.e., self-contained); (*b*) problems relating to systems and their environments; and (*c*) problems related to the interaction of two or more systems. Each of these categories or levels requires a different approach and each will be discussed in turn below.

Level 1: the component or system

This type of problem exists within the component's or the system's own world. It is a simple, standard fault with a simple, standard solution. This is the normal, day-to-day activity for the problem solver. The troubleshooting charts or common sense is usually enough to resolve these problems.

This system or component is malfunctioning or has failed completely. Check inputs, outputs, etc. Troubleshoot within the unit/system. Know how the system works and follow normal troubleshooting practices.

---

[*] Book jacket comment by Library Journal concerning the book *This Is Your Captain Speaking* by Captain Thomas M. Ashwood, National Chairman Flight Security, Airline Pilots Association, Published by Stein and Day, Briarcliff Manor, New York, 1975.

Level 2: the system and its environment

A system fails or "acts up" during some portion of its operation. It may recover and exhibit no more symptoms or may falter intermittently. It may work fine on the ground or in the shop when tested but the malfunction still reoccurs in the air during normal flight operation.

Troubleshooting these problems requires knowledge of and investigation of the primary system or component as well as its inputs and outputs, but the external environment and its effect on the system must also be considered. This includes investigation of how the system or equipment was operated (correctly or not?) and what else was happening during the time of the malfunction (extraneous inputs).

Level 3: the interaction of systems

Something happens in one system when another system is exercised. The two systems may or may not be interrelated or interconnected. Here, assuming that other standards of troubleshooting have failed, you look for some mechanical interference, such as rubbing of parts, or electromagnetic interference coming from a nearby unit, electrical cable, or other system. As a last resort, you look for interference from radiated fields (high or low intensity, any frequency). These are emanations from on-board or off-board systems that interfere with the problem system. This is occurring more and more with the composite (nonmetallic) materials used in airplanes. The composite materials used in modern aircraft do not provide the electromagnetic shielding that the old, metal frames and fuselages used to provide.

Again, the span of knowledge needed to pinpoint these problems is broader than the simple component or system failure discussed above. Knowledge of this type of interaction between (and among) systems may only come with time and experience but it is necessary to gain that insight as you progress through the ranks from maintenance helper to master mechanic and troubleshooter. Once you have achieved this, you are an artist.

Knowledge of Malfunctions

There are a few general concepts of problem solving and troubleshooting that one must understand before we get into the process itself. These are discussed briefly below.

What kinds of things can go wrong?

Most systems will have a set of known things that can and will go wrong with them. The same failures will come up over and over again. Experience with these component or system characteristics will aid the troubleshooter more and more as his or her knowledge base is developed. Armed with this knowledge, the mechanic can sometimes skip certain steps and checks in a troubleshooting chart or procedure and go straight to those steps that are directly related to the problem at hand. Without this prior knowledge of failures, however, a good troubleshooter can still zero in on problem areas by knowing what kinds of things might go wrong with the system. Discussion with others who have worked the same system, and possibly had similar problems, is most useful.

Experience is the best teacher

The expression "experience is the best teacher" is so common that it is almost a cliché and is often treated as just that. However, it is not an untruth. Until you get too old to remember things, remembering, in the maintenance field, can be one of your greatest and most useful assets. The same problems keep coming back. If the problem is the same then the solution is the same. Troubleshooting gets easier as you go. But there is always that bugger of a problem that stymies even the best troubleshooter and that is where all that experience, understanding, and luck have to be called upon. Without any of these, you're out of it.

No fault found

No discussion about troubleshooting will be complete without mention of the concept of *no fault found* (NFF). It is a common action in maintenance to sign off a problem in the airplane logbook with the comment "No fault found" after ground checks have failed to reveal any problem. The NFF conclusion may also be used after an unsuccessful troubleshooting session. This NFF entry seems to be a catchall for ineffective or poor troubleshooting. If the flight crew wrote up an item in the logbook, then there must be some sort of problem. The fact that the mechanics cannot find the source of the problem does not mean that the write-up is in error. If you cannot find the problem through conventional processes, it will be necessary to use a different approach. The NFF result is not the end of troubleshooting; NFF is a signal to regroup, to start a different tack in the troubleshooting process. It may mean moving into a level 2 or level 3 approach.

Rogue units

There is a special category of high–failure rate items generally referred to as "rogue units." These are not unit types (i.e., black boxes, component parts, etc.) that have high failure rates but rather individual units of a type (serial numbered or not) which seem to fail regularly. As an example, suppose you have 25 black boxes (radios, for example) and you have failures in 10 of these boxes over a month. Each time the failure occurs it is a different box or a different aircraft. This may be considered a high failure rate for the system or unit but it is not referred to as a rogue unit. On the other hand, if most or all of the failures involve a single unit (serial numbered or not) then that specific unit might be considered a rogue.

In Chap. 1, we talked about tolerances and their effect on reliability. There is another consideration concerning tolerances we must address. Even though components are built to within design specifications, there can be some differences in how the overall unit performs. Pistons and piston bores in an automobile engine block are built to specification which define an ideal diameter with a specified tolerance that allows these parts to fit together and work together.

If the piston is at one end of this tolerance band and the bore is at the other end, the actual fit may be tight or loose depending on the individual case. Although these parts are within tolerance in both cases, their performance may differ because, in one case, the parts are tight, resulting in more friction and thus more heat generation and wear out; while, in the other case, the fit is loose, causing some energy loss due to undesirable side motion (slop). Thus, although the parts are built to within the allowable tolerance, there may be some detriment to efficient operation in extreme cases. When there are several of these "detrimental tolerance conditions" in a given system, or interacting parts of connected systems, they can be additive; the system can perform poorly; and the system can break down more frequently than another unit built to the same specifications with less extreme variation in tolerances. We generally call this unit a lemon or a rogue.

A rogue unit can sometimes be fixed if you know what components are causing the problem and these components can be exchanged or reworked. This task is usually left to the manufacturer, but it is often too expensive or even impossible to do. In most cases of rogue units it is more sensible to remove the errant unit from the supply system. Although this may be difficult to do with units as expensive as those used on modern aircraft, that cost must be compared with the cost of continual maintenance as well as with the cost of rebuilding the unit.

Bogus parts

Rogue units should not be confused with bogus parts. Bogus parts are those parts built by vendors or contractors that are not up to the original manufacturer's specifications and, very often, those parts that are built without authorization by the original manufacturer or the regulatory authority. These parts are usually cheaper, which is the primary attraction, but they are also inferior. Generally, they have high failure rates, poor wear-out properties, or other detrimental performance characteristics. Although there is a considerable difference between rogue units and the bogus units, the airline's reliability program should be able to find and eliminate both types.

Other significant differences

Experience has shown that maintenance people address problems differently based on their training and experience. Mechanics tend to look for previous write-ups or they observe the equipment in operation prior to using any troubleshooting charts or procedures. Avionics technicians, on the other hand, tend to go straight to the charts or procedures. The primary difference here is in the nature of the malfunctions. Avionics equipment (electrical and electronic) looks essentially the same whether it is working properly or not. But many mechanical faults can be seen or felt by simple operation or they can be gleaned from the crew's description of what happened. Not all mechanics or avionics technicians work the same and not all problems warrant the same approach, but it is possible that many problems can be addressed by using the senses; others must go straight to the theory. This, of course, differs from problem to problem and from person to person.

Knowledge is Power

The most important tool you can have to assist you in troubleshooting is a solid understanding of how the equipment works and how it is supposed to be used by the operator or user. Improper operation can occur in one of two different ways and this needs to be distinguished during the troubleshooting process.

If an operator does not get the desired results from the system, he or she usually writes a discrepancy. The operator may not be aware of the fact that the system was operated incorrectly or that some switch was in the wrong position. It is for him or her a valid write-up.

Certain misuses of the equipment could cause erroneous results and, at times, could actually damage the equipment. Although, in the latter case, the equipment must be repaired or replaced, the solution to the problem (misuse) must also be addressed. The error and its effect on the equipment can also be logged away in the knowledge bank for reference in future troubleshooting.

Know the system

Troubleshooting is essentially a thinking process. It starts with a thorough understanding of how the system works. Know the theory of operation of the equipment or system. Know all the functions and modes of operation, if there is more than one. Understand what components or circuits are common to various operational modes and what ones are specific to each mode. Understand what other systems have to be operating for your system to get all its required inputs.

Know the fault indicators

Know what fault balls, fault messages, flight deck effects, etc. relate to the system and understand which indications can and cannot appear in each operational mode. Know how to address specific problems without starting at the beginning of a fault tree and performing a series of unnecessary or unrelated steps. Understand what circuit breakers, fuses, and auxiliary systems (hydraulic, pneumatic, electrical, etc.) are required for operation of your system.

Know what kinds of things can go wrong
with your system

This, of course, would vary with each system. Use your past experiences; use the experiences of others; use any applicable data available from condition monitoring programs or reliability programs; use information from service tips, service letters, and service bulletins; talk to mechanics, technicians, or engineers from other companies using the same equipment. In other words, know your equipment intimately.

Know the interfacing systems

In addition to knowing what systems must be operating to allow yours to work properly, you must also understand how these other systems or equipment interface with yours. Understand what circuit breakers, fuses, and auxiliary systems (hydraulic, pneumatic, electrical, etc.) are required for operation of these interfacing systems. Know and understand the effect each of these systems has on your system. Know what the consequences are if the inputs from these interfacing systems (logical, electrical, mechanical, pneumatic, or electromagnetic) are not present or are present but not correct.

Know what fault indications would exist for these systems and determine if any of them were malfunctioning. Know what this malfunction does to your system. Know if fixing the interfacing system problem will likely reduce or eliminate your problem.

Know how the system is used

Know how the operator uses the system and what he or she expects of the system during that operation. Their usage, right or wrong, may affect the system's operation as well as your troubleshooting efforts. Common errors of operators or users are (*a*) failure to turn equipment on; (*b*) failure to select correct mode; (*c*) failure to check for correct settings; (*d*) failure to check CBs or fuses. (*Note*: Some of these are not requirements of the user but some are. It depends on the equipment and the operation.)

There are three types of people that interface with equipments and systems—users, operators, and maintainers (see Table C-1). They each have a different

TABLE C-1   Definitions

User: One who benefits from the equipment or system: a passenger in a vehicle, a viewer of television, a listener of radio or recorded music, a home or apartment dweller enjoying the benefits of any number of modern conveniences. They don't have to know how the devices work, they just need to know how to use them for their own advantage, and how to recognize when they are not working properly.

Operator: One who operates or drives the equipment: a pilot of an airplane; the driver of a truck, bus or automobile; a diesel generator engineer who provides electrical power to a facility. These people may have varying degrees of knowledge of how the system works, or is how it is supposed to work, but the details are not important. When an operator uses a piece of equipment, he or she expects certain responses, certain indications, and certain results. If they don't get that they consider the unit to be malfunctioning. They don't have the time or, in some cases, the knowledge, to figure out what's wrong. That is the job of maintenance.

Maintainer: One who is responsible for the maintenance and repair of the system: his or her relationship to the equipment is quite different from the operator or user. The maintainer not only covers the detailed theory of operation of the system and its many components and subsystems; he or she must know about and understand failure, failure modes, and other equipment anomalies. The maintainer also has to understand how to troubleshoot the system, how to test it, how the test equipment works, and on and on. Added to this, to be able to carry out the test and validation process after repair has been made, he or she must also know how to operate and use the system.

view of the equipment or system and a different relationship with it. Therefore, what they know about it and what they need to know about it varies widely.

Don't let the theory get in your way

Too much theory can be a detriment to the troubleshooting effort. Look for the simplest, most obvious problems first: equipment not turned on, proper mode not selected, blown fuses or tripped circuit breakers, improper operation, unit not plugged in. Perform tests and measurements on those problems that are not so obvious. Are inputs and outputs correct? Are proper signals being received from other units? Sometimes it is easy to get bogged down in schematics, wiring diagrams, and maintenance manuals when you've overlooked some simple thing.

Building Your Own Knowledge Base

Many of the modern aircraft maintenance organizations have extensive computer systems that are used for the logging of maintenance data such as pilot write-ups, reliability program data, and problems found during routine maintenance. The records show the discrepancy, corrective action taken, parts replaced, tests performed, and even the flight, cabin, and maintenance crews involved. Other data tallied include flight information (aircraft type, origin/destination, flight phase where discrepancy occurred). This database can be accessed whenever a problem occurs in order for the mechanic or technician to determine if the same or a similar problem has occurred previously. Corrective actions taken on these previous faults may be used in the solution of the current write-up.

A good mechanic or technician, however, often remembers his or her own experiences with past problems and the solutions they ultimately employed. In most airline operations, however, mechanics go from one airplane to another, one type to another, in the course of a day's (or night's) work. Keeping track of each airplane and each failure is difficult if not impossible. However, shift supervisors, maintenance control center personnel, as well as maintenance and reliability engineers should be able to amass a certain amount of this knowledge based on their positions and experience—with considerable help from the computer. There are few problems that should be a complete mystery to everyone in the organization.

Experience

Part of the education of maintenance people is the formal training received in various technical and vocational schools. Part of it is semiformal; that is, special training established within the work unit and training classes conducted by manufacturers or other airlines. The final aspect of training for maintenance personnel is personal. The mechanic's personal efforts throughout his or her career will consist of ongoing education—formal as well as informal study—interaction with other maintenance people, and the competitive effort to get ahead of coworkers.

Much of this education will come from experience. Working on the same equipment day after day lets you learn the easy way, by sheer repetition.

Keep track of the faults that occur on your system, equipment, or vehicle. In spite of the complexity of some modern systems, the same faults often keep coming back. What went wrong the first time was fixed the first time so, if the problem recurs, the same solution should fix it. However, if the fault was not adequately addressed or if it recurs often and at short intervals, perhaps the repair action taken was insufficient. It is necessary in those cases to retroubleshoot the problem. Come up with a better fix—even if you have to call in management or engineering—and then remember the new fix.

Continuing education

The continuing education of a mechanic or technician takes place in several venues: at work, at home, on the job, and in the classroom. At work, you have the day's work and the interaction with others working on the same or similar problems. You always have copies of the maintenance manuals close by. One of the "arts" used in troubleshooting is "brainstorming." Just talk about the problem with other people. Hypothesize about the problem. Suggest some possible solution and discuss why that could be the answer or why it cannot be the answer. You can get as far-fetched as you want (if time permits), because this gets the mind working and helps create new ideas. Soon the "right" answers start poking through the fog.

At home, you have time to relax and let your mind deal with other things. That would be your conscious mind, of course. Fortunately (or not), your subconscious mind continues to work on any problems you have posed to it. With a well-organized storehouse of knowledge and information, your subconscious mind can develop solutions for you while you are at play. Be careful, though: they may pop out at inconvenient and embarrassing times. Nevertheless, a well-organized mind is one of your best tools for troubleshooting.

In class, whether it is a formal course, a company training class, or on-the-job training; whether it is new material or refresher training; you have the chance to learn, relearn, and fill in the gaps in your knowledge from previous studies. You can always learn more even if all you are doing is repeating what you already know or you are explaining something to a coworker. What you know is one thing; putting that into words for others to hear or read is another. An electrical engineering professor this author had in college told the class "If you want to know how much you really understand about this stuff, try to explain it to someone who does not have any technical background at all. If you can do that successfully, then you know your subject."

Understanding the Sequence of Events

There are several sequences of events associated with nearly every system you will encounter in your maintenance and troubleshooting activities and you need to understand them all. The first is the sequence of turning on and setting up a system for use. The second is the operational sequence of a properly operating system while in use and while being switched between operational modes. The third and final sequence to understand is the sequence of events leading up to the current failure. More specific explanation follows.

Sequence of events to engage the working system

Know how the system is turned on, powered up, tuned in, adjusted, positioned, etc. by the operator or user at the start of operations as well as during normal, ongoing operations. This includes switches and CBs being in the correct positions as well as other equipment being turned on or off. It is important to know this sequence and to compare it with that actually used by the operator. As we said before, incorrect procedure may be the operator's problem and training the operator or user may be the solution to the problem. On the other hand, improper use of the system may cause the equipment or system to be damaged or impaired. The troubleshooter must know this and know how to determine if this is the case for the particular system he or she is working on.

Sequence of events within the operating system

Know how the system operates internally; that is, know the normal sequence of events occurring during normal operation or use of the system. Know what it does while in operation, when it does it (e.g., in flight, on ground, in conjunction with certain other actions performed, or with other equipment in use), and know in what portion of the sequence certain actions, responses, and fault indications can and cannot occur. Know the sequence of events in each mode and the sequences involved in transition from one mode to another. This can be useful in following up on the user's explanation of how the system performed just prior to the malfunction (see next section).

Sequence of events leading up to the malfunction

Know the sequence of events leading up to the degraded performance, failure or malfunction. This must be obtained from the user or operator who was "at the controls" of the system when the dysfunction occurred. It is very important to know this sequence in many troubleshooting efforts, because this sequence of events may reveal a developing pattern or an indication, not only of the fault, but also the possible location of the fault.

Eight Basic Concepts of Troubleshooting

Part of the troubleshooting process is knowledge and experience; the rest is a combination of logical procedure, innovation and, sometimes, luck. The simplicity of certain equipment or systems may permit the omission of some of the following steps while the complexity of others may require a more detailed procedure.

The following eight concepts should cover the bulk of your troubleshooting efforts.

1. *Know your equipment.* When it comes to troubleshooting any system—no matter how simple or complex—nothing will serve you better than a good understanding of how the system works. Know all its functions, its operational modes, and the failure modes and their effects in each mode and function.

2. *Know how the controls and displays work.* The troubleshooting process often requires you to operate and adjust the various controls and switches on your equipment, to turn it on, run it through various tests, and check out its overall operation. Know how the operator uses the equipment and what modes or configurations he or she uses. This will help you understand what they tell you in the malfunction reports which are given to you.

3. *Know how other equipment interfaces with your own.* Know what ancillary equipment is connected to the system or equipment you are working on (including BITE). Many of today's avionics systems rely on inputs from other systems. Sometimes electrical, electronic, and/or mechanical inputs from ancillary equipment affect the operation and function of your own system. These interactions must be known and their effects must be known, both the effect on your system when the interfacing equipment is working properly and when is not. The effect on your system when the input signal is not there or is incorrect must also be known.

   Know the outputs from your system and where they go. Understand how other equipment receiving your outputs can effect your own equipment. Bad or missing inputs from your system can affect return data; shorting out or blocking of inputs from your system by the ancillary equipment could also affect your system. These differ from system to system.

4. *Know and understand the maintenance documents.* The maintenance, schematic, and wiring diagram manuals provided with the equipment are your best source of information about how your equipment or system works. They also provide data on equipment that interfaces with yours and how these work. The documents will tell you how to turn on and operate the equipment (yours and theirs) and what prerequisites and precautions are necessary for safe operation; that is, electrical, hydraulic, or pneumatic systems that need to be "on" or "off," what circuit breakers need to be "in" or "out," and similar setup requirements during testing and troubleshooting.

5. *Approach the problem in a systematic and logical manner.* Once the necessary preparation has been taken to accommodate the above steps, the actual troubleshooting can begin. You must proceed systematically and logically from the known symptoms to the cause. This is easier said than done of course. The first approach would be to follow the obvious track, then the not so obvious, and finally, if those do not work, start addressing the improbable or the seemingly impossible.

6. *Analyze the information available in light of equipment operation.* Some basic determinations should be made at the outset of troubleshooting in order to establish the plan of attack. The following five steps are guidelines:

(*a*) Determine what is and is not working properly. If two or more modes or functions are faulty, determine if there are any commonalities between (or among) these and look for a common cause.

(*b*) Determine whether or not the equipment is operating correctly but inaccurately, or determine if it is operating incorrectly or not at all.

(*c*) Determine if one, several, or all modes of operation are affected. Zero in on the appropriate problem area by determining what area(s) the problem could (or must) be in based on those symptoms.

(*d*) Identify what other systems interface with yours and determine their effects (if any) on the problem at hand.

(*e*) Analyze the manner in which the equipment is used or operated.

Table C-2 lists a number of specific questions that should be asked and answered in the effort to pinpoint a problem but not all questions would be required in every case. Determining which ones to ask and to answer, of course, is part of the "art" of troubleshooting.

7. *Be able to perform complete checkout procedures on the equipment and understand the results.* There are usually established procedures for checking out a system: (*a*) ground checks on the aircraft (operational checks, functional tests); (*b*) bench checks in the shop; (*c*) built-in test equipment (BITE) in the unit itself. The BITE system may have an internal fault that results in an

---

TABLE C-2   Questions to Ask in Troubleshooting

Problem history: Are there any records—on paper, in the computer, or in human memory—of any previous failures or malfunctions that are the same or similar to the one you are investigating? If so, what were the similarities? Did the corrective action taken correct the problem? If not, why not? If this was the correct fix for the previous problem, would it apply to the current problem?

Operation: Was the faulty equipment turned on? Were all the necessary circuit breakers closed and/or fuses installed and serviceable? Was the system being operated correctly when the problem occurred?

Power/signal cables: For electronics equipment, was the black box properly seated in its rack (racks incorporating connectors)? Were all connectors properly attached and secure? Are there any blown fuses or tripped circuit breakers in the faulty equipment? If these are replaced or reset, does the problem go away? (Original failure could be due to a power surge and not a malfunction. That is what fuses and CBs are for.)

Multiple systems: If the system or equipment you are investigating has input from and/or outputs to other equipments or systems, were these equipments or systems operating correctly? Were they properly engaged? Check fault balls, fault messages, write-ups, etc. related to these other systems.

Interfacing systems: Were all electrical, hydraulic, and/or pneumatic systems required for operation of your system properly engaged and functioning?

Environment: For systems that rely on information from a ground station, was the ground station up and running properly? Was the aircraft within range of the ground station? Was there any interference (i.e., high-or low-intensity radiated fields) in the vicinity that could cause the problem with your equipment?

erroneous indication. In all cases, you must understand what these procedures will and will not tell you.

8. *Be able to use the proper tools and test equipment needed for the job.* Many troubleshooting activities are assisted and enhanced by the use of common or specialized tools and/or test equipment. Knowledge and understanding of how these tools should be used and how this equipment works is essential to effective application of them to problem solving. Know the capabilities and limitations of these tools and this equipment as well as that of the system you are troubleshooting. It is equally important that you are able to determine whether or not the tools and test equipment are working correctly.

Summary

Troubleshooting is not guesswork, it is not a haphazard approach to problem solving, and it is not a shotgun or a shot-in-the-dark technique. If you don't understand this, you've missed the point of this appendix. If you don't know this, you will have difficulty in troubleshooting and fixing complex systems.

We define a troubleshooter as one who pinpoints and resolves problems. Troubleshooting, then, is the art and science of pinpointing problems. The key word in both of these statements is "pinpoint." One has to search, to zero in on the problem using systematic and focused techniques. Of course, once you've found the problems you are able to correct them.

The term "shotgun troubleshooting" is a four-letter word. I know, it's two words and it's 22 letters; but, still, it is a dirty, obscene, and unacceptable term. The shotgun approach implies blasting away with a wide pattern of shot and hoping to hit something. It is a sign of a poor troubleshooter, a sign of someone who has given up and is groping around in the dark for an answer.

From this point on, you must consider troubleshooting as a systematic approach to finding problems (troubles). You will know your equipment, you will know your profession (that of a troubleshooter), and you will get better and better at both the art and the science as you pursue your career.

Good luck and may all your troubles be pinpointed.

Investigation of Reliability Alerts

Introduction

During a visit to a small but prominent international airline to help with their reliability program, the author was asked by the head of the engineering department—who was new on the job and not too many years out of college—"Just how do I go about investigating these reliability alerts?" It was not a question to be answered quickly or briefly. The assumption that engineers would know what to do is not always a valid one because finding a problem is difficult enough, and knowing where to start and how to proceed is often no easier. The answer given was general but acceptable. Later, when writing this book, the author expanded the explanation to the material in this appendix. The process that resulted will not find all the answers, and it will not provide you with cut and dried procedures, but it should help you in zeroing in on the unique problems you will be required to solve in these reliability investigations. We will begin with a review of reliability and a quick discussion of the cross-functional process of reliability investigations shown in Fig. D-1. That discussion will be followed with the processes of preliminary and detailed investigations in Figs. D-2 through D-5.

A Review of Reliability

A reliability program is a set of rules and practices for managing maintenance and controlling the maintenance program. Reliability programs provide continuous audits of maintenance activities and establish standards for determining intervals between overhauls, inspections, and checks of airframes, engines and appliances. The reliability program measures equipment performance against established standards to identify problem areas and initiate corrective actions.

For midsized to large airlines (10 airplanes or more) a reliability program based on statistical analysis is usually employed. In this statistically oriented program, the utilization of alert levels and trend lines aids the operator in limiting the number of items to be investigated. For airlines with a small number of airplanes, a statistically oriented reliability program is not really feasible because of the small amount of data available. For these smaller airlines, one approach is to review and investigate all malfunctions and removals. This is called an event-oriented reliability program; that is, every event is investigated. Another option is to use historical data; that is, data from previous years (or months) to judge the current performance. In either case, a systematic approach to the problem is required.

All alerts generated by the statistically based reliability program must be investigated and acted upon as appropriate. This function is usually provided by engineering. Engineers responsible for each area—components, airframe, systems, and power plant—should provide analysis and corrective action recommendations to the maintenance program review board (see Chap. 19 for makeup of the MPRB). These corrective actions can vary from one-time actions to fleet-wide improvements to changes in the maintenance program. Alerts commonly result in modifications of equipment; correction of shop, line, or hangar processes; disposal of defective piece parts; additional mechanic training; or changes in maintenance intervals. Since each problem is unique, each solution is also unique.

Alert Investigation—A Cross-Functional Activity

Figure D-1 is a cross-functional chart depicting the identification and processing of a reliability alert. This is not something done exclusively by the reliability department or by the engineering department. It involves various units within the maintenance and engineering organization working together to assess the problem and develop a satisfactory solution. This is just one example of the need for cross-functional cooperation in daily activities we discussed in Chap. 7. A brief explanation of the process is given below. Numbers in parentheses refer to the block numbers in Fig. D-1.

The reliability (1) section collects and tabulates data submitted by the various M&E work centers (9) on a continuing basis. Monthly, these data are charted and analyzed (2) to determine possible problems in the maintenance activity. Such problems are submitted to engineering (3) whose responsibility it is to analyze the problem in detail (5), using additional inputs as necessary from various M&E work centers (10), and develop a corrective action plan (6) to resolve the problem. This plan is reviewed by the maintenance program review board (14) that includes people from the affected work centers (11). If necessary, the MPRB will contact the regulatory authority (15) for approval (16). Once approved by the MPRB, the corrective action plan is returned to engineering and the plan issued in the form of an engineering order (EO) (7) to all applicable work centers. Each work center performs its portion of the corrective action plan (12), coordinating as required with other work centers, and notifies engineering (13) when this has been completed. When all work centers have reported completion of their portion of the work, engineering closes out the EO (8) and notifies reliability of such action. Reliability then continues to monitor the parameter to determine the effectiveness of the corrective action (4).

Each problem, of course, is unique, and the work centers involved in developing and/or implementing the solution will vary, but the process is essentially the same. The bulk of responsibility lies with engineering since they are the technical experts of M&E and also the developers of the maintenance program. The following sections discuss reliability's preliminary and engineering's detailed investigative processes in detail.

Zeroing in on the Problem

Not all problems will require the same course of action. Very often, the nature of the problem or the location of occurrence of the problem will determine the course of action. For example, say an alert exists in ATA Chapter 33, Lights. The first step in the investigation would be to review the reliability data generating this alert and determine if the excessive rate is related to a specific lighting system (panel, strobe, landing, etc.) or is distributed throughout the chapter (i.e., all lights, all subchapters). Some ATA Chapters, such as 33 or 25, contain many types of systems while others, say Chapter 29 or 32, are more limited. In any case, the investigation could proceed in various ways based on distribution of malfunctions in any given chapter.

In the case of the problem being concentrated in one area (one or two sections of the ATA Chapter), the problem investigation should proceed to the equipment type involved. Check the maintenance history of the item to see what has occurred in the past in terms of failures and repair actions. Check the adequacy of these actions. Check the current paperwork to see if the maintenance and inspections (if required) were done correctly. If maintenance procedures appear to be inadequate or appear to have been performed incorrectly, evaluate the procedures to determine if there is a discrepancy in the procedure or query the mechanics to determine if there is a misunderstanding on their part as to how the procedure should be performed. The corrective action required may be in the form of rewriting and improving procedures or providing the mechanics with additional or remedial training on the equipment and/or procedures.

In the case where the failures (removals, etc.) are distributed throughout the subchapters of the ATA Chapter, the implication is that there is a common problem through all the chapter's activities. This could mean that there is something wrong with shop, line, or hangar procedures or with the mechanics or specialists who work on this equipment. There could also be a parts problem from some common source (manufacturer, vendor, supplier, or repair facility).

Another area in which to focus the initial investigation is to determine whether or not the problem is related to a specific airplane (i.e., aircraft tail number), a specific airplane model, a specific engine type, a specific station (line or home), or even a specific shift, crew, or mechanic. Again, the course of action would be dictated by these conditions.

One final note: the approach to analysis differs for systems, components, and events. Some guidelines of these various approaches are given in the following discussion.

About the Alert Analysis Flow Charts

The process of investigation has been broken down and displayed on four, interconnected flow charts (Figs. D-2 through D-5). The first, Fig. D-2, is the overall chart. It refers to each of the others for details of specific parts of the process. We will discuss the process, step by step, moving from one flow chart to another as necessary. This will give you a feel for the total flow process. Each possible alert will result in a different track through the charts and may involve more or less action at the various steps. For reference, blocks in the flowcharts are numbered. These numbers are shown in parentheses in the text; e.g., block (7).

Figure D-2, block (1): reliability has identified a possible problem area based on the alert level established for the parameter and on the event rates for the current and the previous month. Figure D-2, block (2): the first step is for reliability to perform a preliminary investigation.

This takes us to Fig. D-3, block (1). The preliminary investigation will involve several actions, depending on the conditions, to determine if this is a valid alert. Consider the current event rate and the overall pattern of the event rates: wide swings of the event rate above and below the UCL and behavior of the monthly and 3-month rates. Determine if this is normal activity (no alert), a condition that needs to be watched (watch for trends), or something that may require further action (possible need for investigation). If the answer to the question in block (3) is "no," the next question, block (2), asks if this is a "watch." If the answer is "yes," reliability identifies it as such on data sheets and in the monthly reliability report (4). For that particular item, then, we return to Fig. D-2, block (3). If it is not a watch, i.e., if the answer to block (2) Fig. D-3 is "no," then go to block (7) directly. This sends you back to Fig. D-2, block (3) with a "no" answer to its question. However, what if the answer to block (3) in Fig. D-3 is "yes" and we do have a valid alert? Proceed to the next question in Fig. D-3, block (5).

Determine if the alert also involves a repeat item. Repeat items are usually defined in the reliability program document or in the Ops Specs as events that occur three times within 5 days (or four times in 7 days). They are to be investigated by MCC on the spot. If a reliability alert item is also a repeat item, the two may or may not be related. This fact must be noted and engineering must do an investigation. It is possible that the MCC procedures for repeat items are ineffective or not properly employed. It is also possible that there is no connection at all between the two conditions. Engineering will determine this later in their detailed investigation.

Whether or not the alert item is a repeat item, reliability continues to analyze the data in block (8) to determine if this alert condition is shown to be in some specific area such as those indicated in the side table "Specific Areas." The manner in which the data are collected can assist in this analysis. For example, data could be tallied by two-, four- or six-digit ATA numbers, by station, crew, etc. If the answer to the question in block (9) is "yes" this information is noted for use in the alert notice sent to engineering (10) to aid in their investigation. For either answer (yes or no) we go to block (11) and return to Fig. D-2, block (3).

Figure D-2, block (3) asks if a detailed investigation is needed. After the preliminary investigation we have determined "yes" so reliability issues an alert notice to engineering (5) specifying the condition and requesting an investigation. If, in Fig. D-3, we identified a possible relationship to a repeat item or identified any specific area of interest, these would also be noted on the alert notice. Block (6) of Fig. D-2 sends us to Fig. D-4, block (1): detailed investigation.

Engineering begins the analysis using conventional troubleshooting techniques, realizing that different problems, due to their nature, will require different approaches. The first step, however, is to identify the problem correctly. It has been said that proper identification of the problem is 90 percent of the solution. If the problem is poorly or incorrectly identified, the subsequent solution will be ineffective.

We concluded earlier that all problems would fall into one of six basic categories: people, procedures, parts, maintenance program, interference, or equipment design (see Chap. 19). For the sake of analysis, we will further break these into two larger categories. The most likely causes are shown in Fig. D-4 as blocks (3) through (6) and those causes that are a little more rare are shown in blocks (9) through (12). Each will be addressed in detail.

People (3): Mechanics may not be performing the tasks properly. This may refer to scheduled as well as unscheduled maintenance tasks. Inadequate troubleshooting skills of the mechanic may also be a problem. If this is determined to be the cause of the high event rate (i.e., the alert) then the solution will most likely be training of the mechanics. This could be anything from a reminder to adhere to proper procedures to full classroom training on some area of maintenance. The exact nature, of course, should be determined through the detailed investigation performed by engineering.

Procedures (4): A second source of trouble may be the maintenance, troubleshooting, or other procedures used to conduct required maintenance and servicing activities. The procedures in the AMM, the MRB report, or the airline's Ops Specs might be wrong or inadequate. This may require consultation with the manufacturer. Procedures used could have been modified or created by the airline and these may be ineffective or incorrect. Also, the procedure could be misunderstood by the mechanic because of the way it is written. These causes would require either rewriting of the procedure, retraining of the mechanic, or both.

Parts (5): Parts can be a source of problems and in several different ways. Improper parts might be used because the procedures for drawing parts from stores allowed the wrong parts to be issued or the part number used was incorrect. This may be a people problem or a materiel problem (or both). Another possibility of a parts-caused problem could rest with the parts suppliers. They could be providing you with parts that do not meet the required specifications (inferior or bogus parts). If the parts are repairable, the repair facility responsible (yours or third party) may not be performing up to par. It is the responsibility of

QA to audit M&E units as well as outside suppliers and repeating that effort may be part of the solution to the alert condition under investigation. Parts could also be damaged during installation or during shipment. Handling procedures by mechanics, materiel personnel, and shippers may be at fault here. In some cases with time-limited parts, the part may have expired without notice by the materiel section or by the installer.

These parts problems could be addressed at several levels: mechanics training on drawing and handling of parts; materiel processing, handling, and storage of parts; parts suppliers and contractors (third party maintenance) procedures. In every case, it is the responsibility of engineering to determine the cause and determine a suitable solution.

Maintenance program (6): Engineering decided at the outset what maintenance tasks would be used, what the task intervals would be (if different), and how tasks and check packages would be scheduled. As might be expected, this original plan may prove to be less than perfect for the actual operational conditions. As stated in Chap. 2, these tasks and intervals, and their combinations and phasing, may need to be changed relative to experience as shown by reliability data. Therefore, engineering's investigation of alert conditions may indicate a need to change this ideal maintenance program. Tasks may be added or removed; intervals may be shortened; new tasks might even be developed. It could also be necessary to incorporate modifications (SBs, SLs, or even ADs) that were previously rejected to resolve the problem that generated the current alert condition.

These areas represent most of the common problems encountered. Block (7) of Fig. D-4 asks if the problem is in one (or more) of these areas. If "yes" you are directed to block (13) and back to Fig. D-2, block (7). If the answer is "no" to this question—which means you have not pinpointed the cause of the alert condition—then proceed to block (8) of Fig. D-4 to identify other possible areas. These are areas that, although rare, are still distinct possibilities. These are addressed in blocks (9) through (12) of Fig. D-4.

Environmental conditions (9): When an aircraft is sitting on the tarmac there are many flight conditions that no longer exist and cannot be duplicated. These are extremes of temperature (high and low), vibration, and the prolonged subjection of installed equipment to these conditions. In normal conditions on the ground and in the "pristine" environment of a shop or a laboratory, the equipment may work perfectly; the result of ground test is "no fault found," NFF (see Appendix C for a discussion of NFF). However, to isolate any problem, one must consider and, if possible, duplicate the exact conditions under which the original fault was encountered. This may require a mechanic, technician, or engineer to fly with the aircraft in order to observe and then resolve the problem. In some (rare) cases a special nonrevenue flight may be necessary to accomplish this.

Other environmental sources of equipment problems could be weather, corrosion, sand, or dust. This may vary from airline to airline depending on where they are based and where they fly. Nevertheless, these are possible causes that must be addressed.

Electrical and mechanical interference (10): Electromagnetic interference (EMI) can come from various sources and can affect various electronics components in a variety of ways. The impact of EMI can be continuous, intermittent, or fleeting and the isolation and resolution of the problem can be quite elusive. Interference can come from the ground (transmitters of various kinds); from other aircraft nearby; or from electronic or computer equipment within the aircraft. In the case of an in-aircraft source, it can be equipment installed in the aircraft that has a shielding or ground loop problem for example, or the interference could be coming from passenger-carried equipment.

Interference of another type could also occur in certain types of equipment. This could be termed *mechanical interference*. Cables, pulleys, and other moving, mechanical parts could be interfering with other equipment on board and causing problems in either system or both. Unlike electromagnetic interference, mechanical interference can usually be seen and sometimes felt. Such observations could help determine the solution.

A third possibility for interference problems may be the sharing of inputs, outputs, power supplies, or power busses by two or more systems. These common connections could cause a malfunction or error in one system to affect performance of another system. Again, this may be rare but it is a possibility. It needs to be considered.

Flight and cabin crew procedures (11): Aviation maintenance people are conscientious. Whenever there is a discrepancy or a write-up related to aircraft systems and equipment, it is assumed to be a maintenance problem first. (Thus, the consideration of the previous blocks.) Occasionally, however, a discrepancy or write-up is the result of flight crews or cabin crews who do not use the equipment in the way it was intended to be used. These problems may be due to the crew's lack of understanding about what the equipment can and cannot do. Sometimes it is improper procedures in operation (knobs/switches in the wrong position; use of wrong mode, etc.) or, in other cases, equipment that is not turned on, not switched to "transmit" or has circuit breakers pulled or not engaged (for various reasons). The flight crews use equipment to provide them with certain information or control. If they do not get that information or do not believe the results they do get, or if they do not get adequate control as they expect, they will, most likely, write it up as a malfunction. The same can be said of equipment operated by the cabin crew. As one pilot told the author, "We don't have time to troubleshoot the system; if we don't get what we are supposed to get, we write it up and proceed to employ some alternate measure."

When maintenance checks out this equipment and finds it working properly, the operational procedures could be suspect. The solution, of course, is to provide the appropriate flight crew or cabin crew members with adequate training or to clarify the procedures.

The need for redesign of equipment (12): In blocks (3) through (6) of Fig. D-4, we have looked at normal, possible problem areas related to the maintenance of these aircraft systems. In blocks (9) through (11) of Fig. D-4, we have looked at other possible areas that relate to the equipment but are not necessarily directly related to maintenance. If the engineering investigation has not shown the problem to be in any of these areas, then one must turn to the final possible source—equipment design. If the reliability standards cannot be met and it has been determined that (*a*) maintenance and operational procedures have been implemented correctly and (*b*) no other outside sources are to blame; then the only alternative is to contact the equipment or airframe manufacturer for a possible fix or redesign.

The first step would be to determine if the manufacturer is aware of the problem and find out if other airlines have had similar experiences. The manufacturer may already have (or be working on) a fix. This may be in the form of an SB, SL or an AD, or some redesign effort may be under way. If not, the problem may be determined to be unique to the airline and its operational conditions (environment). In this case, the airline and the manufacturer should work together to obtain a solution. In any case, the airline may need to provide the manufacturer with data on event rates and other aspects of the problem to assist in the solution of the problem.

Figure D-4, block (13): Regardless of where the problem lies—blocks (3) to (6) or blocks (9) to (12)—return to Fig. D-2, block (7) to determine the corrective action required. This will direct you to Fig. D-5, block (1).

Figure D-5, block (1): After determining the problem, the corrective action should be defined. What should be done and who should do it (1) will be outlined in detail on a draft engineering order. The corrective action plan will also include parts, manpower, etc., required to accomplish this (2). The corrective action plan will then be discussed in the monthly (or a special) meeting of the MPRB (3). Attending this meeting will be the permanent members of the MPRB and any others involved with the particular problem (see Chap. 19). This committee will review the order for accuracy and feasibility. Once the MPRB agrees on the corrective action plan and the implementation schedule, block (4), returns you to Fig. D-2, block (8).

Figure D-2, block (8): The EO is finalized and issued by engineering to all affected organizations. Each organization notifies engineering of completion (9). When all action has been completed (10), engineering closes the EO and reports completion to reliability, the MPRB, and the regulatory authority as necessary (11). Reliability then continues to monitor parameters as usual to determine the effectiveness of the corrective action (12).

Thus, the loop is closed and all (hopefully) is well. If reliability determines through subsequent data collection that the corrective action has not been effective in reducing the event rate, the process will be repeated.

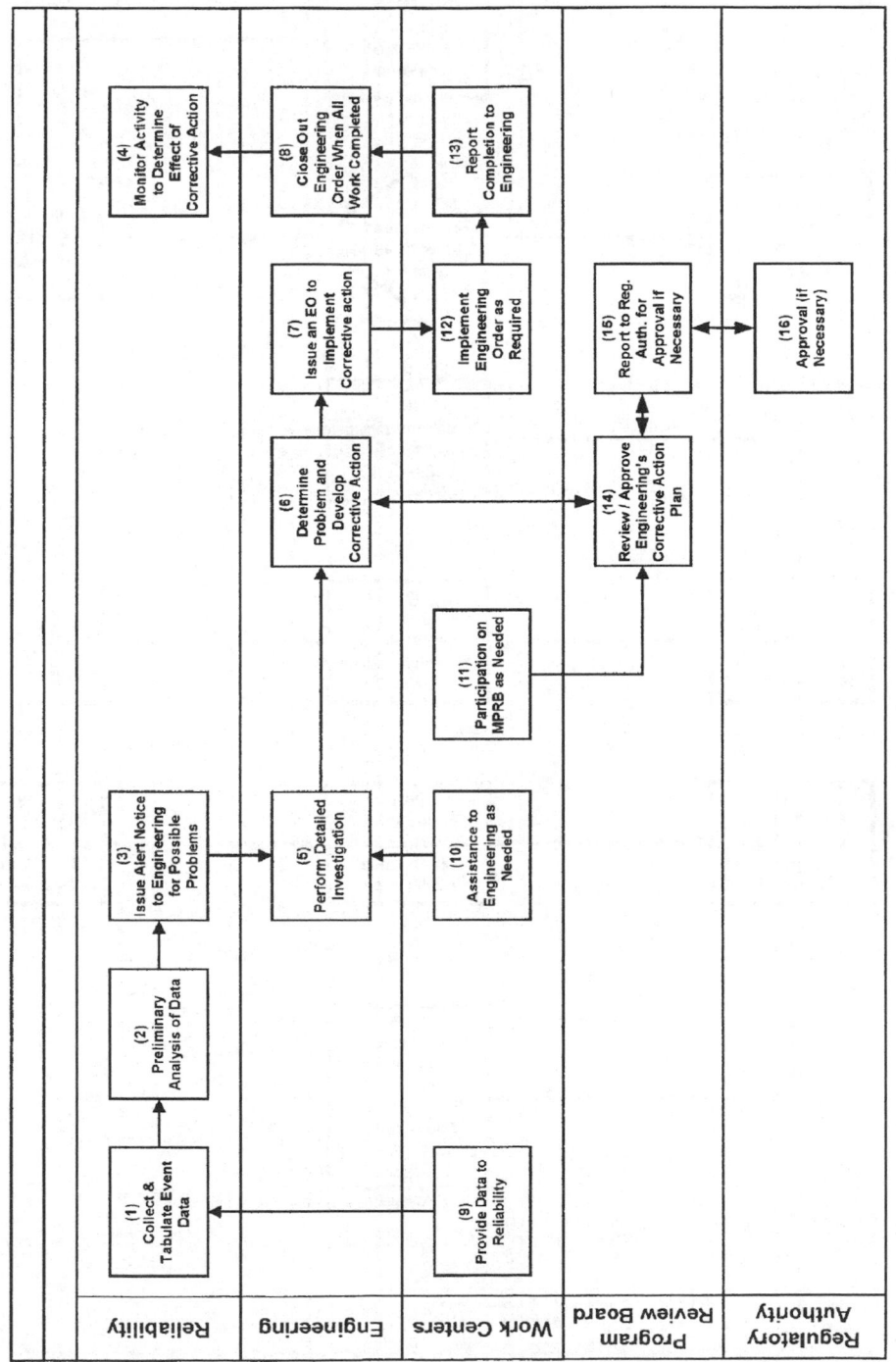

Work Centers means any and all work centers involved with a given problem, including the airline and outside contractors.

Figure D-1 Reliability alerts—a cross-functional process.

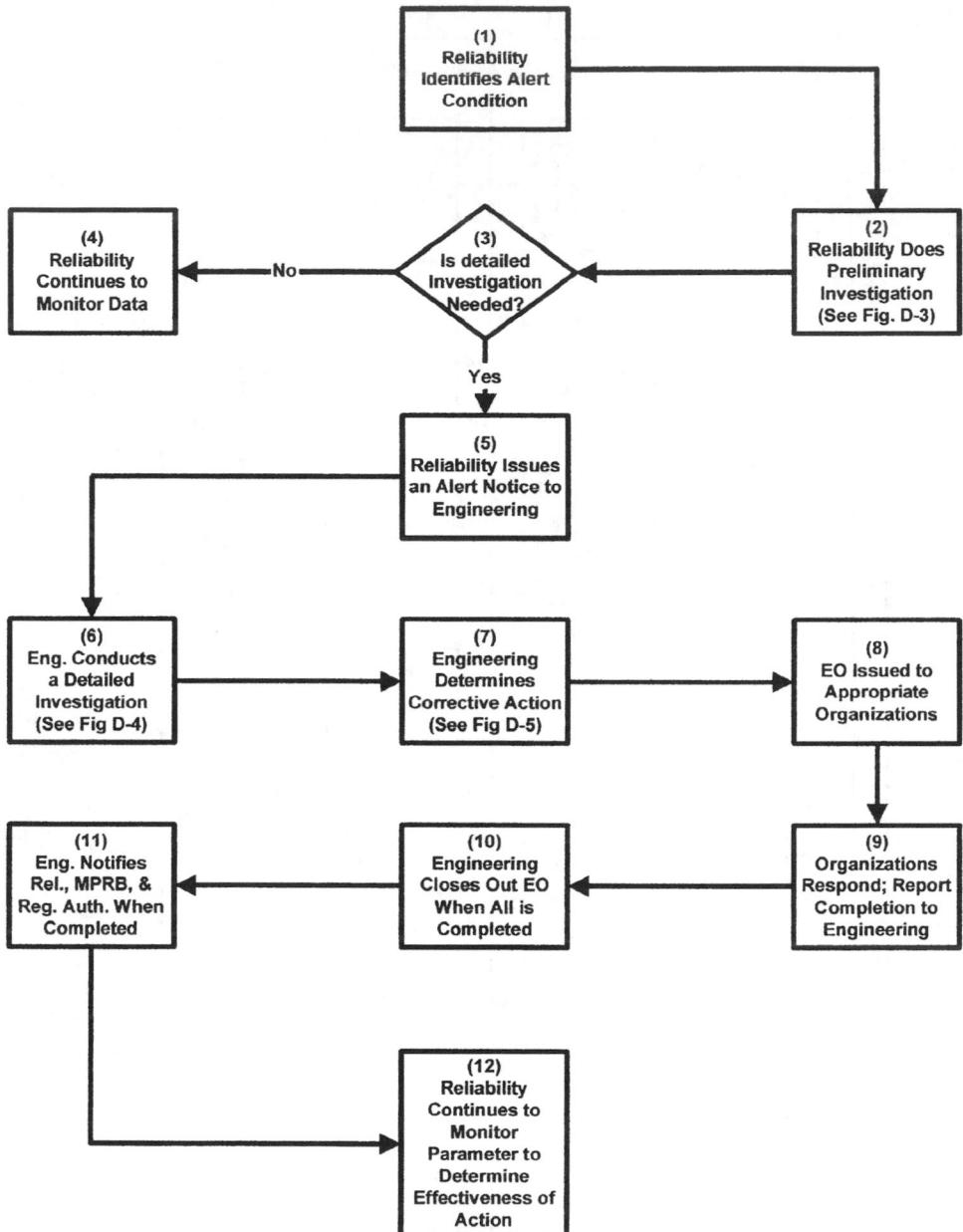

Figure D-2   Analysis of reliability alerts.

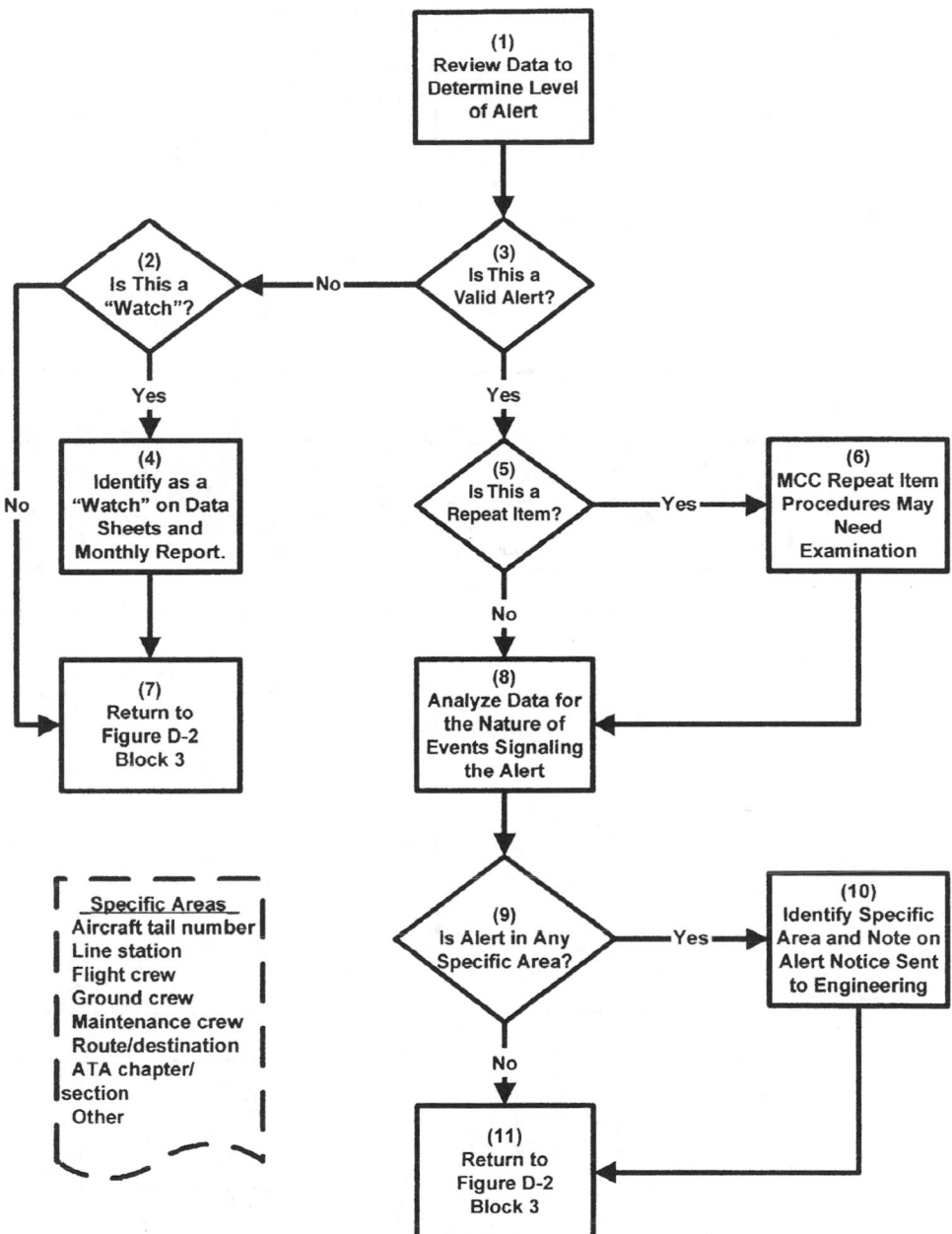

Figure D-3   Preliminary investigation of alert conditions.

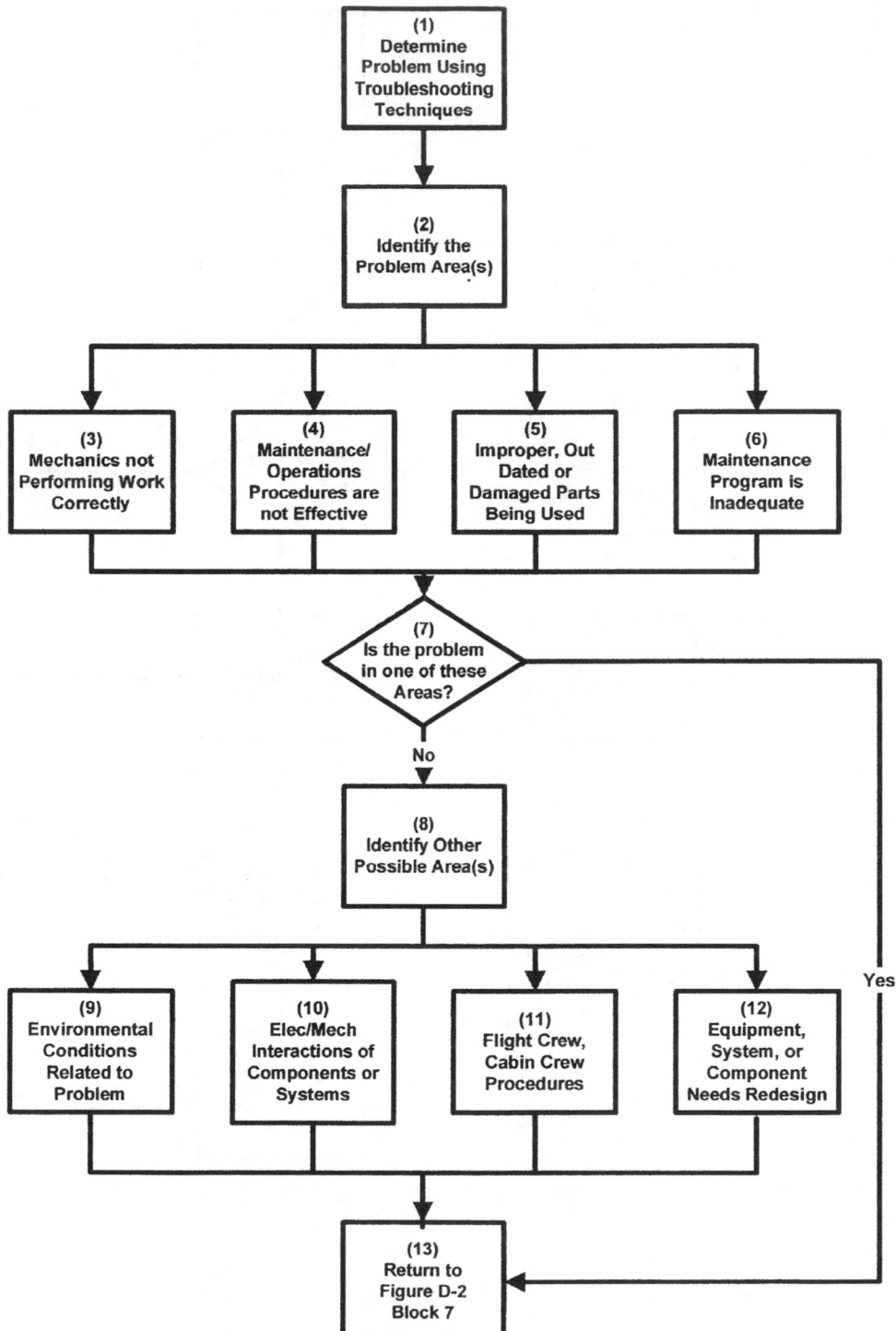

Figure D-4   Detailed investigation of alert conditions.

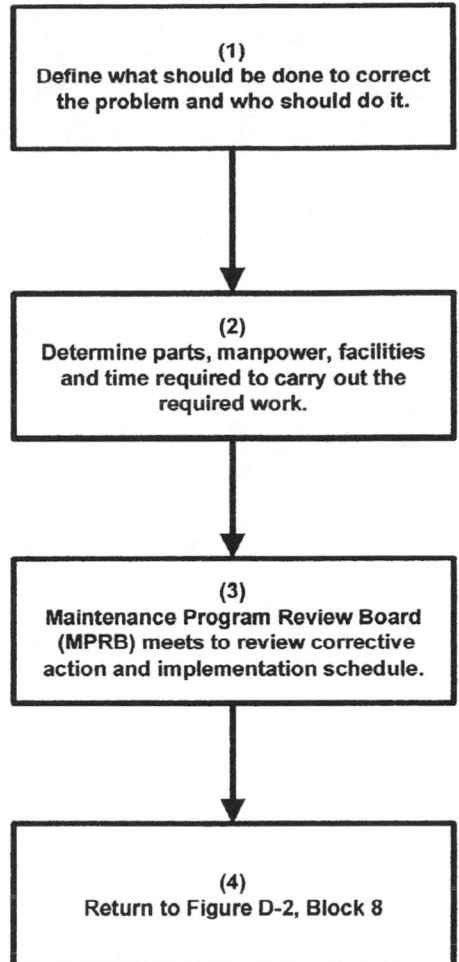

Figure D-5   Determination of corrective action.

Extended Range Operations (ETOPS)

Introduction

The commercial aviation industry has been flying extended range operations (ETOPS) for more than 15 years but there is still some confusion about what ETOPS is all about and what is required of the airline operator to fly ETOPS. This appendix will provide some history of the development of ETOPS and identify just what is required to accomplish this new approach to aircraft operations and maintenance.

Background

In the mid-1950s, the FAA established a basic rule for two- and three-engine airplanes (except three-engine turboprops), which still exists today. That rule is FAR 121.161 and states, in part, the following:

> Unless otherwise authorized by the Administrator, based on the character of the terrain, the kind of operation, or the performance of the airplane to be used, no certificate holder may operate two-engine or three-engine airplanes (except a three-engine turbine powered airplane) over a route that contains a point farther than one hour flying time (in still air at normal cruising speed with one-engine inoperative) from an adequate airport.[*]

The FAA further states in an Advisory Circular on ETOPS, "It is significant to note that this rule is applicable to reciprocating, turbopropeller, turbojet, and turbofan airplanes transiting oceanic areas or routes entirely over land."[†]

At the time the rule was written, essentially all two-engine airplanes were powered by reciprocating (piston) engines with propellers. These internal combustion

---

[*] Federal Aviation Regulation 121.161.

[†] FAA Advisory Circular AC 120-42A, Extended Range Operations with Two-engine Airplanes (ETOPS), December 1988.

engines were subject to in-flight failures and shutdown; and adding more engines to the aircraft did not appreciably improve the situation. However, the three- and four-engine airplanes usually had enough power to sustain safe flight with one engine out. Thus, the three- and four-engine airplanes could fly farther away from the alternate airport with safety. The two-engine airplanes were required by FAR 121.161 to remain within 60 minutes of the alternate airport in case one engine would have to be shut down.

When the jet engines were introduced, they were tremendous improvements over the reciprocating engines and they had much better safety and performance records. Over the years since the jet engine was first employed, these engines got better and better.[*] When the modern "glass cockpit" airplanes (B757, B767, A300) were introduced in the early 1980s, operators wanted to use these airplanes on their North Atlantic routes from the United States to Europe. The problem, however, was that the two-engine rule required them to remain within 60 minutes of a suitable, alternate airport throughout the entire flight. This meant flying over Greenland from NY to London and other European destinations while the three- and four-engine airplanes could fly the North Atlantic tracks which allowed them to fly a shorter route over the southern tip of Greenland.

To alleviate this discrepancy, the industry asked the FAA to change the 60-minute rule, citing significant improvements in engine technology and performance along with better navigation systems of the day. The FAA, instead of eliminating or changing the 60-minute rule, produced an Advisory Circular in 1985 that provided guidelines allowing an operator to obtain approval from the FAA to "deviate from the rule." This gave an operator, after meeting certain requirements (to be explained later), permission to fly up to 120 minutes from a suitable, alternate airport. This allowed ETOPS approved operators of twins to use the North Atlantic tracks—a shorter, more competitive route.

Later (1988), when operators sought other world routes for the twins, the AC was revised (AC 120-42A) and allowed operators who complied with some additional requirements the privilege of flying up to 180 minutes from a suitable, alternate airport. This revision to the AC made it possible to fly two-engine airplanes almost anywhere in the world.[†] Operators in the North Pacific region, however, were limited by the availability of suitable alternate airports. In recent years, FAA permission to fly more than 180 minutes from a suitable alternate airport was extended to 207 minutes (a 15 percent extension over 180) for these operators. This not only closed up the holes (except Antarctica), it allowed twins operating in the North Pacific a better choice of alternates.

---

[*] One engine on the B777 twin-jet delivers more thrust than all four engines of the original B707, i.e., 80,000 to 90,000 pounds thrust on each engine for the B777 versus 18,500 pounds of thrust for the original B707 (74,000 pounds total).

[†] At 120 minutes diversion time, twins could not fly over Antarctica, a large area of the Pacific Ocean, and a number of other isolated areas throughout the world. These areas were closed up, for the most part, by the 180-minute approval. A section of the Pacific Ocean and Antarctica were still unavailable to twins.

The airplane, in order to qualify for 207-minute ETOPS, had to be originally designed for ETOPS and the approval would be given on a case-by-case basis. As of the date of writing this text (December 2003) the AC has not been changed to address this 207-minute operation. There are also, at this time, discussions to extend ETOPS diversion time to 240 minutes (i.e., 4 hours). This extension would not open up any significant airspace for twins, but it would allow all operators with such approval a better selection of alternate airports. This would allow carriers to provide improved passenger comforts in the event of a diversion.*

Deviation from the 60-Minute Rule

Although the basic rule, FAR 121.161, has never been changed, the FAA has established requirements for approval to deviate from the rule. These include specific changes to the equipment and to the airlines' maintenance and flight operations programs.

Equipment modification

The primary requirement for ETOPS was to change the airplane engines to meet a higher standard of reliability, which resulted in a number of engine modifications. Other modifications were incorporated in on-board equipment. The auxiliary power unit (APU), originally designed to operate on the ground to provide AC power when the engines were not running, was modified for ETOPS to serve as a backup power source in the event one engine had to be shut down in flight. This modification assured the APU would start and run at altitudes up to 41,000 feet. In addition, a hydraulic motor generator (HMG) was installed on some models to provide an additional source of AC power in case the APU was inoperative.

All of these modifications were identified by service bulletin (SB) and compiled in an FAA approved document called the configuration maintenance and procedures (CMP) standard. This document also included any maintenance or operations procedures that may have been needed. These SBs, although optional to non-ETOPS operators, became mandatory for ETOPS through the FAA approved CMP. Thus, for ETOPS operators, these SBs had the status of airworthiness directives (ADs). Generally, these modifications would differ from one engine type to another and by airframe. Thus, a CMP was created for each model and included information for all engine and APU units available for that airframe. These modifications, in the beginning, would take up to a year to incorporate in the operator's fleet. This period gave the operator time to get acquainted with the airplane and develop the ETOPS program. In later years, an operator could buy or lease the airplane in ETOPS configuration.

---

* The "suitable, alternate airport" designation refers to the suitability for aircraft landing and taking off. Some of these airports, however, may not have adequate passenger amenities.

Flight operations requirements

The ETOPS Advisory Circular states that the workload for the flight crew should not increase due to ETOPS. That is, flying further than 60 minutes from a suitable alternate airport or flying to an alternate airport on one engine should not require any additional crew duties over those of a conventional flight. There are, however, additional requirements for the airline in preparation for ETOPS flights.

Once the origin and destination of the ETOPS flight are determined, alternate airports must be identified and the route plotted. The distance from each alternate is determined based on the airframe/engine combination and the area where the flight will take place. The altitude to be flown with one engine out is determined by the actual terrain over which the flight will be flown and the altitude necessary for optimum fuel burn. The flight speed is determined for these conditions and the time to the alternate is calculated and translated into distance. This is the distance from the alternate that can be flown per FAA approval.* This route and corresponding flight path and altitude will remain the same throughout the operation. However, for each flight, dispatchers at the airline must determine winds and weather on the route (standard procedure) as well as conditions at the chosen alternate(s). The fuel reserves needed to accomplish the diversion to an alternate are then calculated and added to basic fuel requirements.

Maintenance program changes

Maintenance experts agree that the FAA requirements for an ETOPS supplementary maintenance program are, essentially, what any good maintenance program should be. The AC states that if the airline's current, FAA approved maintenance program does not include the processes and actions stated in the AC, then the program should be upgraded to include them or other processes and actions that will achieve the same goals must be employed.

The supplemental maintenance program outlined in the AC identifies a number of actions. There are six items which directly affect the day-to-day maintenance activities on the flight line: items 1 to 6 in the list that follows. There are four other requirements, items 7 through 10, which should be included in the maintenance management activities to aid in the implementation of ETOPS program. The following items constitute the ETOPS supplemental maintenance program.

1. *Predeparture service check.* An ETOPS service check to be performed prior to each ETOPS departure. Consists of normal transit check, oil consumption monitoring tasks, and any additional checks deemed necessary for ETOPS.

---

* This distance is determined assuming still air. During an actual flight, prevailing winds may alter flying time but does not alter the approval to fly the area.

2. *Oil consumption monitoring program.* A monitoring program to identify engine and APU oil consumption rate for each flight leg for an ETOPS airplane, whether an ETOPS flight or not.

3. *Engine condition monitoring program (ECM).* A program to (*a*) ensure that engine parameters are not exceeded and (*b*) to address problems before they cause degradation or shutdown. Use this in conjunction with the oil consumption monitoring to monitor overall engine health.

4. *Propulsion system monitoring program.* A program to monitor in-flight shutdown rates for the ETOPS airplanes and to ensure that action is taken to restore the engine and also to determine if the recurrence of the problem can be avoided or reduced in the future.

5. *Resolution of discrepancies program.* A program to ensure that proper and expedient corrective action is taken following an engine in-flight shutdown, an ETOPS significant system failure, and any adverse trends indicated by the oil consumption and/or engine condition monitoring programs. Check out the repaired system after maintenance to ensure the effectiveness of the corrective action before releasing the airplane for flight.

6. *Maintenance of multiple, similar systems.* A program to avoid doing maintenance on both units of a dual system such as engines, fuel lines, etc. at the same maintenance visit. Different crews can be used on the separate systems if the work must be performed at one visit.

7. *ETOPS parts control program.* A program to ensure that only ETOPS authorized parts (as identified in the CMP or other SBs or ADs) are used on an ETOPS airplane.

8. *APU high altitude start program.* A program to ensure adequate high altitude start capability for the auxiliary power unit. Usually done during the first 2 months of operation. The operator should establish a 95 percent or higher start rate during this period. This will ensure that the modifications and maintenance actions are adequate.

9. *ETOPS training.* All personnel involved with the ETOPS maintenance program must receive training on the philosophy of ETOPS and on the specific requirements, with emphasis on the differences from the normal operation.

10. *Identify ETOPS significant systems.* This is a list of systems, created by the operator for his specific operation, which identifies those systems that are directly related to ETOPS operation. These are the systems of concern in the other supplemental activities.

ETOPS Maintenance Versus Conventional Maintenance

As stated earlier, these AC requirements for ETOPS maintenance do not constitute a substantial change in the conduct of maintenance. The proposed program is no more than a different approach to maintenance—what might be called the "real time" maintenance approach.

Conventional maintenance activity is primarily reactive and predictive. The reactive approach involves addressing malfunctions when they occur or, in some cases, deferring maintenance to another, more convenient time or passing the problem on to the crew at the next station. The predictive approach involves data collection and analysis of the discrepancy, after the fact, with an effort to predict when or how often such problems will likely occur so as to create certain maintenance actions to address these problems on a scheduled basis. Of course, experience has shown that different items require different approaches and most maintenance programs include both reactive and predictive maintenance.

The real time approach to maintenance is more proactive. The main feature of real time maintenance is to react promptly and effectively to malfunctions and to monitor certain functions to identify any trends that show an impending problem. Thus, action can be taken before the condition escalates into a more serious problem. As an example, the oil consumption and engine condition monitoring requirements of ETOPS will show engine problems as they develop. Maintenance action can be taken to correct the deficiency before a failure or engine shutdown occurs. The resolution of discrepancies concept of ETOPS is an effort to react promptly to problems and to ensure that the action taken has been effective.

The proactive approach is not necessary for everything on the airplane, nor are the reactive and predictive approaches needed universally. The three approaches should be used selectively for any good maintenance program. This is not a drastic change in maintenance philosophy; it is just a more conscientious approach to maintenance.

ETOPS for non-ETOPS Airplanes

Two-engine airplanes not used for ETOPS, and three- and four-engine airplanes, can benefit from this real-time approach to maintenance as much as ETOPS configured airplanes. Although the modifications for ETOPS may or may not be included in a particular airplane (or even available for some models), the maintenance efforts listed above can be applied to all aircraft. The oil consumption monitoring and the engine condition monitoring programs will provide an ongoing view of engine health for all engines on all aircraft. The quick resolution of discrepancies and immediate validation of the corrective action taken can also have benefits to all aircraft whether ETOPS or not. The ETOPS efforts for monitoring all important systems to track and respond to trends are appropriate and effective for all aircraft types. The attitude of being on top of the status of equipment and reacting quickly and responsibly to problems can benefit any maintenance activity (even your car and other ground equipment). In the long run, it can save money in preventing or reducing the number of major problems.

Some airlines configure all airplanes of a given type for ETOPS so that equipment can be swapped between ETOPS and non-ETOPS service quickly to the benefit of scheduling and on-time performance. Other airlines flying both kinds of flights will configure all the engines for a given type airplane for ETOPS so that the engine buildup process can be simplified. This also requires fewer spare engines; i.e., there is no need to have a spare engine for each configuration.

Airplane manufacturers can provide airplanes in either ETOPS or non-ETOPS configuration as the operator desires but the trend is to build all airplanes as ETOPS ready. This could be the final step in ETOPS evolution: the elimination of the differences in ETOPS and non-ETOPS operations.

Summary

The ETOPS supplemental maintenance program is a real-time approach to maintenance that allows the operator to stay on top of equipment condition and monitor any adverse trends. By responding promptly to maintenance problems and by performing validation checks on the maintenance action to ensure an adequate fix has been employed, the airline can ensure a better flight time to maintenance downtime ratio. In the long run, this will be a cost saving for maintenance by avoiding major problems and minimizing downtime.

"A" Check   A maintenance check performed approximately every month (every 300 flight hours, for example).

A&P   Airframe and power plant

AC   Advisory Circular—Information issued by the FAA to identify ways in which an operator can meet the requirements of certain aviation regulations.

AC   Airworthiness certificate—A certificate issued by the FAA to each aircraft built to assure that it has been built to type certificate (TC) standards and delivered to the customer in an airworthy condition.

Accidental Damage   The physical deterioration of an item caused by contact or impact with an object or influence that is not a part of the airplane; damage as a result of human error that occurred during manufacture, operation of the vehicle, or performance of maintenance.

AD   Airworthiness directive—A document issued by the FAA whenever an unsafe condition exists in an aviation product. ADs may prescribe inspections, modifications, conditions, or limitations under which the product may continue in operation. Incorporation of an AD is mandatory.

Alert   An arbitrary level of failure (or removal, etc.) rate set by reliability to call attention to a possible problem area. Must be established by the analyst to provide useful guidelines.

AMM   Airplane maintenance manual—Manual produced by the airframe manufacturer containing pertinent information about the aircraft and its installed equipment.

Airworthiness   Meeting the FAA established standards for safe flight; equipped and maintained in a condition to fly.

AMT   Aviation maintenance technician—Latest terminology for aircraft mechanic; includes those trained and qualified in airframe, power plant, avionics, etc.

AOG   Aircraft on ground—An aircraft that is out of service (i.e., grounded) waiting for a part or parts before it can be returned to service.

APU   Auxiliary power unit—A turbine engine used to generate electrical power on the ground when aircraft engines are not operating. Sometimes used in flight when one engine is out (ETOPS) to replace the inactive engine-driven generator.

ATA   Air Transport Association of America—A U.S. trade organization for commercial aviation operators.

ATC   Air traffic control—An FAA service to promote the safe, orderly, and expeditious flow of air traffic.

Backshops   Another name for overhaul shops for maintenance and repair of off-aircraft equipment.

BITE   Built-in test equipment—Special equipment associated with certain systems to monitor health and operation of those systems and to aid in fault location efforts.

Block Hours   Hours measured from the time aircraft leaves the gate (wheel chocks removed) to the time aircraft stops at the destination gate (wheel chocks in place) (see also Flight Hours).

"C" Check   A maintenance check performed approximately every 12 to 18 months (every 4000 flight hours, for example).

CAMP   Continuous airworthiness maintenance program—The FAA approved maintenance program for a commercial aircraft operator.

CASS   Continuing analysis and surveillance system—A program (or programs) established by the operator to ensure that the maintenance and inspection programs of the carrier's Ops Specs are effective.

CDL   Configuration deviation list—An amendment to the TC that identifies airframe and engine parts that can be missing at dispatch provided that they are not safety related and the aircraft is dispatched with limitations as identified in the CDL for that deviation.

CFR   Code of Federal Regulations—A codification of general and permanent rules published by executive departments and agencies of the U.S. government.

CM   Condition monitoring—A primary maintenance process for items that do not have characteristics that would allow the establishment of HT or OC intervals to determine serviceability. CM items are operated to failure.

Critical Failure   Failures involving a loss of function or secondary damage that could have an adverse effect on operating safety.

CRT   Cathode ray tube—A type of electronic display device using a vacuum tube similar to a conventional TV screen.

CSDD   *Common Source Data Dictionary*—Document issued by ATA containing standard aviation definitions.

Daily Check   A maintenance check performed every day or any time the aircraft has sat on the ground for more than 4 hours. For recent aircraft models, this has been changed to a 48-hour interval.

D&O   Description and operation—Part of the AMM that describes how the aircraft's various systems work.

DDG   Dispatch deviation guide—Maintenance guidelines necessary to properly configure for safe flight those items that have had maintenance deferred by MEL action.

Dedicated Inspector Person assigned as a QC inspector full time. May be in QA, QC, or work center.

Delegated Inspector Person assigned as a QC inspector for specific inspections or a specific work center only; a part-time QC inspector.

Designated Inspector Same as a delegated inspector.

Detailed Inspection An intensive visual inspection of a specified detail, assembly or installation using adequate lighting and, where necessary, inspection aids such as mirrors, hand lenses, etc.

Discard The act of removing a component from service permanently after a specified lifetime.

DMI Deferred maintenance item—A maintenance item deferred by MEL or CDL rules to be accomplished at a later time.

DOC U.S. Department of Commerce—Sets standards for air commerce.

DOL U.S. Department of Labor—Parent organization for the Occupational Safety and Health Administration (OSHA).

DOT U.S. Department of Transportation—Sets standards for U.S. transportation systems. Parent organization of FAA.

EBU Engine Build-Up—The process of adding components to a basic engine to configure it for installation on a specific aircraft and position. Allows for quicker engine changes (see also QEC).

Engine Cycle Operation of the aircraft engine from start-up to shutdown.

Engineer A problem solver; a technical expert in the M&E organization.

Entropy Unavailable energy; the difference between the theoretical system and the practical one.

Environmental Deterioration The physical deterioration of an item's strength or resistance to failure as a result of chemical interaction with its climate or environment. May be time dependent.

ETOPS Extended range operations with two-engine aircraft—Allows two-engine aircraft operator to fly up to 180 minutes (or more) from a suitable, alternate airport.

Evident Failure A failure of an aircraft system or component that is noticeable to the flight crew.

FAA U.S. Federal Aviation Administration—Component of the U.S. DOT responsible for aviation and air transportation.

Failure Effect The effect that a specific failure has on the operation of a system.

Failure Mode The manner in which a system or component can fail.

FAK Fly-away kit—A collection of parts/supplies carried on board the aircraft to facilitate maintenance at outstations where such parts/supplies are not available.

FAR Federal Aviation Regulation—Term used to identify U.S. Code of Federal Regulations (CFR) relating to aviation.

Fatigue Damage The initiation of a crack or cracks due to cyclic loading and subsequent propagation of such cracks.

FH Flight hours

Flight Hours Actual flight time measured from takeoff (wheels up) to landing (touchdown) (see also Block Hours).

FSDO Flight Standards District Office of the FAA.

Functional Check A quantitative check to determine if each function of an item performs within specified limits. This check may require use of auxiliary equipment.

General Visual Inspection A visual examination that will detect obvious, unsatisfactory conditions or discrepancies.

GMM General maintenance manual—Another name for the airline's technical policies and procedures manual.

Goal A goal is a point in time or space where you want to be; a level of accomplishment you want to achieve.

GSE Ground support equipment—Equipment used in the maintenance and servicing of the aircraft and its equipment.

HF Human factors

HFM Human factors in maintenance

Hidden Failure A failure of an aircraft system or component that is not evident to the flight crew.

HMG Hydraulic motor generator—An AC generator, powered by the hydraulic system, to provide an additional source of power for ETOPS operation.

HMV Heavy maintenance visit—A maintenance check that involves structural inspections, major modifications, and other major repairs. Usually extensive downtime.

HT Hard time—A primary maintenance process that requires replacement of a component at specific intervals (lifetime).

IATA International Air Transport Association—An international Aviation Trade Organization.

IDG Integrated drive generator—An aircraft engine–driven electrical generator.

IFSD In-flight shutdown (of an aircraft engine).

Inherent Reliability The "designed-in" reliability of a component or system. This reliability is a combination of design and preventive maintenance efforts.

Inspection An examination of an item and comparison against a specific standard.

ISC Industry Steering Committee—Experienced representatives of manufacturers and operators who oversee the activities of the maintenance steering group (MSG) in generating an aircraft maintenance program.

ISO International standards organization—An international organization responsible for establishing standards throughout the world.

IWG Industry working group—A group of aviation industry experts developing the maintenance program for a new or derivative aircraft.

JAA Joint Aviation Authorities—An association of European Aviation Authorities working to standardize regulations throughout Europe. Not a regulatory authority.

LCD   Liquid crystal display—Type of instrument display device.

LEP   List of effective pages—Identifies pages in a document that comprise the latest revision (helps to identify missing or added pages).

Letter Check   Standard check cycles for certain maintenance efforts. May be called A, B, C, etc. Airlines may use other names. Frequency varies from aircraft to aircraft and from operator to operator. Can be measured in flight hours, flight cycles, or calendar time.

LRU   Line replaceable unit—An aircraft component designed for quick removal and installation to reduce maintenance downtime and minimize flight interruption.

Lubrication   An act of replenishing oil, grease, or other substances used for the purpose of maintaining the inherent design capabilities of a unit or system by reducing friction and/or conducting away heat.

M&E   Maintenance and engineering—The airline organization responsible for all maintenance and servicing of aircraft and any engineering activities related to that maintenance.

Maintenance   The process of ensuring that a system continually performs its intended function at its designed-in level of reliability and safety.

Maintenance Zone   Identified area on an aircraft where visual inspections are performed on all elements within the zone.

MCC   Maintenance control center—The hub of maintenance activities on the flight line for in-service aircraft.

Mechanic   An FAA certified technician or mechanic

MEL   Minimum equipment list—A list of equipment that flight crews agree to accept as inoperative for short periods. Time intervals set by FAA and airframe manufacturer in the MMEL. Operator creates an MEL unique to his or her own configuration.

MIDO   Manufacturing Inspection District Office—FAA organization that is responsible for inspecting airframe, engine, and appliance manufacturers for capabilities and for issuing the production certificate.

MMEL   Master minimum equipment list—Master list of MEL items. Includes all related items available for the aircraft type whether installed on operator's vehicle or not. Developed by airframe manufacturer and FAA approved.

MOE   Maintenance organization exposition—Another name for the airline technical policies and procedures manual.

MPD   Maintenance planning data document (Boeing and Airbus) that identifies MRB and other recommended maintenance tasks for a given model aircraft (see also OAMP).

MPRB   Maintenance program review board—The governing body of the airline's CASS Program; made up of directorate and work center managers.

MRB   Maintenance review board—The FAA organization that oversees the development of aircraft maintenance programs created by the MSG process.

MRBR   MRB report—FAA approved maintenance program, developed by the industry through the MSG process, that identifies maintenance requirements for a given aircraft.

MSDS   Material safety data sheet—An information sheet for chemical substances that provides data on the potential hazards of the product, the required safety standards to be used, and any emergency actions necessary for handling the product.

MSG   Maintenance steering group—Oversight group, consisting of manufacturer, operator, and regulatory personnel, responsible for creating the maintenance program for new and derivative aircraft.

MSI   Maintenance significant item—An item, determined by the manufacturer, whose failure would either affect safety, would be hidden from the flight crew, or would have an operational or economic impact.

MTBUR   Mean time between unscheduled removals (repairable equipment)

MTTF   Mean time to failure (nonrepairable equipment)

MTTR   Mean time to repair (time in shop for maintenance)

NDI   Nondestructive inspection—Inspection technique that does not alter the unit being inspected.

NDT   Nondestructive testing—Testing technique, which does not alter the unit under test.

NDT/NDI or NDT/I   Nondestructive test and inspection

NFF   No fault found—Negative result of a troubleshooting action. Not necessarily the end of the investigation.

NFPA   National Fire Protection Association—An organization to reduce the burden of fire and other hazards; provides scientifically based codes and standards, research, and education in fire safety.

NIST   National Institute of Standards and Technologies—Establishes various standards of measurement including those used to calibrate tools and test equipment.

OAMP   On airplane maintenance program (McDonnell-Douglas) that identifies MRB and other recommended maintenance tasks for a given model aircraft (see also MPD).

Objective   An objective is the action or activity you employ in order to help you achieve a goal.

OC   On condition—Primary maintenance process that schedules periodic inspections or tests to determine remaining serviceability of a component or system.

OC   Operating certificate—Certificate issued by the FAA allowing the holder to engage in air operations.

OJT   On-the-job training—Training given while working at the normal job as opposed to classroom training.

OSHA   Occupational Safety and Health Administration—U.S. Department of Labor organization responsible for establishing the health and safety regulations for business and industry.

Operating Cycle   Take-off, flight, and landing of an aircraft.

Operational Check   A task to determine if an item is fulfilling its intended purpose. This is a failure-finding task and does not require quantitative tolerances or any equipment other than the item itself.

Ops Specs   Operations specifications—An airline, model-specific document that identifies the operations and maintenance programs of the airline in detail. Must be approved by FAA.

Oversight Functions   Those elements of the M&E organization that monitor the performance of the other M&E activities.

PAI Principle avionics inspector—An FAA representative assigned to an airline for liaison and assistance in matters related to avionics systems.

PC Production certificate—A certificate issued by the FAA to the manufacturer of an approved aircraft model.

PERT Program evaluation and review technique—A graphical planning and scheduling technique for complex projects. Identifies each item to be accomplished, the sequence in which items should be performed, and any conflicts which may arise.

PIC Pilot in command—Senior officer of an aircraft flight crew.

PIREP Pilot report—A logbook entry or other report (verbal or electronic) by a flight crew member concerning an aircraft discrepancy or malfunction.

PMI Principle maintenance inspector—An FAA representative assigned to an airline for liaison and assistance on maintenance matters.

POI Principal operations inspector—An FAA representative assigned to an airline for liaison and assistance in matters related to flight operations.

PP&C Production planning and control—The M&E organization responsible for planning and scheduling all maintenance activity at the airline.

Program Module Part of a computer program designed to provide specific operations/manipulations of stored or input data.

QA Quality assurance—The M&E organization responsible for setting standards of operation and for monitoring the operator units to ensure that such standards are met.

QC Quality control—The M&E organization responsible for conducting inspection of maintenance work (when required) and for calibration of tools and test equipment. QC inspectors can be dedicated (full time) or delegated (part time).

QEC Quick engine change—The process of removing and replacing an aircraft engine with a minimum of downtime. All engine build-up (EBU) activities have been done prior to the QEC to facilitate quick removal and installation.

RCB Reliability control board—The governing body of the airline's reliability program; made up of all affected work center managers.

R&I Removal and installation—Procedure for removal and installation of aircraft parts or systems designated as LRUs.

Redundancy The use of two or more items in parallel or in a primary/secondary arrangement to ensure full support in case one unit fails.

Reliability The probability that an item will perform a required function, under specified conditions without failure, for a specified amount of time.

Reliability Program A set of rules and practices for managing maintenance and controlling the maintenance program.

Residual Failure A failure mode that remains if a proposed modification of the unit or proposed change of maintenance program were rejected. Cost of these failures must be considered in the decision to incorporate or not to incorporate the modification.

Restoration That work necessary to return an item to a specific standard. Restoration may vary from cleaning the unit or replacing a single part up to and including a complete overhaul.

RII   Required inspection item—Those items that could result in unsafe operation of the aircraft if maintenance is not performed correctly or if improper parts are used.

SB   Service bulletin—Document issued by the manufacturer to modify or improve operation of an aircraft component or system. Could include substitution of parts; special inspections or checks; or a change in life limits. Incorporation by airline is optional.

Scheduled Maintenance   Simple maintenance and/or servicing activities designed to maintain the inherent level of safety and reliability of a system; done at specified intervals.

SD   Standard deviation—A statistical parameter identifying the relative dispersal of data points about a mean value.

Servicing   An act of attending to basic needs of components and/or systems for the purpose of maintaining the inherent design capabilities.

SL   Service letter—Document issued by the manufacturer to identify a maintenance tip or new procedure. Incorporation is optional.

Special Detailed Inspection   An intensive examination of a specific location; similar to the detailed inspection but with the addition of special techniques.

SSI   Structurally significant item—Any detail, element, or assembly which contributes significantly to aircraft loading and whose failure could affect the structural integrity necessary for safety of the aircraft.

System   A collection of components designed to work together to efficiently perform a certain function.

System Boundaries   The limits of consideration for a study, analysis, observation, or usage of a collection of components.

System Element   Any component that can be assigned a function or an attribute within the context of the defined system

System Interface   A point where two systems or two elements or subsystems connect or interact. This interaction can be direct or indirect; it can be electrical or mechanical; it can be through hard wire, sensory, or transmission devices.

Systematic Approach   A step-by-step process; an essentially linear process or procedure where one accomplishes some goal by performing one step at a time, in sequence, until the desired result or goal is achieved.

Systems Approach   An approach to the study of a complex system considering all parallel and interacting aspects at once as opposed to the systematic approach, which is a linear process.

Systems Engineering   The application of engineering principles to the study and development of a system.

TC   Type certificate—A certificate issued by the FAA that identifies a specific, approved aircraft design.

Third Party   Any person or organization outside the airline performing service or maintenance activities for the airline.

Transit Check   A maintenance check performed prior to each flight (i.e., at aircraft turn-around).

Troubleshooting   The process of studying and analyzing a problem in order to pinpoint the cause and resolve the trouble.

TN   Tail number—Aircraft identification number, usually painted on the tail.

UCL   Upper control limit—A statistical parameter used in establishing a reliability alert level (a mean value plus some multiple of the SD).

Unscheduled Maintenance   Maintenance performed to restore an item that has failed or deteriorated beyond usable levels to its inherent (designed-in) level of reliability and safety.

Validation   Accepting a test procedure after actually performing it successfully.

Verification   Accepting a test procedure based on knowledge of the unit under test and understanding of the procedure. (Procedure is not actually performed.)

Visual Check   An observation to determine if an item is fulfilling its intended purpose. This is a failure-finding task and does not require quantitative tolerances.

Zonal Inspection   Several visual inspection tasks performed in a specific area (zone) of the aircraft.

Index

ACARS system (ARINC
Communications and
Reporting System), 148
accident/incident reporting, 186
accident and injury reporting, 227
"A" check:
during downtime, 150
planning, 117–118
accidental damage, 24
adjusting the plan, 111
AD and SB compliance, 186
advisory circulars (ACs), 62
Airbus Industries, 29
Air Carrier Maintenance
Programs, 75–76
aircraft:
approved operator repairs, 70
check, 65
cleaning/painting/washing, 70
configuration, 61
delivery inspection, 49–53
and engine data, 137
failure, can occur at random, 13
hydraulic fluid level, 30
interior modifications, 155
logbook, 148
maintenance of, in flight, 91
maintenance logbook, 138,
147–148
maintenance management, 90
maintenance program (OAMP), 90
model, 59–60
system configurations,
104–105
zone diagrams, 28
aircraft certification:
airworthiness certificate, 49
production certificate, 46
type of certitficate, 45

airframes:
manufacturer, 59
and power plant (A & P) license,
129
structure maintenance checks,
30
airhome manufacturer, 61
airlines:
activities, that should be audited,
182–186
libraries, 126
maintenance manual (AMM),
58–59, 66–73, 149
maintenance reliability program,
168
manual, 70–73
with mixed fleets, 156
public transport operation, 75–77
RII program, 64
training, 129–134
airline certification:
to operate as a commercial air
transport company, 87
Ops Specs document required by
the FAA, 64
and self-monitoring, 87
airplanes:
check after landing, 29
systems maintenance. *See*
maintenance
tire pressures, 185
Air Transport Association of
America (ATA), 55
airworthiness:
condition at delivery, 78
directive (AD), and hangar
maintenance, 155
directives (ADs), 62–63,
104–105

Airworthiness Certificate (FAA form
8100-2), 49
ATA document standards,
66–73
attitude display indicator (ADI),
167
audits, prescription of, 185
aviation:
component parts of the industry,
54–55
laws, 62
vs. other transportation
industries, 45
still needs attention, 13
uses of the computer in
maintenance, 135
Aviation Industry Interaction,
54–55
Aviation Maintenance Program
Outlines, 75–76
Aviation Maintenance Technician
Schools, 80
avionics, 101
shops, 166–167

battery shop, 166
BITE test, 69
Boeing:
chief mechanic for the design of
the 777
document for maintenance
planning, 28
boroscopes, 196
brake wear indicator pins,
20–21
budgeting efforts, 176
buyback policy, 195
buyer furnished equipment (BFE),
59

ABOUT THE AUTHOR

HARRY A. KINNISON, PH.D., worked for the Boeing Company for 20 years, 10 as a specialist in the Maintenance and Ground Operations Systems Group of the Customer Services Organization. Specifically, he represented Boeing to airlines on the ETOPS (extended-range twin-engine operations) program, participated in airline maintenance evaluations, and helped airlines develop reliability programs. Since his retirement from Boeing in 2000, he has taught aviation maintenance management courses at Embry-Riddle Aeronautical University in Daytona Beach, Florida. He developed this book because no suitable text for courses such as his existed.